*The National Lawyers Guild:
From Roosevelt through Reagan*

The National Lawyers Guild:

From Roosevelt through Reagan

Edited by
ANN FAGAN GINGER
and EUGENE M. TOBIN

Foreword by Ramsey Clark

TEMPLE UNIVERSITY PRESS
Philadelphia

Temple University Press, Philadelphia 19122
Copyright © 1988 by Temple University. All rights reserved
Published 1988
Printed in the United States of America

The paper used in this publication meets the minimum
requirements of American National Standard for Information
Sciences—Permanence of Paper for Printed Library Materials,
ANSI Z39.48-1984

Library of Congress Cataloging-in-Publication Data
The National Lawyers Guild.
   Includes index.
   1. National Lawyers Guild—History.
I. Ginger, Ann Fagan. II. Tobin, Eugene M.
KF294.N33N38 1988   340'.06'073   87-1975
ISBN 0-87722-488-9 (alk. paper)

To those who first committed
the National Lawyers Guild
"to function as a social force in the service of the people
to the end that human rights
shall be regarded as more sacred
than property rights";
to those who have joined the Guild
to carry out this commitment;
to those clients, individual and collective,
who inspired the Guild, and all society,
to carry forward this work;
and to their progeny,
this book is dedicated

Contents

Preface	*xvii*
Foreword by Ramsey Clark	*xxv*

ONE   **The National Lawyers Guild and the Great Depression (1937–1938)**   3

    The Birth of the Guild, *by Maurice Sugar*   7
    Organizing Lawyers to, Inter Alia, Pack the Supreme Court, *by Ann Fagan Ginger*   9
    National Lawyers Guild Constitution: Preamble and Article I   11
    Wheeling and Dealing with the New Deal, *by Morris L. Ernst, Frank P. Walsh, and Franklin D. Roosevelt*   12
    Origins of the National Lawyers Guild, *by Mortimer Riemer*   14
    Taking Hold of the Present: Who Joined the Guild? *by the Editors*   17

TWO   **Lawyers in the Struggle for Industrial Unions (1936–1940)**   22

    The Call for a Liberal Bar, *by Robert H. Jackson*   23
    The New Deal Lawyer: Thomas I. Emerson and the National Labor Relations Board, *by Thomas I. Emerson, with the assistance of Joan P. Emerson*   24
    Defending Unpopular Causes: The Danger of Contempt and Disbarment, *by Edward Lamb and Robert H. Jackson*   26
    Civil Liberties and the NLRB—1940, *by Nathan Greene*   27

THREE   **Shadows of War and Fear (1937–1941)**   30

    The Third Annual Convention: 1939 in Chicago, *by Ann Fagan Ginger*   31

Resignations from the National Lawyers Guild, *by Martin Popper*   34
FBI Operations, 1940–1941, *by Michael Krinsky, Jonathan Moore, and Ann Mari Buitrago*   36
Neighborhood Law Offices, Women Lawyers, and Working Wives, *by Robert D. Abrahams and* The Guild Lawyer   38

FOUR **"V" For Victory over Fascism (1941–1945)**   42

Statement of Policy, February 22, 1941, *by the National Executive Board*   43
Negro Discrimination and the Need for Federal Action, *by William H. Hastie and Thurgood Marshall*   44
The Participation of Negro Labor in Our War Effort, *by Earl B. Dickerson*   45
Discrimination and Racism Produce Riots: Harlem, Los Angeles, and Detroit, *by* The Guild Lawyer, *Carey McWilliams, Alan Brown, and Ned Smokler*   47
Harry Bridges, the Guild, and the FBI, *by the Editors*   51
The Guild's Democratic Tax Program, *by Joseph H. Crown*   54
Rosie the Riveter's Eight-Hour Orphans: The Guild Supports Child Care, *by the Committee on Social Legislation, New York City Chapter*   55
Calls for a United Nations Bar Association, *by* The Guild Lawyer   57

FIVE **Moving Toward Peace, Jobs, Security, and Justice (1944–1947)**   60

The Human Aspects of the Transition from War to Peace, *by the Guild Committee on Post-War Planning*   61
A Social Security Charter for Peacetime America, *by the Guild National Committee on Social Legislation*   62
The 1946 Convention, *by Ann Fagan Ginger*   65
Civil Rights Legislation from the Fourteenth Amendment to an Anti-Lynching Law, *by W. E. B. Du Bois*   68
The Morass of Reconversion: Understanding the Postwar Strikes, *by Victor Rabinowitz*   69

SIX **The End of the Grand Alliance (1945–1948)**   72

A New World Born: The Guild at the Founding of the United Nations, *by Martin Popper*   73
The NLG and the FBI at the UN San Francisco Conference, *by Michael Krinsky, Jonathan Moore, and Ann Mari Buitrago*   75
Try the War Criminals Now, Lawyers Urge, *by Martin Popper*   75
War Crimes and Cold War Conspiracies, *by Mary M. Kaufman*   76

	The International Association of Democratic Lawyers, *by Martin Popper*	79
	The Jewish People and Palestine, *by the Guild and Bartley C. Crum*	80
	The State of American Foreign Policy, *by the Guild Committee on International Law and Relations*	82
	The European Recovery Program—The Martial Plan, *by the Guild Committee on International Law and Relations*	84
SEVEN	**The Cold War Begins (1947–1953)**	*86*
	Robert J. Silberstein Looks Back on the Seven Lean Years, 1947–1954, *by Robert J. Silberstein*	86
	The Constitutional Right to Advocate Political, Social, and Economic Change—An Essential of American Democracy, *by the Guild National Constitutional Liberties Committee*	87
	Harvard Law School Seminar on Civil Liberties (Spring 1948), *sponsored by the Harvard Law School Chapter of the Guild*	89
	Report on Certain Alleged Practices of the FBI, *by a Special Committee of the Guild, with an introduction by Michael Krinsky*	91
	The Keynote Address of the 1950 Guild Convention, *by Clifford J. Durr*	93
	Cold War Foreign Policies Stir Internal Debate: Yugoslavia and Korea, *by the National Lawyers Guild*	94
	The Rosenberg Case, *by* The New York Guild Lawyer	96
	Loyalty to the Bill of Rights, *by Delbert E. Metzger*	98
EIGHT	**Bread-and-Butter Issues (1947–1956)**	*100*
	The Availability of Legal Services—The Guild Position, *by the Guild Committee on Professional Problems*	100
	Guild Student Chapters Address Bread-and-Butter Issues, *by* The Guild Lawyer *and* The Guild Law Student	102
	The Thompson Case: A Real Life Bread-and-Butter Struggle, *by Annie Stein*	104
	Vindication of the Guild Position, *by* The New York Guild Lawyer	106
	Mandatory versus Voluntary Social Security Coverage for the Bar: The Last Obstacle to the Achievement of Social Security Protection for Self-Employed Lawyers, *by Leo J. Linder*	107
	Guild Activity at Conference of State Bar Delegates, *by* The Guild Lawyer of California	109
	Detroit Chapter Trains Lawyers and Fights for Comparative Negligence, *by the Editors*	110

The National Lawyers Guild versus Sexism: The First Step, *by*
  Ann Fagan Ginger — *111*

NINE Cold War against Lawyers (1947–1957) — *113*

The National Lawyers Guild in 1950–1951, *by* Thomas I.
  Emerson — *113*
Testimony of Robert W. Kenny before HUAC, October 27, 1947 — *114*
Report on the National Lawyers Guild: Legal Bulwark of the
  Communist Party, *by the House Committee on Un-American
  Activities* — *115*
The National Lawyers Guild: Legal Bulwark of Democracy, *by
  the National Executive Board* — *119*
Loyalty and Lawyers, *by* Fowler V. Harper — *121*
Testimony of Ben Margolis before the House Un-American
  Activities Committee, October 1–2, 1952 — *122*
The Trials of Harry Sacher and Abraham Isserman, *by* The New
  York Guild Lawyer — *124*
The 1954 Chicago Guild Convention, *by the Chicago Red Squad* — *129*
Testimony of Ruth Weyand before the House Committee on
  Un-American Activities, February 23, 1956 — *130*
Schware, Konigsberg, and Independence of the Bar, *by* John T.
  McTernan *and* The New York Guild Lawyer — *132*

TEN The ABA and the *Attorney General v. NLG* (1953–1958) — *136*

FBI Activity and Executive Order 10450, *by* Michael Krinsky — *137*
Test Oaths: Henry VIII to the American Bar Association, *by*
  Samuel M. Koenigsberg and Morton Stavis — *138*
The American Bar Association, Attorney General Brownell, and
  the National Lawyers Guild in Time of Crisis, *by the Editors,
  Lawyers Guild Review* — *139*
Amended Interrogatories of the U.S. Attorney General
  Concerning Guild Activities in the Matter of the Proposed
  Designation of the National Lawyers Guild Pursuant to
  Executive Order No. 10450 — *141*
Extracts from Briefs to the United States Court of Appeals in
  National Lawyers Guild v. Herbert Brownell, Jr., Brief for
  Appellant, *by* Osmond K. Fraenkel, Earl B. Dickerson, and
  Joseph Forer — *143*
The Leo Sheiner Case: No Disbarment for Use of Fifth
  Amendment, *by* The New York Guild Lawyer *and* Lawyers
  Guild Review — *144*
Living with a Subpoena, *by* Vivian Mandel — *145*

Liberty and Peace: The Role of a Free Bar, *by Malcolm P. Sharp*	147
Report of the Administrative Secretary, *by Jessica Davidson*	149
Selecting Priorities for Guild Work While under Attack: The Ginger Strategy, *by Leo J. Linder*	149
The Guild Honors Defenders of the Bill of Rights, *by* The New York Guild Lawyer	150
A Testimonial to the Struggle for Civil Liberties, *by* The New York Guild Lawyer	152
The Justice Department Ends *Brownell v. NLG*	158
A Promise and a Prophecy, *by the Board of Editors,* Lawyers Guild Review	159

ELEVEN **Moving from Victory to Affirmative Action (1958–1961)**   *161*

The Role of the United States Supreme Court, *by John M. Coe*	161
Attack by Un-American Committee on Guild, *by* The Guild Lawyer	163
Report of the National Lawyers Guild on the Recommendations of the American Bar Association, *by the National Executive Board*	165
The Guild and the Court: Mass Admissions and Amicus Briefs, *by* The Guild Lawyer	166
Facing the Hard Realities: Chapter Pledges and Payments, *by David Scribner*	168
COINTELPRO, *by Michael Krinsky, Jonathan Moore, and Ann Mari Buitrago*	169
Leading Labor Lawyer Urges Fresh Start in Labor Legislation, *by Harold Cranefield*	171
Creative Legal Research, *by Sam Rosenwein*	172
The Central Thesis of the First Amendment: Oral Argument in *Yellin v. U.S.* (1961), *by Victor Rabinowitz*	173
Who Won the Cold War, *by Joseph Forer and the Editors*	175

TWELVE **Civil Rights Moves the Guild (1961–1963)**   *178*

Interposition Interposed, *by Mitchell Franklin*	179
Black People Don't Have Legal Problems, *by Edward A. Dawley*	182
A Cry for Help: Norfolk to Berkeley to New York to Detroit, *by the Editors*	185
Report on Initial Activities, *by Committee To Assist Southern Lawyers (CASL)*	188
The FBI Intrudes on Guild-ABA Relations, *from the FBI*	190

A Report of CASL, *by George W. Crockett, Jr., and Ernest Goodman* 191
Tributes and Deceptions in New York, *by Charles McKinney, Hope Stevens, and the FBI* 192
The Guild Publishes Its First Book, *by the Editors* 194
Albany Journal—Summer 1963, *by Dennis Roberts* 194
Lawyers Arrested at Guild Workshop in New Orleans, *by the Editors* 197
A Stormy National Executive Board Meeting in New York, *by Ernest Goodman* 199
Into the Streets of San Francisco, *by the Civil Liberties Docket* 202

THIRTEEN   The Guild Goes South (1964–1965)   203

The 1964 Convention and the Mississippi Project, *by the Editors*   205
The FBI Meets with Some Civil Rights Organizations, *by the FBI*   206
The Goodmans and Schwerners Go to the Oval Office, *with Martin Popper*   207
Mississippi and the FBI Retaliate, *by the Guild CLAS and from the FBI*   209
Resolutions by the ABA and Mississippi Bar Association, *by the Committee for Legal Assistance to the South*   210
The Guild Looks at Its Budget, Closes, and Reopens, its Jackson Office, *by the Editors*   211
The Guild Goes to the Polls in Michigan, *by the* Guild Newsletter   212
The Mississippi Freedom Democratic Party Challenge, *by Morton Stavis*   212
Storming the Palace in San Francisco, and the Guild Response, *by Paul Harris and the San Francisco Chapter*   214
The Watts Revolt and the Los Angeles Chapter Response, *by the* Civil Liberties Docket *and Leo Branton, Jr., Seymour Mandel, and Ben Margolis*   216
Pondering the Future: Len Rosenthal, Claudia Shropshire, and Ben Smith, *by the* Guild Newsletter, *the Editors, and the Subjects*   218
Whose Rights? What Danger? *by Michael E. Tigar*   221

FOURTEEN   Representing "Hell, No! We Won't Go!" (1965–1968)   228

The Constitutional Right to Object to War, *by the* Civil Liberties Docket *and* The New Draft Law   230

CONTENTS / xiii

The Guild Learns, Teaches, and Organizes Draft Law, *by the Editors*	232
Trying a Case under the Selective Service Law, *by Ben Margolis*	233
Special Problems of Black Draftees, *by E. A. Dawley*	234
Formation of the San Francisco Selective Service Panel, *by the Panel*	237
The Individual's Duty under the Law of Nürnberg, *by Mary Kaufman*	239
Summing Up the Guild's Role in the Vietnam War, *by the Guild Convention, Samuel Neuburger, and Paul Harris*	243

FIFTEEN Confronting the War at Home (1965–1969)   246

How Woman's Work Is Sometimes Done, *by Ann Fagan Ginger*	247
Pioneer's Reports on Poverty Law, *by Simon Rosenthal*	249
The Detroit Recorder's Court and the 1967 Civil Disturbance, *by George W. Crockett, Jr.*	251
"What Did You Do in the Riots, Daddy?" *by John Houston*	255
A Debate on the Definition of "Radical Lawyer," *by David Freedman and Victor Rabinowitz*	257
National Officers and Chapters of the Guild before the 1968 Convention	259
The Confrontational Convention in Santa Monica, 1968, *by Joan Andersson, Dan Lund, David Rein, Bruce Waltzer, James Herndon, Norman Leonard, Rudolph Schware, and Fay Stender*	261
Guild Lawyers at the Chicago Democratic Convention of 1968, *by Dan Lund*	266
Minimizing Racism in Jury Trials, *by Charles R. Garry*	267

SIXTEEN Movement Lawyers and Clients, and the Courts (1968–1976)   270

New Style Law Offices, *by Anne M. Garfinkle and David Finkel*	270
The Role of the Radical Lawyer and Teacher of Law, *by Arthur Kinoy*	272
You Don't Have To Love the Law to Be a Lawyer, *by Paul Harris and Gene Ann Condon*	275
The Class Role of U.S. Courts, *by Doris Brin Walker*	281
The Guild Military Office in the Philippines, *by Howard DeNike and Bob Hilliard*	285
William O. Douglas: In Retrospect, *by Leonard B. Boudin*	289
Boycotting Wine on Interstate 99, *by Barbara Rhine*	291
The Shango Trial: The Lawyer, the Client, and the Jury, *by Ernest Goodman*	293

SEVENTEEN Young Lawyers Take Hold (1970-1979) — 299

The 1970 Convention in Washington, *by Dan Lund*	299
The President's Analysis, *by Doris Brin Walker*	301
The 1971 Convention in Boulder, *by Dan Lund*	303
The FBI Blacklist of Bar Applicants, *by the Editors*	306
Practicing Labor Law, *by Marijana Relich*	308
The National Lawyers Guild as an All-White Organization, *by William Goodman*	309
Sketches of Guild Presidents Larson, Weinberg, and diSuvero, *by the National Guild Banquet Committee*	315
Limiting Access to Federal Courts, *by Frank Askin*	316
When the Defendants Are Foxes Too: The Need for Intervention by Minorities in "Reverse Discrimination" Suits like Bakke, *by Charles Lawrence*	318
Internal Struggles, *by William Goodman*	321

EIGHTEEN Let Theory and Practice Bloom (1977-1980) — 324

Mammon and Caesar, *by Peter Weiss*	324
Resolution on the Middle East, *by the 1977 National Convention and the Middle East Task Force*	328
The Right to Equality: A Marxist Analysis, *by Barbara Wolvovitz and Jules Lobel*	331
National Lawyers Guild v. Attorney General, *by 1986 Guild Annual Report and Michael Krinsky*	336
Opposing Right-Wing White Supremacist Groups, *by Fania Davis, Doris Brin Walker, Ann Fagan Ginger, and the National Executive Board*	338
State of the Guild Speeches, *by Paul Harris and Mary Alice Theiler*	340
Handling My First Constitutional Law Case—1981, *by Colleen Rohan*	344
The Legal Right to Peace Demanded by Our Clients, *by Ann Fagan Ginger*	346

NINETEEN The Challenge of the Eighties (1981-1984) — 350

Rethinking Indian Law, *by Steven Tullberg and Robert T. Coulter for the Guild Committee on Native American Struggles (CONAS)*	351
From National Committee to Combat Women's Oppression (NCCWO) to Anti-Sexism Task Force, *by Elizabeth Schneider, Patti Roberts, and Barbara Dudley*	353

Looking Back and Looking Forward, *by Gerald Horne and Doris Brin Walker* ... 356
Economic Rights as Human Rights, *by Ramsey Clark, Arthur Heitzer, Melinda R. Bird, and Sam Rosenwein* ... 359
Waging the War against Union Security, *by Barbara Kraft* ... 366
Carrying Out the Guild Resolution on Fighting Racism in the Guild, *by the 1979 Guild Convention* ... 367
Sketch of People's Lawyer R. Samuel Paz, *by Roberto Velasquez-Rodriguez* ... 369
The Status of Nuclear Weapons under International Law, *by Elliot L. Meyrowitz* ... 370
Civil Disobedience: Defenses That Keep Issues at the Fore, *by Peter Goldberger* ... 373
Guild Presidents Sound the Alarm, *by Michael Ratner and Barbara Dudley* ... 376

TWENTY **The Future Lies Ahead (1984–   )** ... 378

Legal Services for the Poor, *by Simon Rosenthal* ... 382
Immigrant Rights and Sanctuary, *by Susan Gzesh and Marc Van Der Hout* ... 384
Respice, Adspice, and Prospice, *by Haywood Burns, introduced by Leora Mosston* ... 387
1980s Civil Rights Work, *by Tom Meyer and Ann Noel* ... 391
State of California v. Stephen Bingham, *by Stephen Bingham* ... 393
NLG Leads Battle at California State Bar, *by the Los Angeles Chapter State Bar Committee* ... 397
International Work, *by the International Committee* ... 399
The Priority of Work on Peace Law, *by 1986 National Convention* ... 400
Freedom Is a Constant Struggle, *by the Editors* ... 402
Looking Ahead, *by Haywood Burns* ... 406

APPENDICES

A: Guild National Conventions and National Officers ... 409
B: National Guild Journals and Newsletters ... 412
C: Winners of National Guild Awards ... 414
D: National Officers, Chapters, Projects, Committees, Task Forces, and Caucuses (1986–1987) ... 415
E: Books Published by the National Lawyers Guild ... 418

Index ... 421

Preface

WE BELONG TO the most legalistic and disputatious society in the history of the world. The people of the United States are taught from childhood to revere a piece of paper, a constitution, rather than a king. This strengthens the divine right of constitution, with its provisions for equal power of the courts and the Congress with the power of the president. It also strengthens the belief that almost any social issue can be raised in court, which leads, ineluctably, to the retention of lawyers.

Litigation and the labyrinthine permutations of our judicial system are intimidating, remote, and expensive for people who work for a living, for women and people of color, for reformers and activists. This has led our people, not surprisingly, into a love-hate affair with the law and lawyers.

Throughout our history popular opinion has characterized the bar as a distinct group, but often in the most ambivalent and, at times, unflattering terms. Foreign observers as distant in time and nationality as Alexis de Tocqueville and Lord James Bryce both noted this underlying tension. Lawyers, Tocqueville observed in the 1830s, were the most prominent members of an American aristocracy. Over a half-century later, Bryce sensed the bar's social and political prestige even as popular hostility and suspicion increased. It is one of the ironies of our culture that we combine respect for the law's traditions with a contempt for its practitioners, especially when they lose an important case.

Are members of the National Lawyers Guild a distinct subgroup within the bar? Certainly the founders of the Guild thought so, according to the selections from their writings included in this anthology. They felt the need for communication and support in the 1930s, when a worldwide economic crisis and the rise of Fascism led to a questioning of the most fundamental principles of democratic society. The law inevitably became a forum for action on the social and political issues sweeping across the United States. Catastrophic human dislocation, massive unemployment, and widespread poverty extending well into the upper reaches of the middle class led many lawyers to join the movement for social change, challenging the rules of corporate capitalism and its standards of professionalism. Inspired by the New Deal, Popular Front, and insurgent activities spearheaded by Marxists and Communists, the Guild wrote into its preamble a dedication "to function as a social force in the service of the people to the end that human rights shall be regarded as more sacred than property rights." From 1937 to the present, the Guild has welcomed into membership those supporting the human rights side of the equation of democratic capitalism, finally spelled out in the United Nations Charter and Nuremberg Principles.

As a group, Guild lawyers reflect the tradition of poor kids becoming the first lawyers in the family, joining a handful of lawyers from prosperous families who got the pro bono spirit in the second or third generation after immigration. From the New Deal/Popular Front days of 1937 until 1963, the Guild was led by an inspired group of East Coast lawyers most deeply concerned with national and international issues, which they sought to move forward by resolutions, analytical reports to Congress, creative amicus briefs, and coalition work with labor unions and left-progressive-liberal groups of all sorts. Their ideology was a mixture of humanism, Marxism, populism, and the democratic tradition. Although Midwesterners, Southerners, and people from the West Coast always participated actively in Guild affairs (Robert W. Kenny served as president while attorney general of California), they did not move to center stage until the mighty Civil Rights Movement of the 1960s was under way.

In 1964, Guild leadership moved to Detroit, which had lived through McCarthyism with fewer casualties than New York and Washington, D.C. had suffered. The new leaders were younger than their East Coast predecessors, more were black, and all felt closer ties to their struggling brothers and sisters in Virginia and Mississippi than to some of the international movements to which New Yorkers felt committed. Many of these practitioners made their livings representing plaintiffs injured in automobile accidents or from the use of defective products, cases requiring a more pragmatic approach and a willingness to gamble on a jury verdict.

While the East Coast Guild, and Marxist lawyers throughout the country, remained active in the organization, Guild leadership moved next to the New Left and anti–Vietnam War activists, who came to span the country in a way never experienced in the days before mass air travel and hippie vans. In the seventies, these groupings faced off against the Anti-Imperialist Caucus and what they considered the Ultra Left, deciding, on their demise, that they would concentrate on actions, not resolutions, on direct representation of clients and movements rather than on amicus briefs to appellate courts on neatly-defined legal issues.

The selections in this anthology illustrate the efforts of Guild members and their clients to take advantage of a combination of legal principles and procedures for the protection of human rights over property rights that make it possible to use the courtroom as a forum for an effective fight. Trained in courtrooms from Scottsboro, Alabama, to the Reichstag Fire Trial, from Flint, Michigan, to Jersey City, early Guild lawyers relied heavily on public trials in civil and criminal cases before juries that represented a cross-section of the community and came to their own independent judgments. As they worked in New Deal agencies and for unions appearing before such administrative bodies, they learned how to write and revise regulations, and to demand their strict enforcement.

During World War II, Guild lawyers who did not join the armed forces got accustomed to being paid by their clients and, after the defeat of Fascism, more Guild lawyers found ways to represent working and poor people who could not afford their fees. Some went into personal injury work, with its contingent fees (unheard of in England and most other countries). Others became public defenders, paid by the state to represent people charged by the state with criminal conduct (unheard of in this country only a few years before). They all used fundamental principles established in the American Revolution, the Civil War, the New Deal, and World War II.

The selections here from the Warren Court era (1954–1969) reflect an increasing reliance on the ability to raise social issues in class action suits in the federal courts, challenging local, state, and federal practices of discrimination against women, people of color, and other oppressed people. These suits against government agencies and transnational corporations were often won in the U.S. Supreme Court on the basis of magnificent language that proclaimed the sacredness of human rights before property rights.

One unusual feature of this anthology is its presentation of examples of lawyering skills that receive little media coverage but are essential to the survival of law offices and legal organizations. While lawyers are taught when to sue and fight an adversary in court, they must also be skilled in the arts of bookkeeping, negotiation, conciliation, and compromise. The artful use of these tools kept the Guild together during difficult policy decisions, from the proper policy on U.S. participation in the Korean War during the 1950s, to the proper line on affirmative action and union security questions in the eighties.

How successful has the Guild been in making human rights more sacred than property rights in its first 50 years? There is no statistical study of the successes and failures of the Guild or its members. We do not know precisely what was won in the New Deal or what effect it had in ending the Depression. We have not counted the costs of the Cold War, the number of casualties, the permanent losses; the price that was paid in lives and imprisonment to achieve some victories in the Vietnam War; the hostility and burnout that accompanied clashes among the New Left, the Old Left, and the Ultra Left in the late sixties and early seventies. This anthology presents some of the raw material from which such an evaluation can be made when we finally feel the necessity to make a score card on enforcement of the constitutional guarantees of human rights.

Certainly, the Guild can boast of its participation—as an organization or through individual members—in every significant effort since 1937 to bring about social change by placing human rights above property rights. It can boast of reclaiming several forgotten laws, and proposing some new ones that have become standard tools for people's movements. Obviously, the Guild prospered best when it represented an active, growing popular movement. Yet it proved able to survive when its causes were under intense attack and seemed doomed. With few exceptions, Guild members stood firm in the face of threatened loss of livelihood, bar cards, and fame—the goads and goals of most Left, as well as mainstream, lawyers. Some Guild members even rose to the occasion with the chutzpah, panache, and sense of gallows humor essential in a Cold War or a Reagan administration. These qualities shine through many of the selections in this book.

How successful has the Guild been in increasing the number and percentage of Guild lawyers or Guild-type law practice? Again, we have collected no statistics. Certainly many more law students and young lawyers today express a desire or determination to work in legal services or public-interest, poverty, or "social impact" law than was true in 1937, before many of these phrases had been coined and made respectable. Professors at top 10 law schools report strong dissatisfaction of lawyers 5 to 15 years after graduation with "their ability to achieve social change" and with "the balance of their career and family lives."[1] Some new lawyers talk publicly about the "golden handcuffs" they put on when they accepted high-paid jobs in large firms, and these themes are popular in television sit-coms depicting life among lawyers.[2] These dissatisfactions have so far led few lawyers with Wall Street firms into the Guild; as time pressures on juniors increase, Guild-type work is being done by traditional bar associations, and Cold War attacks on the Guild are occasionally renewed. Still, the Guild boasts over 8,000 members and has become truly national, with 83 chapters of lawyers and legal workers, 102 chapters of law students, and 12 jailhouse lawyer chapters in 42 states and the District of Columbia.

We used several criteria in the selection of material for this book, striving for well-written pieces on interesting subjects of continuing as well as historical interest by a variety of authors from many jurisdictions, viewpoints, and generations. We have tried to let the documents speak largely for themselves, confining our comments to the chapter introductions. For example, we have presented material from unevaluated FBI reports garnered in *National Lawyers Guild v. Attorney General* (also known as *NLG v. FBI*) and testimony before Congressional committees, only occasionally noting an obvious inaccuracy. We have presented portions of resolutions (and what might be called diatribes) by active

---

[1] David L. Chambers, "Back to the Future," *University of Michigan Law Quadrangle Notes* 31, no. 1 (Fall 1986): 15.

[2] Michael Harris, "Golden Handcuffs Lure Young Lawyers," San Francisco *Chronicle*, Jan. 13, 1987, 19.

participants in various disputes that may read somewhat differently today than they did in the heat of the contest.

This book could more easily have been two or three times its size. In order to squeeze as many voices and issues as possible into these pages, we have cut selections ruthlessly and, we hope, judiciously. Our files are bulging with excellent, well-written material that could not be crammed into these pages. We have similarly cut the repetition of rhetorical devices used in speeches and reports without, we believe, diminishing the effectiveness of presentation.

This leads to the question of ellipses. If this were a book for academicians based solely on scholarly, footnoted work, we would, of course, have included an ellipsis whenever we deleted anything. Many of these selections, however, are speeches made on the spur of the moment at a convention or seminar; some are reports or oral histories. They would not read well if every cut were marked by ". . . ." For this reason, we encourage interested readers to go back to the full texts in the original sources cited in the source notes. We would also like to explain our use of brackets. Some authors have changed a few words in this version of their articles or speeches, correcting errors in the original publication. These are marked by brackets, as are the phrases the editors used to shorten a long discussion. Again, for the pristine prose, please see the original sources. The few articles that originally appeared in law reviews with footnotes have been permitted more ellipses and brackets than the less formal pieces.

■

This anthology is the culmination of a discussion that occurred on a sunny June morning in 1985 as two strangers sat on a front porch in Berkeley, California. One was a lawyer and peace activist, a proud, indefatigable spokesperson and participant in progressive movements for over four decades. Her companion was a younger, admittedly more conservative historian who cared as much about the Old Left as the New. They discovered that they shared a mutual passion for history and interest in the National Lawyers Guild, which indirectly had brought them together. This then is a collaboration between a practicing lawyer and a practicing historian, each with her and his own agenda. If this had been either a brief or a monograph, it might never have been completed. We have fought and argued, compromised and negotiated, shared birthdays and anniversaries, and exchanged more long-distance telephone calls than we could ever admit to our spouses, Jim and Beverly. But we did not compile this anthology without accumulating a great many debts that can never be adequately repaid or suitably acknowledged.

Our greatest obligation, of course, is to our contributors, whose work makes up this book. Editing and compiling an anthology is a very humbling experience. We wish to extend our deepest respect for the men and women who wrote, and often lived, the pieces we have collected. The bulk of the materials were carefully collected and catalogued in the NLG Archives at Meiklejohn Civil Liberties Institute in Berkeley (location given simply as "MCLI" in footnotes), where they had been processed under a grant from the National Historical Publications and Records Commission in 1980. We found "The National Lawyers Guild: An Inventory of Records 1936-1976, An Index to Periodicals 1937-1979," published by Meiklejohn (1980), an invaluable tool. David Christiano and his exceptionally talented colleagues at the Institute found room for us to work in its crowded quarters, and really made possible this anthology.

In addition, activists and librarians across the country have graciously corresponded with us, opened their doors, answered our questions, and facilitated our work with warmth and professionalism. We would especially like to acknowledge the assistance of Raymond Teichman of the Franklin D. Roosevelt Library, Hyde Park, N.Y.; Judith A. Schiff and Lynn J. Stewart of Yale University's Sterling Memorial Library; Bonnie Hardwick of The Bancroft Library at the University of California, Berkeley; Nancy Bressler of Princeton University's Seeley G. Mudd Manuscript Library; Cathy Henderson of the Harry Ransom Humanities Research Center at the University of Texas at Austin; and Ronald G. Grele and his colleagues at Columbia University's Oral History Research Office. Joan T. Wolek and Karolyn G. Crockett of Hamilton College's Burke Library responded as always with skillful professionalism and enthusiasm to our inter-library loan requests.

One of the most rewarding and satisfying aspects of compiling this book has been the opportunity to meet and work with hundreds of members, officers, and friends of the National Lawyers Guild. While we have enjoyed their fullest support and understanding, we have also exercised complete editorial control and independence of judgment. It is not possible to mention everyone by name, but we do want especially to thank Barbara Dudley, Haywood Burns, Martin Popper, Victor Rabinowitz, Ernest Goodman, Mary Alice Theiler, Marc Van Der Hout, Joe Popper, Howard DeNike, Michael Ratner, Doris Brin Walker, Bill Goodman, Rudolph Schware, Michael Krinsky, the Emersons (Thomas, Ruth, and Joan), Harry Lore, Ann Mari Buitrago, Jonathan Moore, Ben Margolis, Corinne Rafferty, Michael E. Tigar, the Honorable Claudia House Morcom, Bill Montross, Leonard B. Boudin, Leon Goldin, Susan Gzesh, Carolyn Patty Blum, Robert Gibbs, Ralph Shapiro, Mary Kaufman, Florence Forer, and Fab Nijhof for their assistance. Ramsey Clark deserves special thanks for writing his insightful and poignant Foreword while flying to trials and appearances from Seoul to St. Georges to the Nevada test site.

It takes sizable amounts of time and money to write books and to publish them. We would like to acknowledge the extraordinary generosity of Gene's institution, Hamilton College, and Ann's, Meiklejohn Civil Liberties Institute, and in particular, the support of Hamilton President J. Martin Carovano and Dean of the College Melvin B. Endy, Jr. A Hamilton faculty fellowship during the winter and spring of 1985 allowed this project to make substantial progress. A stipend from the Williams-Watrous-Couper Endowment Fund enabled Gene's family,

Beverly, David, and Leslie to spend the summer of 1986 in Berkeley and Palo Alto. Participation by Gene in a National Endowment for the Humanities summer seminar on the New Deal at Stanford University, under Otis L. Graham, further stimulated our research. We also take pleasure in acknowledging the support and professional judgment provided by our publisher, Temple University Press, and Janet M. Francendese, Doris B. Braendel, Jennifer French, and JoAnne Mottola. Their enthusiasm for this scholarly but nonacademic project has made it a pleasure to work with them.

Finally, we hope that our dedication indicates our pride in the men and women who took pen to paper when they felt the interests of society so intertwined with their own self-interest that they would risk their time and professional standing to make real their promise to make human rights more sacred than property rights. Their courage and commitment remind us that brave people are the conscience of every generation, and that some of them are lawyers.

Ann Fagan Ginger
Eugene M. Tobin

Foreword BY RAMSEY CLARK

OF COURSE THERE would be no lawyers in Utopia. Nor would there be doctors, merchants, chiefs, rich men/women, poor men/women, beggarmen/women, or thieves. No contract with Dick the Butcher would be necessary to achieve that lawyerless estate. Lawyers would simply lay down their yellow pads, bifocals, stentorian tone, fat fees, litigious contentions, and monopolization of unnecessary knowledge in order to avoid the hearse horse's snicker.

But we do not live in Utopia, which may be the best thing to be said for the world as it is. We would die of boredom.

While nothing can be clearer than the vast need for lawyers' skills if social justice is a great concern of humanity on this earth, it is instructive to inquire whether on the whole lawyers do more good or harm.

If a lawyer's time is her stock in trade, then the Surgeon General should require a large label on all the cans proclaiming in bold face type that the contents are deleterious to health. A small shelf in the back of the store might be excepted. Too often legal services are merely the continuation of violence by other means. Overwhelmingly they are a glaring revelation of our consuming materialism and lust for power. Top law graduates make Faustian bargains for $80,000 their first year with huge conglomerate law firms that dominate the practice, while a handful of lonely impecunious practitioners seek to serve the powerless with laws that are largely irrelevant if not antagonistic to their needs.

With rare exceptions lawyers inflicted cruel and unusual punishments on all parties, more painful than a dentist's visit, when the Guild was aborning. They rarely saved a tooth that was in trouble, though they often pulled a good one. Wisdom dictated that one suffer any wrong before entering those lists. Perhaps law has always been a mere tool with which the powerful enforce their will, a means by which moneyed might wearies out the right.

Still, law can be a major instrument for social change, a protector of life, provider of liberty, an engine for the pursuit of happiness. Law offers ways for people who want a life of principle to pursue it. Law is inherently involved as a major potential for the solution of the graver problems afflicting the planet. Attention must be paid to what law can and ought to do.

How can the United States liberate itself from the governing plutocracy and become the democracy we say we are without law? Over the course of 200 years we have slowly and grudgingly extended through law the right to vote without account of race, to women, the poor, illiterates, new residents, young people. The Voting Rights Act of 1965 is a modest illustration of the capacity of law to involve the people in the political process. Money, which dominates politics and through politics government, can be driven from the temple of democracy by law. Our individual capacity to affect our common destiny through the electoral process can be made more nearly equal. Beyond mere voting, a minor aspect of a vital democracy, far more responsive government can be provided through law, both seeking and reflecting the will of the people. These democratic rights, protective as they are of other rights, remain a priority of domestic tranquility.

Freedom from want, asserted by F.D.R. in harmony with the spirit of the first decade of the Guild, involves the most elemental human needs. If right is freedom as idea, Hegel's view, then law must imagine and model rights and governmental methods securing freedom from want. The New Deal and Poverty programs of the 1930s and 1960s were tentative efforts. Tax policy and government programs, both creatures of law, through a vast, flexible, sensitive, efficient redistribution of wealth that retains maximum individual choice, can create freedom from want. Ten million infants starved to death last year for want of food. One billion more people will populate the planet within a decade, overwhelmingly dark skinned and desperately poor. International institutions such as a World Food Bank, capable of providing proper food in any emergency anywhere, while supporting programs for food independence throughout all regions and people and eliminating the cruel and violent use of food as a weapon, will be essential.

Law alone can address the corrupt use of criminal enforcement power and processes to control segments of the population, primarily young, poor, male minorities, and to reorient crime control to address devastating economic crime by the wealthy. Law can provide prevention programs for the young and poor with alternatives to incarceration where prevention fails.

Human rights and civil liberties require legal protection and affirmative action for fulfillment. Legions of lawyers ought to be employed in their zealous pursuit. The small gesture law made for the Scottsboro boys' right to counsel must be expanded to assure real and effective assistance of counsel for every person accused of crime and full access to counsel to achieve or protect basic civil rights. With more than 1800 people on death rows across the country, most of whom did not have effective counsel, lawyers who want Equal Justice Under Law to be more than a cynical slogan must rise to the defense. But abolition of the death penalty is essential to make law more than a murderer itself.

Similarly, while lawyers defending Central Americans and others seeking sanctuary from tyranny in their native land are present day heroes, an underground railroad leading to a courtroom and threatened deportation cannot adequately protect human rights. A Freedom Express founded in law and supported by our government ought to speed brutalized peoples to safe asylums until a decent foreign policy demanded by the American people and inscribed in our laws helps create conditions abroad from which people need not flee, and conditions here that are loving and generous to the oppressed who reach our shores. This will require cancellation of Third World debt that exploited poor people when loaned and takes food from the mouths of their hungry children when repaid. It will require the United States to stop supporting dictatorships that tyrannize their people.

Lawless acts by our own government can be prevented with enforcement of law, the lone non-violent means. Insurrection, revolution, and war must wait for their chance. The invasion of Grenada; training, financing, and motivating murderous Contra forces in Nicaragua; bombing Libya only happen in the absence of national commitment to constitutional principles. Lawyers must play a major role in the conceptualization and expansion of such a commitment and in assuring impeachment or criminal prosecution of leadership that violates the law. This is the highest enforcement priority of a principled government.

Aside from these modest challenges is the question of omnicide, the destruction of life on the planet by the species that produced Mencius, Francis of Assisi, Bartolome de las Casas, Ghandi, and Martin Luther King. One Trident II nuclear submarine can launch twenty-four missiles simultaneously while submerged, each missile containing seventeen independently targeted maneuverable warheads, each nuclear warhead with a weapon ten times more powerful than the bomb dropped on Hiroshima, a range of 7000 nautical miles, and the ability to strike within 300 feet of a pre-determined target. One launch from one finger can obliterate 408 centers of human population and perhaps bring nuclear winter and a lifeless planet.

It is the "care to preserve society" that is "the source of all law," Grotius believed. Such a weapon could not be legal by any imaginable moral standard. Yet we build the Trident II and three to five additional nuclear warheads every day. Unless world law is quickly created to control such monstrous capacities for violence we will continue to run intolerable risks of self destruction. War is inevitable among sovereign powers not governed by positive law. Aquinas and Einstein are only recent observers of this obvious truth.

Lawyers, get to work.

What this has to do with the National Lawyers Guild may not seem clear. Except having been born in a household of lawyers, I can attest from my earliest years that when a radical cry for social justice was most dangerously and desperately needed a Guild lawyer was most likely to give it: lynchings, Scottsboro, the struggle against fascism in Spain, concentration camps for Japanese Americans. Later as I wandered among the world's woes my most frequent encounters with lawyers where they ought to be were with Guild members: Bobby Sands in prison, Kent State, South African depredations in southern Angola, the Attica penitentiary rebellion, Nicaragua modeling a constitution, Chile seeking desaparecidos, the occupied territories of the West Bank and Gaza. Lawyers in the Guild have more nearly reflected the conscience of a people in struggle for social justice than any other lawyer group in America.

One cannot do good with impunity, but it has its satisfactions, perhaps the best. Read their story.

*The National Lawyers Guild:
From Roosevelt through Reagan*

■ ONE

The National Lawyers Guild and the Great Depression (1937–1938)

FIFTY YEARS AGO almost half of the attorneys in the United States earned less than $2,000 annually when $2,500 was considered the poverty line for a family of four.[1] By 1935 over 1,200 of New York City's unemployed attorneys joined the Lawyers Security League to pressure the New Deal's Works Progress Administration (WPA) into providing public employment opportunities for distressed members of the bar. Nationally, lawyers at the bottom of the professional ladder were among the one-third of the nation that President Franklin D. Roosevelt said were "ill-clad, ill-housed, and ill-nourished."[2]

Fifteen million people in the United States were unemployed—25 percent. Thousands of families were evicted from their homes and farms by foreclosures and Dust Bowl storms, becoming refugees in their own country. At least one million homeless men and women roamed the nation's highways and rode freight trains in desperate pursuit of food and shelter. Americans scavenged in restaurant garbage cans and made Hooverville shacks out of tar paper from city dumps. Hungry children stood silently on bread lines while their parents grimly gathered at factory gates, down at the docks, or in migrant labor camps looking for a day's pay. Those fortunate enough to find jobs were victimized by low wages, long hours, unhealthful working conditions, and company unions and other union-busting tactics, and faced sweeping labor injunctions when they went on strike.

Primarily concerned with economic survival, these men and women also had

---

1. Isidor Lazarus, "The Economic Crisis in the Legal Profession," *National Lawyers Guild Quarterly* (hereinafter *NLG Quarterly*) 1:1 (Dec. 1937), pp. 18–19; American Bar Association, *The Economics of the Legal Profession* (Chicago, 1938), p. 47; and Jerold S. Auerbach, *Unequal Justice: Lawyers and Social Change in Modern America* (New York: Oxford University Press, 1976), pp. 158–59.

2. Samuel Rosenman (ed.), *The Public Papers and Addresses of Franklin D. Roosevelt* (13 vols., New York, 1938–50), VI, p. 4.

legal problems. They needed lawyers at bankruptcy and eviction proceedings, in negligence and worker's compensation cases, and as speakers and organizers. But few could afford to pay a fee. When participants in hunger marches, rent strikes, and farm-price strikes discovered they had few legally recognized rights, they joined the movement to organize industrial workers and the unemployed, to inaugurate a major political realignment in the 1932 election.

Beginning in March 1933, with Franklin Roosevelt's first one hundred days in office, the American people enthusiastically embraced a heterogeneous array of programs that attacked the nation's economic and spiritual paralysis. If New Deal solutions were often temporary and sometimes unsuccessful, they nonetheless addressed the new agenda for public policy demanded by the mass movement and enunciated by the most articulate: public works spending, unemployment compensation, labor's right to organize and bargain collectively, securities regulation, and child labor reform. Political radicals and intellectuals of many stripes demanded that two additional items be placed on the nation's agenda: national economic planning to avert future depressions, and a struggle against international Fascism as increasingly exemplified by Adolf Hitler and Benito Mussolini.

The New Deal's crusading spirit arose out of necessity, and stimulated further social consciousness. It awakened a national commitment to public service that addressed the concerns of industrial workers and family farmers, just as it nourished the professional needs of writers, musicians, and artists. No group of professionals, however, was more directly affected by the combination of depression economics and New Deal reforms than lawyers.

The American Bar had always been a highly stratified profession. At the very top stood the elite minority of large corporate law firms whose white male partners catered to the needs of international financiers and corporations. These established lawyers vigorously guarded access to the privileged levels of their fraternity. Law-school graduates were hired on the basis of their social background and institutional affiliations. Blacks and women were automatically excluded; the more liberal law firms accepted a token percentage of Jews. This legal elite dominated state Bar associations, controlled character and fitness committees that regulated admission to the Bar, and shaped the rigidly conservative policies of the American Bar Association (ABA) in the interest of corporate America. Its leaders saw no distinction between reform and revolution, and viewed government regulation with unmitigated horror. The ABA attacked the growth of administrative law, denied the constitutionality of New Deal regulatory agencies, and was openly hostile to passage of the child labor amendment to the Constitution.

Most lawyers belonged to a much different legal fraternity, one of solo practitioners or small partnerships whose catch-as-catch-can practices depended on the steadily declining number of clients who could afford even minimal legal fees. These attorneys represented their families and friends, whose legal problems were the problems of the working poor: criminal cases where fees were low, and personal injury cases in which inadequate fees were compounded by low rates of recovery. The few black lawyers operated under even more difficult conditions. In the North, black lawyers in Cleveland, for example, were denied rental space in downtown office buildings. In the South, black lawyers were not allowed to use local law libraries. All were barred from membership in the segregated ABA at a time when a courageous minority of black and white attorneys were fighting against poll taxes, lynching, and discrimination in public accommodations.

All these lawyers desperately needed the professional recognition, enlightened leadership, and sense of purpose that only a national progressive Bar association could provide. They also sought recognition of their need for economic security and drafted a plan to achieve it. In the New Deal year of 1936, with Roosevelt's popularity at its apex, the creation of a liberal lawyers' organization seemed not only possible but inevitable. The New Deal was very much a "lawyer's deal," needing counsel to provide its structure and shape its content. The legislation proposed by FDR's brain trust, which was to be passed by Congress and administered by the federal government, generated enormous jobs of drafting statutes and regulations. Later, lawyers had to become administrative law judges to settle disputes arising under the new statutes and regulations.

The newspapers trumpeted the common fear that the country was in for either reform or revolution. The New Deal represented reform, and reform meant change by law. The unprecedented growth of the federal government's regulatory responsibilities over industry, labor, and agriculture placed a premium on legal skills and values. "The plague of young lawyers" who descended on Washington "with their hair ablaze" found work with the National Recovery Administration (NRA), Agricultural Adjustment Administration (AAA), and National Labor Relations Board (NLRB).[3] New agencies were being created and new policies determined. Young lawyers unable to find apartments slept on office couches or in hotel rooms hired for government meetings. It was an extraordinarily exciting time in which to live and work.

These young lawyers were members of a distinctive generation shaped by the exigencies of the Great Depression and the exhilaration and commitment engendered by the unprecedented mass movement which found its expression in the New Deal. The older lawyers, who had experienced the Great War, the Palmer Raids, and the anti-labor thrust of the 1920s, had learned that the law is both a framework and a tool. Despite legal protections for property rights, some gains may be won for the people's needs through the structure of the court system and its procedural rules. The court system gives lawyers and clients a framework or forum in which to demand justice, and provides guidelines for drafting documents demanding specific relief. The content of the law provides arguments and

---

3. George Peek, *Why Quit Our Own* (New York: Van Nostrand, 1936), p. 20, as quoted in Peter Irons, *The New Deal Lawyers* (Princeton: Princeton University Press, 1982), p. 10.

precedents—tools—to use in this legal forum, if the lawyer looks hard enough and the mass movements are powerful enough.

By 1936 most of these lawyers were not pursuing law careers solely out of self-interest or from some vague hope for upward social mobility. A significant but small minority had become Marxists, Communists, and Socialists, having come to believe in the power of the working class. They considered it their role, as lawyers, to study the contradictions inherent in the operation of a capitalist economic system housed in a democratic form of government. They believed in helping the mass movement by using provisions in the Constitution and laws passed by Congress during earlier progressive periods, and they were anxious to draft new laws for Congress to pass in its present New Deal mood.

Many lawyers got their start working against lynchings, legal and otherwise, in the cases of the "Scottsboro Boys" and Angelo Herndon, and representing people arrested in demonstrations called by the Unemployed Councils. Some came out of a populist tradition, and a great many were organized Democrats whose legal heroes had long been Clarence Darrow and Frank P. Walsh. They sat on the boards of the American Civil Liberties Union (ACLU), International Labor Defense (ILD), and International Juridical Association (IJA). They lent their time and efforts to the American Committee for the Protection of the Foreign Born and the American Labor Party. They used their legal skills to fight Fascism at home and abroad, representing veterans of the Abraham Lincoln Brigade returning from Spain and others arrested for deportation because of their political beliefs and activities. They attacked the Ku Klux Klan and supported anti-lynching legislation, defended hunger marchers and the unemployed, and lobbied in behalf of worker rights, civil liberties, racial equality, and low-cost legal services.

These lawyers were imbued with a strong spirit of reform and believed in the new regulatory state. Most resented the ABA's undisguised hatred of the New Deal. Some wanted a new lawyers' association that would defend the Roosevelt administration from attacks by legal conservatives. Most were appalled by the organized Bar's commercialism, preoccupation with corporate clients, and indifference to the changing imperatives of twentieth-century urban and industrial life. Many had studied law under the direction of the new "legal realists" and the advocates of "disinterested government service." Jerome Frank, Thurman Arnold, and William O. Douglas at Yale, Adolf A. Berle, Karl Llewellyn, and Walter Gellhorn at Columbia, Thomas Reed Powell and Felix Frankfurter at Harvard, Alexander Frey at the University of Pennsylvania, Felix Cohen at the New School for Social Research, Malcolm Sharp at Chicago, and others tried to demonstrate how to use the law in the interest of social change. They wanted to move their profession away from the stultifying, inflexible veneration of Supreme Court precedent and to direct Anglo-American common law toward a recognition of U.S. law as a social institution based on the Bill of Rights, Reconstruction Amendments, and acts of Congress. Beyond that, they wanted to fight openly for human rights over property rights.

The stock market crash gave their views a wider, more receptive audience; the New Deal provided a vehicle for their political expression. When reform-minded lawyers of the depression generation agreed that the law must serve the public interest as an instrument for social change, the conditions for the emergence of the National Lawyers Guild were in place.

THE BIRTH OF THE GUILD
By Maurice Sugar

[Maurice Sugar, the veteran Marxist labor lawyer from Detroit who became chief counsel of the United Automobile Workers of America, first proposed creation of a progressive Bar association in the early 1930s.]

In 1933, when I had just returned from the Soviet Union, I accepted an invitation to make a national lecture tour under the auspices of an organization called Friends of the Soviet Union. I spoke in some 33 cities from New York to Seattle.

I met attorneys who were attracted by my labor union connections. All were having experiences similar to mine. Many were suffering virtual ostracism because of their defense of those who otherwise would have been defenseless. Most had contributions to make, but there was no clearinghouse—indeed very little contact at all. The handicaps were great because so many of the problems were not merely local ones; they were of national import and could be tackled effectively only on a national scale.

By the time I returned to Detroit I had worked up an outline for a national bar association of liberal lawyers:

Suggestion for Association of Lawyers

1. A national organization of progressive, liberal, radical attorneys— with state and local units
2. Each unit, national, state and local, to elect its own officers
3. Each unit to concern itself with the problems of its own community— and, through correlation by the national office, with national problems
4. Annual dues—modest in amount, perhaps $2.00 or $3.00 per year— to be divided among the three units for the purpose of meeting clerical expenses, cost of stationery, and periodic publication of a bulletin
5. A national executive committee, with nationally known legal figures, active if possible, otherwise honorary (such as Darrow, Chafee, Frankfurter, Pound, Walsh, etc.)

"The Birth of the Guild," by Maurice Sugar, unpublished autobiography, Maurice Sugar Papers, Meiklejohn Civil Liberties Institute, Berkeley, Cal. (hereafter MCLI).

Suggested Divisions for Pursuance of Activities

1. Research Division
2. Legislative Division
3. Division of Civil Liberties and Democratic Rights
4. Lawyers Protective Division
5. Division of Economic Security for Lawyers

Benefits Flowing from Such an Association

1. Development of a united front in anti-Fascist struggles among lawyers of various degrees of political and economic education
2. The bringing of lawyers closer to the labor movement
3. Stimulation of lawyers in progressive, political activities such as the Farmer–Labor Party movement
4 Augmentation of ranks of lawyers available for work in labor defense, civil rights struggle, drafting of legislation, appearance before legislative committees
5. Furnishing national support to lawyers subjected to oppression in the pursuit of their labor, progressive, and liberal activities
6. Inspiration to sympathetic lawyers now isolated and discouraged
7. Education of lawyers to increase their efficiency in labor work
8. Utilization of lawyers for effective work in their spheres of influence

I felt that the place to get the best start would be in New York, and I sent the outline to some New York lawyers of my acquaintance. The idea was seriously considered by them. They agreed that there was need for such an organization but they doubted that the time was opportune to initiate it.

I was disappointed. As time went on I felt even more strongly that we must have such an association if we were to advance the progressive causes in which we were all interested, and if we were to give effective support to the New Deal measures which had been making their appearance and which, while capturing the imagination of the American people, were vigorously attacked by big business and their conservative legal representatives—prominent members of the American Bar Association.

So in the winter of 1935 I went to New York and met with a group of attorneys to give renewed consideration to the project. They were for it, but since theirs would be the task of launching it, they needed time to survey the situation and be properly prepared to do the launching. Finally, in December 1936, I received a letter from New York headed "Re: National Lawyers Guild," signed by the executive secretary who had been present at our meeting. He wrote, "Many of us in New York have been discussing and formulating plans for launching the organization you have in mind." He said that simultaneously others in the same city, unknown to them, "had been doing some thinking about the same thing." He said they got together and the result was a meeting of a group of liberal and progressive lawyers at which the National Lawyers Guild was launched.

The response was overwhelming. In February 1937, 600 lawyers from all over the country attended the founding convention. Among the founders were two federal judges, justices of two state supreme courts, two members of Congress, two state governors, and five law professors.

A temporary executive committee of 14 members included five incumbent judges; the governor of Wisconsin, Philip F. La Follette; the senator from Washington, Homer T. Bone. The distinguished Frank P. Walsh was the temporary president. The Guild's second president was Justice John P. Devaney of the Supreme Court of Minnesota. The solicitor general of the U.S., Robert H. Jackson, later to become a Supreme Court justice, was an early Guild member.

The first National Executive Committee included counsel for the ACLU; a justice of the Domestic Relations Court of New York; the counsel for the AFL; and a judge of the United States District Court at Chicago. They put me on it, too.

ORGANIZING LAWYERS TO, INTER ALIA, PACK THE SUPREME COURT
By Ann Fagan Ginger

The legal and commercial press reported the first meeting of the New York City Chapter on December 22, 1936, when Frank P. Walsh called to order the 600 lawyers who attended. They reported Walsh, Chairman of the New York Power Commission and a long-term member of the ABA, saying that the ABA, representing only a small minority of the nation's attorneys, "has degenerated into a sort of lawyers' trust." Dr. Karl N. Llewellyn, of the Columbia University Law School, said the position of a group of lawyers on such questions as a constitutional amendment to prohibit child labor was of no more value than that of a group of plumbers. "The abomination of abominations of the American Bar Association," he declared, "is not that they have been completely blind on every public question, but that they have been such lousy lawyers, such incompetent advocates of the position they maintain." Morris Ernst said he had refused for 20 years to join the ABA, ever since he

---

"Organizing Lawyers to, Inter Alia, Pack the Supreme Court," by Ann Fagan Ginger, in forthcoming biography of Carol King.

learned that it elected a Negro to membership "by mistake." He got into the habit of replying to the Association's annual invitation to join by asking whether Negroes can belong. Each year the ABA replied: "We're sorry; we didn't know you were a Negro."

The meeting ended with a great deal of enthusiasm and pledges to sign up new members. Among the recruits, Osmond K. Fraenkel, a noted ACLU lawyer, especially remembered Joe Brodsky, who had fought vigorously as attorney for the Communist Party, as a leader in the International Labor Defense, and as founder of the International Workers Order (IWO), a fraternal benefit society for foreign-born and poor working people. Fraenkel also mentioned S. John Block, old-time Socialist candidate for public office, and Felix Cohen, then in the Department of Interior, who was active in international matters and devoted to the welfare of American Indians.

On February 15, 1937, in preparation for the Guild's first national convention, the New York Chapter met at the Bar Association building to debate its stand on Roosevelt's plan to "do something" about the recalcitrant Supreme Court, which refused to uphold as constitutional much New Deal legislation. Three hundred lawyers attended the discussion on the President's proposal to "pack the Court" with enough additional justices to defeat the reactionary majority. The Guild went on record in favor of FDR's plan and agreed that "It is essential to the public interest to limit the power of the judicial review of legislation." The discussion then turned to the methods for amending the Constitution to limit the power of the judiciary.

Four days later the national convention opened in Washington, and the full range of the delegates' concerns became clear. The court-packing plan was approved but so, too, was a resolution urging passage of a constitutional amendment to protect social legislation from judicial veto. The convention endorsed the Child Labor Amendment, called for the enlargement and extension of Social Security benefits, continuation of public works and relief programs, wider employment opportunities for lawyers, and a new code of legal ethics acknowledging the responsibilities of the lawyer to society. Delegates overwhelmingly supported calls for a federal anti-lynching statute, an end to poll taxes and other discriminatory restrictions on voting. On civil liberties, the convention opposed censorship, teachers' loyalty oaths, and "all legislation making criminal the advocacy of the doctrines of, or membership in, any political party." The delegates also endorsed asylum for political refugees and urged the revision of U.S. immigration laws. The work of the Senate's La Follette Civil Liberties Committee was praised, and the convention strongly supported labor's right to bargain collectively and all legislation to protect that right.

At the end of its first year, the Lawyers Guild boasted 5,000 members from among the 175,000 lawyers in the country. Organized in part to support the court reorganization plan, the Guild was well on its way to becoming a large, broad-based, and influential voice for social justice.

NATIONAL LAWYERS GUILD
Constitution

PREAMBLE

Recent and developing social and economic changes are profoundly disturbing our nation and make new legal attitudes imperative. The legal profession must necessarily play an important role in shaping our changing legal structure. Having in mind these conditions and responsibilities, the National Lawyers Guild aims to unite the lawyers of America in a professional organization which shall function as an effective social force in the service of the people to the end that human rights shall be regarded as more sacred than property rights. This organization aims to bring together all lawyers who regard adjustments to new conditions as more important than the veneration of precedent, who recognize the importance of safeguarding and extending the rights of workers and farmers upon whom the welfare of the entire nation depends, of maintaining our civil rights and liberties and our democratic institutions, and who look upon the law as a living and flexible instrument which must be adapted to the needs of the people.

ARTICLE I—Name and Objects

Section 1. The name of this organization shall be the National Lawyers Guild.

Section 2. The objects of the organization shall be:

a. To aid in making the United States and the State constitutions, the law, and the administrative and judicial agencies of government responsive to the will of the American people;
b. To protect and foster our democratic institutions and the civil rights and liberties of all the people;
c. To promote justice in the administration of the law;
d. To aid in the establishment of governmental and professional agencies to supply adequate legal service to all who are in need or cannot obtain it;
e. To aid in the adoption of laws for the economic and social welfare of the people;
f. To keep the people informed upon legal matters affecting the public interest;

g. To advance the economic well-being of the members of the legal profession, and to improve the relations between the legal profession and the community at large;
h. To encourage, in the study of the law, a consideration of the social and economic aspects of the law; and
i. To improve the ethical standards which must guide the lawyer in the performance of his professional and social duties.

WHEELING AND DEALING WITH THE NEW DEAL
By Morris L. Ernst, Frank P. Walsh, and Franklin D. Roosevelt

[From the very beginning, the Guild was a significant and very visible supporter of the Roosevelt administration. One of the Guild's most well-known movers and shakers, New York attorney Morris L. Ernst, prided himself on his connections with prominent New Dealers and on his access to the President. Ernst's letter to Roosevelt implicitly links the new Lawyers Guild to a concurrent attempt to reform the Constitution. On February 5, 1937, Roosevelt shocked the nation by sending his court-packing plan to Congress, a proposal strongly endorsed by the Guild. Two weeks later FDR sent his "warm personal greetings" to the first annual convention.

[Frank P. Walsh, the NLG's first honorary president, was a veteran labor lawyer whose distinguished career included service as chairman of the U.S. Commission on Industrial Relations, co-chairman of the War Labor Board, chairman of the New York Power Authority (appointed by Governor Franklin Roosevelt), and chairman of the National Public Service Commission.]

January 18, 1937

Hon. Franklin D. Roosevelt,
The White House,
Washington, D.C.

My dear Governor:

I am writing to ask whether I could see you sometime for a few moments. I want to lay before you two matters which no doubt will be of interest to you:

"Wheeling and Dealing with the New Deal," by Morris L. Ernst, Frank P. Walsh, and Franklin D. Roosevelt, President's Personal File, Box 4411, Franklin D. Roosevelt Papers, Roosevelt Library, Hyde Park, N.Y.

1. Senator [George] Norris has agreed to preside at a convention in Washington the early part of March, at which there will be a wide exploration of the innumerable suggestions made for amending the Constitution. The Consumers League, labor groups, farm groups, and leading college professors will no doubt be in attendance. We hope to have a fair sprinkling of congressmen, governors, and judges. The implications of the conference may be more than subtle.

2. National Lawyers Guild is well under way with Frank Walsh as President. Its convention will be held in Washington on February 22. This is the first national answer to the Liberty League and the American Bar Association, being the main spokesman for the 175,000 lawyers in the United States. If you take the resolutions of the American Bar Association for a decade and put them in reverse, you will come fairly close to the program which the National Lawyers Guild will possibly promulgate at the Washington Birthday convention.

I stopped in last week one day and tried to see Steve Early in order to give him this data so that he could forward it to you. Both groups, however, would very much appreciate your slants on the two movements.

Respectfully yours,

[Signature]

Morris L. Ernst

MLE:DF

THE WHITE HOUSE
WASHINGTON

February 18, 1937

My dear Frank:

I wish much that I could have accepted the cordial and insistent invitation extended to me to take a part in this gathering of the National Lawyers Guild.

Since that was not possible I hope you will convey to all your associates my very warm greetings. I am sure that the results of this meeting will be well worth while. It is a time for progressive and constructive thinking, and having known most you intimately for many years I have every confidence that your deliberations will affect the welfare of your own profession and the well-being of the country at large. I send to all of you my hearty felicitations and warm personal greetings.

Very sincerely yours,

[Signature]

Franklin D. Roosevelt

Mr. Frank P. Walsh
President,
National Lawyers Guild
Shoreham Building,
Washington, D.C.

ORIGINS OF THE NATIONAL LAWYERS GUILD
By Mortimer Riemer

[On December 14, 1955, Mortimer Riemer, the first executive secretary of the Guild, appeared as a "friendly" witness before a HUAC subcommittee investigating Communist infiltration of the government. He renounced his own past Communist associations and identified former friends and colleagues in the Guild and NLRB as having once been members of the Communist Party. Even in the course of "naming names" and thus betraying the trust and confidences of past relationships, Riemer's testimony offers a powerful economic and social explanation of the forces that led to the creation of the National Lawyers Guild.]

TESTIMONY OF MORTIMER RIEMER, ACCOMPANIED BY COUNSEL, THOMAS A. BURKE

MR. TAVENNER: Will you state your name, please, sir?
MR. RIEMER: Mortimer Riemer.
MR. TAVENNER: What is your occupation or profession?
MR. RIEMER: I am an attorney.
MR. TAVENNER: Will you tell the committee, please, what your formal educational training has been for your profession?
MR. RIEMER: I graduated from the Syracuse, N.Y., Central High School in June of 1921. I graduated from Syracuse University in June, 1925,

---

"Origins of the National Lawyers Guild," testimony of Mortimer Riemer, "Investigation of Communist Infiltration of Government—Part 2," Hearings before Committee on Un-American Activities, 84th Cong., 1st sess. (Washington, D.C., 1956).

and graduated from the Law School of New York University in June of 1931. I was admitted to the New York Bar in 1932.

MR. TAVENNER: What was your first employment after engaging in the practice of law for a period of approximately 4 or 5 years?

MR. RIEMER: While I was still engaged in the practice of law in New York City, I became the executive secretary of the National Lawyers Guild.

MR. TAVENNER: Were you its first executive secretary?

MR. RIEMER: That is correct . . . in the late fall of 1936.

MR. TAVENNER: How long did you remain executive secretary of the National Lawyers Guild?

MR. RIEMER: Until the fall of 1939.

MR. TAVENNER: Will you tell the committee when you became a member of the Communist Party, and under what circumstances?

MR. RIEMER: I became a member of the Communist Party late in 1935 or early in 1936. I cannot give this committee the exact date of that step. But, as this committee knows, the mid-1930s was a period of great unemployment, unrest, confusion, and indecision, and I was particularly disturbed by those conditions domestically, and I was disturbed by events abroad, particularly in Germany. As a Jew, I was deeply concerned. And it was represented to me that the Communist Party had a program, an effective one, to contribute to a solution of some of those ills, and I was solicited to join and I did so.

I am glad now of the opportunity to make known what I did, and to explain to the committee how and under the circumstances it occurred.

MR. TAVENNER: Where was this group or cell of the Communist Party of which you became a member located in the city of New York?

MR. RIEMER: Some time after I became a member, I was assigned or directed to a lawyers group.

MR. TAVENNER: In what area?

MR. RIEMER: It was in Manhattan—I know that.

MR. TAVENNER: Before we go further I think that you should tell the committee by whom you were recruited into the Communist Party.

[The witness answered the question.]

MR. TAVENNER: Will you give the committee the names of those who were members of this Communist Party group with you?

[The witness answered the question.]

MR. TAVENNER: Did this group of the Communist Party become interested in any project in which the legal profession was particularly involved and concerned?

MR. RIEMER: Some time in 1935, I believe, there was organized in New York City an outfit called the Lawyers Security League. Now, who organized it and how it was organized and when it was organized, I do not know. I did not become a member of it until, I would say, the spring of 1936. Its primary function, as I later learned, was to secure employment for lawyers, and, due to the then economic condition of the Bar in New York City, the encroachments made upon the practice by the unauthorized practices of others, I would say there were literally thousands of lawyers who were either unemployed or just could not exist professionally.

MR. SCHERER: Do you happen to recall some of the other objectives in which the league was interested?

MR. RIEMER: It was primarily concerned, Mr. Scherer, with job opportunity.

MR. TAVENNER: Did it finally develop to the point where representatives were sent to the American Bar Association to promote certain of the worthwhile principles advocated by the league?

MR. RIEMER: Here is how that came about: I was at that time a member of the American Bar Association, and, prior to the year 1936, I had considered going to the Boston convention of the American Bar Association. I discussed with this committee of which I was chairman the possibility of some or all of us going to that convention. . . .

We were principally interested in getting the American Bar Association to endorse the idea of WPA projects for lawyers, making a study of the economic condition of the Bar, concerning which there was no real available data, or statistics at that time, or doing more about the unauthorized practice of law and issues of that nature.

MR. MOULDER: As I understand, your testimony is now concerning activities which are in no way related to the Communist domination or activities with which this committee is interested. Those are all worthwhile objectives that you had.

MR. TAVENNER: Did the Lawyers Security League develop later into another organization?

MR. RIEMER: Yes.

MR. TAVENNER: Just tell us briefly.

MR. RIEMER: Subsequent to the American Bar Association convention, there was a meeting in New York City held at the Association of the Bar of the City of New York, of the Lawyers Security League, at which I rendered a report on what had occurred at the American Bar Association convention. I said it seemed to me that the American Bar Association was not going to do too much about the economic condition of the Bar. It was not primarily concerned with that. I said that another approach had to be taken or other means devised if lawyers were going to do anything about their economic conditions in the profession at that time. At the meeting somebody urged a resolution that the committee be continued in power, and authorized to develop a program leading towards a meeting perhaps on a national basis to be held sometime around Thanksgiving of 1936, to see if it could evolve a program concerned with those conditions, which made it difficult, and in some cases almost impossible, for lawyers to gain a living professionally. So we undertook such a program, this committee of which I still continued to act as chairman. We attempted to contact people in other cities.

MR. TAVENNER: And that led, I am told, to the call for the first meeting of the National Lawyers Guild?

MR. RIEMER: That is right. That germ, or that idea that was thrown out, led to the thought or the idea of the National Lawyers Guild, and it was really the start of it. The idea was that if we confined or restricted ourselves to an economic program, you could not get liberal and progressive lawyers who were interested in other things to join with you, and that you had to have a well-rounded program incorporating a lot of things, in addition to such dry and dull subjects as the unauthorized practice of law.

TAKING HOLD OF THE PRESENT: WHO JOINED THE GUILD?
By the Editors

Joining the National Lawyers Guild in the late 1930s was an act of faith—that law could become a living instrument for social change—and an act of protest—against the staid reactionary policies of the legal establishment. It would be impossible, however, to compile a set of common characteristics shared by Guild members. In fact, what is most remarkable about this first generation is the heterogeneity of their personal background, cultural outlook, race, gender, and life-style. Just as it would be foolish to classify them by religion or class, it would be equally misleading to search for a common political perception beyond a general commitment to an activist government. What many did share was a willingness to confront and change current injustices by becoming founding members of the National Lawyers Guild.

Who joined the Guild?

JUSTINE WISE POLIER, daughter of Rabbi Stephen S. Wise, followed her graduation from college by working in the textile mills of Passaic, New Jersey. Blacklisted for union organizing convinced her that a law degree would be a powerful weapon against company thugs and employer espionage. She entered Yale Law School in 1925, one of only five women in a class of approximately 120, but continued to aid Passaic's workers during the 1926 textile strike.

Polier pursued her interest in labor law as a Workmen's Compensation referee and later helped develop the beginnings of New York's unemployment insurance system. Meanwhile, her political work brought her in contact with attorney Carol King and the group of lawyers who wrote about labor, civil liberties, and civil rights issues for the *International Juridical Association Bulletin.*

Justine Wise Polier once was asked to explain why a young New York lawyer would spend night after night working on something that had happened in Georgia or Alabama. Her response reveals much about the kind of person who joined the Guild:

> I think that younger people at that particular time had a much deeper sense of the terrible suffering that was all around them, and also the wonderful optimism that, if they worked hard enough, they could change things. . . . So, one lived two lives—one worked during the day at one's job, and then pitched into the things that seemed most important at night.

As New York state family court judge for four decades, president of the Field Foundation, and Chairman of the Eleanor Roosevelt Institute, Justine Polier continued to reflect such concerns.

CHARLES H. HOUSTON, descendant of free blacks and slaves, was born in Washington, D.C. He attended Harvard Law School, was the first black elected to the editorial board of the *Harvard Law Review*, and graduated with honors. After his admission to the Bar in 1924, he joined his father in practice and in teaching at Howard University. He worked as Dean of Howard University Law School to make it an accredited, nationally respected institution.

He was the architect and dominant force of the NAACP legal defense program and deliberately prosecuted the series of cases that culminated in *Brown v. Board of Education.* In speeches and writings on the condition of black Americans, Houston emphasized that the use of the law was an unparalleled tool for an oppressed minority. His encounters with the government, however, convinced him that political and economic realities worked against the elimination of institutional racism. Therefore, he devoted much of his life to protest as well as to litigation. In February 1937, Houston was elected to the executive board of the Guild, then the only integrated national Bar association in the United States.

LOUIS B. BOUDIN was born in Russia and came to the United States in 1891. He received his master's degree from New York University Law School and was admitted to the New York Bar in 1898. After a few years in general practice, he specialized in labor and constitutional law. Representing rank-and-file union members and international unions, both AFL and CIO, he worked to shape the law on many critical questions, particularly to extend constitutional guarantees of free speech and association to essential union activities—picketing, boycotts, and strikes.

Boudin was an extraordinarily gifted and productive scholar; his *Theoretical System of Karl Marx* (1907) remains a classic in Marxist philosophy. His *Government by Judiciary* (1932) established the tone for New Deal liberalism by rejecting the power of the courts to assert supreme authority over Congress, the President, and the people. As chairman of the Guild's Labor Law Committee, he helped write a number of authoritative briefs and reports that influenced legislation and litigation.

PEARL M. HART, born in Traverse City, Michigan, grew up in Chicago, earned her law degree from John Marshall Law School, and was admitted to the Illinois Bar in 1914. Heavily influenced by the national progressive movement for social reform and by the work of the remarkable women of Hull House, Jane Addams, Julia Lathrop, and Grace and Edith Abbott, Hart devoted herself to the problems of juvenile delinquency and child welfare.

She also made a lifelong commitment to protect the rights of the foreign-born against hounding by the Immigration Service, and counseled witnesses called before the House Un-American Activities Committee. In 1935 Eleanor Roosevelt named her one of only ten women in the country qualified to serve as president. She was the first national treasurer of the Guild, was long associated with its Civil Liberties Committee, and later served as president of the Chicago chapter.

HARRY SACHER, a fiery, caustic, brilliant trial lawyer, was born in 1902 in the Brownsville section of Brooklyn. He practiced law at the cutting edge of the social issues of his time and devoted his life to protecting the rights of the working class. During the 1930s he courageously represented the fledgling Transport Workers Union of New York City and never abandoned his commitment to radical unions and causes.

It was not in his nature to remain impartial, aloof, or restrained in representing his clients. In 1949, he was one of five lawyers in the nine-month trial of Communist Party leaders for violating the Smith Act. The jury convicted all the defendants, and the judge cited all the lawyers for conspiracy to disrupt the trial and for contemptuous behavior. Sacher was sentenced to six months in federal prison and was subsequently subjected to a protracted disbarment proceeding.

Called before the Senate Internal Security Subcommittee in 1955 to answer questions about whether he was a member of the Communist Party, he delivered an unforgettable speech:

I refuse to bend the knee to an inquiry concerning my innermost thoughts and beliefs, whether they be on politics, religion, or anything else. My conscience dictates to me that I shall not, under compulsion, answer today any more than John Freeborn Lilburn answered in the 1640s to the Court of Star Chamber and on the same grounds, Mr. Chairman . . . that it is incompatible with the dignity of the individual to make compulsory disclosure of his thoughts and his ideas and his beliefs.

Harry Sacher was elected to the first executive board of the Guild in 1937.

CAROL WEISS KING graduated from New York University Law School in 1920 at the height of the Red Scare's hysterical attacks on immigrants and other dissenters from "100 percent Americanism." She threw herself into the task of defending the dispossessed and the underprivileged. Her law practice was designed to aid people at the bottom of society, especially those who joined together to help themselves in unions and later in the American Committee for the Protection of the Foreign Born.

She worked on some of the most momentous legal issues of her time, playing a crucial role behind the scenes in the Scottsboro cases, *Herndon v. Lowry,* the repeated deportation trials of Harry Bridges, the Schneiderman case, and the Ellis Island hunger strike cases during the Cold War.

At the same time, Carol King was the principal organizer of the *International Juridical Association Bulletin.* For ten years she saw to it that the *Bulletin* kept the legal community abreast of the major issues involving labor, civil liberties, and civil rights. She quickly became the resident expert on immigration and naturalization law within the Guild. It was largely through her efforts that the courts held that the Administrative Procedure Act of 1947 applied to the Immigration and Naturalization Service, unless Congress expressly voted otherwise.

SAMUEL ROSENWEIN grew up in Brooklyn, New York, the product of the public schools and city street corners. After graduating from New York University Law School he joined the International Labor Defense and devoted himself to the protection of workers' rights. In 1941, he defended some of the teachers involved in the Rapp-Coudert committee attack on academic freedom in New York City. During World War II Rosenwein served as senior trial and appellate attorney in the Office of Price Administration. He was the executive secretary of the New York City Guild chapter between 1943 and 1945.

As the Cold War heated up in 1947, Rosenwein was one of the attorneys representing the Hollywood Ten before HUAC; and he also served as counsel for Bertolt Brecht, one of the nineteen "unfriendly witnesses" originally subpoenaed by the committee. Through the worst years of the McCarthy era, Rosenwein fought government oppression. He moved to Los Angeles and assisted in the appeal of *Yates v. United States,* the first in a line of cases that vitiated the Smith Act. In later years he formulated a paper on the illegality of U.S. involvement in Vietnam and testified before Bertrand Russell's War Crimes Tribunal on U.S. violations of the United Nations Charter.

In February 1937, Rosenwein became one of the brief-writing founding members of the National Lawyers Guild.

ELMER McCLAIN was anything but a typical Guild member. He did not live in New York City or specialize in either labor or personal injury law. But he was a very active member of the Guild who delighted in reminding his eastern friends that his home was in Lima (lī′ma), Ohio, and not Lima (lē′ma), Peru, as his more urbane colleagues pronounced it. No Guild convention was complete without McClain's impassioned and knowledgeable discussion of the farm problem.

■ TWO

Lawyers in the Struggle for Industrial Unions (1936–1940)

IN THE MID-1930s workers insisted that their right to organize and bargain collectively was as important as the employer's property right of ownership and control. This understanding emerged as the CIO succeeded in organizing the mass production industries, curbing the untrammeled power of major corporations in their dealings with employees. Worker militancy arising out of the Great Depression pushed the President and Congress into passing New Deal legislation that marked a basic change in industrial relations and transformed labor law into a major legal specialty. In the first hundred days of the New Deal, Congress passed Section 7a of the National Industrial Recovery Act, setting forth the right of workers "to organize unions of their own choosing" and to engage in collective bargaining. Though certain powerful elements on the political Right feared that the nation faced revolution, Congress did not provide workers with the legal protection to enforce Section 7a. Many employers responded to this political gesture with company unions, strike-breakers, lockouts, labor spies, and private police equipped with military arsenals.

Lawyers were in the forefront of these battles. Union attorneys defended workers' demands for union recognition; government lawyers working for the National Labor Board and its successor, the National Labor Relations Board (NLRB), tried at first through mediation and persuasion, and then through the Wagner Act's enforcement authority, to place the full weight of the federal government behind workers' right to organize and bargain collectively.

The Guild and its members played an important role in these struggles. Abraham Isserman, attorney for major CIO unions and the ACLU in New Jersey, filed early suits culminating in *Hague v. CIO,* in which Arthur T. Vanderbilt, former president of the ABA, representing the CIO, overturned antiunion city ordinances in a major Supreme Court decision. The Guild founding convention, coinciding with the United Automobile Workers successful sit-down strike in Flint, Michigan, enthusiastically endorsed both the campaign for industrial unionism and the preservation of civil liberties. Many of the attorneys representing the new CIO unions, such as Maurice Sugar, Lee Pressman, Edward Lamb, and William Standard, were Guild activists. Most of the NLRB lawyers, including two chairmen, Lloyd Garrison of the pre-Wagner Act Board and Warren Madden, as well as chief counsel Charles Fahy, Board secretaries Benedict Wolf and Nathan Witt, and Thomas Emerson, were also Guild members. The Guild endorsed the work of the NLRB, championed its recommendations for wage and hour legislation, and defended the agency against crippling amendments proposed by employer groups. The Guild also supported the Senate La Follette Civil Liberties Committee investigation of employer violence and worked to expand workers' legal rights while protecting their civil liberties.

THE CALL FOR A LIBERAL BAR
By Robert H. Jackson

[Robert H. Jackson was one of the New Deal's most effective legal advocates. In 1938, at the time of this address to the Guild's second convention, he was solicitor general and well on his way to a seat on the United States Supreme Court. This excerpt from his speech represents a clearly articulated vision of the New Dealers' commitment to the rights of working people and to the use of law for achieving social change.]

The history of progress in society is a story of struggle for better law. It has been one of the tasks of lawyers to translate the aspirations of our people into law, and into living institutions. In this their function has been vital to progress, and the call for their service is a continuing one....

Social and economic objectives belong to society, not alone to our profession. It is not the lawyer's function, though it is his right as a citizen, if he desires, to arouse or to stay the social forces that are driving for reform. We have no special call or competence for directing them. But it is our function to know those forces and to understand those movements which a restless day is fathering. It is not enough that we know the forces which brought about *Magna Carta* in the beginning of the thirteenth century, we must also understand the forces of today which demand social security and economic justice.

If we look understandingly at the liberal movement of the present we see that it is concerning itself more with economic rights and privileges than with political rights and privileges. Our generation is groping toward an economic bill of rights that will protect our people from irresponsible exercise of economic power, just as past generations worked toward the constitutional bill of rights which has long restrained the irresponsible exercise of political power....

"The Call for a Liberal Bar," by Robert H. Jackson, *NLG Quarterly* 1 (1937).

Still in the field of debate are other ideas which liberal men everywhere are trying to put into workable laws: collective bargaining for labor, the right to work free from industrial espionage, the ending of the oppression of starvation wages and sweatshop hours, the right of the willing to work, the right to a living when work is not available, the right to some shelter from the cruelties of impoverished age.

We begin to see that political rights, valuable as they are, too often depend on other rights. Due process of law loses much of its practical value to a man who cannot hire a lawyer. The franchise to vote for a mayor of a city may mean less than the right collectively to bargain for a fair wage. We must guard political rights by guarding the economic independence necessary to assert and defend those rights. These things our generation is trying to write into the law. . . .

The call of the liberal movement for counsel is to those free enough to think as part of the general social structure, and to place commonwealth before wealth in their intellectual interests. . . .

To such service the hopes of a people seeking counsel and leadership call us. To such service the liberal Bar will dedicate itself.

THE NEW DEAL LAWYER: THOMAS I. EMERSON AND THE NATIONAL LABOR RELATIONS BOARD
By Thomas I. Emerson, with the assistance of Joan P. Emerson

["To young radical-minded lawyers," as Tom Emerson reminds us in this memoir, "the NLRB was the glamour agency of the New Deal." The exhausting hours, frenetic pace, and extraordinary intellectual and emotional demands were intoxicants to the young idealistic lawyers who relished the personal responsibility and opportunity to shape policy and litigation strategy. Emerson arrived in Washington in 1933 after graduating from Yale, spurning offers from prestigious Wall Street law firms, and joined Walter Pollak's office, where his first case was *Powell v. Alabama* (1932), the landmark appeal in the "Scottsboro Boys" case. He spent a year with the National Recovery Administration before joining the NLRB, where he helped draft the brief in the Jones and Laughlin Steel case.]

Under the new National Labor Relations Board established by the National Labor Relations Act I was sent to Atlanta to handle the southern region. My second case involved the Clinton Cotton Mill in South Carolina. The textile union had filed charges under the Act alleging interference with union activities. I went to Clinton to investigate the matter.

"The New Deal Lawyer: Thomas I. Emerson and the National Labor Relations Board," by Thomas I. Emerson, with the assistance of Joan P. Emerson, Columbia University Oral History Collection, N.Y. Courtesy of the Emersons and Columbia University Oral History Collection.

The town seemed to be run by the mill and bank, with little objection from employees, union, or anyone else. I spent several days talking with union members, trying to find out what had actually happened in the situation. I made no attempt to contact the company or obtain a settlement. We then issued a complaint charging the company with unfair labor practices, and a hearing was held.

A male employee had circulated a petition in support of the company union. Attempting to demonstrate that this petition had been signed under pressure from foremen and other company agents, I seemed to be getting nowhere. After I had given up and we were about to adjourn, the trial examiner asked a simple question: "Isn't it true, Mr. Witness, that anyone who didn't sign this paper would have been discharged?" He answered, "Yes." One direct question established the proposition that I had been pussyfooting around for a half hour.

I had known this trial examiner in Washington. After the sessions were over each afternoon my wife and I went to the trial examiner's room for a drink and then we all went out to dinner together. As a matter of fact, the trial examiner would adjourn the hearings promptly at ten minutes of five. I was puzzled as to why he insisted on stopping at that precise time. It turned out that he had discovered the liquor stores closed at five o'clock and he wanted to supply himself with a bottle of Old Overholt for our cocktail hour. Later such "fraternization" of trial examiners and trial attorneys was strictly prohibited by the Board.

During my five or six months in the South I covered a good deal of South Carolina, Georgia, Alabama, and Tennessee. There was no doubt about the general anti-union atmosphere of the whole territory. Union organizers were chased out of town, or occasionally beaten up or subjected to other violence. I was never personally threatened, but company spies seemed to be present at all my dealings with the unions which involved any large gathering.

The labor groups were quite disorganized. I did not have the impression that there was any organized opposition to what we were doing in the various towns except from the parties involved in the case. Neither political support nor much interference for the Board's policies existed, except from the employer groups fighting the cases. No general effort was made to smear the Board or its agents by accusing them of subversive activities.

I was impressed by the poverty. Company houses were deteriorating, badly in need of paint, very drab and desolate. I have never been so cold as I was sitting in some of those houses without cellars. People seemed to be washed out at an early age. . . . The wages were extremely low. I saw pay envelopes for 3 cents and 27 cents because of deductions for rent, groceries, loans, etc.

Racial issues were surprisingly absent in our work. Negroes were not allowed to work in any of the industries I dealt with, except as loaders outside the plant. Overwhelmed with other issues, the unions were not thinking about creating employment for Negroes in the plants.

I was fascinated by this experience in the South. I look back on it as one of the most significant experiences in my whole career, partly because I was engaged in dramatic legal work, but also because I had contact with the grass-roots as trends and procedures were developing. I felt a sense of mission, a sense of active struggle against opposition, and a sense of accomplishment. I had believed from the very beginning that the National Labor Relations Act was the key piece of legislation in the New Deal. By establishing the power of labor to organize into associations, the Act was creating an institutional force which would support the liberal measures that the New Deal advocated.

DEFENDING UNPOPULAR CAUSES: THE DANGER OF CONTEMPT AND DISBARMENT
By Edward Lamb and Robert H. Jackson

[The independence of the Bar is a fragile commodity inordinately dependent on community mood and judicial tolerance. The explosive nature of the CIO's drive for industrial unionism and the NLRB's intervention in behalf of workers' rights disrupted the complacency and awakened the parochialism of one-industry towns.

[In August 1937, a judge in Portsmouth, Ohio, cited for contempt Edward Lamb, regional attorney for the CIO and executive vice-president of the National Lawyers Guild, for his vigorous objections to issuance of an anti-strike injunction. A specially appointed three-member committee then recommended disbarment on grounds that Lamb's conduct had been unprofessional, disrespectful, and had stirred up class hatred.

[The Guild immediately mobilized a National Defense Committee composed of such nationally prominent jurists as Federal Judge William H. Holly, Solicitor General Robert H. Jackson, and Assistant Attorney General Thurman Arnold. The following selection includes an excerpt from Lamb's closing statement at his disbarment hearing and portions of a letter written in his behalf by Jackson.]

May it please the Court:

I am a lawyer for labor and various other democratic causes. Today I am faced with disbarment charges.... I am charged with "moral turpitude" because I aggressively bespoke the rights of my trade union client, the United Shoe Workers, who were on strike against the Williams Shoe Manufacturing Company at Portsmouth, Ohio....

It is difficult for a lawyer to speak without feeling when faced with

---

"Defending Unpopular Causes: The Danger of Contempt and Disbarment," by Edward Lamb and Robert H. Jackson, NLG Pamphlet, 1938.

the possibility of being stripped of his profession. . . . My life has been devoted to the cause of unpopular clients and of persons whose civil liberties have been stripped away. And all my life I shall continue fighting the battle of the underdog. My devotion to the cause of labor shall not be determined by a single defeat or victory—I have enlisted for the course of the war. Many have said that these proceedings were instituted against me because I defended a labor union client. I can only assure my friends and my family that a man of honor and character who enters the legal profession with the intent of preserving the democratic process must remind himself that his task must ever be that of a bulwark against oppression. . . .

I deem it necessary to retain a clearness of vision so that when labor enters the courts it may be represented by attorneys who are not terrorized or discriminated against because of veiled threats to their professional liberty. I therefore conceive it to be the duty of this Court to dismiss the charges filed against me with a clear and courageous statement as a reassurance to the members of our profession that causes of every nature shall be given an adequate defense in court.

[When Solicitor General Robert Jackson was attacked for defending Lamb, he issued this forceful reply.]

I usually ignore criticisms, on the theory that friends require no explanation, enemies will accept none, and others do not care. Since your criticism has been so painstaking . . . I shall depart from my usual rule. . . . You suggest that the defense of Lamb proceeds from a desire to break down the judicial system. This, it seems to me, shows a lack of understanding. . . . We cannot have a worthy judicial system unless we protect the right of advocates to champion the cause of any person who becomes involved in the machinery of the law. I know of no group today that needs competent lawyers to defend it in the courts more than labor. . . . I, with the other members of the Lamb Defense Committee, will leave no stone unturned to see that this effort does not succeed, and to focus public opinion on the effort if it is persisted in.

[On June 30, 1938, Edward Lamb expressed "regret" for certain "discourteous" remarks. The Court accepted the apology; all charges were dismissed.]

CIVIL LIBERTIES AND THE NLRB—1940
By Nathan Greene

[The Supreme Court decision upholding the constitutionality of the National Labor Relations Act did not stop employer attacks on the NLRB. Employers'

"Civil Liberties and the NLRB—1940," by Nathan Greene, *National Lawyers Guild Practitioner* (hereinafter *NLG Practitioner*) 38:4 (Fall 1981).

associations, aided by a conservative, anti-union Congress, launched a powerful counteroffensive aimed at emasculating the NLRB's authority.

[In this 1940 speech, Nathan Greene, editor of the *International Juridical Association Bulletin,* argues that employers' right to free speech must be judged against their workers' right to human dignity and freedom from fear.]

We have special reasons these days to cherish liberty and a special obligation to defend it. Any man or group of men or institution, inside or out of the government, which is loyal to the demands of this concept must be given quick and whole support; and any man or institution which challenges this concept must be exposed and fought. I propose briefly to inquire whether, from this projection, the NLRA and the NLRB merit support or merit rebuke.

Prior to April 12, 1937, the date of the Supreme Court decisions upholding the constitutionality of the NLRA (301 US 1), the Jones and Laughlin Steel Corporation freely exercised a liberty, in the town of Aliquippa, which it deemed fundamental and which it was entitled to believe was a basic item in the Bill of Rights. The content of that liberty was expressed by a writer for the *St. Louis Post-Dispatch* in this way:

An elaborate system of espionage permeated not only the plants but extended into the schools, churches, lodges, and even the homes. Nothing was too small to pass unnoticed. The most innocuous remark was apt to be carried to the boss, perhaps twisted in the telling. A check was put against a man's name at the first offense, but if too many checks accumulated he was likely to find himself out of a job, perhaps run out of town.

What happened to this liberty we all know. First the Act struck it down; then the Board struck it down; finally the odd man on the Supreme Court struck it down.

Prior to April 12, 1937, the Republic Steel Corporation exercised a liberty which it deemed fundamental and which it was entitled to believe was a basic item in the Bill of Rights. An extract from a Board decision will serve to illuminate that liberty:

By its espionage, shadowing, and beatings of organizers and active members of the Union; its announcements, before and after the presentation by the Union of its proposed agreement, that it would not sign any contract with the Union; its statements to its employees attempting to vilify and discredit the Union; its threats to discharge union members and to close its plants before recognizing the Union; its attempts to turn civil authorities, business, and other interests against the Union in order to further its own anti-Union activities; its incitement of violence and hysteria, in order to terrorize union adherents.

What happened to this liberty we all know. First the Act struck it down; then the Board struck it down; then a Court struck it down.

These are but a few samples of dead liberties. Other like liberties also have been trampled under foot by the Labor Board in glass, in rubber, in autos, in textiles, in the lead-dust of Tri-States, on the water, on the waterfront and back of the waterfront in the East, South, West, and the Great Lakes. Yes, the Labor Board has been poison to an employer's liberty to intimidate, to harass, to coerce, to black-list, to spy upon, to discriminate against, to favor, to dominate.

What may we say in fair summary of what the Act and the Board have done *to* liberty and *for* liberty? To liberty: they have in many places checked the employer's freedom to run his business in his own way; they have in many places checked the employer's "inalienable" freedom to hire and fire; they have, as Judge Hand reminded us only the other day, checked the employer's freedom to turn his back upon a labor union; and, also in other ways, they have narrowed the employer's freedom to be irresponsible in the use of his economic power. For liberty: they have raised millions of workingmen to the dignity of free human beings; they have given millions of workingmen access to freedoms about which they had become deeply cynical; they have lifted from freedom's *use* by these millions the paralyzing terror of economic degradation.

I have heard an important person in this city defend what he called Henry Ford's right of free speech in the cases I have discussed, in this way. He said, "I am for free speech though the universe shall smash." Forgive the IJA. We are for free speech in an unsmashed universe, or, to narrow the figure just a little, in an unsmashed world. We believe speech and the other civil liberties are meaningful only to men who dare to use them. And that before "daring" come bread and water, come roots in the community, comes respite from fear. Only a reasonable whole world, not a "smashed" world, will ever tolerate free speech.

■ THREE

Shadows of War and Fear (1937–1941)

WITHIN A YEAR of its founding the Guild faced a more hostile political climate. Liberals were on the defensive, unable to counteract a conservative backlash fueled by middle-class alarm over the CIO-led sitdown strikes, an economic recession that saw breadlines return and relief rolls soar, and hostile reactions to the court-packing plan.

A darker side to conservative (and some liberal) frustration was reflected in the creation of the House Committee on Un-American Activities (HUAC) under the leadership of Martin Dies. The Guild vigorously denounced the Dies Committee's assault on all progressive movements. Its Civil Liberties Committee fought passage of the Smith Act for attacking the rights of citizens and aliens to advocate social change. When friends and veterans of the Abraham Lincoln Brigade were accused of criminal activity, Guild lawyers rushed to their aid. After the American Legion, HUAC, and state "Little Dies" committees barred minority parties from the ballot, Guild lawyers documented official misconduct and urged the Justice Department to take action.

This refusal to surrender to the assault on human rights manifested itself in other ways. The Guild introduced the concept of low-cost neighborhood law offices to address needs of community residents and underemployed lawyers. It supported expansion of the civil service system to include government legal positions and welcomed creation of law-student chapters to help demystify the law. According to Hubert T. Delany, City Commissioner of Taxes and Finance, the New York Chapter hosted the National Bar Association convention in 1939, which marked a significant gain for democracy and civil liberties. The Guild campaigned for a separate Civil Liberties division within the Justice Department and worked effectively for an investigation of the activities of the FBI.

The Guild's growing public involvement with domestic and foreign policy questions stimulated a vigorous debate over the kind of association the Guild should be and on what subjects it should express opinions. Should the Guild avoid controversial issues and confine itself to what had been defined as strictly legal questions? What was the relationship between politics and professionalism? Were domestic politics and international diplomacy appropriate areas of Guild concern? These were just some of the issues facing the Guild as it entered a period of war and fear.

THE THIRD ANNUAL CONVENTION: 1939 IN CHICAGO
By Ann Fagan Ginger

[The infectious spirit and commitment to common goals that had allowed the Guild to submerge internal differences during its first two years began to wane by the end of 1938. The national mood reflected a backlash against liberalism—whether it was the militant organizing drives and sitdown strikes led by the CIO, or the increased suspicion of Communist participation in liberal organizations.

[In the following selection, Ann Fagan Ginger recalls the 1939 Chicago convention meetings of the National Executive Board (NEB) as Guild leaders debated the merits of a resolution that denounced dictatorships of the Left and Right.]

On Friday morning, under "new business," Morris Ernst, who had helped start the Guild, told NEB members that he had come to the conclusion that the greatest obstacle to growth of the Guild was the fact that the public had misconstrued the position of the Guild. "Therefore, I intend to present a proposed amendment making clear that we are for democracy, and the Bill of Rights, and we are opposed to Communism, Fascism, and Nazism." He was not going to ask that it be adopted by the Board, but he thought that "short of such a declaration by us, we are going to have a hard time clearing our record before the public."

So began three days of intense discussion and parliamentary maneuvering by the diverse elements making up the Guild. The members had to deal with the substantive issue raised by Ernst, the opposition to his approach, and the procedural questions of who should resolve the issue and how this could be done with the least negative impact on the Guild.

The Board met again Friday at 4:00 P.M. Ernst raised his issue a second time. He proposed that the following language be added to the Guild constitution:

The National Lawyers Guild is deeply concerned at this time with the organized attacks which are being made in this country upon the fundamentals of our democratic processes. We therefore reaffirm our faith in the Bill of Rights, in freedom of speech, press, assembly, and religious worship. We are opposed

---

"The Third Annual Convention: 1939 in Chicago," by Ann Fagan Ginger, in forthcoming biography of Carol King.

to dictatorship of any kind, whether Left or Right, whether Fascist, Nazi, or Communistic.

Ernst said that, as to the merits of his proposal, there could be no possible objection "other than from persons who believe in dictatorship." He believed that thousands of lawyers "are ready to join the National Lawyers Guild as soon as we make this pronouncement," and that President Ferdinand Pecora said he had been talking to leading government lawyers, who had clearly indicated that they were reluctant to join because of the misconception that the Guild possibly had a preference for some kind of dictatorship rather than the Bill of Rights and democratic process.

Ernst said, "I am told that this is a form of red-baiting," but he added that he was not afraid of this charge.

After the Ernst motion was seconded, President Pecora adjourned the heated meeting so that everyone could attend the convention banquet. A large number of delegates had been told about the "Ernst issue" by this time, and listened to Pecora's remarks with that dispute in mind:

The National Lawyers Guild stands four-square behind democracy. Directly and by all the implications of our Constitution, we are pledged to the protection of our democratic institutions. That means that we oppose any and all ideologies or political philosophies which challenge them; whether from the Right or from the Left. Communism, Fascism, Naziism—any "ism," be it of native or alien origin—which seeks to supplant our democracy is a target for our attack. We denounce and will combat any system subversive of the principle of democracy upon which America is bedrocked.

Having heard these words, the NEB reconvened at 10 P.M., with 28 members present, surrounded by a roomful of delegates who had heard about Ernst's proposal. There was some sparring about how the issue should be brought to the convention, and whether the Board should be discussing the issue in front of so many non-Board members. But Professor Alexander Frey, of the University of Pennsylvania Law School, soon confronted the real issue. Describing himself not only as a Guild member but also as chairman of the Philadelphia chapter of the ACLU, he opposed the Ernst motion. Any change in the Guild constitution, he believed, would suggest that there was some justification for the charge that the Guild had been favoring a dictatorship from the Left.

Lawyers who were in or near the Communist Party opposed Ernst's proposal for many reasons. They saw it as divisive because it would require people to define their attitudes toward Fascism and Communism at a time when the important task of New Dealers and all democratic forces was to join together to oppose Fascism. They did not think it would help to discuss in the NEB the underlying issues: Do U.S. Communists favor or oppose democracy? What is their stand on dictatorship? They had debated these questions with their fellow lawyers many times through the years. Now it was time to stand on their records as civil liberties and labor lawyers, to limit the debate, to defeat the proposal, and to move forward on the Guild program.

The argument continued until Ernest Cuneo offered a substitute for Ernst's motion. Cuneo moved that President Pecora's banquet address "be by acclamation declared the will and intent of the purposes of the Guild" and that a copy be mailed to each member and to the public.

After another midnight hour of hot debate, Professor Malcolm Sharp, of the University of Chicago, proposed that the Board thank President Pecora for his address, record their general agreement with the position there stated, and ask the editors of the *Lawyers Guild Quarterly* to print the address in their next issue. The Board unanimously adopted Sharp's motion, and the meeting adjourned at 1:30 A.M.

But the matter was not over.

On Sunday morning the Board met again to reconsider the motion passed early Saturday morning. Osmond Fraenkel, a firm but quiet leader in the Guild and the ACLU, said bluntly: "I want it understood that the adoption of this resolution is going to put an end to this controversy which was precipitated by Mr. Ernst's resolution. If so, vote for it. If not, vote against it."

Lawyer after lawyer took the floor in short, eloquent speeches worthy of the summation in a big case to a judge or jury. Finally, Judge Patrick H. O'Brien of Michigan spoke. A portly white-haired Irishman originally from the Upper Peninsula, he had missed Pecora's speech, but had read it Sunday morning. "When I joined the Guild," he said, "it may be I have a very hazy conception, but I thought it stood for the utmost freedom of conscience in the very broadest sense of the term. And I hoped that when I came here I would meet in the Guild and be able to cooperate with men of many different philosophical views."

Judge O'Brien said the Guild chapter in Detroit had faced the same sort of proposition Ernst had just presented. It had found a lot of opposition. Some men who had been New Dealers withdrew, and there was a gradual swing away from the Guild by those who said the Guild was Communistic and so forth, and felt that the Guild would be a fine place if it did not have this or that fellow as a member.

"We went through that whole business. We conquered it, and we now have a number of conservative lawyers who have joined us." O'Brien said the Guild should be willing to welcome anyone, feeling that "nothing human is alien to us."

He wanted to see Pecora's speech printed but did not want to say whether he agreed with it until he had studied it. "That is not important.

The Guild is known now as a liberal organization of lawyers," as an organization that is "free intellectually," that is attempting "to interpret some of the social and economic views of the more radical thinkers. . . . If it is going to be just another American Bar Association, I do not want to belong to it. If our purpose is to defeat legally any sort of social or legal progress, then we are not going to develop and train our members so they can advance social progress."

Isidor Lazarus stated the view of another group: "It is a fact that many people in many fields have been overenthusiastic in the Guild in the past and have tried to use the Guild, with the most idealistic motives, to advance political philosophies of one kind or another. Mr. Ernst has done us a service in calling attention to dangers" in this approach and asking whether we are willing to concentrate on Americanism, whether we are "willing to tackle problems we already have under our present institutions." Lazarus said he was thankful to Judge Pecora, and endorsed his speech 100 percent, "although I would not write it that way. It is the spirit that we are opposed to using the Guild for political attacks upon the American system of doing business."

Harry Sacher, the short, feisty New Yorker, said that the discussion had disclosed that "our fundamental concern is not really the resolution but appreciation on our part that we are not confined to purely professional problems." Some rose to warn against the idea that men would resign from the organization if their position on this motion did not prevail; others assured the body that this, of course, would not occur.

Finally, President Pecora called for a vote on the motion to publish his speech in the Guild *Quarterly* and send it to all members who subscribe. Those in favor rose: 28. None opposed. One lawyer abstained. The NEB members returned to the Convention, which in due course elected Judge John Gutnecht of Chicago president.

But the matter was still not over.

RESIGNATIONS FROM THE NATIONAL LAWYERS GUILD
By Martin Popper

[The anti-Communist issue that had so disrupted the Guild's convention in February 1939 would not go away. News of the Nazi-Soviet Non-Aggression Pact in August and the start of war in Europe in September allowed a powerful number of New Deal insiders to resurrect the "Red" question. Led by Securities and Exchange Commissioner Jerome Frank, his former law partner Morris Ernst, and one-time Assistant Secretary of State Adolf A. Berle, Jr., power struggles developed in the New York and Washington chapters.

"Resignations from the National Lawyers Guild," by Martin Popper, Oral History Memoir, MCLI.

[In the following oral history memoir Martin Popper, newly elected as Guild executive secretary, recalls the 1940 convention, the departure of the organization's most recognizable political figures, and Robert W. Kenny's first days as Guild president.]

The Guild was involved in an enormous controversy at that time about the insistence of a segment of the membership that we adopt a resolution equating Germany and the Soviet Union—Fascism and Communism in some form. It was probably one of the things which resulted in Bob Kenny's becoming President. There were many people who would otherwise have been willing to serve who were not then. But Bob Kenny was at that time a state senator from Los Angeles County and already a leading member of the Democratic Party in California. He realized the Guild was in difficulty as a result of this controversy, didn't duck the difficulty, and was willing to take on the post of president.

I had not known Bob before then. We met each other at the convention. The office was in Washington at that time, and we went down together right after the convention. When we got there we went to the Guild office and found a closed door, with a stack of telegrams and letters, from the floor to the top of the door, of resignations. That was our introduction to our officership. Well, I went back to Bob's hotel with him. It was a hot summer day. Bob lay on his bed in the nude; there was no airconditioning in those days, and they had fans on the ceiling that circulated air—so he lay on his bed.

We talked about problems of the Guild because he was going back to California the next day. He got a telephone call from either Jerome Frank or Berle, and they said, in effect, that there were a lot of problems in the Guild now. They were representing a group of very important officials in the Roosevelt administration. There was Robert Jackson and Berle and Frank, and I guess by that time Abe Fortas was involved, and they were associated in this group in New York with Morris Ernst. They said to Bob, "Look, we have a lot of problems, especially here in Washington, and we are so busy that we can't pay attention to those problems in the chapter particularly, and we think there's a lot of Communist domination in the chapter. What we think we ought to do is resign as members of the chapter and remain as members-at-large."

Bob's immediate reaction, and mine too, was: "Well, O.K., I mean if that's the limit at which you feel you can remain in the Guild, by all means remain in the Guild and don't get out, if you want to be members-at-large." And so Bob said, "Fine," and they said, "We'll get back to you." And then some time later whoever it was who called in the first place, called again, and said, "Look, we've talked about it among ourselves, and we're willing to do that, provided the following people resign from the National Board," and they gave a group of people whom they wanted to resign on the ground that they were too Left or too influenced by Communist thoughts, or whatever the phrase. Bob's immediate reaction was we couldn't do anything like that, so the deal fell through.

FBI OPERATIONS, 1940–1941
By Michael Krinsky, Jonathan Moore, and Ann Mari Buitrago

[On February 6, 1940, a series of events began that apparently led to the first FBI surveillance of the Guild. Eleven people were arrested in Detroit for conspiracy to violate the Enlistment in Foreign Service Act for having allegedly recruited people to fight in defense of the Spanish republican government. On February 16, the new attorney general, Robert Jackson, ordered dismissal of all charges. Ernest Goodman, their Guild lawyer, celebrated the victory and worked with New York attorney Max Lowenthal and Senator George Norris (Rep.-Neb.) for a Justice Department investigation of the FBI. This ended in a whitewash report on May 3, submitted by Jackson to Norris, who responded in his last major speech: "It is my humble judgment . . . that Mr. [J. Edgar] Hoover is doing more injury to honest law enforcement in this country by his publicity-seeking feats than is being done by any other one thing connected with his organization."

[On June 19, 1940, Walter Winchell's syndicated column reported a speech by Goodman attacking the FBI. Goodman wrote Winchell, emphatically denying the statement attributed to him, and sent a copy to Winchell's editors. Winchell did not respond to Goodman, but sent Goodman's letter to the Associate Director of the FBI. Hoover responded to Winchell's possible problem with his editors by confirming the accuracy of the remarks Winchell attributed to Goodman, based on a "confidential informant who heard his speech."]

Comparison of all the relevant material in the FBI files suggests that this quotation, taken from the June 10th report of "New York Paid Confidential Informant Gunther Reinhardt," was sent on that same day to the Attorney General and to Winchell for use in his June 19th column.

Thus, the first use the FBI made of information gathered on the NLG was to neutralize Guild criticism of the FBI by engineering a public attack on the NLG and to shore up Hoover's allies in their attacks upon the Guild. It should be noted that the director's desire to supply FBI information in aid of an attack on the NLG was strong enough to overcome the frequently proclaimed policy that FBI files were confidential.

"FBI Operations, 1940–1941," by Michael Krinsky, Jonathan Moore, and Ann Mari Buitrago, Plaintiff's Principal Factual Papers in Opposition to the Motion of the United States of America for Partial Summary Judgment Dismissing the Damage Claims Arising from the FBI's Conduct and in Support of Plaintiff's Cross-Motion for Partial Summary Judgment, volume 1, National Lawyers Guild, Plaintiff, against Attorney General, et al., Defendants, Sept. 26, 1984.

Six months after the Goodman/Winchell incident, the FBI's Washington Field Office (WFO) surreptitiously entered the NLG's national office in Washington, D.C., and photographed the entire corpus of the Guild's files. This material was retyped into a 775-page WFO Report, dated May 15, 1941 and known by its author's name as the Dawsey Report.

It is clear that this material could have been copied only *inside* the NLG's offices. There are specific references in the Dawsey Report to the sources of this material, e.g., the Minute Book of the NLG Executive Committee and the ledger cards at NLG headquarters, and it concludes with the following comment: "The information quoted in this report was obtained from photographic or mimeographed copies of correspondence obtained through a *highly confidential source* and from publications issued by the National Lawyers Guild." The words "highly confidential source" represent language used by the FBI to indicate warrantless burglaries. This burglary was conducted at a time when the FBI did not even have Department of Justice authorization to *investigate* the Guild.

Just prior to the break-in, Hoover had made an unsuccessful effort to secure authorization to investigate the Guild. He wrote to a Department of Justice official on December 20, 1940, requesting authorization to initiate an "investigation of the alleged Communist connections, affiliations, direction, and control" of the NLG and ten other organizations. The letter was addressed to Lawrence M. C. Smith, who had just been appointed head of a newly created Special War Policies Unit. The Attorney General had assigned to that Unit responsibility for "departmental planning for the war, as well as analysis and evaluation of FBI intelligence reports and the review of names placed on the Custodial Detention List."

Hoover's letter to Smith stated: "From time to time newspaper dispatches indicate that the several organizations named hereinafter are Communist-dominated or controlled. In view of these allegations I would appreciate being advised whether the Bureau should conduct investigations for the purpose of determining the foundation of these charges."

The FBI received Smith's reply on January 13, 1941:

It would seem to me that a mere charge in a newspaper, particularly in the absence of any indication in those dispatches or of any facts now in your possession reflecting the possibility of a violation of a federal criminal statute by those organizations in connection with which a knowledge of the alleged Communist connections, affiliations, direction, and control would be useful, is *not sufficient grounds for an investigation.*

The FBI understood that this exchange had the effect of denying it authorization to investigate the Guild. In fact, during this period, and the many years thereafter in which it sought such authorization, the FBI repeatedly asserted that no investigation of the Guild had ever been conducted. However, when FBI Director William Webster looked at the files in 1979, he reported that the FBI had been investigating the Guild since 1941.

NEIGHBORHOOD LAW OFFICES, WOMEN LAWYERS, AND WORKING WIVES
By Robert D. Abrahams and The Guild Lawyer

[The Guild continued to demonstrate its commitment to social and economic reform in spite of the growing illiberal mood of the time. We begin this selection with an evaluation by Robert Abrahams of the neighborhood law office experiment in Philadelphia, followed by a questionnaire required of all lawyers interested in starting such offices in New York City. The final two documents reflect Guild interest in the problems of women as workers and as lawyers.]

■

By Robert D. Abrahams

1. There is a large section of the public, in the lower-income group in Philadelphia, which does not now find readily available a proper legal service at a fair price.

2. This public will respond readily to a service brought to it in the neighborhood in which it lives.

3. The neighborhood lawyer, in order to establish his practice, must be more than a man who merely sits in his office wishing he were downtown. He must participate in the life of his neighborhood in the same way as the lawyer in the small town participates in the life of the town.

4. Above the relief neighborhoods, the poorest neighborhood is the best one for neighborhood practice. Neighborhoods of higher income groups prefer offices with more "front."

5. There is a vast amount of preventive law work to be done, and very little such work is being done at the present time—by lawyers.

6. The five maxims of practice we set up for the participants have proved their worth.

   (a) Preventive law is to justice what preventive medicine is to health.
   (b) It is the dignity of the client, not that of the lawyer, which counts.
   (c) The lawyer should not be remote from his client either in geography or in understanding.

"Neighborhood Law Offices, Women Lawyers, and Working Wives," by Robert D. Abrahams, *Lawyers Guild Review* 1:1 (Oct. 1940), and the *Guild Lawyer* editors, *Guild Lawyer* (Sept. 1939, Sept. 1940, and Oct. 1940).

(d) The lawyer who makes a mystery of his fees makes a critic of his client.

(e) The lawyer who gives a service earns a fee.

7. The Canons of Ethics, with regard to advertising, need drastic revision. The whole Bar must tell the whole public what services are available and where. If the whole Bar won't do it, then individual Bar associations or committees must undertake to do the job. It is unfair to the public to establish clinics, neighborhood offices, or any other legal service projects and not let the public know about it.

The Guild has a great opportunity in the Legal Service field. What can be more worthy than the efforts of any Guild chapter to try to bring the lawyer and his proper clientele together? Don't follow the Philadelphia Plan. Devise your own, but, by all that's holy, don't talk about it — do it!

∎

By The Guild Lawyer, *October 1940*

The following information about each selected district will be required before approval of the locality.

I. Describe physical character of neighborhood where office is proposed.

II. Describe the character of the population.

Describe national, racial, religious, and language groupings.

Determine so far as possible what proportion of the population is engaged in business, in practicing professions; or employed by others and describe nature of business, professions, and employment.

Determine so far as possible what portion of the employed group are white-collar workers, skilled labor, unskilled labor, or government employees.

Determine what proportion of the population of the neighborhood is employed by WPA, NYA,* or other relief projects.

What portion of the neighborhood is on relief?

Determine so far as possible the educational and cultural background of the population.

Locate and describe civic, political, and other organizations of general interest, if any.

III. Describe courts and legal facilities already in neighborhood.

(Name and location of court or courts. Type of litigation handled in such court or courts.)

---

*Works Progress Administration and National Youth Administration

Locate and describe law offices presently existing in the neighborhood.

Describe so far as possible the nature of the practice now carried on in such offices.

Locate and describe such agencies as may be rendering legal or quasi-legal services, such as notaries public, steamship ticket agents, undertakers, marshals, real estate, insurance or business brokers, banks, trusts or title companies, stationery stores engaged in selling legal blanks, Legal Aid Societies, etc.

IV. Describe nature of law business anticipated in proposed office such as:

(a) Advice
(b) Workmen's Compensation
(c) Social Security
(d) State Workmen's Unemployment Insurance
(e) Wages and Hours
(f) Immigration and Naturalization
(g) Small Claims and Wages
(h) Domestic Relations
(i) Negligence matters
(j) Legal instruments
(k) Notary's services
(l) Civil Service matters
(m) Criminal and Quasi-Criminal matters
(n) Landlord and Tenant matters
(o) Any others, etc.

Give reasons for such anticipation.

V. Reasons for choosing specific locations.

VI. Any other pertinent information.

■

Woman Lawyer Committee Active

September 1940

The Committee on The Woman Lawyer of the National Lawyers Guild, of which Minna F. Kassner is Chairman, participated in Women Lawyers' Day at the World's Fair held on September 14th, 1940. Other participating organizations included the National Association of Women Lawyers, the Brooklyn Women's Bar Association, Queens County Women's Bar Association, Nassau County Women's Bar Associations, Bronx Women's Bar Association, New York Women's Bar Association, and the New Jersey Women Lawyers Club.

Women attorneys from almost every State of the Union were present, and a number of prominent women judges took part in the program. The final event was a dinner at the National Advisory Committee's Building on the fair grounds. The Chairman was Vesta J. C. Skehan, a New York City attorney. Magistrate Anna Moskowitz Kross presided as Toastmaster.

The Committee on The Woman Lawyer of the Guild has again shown its interest in concerted action on the part of women lawyers' groups. It is hoped that such action will be possible in the future along the lines of furthering progressive legislation and improving the status of women generally throughout the country.

Justice Kenyon Defends Right of Wives to Jobs

September 1939

A near riot occurred at a meeting of the Institute of Human Relations in the course of a debate on the right of married women to hold jobs, held at Williamstown, Mass.

Justice Dorothy Kenyon heatedly defended that right. Mrs. Cornelia Straton Parker just as heatedly opposed. The audience booed and cheered—depending on their age, the old apparently agreeing with Mrs. Parker. Even the unmarried women in the audience had decided opinions, and were very willing to express them.

Justice Kenyon said that most women are working for the same reason that every one else works—they need money. She said in part: "If our economic system were so geared that their husbands could earn enough to support a family, these women would not need to work. Most of them would be glad to be able to spend their time in comfortable, secure homes. It would be a terrific hardship to many homes if married women were deprived of the right to work."

Mrs. Parker thought otherwise. She said, in part: "The most important thing that any woman can be in this world is a successful wife, mother, and homemaker. I concede there may be an infinitesimal group of women in this country who can be all three, but I never met any of them.... Any married woman who likes a job is a living example of the failure of our economic system to pay men enough to support a family."

The meeting broke up at lunch.

■ FOUR

"V" for Victory over Fascism (1941-1945)

AT THE START of U.S. participation in the Second World War, many liberals expressed a willingness to postpone their commitment to reform in the interest of national security. The Guild strongly dissented from that view. Its leaders argued that reform was compatible with wartime demands—in fact, it was necessary in order to win. Victory over Fascism would be meaningless if reaction triumphed at home. "Our entire history," Martin Popper told the delegates to the War Convention in February 1943, "is a record of support for democracy and opposition to reaction."

In pursuit of that goal, the Guild NEB sponsored a panel on "The Role of the Lawyer in Defense of the United States." The Chicago and New York chapters offered to represent tenants and consumers against Office of Price Administration (OPA) violators and to donate their legal services to the Red Cross. In San Francisco Guild lawyers mobilized local attorneys for defense work. All across the country individual Guild members served in the military, registered as blood donors, acted as air wardens, spoke in behalf of war-bond drives and Soviet-American friendship, and did what seemed expected of responsible citizens.

What distinguished the Guild from other Bar associations was the role it played in shaping social, economic, and political policies. Though Guild labor lawyers accepted the wartime no-strike pledge and voluntary arbitration, they publicly denounced proposals aimed at regulating unions, arresting strike leaders, or permitting the government to seize struck defense plants. (When the OPA rejected a wage increase, one union boasted that their lawyer, Harry Sacher, had invented and fought for a welfare fund to provide more income, which came to be known as fringe benefits.)

In the area of race relations, the Guild was notably active and influential. It lobbied extensively so that black lawyers would have the opportunity to serve as commissioned officers in the military and as civilian attorneys in such agencies as the Justice Department, OPA, and the War Production Board. The Guild strongly supported creation of the Fair Employment Practices Committee and campaigned successfully for the appointment of Guild leader Earl Dickerson to the Committee. Acting on the advice of such distinguished black lawyers as William Hastie and Thurgood Marshall, the Guild pressed the President and Attorney General to prosecute acts of violence against black soldiers, and further proposed that crimes against members of the armed forces come under federal jurisdiction. In New York City, the Guild chapter cooperated with the Harlem Lawyers Association in investigating exaggerated reports of the so-called "Harlem Crime Wave." The Los Angeles and Detroit chapters closely monitored police behavior during racial riots in those two cities and urged thorough investigations of the underlying causes of such unrest.

When the Guild began its wartime work in 1940-1941, the resignations of its most prominent New Deal members had seemed a crippling blow. Yet, less than four years later, Secretary of State Edward Stettinius invited the Guild to participate as a "consultant" organization at the founding of the United Nations in San Francisco.

STATEMENT OF POLICY, FEBRUARY 22, 1941
By the National Executive Board

[Throughout this nation's involvement in World War II, the Guild insisted that victory over Fascism abroad required the preservation and expansion of change at home. Meeting in Washington, D.C., at the beginning of 1941, the NEB formulated a policy in which national defense depended on an unfaltering commitment to civil rights and civil liberties.]

At this time of crisis we rededicate ourselves to the defense of our democratic institutions and the social and economic well-being of the American people.

That is why we view with deep concern the efforts now being made to break down our civil liberties, the rights of labor, and the whole fabric of social legislation. We repudiate the proposition that our democracy can be protected or our national defense served by the destruction of democracy itself.

We oppose all attempts to curtail labor's rights to organize and to strike or to impose upon labor any form of compulsory mediation or arbitration. We oppose pending legislation to legalize wire tapping and the so-called "model" bills recently introduced in several state legislatures, which under the guise of national defense against sabotage might provide an effective instrument for interference with free speech and labor's rights.

"Statement of Policy, February 22, 1941," by National Executive Board, *Lawyers Guild Review* 1:4 (1941).

We urge the inauguration of an unswerving policy of non-discrimination against the Negro people in every phase of public life. It is of the utmost importance that all manifestations of Jim-Crowism be eliminated from the War and Navy Departments.

Our social legislation is also under severe attack. Efforts to amend or repeal the Wagner Act and the Wage-Hour Act, curtailment of relief and unemployment benefits, and the virtual abandonment of a national health and housing program, all these are danger signs which require vigilant attention by those who would serve the general welfare. We reiterate that we regard the preservation and improvement of the social and economic well-being of our people and the protection of their democratic rights as an essential part of a real national defense program.

We urge the unimpaired protection of all labor legislation and labor's rights. We, therefore, urge the continuance and extension of social legislation, particularly in the fields of unemployment, relief, health, and housing.

Finally, we urge that the cost of national defense be equitably distributed by taxation according to the ability to pay, by the enactment of a more democratic tax program which will stop the amassing of huge war profits resulting in an increased cost of living.

NEGRO DISCRIMINATION AND THE NEED FOR FEDERAL ACTION
By William H. Hastie and Thurgood Marshall

[The discrepancy between wartime ideals and daily realities was nowhere more glaring than in the experience of black Americans. In the following selection, a report submitted to the Guild's National Executive Board in November 1942, Howard University Law School Dean William Hastie and NAACP counsel Thurgood Marshall are sharply critical of the Justice Department's inaction on lynchings, violence against black servicemen, white primaries, and poll taxes.]

It should be recognized at the outset that while other Americans are taking steps to protect their basic civil rights, Negro Americans are faced with a two-fold problem, namely, to obtain basic civil rights which have been denied them in the past and to protect such few rights as have heretofore been accorded them.

Constitutional guarantees and laws guaranteeing civil rights are worthless scraps of paper to the people who are prevented from exercising these rights by the constant threat of violence. The recent outbreaks of mob violence again emphasize the fact that only federal action

---

"Negro Discrimination and the Need for Federal Action," by William H. Hastie and Thurgood Marshall, *Lawyers Guild Review* 2:3 (1942).

will protect us from lynchings and the threat of lynchings. It is significant that lynchings have increased and decreased as the enactment of federal legislation has seemed remote or imminent.

An attack on a Negro soldier or sailor in uniform is a direct attack on our government. Unless the federal government is willing to protect its soldiers and sailors on leave and while on duty, it is impossible to maintain the proper morale among Negro soldiers and sailors and their families, and the authority of the government itself is undermined.

The Poll Tax issue in eight southern states prevents large numbers of Negro and white citizens from qualifying as voters. Negroes in several of these states and in other southern states without Poll Tax provisions are prevented from voting by being excluded from voting in primary elections. The system of "white primary" is prevalent throughout the deep South. It is an admitted fact that in these same states nomination at the Democratic primary is tantamount to election at the regular elections. The refusal to permit Negroes to vote at this stage of the election process excludes Negroes from voting at the only stage that their votes would have any effect.

It is up to the U.S. Department of Justice to institute criminal proceedings against the officials who refuse to permit qualified Negroes to vote in primary elections solely because of their race or color. Instead of helping in the civil case now pending and also bringing criminal procedure in these cases, the U.S. Department of Justice at the present time seems to be doing nothing on this question.

THE PARTICIPATION OF NEGRO LABOR IN OUR WAR EFFORT
By Earl B. Dickerson

[Many scholars trace the origin of the modern Civil Rights Movement to the threatened March on Washington that pressured President Roosevelt to create the Fair Employment Practices Committee (FEPC). The author of the next selection, Earl Dickerson, a black Chicago alderman and one-time president of the city's Guild chapter, received a presidential appointment to serve on the FEPC.]

Eight million additional employees must be added to our national labor force this year if we are to meet the production quotas promised to our armed forces and those of our Allies. Where are these workers to be found? Negroes constitute 11 percent of America's gainfully employed workers and even a greater percentage of America's unemployed labor

---

"The Participation of Negro Labor in Our War Effort," by Earl B. Dickerson, *Lawyers Guild Review* 2:3 (1942).

supply. Yet more than half of the companies holding war contracts, throughout the country, have informed the United States Employment Service that, war or no war, they will not employ Negro workers on production jobs! The Axis radio belittles our democracy; fifth columnists whisper that we don't actually believe in racial equality. Thus, the problem of Negro labor's status challenges us from innumerable angles. Is discrimination going to be allowed to slow down our re-arming? Can't Negro Americans share the fight against Fascism? What kind of a democracy are we going to have when the war is over?

The social ostracism of the Negro and his disfranchisement in large sections of our country today is the subject of much attention. We are not so familiar, however, with the efforts of the Negro to find work, with his struggle to become integrated into the industrial life of America. Nevertheless, the exclusion of the Negro from America's productive activity has been even more complete than his exclusion from its social and political life. And only with a firm economic base can the Negro hope to assume his place in the social and political spheres of American life.

Those of us vitally interested in the integration of Negroes into our industrial life know that the prejudice and discrimination encountered there by the Negro is part of the intolerance which pervades the whole of our American life. Therefore, no law or order like Executive Order No. 8802, no man or group of men like the FEPC, can alone solve the problem.

It remains to be seen whether the FEPC can devise orders that will end discrimination and, if such orders are devised, whether they can be enforced. Based as the Committee is on the war powers of the President, it would seem to be strategically equipped, as far as legal theory and patriotic sentiment could make it, to see that our war effort on the industrial front does not lag by reason of color prejudices. If necessary the same sanction used by the President to enforce recommendations of the War Labor Board that employers bargain collectively, namely, government seizure and operation of the plant, should constitute the ultimate authority to enforce utilization of all available labor, regardless of its color, for the war effort.

Just as the right of labor to organize and bargain collectively was first accorded national recognition by executive orders and boards operating thereunder, with little or no effective enforcement machinery and within a few years' time, became established by federal legislation and effective administrative machinery, so a continuous movement forward in the establishment of the right to employment without racial discrimination may follow an analogous course.

The new right which has grown up during the New Deal days—the right to a job, freedom from want—has received international recognition in the Atlantic Charter. That right must be guarded against many infringements. Today the right to a job cannot be denied because of union membership. The policy to recognize that right as against encroachments of racial prejudice has received national definition in Executive Order No. 8802. The next step is to make the right to a job without regard to race, color, or religion a reality in American life. The steps ahead are clear. The people must come to believe in that right. The federal government must be willing to put all its power into protecting that right from those who through ignorance, bigotry, or prejudice would destroy it.

DISCRIMINATION AND RACISM PRODUCE RIOTS: HARLEM, LOS ANGELES, AND DETROIT
By The Guild Lawyer, *Carey McWilliams, Alan Brown, and Ned Smokler*

[Executive Order 8802, creating the Fair Employment Practices Committee, did not mean that ignorance, bigotry, and prejudice would disappear from life in the United States. In fact, throughout the war local Guild chapters repeatedly called attention to discrimination, festering racism, and irrational prejudice in their communities. On occasion, as in the first selection about Harlem, the Guild proposed an investigation of conditions to alleviate the worst abuses. More often, however, as in the descriptions of riots in Los Angeles and Detroit, the Guild responded after the violence had erupted.]

■

Constitutional Liberties Committee Projects Harlem Investigation

November 1942

The Committee on Constitutional Liberties has been engaged in the formulation of a comprehensive project for the holding of public hearings in Harlem, to which Negroes and others may come to testify before a jury of distinguished citizens concerning all aspects of the problems of the Negro people. The project has received thorough consideration by the committee, and it is felt that it is necessary and feasible. Very little need be said concerning its necessity. The war effort makes imperative the full participation of the Negroes in our fight against Fascism. National unity demands equality of treatment and understanding of the Negro people by all other groups. The newspaper emphasis on juvenile

---

"Discrimination and Racism Produce Riots: Harlem, Los Angeles, and Detroit," by *The Guild Lawyer*, Carey McWilliams, Alan Brown, and Ned Smokler, *Guild Lawyer* (Nov. 1942, June/July 1943, Sept. 1943).

delinquency and "muggings" in Harlem has served to cast unwarranted reflection on the hard-working, respectable mass of Negro people in that area. Newbold Morris told a Harlem audience on October 11th: "There is no Harlem crime wave except in the columns of a few newspapers."

Whatever the statistics on the increase of crime in Harlem, it is clear that the Negro people resent the callous disregard by the press and police of the underlying factors peculiarly responsible for delinquency in Harlem. Instead of sympathetic awareness and understanding of the sociological causes, the Negroes encounter police suspicion, violence, and brutality to a point where the civil liberties of that whole section of our population have been restricted and often grossly violated.

■

Los Angeles Reports
By Carey McWilliams, President, Los Angeles Chapter

June/July 1943

Immediately upon the outbreak of the riots in Los Angeles, on June 5th, 6th, and 7th, the Guild's national president and attorney general of California, the Hon. Robert W. Kenny, directed the law enforcement machinery of the state and was named chairman of the governor's investigating committee to determine its cause.

At the request of a number of citizens, I headed a citizens' committee which worked in close cooperation with Mr. Kenny. Our national executive secretary, Martin Popper, conferred in Washington with Ugo Carusi, assistant to Attorney General Biddle, Nelson Rockefeller and other Washington officials to urge that the Department of Justice prosecute Los Angeles police officials for alleged violations of the federal civil rights statutes in detaining Mexican-American youths without preferring charges. Popper also requested the OWI to intervene on the ground that the Hearst papers in Los Angeles were jeopardizing the war effort through a distorted and unfair presentation of the situation.

The riots were large-scale *race* riots. They involved wide areas of the city and included riots by service men on virtually every large downtown motion picture theater. Temporarily, the Armed Forces declared Los Angeles "out of bounds." Over fifty people were seriously injured and some four hundred Mexicans were jailed.

POLICE CULPABLE

The evidence clearly indicates that the police stood by laughing and kidding while the mob beat, insulted, and humiliated every Mexican they could lay their hands on (including also Negro youngsters). The newspaper stories about "Zoot-Suit Gangsters" are nonsense. Not more than one-third of the persons seized by the mobs were even wearing "zoot-suits." It was Mexicans they were after. The evidence also indicates that the military police, when they did take soldiers and sailors into custody, patted them on the back and laughed and joked with them.

I feel that the Republic of Mexico should be encouraged to make the strongest representations, even to the point of closing the border and forbidding the importation of further agricultural labor and closing the Los Angeles consulate as a protest.

Some seem to feel that a high-toned "cultural" program is all that is needed. There is no doubt that there will be further trouble and the Administration can anticipate nothing but continued embarrassment unless it actively intervenes. To call this situation a "local problem" is absurd.

BIDDLE ASKED TO ACT

As soon as our investigation disclosed the true character of the riots, the Los Angeles Chapter sent the following telegram to Attorney General Biddle:

Request following immediate action your office (1) that you assign representatives from Washington office, Civil Rights Unit, to Los Angeles for a full investigation of the extensive race riots which occurred here June 5th, 6th, and 7th; (2) that such investigation be made jointly with representatives of Office of War Information, Coordinator of Inter-American Affairs, Fair Employment Practice Committee, and Naval and Army intelligence officers in this area. These riots were not isolated, spontaneous incidents. Evidence indicates that week-end violence represents logical culmination of provocative and discriminatory policies pursued by local police officials toward the Mexican section of the community during last eighteen months. Characterization of riots in press as "indignation of service men against Mexican gangsters" is fundamentally at variance with background of factual situation. Continued repetition of such incidents constitutes direct interference with war effort, disrupts national unity, and jeopardizes President's Good Neighbor Policy. Feel that full federal investigation essential to prevent occurrence of similar disgraceful manifestations of race prejudice in the future. Your prompt attention to this wire is imperative.

■

Detroit Reports
By Alan Brown and Ned Smokler

Not only the recent Detroit race riot, but its aftermath, the railroading of Negroes to 90-day prison terms, is a cause of serious concern.

We feel that the manner of determining guilt and the imposition of maximum sentences on the defendants involved in the riots, without due regard to their fundamental rights, will not cure the existing causes of racial hatreds and deep-seated prejudices, but, on the contrary, will cause even greater racial tension than heretofore existed. If a defendant was unwittingly and unwillingly drawn into a mob, or defended himself from attack, his imprisonment for 90 days would only cause greater resentment and ill feeling which he will blame on color discrimination, intolerance, and injustice by the courts. This is particularly true in light of the fact that the overwhelming percentage of defendants are Negroes. Under no circumstances should the mob hysteria of the public streets or even an appearance thereof be permitted in the halls of justice. This situation is one we feel the courts are overlooking.

It is important that people preserve their respect for law and order and the proper dispensation of justice in the courts; while the Guild cannot hope to attempt a cure of all the ills that attend this nightmarish spectacle, we can contribute in some measure to a more respectful feeling for the orderly processes of the courts. Many lawyers in the Guild have volunteered their services, without charge, to indigent worthy defendants in misdemeanor cases, making only the reservation that they have the right to refuse assistance if, in the opinion of the attorney after investigating the cause, such defendant was either a ring-leader or an aggressive participant in the rioting.

Hon. Patrick H. O'Brien, honorary chairman of the Detroit Chapter, as head of a Citizens Committee to investigate the causes of the riots, worked closely with the Wolverine Bar Association—an association of Negro attorneys—which established panels of both bar associations to represent defendants—mostly Negroes—who were held incommunicado by the police. Thirteen hundred persons were arrested.

The riots have given direct material support to the enemies of the United States in the loss of production of weapons and munitions at the first moment in the war when shipping capacity exceeds available cargo and on the eve of great offensives.

THE CAUSES

In respect to the immediate causes we deplore the apparent readiness of FBI and other officials to assume without investigation or upon an obviously hurried and superficial investigation that the disorders were not precipitated by enemy action or treasonable conspiracy. We remind Detroit of well-known facts which indicate the extreme likelihood that such was the case: the known existence of the Ku Klux Klan in this city; the known affiliation of the Ku Klux Klan with seditious and fascist sympathizing groups; the indictment of Chambers and Alderman for active incitement of similar disorders at Sojourner Truth (and why haven't they been brought to trial, Mr. Attorney General Biddle?); and, more significantly, the fact that similar disorders have been "spontaneously" occurring in other vital centers of war production during recent weeks—at the precise time when internal disunity and disruption of our production are of the most urgent importance to our enemies. Such other outbreaks have occurred *recently* in Pascagoula, Alabama (shipbuilding), in Los Angeles, California (aircraft), in other shipbuilding centers in Florida and Texas, and at the munitions and chemical centers of Chester, Pennsylvania, and Newark, New Jersey. The press reports plausible accounts of many evidences of systematic organization and supply of the mobs in Detroit.

The Guild was the only Bar association of Michigan that presented a program on the question of race discrimination in employment, housing, education, and in the armed forces. The resolution on race disorders stressed the need for national unity on the eve of the greatest offensive in this country's history; the need to marshal all our forces if victory is to be attained; the fact that membership of the State Bar consists of many races and national origins; that the resolution vitally affected not only our members but the community as a whole; that the people of Michigan were looking to the State Bar for effective leadership in preventing further recurrence of race disorders; that its passage and adoption would be a unique contribution to winning the war.

HARRY BRIDGES, THE GUILD, AND THE FBI
By the Editors

[Communism has frequently been identified with immigrants, and subversion with the foreign-born, despite the importance of native-born radicals from Eugene Debs to Elizabeth Gurley Flynn. The image of the radical alien coalesced during the early 1940s around the seemingly endless efforts by Congress, the Labor Department, and Attorney General Francis Biddle to deport Harry Renton Bridges, the Australian-born president of the International Longshoremen and Warehousemen's Union. He was accused of no crime. His deportation was simply said to be "in the best interests of the United States."

[The Guild vigorously opposed these efforts and filed briefs at every stage of the deportation procedure. Guild lawyers Carol King of New York and Richard Gladstein and Aubrey Grossman of San Francisco represented Bridges. The documents in this section reveal the range of concerns and strategies pursued by the FBI, the Justice Department, and Guild lawyers.]

"Harry Bridges, the Guild, and the FBI," by the Editors, from *Guild Lawyer* (June 1942); Richard Gladstein letter to Grossman, Margolis & Sawyer, Sept. 29, 1941; and "Memorandum for Hugh B. Cox, and J. Edgar Hoover," Carol King Papers, MCLI.

Labor Law Committee Condemns Bridges' Ouster as Blow at War Effort

The order of the Attorney General directing the deportation to Australia of Harry Renton Bridges, President of the International Longshoremen and Warehousemen's Union, CIO, Director for the State of California and member of the National Executive Board of the CIO, constitutes a reversal of the unanimous decision of the Board of Immigration Appeals, which held that the evidence did not establish that Bridges was a member of an organization seeking to overthrow the government of the United States by force and violence.

This action will further interfere with the war effort because of its effect on labor generally, and it will aid the disruptive elements both in and out of the ranks of labor.

It represents a capitulation to the dangerous forces of appeasement, reaction, and anti-unionism. It is a blow to national morale. It subverts the fundamental standard repeatedly set by President Roosevelt that national unity must be preserved and strengthened in this period of war crisis.

For the foregoing reasons, the New York Labor Law Committee of the National Lawyers Guild demands that the order of the Attorney General directing the deportation of Harry Renton Bridges be reconsidered and revoked.

■

[Gladstein discusses the political and strategic aspects of the Bridges case with his law partners.]

September 29, 1941

Dear Everybody:

Yesterday and this morning I held some conversations with people whose judgment I very much respect, and the result is that the question of a Guild resolution on the Bridges case has taken on complications. Here is the situation.

Obviously, we do not want merely a reiteration of the resolutions passed by the last Guild convention which were two in number: one demanding cancellation of the warrant and of all further proceedings against Bridges; and the other attacking the FBI, urging the removal of Hoover, and demanding that the FBI's jurisdiction be limited so as not to invade labor's rights or civil liberties. Before Aubrey left, we agreed that the usefulness of a Guild resolution at this time would be its potential influence on certain Senators who we hope will raise a demand in Congress for an investigation of the FBI; and we also were agreed that our main strategy must be to isolate the FBI from Biddle and the administration. Both of these views took into consideration the important problem of refraining from making a frontal assault on the administration itself, and of properly utilizing material being prepared in Washington which demonstrates the Gestapo activities of the FBI. This is not, however, to say that a resolution on the FBI as such has been ruled out, but apparently it will be necessary for me to prepare two resolutions, one on the case itself and another on the FBI, with fair assurance of the passage of the first and no assurance at all on the second.

One more thing. In the light of our desire to get a congressional investigation of the FBI, it seems clear that the wiretapping against Harry would be our best springboard, and that a Guild resolution on wiretapping might serve our purpose. Here again the view was put forward that wiretapping as such is not a bad thing, since it can be used and has been used for purposes of which we approve, such as in the present trial against the Nazi spies. It is stated that the President, Jackson, and Biddle, as well as others of a liberal tinge with whom it is hoped to establish contact, have expressed themselves in favor of restricted wiretapping, and if the Guild should now take an unqualified opposition stand to any kind of wiretapping, the difficulties of establishing contact will be enhanced.

In other words, the whole question is no picnic at all, and it is difficult to decide exactly what should be done.

■

MEMORANDUM FOR HUGH B. COX, ASSISTANT
ATTORNEY GENERAL, AND J. EDGAR HOOVER, DIRECTOR,
FEDERAL BUREAU OF INVESTIGATION
By the Attorney General

July 16, 1943

I refer to Mr. L. M. C. Smith's memorandum to me dated June 28, 1943, which reviews the history, development, and meaning of the Special Case work and of the danger classifications that were made as a part of that work.

After full reconsideration of these individual danger classifications, I am satisfied that they serve no useful purpose. The detention of alien enemies is being dealt with under the procedures established by the Alien Enemy Control Unit. The Special Case procedure has been found to be valueless and is not used in that connection. There is no statutory authorization or other present justification for keeping a "custodial detention" list of citizens. The Department fulfills its proper functions by investigating the activities of persons who may have violated the law. It is not aided in this work by classifying persons as to dangerousness.

Apart from these general considerations, it is now clear to me that this classification system is inherently unreliable. The evidence used for the purpose of making the classifications was inadequate; the standards applied to the evidence for the purpose of making the classifications were defective; and, finally, the notion that it is possible to make a valid determination as to how dangerous a person is in the abstract and without reference to time, environment, and other relevant circumstances, is impractical, unwise, and dangerous.

For the foregoing reasons I am satisfied that the adoption of this classification system was a mistake that should be rectified for the future. Accordingly, I direct that the classifications heretofore made should not be regarded as classifications of dangerousness or as a determination of fact in any sense. In the future, they should not be used for any purpose whatsoever. Questions raised as to the status or activities of a particular person should be disposed of by consideration of all available information, but without reference to any classification heretofore made.

A copy of this memorandum should be placed in the file of each person who has hitherto been given a classification. In addition, each card upon which a classification appears should be stamped with the following language:

THIS CLASSIFICATION IS UNRELIABLE. IT IS HEREBY CANCELLED, AND SHOULD NOT BE USED AS A DETERMINATION OF DANGEROUSNESS OR OF ANY OTHER FACT. (SEE MEMORANDUM OF JULY 16, 1943, FROM THE ATTORNEY GENERAL TO HUGH B. COX AND J. EDGAR HOOVER).

THE GUILD'S DEMOCRATIC TAX PROGRAM
By Joseph H. Crown

[The Second World War caused an enormous increase in governmental expenditures, creating the need to find new sources of revenue. The Guild's Committee on Taxation, led by Randolph Paul, labored to insure that the burden of financing this pay-as-you-go war would fall on the shoulders of those with a high personal income and corporate taxpayers rather than on working people in the form of excise and sales taxes.]

To capture the flavor of the tax programs projected by the Guild's National Committee on Taxation, we set out below the peroration to a "Democratic Tax Program for the American People," which the Taxation Committee issued in 1941 in response to the Treasury's proposals to raise $3.5 billion in new taxes.

"The Guild's Democratic Tax Program," by Joseph H. Crown, *NLG Practitioner* 33:1 (Winter 1975).

Democracy in taxation and the maintenance of a stable economy through increases in the purchasing power of workers and farmers require that taxes be collected from those able to pay, and especially from those corporations which are reaping swollen profits from the armament program.

To achieve a defensible tax program, proposals such as "consumption" taxes, excise taxes on consumer necessities, sales taxes, taxes on salaries and wages, which would increase the tax burdens on persons whose present incomes do not permit a minimum standard of living, must be repudiated and defeated. Instead the increased tax burdens should be placed on the shoulders of those best able to carry them.

An effective excess profits tax should be enacted. The amortization privilege should be repealed, and stringent profits limitations on government contracts should be adopted. The undistributed profits tax should be restored to reduce opportunities for tax avoidance. The income from federal, state, and local securities (outstanding and future issues) should be taxed.

The $2,500 and $1,000 personal exemptions should be restored. The Joint Committee proposal to increase personal income surtax rates should be modified by increasing the surtax exemption to $2,500 and increasing surtax rates above $100,000 by 10 percent in each bracket. Capital gains should be taxed at full rates and capital loss deductions against ordinary income should be disallowed. The federal estate tax and gift tax should be integrated into a single tax system, with a single exemption and a single set of graduated rates drastically increased for all brackets, so as to prevent estate tax reductions through gifts. Finally, no increase can be tolerated in the tax burden imposed on the millions of people who are "ill-fed, ill-clad, and ill-housed" until persons with "comfortable and large" incomes have been taxed to the very limit of their capacity to pay. Such would be the direction of a democratic tax program.

ROSIE THE RIVETER'S EIGHT-HOUR ORPHANS: THE GUILD SUPPORTS CHILD CARE
By the Committee on Social Legislation, New York City Chapter

[Six and one-half million women, most of them over thirty-five and married, entered the labor force between 1941 and 1945. Over seven million changed their county of residence. Most went through these changes without meaningful

---

"Rosie the Riveter's Eight-Hour Orphans: The Guild Supports Child Care," by the Committee on Social Legislation, New York City Chapter, *Guild Lawyer* (1943).

help from government or industry to accommodate the special needs of working mothers. The New York City chapter addresses this problem in the following 1943 selection.]

The greatly increased employment of women in war industries and their greatly expanded participation in such work in the near future is essential to this country's efforts to win the war. That participation has created important problems in relation to child care. The country owes these women the responsibility of caring for their children who are left without the maternal care that they need while their mothers are at work.

CARE FOR PRE-SCHOOL CHILDREN

It is recommended that a registration center be established in each borough for working women whose children need day care; that funds be provided for the care of such children in accordance with adequate education and health standards; that WPA increase its non-relief personnel to approximately 45 percent as it has done in other states so that permanent qualified head teachers can be provided for each nursery school; and that hours of public schools and kindergartens be lengthened to provide full day care for children of working mothers.

EDUCATION AND RECREATION

It is recommended that vacancies in the school system be filled; substitute teachers be placed on the same salary schedule as regularly appointed teachers; overcrowded classes be eliminated by employment of additional teachers; part-time schooling be ended; free hot lunches be provided for all needy children and at minimum cost for those who can pay; an adequate number of supervisors be provided so that full use be made of baths and swimming pools; the all-day school program be extended so children of working mothers will have supervision during the hours their mothers work; and that schools be kept open until 10 o'clock at night so they may function as community centers.

JUVENILE DELINQUENCY AND CRIME

There was a 14 percent increase in juvenile delinquency in the first six months of 1942 compared to the first six months of 1941, and there was an increase of 20 percent in commitments to correctional schools of New York City children during the same period. There was an increase of 30 percent in wayward minor cases during the first nine months of 1941. The temporary shelters of the Society for the Prevention of Cruelty to Children used by the city are overcrowded and state schools for delinquent boys and girls have had to stop new admissions for extended periods. The Children's Court is understaffed and has not even secured replacements to its probation staff. Despite the growing number of children in need of individual care and supervision, the case-work division of the Juvenile Aid Bureau has been practically abolished. It is recommended that the Children's Court be adequately staffed and vacancies filled; a larger number of foster homes be found for children whose parents are unfitted or unable to care for them; the case-work division of the Juvenile Aid Bureau be re-established; and that all other recommendations above be carried out because they are essential to stem the rise in juvenile delinquency and crime.

We should learn from the experiences in England, where social services have been expanded as the war progressed, while in New York education and social services are being curtailed. Even the meager existing budgets for essential services are not being filled. Care must be taken not to take mothers of young children away from their young children by influencing them to go into war industry until the need for their services cannot otherwise be filled, because it is important that very young children not be separated from their mothers. To that end it is necessary that adequate personnel be provided in registration centers to advise mothers; and that, where mothers seek employment because of need, supplementation of income should be provided to enable them to remain at home.

It is urged that all members of the Guild sign petitions to the Mayor and that the Guild cooperate with the Committee for the Care of Young Children in War Time in their effort to provide the care and facilities needed for safeguarding the health, welfare, and education services to the children of the City of New York.

CALLS FOR A UNITED NATIONS BAR ASSOCIATION
By The Guild Lawyer

[One underlying goal motivated the Guild throughout the Second World War: maintaining a united front against Fascism both at home and abroad. Toward that end Guild leaders actively worked to create international coalitions in support of the Allies. One example of this alliance-building was the effort to create a United Nations Bar Association. The following selections document the intensity and enthusiasm with which the Guild pursued a united front.]

"Calls for a United Nations Bar Association," by *The Guild Lawyer* (March 1943).

March 1943

Convention Calls for United Nations Bar Association

Formation of a United Nations Bar Association was urged in the final session of the war convention in a resolution which declared that such an international association would be a symbol of the real unity of the nations at war with the Axis and a means of winning the struggle and achieving a lasting peace.

In presenting the resolution. Martin Popper, executive secretary, said: "If this war is to have a basic meaning for us now and in the future, it must be the means toward eliminating the causes of international friction. The Bar has a function and a duty to originate and give impetus toward international cooperation."

A United Nations Bar not only presents the opportunity to function effectively in the legal field on an international scale, but it offers the opportunity to learn the legal systems of the different countries.

Inter-American Bar Admits Guild to Membership

The National Lawyers Guild proudly announces its membership in the Inter-American Bar Association. The Guild will be represented at the Inter-American Bar Conference in Rio de Janeiro in August. Greetings from William Roy Vallance, secretary-general of the association, were read to the convention. Mr. Vallance's letter stated:

"On behalf of the Inter-American Bar Association, it gives me great pleasure to welcome the National Lawyers Guild as one of the new members of our Association, which at this time has a membership of sixty-six associations, composed of national, state, local, and special bar organizations in nineteen countries. The Inter-American Bar Association extends good wishes for the success of your War Convention.

"The next Conference of the Inter-American Bar Association will take place in Rio de Janeiro beginning August 7, 1943, on the occasion of the 100th anniversary of the Brazilian Bar Association. The need for solidarity of lawyers in the American hemisphere has never been more urgent than at the present time, and we hope with your help to exert a substantial influence in the policies which shall lead to the establishment of peace and the reign of law."

THE WHITE HOUSE
WASHINGTON

March 15, 1944

Dear Mr. Kenny:

I am glad to learn from your letter that one of the purposes of the meeting of the National Executive Board of the National Lawyers Guild will be to lay plans for helping to initiate forms of permanent collaboration between associations of lawyers of the various members of the United Nations in working for international cooperation.

Bar Associations in all countries can do a great deal to further the cause of cooperation and peace in the world. Much can be accomplished by exchange of information and knowledge of the different systems of law prevailing in the several United Nations.

I wish you well in this project.

Very sincerely yours,

[Signature]

[Franklin D. Roosevelt]

Honorable Robert W. Kenny,
President,
National Lawyers Guild,
University Club,
Washington, D.C.

"The White House," letter from Franklin D. Roosevelt to Robert W. Kenny, March 15, 1944, Kenny Papers, Bancroft Library, University of California, Berkeley.

■ FIVE

Moving Toward Peace, Jobs, Security, and Justice (1944–1947)

THE NATIONAL LAWYERS Guild emerged from the war confident that it had become a permanent part of the nation. The sense of mission that had driven the organization's efforts against Fascism was soon directed toward building a prosperous society free from discrimination and injustice. New members were recruited, chapters were reorganized, a new student component was created, and an administrative secretary was hired.

Programmatically, Guild leaders identified full employment, civil rights, national health insurance, public housing, and the expansion of social security as primary domestic goals. Guild committees lobbied friends in Congress, drafted reports, sponsored conferences, and invested time and energy in such urgent questions as reconversion, demobilization, and labor-management relations. An analysis of Guild domestic activities during the period from 1945 to 1946 testifies to the extraordinary optimism and confident belief that this progressive bar association had finally arrived. The Guild's commitment to economic rights foreshadowed concerns of our own generation, as did its emphasis on legislative work.

In retrospect, the Guild was clearly overconfident. The substance of the law gives the appearance of majestic equality, but the procedures all favor the well-to-do, as George Olshausen demonstrated in his seminal article, "Rich and Poor in Civil Procedure," published in 1947. The experience of 110,000 Japanese-Americans interned in government relocation camps during the war, a decision supported by the Guild, was an ominous portent of the future. It was mitigated somewhat by the Supreme Court's unanimous decision in 1944 in *Ex Parte Endo* that Mitsuye Endo, a Japanese American, was entitled to unconditional release from the War Relocation Center, an act applauded by A. L. Wirin as editor of the *Los Angeles Guild Lawyer*. But the impunity and indifference with which the white South violated the legal and human rights of blacks continued. Congressional and presidential reluctance to embrace Roosevelt's dream of an economic bill of rights suggested that Guild efforts in behalf of social welfare legislation would not be easy to fulfill. Finally, the Attorney General's 1946 attack on "legal ideologists" and "revolutionaries" offered a glimpse of a fearful present.[1]

THE HUMAN ASPECTS OF THE TRANSITION FROM WAR TO PEACE
By the Guild Committee on Post-War Planning

[The following report was presented at a special National Conference on Post-War Problems in December 1944. Note the early emphasis on full employment, retraining, and the expansion of social security.]

Our primary goal must be full production and full employment. The objectives of sixty million jobs for the post-war period, the replacement of war work with civilian production, the substantial increase of the domestic and foreign markets, the maintenance of a national income of at least one hundred and fifty billion dollars a year: these are the bold and practical measures which will provide a firm foundation for a prosperous post-war economy. If measures for achieving these objectives are taken now, the inevitable hardships of the transition period will be sharply reduced. These hardships cannot be wholly eliminated, however, and consideration must, therefore, be given to solution of the problems of the period of transition from war to peace, which will affect the human beings whose energies and skills have been devoted to the war.

During the transition from the temporary economy of war to the establishment of a permanent economy of peace, these problems will be faced both by the men and women in the armed forces, who will be demobilized, and by the men and women producing the things with which the war is being fought, whose jobs will end with the war. There are over ten million men and women in the armed services. There are several times that number in war production. A very large proportion of both will require assistance in reestablishing themselves in peacetime work. It is important that plans be made now, before the full tide of the need is upon us, to take care of all who are helping to bring about victory. We cannot wait until the war is over, because the problems will not wait. To a considerable extent, they are with us now.

War workers, unlike veterans, have no legal right to the civilian jobs they may have left to go to war plants, although President Roosevelt recommended that employers maintain the seniority of employees who

---

[1] Tom C. Clark, "Civil Rights: The Boundless Responsibility of Lawyers," *American Bar Association Journal* 32 (August 1946): 456–57.

"The Human Aspects of the Transition from War to Peace," by the Committee on Post-War Planning of the NLG, *Lawyers Guild Review* 5:1 (Jan.–Feb. 1945).

left to take war jobs. The primary protection of workers now employed in war work against unemployment in the transition and post-war periods is full employment.

No provisions have been made for the retraining of war workers where necessary for jobs in peacetime industry. The Murray-Kilgore Bill, which the National Lawyers Guild approved, sought to accomplish this objective among others, but it failed of passage. The speedy enactment of legislation to provide for retraining and reemployment of workers is imperative to meet the needs of the period following V-E Day.

The Guild is committed to an unemployment insurance program that would adequately cover all workers; that would provide benefits for the duration of unemployment in amounts that would guarantee to each worker not less than the minimum subsistence for himself and family, but not more than previous wages.

The period of transition from war to peace and the period of peace and prosperity which we should have when victory is won must have a nation that is protected by an adequate social security system, which will assure its people employment after the war and tide them over between jobs and during sickness. Provision must be made for medical care and hospitalization, disability benefits, adequate systems of unemployment insurance and old age and survivors insurance, maternity benefits, and a unified public assistance program, to assure freedom from want for all the people, one of the Four Freedoms for which this terrible war is being fought.

In the midst of this war, in which the people of Great Britain are in the front lines, their government has proposed the enactment of such a system of social security for all their people. The people of our country should follow their example by enacting now a system of social security, even broader and more liberal than that proposed for the people of Britain, commensurate with our greater resources and prosperity.

A SOCIAL SECURITY CHARTER FOR PEACETIME AMERICA
By the Guild National Committee on Social Legislation

[Few progressive organizations devoted as much planning and consideration to the problems and possibilities of the post-war society as the Guild. Its committees were both active and influential in shaping the legislative agenda of the Democratic Left. The unquestioned leader in the field of domestic social welfare

---

"A Social Security Charter for Peacetime America," by the National Committee on Social Legislation of the NLG, *Lawyers Guild Review* 5:4 (July–Aug. 1945).

proposals was the Committee on Social Legislation, led by its chairman Leo J. Linder and secretary Morris A. Wainger.]

The end of the war confronts America with gigantic problems.

The millions of men who have made sacrifices and endured privations in the armed services want employment and security. Their imaginations have been stirred by the war aim of achieving freedom from want. They will not want to come home to unemployment and frustration. The millions of war workers who must find work in civilian production are equally concerned with the urgent need for jobs and security. They understand that unemployment threatens the standard of living of the entire nation. Assurance of continuity of income is required by the national welfare.

Social insurance provides the means by which Americans can be assured against the immediate hazards of unemployment, sickness, old age, and the death of the family breadwinner. It provides the means whereby purchasing power can be maintained between jobs in the interest of stabilizing the national economy. But our present social insurance provisions are inadequate to provide security for American workers; they are inadequate to stabilize our economy. This inadequacy derives from the fact that almost one-half of civilian jobs are not covered by our existing social security laws, and that those who are covered receive benefits which are inadequate both in amount and duration. The most serious deficiency of all is the fact that the American people are without protection against the hazards of sickness: the costs of adequate medical care and loss of income resulting from sickness. Most Americans need this protection.

The Wagner-Murray-Dingell Social Security Bill of 1943 was a concrete proposal, presented during wartime, to rebuild our social security system in preparation for peace. Its prompt enactment would have enormously improved our social insurance and would have enabled us to meet the problems of reconversion with more adequate tools. The National Lawyers Guild supported that Bill as did labor organizations and progressive organizations throughout the country. It died in Congress.

The new Wagner-Murray-Dingell Social Security Bill of 1945 is a greatly improved revision of the 1943 Bill.

THE SINGLE, COMPREHENSIVE SOCIAL INSURANCE SYSTEM PROPOSED BY THE BILL

The Bill would create a single national social insurance system financed by a single social insurance tax and integrating within one unified system a new health program, a federalized unemployment insurance program, and an expanded and improved program for the aged and survivors.

The Bill would thus provide one comprehensive, basic system affording insurance against involuntary loss of earnings for all the causes not within the control of individual workers—involuntary unemployment, temporary and chronic sickness, old age, the death of the breadwinner. It would provide a vast health program insuring needed medical, hospital, dental, and nursing care, and would insure the effective administration of these services by making possible construction and improvement of hospital and health facilities, as well as by expanding the public health program.

The inclusion of this protection against all these risks in a single system would avoid the gaps, the overlappings and the wastes which characterize our present congeries of inadequate systems. It would achieve the economy and simplicity of a single administrative mechanism. It would extend protection against all these risks to virtually all gainfully occupied persons, bringing old age and survivors insurance and health insurance benefits for the first time in our country's history to the self-employed, the small business man, professional man, and the farmer. And it would cover virtually all persons working for wages or salaries against all these risks. It would thus bring for the first time within the protection of the system millions of persons now excluded—agricultural workers, domestic workers, and employees of non-profit institutions.

The Bill would create a new unified Federal-State program of public assistance to provide for the needy of the country not covered by the social insurance program. It would help the poorer states by larger federal contributions. By compelling the abandonment of restrictive residence eligibility qualifications now imposed by most states, it would largely guarantee that Americans, wherever they live in the nation, could be assured a reasonable minimum of subsistence.

The Bill is one of the most important legislative proposals before the American people. Its enactment would be a national safeguard against economic disaster. It would provide a foundation of minimum purchasing power upon which the economy could rest. It would add to the productivity of the nation by avoiding the stupendous economic waste caused by the cessation or interruption of purchasing power because of unemployment and ill health.

The Bill is a legislative proposal of paramount importance to every American. It presents a bold challenge to our country. For it is a proposal to improve the economic security of most American families. The Bill would completely overhaul our social insurance system. It would bring its protection virtually to all American wage earners and their families and would provide an assurance of minimum income to all primary dependents of a family breadwinner upon his or her death. It would reorganize and enormously improve a supplementary system of public assistance to provide for those who are not protected by the social insurance system.

Enormous as these advances are, they are equalled by the vast significance of the health proposals of the Bill. The majority of American families cannot afford adequate medical care. Large areas of the nation have too few doctors, hospitals, or health facilities; yet we spend billions annually on health services and the best medical knowledge and skill in the world are at hand in our own country. What is so urgently needed is that we organize the distribution of the costs of medical care to bring its benefits within the range of all, and, at the same time, organize the distribution of health facilities so that they will be everywhere available. The Bill, at long last, proposes to do these things. It would assure medical care virtually to every person engaged in productive work, whether as an employee or employer, and to their families, as social insurance beneficiaries, and to many if not all public assistance recipients.

The Bill is thus truly a social security charter for peacetime America.

THE 1946 CONVENTION
By Ann Fagan Ginger

[The Guild's 1946 convention, held in Cleveland, Ohio, over the July 4th weekend, represented both the high- and low-water marks in its still young history. In this selection, Ann Fagan Ginger, fresh from law school, recalls her first convention.]

In January 1946, 750,000 steelworkers went on strike in an unprecedented show of unity, and other large strikes were expected as soldiers returned from World War II to industrial production, demanding higher wages and a different approach to negotiations than before the war. On March 5, at the request of the Missouri politician who sat in the White House, Sir Winston Churchill came out of retirement to tell the United States what its foreign policy should be. At Fulton, Missouri, the man who had actually presided at the setting of the sun on the British Empire rose again to fashion an Iron Curtain against the Soviet Union, wartime ally of Britain and the United States against Hitler Germany.

In the spring, while working on a new spate of post-war deportation cases, Carol King got notice that the Lawyers Guild was going to hold its first convention since 1941, its seventh convention since its founding

---

"The 1946 Convention," by Ann Fagan Ginger, in forthcoming biography of Carol King.

in 1936–1937. She looked forward to a reunion with all her "boys" who had been away in the Service, and began preparing resolutions on immigration for the convention. Others in the Guild had been preparing and printing reports by individual members and the Guild Committee on Post-War Planning on numerous questions: the trials of war criminals, the human aspects of the transition from war to peace, and the disposal of surplus government (war) property. The Guild was also deeply concerned with the attacks on black militants trying to register and vote in Columbia, Tennessee, and in Mississippi.

Attorney General Tom Clark was preparing remarks at the same time for an address before the Chicago Bar Association on June 21, 1946. He charged that this country was the target of a sinister and deep-seated "plot" on the part of "Communists," "outside ideologists," and "small groups of radicals." The plot was, he said, directed at the seizure of our country through a division of national unity. This objective was being forwarded through the capture of important offices in labor unions, the fomenting of strikes, and the raising of barriers to the efforts of lawful authorities to maintain civil peace. He said he had been "told" that in the councils of many labor unions, "wherein deliberations are screened from the public," these "plotters" connive to seize power.

Another aspect of the plot consisted of protests by the plotters that civil rights of minority groups are being abridged. Clark cautioned lawyers: "We must be alert as officers of the court to see the difference between sincere and honest protest of groups of our citizens against injustice and the effort of these outside ideologists to stir up trouble according to the old plan of 'divide and rule.'"

One year after the United States, Great Britain, and the Soviet Union defeated the Fascist powers, the Attorney General said bluntly of Fascism and Communism, "I see no difference in them." And he concluded:

> I do not think there is anyone more subject to censure in our profession than the revolutionary who enters our ranks, takes the solemn oath of our calling, and then uses every device in the legal category to further the interests of those who would destroy our government by force, if necessary.
>
> I do not believe in purges because they bespeak the dark and hideous deeds of Communism and Fascism, but I do believe that our Bar associations, with a strong hand, should take those too brilliant brothers of ours to the legal woodshed for a definite and well-deserved admonition.

Martin Popper, Executive Secretary of the Guild, and the Convention planning committee responded to this attack by working even harder to build support for the Guild. When the Convention opened on July 4, messages of greeting were read from four Justices of the Supreme

Court. I remember how impressed I was, listening to messages from Hugo Black, Wiley Rutledge, Stanley Reed, and Frank Murphy extending their best wishes for a successful convention and praising the Guild's commitment to forward-looking progressive causes.

And I was inspired by a short speech by Shad Polier on Law, Conscience, and Society in which he said:

Law merely "on the books," that is "idle" law, is no social force. Only if the three law-making phases—enactment, construction, and enforcement—are conceived of as a continuing process to secure new enactments, to obtain sound interpretation, to assure vigorous, intelligent, and constructive enforcement, can law become and remain a social force. . . . Law is not a solution; it is a way of solving. It is not a guaranty; it is an opportunity. It is not even an answer; it is a way of demanding.

Attorney General Clark's "woodshed" speech was mentioned repeatedly during the Convention, and the delegates finally passed a resolution committing themselves to fight back:

The National Lawyers Guild stands ready to protect and assist to the full extent of its ability any member of the bar against whom an effort is made by Tom C. Clark or any person or organization acting at his instance, to take any such lawyers "to the legal woodshed" as threatened in Mr. Clark's Chicago speech.

We call upon lawyers everywhere to repudiate the reactionary position of the Attorney-General and in the tradition of free lawyers in a free society continue in their fight to preserve and safeguard the rights of the people.

The resolution recommended that the Guild send a committee to submit its views on Clark to President Truman, including its rejection of Clark's explanation for his failure to protect the civil liberties of Negroes seeking to vote in the South. The resolution also demanded "the immediate strengthening of the Department of Justice by the addition of liberals, both Negro and white, in positions of high responsibility." It also demanded "the immediate reorganization of the FBI and the addition of liberals both Negro and white in policy-making and general investigatory positions."

The Convention discussed, amended, and finally passed a great many resolutions on a variety of subjects, from "The Problem of Full Production and Employment in the Post-War Economy" to "American Foreign Policy, Utilization and Control of Atomic Energy," and "Extension of Legal Services to Low Income Groups."

This was heady stuff for someone like me, coming straight from traditional classes on Bills and Notes taught by pre-war professors in the medieval quadrangle at Ann Arbor.

CIVIL RIGHTS LEGISLATION FROM THE FOURTEENTH AMENDMENT TO AN ANTI-LYNCHING LAW
By W. E. B. Du Bois

[On January 25, 1947, Dr. Du Bois, the distinguished scholar and director of special research for the NAACP, addressed the Legal Conference on Federal Power to Protect Civil Liberties. The legal history of black Americans, he noted, was a conflict between ideals and prejudice. If the citizens of this country really wanted democracy, the Fourteenth Amendment had to be enforced and a federal anti-lynching act passed.]

During the Civil War and Reconstruction the whole relation of federal and state legislation began to change.

Then came the revolution instituted by the Reconstruction Acts and the 14th Amendment and a new relation of citizens to the federal government. Some Southern states passed Civil Rights legislation and then came the federal Civil Rights Act of 1866. In 1868 came the 14th Amendment.

The counter-revolution came in 1876, and from 1875 to 1883 we have a new era. Delaware in 1873 and Tennessee in 1875 tried to take away most civil rights, and all Southern states practically nullified enfranchisement by lawlessness and intimidation. Here arose the new problem of lynching. Mob murders reached their climax in 1892, and the helplessness of the federal government under law and decision was clear. Between 1883 and the early part of the twentieth century, the Civil Rights Bills passed by the Reconstruction Administrations in the South became inoperative or were repealed. The 14th Amendment was emasculated in 1872. The federal Civil Rights Bill of 1875 was declared unconstitutional in 1883.

Then followed the bulk of state civil rights legislation in the North.

This legislation for the most part forbade discrimination in restaurants, public conveyances, and in places of public amusement and accommodation, including barber shops and theaters. Less often they mentioned hotels, soda fountains, and saloons.

For the most part violation of these laws was punished by a fine and regarded as misdemeanors. Usually courts enforced these laws reluctantly and demanded specific statements as to just what the legislation meant and applied to do. In fact the legislation of this period was far in advance of public opinion and had no federal sanction back of it.

During the twentieth century, the state Civil Rights laws have been amended in various ways and now exist in sixteen different states.

"Civil Rights Legislation from the Fourteenth Amendment to an Anti-Lynching Law," by W. E. B. Du Bois, *Lawyers Guild Review* 6:5 (Nov.–Dec. 1946).

The most radical forward step in this era has been the Fair Employment Practice Legislation originating in Roosevelt's war order and then implemented by state action in New York and elsewhere. Whereas civil rights previously had touched largely matters of comfort and recreation, it now entered the vastly more important and fundamental field of earning a living. Its progress here especially by federal legislation will be crucial.

What we really see in this civil rights legislation is a conflict between ideals and prejudice; between the attempt to establish democracy upon equal treatment under the law, and at the same time the refusal of a large number of persons to treat persons of Negro descent on any real basis of equality. The result of this dichotomy is a tendency to let the laws fall into disuse; or to enforce them lightly; and, on the part of the Negroes, disinclination to call them into effective action. They represent therefore on the whole not the expression of a clear public opinion but an attempt to force public opinion to take a stand, which this same opinion recognizes as ethically right.

Considering this whole matter, we are faced by several considerations: how far can a nation maintain a high ideal of political and social action, when the majority of persons in that nation are disinclined to its application in particular cases? This is primarily a matter of education and of advance in ethical standards. It calls for careful consideration on the part of the nation as to just how far its ideals are worthwhile. Do we want democracy in the United States, and if so what are we willing to pay for it?

Today the fight for civil rights lies first in the field of appealing to public opinion. Beyond this is a clear call for a positive federal law against lynching, against discrimination in work and education, and against disfranchisement. The restoration of the 14th Amendment and further laws based on its original meaning are demanded.

THE MORASS OF RECONVERSION: UNDERSTANDING THE POSTWAR STRIKES
By Victor Rabinowitz

[For millions of Americans the post-war upheaval was a nightmare that would bring unemployment and either inflation or deflation. They recalled the recession of 1921 and, of course, were scarred by memories of the Great Depression. Trade unionists had an added concern that the wave of strikes following World War I would produce the same repression and anti-union climate in 1946.

"The Morass of Reconversion: Understanding the Postwar Strikes," by Victor Rabinowitz, *Guild Lawyer* (Jan.–Feb. 1946).

In the next piece, the General Counsel for the American Communications Association–CIO discussed the problems of reconversion.]

The analogy between the present industrial struggles and those after the First World War is clear. Once again, we have major strikes in almost every large American industry. Once again, the causes of those strikes seem to arise from the sharp increase in the cost of living, together with a determination on the part of big business to destroy or at least weaken the trade union movement.

The differences between 1919 and 1945 are, however, most significant. In the first place, organized labor is twelve million strong today. Organization is industrial, including millions of Negroes and women who were generally left out of the trade union movement two decades ago, and constituted the bulk of strikebreakers in the steel and other strikes in 1919. Those groups are today as well organized as the skilled craftsmen.

In the second place, labor, today, has political power much greater than at any previous time in our history.

In the third place, Big Business has completely failed in its efforts to rally returning veterans behind an anti-union movement. Experience in every large strike in the country since the war has demonstrated that the leadership is frequently taken by militant returned veterans who are determined to fight for a higher standard of living. The importance of this is seen by recalling that in 1919 the American Legion was one of the most active forces in the anti-union front. Due partly to the fact that a much greater proportion of the population is actually engaged in labor disputes, public opinion, likewise, has not responded to the propaganda of employers in the same degree as at the end of World War I.

As a final distinction between 1919 and 1946, we find a much more mature and politically developed trade union leadership. Today, and for the past eight years, unions have paid much attention to problems of education, both of their membership and of the general public. Public relations now form an essential part of any union organization. A more enlightened approach toward the public interest and toward intelligent political action is, likewise, noted.

The stake of our entire population in the present wave of strikes is clear. Full employment is impossible unless purchasing power is maintained and even increased, and such results are possible only through increases in wages. Because the productivity of labor has increased tremendously in the last decade, the worker today is entitled to a proportionate increase in his standard of living. Any other premise is economically disastrous and will inevitably result in the complete collapse of our economic system.

Industry is, similarly, striving to increase its proportion of the national income. Because of the peculiar features of the Tax Law, together with the confusion necessarily attendant upon reconversion and demobilization, the present evidently seems to be, to Big Business, a propitious time for a determined assault on the labor movement.

The interest of the average member of the public should be clear. A victory for labor will mean increased prosperity for the masses, whether they may be members of trade unions or not. Destruction of the trade union movement will mean, as it meant after the last war, economic depression and a return of the chaos of the early thirties.

■ SIX

The End of the Grand Alliance (1945-1948)

THE UNITED STATES emerged from World War II as the most powerful nation on earth. It possessed a monopoly over the prime weapons of destruction —the atomic bomb—and reconstruction—foreign aid. Nonetheless, the Guild entered the post-war years hopeful that it could nurture mutual accommodation between the United States and the Soviet Union. It spent an enormous amount of intellectual and emotional energy on the new United Nations. Its representatives actively participated at the organization's founding conference in San Francisco and urged the Truman administration to adopt foreign policies consistent with the UN Charter. Whenever possible, Guild leaders and committees supported international efforts at cooperation, particularly with respect to atomic energy, reconstruction of war-torn Europe, the war crime trials at Nuremberg, and the unrestricted access of Jews to Palestine.

But the Truman administration, already tied to the new military-industrial complex, rejected the One World and UN approach of Wendell Willkie and Franklin Roosevelt to pursue the related goals of economic expansion, national security, and unquestioned international influence. The pursuit of these goals was characterized by unilateral action, an arrogant diplomatic style, and an apparent willingness to allow resolvable issues to escalate into full-scale confrontations.

The speed with which the wartime alliance between the United States and the Soviet Union disintegrated came as an alarming and sudden shock. What emerged was a new international order. The UN itself became a battleground. Heated rhetoric, mutual suspicions, and the danger of atomic war inaugurated a new Cold War atmosphere.

A NEW WORLD BORN: THE GUILD AT THE FOUNDING OF THE UNITED NATIONS
By Martin Popper

[Writing in 1985, Martin Popper, executive secretary of the Guild between 1940 and 1947, recalls the organization's role in the founding of the United Nations.]

I remember hearing or reading somewhere that the State Department had decided to designate a number of organizations as Consultants to the United States delegation. In my opinion, the public interest required that the Guild should be selected as a consultant organization. I went to the State Department and presented our case. Ultimately, 42 organizations were invited, and the Guild was one of them.

Representing the Guild was NLG President Robert W. Kenny, with myself and National Vice-President Bartley Crum as alternates. Kenny was California's attorney general at that time, and he made his San Francisco offices available to us for the duration.

The Consultants were admitted to all the deliberations of the conference and had ready access to the United States delegation, as well as to the representatives of the media, who were present in the thousands.

The Guild Consultants made singular contributions to the work of the conference in two areas. One related to the composition of the International Court of Justice (the World Court); the other involved the manner in which the powers of the Security Council were to be exercised.

Some delegates and influential members tried to persuade the conference to continue the existing World Court, established by the League of Nations. That body included judges from the Axis Powers and Franco Spain. The Guild urged the creation of a new Court. We published and distributed our brief on the subject to each of the fifty participating government delegations. The scholarly quality of our presentation rendered a genuine service to the delegates and it was the majority view.

On the matter of the Security Council, possibly the most fundamental issue before the conference, the Guild advocated the adoption of the unanimity principle: the right of veto by the permanent council members on issues of the conference. We recognized that without the unanimity principle there would be no United Nations—or at least no United Nations that the United States and Soviet Union would join.

The manner in which we NLG representatives conducted our work is worth recounting. There was a core of U.S. establishment organizations cooperating with each other. They had developed close relations

---

"A New World Born: The Guild at the Founding of the United Nations," by Martin Popper, *Guild Notes* (Summer 1985).

with the State Department. We were not part of this group. We were compelled to develop our own methods for publicizing our views.

We were particularly effective in press relations. The *New York Times* (which published a special daily UN edition) and *San Francisco Chronicle* printed several major articles based on our releases and press conferences. The delegates read these papers avidly. We also utilized the presence of the international press corps to indicate our support for the Nuremberg War Crimes Charter, and our demand that the leaders of Japan, including the Emperor, be indicted and tried by an international tribunal.

What distinguished our work from that of the other Consultants was our emphasis on the legal aspects of the issues at hand. We decided that our primary contacts would be with the lawyer members of the various delegations, and were able to establish strong ties with many of them.

The Consultant organizations were responsible for several lasting contributions. It is largely due to their sponsorship that the preamble of the Charter emphasizes the promotion of and respect for human rights and equal rights of men and women. Their efforts also led to the enactment of Article 68, which required the Economic and Social Council to establish a Human Rights Commission, and Article 71, which established the right of consultation between non-governmental organizations and the Economic and Social Council. Unfortunately, the Guild has not yet taken advantage of Article 71.

Secretary of State Stettinius's "Report to the President on the Results of the San Francisco Conference" contains this reference to the work of the Consultants: "Their presence in San Francisco meant that a very large body of American opinion which had been applying itself to the problems of international organization played a direct and material part in drafting the constitution of the United Nations."

Our effectiveness was demonstrated when the San Francisco chapter (a force in the community) invited the San Francisco Bar Association and Lawyers Club to jointly sponsor a dinner in honor of all the lawyer delegates to the conference. Most of those delegates and about 500 area lawyers attended the affair at the Palace Hotel. There were speeches, of course, and some were undoubtedly eloquent. But what I remember most is the genuine 100-proof bash that followed—500 lawyers and judges of all persuasions and nationalities spontaneously and uninhibitedly celebrating their one-world togetherness. It was international amity at its zenith.

Forty years later, the United Nations Charter remains a document of preeminent historical importance. The principles set forth therein express the hopes of humanity that aggression, dependence, poverty, and repression shall be eliminated from the face of the earth. These aspirations are now codified as integral parts of our international and domestic law. We must expose and resist every effort by our government to violate its provisions and to undermine its institutions. As lawyers, we should utilize the Charter in every available forum, to defend the victims of repression, to affirm the right of self-determination and independence, and to oppose every form of inequality.

THE NLG AND THE FBI AT THE UN SAN FRANCISCO CONFERENCE
By Michael Krinsky, Jonathan Moore, and Ann Mari Buitrago

["For most of its life," writes Michael Krinsky, "the Guild has been relatively an open book to the FBI." The Bureau's information was obtained through a variety of "investigative techniques," all of which were designed to destroy the Guild and discredit the reputation of its members.]

In 1945, the FBI apparently used information obtained from a wiretap on the Guild to disrupt the organization's efforts at the founding sessions of the United Nations. By means of this wiretap, the FBI monitored the activities of Guild members who were in San Francisco serving as official advisors to the U.S. delegation to the UN at these sessions. The FBI listened in as Guild members organized and recruited prestigious speakers for a series of six seminars on topics currently on the UN's agenda, for example, Constitutional Aspects of Dumbarton Oaks, Bretton Woods, the post-war role of China and Japan. Speakers included a Stanford University professor, a Stanford Law School professor, the chief counsel of the U.S. Treasury Department, and Dr. Avra Warren of the State Department. Dr. Warren subsequently cancelled his appearance. The inference to be drawn on the present record is that the FBI, forewarned by its wiretap, approached the State Department.

TRY THE WAR CRIMINALS NOW, LAWYERS URGE
By Martin Popper

[In the following excerpt from his oral history memoir, Martin Popper recounts the Guild's role at Nuremberg.]

"The NLG and the FBI at the UN San Francisco Conference," by Michael Krinsky, Jonathan Moore, and Ann Mari Buitrago, counsel for plaintiff, in Plaintiff's Principal Factual Papers in Opposition to the Motion of the United States for Partial Summary Judgment Dismissing the Damage Claims Arising from the FBI's Conduct and in Support of Plaintiff's Cross-Motion for Partial Summary Judgment, vol. 1, National Lawyers Guild, Plaintiff, against Attorney General, et al., Defendants, Sept. 26, 1984.

"Try the War Criminals Now, Lawyers Urge," by Martin Popper, Oral History Memoir, MCLI.

Later the National Lawyers Guild and the American Bar Association were invited by Mr. Justice Jackson each to send two official observers to the Nuremberg Trials.

Why were you invited, do you think?

That's very interesting, because Jackson had been a member of the Guild and had resigned years before. He considered that the Guild's position, I imagine, on the War Crimes Trial on Nuremberg was important, and he wanted us to observe the trial and to make our observations known to the American legal profession. He knew that our general views of the world and the American Bar Association's were different, and he felt it apparently fair and reasonable that both those views should be represented. It turned out that our views were more helpful to him than the American Bar Association's. There was an awful lot of discussion in the legal profession as to whether the crimes were legal, under international law.

Anyway, we went to Nuremberg, Bob Kenny and I. It took us two nights. We got to Paris in the middle of the night, so we had to stay in the airport till the next morning, because we had to get a plane to Nuremberg; we traveled on U.S. Army planes because we had been invited by Justice Jackson. When we got to Nuremberg we were pretty damn tired, and Jackson asked me when we met with him, "Where have you been? Didn't you know that I'd sent a plane to pick you up in Paris?"

I gave several press conferences on our reaction to what we were seeing. One was covered in the *New York Times*, in which I indicated that in some respects the court was bending over backwards to see to it that the defendants were given their rights. That pleased Justice Jackson; he told me so. And then I either gave another interview or wrote an article after I came back for a newspaper called *P.M.*, I believe it was, critical of the fact that they had not included among the defendants and that there was no plan to try the Nazi industrialists and financiers. That I don't think did please Justice Jackson.

WAR CRIMES AND COLD WAR CONSPIRACIES
By Mary M. Kaufman

[Constitutional and international lawyer Mary Kaufman was a prosecuting attorney in the U.S. War Crimes Trial of I. G. Farben at Nuremberg.]

I was working with the Wage Stabilization Board in Washington, D.C., in 1946, and that agency was closing down because the war was

---

"War Crimes and Cold War Conspiracies," by Mary M. Kaufman, from *The Relevant Lawyers*, Ann Fagan Ginger, ed. (New York: Simon & Schuster, 1972).

over. Somebody who was in Nuremberg and was scouting around for talent for the American prosecution team asked would I go. I said I would be delighted.

I went in February 1947 as a civilian employee of the United States Army. I had to leave my five-year-old son behind until I found a house in Germany—Army rules. My parents brought him to Nuremberg in September, and they stayed and took care of him while I worked. I couldn't have done it without them.

I was to help prosecute one of the major industrial concerns—an international cartel: I. G. Farben. The people in the dock were its board of directors. This was the second echelon of war criminals, being prosecuted in separate trials in each of the occupied zones.

I was going there to be a trial lawyer, to be a prosecutor. The team for the I. G. Farben trial had already been more or less settled when I arrived. And I found myself waging a real battle, not with the head of the team, who was a rather nice guy, but with the subhead of the team. I think it was because I was a woman. While it's true I came there with very limited trial experience, I had a background of considerable mature legal experience and skill. I simply didn't yield, and I was assigned as a trial lawyer.

I. G. Farben was charged with all the war crimes. We had a staff of six or seven prosecutors. There were twenty-four defendants in the dock, and they had about fifty German lawyers representing them, Nazi-oriented in the main. I witnessed quite an interesting development in these lawyers. In the beginning they would come walking into the courtroom very obsequiously, all fifty of them, bowing. But as time, and the Cold War, progressed, they stood more upright, became bolder, until they were arrogantly projecting the Nazi ideology and reaffirming the pretext for the whole Nazi invasion, namely the need to defeat the Communists.

The Cold War was having a profound effect on the prosecution side as well. We found ourselves in the peculiar position of working very hard to prosecute the industrialists and being impeded in every way by the failure of the State Department to support us. We didn't have adequate materials; our orders were countermanded; there were numerous incidents.

By the time the verdict against I. G. Farben came out, the Cold War was in full blast. The Berlin airlift had already begun. So the Farben people first were acquitted of all charges of waging aggressive war, in spite of overwhelming evidence of their participation in it.

When it came to property rights, it is interesting to note that the tribunal was not so generous. It convicted all of the defendants for the war crime of plundering property in occupied Europe. Human beings did not figure so high in the scale of justice—at least for the two majority members. They found only some defendants guilty of the crime of the use of slave labor, although, as the dissenter pointed out, the evidence was abundant to convict all. The sentences ranged from one and a half years to a maximum of eight years. A range of four to eight years was given to those who participated in the crime of annihilating thousands of human beings.

These were the people whom even a Cold War tribunal found guilty of war crimes and crimes against humanity. These were the makers of the gas used for extermination; the procurers and users of slave labor from the infamous Auschwitz and elsewhere—used by Farben to the point of exhaustion—and then sent to the extermination chambers. Even the two members of the tribunal who voted acquittal on some of these charges said, "With knowledge of the abuse and inhumane treatment meted out to the inmates by the SS, Farben aggravated the misery of these unfortunates in the way in which they used their labor." The not so respectful dissenter on the tribunal, who voted to convict, said that "it was no overstatement to conclude that Farben's working conditions resulted in the death of thousands of human beings."

When they read the judgment to us, we were in a state of utter shock.

Of course, the Allies had made agreements that never again would these industrial powers, I. G. Farben and Krupp, be allowed to emerge in that strong a form. And the Allied Control Commission had responsibility to see that the military forces were not rebuilt. But these agreements were not carried out. Today I. G. Farben and Krupp are as powerful as they ever were.

I don't know where historians trace the beginning of the Cold War, but I know from personal experience that at the very moment when the principles of Nuremberg were being fashioned, the seeds of the Cold War were already sprouting: we had used that atom bomb on a civilian population for the purposes of intimidating the Soviet Union in the peace negotiations that followed.

The prosecutions of war criminals were motivated by three forces. The world was horrified by the excesses of the war, particularly the barbarities of the German forces. In addition, our explosion of the atom bomb over Hiroshima and Nagasaki was so terrifying for many people all over the world that there was an enormous public clamor for some brake, some deterrent force to be exerted against potential future wars. The other force was the usual attempt of the victor to obtain control over the vanquished.

If we are concerned with the application of principles of law to everybody, not just to the losers, the basic and fundamental meaning of Nuremberg is that we must assume some personal responsibility for its enforcement.

THE INTERNATIONAL ASSOCIATION
OF DEMOCRATIC LAWYERS
By Martin Popper

[The Guild's commitment to the creation of an international bar association finally reached fruition in the fall of 1946.]

For some time the National Lawyers Guild has endeavored to establish the closest relations among the lawyers of the United Nations as a means of contributing towards the development of an effective international law as well as unified activity in the interest of lasting peace and democratic advancement.

An important step in this direction has just been made by the formation of the International Association of Democratic Lawyers. This new bar association was formed by the unanimous decision of the lawyers and judges of twenty-four nations who took part in the recent International Congress in Paris, October 24–28, 1946.

In a large sense the Paris Congress was the culmination of the sustained efforts of the Guild which during all the war years had urged the creation of such an international bar association. The foundations were laid in the conferences of United Nations legal representatives at San Francisco and through personal contacts by Guild officials in visits to countries of Europe and Latin America. The pioneering work of the Guild in the field of war crimes and as a consultant organization to the United States delegation at San Francisco was a significant factor in defining the implications of international cooperation among jurists.

The Paris Congress brought together for the first time the foremost lawyers of those nations which played a leading part in the defeat of Nazi Germany. The spirit which permeated every report and speech indicated that these colleagues of ours felt deeply about the responsibility of our profession to safeguard democratic liberties, to make international law an instrument for peaceful relations among nations, and to fully explore the meaning of such new legal developments as the Nuremberg Trial. The unfinished tasks of post-war democracy were dramatized by the presence of delegations representing Republican Spain and the lawyers of the EAM, counsel for Greek freedom.

The United States delegation was composed of five members of the Guild. The National Bar Association accepted the invitation to the Congress but at the last moment, due to illness, its delegate was unable to attend. It is expected that this association will become an affiliate in the near future. The American Bar Association was invited but did not send any representative.

"The International Association of Democratic Lawyers," by Martin Popper, *Lawyers Guild Review* 6:4 (Sept.–Oct. 1946).

If we grasp the fact that in the creation of the International Association of Democratic Lawyers, a forum exists from which the viewpoint of the Guild in international law and relations can be stated, we shall at the same time serve to increase our strength and prestige among the lawyers of our own country. We exercised an influence during the San Francisco Conference. As part of the new Association, we can be even more effective at the capitol of the United Nations.

THE JEWISH PEOPLE AND PALESTINE
By the Guild and Bartley C. Crum

[Few issues caused more anguish for the Guild than the fate of the survivors of the Holocaust. What follows is the Guild's policy statement and a report by Bartley Crum, Guild vice president and member of the Anglo-American Committee of Inquiry.]

The tragedy of the Jewish people is a burden on the conscience of all mankind. Events make essential that the National Lawyers Guild, as an organization of forward-looking lawyers and jurists in the United States, express the rights of the Jewish people in the international field and that the obligations of all nations to them be clearly established. Accordingly, this brief statement of Guild policy with respect to the Jewish people and particularly to those surviving the Nazi program of extermination who are commonly known as Displaced Persons is presented.

We are concerned with three rights: the right of haven in the United States; the right of return to and security in European homes; and the right of entry into Palestine. These are not privileges to be conferred as a matter of grace, but rights to be recognized by international law.

The American obligation to displaced persons was partly recognized by President Truman's directive on December 22nd, 1945, for the application of available quotas of Central European nations for the benefit of displaced persons. The Anglo-American Committee of Inquiry recognized that nations could not in good faith demand the opening of the doors of Palestine to Jewish immigration without themselves making some contribution to the solution of the problem by liberalization of their own immigration laws and procedures. It therefore recommended that the American and British Governments together with other countries should endeavor immediately to find new homes for all displaced persons seeking admittance.

While it is recognized that the United Nations embody the promise of a system for the universal protection of human rights, the new orga-

---

"The Jewish People and Palestine," by the NLG and Bartley C. Crum, *Lawyers Guild Review* 6:2 (May–June 1946), and *Guild Lawyer* (July–Aug. 1946).

nization has not as yet been given power to protect or safeguard human rights nor does it possess the machinery or the competence to take over the tasks of restitution, rehabilitation, and resettlement for which provision can be made in the peace treaties. The minimum concepts of decency and justice demand, therefore, that the peace treaties between the United Nations and the former enemy countries contain appropriate provisions for the righting of these wrongs and the redressing of these grievances, and, above all, for securing for the Jewish people remaining in the European countries the right to a free and peaceful life.

The League of Nations, by unanimous approval of its members, and with the acceptance of the United States, by separate convention in 1924, mandated the area known as Palestine to Great Britain. Among other provisions it specifically directed that the Mandatory facilitate Jewish immigration and land settlement in Palestine.

In the Munich era of 1939, Great Britain's continuous violation of the basic tenets of the Mandate reached its climax with the promulgation of the White Paper. By the terms of this paper, issued without consultation or approval of the League of Nations or any of its members, the future immigration of Jewish people into Palestine was to be limited to 75,000, spread over a period of five years. It provided further that the British Government would do "everything in their power to create conditions which will enable the independent Arab State (of Palestine) to come into being within ten years."

This action by Great Britain was the culmination of a course of conduct which demonstrates clearly that she has violated and sabotaged the terms and principles of the Mandate. She has done this with the connivance and through the use of reactionary Arab puppets who have always acted against the best interests of the common people of this area.

We maintain that the few potentates who at present raise their voices in opposition to continued Jewish immigration do not speak for, and have no right to speak for, the vast Arab population who have been held in complete subjugation by the so-called "spokesmen."

The end of the war has revealed that barely one and one-half million of the seven million Jews of Europe have survived the slaughter. Many of these are still living in desperate conditions in refugee camps, buoyed up by the sole hope that they will be able eventually to reestablish their lives among their own people in Palestine. Many others are no less determined to leave countries in which anti-Semitism continues a potent and vicious factor. In the overwhelming majority they, too, look to Palestine as their one hope of a dignified self-respecting existence.

These facts were confirmed by the unanimous Report of the recent Anglo-American Committee of Inquiry, which, in recommending the immediate admission of 100,000 Jews into Palestine as well as the removal of the unwarranted restrictions on Jewish settlement in Palestine, repudiated the policy of the 1939 White Paper.

The continued delay in fulfilling those two recommendations of the Anglo-American Committee of Inquiry is open to the gravest criticism.

Great Britain's unilateral action of dividing the area of Palestine and setting up an alleged independent state of Trans-Jordan further violated the terms of the Mandate. In addition, her very recent suppression of the civil liberties of the Palestinian settlers, and the imposition of martial law, are not only contrary to the terms of the Mandate, but violate every concept of decent, democratic government.

We therefore propose that the U.S. disassociate itself from the attitude of the British Government toward Palestine and exercise its influence toward the following objectives:

1. The immediate lifting of martial law and the restoration of civil rights of the settlers of Palestine.
2. The immediate issuance of 100,000 entry visas to the displaced persons of Europe.
3. The immediate allowance of unrestricted immigration and land acquisition in Palestine.
4. The removal of the Mandate of Palestine from Great Britain and the transfer of the administration of Palestine to the jurisdiction of the United Nations.
5. The determination of the ultimate peaceful solution of the status of Palestine by all the people of Palestine.

THE STATE OF AMERICAN FOREIGN POLICY
By the Guild Committee on International Law and Relations

["No dispute," Guild Vice-President Osmond Fraenkel wrote UN Secretary-General Trygve Lie in March 1946, "is of so great magnitude as to warrant the disruption of the unanimity of the Great Powers." The U.S., he affirmed, must not violate the UN Charter, and the UN Security Council must gain control of atomic energy.]

The years between World War I and World War II, which saw the rise of Fascism, were a period of chaos in international relations and international law. The inability and unwillingness of the Western Democracies to establish a system of collective security against the menace of Nazi Germany led to the increasingly rapid development of the infamous appeasement policy which reached its climax at Munich. The League of

---

"The State of American Foreign Policy," by the Committee on International Law and Relations, *Lawyers Guild Review* 6:1 (Jan.-Feb. 1946).

Nations served merely as the vehicle for the furtherance of these antidemocratic doctrines.

It is now evident that the United States shared responsibility for the crises in world relations ending in World War II. Our isolation from the League of Nations indicated an unwillingness to participate in collective action for peace. The Embargo Act aided the Axis conquest of Republican Spain. The continuation of "commercial relations with Japan" helped the Axis in its war against China. Our policy of antagonism towards the Soviet Union was part of the pattern of appeasement.

It was only in the midst of actual war for survival that we adopted the new policy which gave us military victory and laid the basis for a durable peace. Step by step this policy has been embodied in various agreements and treaties which comprise the new international law.

We may recall these steps. The Atlantic Charter with its declaration of certain fundamental war aims; the formation of the United Nations as a military alliance; the Moscow and Teheran Agreements, which gave formal expression to the Big Three coalition for war and peace; and the Yalta Agreement, projecting the idea of a United Nations organization and embodying in legal terms President Roosevelt's unanimity formula.

It was at San Francisco soon after the present administration took office that the country first witnessed a whole series of official actions constituting a departure from the policies to which the United States had subscribed in the Atlantic Charter and at Moscow, Teheran, Yalta, and Dumbarton Oaks.

At the very beginning, the United States delegation threatened the success of the Conference by sponsoring the admission of Fascist Argentina and, again, by challenging the authority of the Security Council as conceived at Dumbarton Oaks through an attempt to establish a Hemisphere Bloc. Then, in quick succession, the United States delegation opposed such democratic objectives for the United Nations Organization as the right of independence for colonial peoples and the right to work. Finally, it cast a decisive vote against advisory representation for the World Federation of Trade Unions.

Such an examination leads to the conclusion that the administration's foreign policy has been violative of the principles which governed the conduct of the United Nations war effort, and which, as incorporated in the UNO Charter, provided the foundations for a lasting peace.

The National Lawyers Guild, as an integral part of the democratic movement of our country, shall continue to carry on its activities in support of a program for world peace. We shall exert our efforts towards compelling a return by our government to the Roosevelt program of Anglo-American-Soviet friendship as the cornerstone of United Nations collaboration.

We urge the following immediate course of conduct by our government:

Take steps to vest the control of atomic energy in the Security Council of the United Nations.

Extend generous credits to nations in need without interference in their internal affairs.

Withdraw all American armed forces from China.

Sever diplomatic relations with Franco Spain—and prosecute Franco as a war criminal.

Exert the full force of our influence in the UNO for the abrogation of the British White Paper and in favor of unrestricted immigation of Jews into Palestine.

Enact legislation acknowledging the right of complete independence for Puerto Rico.

THE EUROPEAN RECOVERY PROGRAM— THE MARTIAL PLAN
By the Guild Committee on International Law and Relations

[In the following report the Guild Committee criticizes the unilateral approach to European recovery adopted by the Truman administration as incompatible with the principles of the United Nations.]

During the war and for some time after the end of hostilities, it was universally recognized that the same cooperation which was indispensable to victory in the war would also be necessary in the peace that followed. The United Nations organization is the embodiment of that principle. It was also recognized that the interdependence of the world economy was such as to make the economic well-being of each part a matter of vital concern to other parts; that only genuine international cooperative action could avoid the plagues of depressions, crisis, and the conflicts of nations and groups of nations, which lead to war.

Our abandonment of these principles, our return to unilateral action, has brought no solution to the critical economic problems of Europe. It *has* served to increase division and hostility among the United Nations which has mounted to a point dangerous to world peace. Moreover, the United Nations has been weakened by our practice of bypassing it to such a point that many begin to lose faith in its value as an instrument for peace.

For these reasons, the Guild has supported consistently the adoption of international, rather than unilateral, measures for the solution of

---

"The European Recovery Program—The Martial Plan," by the Committee on International Law and Relations, *Lawyers Guild Review* 8:1 (Jan.-Feb. 1948).

world or European political or economic problems. It has also opposed the employment of relief or other aid for political purposes. We must view the European Recovery Program in the light of these principles.

The historic speech by General Marshall on June 5, 1947, at Harvard University did not present the details of a plan for European reconstruction; that speech was simply a "suggestion" that the countries of Europe agree among themselves as to the "requirements of the situation," and carried the notion that the United States would then proceed to give friendly aid in the drafting of a European program, to be supported later by the United States within the limits of its ability. Our policy, he explained, "is directed not against any country or doctrine, but against hunger, poverty, desperation, and chaos."

The decisive and controlling aspects of the plan consist of these factors:

1. The Administrator will decide, commodity by commodity, and country by country, what, if any, aid shall be given to any participating country;
2. Relief and credit will not be granted in a lump sum, but will be allocated *from month to month;*
3. The United States may terminate relief or the further extension of credit at any time; and
4. The recipient countries are required to enter into a contract binding them to comply with a series of conditions precedent to the granting by the United States of any form of assistance.

The imposition of such conditions, taken together with the fact that the proponents of the program have constantly emphasized its anti-Soviet or anti-Communist function, establish that the program necessarily and inescapably involves interference by the United States in the internal economic and political affairs of the participating countries. This is true even though the governments concerned may consent to their subjection to these conditions. It is the basic premise of the program that their condition is desperate; that unless they receive this assistance some of the participating countries will soon suffer complete economic collapse. Under these conditions, consent cannot have meaning.

■ SEVEN

The Cold War Begins (1947–1953)

ROBERT J. SILBERSTEIN LOOKS BACK ON THE SEVEN LEAN YEARS, 1947–1954
By Robert J. Silberstein

THE NATIONAL LAWYERS Guild Convention that began on April 13, 1947, followed closely on an ominous blow to First Amendment rights. On March 21, 1947, President Harry Truman had issued Executive Order 9835, instituting a so-called loyalty program in the executive department. The National Executive Board committed the Guild to fulfill its responsibility to defend the individual victims of the "loyalty" program and to explain to the general public and to the Bar the value of civil liberties, their grave peril, and the need to defend them.

Despite the intensity of the attack on First Amendment rights, the Guild did not lose sight of other issues of compelling importance. We opposed universal military training and the draft as dangerous to the welfare of the nation. We opposed the Taft-Hartley Act as threatening the labor movement through its prohibitions of the closed shop and of contributions in primaries and federal elections, and because it established political tests for holding union office. The Guild was active in urging a meaningful national housing bill, federal rent controls, and a national health insurance bill. We urged and worked for legislation to guarantee fair employment practices, an adequate minimum wage, anti-lynching, and anti-poll tax legislation—to permit poor people, especially blacks, to vote in several states.

In May 1948 the biggest and most far-reaching repressive effort was launched. The so-called Mundt-Nixon Bill, the Subversive Activities Bill, was quickly

---

"Robert J. Silberstein Looks Back on the Seven Lean Years, 1947–1954," *NLG Practitioner* 33:1 (Winter 1975).

passed in the House to extend the loyalty oath program to all the people and the organizations through which they could express their views and hope to influence the policies of the government. It authorized the attorney general to list organizations as "Communist political" or "Communist front," defined as groups utilized by the World Communist Movement or by a "Communist political organization." The Guild opposed the bill in the Senate. Professor Thomas I. Emerson, of the Yale Law School, testified against the bill and filed a Guild brief on its unconstitutionality, which was distributed to all members of the Congress and to hundreds of organizations. We lobbied against the bill and assisted Senators who worked against the bill through the years of the fight, including the final unsuccessful filibuster, one of the few in which distinguished liberal Senators participated. [The bill passed in 1950 as the Subversive Activities Control Act or the McCarran Internal Security Act.]

THE CONSTITUTIONAL RIGHT TO ADVOCATE POLITICAL, SOCIAL, AND ECONOMIC CHANGE—AN ESSENTIAL OF AMERICAN DEMOCRACY
By the Guild National Constitutional Liberties Committee

[On March 21, 1947, only nine days after delivering the "get-tough" anti-Communist Truman Doctrine speech, the President promulgated Executive Order 9835, requiring a loyalty investigation of all civilian employees in the federal government. The Guild responded immediately with this report denouncing the abridgement of civil liberties.]

It is incumbent upon those who love liberty at all times to be alert for any effort which might tend to subvert it. We cannot ignore any attempt to restrict the political rights of the American people. In recent months, the nation has been deluged on all sides with legislative proposals, executive orders, and even judicial decisions which again, as in similar historical periods in our nation's existence, threaten the keystone of our democracy—the Bill of Rights.

To speak freely means to a workingman the right to agitate for better wages and a higher standard of living; to a Negro, the right to struggle for equality of opportunity in every sphere of life; and for every person who values the dignity of human beings, it means the right to advocate social changes which will broaden the vistas of man's progress.

Thus the President of the United States has issued an executive order creating a loyalty commission, designed to investigate the backgrounds

---

"The Constitutional Right to Advocate Political, Social, and Economic Change—An Essential of American Democracy," by The National Constitutional Liberties Committee, *Lawyers Guild Review* 7:2 (March–April 1947).

and political opinions of all federal employees and to discharge those considered to have "Communist leanings." The order empowers the Attorney General, without any restriction, to designate those organizations in the United States which shall be considered as subversive and the members of which shall be regarded as disloyal.

It is, therefore, fitting that these matters should receive the serious consideration of the National Lawyers Guild. One of the Guild's primary functions is vigilantly to defend the civil rights of the American people, of the Negroes, of political parties, of trade unions, and of the foreign-born, to the end that the democratic process may be strengthened and the American way of life preserved. The Guild has always believed that all of these rights are cognate rights, indissolubly linked together, and that to strike at one is to strike at all.

It is apparent from the foregoing that the Executive Order of the President is offensive to our constitution in many respects. It:

1. Constitutes an unwarranted intrusion of the executive into the sphere reserved for the legislative branch;
2. Denies the constitutional safeguards of a fair hearing;
3. Sanctions the unconstitutional doctrine of guilt by association;
4. Sets up the Attorney General as a high priest of political orthodoxy;
5. Violates the constitutional doctrine that standards for punishment be precise and definite.

We are living today in a period of rising opposition to the civil rights of minority groups. Not since the post-war days of the First World War have we seen so strong a movement to deny constitutional rights to those who hold unorthodox views. It would be foolhardy to suppose that so serious a deprivation of constitutional rights and the freedom of opinion can be stopped at the point of federal employees. The analogy is too clear, its logic, if once permitted, too irrefutable, to prevent its extension to other fields. If these indeed be standards of loyalty to our government, why should they not be extended to state and municipal employees, to officials of our quasi-public institutions such as schools, universities, or labor unions? They may well be extended to employees in public utilities or essential industries, who by presidential edict may be declared to be government employees. The object lessons of Fascism are too close upon us to permit us to forget that just such a step of requiring political orthodoxy among government employees was among the first taken by Hitler upon his accession to power in 1933.

To those who urge that we sit back and wait to see how the order is administered, we can answer that we may learn by waiting, but at too late a time and too great a cost.

HARVARD LAW SCHOOL SEMINAR ON CIVIL LIBERTIES (SPRING 1948)
Sponsored by the Harvard Law School Chapter of the Guild

[This syllabus is testimony to the Guild's interest in law students as well as to the Harvard chapter's ties to its prestigious faculty.]

Seminar Course on THE LAW PROTECTING CIVIL LIBERTIES AND RIGHTS

This course has been organized to meet for one two-hour seminar each Tuesday throughout the spring term at Harvard Law School. Assignments consist of two- to three-hour readings of leading cases on the subject of the particular seminar. Admission is open to all Harvard Law students, but the size was originally limited to 30 members. Instructors are drawn primarily from members of the Harvard Law faculty.

The course is aimed primarily at providing the substance of the law now protecting civil rights and liberties. It is sponsored by the Harvard chapter of the National Lawyers Guild, and was organized by a committee of students headed by George Spiegel and including Lloyd H. Reed, Irving Ferman, Bernard Frank, Richard Gyory, and Arnold Parker. The final assignments are the result of consultation with the instructor handling the particular seminar.

Agenda:

I. Scope and Sources of Law Protecting Individual Liberties and Rights. Professor Mark DeWolfe Howe, Feb. 10
II. Freedom of Assembly and Association. Charles Anderson, Graduate student, Feb. 17
III. Freedom of Speech and Press. Professor Thomas Reed Powell, Feb. 24
IV. Freedom of Religion; Separation of Church and State. Professor Robert R. Bowie, Mar. 2
V. Search and Seizure. Professor Edmund Morgan, Mar. 9
VI. Elements of a Fair Trial. Professor Edmund Morgan, Mar. 16
VII. Rights of Government Employees; Limits on Legislative Inquiry. John L. Saltonstall Jr., Boston attorney, Mar. 23
VIII. Citizenship, Suffrage, and Political Parties, Mar. 30
IX. Procedures by Which Civil Liberties Issues Are Raised. Osmond K. Fraenkel, Am. Civil Lib. U., Apr. 6

"Harvard Law School Seminar on Civil Liberties (Spring 1948)," sponsored by the Harvard Law School Chapter of the NLG, Ann Fagan Ginger Papers, MCLI. Guild Law Student Chapter Activities from the *Guild Student Bulletin* (May 1947).

X. Denial of Equal Protection by Federal and State Governments. Professor David F. Cavers, Apr. 13

XI. Federal Intervention Against the Denial of Rights by State Officials and by Individuals. Professor Paul A. Freund, Apr. 20

XII. Rights of Aliens. Professor Ernest J. Brown, Apr. 21

XIII. Suspension of Civil Rights in War Times, May 4

[Harvard Law School was not the only Guild chapter in which progressive-minded law students could be found. The following items are drawn from *The Guild Student Bulletin* for May 1947.]

New York University

N.Y.U. cosponsored a meeting with Columbia Law School chapter at which O. John Rogge, former Chief of the Civil Rights Division of the Department of Justice, spoke. With membership approaching the seventy mark, the N.Y.U. chapter is winding up its first semester. In addition to other activities, the chapter is completing a "Career Series."

University of Michigan

The chapter, which has 37 members, has conducted an active program of lectures and student seminars. In addition they have cooperated actively with the Detroit chapter of the Guild in behalf of the state Fair Employment Practices and Fair Education Practices Bills. They also have done an important piece of work in preparing 150 questions and answers designed to help potential voters of the State of Alabama gain the right to vote in local and federal elections. Literacy requirements are very burdensome in that state.

Howard University

On April eighteenth, David Rein, Secretary of the District of Columbia chapter of the Guild, Charles Wilson, and Charles J. Morris of Columbia University addressed the student body of the Law School. The students displayed genuine interest in the Guild Student Section, and it is apparent that the organization of a chapter has been delayed only by the expressed preference of the students for a District of Columbia chapter rather than a chapter at Howard itself. Efforts to enroll a group at George Washington Law School are in progress, and it is expected that a District of Columbia student chapter will come into being following the period of examination.

Columbia

Finding its treasury in a rather shaky condition, the Columbia Division launched a very successful social program that helped its members to become acquainted and added almost one hundred dollars to its operating funds. Membership at Columbia is approaching 90.

University of California, Hastings Chapter

The Hastings chapter, which had 70 members, has been much concerned with school and veteran student problems. They voted against permitting veterans with one year's training at law prior to service to enter the Bar on motion after graduation without taking a Bar examination. The reason was that they opposed special favors for selected individuals. They also opposed the enactment of the notorious Tenney anti-education bills as an unjustified intrusion on academic freedom. They recommended defeat of the pending bill to lower legal educational standards by extending the same privileges to unaccredited law schools as are now enjoyed by accredited schools.

Wayne University

The Wayne chapter, which has 65 members out of the 200 day students, is firmly established. Its activity has consisted of lectures by prominent members of the Detroit chapter who are either specialists or judges of the circuit court. They arranged a very successful "coffee hour" to introduce the students to the faculty. They are about to commence publication of a Guild student bulletin.

REPORT ON CERTAIN ALLEGED PRACTICES OF THE FBI
By a Special Committee of the Guild,
with an introduction by Michael Krinsky

[Americans of the Cold War generation trusted and admired the FBI. The Bureau's exploits were celebrated in everything from comic books to government reports. "G-Men," as portrayed by actors James Cagney and Edward G. Robinson, captured public enemies, whether gangsters or Nazi spies; they did not engage in wire-tapping, illegal searches and seizures, nor did they pry into opinions and beliefs. Or did they?]

On June 14, 1949, the Bureau learned from its tap on the Guild office that Executive Secretary Silberstein, Vice-President Thomas Emerson, and Guild President Clifford Durr were preparing to issue a press release calling on President Truman to appoint a committee of prominent citizens to investigate the FBI. The FBI also learned from the tap something not included in the press release: the Guild's NEB had instructed that in the event Truman failed to appoint a committee, the Guild "will undertake to form such a committee itself to make the

---

"Report on Certain Alleged Practices of the FBI," by a Special Committee of the NLG, *Lawyers Guild Review* 10:1 (Winter 1950).

best type of study" possible. The stimulus for the Guild's actions was the revelations of FBI surveillance in the recent Judith Coplon espionage trial.

For once the Bureau was on the defensive, the fragmentary disclosures in the *Coplon* case of FBI spying on citizens' political activities having become front-page news, and Hoover feared the impact of this high-level Guild report. He followed the Guild committee's work closely through repeated burglaries of the Guild office.

Although the Attorney General did indeed reject the Guild's forthcoming report even before its issuance, he would not take the ultimate step Hoover had been urging of listing the Guild as a subversive organization. Hoover arranged for the next best thing: a public branding of the Guild as a subversive organization by the House Committee on Un-American Activities. On the very eve of the Guild's release of its report criticizing the FBI, Hoover had Congressman Richard Nixon publicly call for a HUAC investigation of the Guild, successfully diverting the press's attention from FBI practices. By the time of the Guild's press conference, press attention had shifted from the Guild's demand that the FBI be investigated to Nixon's demand that the Guild be investigated. The press and broadcast coverage the following week coupled the two stories, thus severely blunting the impact of the Guild's Special Report.

■

Report on Certain Alleged Practices of the FBI

The practices and policies of the FBI violate our laws, infringe our liberties, and threaten our democracy. Remedial action is required immediately, as follows:

(1) The Attorney General should immediately issue a directive directing the FBI to cease engaging in practices which violate federal law, including wiretapping, mail opening, illegal searches. It should be plain that there should be no exceptions to this directive.

(2) The Attorney General should immediately direct the FBI to confine its investigations to cases where there is reasonable basis for belief that federal crimes have been or may be committed, and to the limited other categories of legitimate exercise of FBI jurisdiction. He should direct the FBI not to investigate persons merely because they are believed to have dissident views and associations. He should direct the FBI to end its fantastic program of investigating, in the name of internal security, the "loyalty" of the population. He should instruct the FBI that persons' views, beliefs, union memberships, other associations, and propaganda activities are not the concern of the FBI so long as no violations of federal law are involved.

He should make it plain that these directions are intended to be obeyed, and that they are not (as some of Mr. Hoover's statements apparently are) intended only for public consumption.

(3) The issuance of directives of cessation is not enough. The President should direct a thorough investigation of the programs, practices, and policies of the FBI. Only then can there be known the full steps which must be taken to correct all improper activities, including any not yet revealed. Such steps should include reorientation of FBI agents and the dismissal of those who are not amenable to the process. Such an investigation should be conducted by a group of able and distinguished private citizens having, by executive authority, full access to FBI files and plenary powers of interrogation.

The plain fact is that the liberties of the American people are not safe so long as the FBI continues on its present path.

THE KEYNOTE ADDRESS OF THE 1950 GUILD CONVENTION
By Clifford J. Durr

[Guild survival during the brutally repressive years of the early 1950s owed much to the courage and skill of its leaders. The presidency of Clifford J. Durr stands out in this regard. He was a Rhodes scholar from Alabama and brother-in-law of Supreme Court Justice Hugo Black. Appointed to the Federal Communications Commission (FCC) in 1941, he established a reputation for integrity, frequently battling Congressman Martin Dies and the FBI. Faced with the choice of a second term as FCC commissioner in 1948 and the obligation of implementing the Truman administration federal employee loyalty program, Durr resigned in protest.]

This particular moment of American history is not a happy one for the lawyer who takes seriously the responsibilities of his profession and the oath he took upon entering it. The rule of law appears to be giving way under the corrosive effect of fear. In the name of loyalty, men are officially empowered and directed to sit in secret judgment upon the minds and emotions of their fellow citizens, to deny them the right to confront their accusers, to try them on the unsworn testimony of unknown witnesses, and to convict them on speculations as to their state of mind. In the name of security, the Attorney General of the United States is authorized by *ex parte* and unreviewable decree to prescribe what organizations we may join; our secret police are given surveillance over our beliefs and associations; agents and informers are sent forth to take down our words and make note of our comings and goings; neighbors

---

"The Keynote Address of the 1950 Guild Convention," by Clifford J. Durr, *Lawyers Guild Review* 10:2 (Spring 1950).

are encouraged to spy upon neighbors; and tattlers and gossips are officially raised to a new level of dignity and power.

Men are being punished for mere "teaching" and "advocacy" unaccompanied by illegal acts, and lawyers sent to prison for vigor in the defense of their clients. The fundamental American idea that people are to be judged on the basis of their own behavior and not the behavior of others appears to be giving way to the alien doctrine of guilt by association. The basic legal principle that every man is presumed innocent until his guilt is established beyond a reasonable doubt is giving way to a weird new doctrine of guilt by accusation, and it looks as if that doctrine in turn will be supplanted by an even newer doctrine of guilt by denial.

What lies behind our loyalty oaths and loyalty programs? What weakness has been disclosed in the American idea that makes it necessary to send men to prison for mere "teaching" and "advocacy" unaccompanied by wrongful acts? What secret menace lies hidden in the guarantee of the right of counsel set forth in the Sixth Amendment to our Constitution that makes it necessary to nullify that right by intimidating lawyers? Have the lessons of history been so completely discredited that we must now honor informers, gossips and tattlers by conferring upon them the badge of true patriotism? Have the American traditions and sacred guarantees contained in our Bill of Rights now become barriers to our freedom and our safety?

COLD WAR FOREIGN POLICIES STIR INTERNAL DEBATE: YUGOSLAVIA AND KOREA
By the National Lawyers Guild

[Secretary of State Dean Acheson remarked in 1950 that there was no longer any distinction between foreign and domestic questions. Guild policy was no exception to that observation, but relative unity on domestic issues did not mean similar agreement on foreign policy. The cases of Yugoslavia and Korea are instructive.

[When the International Association of Democratic Lawyers expelled the Yugoslavian delegation in October 1949, many Guild members were shocked to learn that their representative had approved the action. In response, the Guild adopted the following resolution.]

Whereas, at a meeting of the Council of the International Association of Democratic Lawyers, held at Rome on October 28, 1949, its Yugoslav Section was expelled upon the ground that the representatives of the Association of Yugoslav Lawyers refused to disassociate them-

---

"Cold War Foreign Policies Stir Internal Debate: Yugoslavia and Korea," statements by the NLG, *Lawyers Guild Review* 10:2 (Spring 1950), and 11:1 (Winter 1951).

selves from the policies of the Government of their country, and the appeal by the Yugoslav delegation was referred to the next Congress of the International Association of Democratic Lawyers to be held in 1950, and

Whereas, such action was taken without prior notice to the National Lawyers Guild, and

Whereas, said action of the International Association of Democratic Lawyers involves accusations and denials concerning an issue which the National Lawyers Guild believes should not constitute a basis for expulsion of a national section,

Be it resolved by the National Lawyers Guild, in Convention assembled, that the National Lawyers Guild disapproves the aforesaid action of the Council of the International Association of Democratic Lawyers and instructs its delegates or representatives to any congress or meeting of the International Association of Democratic Lawyers to vote to restore the Yugoslav section to membership.

[The Korean War, which began on June 25, 1950, presented a much more difficult problem. When the National Executive Board convened in early September, sharp differences were apparent. Some NEB members endorsed a statement denouncing the North Korean invasion. Others did not agree that North Korea had been the invader, and called for a cease-fire and settlement, but refused to support the United States–sponsored UN counteroffensive. The carefully crafted compromise that was reached reflected the participants' understanding that the causes of the conflict were inextricably linked to the Cold War at home.]

We support the action of the United Nations in opposing the aggression of North Korea against South Korea. We hope that this action will strengthen the authority and prestige of the United Nations and prove a deterrent to future aggression.

In our judgment the conflict in Korea today is the result of the cold-war policy—a policy of blind opposition to Communism which ignores the economic, social, and political problems of the ordinary people of the world who are struggling to obtain a better lot in life. An intelligent policy of helping the people of Korea to solve these problems through democratic methods, rather than supporting corrupt and reactionary forces merely because they were opposed to Communism, would almost certainly have avoided the tragic loss of life in Korea today. Nevertheless, we must oppose the resort to arms by the North Koreans, with at least the acquiescence of the Soviet Union, which has subsequently supported the North Koreans in the United Nations.

Whatever differences develop between the two great rival systems represented by the United States and the Soviet Union, those disagreements must be settled by peaceful methods. The only alternative is a third world war that will spell the end of humanity as we know it today.

For this reason we support the action of the United Nations in resisting the aggression of North Korea. The United Nations remains the one last hope for a peaceful adjustment of world tensions, and its efforts toward promoting world peace and progress will have our fullest support.

For the same reasons we cannot now, any more than in the past, approve those aspects of United States foreign policy which in our judgment undermine the United Nations and increase the likelihood of world conflict. Hence we do not approve the action of the United States in ordering military intervention in Korea unilaterally before the United Nations acted, in refusing to recognize the present regime in China, and in interfering unilaterally with military force in Formosa.

We believe it imperative that efforts be made at once to settle the Korean conflict. This can be done only through a fully representative United Nations. Without the admission of the present government of China, which rules over 400 million Asiatic people, the United Nations cannot hope to achieve a peaceful settlement of the Korean conflict.

We support also the efforts of Prime Minister Nehru to obtain an end of the fighting through mediation and negotiation. We hope that these efforts will be continued and that they will result in the adoption of measures by the United Nations which will assure a unified Korea, democratic elections, and economic assistance. The Korean people have struggled for years to obtain a free and united country in which they can build a better life for all their citizens. This is the basic issue in the Korean problem and the ultimate solution can only be one which recognizes that fact and which will assist the Korean people in the achievement of their legitimate aspirations.

THE ROSENBERG CASE
By The New York Guild Lawyer

[The Cold War mood of suspicion and conspiracy, leading to anger and fear bordering on terror, made the trial and execution of Ethel and Julius Rosenberg the ultimate political case of the era. The Guild participated organizationally through submission of amicus curiae briefs and through the valiant efforts of individual members Emanuel Bloch and Gloria Agrin, who represented the Rosenbergs.

[Extracts from the Guild brief appeared in *The New York Guild Lawyer* (January 1953).]

The Guild brief stresses the point that this case involves issues of fundamental character touching the heart of the law or its fair and impartial administration; that it has been cast into national prominence by widespread publicity and intense excitement concerning atom-bomb spying on behalf of the Soviet Union.

The brief asserts that the atmosphere in which the case was tried was so hostile that the question has arisen in the minds of many people whether a fair trial was possible under the circumstances. Even more compelling was the question "whether the extreme sentences were the result of the improper influence of extraordinary public clamor upon the judicial process."

Before the trial the press and radio had created in our midst a pervasive atmosphere of intense fear and insecurity based on allegations that our country was menaced with the threat of atomic attack from the Soviet Union, which had acquired the bomb due to the acts of spies who had made our atomic "secrets" available to it and might at any time devastate our cities by its use.

The proposed brief says that when "political and international issues" are involved in criminal prosecutions the public discussion of these issues in a democracy may develop intense heat which enters the courtroom. But "it is a paramount function of the courts and of associations and members of the Bar to exert their utmost effort to make certain that the judicial process rises above this clamor to mete out impartial justice to all. We must be on guard to assure that the judicial process is moved by calm and deliberate evaluation of proven facts and not by extraneous heated discussion and emotion fanned by the media of mass communication."

"We have been unable to resist the conclusion that however much the trial judge may have endeavored to resist the impact of public clamor, the very magnitude of these sentences reflects the impact of this public clamor."

This conclusion is reinforced by an evaluation of the validity of the statement by the trial judge in announcing the death sentences that: "In putting into the hands of the Russians the A-bomb years before our best scientists predicted Russia would perfect the bomb, has already caused, in my opinion, the Communist aggression in Korea, with the resultant casualties exceeding 50,000, and who knows what but that millions more of innocent people may pay the price of this treason. I feel that I must pass such sentence upon the principals in this diabolical conspiracy."

The Guild memorandum states: "We must conclude that the trial judge's assertion that the Rosenbergs put into the hands of the Russians the atom bomb, is entirely unfounded. It follows that the responsibility which the trial judge placed upon the Rosenbergs for all the casualties which had occurred and would occur in Korea must be removed from them, since that responsibility rested upon the erroneous assumption that the Rosenbergs had given the atom bomb to the Soviet Union. We would add that even if the Rosenbergs had given the atom bomb to the Russians it would require the exercise of almost pure conjecture to trace the origin of the Korean war to these circumstances alone."

The brief concludes: "It is not on conventional grounds that the sentences are excessive that the Guild has intervened. We believe this case exemplifies the great injuries that can be done to a law-governed society and to the true administration of justice when public passion and prejudice, politics or propaganda operate or seem to operate to influence the judgment of courts.

"We believe that the interests of justice will be well served and the spirit of our law invigorated if the sentences imposed on these three defendants are freshly reviewed in the light of the presently known facts, with calmness and greater objectivity. We are convinced that such reconsideration should result in a reduction of the sentences."

LOYALTY TO THE BILL OF RIGHTS
By Delbert E. Metzger

[The Guild has always had the foresight and ability to turn external criticism into internal solidarity. While the methods have varied, Guild leaders have usually chosen to honor one of their own members or to bestow an award on a deserving, courageous citizen of the larger community. In honoring such qualities, the Guild honors itself and the ideas to which it is committed.

[In February 1953, the political climate was frigid. A new Republican Attorney General seemed more responsive to placing the Guild on the subversive list. The ABA was actively pursuing disciplinary action against lawyers who claimed their privilege against self-incrimination guaranteed in the Fifth Amendment. The right to counsel and counsel's rights were seriously threatened. In these circumstances, the Guild chose to bestow its highest honor, the Franklin D. Roosevelt Award, on Delbert Metzger, a retired U.S. District Judge from the territory of Hawaii, where Myer Symonds and Harriet Bouslog had been keeping the faith with the Guild since 1946.

[Judge Metzger's entire career was a testament to the protection of civil liberties. Two particular issues concerned the Guild. He was the first judge to uphold the rights of witnesses to refuse, under the Fifth Amendment, to testify to their political beliefs before HUAC. Metzger had also ordered a reduction of bail for Smith Act defendants in spite of strong public opposition.]

I labored, until recently, for upwards of twenty years in the field of jurisprudence. I am no longer a Judge. I do not know precisely why, for I know I was a better judge when I quit than when I began.

There exists today, as much as ever before, the urgent need for

---

"Loyalty to the Bill of Rights," by Delbert E. Metzger, *Lawyers Guild Review* 13:1 (Winter 1953).

courageous lawyers to speak out against encroachments by Congress and the courts in the destruction of our Bill of Rights, and in the curbing of Civil Rights generally.

I cannot agree with Judge Learned Hand that the advocacy of ideas by 30,000 American Communists, out of a population of 160,000,000 Americans, constitutes a "clear and present danger" to the people of the United States.

My remarks, I suppose, make it clear why I was not reappointed to my federal judgeship, particularly when judges who preside over Smith Act trials, where there are convictions, are promptly promoted, and Smith Act prosecutors are made judges. I gained the displeasure of higher-ups in the Department of Justice and several men in Congress because I could not agree with their ideas of what dictation a judge should take and conform to. Finally, I was *liquidated,* but I am still happy, and still free, I hope, to be able to continue, loyally and helpfully, in some service to my beloved America, and the principles upon which it was founded.

It is a great pleasure to be among a group of lawyers who have the courage and intent in these times of almost universal fear to struggle to preserve the Bill of Rights.

■ EIGHT

Bread-and-Butter Issues (1947–1956)

FROM ITS FOUNDING in the New Deal period, the Guild was concerned with the day-to-day efforts of individual Guild members to win bread-and-butter cases for their clients, or at least to present the best case possible. The organization continuously functioned as a guild of skilled workers engaged in practicing their craft; some lawyers considered it their union. Local chapters addressed basic professional needs while also participating in debates and actions on national and international issues, which consistently received coverage in Guild publications.

This two-level concern continued during the Cold War period. The Guild leadership and membership saw to it that its commitments never faltered: to social security for lawyers, comparative negligence recoveries for injured parties, group insurance, and equal justice under law. Indeed, some of these issues received new emphasis in this repressive period, and on some the Guild achieved partial victories. Facing virulent attacks on several fronts, the Guild found this two-pronged approach necessary to its survival.

At the same time, some of the personal injury (PI) lawyers most active in the Detroit and Cleveland Guild Chapters helped found what became the American Trial Lawyers Association, to work exclusively on the problems of lawyers representing injured people seeking damages or workers' compensation. They were joined by some labor lawyers who had lost their union clients due to Red-baiting and who had shifted into PI work.

THE AVAILABILITY OF LEGAL SERVICES—
THE GUILD POSITION
By the Guild Committee on Professional Problems

[From its inception, the Guild recognized the inter-relationship between providing equality before the law and the needs of the legal profession. Sparked

---

"The Availability of Legal Services—The Guild Position," by the Committee on Professional Problems, NLG, *Lawyers Guild Review* 10:2 (Spring 1950).

by Robert J. Silberstein, Guild members Gloria Agrin, George Olshausen, Robert Abrahams, Alex Elson, Sol L. Firstenberg, Isaac C. Donner, and Henry Wolf prepared a major report in June 1950 on the need for legal services by "one hundred million clients."]

For more than half a century the problem of providing legal assistance for those unable to buy it has engaged the attention of the Bar of this country.

Our law contemplates a solicitousness for the rightful claims of every man or woman, whether rich or poor, whether of high estate or low. The ideal of the law is to render exact justice to every person who lives within the jurisdiction of the United States, whether a citizen or an alien, and regardless of race, color, or creed. It is the mandate of the constitutions of the States; it is the mandate of the United States Constitution: that every person is equal before the law and is entitled to the equal protection of the law.

The Supreme Court has already recognized, in criminal cases, that the right to effective counsel is a constitutional prerogative. It cannot be less true, in civil cases, that a person, under a system of laws becoming more complex and intricate each day, who, because of lack of funds, is compelled to dispense with the assistance of a skilled attorney, is denied an equality of treatment with his wealthier opponent. Nor can litigation expenses, which constitute a price of admission too high for all but the economic elite, but make a sham of equal protection of the law.

We accept the proposition stated by Reginald Heber Smith: "that the state is bound to see that its citizens receive justice," with all its implications. The responsibility to assure the availability of legal aid and advice, and full access to the judicial processes to those who cannot financially provide it for themselves, belongs to the government. The fulfillment of this responsibility is an essential part of the government's function to administer justice in our land.

It is the special responsibility of the Bar, as a part of the judicial structure, to provide leadership in the shaping of the measures to be adopted, and to help assure that the right of the people to have counsel of their own choice, and vigorous legal prosecution and defense of their rights, is maintained in any proposals adopted.

We are concerned here with the measures which should be taken to translate the promise of equality before the law into a reality; with the means by which the governments, National and State, might properly fulfill their responsibility to assure equal justice to all the people. We do not intend, however, to elaborate a specific plan or bill. That is essentially a governmental responsibility in the fulfillment of which the advice of the Bench, the Bar, and representatives of interested lay agencies should be sought.

Because of the special responsibility of the Bar to provide leadership in the effort to find a speedy, just, and sound solution, we deem it appropriate to set out some of the principles we believe should be incorporated in such a solution, and to discuss several possible approaches to a solution worthy of consideration.

1. No person ought to be deprived of advice or, if necessary, legal representation because of his financial inability to pay for it.
2. No person ought to be denied full access to the judicial processes by his financial inability to pay costs or charges ordinarily imposed by the Courts, or expenses ordinarily incurred in litigation for the protection of his rights.
3. Those who can afford to pay nothing should receive legal aid free. Those who can afford to pay some, but not all, legal expenses, should contribute to the costs in proportion to their ability.
4. Lawyers should be paid for their services to assisted persons at a fair and reasonable rate. The lawyer and the client should be assured the traditional lawyer-client relationship, and, to the largest extent possible, the client, counsel of his own choosing.
5. Legal aid and assistance should be financed, insofar as any system adopted is not self-liquidating, not by public or private charity, as a matter of grace, but by the government as a matter of right.
6. All legal aid or advice should be administered without discrimination in regard to race, creed, color, or sex.

GUILD STUDENT CHAPTERS ADDRESS BREAD-AND-BUTTER ISSUES
By The Guild Lawyer *and* The Guild Law Student

[Few professional organizations were as diligent in recognizing the special needs and concerns of their future colleagues as the Guild. Its national conventions addressed students' intellectual and political interests. At the same time, law student chapters revealed an unexpected degree of independent progressive activism that forcefully counters the image of a "silent generation."]

∎

BREAD AND BUTTER TOPICS

[Spring 1949]

The resolution on lawyer and law student cooperation acknowledged the need for the addition of "bread and butter" subject matter to law

---

"Guild Student Chapters Address Bread-and-Butter Issues," by *The Guild Lawyer* (Spring 1949) and *The Guild Law Student* (Sept. 1951).

school curricula. Need for an effective job placement service was also expressed. Recognizing the tightening economic picture and still unfilled need for legal services by the low income group, the panel recommended a study designed to assure that every American has the legal advice and representation he needs, regardless of his economic situation. The desirability of making it possible for the lawyer to accept positions with broad clinics, together with members of other professions, organized by trade unions, community groups, neighborhood councils, and church organizations was also indicated. The panel advocated a re-examination of the On-the-Job training program of the Veterans Administration to afford broader opportunities for this type of training to qualified veterans either before or after graduation from law school.

Judge Ira W. Jayne chaired the panel on Law Reform, in which Ronald H. T. Whitty, fraternal delegate from England representing that country's Haldane Society, read the report on the British Legal Aid and Assistance Bill to establish a system of free and subsidized legal services to those unable to pay. The report aroused widespread interest among the delegates. The conviction was evident that the principles of governmental responsibility embodied in the Bill were equally applicable to a demonstrated need for such services in this country.

■

SD Asks NYU Remove "Religion" [and] "Race" Queries; Wide Support Grows

[September 1951]

Students at New York University Law School were urged, on the opening day of registration for the Fall Semester, to refuse to answer questions concerning "race" and "religion" on school registration forms. The request came in a letter mailed each student by Mark Lane, Executive Secretary of the Student Division. The letter pointed out that the information gathered from the questions "was not necessary for any legitimate reason and could provide a basis for discrimination as regards awards, degrees, scholarships, employment by the university, and recommendations by the university for study and employment elsewhere."

Student organizations at NYU and elsewhere have voiced their desire to cooperate with the Guild-initiated effort.

NYU Law School . . . overcame administration refusal to allow meetings on campus by offering, at a nearby hotel, the series "From Casebook to Law Office." Guild students at NYU also presented a debate on censorship.

YALE

March 1951. "The Availability of Legal Services for Low Income Groups" was discussed by Thomas R. Robinson, Public Defender of New Haven County. Francis Vallat, Esq., Legal Adviser to the United Kingdom Delegation to the UN, discussed socialized legal services in Great Britain. The plan of the Guild was presented by Executive Secretary Robert J. Silberstein.

May 1951. The last meeting of the year was on a subject of great interest perhaps not to *all* law students, but to all but some 10 percent at each school: "Job Opportunities for Non-Journal Law Students," on the theory that law students who make their school's law journal or law review will have no difficulty in obtaining employment. The participants in this discussion were the Director of Placement at Yale and David Weissman from the Guild's committee dealing with the subject.

THE THOMPSON CASE:
A REAL LIFE BREAD-AND-BUTTER STRUGGLE
By Annie Stein

It is hard for Washingtonians today to imagine or for older residents to remember what the Nation's Capital was like in 1947. Except for seating in the bus, Washington was a Jim Crow town. Black residents could not eat in any private downtown restaurant. No hotel outside the black ghetto would provide lodging or a meeting space. Most department stores would not sell to blacks. Downtown movies, the National Theatre, public swimming pools, hospitals, schools were rigidly segregated.

A Presidential Commission in 1947 was at work on the report "To Secure These Rights." Charles E. Wilson, who headed the Commission, reported that in their researches they had found that in 1872 and 1873, the Legislative Assembly had passed laws forbidding discrimination against any "respectable person" in hotels, restaurants, barber shops, and the like.

The Progressive Party's anti-discrimination committee asked the Lawyers Guild to study the question, and Joe Forer was put on the job. Seventy-five years after the passage of these laws, Joe holed up in a law library for a week and came up with the answer. He wrote the Guild opinion that was to make history. He found that:

1. The laws had been enforced at least once, against the prestigious

---

"The Thompson Case: A Real Life Bread-and-Butter Struggle," by Annie Stein, in *NLG Tribute to Joseph Forer*, banquet journal (1979).

Harvey's Restaurant in 1874. Harvey's had to close its doors for several years because it refused to serve a respectable black patron.
2. The laws of 1872 and 1873 had never been repealed, but had simply been ignored in the 1909 codification.
3. A precedent existed to show that the laws were still valid and in effect in 1947.

A committee was promptly organized, headed by the distinguished black educator and civic leader, Mary Church Terrell, then eighty-six years old.

A test case was begun in 1948. The restaurant chosen was Thompson's, for the good and sufficient reason that it was in the same building on 14th Street where Forer and Rein had their office. Mrs. Terrell and the Reverend Dr. W. H. Jernagin, also an octogenarian, moved their trays down the cafeteria line and were told by the manager in the presence of witnesses (David and Joe, of course) that they could not be served because they were "colored." There was no doubt that they were eminently "respectable."

The complaint was then formally filed with the Corporation Counsel, whose duty it was to argue on behalf of the two complainants. The Thompson Restaurant Case was launched, based on the precedent and argument in the Guild Opinion.

The Coordinating Committee for the Enforcement of the Anti-Discrimination Laws of 1872 and 1873 spent the next five years on picket lines, testing restaurants and arguing with restaurant owners while the case went from appeal to appeal. Thousands of Washingtonians walked those lines under Mrs. Terrell's indomitable leadership, breaking down segregation at Kresge's (nine months), Murphy's (six months), and most valiantly at the Hecht Company lunch counter after nine more months of picketing. Dave and Joe were active throughout the five years, working on the court case, in the meetings and on the picket line.

In 1953, the U.S. Supreme Court acted on the Thompson Restaurant Case, declaring that the old anti-discrimination laws of 1872 and 1873 were still in force and that all segregation in restaurants and hotels must cease forthwith.

That case cracked the dam of Jim Crow in the District. Movies and stores followed within a month, and all places of public accommodation. In 1954, the schools desegregated, restrictive housing covenants were shortly ended, jobs in stores, buses, and the government service soon followed.

It was a glorious victory and foreshadowed the great struggles of the early 1960s that ended Jim Crow in public accommodations throughout the South.

VINDICATION OF THE GUILD POSITION
By The New York Guild Lawyer

[The Guild has had many monumental battles with the ABA. One of the most important was the fifteen-year struggle to overcome ABA opposition to compulsory social security coverage.]

On the basis of a unanimous recommendation of its Board of Governors, the House of Delegates of the ABA on February 21, 1955, adopted a resolution favoring "voluntary coverage under the Social Security Act for lawyers and such of the professional groups as desire to be included." The resolution declares that the action is taken "in view of the present sentiment of the members of the legal profession in favor of voluntary social security coverage."

The ABA, at the same time, made public the results of questionnaires sent to the presidents of bar associations throughout the United States, as well as the result of polls taken by hundreds of state and local Bar associations. 607 bar presidents were polled for their "personal opinions." 490, or 80 percent, personally favored inclusion. The ABA further published the results of 366 polls taken by state and local associations who had polled their members. 364, or 83 percent of such polls showed that the members favored inclusion.

Thus, at long last, the ABA, with its 50,000 members throughout the United States, has recognized the dire need and the desire of the Bar for social security protection, and has placed its great weight and its prestige and influence behind the effort to obtain this protection.

For fifteen years the Guild has urged that all employed and self-employed persons had a right to economic security and that the economic interests of the nation, as well as the protection of the health and welfare of its citizens, required universal coverage under the social security system. The Guild has urged that self-employed lawyers were as economically insecure as other employed and self-employed persons and that they and their families needed social security protection and that there was no justification for discriminating against them.

In 1950, at the time of the great revision of the Social Security Act, when Congress recognized the injustice of excluding self-employed persons and extended coverage to some four and a half million self-employed persons, the Guild urged that self-employed lawyers should be covered as well. The leadership of the ABA resisted such coverage. Congressional leaders declared that the Bar was not covered because the Bar did not want coverage.

Since social security protection was thus being denied the profession

---

"Vindication of The Guild Position," by *The New York Guild Lawyer* (March 1955).

because the Congress believed that the Bar did not want it, the Guild endeavored to obtain the opinion of the Bar. Seven years ago, in July 1948, the New York City Chapter conducted a questionnaire survey on the subject. At that time, of 2,378 lawyers, 2,145, or 90 percent, voted in favor of coverage. In September 1951, Senator Henry Cabot Lodge of Massachusetts took a poll of his own of the Massachusetts Bar and of 1,669 replies he reported to the Senate that 1,481, or 88 percent, "declared themselves most emphatically in favor of coverage." In 1952, the Guild decided to conduct a national poll to obtain an expression of the opinion of the Bar as a whole. A ballot was mailed to every tenth lawyer in the United States. Of 3,163 ballots received, 2,276, or 72 percent expressed themselves in favor of coverage.

The Guild then addressed the state and local Bar associations throughout the United States. The Guild brought to them the results of its poll, as well as a statement of the Guild members. The Guild urged the associations to obtain the opinion of their members. This effort continued all through 1952, 1953, and 1954.

The ABA official position favors coverage on a voluntary basis. This position is taken according to the Board of Governors' recommendation "in view of the present sentiment of the members of the legal profession in favor of voluntary social security coverage."

The Guild believes that mandatory coverage is both in the national interest and in the interest of the Bar. If the choice were voluntary coverage or no coverage at all, by all means the coverage should be on a voluntary basis.

MANDATORY VERSUS VOLUNTARY SOCIAL SECURITY COVERAGE FOR THE BAR: THE LAST OBSTACLE TO THE ACHIEVEMENT OF SOCIAL SECURITY PROTECTION FOR SELF-EMPLOYED LAWYERS
By Leo J. Linder

[It is only fitting that this final selection on Social Security for lawyers be written by the long-time chair of the Guild Committee on Social Legislation. For over twenty-five years he devoted his life to a succession of social welfare measures that have benefited generations of citizens.]

It would seem gratuitous at this late date to argue the advantages of protection under the Social Security Act.

Yet, a minority of the Bar still opposes such coverage. Opponents

---

"Mandatory versus Voluntary Social Security Coverage for the Bar: The Last Obstacle to the Achievement of Social Security Protection for Self-Employed Lawyers," by Leo J. Linder, *Lawyers Guild Review* 15:3 (Fall 1955).

have contended that lawyers do not need coverage and that in any event the benefits are too small to be valuable. Now that it is clear that most lawyers think they need coverage and regard the benefits as valuable, the opposition of the Bar associations has shifted to opposition only to "compulsion." . . .

From the standpoint of the national interest, it would be better to bring all lawyers and all the professions in on a compulsory basis. The representatives of the U.S. Chamber of Commerce, appearing before the Congressional Committees on hearings on social security, understood this when they urged universal coverage on a compulsory basis. It is unsound that those who need the protection most and are perhaps the poorest risks should come in while the best risks stay out. Those who are nearest the retirement age or whose longevity is shortest because of age or poor health would come in; they would pay the least and take out the most. On a voluntary basis, the healthiest, the best circumstanced, those who would pay the most and probably take out the least, would stay out.

From the standpoint of sound social insurance principles, voluntary coverage is wholly inappropriate. A private insurance company can adjust premiums so that the best, the youngest, and healthiest risks pay small premiums and the poorest, the sickest, and the oldest pay more. But in social insurance each pays at the same rate based upon income, and each takes out benefits again based to a certain extent on contributions.

From the standpoint of the economic interests of the Bar itself, the argument for mandatory coverage is, we think, unanswerable.

If social security were on a voluntary basis, well-to-do lawyers who think that they do not need the benefits would stay out. They would lose the tax advantages of the tax-exempt income involved. But the greatest loss would be the social loss in that the national fund would lose the taxes they would pay. There is, however, the danger that young lawyers and improvident lawyers of any age might forfeit the benefits for themselves and their families by reason of the folly of saving $100 or so a year in taxes. That they would suffer in their old age and that there would be a social burden in protecting them in destitution would be bad enough. But that their families should suffer for this improvidence and that our country—that is, all of us—should have to pay for this improvidence, as we surely would have to, simply makes no sense at all.

All lawyers owe it to themselves to raise the matter in their Bar organizations and to inform Congress of their wishes. If this occurs, there cannot be any doubt but that at the next session of Congress, in 1956, lawyers and their families will finally achieve retirement pension and old age and survivors' insurance protection under the Social Security Act.

[On August 1, 1956, President Dwight D. Eisenhower approved the Social Security Amendments of 1956, extending benefits to self-employed lawyers. Linder's grand scheme also led, decades later, to the popular Individual Retirement Accounts (IRAs), through which many taxpayers seek greater security in their senior years.]

GUILD ACTIVITY AT CONFERENCE OF STATE BAR DELEGATES
By The Guild Lawyer of California

[The Guild has always functioned as a Bar association. Its chapters and members carried the organization's message and concerns into their communities, voluntary associations, and professional societies. From the beginning, Guild chapters in San Francisco and Southern California effectively advanced progressive proposals through the Conference of Delegates of the California State Bar Association. Some highlights of Guild activities in 1953-1954 are provided below.]

The delegates to the 1953 Conference of State Bar Delegates, which met in Monterey on October 5 and 6, acted favorably with respect to several of the resolutions submitted by the California Guild Chapters.

1. Campaign to eliminate the doctrine of contributory negligence and substitute the principle of comparative negligence.
    The Guild first proposed this before the last war. The principle was adopted by the Conference in 1950 and became part of the state Bar legislative program in 1953. It is now under study by an interim committee of the State Senate.
2. Proposals to liberalize the California Workmen's Compensation statute to increase protection for the injured worker.
3. Measures to broaden the base of the jury system by raising jury fees to approximate a fair day's pay so that working people could afford to serve.
4. Proposed legislation to make justice more available for poor litigants by charging jury fees to general county funds and doing the same for other litigants' costs where the party satisfied a poor litigant's test.
5. A campaign conducted from 1946 to establish as a condition of participation in our integrated Bar that local Bar associations not discriminate as to terms or conditions of membership on account of race or color. Just this year the Board of Governors adopted this proposal.
6. A comprehensive legal assistance statute designed to bring legal ser-

---

"Guild Activity at Conference of State Bar Delegates," by *The Guild Lawyer of California* (Jan. 1954).

vices within the reach of individuals otherwise unable to pay and assure at least a modest but reasonable return for the lawyer who performs such services.
7. A proposal to include lawyers in the national social security program.

The San Francisco Chapter proposed to end the illegal practice of "en route" arrests by making offending officers liable in damages to persons so held. The Conference approved, in principle, this protest against the practice of making such arrests but did not approve the proposed legislation.

A resolution presented by the San Francisco Chapter to the 1952 Conference was the source of the item to which the 1953 Conference gave the most attention. This resolution proposed to the 1952 Conference that it endorse repeal of the Emergency Detention Act of 1950 (Title II, Internal Security Act of 1950, 50 USC 811). After considerable discussion, the Conference finally decided to refer the entire matter to an interim committee for further study and report to the 1954 Conference.

The delegates also acted favorably upon the proposal of the Los Angeles Chapter that defendants in personal injury and property damage cases be required by law to disclose the particulars of any liability insurance policies covering the loss for which damages are sought. Legislation to this end will continue to be sponsored by the state Bar.

DETROIT CHAPTER TRAINS LAWYERS AND FIGHTS FOR COMPARATIVE NEGLIGENCE
By the Editors

Through the years the Detroit chapter demonstrated the most consistent interest in bread-and-butter issues. Its members' ties to the union movement and specialization in personal injury and workers' compensation made them good teachers. In the later 1940s and early 1950s, Dean Robb, Barbara Robb, Harry Philo, and others started a weekly class in personal injury law and the medical knowledge needed to convince juries to make appropriate damage awards to people injured in accidents. John and Nathan Conyers and many other young black lawyers attended, making lasting friendships among individuals and between the Wolverine Bar Association and the Detroit Guild chapter.

This led to chapter work in the legislative arena. Harold Norris, executive secretary of the chapter, testified before the House Judiciary

---

"Detroit Chapter Trains Lawyers and Fights for Comparative Negligence," by the Editors; Harold Norris' testimony in Norris, *Some Reflections on Law, Lawyers, and the Bill of Rights* (Detroit: Michigan Law Book Publishing, 1984).

Committee in Lansing in March 1951 in support of comparative negligence. He argued that:

The present rule of contributory negligence is antiquated, unfair, and unjust. The purpose of the law of negligence is to provide an equitable and effective system of loss distribution. The present rule bars from recovery a plaintiff whose degree of negligence may be only 10 percent responsible for a collision, and permits the defendant whose degree of negligence may be 90 percent responsible to escape liability.

An inequitable rule of law undermines the faith, respect, and confidence of the public in our laws and in our courts.

The present rule of contributory negligence unjustly bars many citizens from recovery who thereby become wards of the state in order to secure medical care and hospitalization and the taxpayer must foot the bill.

House Bill #178 provides for a division of the total damages in accordance with their respective degrees of negligence; for the joining of all parties who have any connection with the loss; for equal liability where the jury finds itself unable to make an exact apportionment, and for the apportionment of the loss among persons other than plaintiff whose negligence is not equal.

THE NATIONAL LAWYERS GUILD VERSUS SEXISM: THE FIRST STEP
By Ann Fagan Ginger

[Cleveland labor lawyer Ann Fagan Ginger submitted the following resolution on discrimination against women to the 1950 Guild Convention Resolutions Committee chaired by Leo J. Linder. His first reaction was that the Guild could not possibly consider every question under the sun. The proponent said she was amazed, furious, and determined. The debate in the virtually all-male committee was short, hot, and (to the proponent's utter embarrassment) tearful. The Committee then approved the resolution, and the Convention adopted it, making the Guild one of the few national organizations to call for legislative action to end sex discrimination.]

The progess of American women has been burdened and impeded by discriminations arising in part from assumptions embedded in the common law. Notwithstanding notable legislative achievements in modern times, there remain in effect statutes, regulations, rules and governmental practices which discriminate unfairly on the basis of sex.

The present is an appropriate occasion to review the political, civil, economic, and social status of women for the purpose of modernizing applicable legal codes and administrative practices, and eliminating the unjust burden of arbitrary distinctions.

"The National Lawyers Guild versus Sexism: The First Step," by Ann Fagan Ginger, *NLG Practitioner* 34:3 (Summer 1977).

The Guild, in keeping with its concern for the welfare of all Americans, particularly those now discriminated against without just cause, supports measures which will alleviate many of these areas of unequal treatment. In particular it will support:

1. Federal, state and municipal legislation specifically prohibiting discrimination in hiring, firing, upgrading, seniority or other terms and conditions of employment on the basis of sex or marital status (except such as are reasonably justified by reasons of health or maternal function).
2. Legislation in the 39 states not now having such laws, assuring equal pay for the same or similar work, including adequate enforcement provisions and funds for enforcement and education.
3. Legislation to repeal existing statutory provisions which disqualify women for unemployment compensation where unemployment results from pregnancy or marital or parental obligations.
4. Revision of income tax regulations which deny working mothers the right to deduct expenses necessarily incident to their employment, for nursemaids, or after-school day care.
5. Legislation to provide protection for the working conditions of domestic workers through coverage under wage-hour, social security, unemployment compensation, and workmen's compensation laws.
6. Legislation making the rights and obligations of women the same as those of men with reference to jury service, wherever distinctions now exist in the state and federal judicial system.
7. S. 1430, the Women's Status Bill, which provides for an immediate declaration of federal policy opposing discrimination against women and the establishment of a commission to make an orderly review of state and federal legislation to remove existing discriminations against women, and make recommendations for their elimination.

■ NINE

Cold War against Lawyers (1947–1957)

THE NATIONAL LAWYERS GUILD IN 1950–1951
By Thomas I. Emerson

WHEN I BECAME president of the Guild in May 1950, the prevailing mood was one of confidence. We had a firm conviction that the problems of the world could be solved. Actually, there was no good reason why we should have been optimistic. The Cold War was raging full blast. Moreover, the Guild itself had suffered much from the anti-Red hysteria of the times. Out of 35 original chapters, only 14 were still functioning. In Washington, where at one time 400 or more government lawyers had been Guild members, not a single government lawyer remained on the rolls.

In September 1950, to our complete surprise, HUAC issued a 50-page report entitled *The National Lawyers Guild: Legal Bulwark of the Communist Party*. It recommended that the Department of Justice put the Guild on its list of subversive organizations. It further recommended that members of the Guild be barred from federal employment, and that the ABA consider whether membership in the Guild, a subversive organization, was compatible with membership in the Bar. The Guild was hard hit by the HUAC report, to put it mildly. We immediately lost many of our members, including some of the most prominent.

Even more important than the resignations was the fact that the Guild now found it almost impossible to recruit new members. Formation of student chapters in the law schools was very difficult. Younger lawyers were afraid that their careers would be blighted by association with an organization designated by the government as a Communist front. It was to be a long time before the Guild was to shake off the effect of the HUAC report.

"Introduction: The National Lawyers Guild in 1950–1951," by Thomas I. Emerson, *NLG Practitioner* 33:2 (Spring 1976).

The Guild was also on the defensive on other fronts. The ABA was proposing that the association "expel from its membership any and every individual who is a member of the Communist Party of the United States, or who advocates Marxism-Leninism"; that state Bar associations do the same; and that the appropriate authorities "immediately commence disciplinary actions of disbarment" against all such lawyers.

The Cold War against lawyers had begun.

TESTIMONY OF ROBERT W. KENNY BEFORE HUAC, OCTOBER 27, 1947

[Few individuals have been as important in the history of the Guild as Bob Kenny. When he assumed the presidency in 1940, a post he would hold for eight years, he was already a major figure in Democratic politics and in progressive legal circles. As state senator from Los Angeles County and then attorney general of California, Kenny established a reputation for integrity and courage. In the following excerpt from testimony before HUAC in connection with the Hollywood Ten case, Kenny's wit and guts clearly come through.]

THE CHAIRMAN: Mr. Kenny, the reason for calling you to the stand this afternoon is a newspaper article which appeared in this afternoon's *Times-Herald*:

Counsel for 19 "defense witnesses" in the House Reds-in-filmland investigation said today he would advise all his clients to invite prosecution by refusing to say whether they are Communists. . . .

Hollywood attorney Robert W. Kenny said he would also advise the other 18 "to walk the plank."

Mr. Kenny, is that a correct quotation?

MR. KENNY: Well, I will have to say that it is not quite correct.

THE CHAIRMAN: Not quite correct?

MR. KENNY: But I have also said that what a witness does in his relation with this committee is a matter between the committee and the witness. The best that we lawyers can do is to give the client the best constitutional advice that we can. And that is exactly what I embraced in the brief, which recited that we felt that this committee was unconstitutional and illegal.

THE CHAIRMAN: But I would like to know, as the chairman of a congressional committee, whether or not you, as the attorney for these witnesses, advised them not to answer questions put to them by this congressional committee or its chief investigator.

"Testimony of Robert W. Kenny before HUAC, October 27, 1947," as reprinted in *NLG Practitioner* 38:4 (Fall 1981).

MR. KENNY: Mr. Thomas, I would be disgraced before every one of 100,000 lawyers in the United States if I answered that question. That is one thing that cannot be answered.

THE CHAIRMAN: Still getting back to the newspaper article, in what way is this article, has the article failed to report what you said?

MR. KENNY: Well now, what I undoubtedly did say is that they are probably going to be invited to walk the plank. I don't advise anybody to walk any plank. I am not that bad a lawyer.

THE CHAIRMAN: I will tell you, Mr. Kenny, as chairman, I want to let you know that you squirmed out of this one temporarily, but if the committee should determine that is a violation of this Conspiracy Act, then the committee will take under consideration referring the matter to the United States attorney.

MR. KENNY: That is right, Mr. Thomas. I might say that the committee has squirmed out of one too, because I am sure that committee did not intend to invade the sacred province of relationship between attorney and client.

THE CHAIRMAN: Oh, no; and neither would you want to commit conspiracy.

MR. KENNY: Neither one of us are intimidated; is that right, Mr. Chairman?

THE CHAIRMAN: We will have the next witness.

REPORT ON THE NATIONAL LAWYERS GUILD: LEGAL BULWARK OF THE COMMUNIST PARTY
By The House Committee on Un-American Activities

[For years after release of HUAC's report, millions of people must have assumed that the Guild's full name was: "National Lawyers Guild: Legal Bulwark of the Communist Party" (see Figure 1). A close reading of the document, however, reveals that this alleged indictment actually represents one of the strongest endorsements ever accorded the Guild by a government agency. Of course, as Guild writer-lawyer Frank Donner noted in *The Un-Americans*, HUAC never had much regard for the truth.]

The National Lawyers Guild is the foremost legal bulwark of the Communist Party, its front organizations, and controlled unions.

A striking example is the present attack by the Guild on the Federal Bureau of Investigation, echoing the current line of the *Daily Worker* and Moscow. The Guild today is crying for an investigation of the FBI,

---

"Report on the National Lawyers Guild: Legal Bulwark of the Communist Party," by the House Committee on Un-American Activities, U.S. House of Representatives, Sept. 21, 1950, 81st Cong. 2d Sess.

Union Calendar No. 1073

81st Congress, 2d Session . . . . House Report No. 3123

REPORT ON

THE
NATIONAL LAWYERS GUILD

Legal Bulwark of the Communist Party

SEPTEMBER 17, 1950
(Original release date)

September 21, 1950.—Committed to the Committee of the Whole House
on the State of the Union and ordered to be printed

Prepared and Released by the
COMMITTEE ON UN-AMERICAN ACTIVITIES, U. S. HOUSE OF REPRESENTATIVES
WASHINGTON, D. C.

Figure 1.

the vigilant guardian of our national security, on the ridiculous grounds that it is a "gestapo" or "political police" whose "practices and policies ... violate our laws, infringe our liberties, and threaten our democracy."

There is no doubt in the opinion of the committee that the National Lawyers Guild attacks on the Federal Bureau of Investigation are part of an overall Communist strategy aimed at weakening our nation's defenses against the international Communist conspiracy.

The National Lawyers Guild has also conducted a malicious campaign against the loyalty program.

The Guild's opposition to the loyalty program was compiled into a 23-page report entitled "The Constitutional Right to Advocate Political, Social, and Economic Changes—An Essential of Democracy," which was sent to government officials, Members of Congress, the judiciary, the Bar, labor and civic organizations. The conclusion of this report charged that "our citizens are denied the right to advocate fundamental social, economic, and political change."

Any legislation which would curb the activities of Communists, regardless of the importance of such legislation to our national security, is faced with bitter opposition from the National Lawyers Guild.

At its first convention, the Guild opposed statutes providing that teachers take a loyalty oath or those "making criminal advocacy of or membership in any political party."

The National Lawyers Guild denounced the anti-Communist provisions of the Taft-Hartley Law on the ground that it was unconstitutional. Leonard B. Boudin, chairman of the labor law committee of the National Lawyers Guild, testified before a labor subcommittee of the House of Representatives concerning the non-Communist affidavit of the Taft-Hartley bill. At that time, Mr. Boudin stated that the non-Communist affidavit was an insult to the American worker because Congress thereby told the workers they were not wise enough to manage their own affairs.

The Guild has opposed the Rapp-Coudert committee investigating subversive activities in the public school system of New York City, for example. It has also opposed the York committee investigating subversive activities among state employees of California; the Ellis committee investigating subversive activities in the New York Civil Service; and the Special Committee on Un-American Activities, predecessor of the present House Committee on Un-American Activities.

Abolition of the present Committee on Un-American Activities is called for by the National Lawyers Guild.

The files of the Committee on Un-American Activities show that the dominant forces in the National Lawyers Guild have been composed of known Communists and fellow travelers.

Thomas J. [sic] Emerson, a law professor at Yale University, was elected president of the National Lawyers Guild at its national convention in New York City in May 1950. Mr. Emerson has been associated with the Guild from its very beginning, and served on the Guild's executive board during its first year, 1937. The records of the Committee on Un-American Activities show that Mr. Emerson has an unusual affinity for Communist-front organizations and that in addition to the National Lawyers Guild he has associated himself with such groups as Civil Rights Congress, Jefferson School of Social Science, Southern Conference for Human Welfare, National Council of the Arts, Sciences, and Professions. He has further associated himself with the Communist-blessed Progressive Citizens of America and with the Communist-dominated United Public Workers of America.

Clifford J. Durr, 1949 head of the Guild, who has appeared before the Committee on Un-American Activities representing clients who declined to answer questions as to Communist affiliations on the grounds of self-incrimination, in August of 1948 attended the World Congress of Intellectuals for Peace behind the iron curtain, at Wroclaw, Poland. In May of 1948, Durr, in a speech before the Federation of American Scientists, charged that United States scientists are forced to "work in an atmosphere of corrosive fear." This was prior to the disclosure regarding the spying of the British atom spy, Klaus Fuchs.

The 1950 vice presidents of the National Lawyers Guild include the following other individuals with significant records of associations with Communist enterprises:

Bartley C. Crum: Associated with California Labor School, National Committee To Win the Peace, National Federation for Constitutional Liberties, Veterans of the Abraham Lincoln Brigade, Joint Anti-Fascist Refugee Committee, American-Russian Institute, American Slav Congress, American Youth for Democracy, American Committee for Spanish Freedom.

Osmond Fraenkel: Associated with Consumers National Federation, American Labor Party, National Committee for the Defense of Political Prisoners, American Student Union, Consumers Union, American League Against War and Fascism, New York Tom Mooney Committee, National Emergency Conference for Democratic Rights, International Juridical Association, National Committee for People's Rights, Medical Bureau and North American Committee To Aid Spanish Democracy, Greater New York Emergency Conference on Inalienable Rights, Film Audiences for Democracy, Films for Democracy, Coordinating Committee To Lift the Embargo, Citizens Committee to Free Earl Browder, School for Democracy.

The Committee on Un-American Activities recommends that the National Lawyers Guild be placed on the Department of Justice subversive list and that it be required to register as an agent of a foreign principal.

It recommends further that members of the National Lawyers Guild be barred from federal employment and that the American Bar Association consider the question of whether or not membership in the National Lawyers Guild, a subversive organization, is compatible with admissibility to the American Bar. It calls on decent lawyers and those sincerely interested in the liberal principles of American justice to warn the younger members of the Bar of the real nature of the Guild, as an arm of the international Communist conspiracy.

THE NATIONAL LAWYERS GUILD: LEGAL BULWARK OF DEMOCRACY
By the National Executive Board

[The Guild's point-by-point rebuttal of the HUAC report got lost in the hysteria of a full-scale Red scare. A succession of shocks beginning in August 1949 with the Soviet detonation of an atomic bomb, the "fall" of China, the Alger Hiss case, the arrest of British physicist Klaus Fuchs, Joseph McCarthy's "I have here in my hand" speech, culminating in the Korean war and the Rosenbergs' arrests, made the public willing to believe anything the government said.]

The essence of the democratic process is that issues be considered on their merits. It is in the give and take of rational discussion—not in name-calling, or impugning of motives, or appeal to prejudice—that the sound and best decision is to be reached.

The Committee on Un-American Activities has flagrantly violated this cardinal principle of democracy. Its report makes no attempt whatsoever to discuss the merits of the issues on which the Guild has taken a position. It does not contain even a statement of what those issues are. Most of the report is simply devoted to showing that, with respect to those matters the Committee touches on, the Guild has taken a position similar to that of the Communist Party or alleged Communist front organizations. The remainder is largely an attempt to show that individual members of the Guild have been "associated" with the Communist Party or with alleged front organizations.

One or two examples will suffice to make the point clear. The report charges the Guild with opposing "any action on legislative or executive levels of the Government which tends to interfere with the Communist

---

"The National Lawyers Guild: Legal Bulwark of Democracy," A Reply to the Report of the Committee on Un-American Activities by the National Executive Board, *Lawyers Guild Review* 10:4 (Fall 1950).

fifth-column operations in this country" (p. 6), and cites as its chief evidence the criticisms made by the Guild of the FBI. The report makes no effort to consider whether the Guild's charges against the FBI are justified. It does not discuss, or even refer to, the evidence offered by the Guild to show that the FBI constantly engages in illegal wire-tapping, mail opening, and other forms of illegal procedures [and] makes extensive investigations into the political beliefs and associations of thousands of Americans not charged with violation of any federal law; the proof offered by the Guild that the FBI standards of loyalty do not admit of any substantial deviation from the government's official foreign policy; or the effect of these FBI practices upon freedom of political expression in the United States. In the eyes of the Committee it is enough to condemn the Guild as subversive that it has attacked the FBI and that the Soviet Union and the *Daily Worker* have done likewise.

The Committee concludes that the Guild is a "subversive" organization, but it nowhere makes explicit just what are its standards for determining whether conduct is "subversive."

Defense of the constitutional rights of Communists or alleged Communist sympathizers is plainly considered subversive. Representation of witnesses called before the Committee is presumptively subversive, and definitely so if the witness is advised to rely upon his constitutional right against self-incrimination. Criticism of the FBI or of the Loyalty Program is per se subversive. Opposition to the Taft-Hartley Law, the Mundt-Nixon bill, Maryland's Ober Law, and the Smith Act is subversive, or at least opposition to *all* of them is. Apparently criticism of the Hobbs Concentration Camp bill, the proposed bill of attainder to deport Harry Bridges, the Voorhis Act, or any phase of our foreign policy except on Spain is likewise subversive, at least if the Communist Party is also critical of the same policy.

On September 20 of this year Attorney General McGrath, addressing the American Bar Association Convention, said: "We appear to be going through a period of public hysteria in which many self-appointed policemen and alleged guardians of Americanism would have us fight subversion by prescribing an orthodoxy of opinion, and stigmatizing all who disagree or oppose them." The Attorney General's statement aptly describes the report of the Committee on Un-American Activities.

Using the very same methods which have contributed so much to the wave of hysteria sweeping the country, the Committee now attempts to intimidate and silence a group of lawyers who have consistently and unswervingly sought to carry out their obligation as members of the Bar to supply legal leadership in advancing the cause of democracy and social progress. Our answer to the Committee is that we will not be intimidated or silenced. We will continue to press forward, to the best of our ability, with the task we have pledged ourselves to perform.

LOYALTY AND LAWYERS
By Fowler V. Harper

[The Sixth Amendment's right to the assistance of counsel and a lawyer's responsibility to exert "utmost learning and ability" in a client's defense were severely strained during the Cold War. In the following speech, Yale Law School Professor Fowler Harper addresses the impact of loyalty oaths on the Bar.]

The men who won our freedom hoped, but did not necessarily assume, that we would keep it. They knew that liberty had to be won over and over again. They set up for us the most revolutionary form of government in history. Compared to *our* political theory the radicalism of Marx-Leninism which the American Bar Association fears so much looks puny, indeed.

All lawyers take an oath to support the Constitution of the United States. Those of us who believe that the right of revolution is a part of our Constitutional heritage are pledged to support that, too.

But this is an oath of allegiance, a general oath, promissory in character. The sub-loyalty oaths are *not* loyalty oaths at all. They are oaths of conformity—conformity to the prevailing bigotry of the time and place, conformity to the notions of patriotism entertained by the American Legion, or the House Un-American Activities Committee, or a Mundt or a McCarthy or a Special Bar Association Committee.

The American Bar Association's proposed oath seems strangely out of the context of the same organization's Canons of Professional Ethics, which makes it the duty of the lawyer to perform his function of advocacy with zeal and courage, without regard to the unpopularity of his client's cause.

What has happened to this strong nation of ours? What are we afraid of? I'll tell you what has happened.

We tolerate suppressive legislation and that faint, feeble murmur you hear is the only protest.

We witness gross violations of academic freedom. Only a handful of professors cry out against them.

We see reputations of decent men blasted and their characters assassinated, but no effective voice is raised in defiance.

"Loyalty and Lawyers," by Fowler V. Harper, *Lawyers Guild Review* 11:4 (Fall 1951).

Bar Associations betray the heritage of their profession. Something has gone out of us because we are a scared people.

TESTIMONY OF BEN MARGOLIS BEFORE THE HOUSE UN-AMERICAN ACTIVITIES COMMITTEE, OCTOBER 1-2, 1952

[As part of its investigation of Communist activities among professional groups, HUAC conducted public hearings in Los Angeles in the fall of 1952. One of the witnesses, Guild founder Ben Margolis, used his appearance to lecture members of the committee on the Bill of Rights.]

MR. TAVENNER: Would you state your name, please?

MR. MARGOLIS: My name is Ben Margolis. Mr. Chairman, I have a statement here, and I wonder if you would permit the reading of a voluntary statement by a witness who has no intention of becoming one of your stool pigeons?

MR. WOOD: The rule of this committee, as you well know, because you have practiced considerably before it, is that we would be glad to have you file with the committee any statement you desire.

MR. MARGOLIS: I also know that stool pigeons are allowed to say anything that they please. If you stand on your knees before this committee, you can talk all you want; if you stand on your feet, you are shut up.

MR. TAVENNER: When and where were you born, Mr. Margolis?

MR. MARGOLIS: I was born in New York City on April 23, 1910, and almost from the first day that I can remember, I have hated tyranny, and that is why I feel the way that I do about this committee.

MR. TAVENNER: Are you now engaged in the practice of law?

MR. MARGOLIS: Yes, I am; I am engaged in the practice of law and in an attempt to uphold the Constitution of the United States at every opportunity available to me.

MR. TAVENNER: Are you acquainted with Mr. Edward Dmytryk?

MR. MARGOLIS: Mr. Tavenner, unfortunately Mr. Dmytryk, according to my knowledge, has become a member of your stable, and I would refuse to answer any questions concerning any such person, on the grounds, first, that it would tend to degrade me to associate myself with any such person.

MR. TAVENNER: And, of course, you know that is no defense to the question.

MR. MARGOLIS: I think it is a very good American defense of this ques-

---

"Testimony of Ben Margolis before the House Un-American Activities Committee, Oct. 1-2, 1952," Communist Activities Among Professional Groups in the Los Angeles Area—Part 3, Hearing before HUAC, House of Representatives, 82nd Cong. 2d Sess.

tion, but I intend to rely upon a number of them, including this one. You will not tell me what I know, Mr. Tavenner. I will tell you what I know to the extent that I feel like telling you, and no further.

MR. TAVENNER: Well, you are familiar with the decisions on the subject?

MR. MARGOLIS: Yes, I am familiar with the decisions on the subject, and I think I know them very much better than you.

MR. TAVENNER: That may be, but I am glad to know that you are acquainted with that one.

MR. MARGOLIS: I will repeat, that I will not admit any association with any person of that character, on the ground that the admission of such association would tend to degrade me; on the further ground that you are attempting to invade my right of association, my right of freedom of speech, and if I were to answer such a question, I would help you to desecrate the Constitution of the United States, which I will not do. I also refuse to answer on the ground that you are attempting to destroy the highest sovereignty in this land, the sovereignty of the people of the United States, to think as they will and to tell them what they should think. This is in violation of the ninth and tenth amendments—do you want me to finish my answer?

MR. WALTER: No.

MR. MARGOLIS: Are you afraid to hear my grounds, Mr. Chairman?

MR. WOOD: No, sir, I am just getting a little weary of your contemptuous attitude.

MR. MARGOLIS: If you get weary, I have nothing but contempt for this committee, and I will show it as long as I am up here.

MR. WOOD: It is entirely mutual, but I am trying my best to keep from showing it to you.

MR. MARGOLIS: Do you wish to withdraw the question?

MR. WOOD: I want you to state any further legal reasons you have.

MR. MARGOLIS: My further reason, legal reason, is that I refuse to answer this question on the ground that no committee, this committee nor any other committee, has the right to tell the American people what they can or they cannot think. On the contrary, it is the function of the American people to tell their Congressmen they should or should not vote, and you are reversing the process of legislation by becoming a tyrannical government, by seeking to make this a tyrannical government instead of the democratic government that it was intended to be. I further refuse to answer this question on the grounds of the fifth amendment, because I will not aid you in your attempts to persecute me and others.

MR. JACKSON: Mr. Chairman, I have no questions, but I think certainly that the testimony of this witness is one excellent reason why the sessions of this committee and every other congressional committee should be carried before the eyes of every American citizen: The arrogance, and the hatred of our institutions and our way of life; yes, and of the Congress of the United States, should be—

MR. MARGOLIS: I challenge you to a public debate on who loves our institutions the most.

MR. JACKSON: I have too much respect for myself and my beliefs to engage in any sort of a debate—

MR. MARGOLIS: You are afraid, and you are scared to death, and you know how you would come out.

MR. JACKSON: Are you opposed to me?

MR. MARGOLIS: Am I opposed to you! And how!

MR. JACKSON: Well, I am glad to hear it. That is the greatest election speech I could ask of anyone.

MR. MARGOLIS: I will be glad to repeat that on a public platform, and I will pay the expenses, and we will argue about who is the better American, you or I.

MR. WOOD: I want to ask you a question as a lawyer. If perjury was committed in 1946, as a matter of law, it would be barred by the statute of limitations now, would it not?

MR. MARGOLIS: Yes, it would.

MR. WOOD: That is all.

Any further questions?

MR. TAVENNER: No.

MR. MARGOLIS: I won't send a bill for that, Mr. Wood.

MR. WOOD: The witness is excused.

THE TRIALS OF HARRY SACHER AND ABRAHAM ISSERMAN
By The New York Guild Lawyer

[The October 1949 Smith Act trial of the eleven leaders of the Communist Party of the United States was a perfect symbol of Cold War hysteria. The jury's guilty verdict against the Party leaders was expected; Judge Harold Medina's summary contempt charges against their counsel was unprecedented. Five defense attorneys were sentenced to terms of thirty days to six months in jail; three were the objects of disciplinary proceedings, and two were disbarred in state and federal courts. For the two lawyers most severely punished, Harry Sacher and Abraham Isserman, the ordeal was a nightmare that prevented them from practicing the profession they loved and had sought to honor.]

"The Trials of Harry Sacher and Abraham Isserman," by *The New York Guild Lawyer* (April 1952).

On March 10, 1952, the Supreme Court affirmed the conviction of Sacher, Isserman, and the other counsel for the defendants in the *Dennis* case. In the meantime, on January 2, 1952, Judge Hincks ordered the disbarment of Sacher and the suspension for two years of Isserman from practice in the Southern District Court.

I.

On October 14, 1949, at the conclusion of the trial of the *Dennis* case, Judge Harold R. Medina, who had been presiding, filed a certificate of contempt under Rule 42 (a) of FRCD against counsel for the defendants for acts and statements occurring during the trial and imposed sentences of imprisonment on all of them, Sacher receiving six months and Isserman four. The certificate consisted of a preliminary statement and forty specifications. The preliminary statement stated that the accusing Judge would have "overlooked or at most merely reprimanded Counsel for conduct which appeared to be the result of the heat of controversy or of that zeal in the defense of a client or in one's own defense which might understandably have caused one to overstep the bounds of strict propriety. Before the trial had progressed very far, however, I was reluctantly forced to the conclusion that the acts and statements to which I am about to refer were the result of an agreement between these defendants, deliberately entered into in a cold and calculating manner, to do and say these things for the purpose of: (1) Causing such delay and confusion as to make it impossible to go on with the trial; (2) provoking incidents which they intended would result in a mistrial; and (3) impairing my health so that the trial could not continue."

Specification I charged that counsel "joined in a wilful, deliberate, and concerted effort" or "plan" to obstruct the trial for the purposes of preventing a verdict by the jury on the issues raised by the indictment and bringing the Court and the entire federal judicial system into discredit, by various means including attacking the Presiding Judge and all the Judges of the Court, the jury system in the District, the Department of Justice, the President, the police of New York City, and the public press of New York and other cities. The remaining thirty-nine specifications refer to particular episodes during the trial, some involving all and others only some of counsel. In the Appellate Courts Specification I was referred to as the "conspiracy" count.

In the Court of Appeals Specification I was reversed on the ground that the accusing judge was without power to make a summary (that is, without notice, hearing, and opportunity to defend) finding of an agreement or plan that did not take place in his hearing and actual presence, as subdivision (a) of the rule requires. The remaining specifications, except two, were affirmed. Judge Clark, dissenting and voting to remand for hearing of all the charges, pointed to the dilemma created by an affirmance of the judgment of punishment for individual acts in the face of "the judge's own statement that he was punishing for the conspiracy." Judge Frank agreed with Judge Augustus N. Hand that the conspiracy charged in the preliminary statement and Specification I should not be read into the other specifications and that they should be treated as "surplusage." In the Supreme Court counsel argued that by so doing the Court of Appeals "in effect rewrote the trial court's judgment to respond to its own reactions."

At first the Supreme Court denied certiorari. On rehearing certiorari was granted.

While the appeal was pending in the Supreme Court, Judge Hincks handed down his opinion in the disciplinary proceeding brought against Sacher and Isserman in the District Court by the Association of the Bar of the City of New York and the New York County Lawyers Association. The charges lodged against Sacher and Isserman in this proceeding, generally speaking, paralleled the certificate of contempt.

It has been noted that the reversal of the conspiracy specification (I) by the Court of Appeals was not a ruling that no conspiracy existed, but only that the accusing judge lacked the power to make it summarily. No one questioned Judge Hincks' power to make a ruling on the merits. His finding, on the merits, was that the proofs before him did "not warrant a finding of conspiracy."

Judge Hincks, however, found Sacher and Isserman guilty of particular episodes and acts and ordered Sacher disbarred and Isserman suspended for two years. He treated the conspiracy charged therein as "surplusage"; and in finding them guilty of these and particular acts charged in the other paragraphs he made no mention of the accusing judge's appraisal of counsels' conduct: that, divorced from conspiracy, it deserved at most a reprimand.

The Supreme Court, in affirming the contempt judgment, divided five to three. Four opinions were written: Mr. Justice Jackson for the majority; and one each by Black, Frankfurter, and Douglas, JJ., dissenting.

The majority opinion held that it was permissible for the accusing judge to proceed as he did. It disposed of the dilemma created by the Court of Appeals' affirmance of the judgment, while reversing the conspiracy specification, by stating that the Court of Appeals "considered the substantive offenses separable and independent, as we do." This is no answer to counsel's argument that this was not the accusing judge's appraisal of their conduct; that he punished them only because of a conspiracy; and that to affirm the judgment is to let the results of his action stand basis for it. The majority did not therefore resolve the dilemma.

None of the minority opinions undertook to resolve the dilemma. Mr. Justice Frankfurter based his dissent on the grounds that, since no overriding necessity of preventing the trial from becoming aborted existed at the time the accusing judge acted, two basic principles were violated by his action: "That no judge should sit in a case in which he is personally involved and that no criminal punishment should be meted out except upon notice and due hearing." Mr. Justice Black agreed with both grounds and, in addition, was of the opinion that counsel were constitutionally entitled to a trial by jury. Mr. Justice Douglas agreed with the other two dissenters that "This is the classic case where trial for contempt should have been held before another judge."

To demonstrate the deep personal involvement of the accusing judge, Mr. Justice Frankfurter annexed to his opinion an appendix containing excerpts from the *Dennis* case to supplement "the meager excerpts in the certificate" and to give "a much more balanced perspective than can be got from the certificate of contempt." Mr. Justice Frankfurter sums up his view of the record as follows: "Truth compels the observation, painful as it is to make it, that the fifteen volumes of oral testimony in the principal trial record numerous episodes involving the judge and defense counsel that are more suggestive of an undisciplined debating society than of the hush and solemnity of a court of justice."

For the purpose of making the same demonstration Mr. Justice Black examined two incidents in the record: One, which was not quoted in the specification; and another, which took place immediately after sentencing of counsel.

Specification XV charged Sacher with having spoken falsely in relation to press releases. The Court of Appeals reversed this specification on the merits on the ground that it was not sufficiently clear that Sacher was attempting to mislead the Court. In the first incident examined by Mr. Justice Black the accusing judge had said to Sacher: "There was an instance in which you deliberately lied to me when they were passing these press releases. You said they were not and you were caught red-handed." After a heated response by Sacher, the accusing judge repeated: "You were caught red-handed." Mr. Justice Black's observation was: "Liar ordinarily is a fighting word spoken in anger to express bitter personal hostility against another. I can think of no other reason for its use here, particularly since the judge's charge was baseless."

The other incident examined by Mr. Justice Black took place immediately after counsel had been sentenced. Mr. Justice Black wrote with reference to this incident:

Sacher asked and was granted the privilege of making a brief statement. This statement was relevant and dignified. Nevertheless the judge interrupted him and used this language to a lawyer he had just abruptly and summarily sentenced to prison: "You continue in the same *brazen* manner that you used throughout the whole trial. . . . despite all kinds of warnings, throughout the case, you continue with the same old *mealy-mouth* way of putting it which I have been listening to throughout this case." (Emphasis supplied.) Candor compels me to say that in this episode the decorum and dignity of the lawyer who had just been sent to prison loses nothing by comparison with others.

Mr. Justice Douglas wrote:

I agree with Mr. Justice Frankfurter that one who reads this record will have difficulty in determining whether members of the Bar conspired to drive a judge from the bench or whether the judge used the authority of the bench to whipsaw the lawyers, to taunt and tempt them, and to create for himself the role of the persecuted. I have reluctantly concluded that neither is blameless, that there is fault on each side, that we have here the spectacle of the bench and the Bar using the courtroom for an unseemly demonstration of garrulous discussion and of ill will and hot tempers.

In his opinion of affirmance of the Dennis case in the Court of Appeals Judge L. Hand observed that "at times he [the accusing Judge] used language short of judicial gravity." This is but a recognition that in a trial of such duration and import no one can completely escape the human condition. In the view of the dissenting Justices in the Supreme Court the accusing judge failed to escape it at all. The appendix annexed to the opinion of Mr. Justice Frankfurter gives evidence that he was not unaware of his own limitations. This awareness may perhaps explain his sympathetic appraisal of counsels' conduct, divorced from conspiracy, and his readiness to overlook it, except for the conspiracy.

But, irrespective of the validity of that explanation, two lawyers are about to go to jail, one is ordered disbarred, and the other suspended for two years for conduct which the judge, in whose presence it was committed and who was most immediately affected by it, said he would have overlooked or at most reprimanded if he had not become convinced, erroneously it has now been found, that it was the product of an agreement or plan.

[Both men went to jail, as did their colleagues in the Smith Act trial. Sacher's disbarment, initiated by the Association of the Bar of the City of New York, was upheld by the Second Circuit. In 1954, the Supreme Court held that permanent disbarment was "unnecessarily severe." Isserman was disbarred in both New Jersey and New York as well as in the federal courts. In 1954 his Supreme Court disbarment was overturned, and five years later he was readmitted in New York. Not until 1961, however, was he allowed to practice in his home state.]

THE 1954 CHICAGO GUILD CONVENTION
By the Chicago Red Squad

[The following document was obtained through the cooperation of the Chicago, Illinois, Red Squad.]

---

document courtesy Chicago Police Department Red Squad

November 22, 1954.

From: Commanding Officer - Security Unit.

To: Commissioner of Police.

Subject: National Lawyers Guild (Legal Bulwark of the Communist Party), 1954 Convention, November 19-21, 1954, Congress Hotel, Chicago, Illinois, $5.50 Per Plate.

Attached comprises report of subject Communist front activity, covered by members of this Unit.

FJH/eww/rtb ← *report*

cc: DC SS

Sgt. Frank J. Heimoski

Subject: National Lawyers Guild (Legal Bulwark of the Communist Party), 1954 Convention, November 19-21, 1954, Congress Hotel, Chicago, Illinois.

This report covers the Annual Banquet held in conjunction with subject Convention. Said banquet was given on Saturday, November 20, 1954, at 7:30 P.M. in the Gold Room of the Congress Hotel.

Subject organization at the present time is frantically maneuvering to prevent the Office of the Attorney General from placing it, said organization, upon the Attorney General's 'subversive list'.

During the banquet there were approximately eight hundred (800) persons in attendance, an apparent over-flow crowd as tables were set-up on the balcony to accomodate those persons who could not be served in the Gold Room proper.

At 9:15 P.M., the Toastmaster for the evening, ▓▓▓▓▓▓ (Communist), President, National Lawyers Guild of Los Angeles, California - in 1949, the Un-American Activities Committee listed Mr. ▓▓▓▓▓▓ as appearing or following the Communist Party line for a long period of time, asked those in attendance to rise and join in the singing of the National Anthem. At the conclusion of the National Anthem, ▓▓▓▓▓▓ asked that the audience remain standing while a prayer was offered. Rev. ▓▓▓▓▓▓ (Communist), Pastor, ▓▓▓▓▓▓, Chicago, Illinois (Communist front), delivered the invocation.

After the invocation ▓▓▓▓▓▓ proceeded to introduced the distinguished guests and prominent members of the National Lawyers Guild who were seated on the dais. These persons were introduced as

---

attorney), Pensacola, Florida - Earl B. DICKERSON, colored, (Communist fellow-traveler), out-going National President, subject organization -

---

At this time the Toastmaster, ▓▓▓▓▓▓ gave a short talk outlining a bit of the history of the Guild. He stated that he was grateful for the opportunity of welcoming the audience at this highpoint of the 1954 Convention. He felt honored to participate in celebrating the Guild's incomparable record of service to the bar and to the people. ▓▓▓▓▓▓ remarked that the Guild has a wide reputation as a liberal bar association, but too few, even among those here tonight, are fully aware of the many signal achievements through which this reputation was gained.

Created in 1937 in the heyday of the Roosevelt era, the Guild was brought into being to give expression to the aspirations of liberal-

"The 1954 Chicago Guild Convention," by the Chicago Red Squad (Banquet tribute to Earl B. Dickerson, 1980, 1983).

> minded lawyers who found hope and promise in the program of the New
> Deal. The Guild has concerned itself, of course, with all the problems
> of usual interest to a bar association - administration of justice, legal
> aid, the welfare of the lawyer, the standards of the profession.
>
> To many traditional problems of the profession it brought
> a fresh approach. The Guild was the first national bar association to
> welcome into its ranks (as well as its leadership) all members of the
> bar, without regard to color. In concluding his remarks, ▌▌ intro-
> duced the outgoing National President, Earl B. DICKERSON.
>
> Mr. DICKERSON also spoke of the achievements of the Guild
> and member lawyers in general. He condemned the attempts of the Attorney
> General to place the Guild on a subversive list - he condemned the tact-
> ics of investigating bodies. Lawyers don't ask religious or political
> beliefs of their clients. Unless lawyers are free, the people become
> victims of the witch-hunts. The people would be in a sad state if
> Jefferson and his men were not free to write the Bill of Rights - what if
> Lincoln, another great lawyer, had been stopped in 1853? The Emancipation
> Act would never have been passed. A highlighted legislative act of the
> present administration, the Desegregation Act, was passed with the aid of
> ▌▌ (Communist fellow-traveler), colored, (endorsed the
> ▌▌, Chicago, 'Communist front' - member
> of presiding committee, ▌▌ now merged with the
> ▌▌ 'Communist front'), from Delaware, who is here
> tonight. ▌▌ is also a member of the Guild. In summing-up,
> DICKERSON stated, "If you here are among those who want the people
> free, then back the National Lawyers Guild."

document courtesy Chicago Police Department Red Squad

TESTIMONY OF RUTH WEYAND BEFORE THE HOUSE COMMITTEE ON UN-AMERICAN ACTIVITIES, FEBRUARY 23, 1956

[Six years after ceasing to be a dues-paying member, Guild founder Ruth Weyand of Chicago was called before HUAC. She refused to disassociate herself from lifelong friends and commitments and, in fact, took the occasion to praise the Guild.]

MR. ARENS: During the course of your employment in the National Labor Relations Board from 1938 until 1950 you maintained at all times your association and activity in the National Lawyers Guild; is that correct?

MISS WEYAND: That is correct.

MR. ARENS: Ma'am, did you continue your affiliation with the Lawyers Guild after it had been cited by the House Committee on Un-American Activities as a legal arm of the Communist Party?

MISS WEYAND: I never paid any attention.

"Testimony of Ruth Weyand before the House Committee on Un-American Activities, February 23, 1956," Investigation of Communist Infiltration of Government—Part 4, Hearing before HUAC 84th Cong., 2d Sess.

MR. ARENS: Ma'am, would you kindly tell us who of these persons whom we have just been discussing—your associates there in the capacities which you have recited—were likewise your colleagues or associates in the National Lawyers Guild?

MISS WEYAND: Joe Robison was treasurer of the Lawyers Guild and David Rein was secretary the year that I was president of the District chapter. We had a very active District chapter, with some 400 Government employees, including local judges and the general counsels of almost every federal agency. I was very proud of my work the year I was president.

MR. ARENS: I take it, Ma'am, your little detour there indicates a degree of pride on your part because of the association with the National Lawyers Guild; is that correct?

MISS WEYAND: I was very proud of the job I did as president of the District chapter that year.

MR. ARENS: Were you proud of the National Lawyers Guild?

MISS WEYAND: I was proud of it.

MR. ARENS: Are you proud of your associations with these persons whom you have just been describing who were your colleagues and also your associates in the National Lawyers Guild?

MISS WEYAND: I certainly was, and I still am.

MR. ARENS: Now, Ma'am, if you please, have you learned since your disassociation from the National Labor Relations Board that each of these persons among others, has been before the Committee on Un-American Activities of the United States Congress and, notwithstanding the fact that sworn testimony has identified them as members of the Communist Party, each has declined to answer questions respecting such alleged affiliation?

MISS WEYAND: I understand that they followed Dean Griswold's theory that the fifth amendment was a haven for people who believe in freedom of speech and freedom of the press. I am not following the same course, but I see nothing wrong with their having followed the dean of Harvard's idea that you can take the constitutional right. Today the fifth amendment is the protector of people who still believe in the democracy and freedom of speech and freedom of the press, and I see nothing wrong with their having followed the dean of Harvard's notion.

MR. ARENS: Would you kindly tell us whether or not you have revised your opinion or estimate of your former colleagues in the National Lawyers Guild and on the National Labor Relations Board in view of what has transpired in the public revelations of their affiliations and activities?

MISS WEYAND: I know nothing in their public revelations that I give any credence to that reflects in the slightest upon my respect for them as lawyers and loyal American citizens.

SCHWARE, KONIGSBERG, AND INDEPENDENCE OF THE BAR
By John T. McTernan and The New York Guild Lawyer

[John McTernan subtitled the following article, "The Return to Reason." Its publication in 1957 appeared to coincide with an end to the cold war against lawyers. Just in case there were any doubters, however, McTernan's final sentence was directed to the Attorney General—"Mr. Brownell, please note."]

The Supreme Court's recent opinions dealing with the exclusion of applicants from the Bar offer substantial grounds for the hope that the political test may be discarded as a qualification for obtaining or retaining a lawyer's license. [*Schware v. New Mexico*, 353 U.S. 532 (1957) and *Konigsberg v. California*, 353 U.S. 552 (1957)].

The rationale of these cases and their inescapable implications indicate that "political loyalty" may no longer measure the individual's right to employment and economic security.

In *Schware,* the applicant had been excluded from admission primarily because of his admitted past membership in the Communist Party, but also on account of his use of aliases and record of arrests in the early mid-thirties. At the outset the Court reiterated the familiar, but in recent years neglected, principle that safeguards the right to pursue a calling, including the practice of law, with the shield of due process and equal protection: "A State cannot exclude a person from the practice of law or from any other occupation in a manner or for reasons that contravene the Due Process or Equal Protection Clause of the Fourteenth Amendment" (353 U.S. 238-239).

The Court quickly disposed of the use of aliases and prior arrests. Schware had used an assumed name once to "forestall anti-Semitism in securing employment or organizing his fellow workers," and again to avoid being fired as a striker when "picked up in a mass arrest during a labor dispute." This was held "certainly not enough evidence to support an inference that petitioner has bad moral character more than 20 years later" (353 U.S. 240-241).

In analyzing Schware's prior arrests, the Court significantly went beyond the obvious observation that none had led to a trial or conviction and therefore showed nothing reflecting upon his moral character. It pointed out that many arrests were made during the bitter Pacific Coast Waterfront strike of 1934, when "great numbers of strikers" were picked up on "suspicion of criminal syndicalism" (353 U.S. 241).

In 1940, Schware was arrested for violation of the Neutrality Act of

1917 on account of his efforts to recruit persons to go overseas in order to aid Spanish Loyalists against Franco. The charge was dropped, but the Court examined its nature more closely and concluded that no moral turpitude was involved: "Many persons in this country actively supported the Spanish Loyalist Government. During the prelude to World War II, many idealistic young men volunteered to help in defending causes they believed right." Numbers aided China and England before our entry into the war, and there was no record that any of them were prosecuted under the Neutrality Act. "Few Americans would have regarded their conduct as evidence of moral turpitude" (353 U.S. 242).

Schware's membership in the Communist Party had extended from 1932 to 1940. The New Mexico court, basing itself expressly upon Justice Jackson's concurring opinion in *American Communications Association v. Douds,* 339 U.S. 382, 422 (1950), had assumed that the Party in that period was dominated by a foreign power and dedicated to force and violence. But Justice Jackson's observations, the Court held, did not purport to be findings of fact and could not substitute for evidence in another case. The Court pointed out that during the period of Schware's membership, the Communist Party "was a lawful political party with candidates on the ballot in most states." In that time, it attracted many people by its "radical solution to the grave economic crisis," its opposition to Fascism, and its program for full employment and racial equality. There was no evidence that Schware engaged in unlawful conduct. Assuming that some members of the organization had illegal aims and engaged in illegal activities, "it cannot automatically be inferred that all members shared their evil purposes or participated in their illegal conduct" (232 U.S. 246).

The Court concluded "there is no evidence in the record which rationally justifies a finding that Schware was morally unfit to practice law," and held that New Mexico had deprived him of "due process in denying him the opportunity to qualify for the practice of law" (353 U.S. 247).

The *Konigsberg* case presents more complex facts. Unlike *Schware,* where the determination to reverse the New Mexico Supreme Court and Board of Bar Examiners was unanimous (one Justice not participating), the *Konigsberg* case was determined by a 5-3 vote (one Justice dissenting on jurisdictional grounds and two on that ground and on the merits). The dissent on the merits was extensive. The fact that there was so thorough a canvassing of the issues involved lends especial weight, we believe, to the result reached by the Court.

The California statutes require that (1) an applicant must have "good moral character" before he can be certified for admission by the Committee of Bar Examiners, and that (2) admission to practice is prohibited to any person who advocates the overthrow of the Federal or State Government by force, violence or other unconstitutional means (353 U.S. 253). Konigsberg, like Schware, had made a "forceful showing" of high moral character. There was some evidence of his past membership in the Communist Party, and he refused, on First Amendment grounds, to answer questions dealing with his political associations or opinions. California denied him admission because he failed to meet both statutory tests. As the Court construed California's action, it was not based merely on Konigsberg's refusal to answer questions. The issue for decision was, "Does the evidence in the record support any reasonable doubts about Konigsberg's good character and his loyalty to the Government of the State and Nation?" In resolving that question the Court held that it must "take into account the (Bar) Committee's contention that Konigsberg's failure to respond to questions was evidence from which some inference of doubtful character and loyalty can be drawn" (353 U.S. 262).

The Court gave short shrift to the evidence of Communist Party membership in 1941. It found the testimony "not very convincing" (353 U.S. 267). But, assuming the fact of membership in 1941, the organization was a recognized political party offering candidates at the elections, and the state attempted to attach no penalty to membership in it. "Those who accepted the state at its word and joined that party had a right to expect that the state would not penalize them, directly or indirectly, for doing so thereafter" (353 U.S. 268). There was no evidence of Konigsberg's agreement with or advocacy of proscribed doctrine. His alleged membership affords no "reasonable basis" for inferring such advocacy (353 U.S. 271). Konigsberg had written editorials in 1950 severely criticizing American participation in the Korean War, actions and policies of leaders of major political parties, the influence of "big business" in American life, racial discrimination and decisions by the Supreme Court in the *Dennis* (Smith Act) case and other cases. The Court held, however, that "because of the very nature of our democracy such expressions of political views must be permitted," and that no inference of bad moral character could be drawn from them (353 U.S. 268-9).

Concerning Konigsberg's refusal to answer questions relating to "political affiliations, editorials and beliefs," the Court refused to draw any inference adverse to him. Declining to pass upon his First Amendment objections to replying, the Court observed that they were "not frivolous," and that there was nothing to indicate that they lacked good faith. The Court held (353 U.S. 270-271):

> Obviously the State could not draw unfavorable inferences as to his truthfulness, candor or his moral character in general if his refusal to answer was

based on a belief that the United States Constitution prohibited the type of inquiries which the Committee was making. . . . On the record before us, it is our judgment that the inferences of bad moral character which the Committee attempted to draw from Konigsberg's refusal to answer questions about his political affiliation and opinions are unwarranted.

TEN

The ABA and The Attorney General v. NLG *(1953–1958)*

On August 27, 1953, U.S. Attorney General Herbert Brownell struck the severest blow at the independence of the Bar: the right of advocacy and the right of those accused to counsel of their choice. In an address to a meeting of the American Bar Association, he stated that he had ordered the Guild to show cause why "it should not be designated on the Attorney General's list of subversive organizations." The effect was immediate and devastating. Within a few weeks nearly 700 members resigned. No Bar association challenged the Attorney General's Action against the Guild. Leaders of the Bar, who were invited to join as co-counsel in *Guild v. Brownell,* either in defense of the Guild, or at least in defense of independence of the Bar, expressed interest and sympathy, but found reasons why they were not able to accept. This default brought serious discredit to the Bar, which demonstrated it was not prepared to uphold the Constitution in a time of peril to the most fundamental freedoms.[1]

THIS WAS THE assessment of Robert J. Silberstein, the Guild executive secretary during this critical period.

The media also stopped publishing all press releases from the Guild, and whenever the Guild was mentioned, added "an organization on the Attorney General's list," although such a listing never occurred. By 1955 the Guild membership had fallen to 500, where it remained for three years.

The Guild leadership, with the strong support of its small membership, pursued an aggressive strategy. Not waiting for hearings, the Guild sued the Attorney General, challenging every legal aspect of the effort to list the Guild and the very concept of a "subversive list." Losing in the three tiers of the federal courts (the Supreme Court refused to hear the case), the Guild then dug in, challenging

---

1. "Robert J. Silberstein Looks Back on the Seven Lean Years, 1947–1954," by Robert J. Silberstein, *NLG Practitioner* 33:1 (Winter 1975).

every step in the administrative proceeding, starting with the questions the Attorney General sought to have answered (some of which appear below in "Amended Interrogatories").

The government's main response was delay. Months, and finally years, went by without any progress toward an administrative hearing. Meanwhile, Guild lawyers were also under individual attack, professional, financial, and political. Many clients came to them in political cases for free and dedicated representation. Sometimes when their cases reached the Supreme Court, they shifted to "respectable" lawyers whom they paid well. And when these political clients had bread-and-butter cases that might generate a fee, some steered clear of their political lawyers, who were themselves being called as witnesses before legislative investigating committees, or getting other bad publicity.

Guild lawyers, and their clients, got a tremendous boost on June 17, 1957, when the Supreme Court handed down the latest in a series of decisions striking down such Cold War totems as sweeping unrestrained HUAC investigations, contempt citations for invoking the Fifth Amendment protection against self-incrimination, and guilt by association arguments used in loyalty-security proceedings. This caused some to want to add up the score in the Cold War, and led to a Guild conference and banquet honoring ninety Guild members for conspicuous service to the cause of civil liberties. "While we are small in numbers compared with the ABA," executive secretary Royal W. France told the audience, "we have been a powerful factor in this important area of our national life."

By the spring of 1958, the Guild was ready to try a bold strategy in its listing case: the Attorney General must put up or shut up. The Guild sued in federal court for dismissal of the listing proceedings for lack of prosecution during four and a half years, which could have fueled a quick public hearing. Instead, the Attorney General prayed for additional time to file an answer. On September 12, 1958, he withdrew the proceedings, in correspondence presented below.

FBI ACTIVITY AND EXECUTIVE ORDER 10450
By Michael Krinsky

The material that FBI Director J. Edgar Hoover put before the Justice Department to move Attorney General Brownell to . . . [announce proceedings to designate the Guild a Communist-front organization] had come overwhelmingly from the burglaries and wiretaps of the Guild office. Between 1947 and 1951 the FBI entered into the Guild's national office no fewer than fourteen times, photographing each time whatever material it had not secured in previous entries. There was no judicial warrant and no attorney general authorization for these entries.

"FBI Activity and Executive Order 10450," by Michael Krinsky, written expressly for this book.

The government's proceedings required the Guild to form a legal assistance committee of ten members for the purpose of consulting with attorneys representing the NLG. True to form, the FBI at the time had an informant on the Guild's Executive Committee who was privy to confidential deliberations by the Guild with its counsel.

Two years prior to Brownell's announcement, Guild attorneys had won a significant Supreme Court victory requiring an administrative hearing before the Attorney General could list an organization as subversive (*Joint Anti-Fascist Refugee Committee v. McGrath,* 341 U.S. 123 [1951]). It is one of the great lessons of the Guild's history that this Supreme Court victory, achieved for others, proved critical to the Guild's own survival.

TEST OATHS: HENRY VIII TO THE AMERICAN BAR ASSOCIATION
By Samuel M. Koenigsberg and Morton Stavis

[The article from which the following selection was taken became the standard reference for lawyers needing some historical background to handle their first loyalty oath case.]

A test oath for all attorneys was demanded by the American Bar Association at its 1950 convention. Its resolution declares it appropriate that loyalty to the government be attested by an anti-Communist oath, and recommends that each member of the Bar be required to file a periodic affidavit disclosing present or past membership in or affiliation with the Communist Party and membership in or support of any organization espousing the overthrow of the government. The resolution further provides that, if such membership is acknowledged, the attorney be investigated by the appropriate authorities to determine his fitness to continue to practice law.

The Canons of Professional Ethics of the American Bar Association call upon attorneys to represent parties fearlessly and regardless of the unpopularity of their cause, and a long honor roll of lawyers testifies to the vigor of this injunction in times past. The era through which we are passing is subjecting the continued vitality of this mandate to an even greater strain. The difficulties of persons involved in cases of a Communist character in securing the services of counsel are a matter of public record. The prospective economic and professional hardship to a lawyer appearing in such cases is of itself a mighty deterrent to the performance by members of the Bar of their traditional duties in unpopular trials.

"Test Oaths: Henry VIII to the American Bar Association," by Samuel M. Koenigsberg and Morton Stavis, *Lawyers Guild Review* 11:3 (Summer 1953).

Even if sufficient courage to appear for the defense is mustered by an attorney, the vigor and firmness with which he performs his duties will inevitably be weighed by him against the possibility that his conduct may be considered contemptuous or otherwise improper, an asserted mark of a Communist or revolutionary lawyer, and that the sanctions of a false oath may be applied to him.

One final thought: The oath will not remain long in the form in which the American Bar Association proposed it. Its committee's report advocating disbarment not only for members of the Communist Party but also for advocates of Marxism-Leninism already suggests additional matter to be foresworn. And history shows us that the disavowals will almost inevitably become more and more minute and increasingly tied to the political necessities of the moment. The direction of the expansion, of course, cannot be foretold. The lawyer who feels free to take the first oath may begin to feel reluctant at some future one, when it will have become an established mechanism. The oath to stop is the first one.

THE AMERICAN BAR ASSOCIATION, ATTORNEY GENERAL BROWNELL, AND THE NATIONAL LAWYERS GUILD IN TIME OF CRISIS
By the Editors, Lawyers Guild Review

[Between 1948 and 1953 the American Bar Association adopted resolutions prohibiting lawyers sympathetic to world Communism from membership; it recommended periodic anti-Communist loyalty oaths for all lawyers, urged the disbarment of attorneys who advocated "Marxism-Leninism," and proposed disciplinary action against those who took the Fifth Amendment before Congressional committees. The editors of the *LGR* offered the following editorial response.]

The National Lawyers Guild is not deceived by the real purposes behind the crusade against the "puny band" of Communists in our midsts. It is no coincidence that the shrillest among the crusaders are also implacable opponents of every measure to improve the well-being of our people. It is clear to us that the enemies of change in America are exploiting the tragic world tensions for anti-social ends. As proof that not the "puny band" but the welfare of our people is their real objective, we would remind labor that the Taft-Hartley Act is still the law of the land; the Negro—and the white as well—that discrimination for race and color still prevail in our country; the millions too poor to obtain medical care that no provision has been made for their needs; the ill-

---

"The American Bar Association, Attorney General Brownell, and the National Lawyers Guild in Time of Crisis," by the editors of *Lawyers Guild Review* 13:3 (Fall 1953).

housed and those who have no housing at all that slums and hovels and trailers are still the homes of too many Americans; and all Americans that prices have reached a new peak and are still climbing.

The Guild is aware that the real purpose behind the crusade is to enforce acquiescence in these conditions and silence protest against them; to brand proposals for change as communistic, socialistic, subversive, and evil. But we shall not be silenced. We shall continue to defend our sacred freedom, including the freedom to criticize, dissent, and propose alternatives so that our people can make the choices that seem to them wisest. We shall continue to defend, as American lawyers from Hamilton to Willkie have in the past, those of our fellow citizens and our colleagues, no matter how hated or unpopular, whose civil liberties or constitutional rights are threatened.

We believe that the principles and intentions expressed in this appeal are in keeping with the finest traditions of American democracy and freedom. Indeed, we believe that those who would silence us are the real un-Americans, that, when these times of tension are past, they will find themselves in the dustbin of history with the prosecutors and judges of the Alien and Sedition Laws of 1798, with the Palmers and Lusks of the post–World War I hysteria, and with all those who have, at one time or another, betrayed the democratic faith.

In the meantime, we appeal to all men and women, in and out of our profession, who are not yet beyond the reach of reason, to help us defend not only the Guild but American liberties. We have no wish for martyrdom. Our most ardent wish is for a truly prosperous and free and peaceful America. We most humbly believe that the latest attack on the Guild is not only one more step away from these consummations but a serious blow to America's moral prestige and standing in the world.

To paraphrase slightly Judge Clark's dissent in *Matter of Sacher* (206 F. 2d 358, 366):

Why must the most serious wounds to our democracy and prestige be self-inflicted?

Are the many men and women of good-will in this nation ready to join us in this struggle to restore the America of Tom Paine and Jefferson, Holmes and Brandeis, Fighting Bob La Follette and Franklin Delano Roosevelt? Or shall it be said of them that they lost their freedom by default?

Amended Interrogatories of the U.S. Attorney General Concerning Guild Activities
IN THE MATTER OF THE PROPOSED DESIGNATION OF THE NATIONAL LAWYERS GUILD PURSUANT TO EXECUTIVE ORDER NO. 10450

[A random selection—it is crucial to remember that the Guild vigorously protested all of these questions, and that it won the right of confidentiality.]

INTERROGATORY (5)

(a) Has the NLG or any of its affiliated branches, locals, clubs, chapters or the officers or members thereof on behalf of the NLG, ever at any time received orders or directives pertaining to the policies or programs of the NLG, directly or indirectly, from the Communist Party of the United States of America (hereinafter referred to as CP, USA), its leaders, functionaries, officials, or members?

(b) If so, describe in detail the orders or directives, when received and from and by whom received.

INTERROGATORY (17)

Is it the official position of the NLG that self-imposed investigations by organizations of their membership for the purpose of effecting the expulsion of Communists constitute a dangerous and anti-democratic development?

INTERROGATORY (30)

Has the NLG taken an official position on the following matters, and, if so, give the date when the official resolution, declaration, or statement was released and furnish a copy thereof?

1. Disarmament (post-World War II)
2. Atomic energy and control of weapons thereof
3. United Nations
4. Admission of Red China to the United Nations
5. American support for Nationalist China
6. Aid to Greece and Turkey by the United States
7. European Recovery Program, Marshall Plan and NATO

"Amended Interrogatories of the U.S. Attorney General Concerning Guild Activities in the Matter of the Proposed Designation of the National Lawyers Guild Pursuant to Executive Order No. 10450," reprinted in *The National Lawyers Guild: An Inventory of Records 1936–1976; An Index to Periodicals 1937–1979*, MCLI Inventory No. 2 (1980).

8. Withdrawal of American troops from Europe and Asia after World War II
9. On the question of maintaining diplomatic relations with Argentina and Spain

INTERROGATORY (37)

Has the NLG taken an official position on the following matters, and, if so, give the date when the official resolution, declaration, or statement was released and furnish a copy thereof?

1. Fingerprinting and requiring of identification cards for all aliens
2. Deportation of aliens
3. Deportation of Harry Bridges
4. Committees of Congress investigating Communism
5. The Federal Bureau of Investigation
6. Loyalty program of the Federal Government
7. Peekskill incident involving Paul Robeson
8. Prosecution of Gerhardt Eisler
9. Non-Communist affidavit in the Taft-Hartley Act
10. University military training
11. The Voorhis Act
12. The Smith Act
13. Communist Party on Ballot
14. Re Peace Information Center as a foreign agent
15. Re the indictment of Maurice Braverman under the Smith Act
16. Re the conviction for contempt of certain attorneys in the Smith Act cases
17. The McCarran Bill affording immunity to Congressional witnesses
18. Legalized wiretapping
19. American Bar Association Loyalty Oath
20. Contempt citations of Communist attorneys in the Dennis case
21. Dismissal of teachers for membership in Communist Party

INTERROGATORY (42)

(a) Submit a list of the current membership of the NLG indicating with which branch, local, club, or chapter each member is affiliated.
(b) Do you know or have you reason to believe that any of the current members of the NLG are now or have ever been members of the CP, USA, or the Communist Political Association, hereinafter referred to as CPA?
(c) If you have such knowledge or belief, identify these members.

EXTRACTS FROM BRIEFS TO THE UNITED STATES COURT OF APPEALS IN *NATIONAL LAWYERS GUILD v. HERBERT BROWNELL, JR.*, BRIEF FOR APPELLANT
By Osmond K. Fraenkel, Earl B. Dickerson, and Joseph Forer

[Writing briefs is a solitary task, but the mark of a lawyer is the ability to leave the law library and confer, discuss, debate, and collaborate with clients and colleagues. Osmond K. Fraenkel, the Guild's executive vice-president and lead counsel in the Brownell case, was a master of brief writing and coalition building, as these excerpts from the Guild's brief to the Court of Appeals show.]

QUESTIONS PRESENTED

Whether there exist substantial constitutional questions as to the validity of the provisions of Executive Orders 10450 and 9835 regarding designation by the Attorney General of organizations thereunder.

Whether the Attorney General's regulations and procedures for designating organizations under Executive Order 10450, on their face and as applied to appellant, violate due process of law.

Whether the Attorney General's proposed proceeding for designation of appellant under Executive Order 10450 will necessarily be invalid by reason of the Attorney General's expression of prejudgment and bias.

Whether a Bar association seeking to enjoin the Attorney General from proceeding to designate it under Executive Order 10450 must exhaust the administrative remedy prescribed by the Attorney General when (a) the association will suffer irreparable injury to constitutionally protected interests if it is required to exhaust the administrative remedy; (b) the Attorney General has publicly prejudged the case against the association and has expressed bias against it; (c) the administrative procedure violates due process of law and the Administrative Procedure Act; and (d) substantial constitutional questions exist as to the validity of the provisions of the Executive Orders authorizing the Attorney General to designate organizations thereunder.

We have said that the injuries threatened are multifarious. They may well be also fatal. In the *Joint Anti-Fascist Refugee Committee* case, supra, Mr. Justice Burton said that the effect of a listing "is to cripple the functioning" of the organization (341 U.S., at p. 139). Mr. Justice Black spoke of it as "practical equivalents of confiscation and death sentences" (p. 142); Mr. Justice Frankfurter wrote that it "drastically

---

"Extracts from Briefs to the United States Court of Appeals in *National Lawyers Guild v. Herbert Brownell, Jr.*, Brief for Appellant," by Osmond K. Fraenkel, Earl B. Dickerson, and Joseph Forer, *Lawyers Guild Review* 14:1 (Spring 1954).

restricts the organizations, if it does not proscribe them" (p. 161); and Mr. Justice Douglas described an organization so listed as "maimed and crippled" (p. 175). This was said of the organizations involved in that case. How much more disastrous are bound to be the effects on an organization of lawyers! For nothing is plainer than that the listing of appellant will not only destroy its own activities in the field of civil liberties and rights, but will frighten thousands of its members, past and present, and no doubt many others, into similar inactivity. How many lawyers, being or once having been members of a proscribed organization, will risk defending Communists or those called Communists?

We believe we have established that the complaint raises substantial questions concerning the power of the Attorney General to carry on the administrative proceeding, both because this impairs First Amendment rights and because the absence of proper standards violates the due process clause of the Fifth Amendment. We have shown also that the administrative procedures are defective, in part because the regulations deny due process, in part because they violate the Administrative Procedures Act, but above all because defendant has prejudged the particular case.

THE LEO SHEINER CASE: NO DISBARMENT FOR USE OF FIFTH AMENDMENT
By The New York Guild Lawyer *and* Lawyers Guild Review

[On July 29, 1955, the Supreme Court of Florida held that an attorney could not be disbarred for exercising the privilege against self-incrimination in response to questions about membership in the Communist Party. The Guild and the ABA's Special Committee on Communist Tactics had filed opposing briefs amicus curiae and presented oral arguments before the court. The great interest in this case was also indicated by the introduction of these briefs into the Congressional Record by Senator William Langer on May 26, 1955. Excerpts from the decision follow.]

The pertinent part of the motion to disbar is predicated on "(a) unprofessional acts which unfit him for association with the fair and honorable members of the profession, (b) deceit or misconduct in his office of attorney, and (c) violating the code of ethics prescribed for members of the bar of the State of Florida," in that he is or has been a member of the Communist Party, that he refuses to answer questions regarding his membership in groups which advocate and teach the forcible overthrow of constitutional government of the United States, bas-

---

"The Leo Sheiner Case: No Disbarment for Use of Fifth Amendment," by *The New York Guild Lawyer* (July–Aug. 1955), and *Lawyers Guild Review* 15 (1955).

ing his refusal to answer on the protection given him against self-incrimination by the First and Fifth Amendments to the Federal Constitution and Sections 12 and 13, Declaration of Rights, Constitution of Florida.

Historically, the privilege against self-incrimination was raised as early as the twelfth century but was limited to inquisitorial proceedings of the Star Chamber and the High Commission of England. It was granted as a protection against religious dissent or other mental convictions, including religious or political heresy. In the colonies the privilege had to do with political inquisitions by prerogative courts. It may, therefore, be reasonably inferred that the inclusion of the privilege against self-incrimination in the fundamental law was to halt unwarranted inquisitions, particularly in cases where political or religious believers were involved.

By training the lawyer is better qualified than the layman to avoid the Communist net. If his preparation for the Bar did not plant in him an allergy for subversive leanings, it fell far short of the mark. If he unwittingly gets sucked into a subversive organization and refuses to testify as to his connection with it for reason of self-incrimination, his claim should be respected if it is properly grounded. Invoking the Fifth Amendment may or may not imply good character; neither does it prove guilt.

After all is said, we are driven to the conclusion that appellant was not accorded due process, in that there is no evidence connecting him with Communistic activities except the Congressional Committee report and inferences that may be drawn from it having to do with activities that took place seven years before this proceeding was brought and the fact that he invoked the protection of the Fifth Amendment. Before the Congressional Committee, appellant was denied the right of confrontation and cross-examination.

LIVING WITH A SUBPOENA
By Vivian Mandel

[During the McCarthy era Guild families felt the sting of disbarment proceedings and the uneasiness of the subpoena server. In the following selection, Vivian Mandel provides a personal recollection of one family's experience in Los Angeles.]

I'm sure you all have heard of many of the people who have been receivers of subpoenas before the Un-American Activities Committee—

"Living with a Subpoena," by Vivian Mandel, *New York Guild Lawyer* (Dec. 1954).

but how many of you know just what it is like to be the wife and family of a subpoenaed lawyer?

Until the time when you receive that ordinary looking pink slip of paper you feel that you are an active liberal thinking person, working hard in community organizations—working successfully to defeat a state bill requiring loyalty oaths of all professionals—and just when you feel you have reached the point of complete exhaustion and are ready to take a much needed rest from such activity—you have a husband and two small children. . . . Just then after 15 years of constant meetings you feel it is time to slow down for awhile. It is at this point you hear that subpoenas have been served to a dozen lawyers. You and your husband discuss them with a detached feeling. You talk of this terrible attack on their civil liberties, but think of yourself as small fry—and who is interested in our thinking anyhow? These things hit only other people.

Suddenly one day you get a phone call from your husband. He tells you that he just received his pink slip. . . . *It happened to us.* . . . I didn't believe it; we were afraid to tell our friends—maybe they wouldn't like us. I wondered what Seymour should do—maybe he could say something that would pacify the committee that wouldn't put him in the limelight and would hush everything. Then I re-read the subpoena—they were investigating subversive activities. I thought what had Seymour done?—he had only been Exec. Secy. of the Guild at one time—but the Lawyers Guild is a recognized Bar association in Calif.—with its members and constitution on record with the state Bar. My husband explained to me that by some fantastic legal situation (with which I was not familiar) that if he would answer even one question about his own thoughts and the thoughts of his friends, he would waive his privilege and would then have to answer any question asked about his friends—and then would he have any friends?

Now I knew the reason for the use of the Fifth Amendment—it is the duty of a lawyer and *his family* to stand and defend every part of the Bill of Rights. He took a lawyer's oath to do just that. What would his clients say if they knew he would betray their confidence and speak of them before the committee? I then began to realize that we had no other choice but to defend the rights of ourselves, our children, and our friends for years to come. What kind of a democratic heritage would I leave to my children if we betrayed our Bill of Rights? *No*—we had to stand together and help defend the rights of all Americans!

Well, soon the hearings were held—I won't give you details about them as no one is prouder than I that we in L.A. really made history in those hearings of Oct. '52—the whole country knew how the lawyers and doctors fought for their rights. I sat in that hearing room for 10 days and saw wonderful men and women of courage—I saw them rise to great heights—some mature in a minute. . . . Because "Courage is Contagious." Those were history-making days, and after it was over I couldn't understand how I was ever able to consider any other course but that we had followed.

Before I close I want to read you a letter of courage—a letter from the wife of a disbarred lawyer:

> I am sorry that I cannot attend the convention. May I just say these few words to the wives of Guild members. My husband has practiced law for twenty years. Law was his profession, his livelihood, and his inspiration. Overnight, he was severed from his profession because he chose not to speak, as was his constitutional right, when words would have meant dishonor. The consequences of his action were heavy upon him, my daughter, and myself. I know, though, that he did the right and honorable thing. I ask you all to take courage. Today's hysteria and fear can only be met this way.—Sincerely, Ada Sheiner.

LIBERTY AND PEACE: THE ROLE OF A FREE BAR
By Malcolm P. Sharp

[On first glance, Malcolm Sharp, the distinguished economic conservative who taught law for over thirty years at the University of Chicago, might seem an unlikely person to lead the Guild from 1954 to 1956. An avowed critic of New Deal tax and social policy, Sharp was at the same time a courageous defender of civil liberties, an ardent foe of racial discrimination, and a powerful voice for a democratic foreign policy. His presidency symbolized the Guild's commitment to unity in support of constitutional rights during the difficult years of the McCarthy era.]

How far I am qualified to strike a keynote for the Guild is doubtful. Those of you who have been at Board meetings will have discovered that my views on economics are quite unorthodox in these circles. When I get to liberties other than the economic ones, I do better. I do pretty well on war and peace. Some of you will have suspected that what I call my philosophy may be a little eccentric.

Violent revolution on any sizable scale is as intolerable as violent war in a society equipped with the modern weapons. It may be indeed that the philosophy of the Declaration of Independence is outmoded by the advance of technology, though it is hardly a disqualification for any public function to think otherwise. Like our own Nathan Hale, spies risk death as do soldiers. Any serious threat of atomic espionage must be taken seriously, and any threat of sabotage with the new explosives must be taken very seriously.

"Liberty and Peace: The Role of a Free Bar," by Malcolm P. Sharp, *Lawyers Guild Review* 14:4 (Winter 1954–55), and 16:1 (Spring 1956).

Nevertheless, exaggeration can do as much harm as neglect. It can lead to fears which will come close to paralyzing the normal activities of life. Exaggeration itself can lead to the warfare which it is expected to prevent. It can lead to a world like that of George Orwell's *1984*, in which not only communication but all the most intimate human relationships are subject to supervision.

The atomic age is doubtless bringing us great advantages. It has solved a problem of industrial energy; it is contributing to the solution of problems of health; it has made war obviously absurd. While we gain the resulting advantages, we shall also doubtless conquer the fears to which the first appearance of the age has given rise. Fears may bring exaggerated hatreds, and hatreds may bring war. It is a safeguard for all we value most to have members of the community who see to it that the great fears and hatreds of the day are subject to critical scrutiny, in the press, the universities, the government, and the courts.

The human desires and values which oppose these tendencies are fostered by the many good Americans who have opposed the exaggerated fears and hatreds of recent days.

There is communication, which, as Socrates knew, is indispensable for any life which is to be called human. There are all the elusive values, which cannot be catalogued or easily named, which depend on communication. There is justice in the elementary sense of safeguards for the individual against destruction by the uncontrolled violence of individuals, groups, or state.

Guild lawyers and other lawyers on the same side may have lost many of their cases, but it would be a mistake to say that they have failed. Fortunately they have won some important cases. Those who were on the losing side in the other cases have made a record which was a safeguard against further extensions of the passing fury, and a means by which historians can in a later day examine the administration of justice in the first years of the atomic age.

The Guild's distinct mission now is to help prevent the spread of loyalty proceedings to the Bar. Its efforts are related in many and various ways to liberty and peace. Much of the emotion that expresses itself in loyalty proceedings is stimulated, as hostility to German-Americans was stimulated in 1917 and 1918, by the fears and hostilities of the Cold War. The resulting domestic fears and hostilities contribute in turn to the stimulation of international mistrust and hatred. The final result is an obstacle to our return to the conditions of security and sanity which are most suitable for the development of a free society. It is the purpose of the Guild, as of the American people generally, to contribute to the creation of conditions in which free societies may thrive.

REPORT OF THE ADMINISTRATIVE SECRETARY
By Jessica Davidson

[Jessica Davidson, the Guild's Secretary in 1954–1955, argues below that the organization's immobilization during the Brownell case would be tantamount to a victory for the Attorney General.]

The Guild is fighting for its life, and a very large proportion of the time and energy and resources of the Guild must, of necessity, be devoted to winning the suit against listing by the Attorney General.

Neither the Guild as an organization nor its members individually can hibernate through the bitter winter of reaction. For this winter will not give way to a brighter spring by the passage of time alone. This climate of fear is man-made and it will last as long—and only as long—as the people, through inaction, suffer it to last. We *are* the people and we *speak* to the people and our influence will be as great as the service we offer.

Above all, let's stop trying to see ourselves as others see us, for they see us through the distorted lenses the Brownells and McCarthys have fashioned. If we accept this picture of ourselves, we will in truth be isolated. If we make no effort to introduce Guild proposals before other organizations because we fear that others will shun the Guild and reject our ideas, we will be carrying out Brownell's purpose more effectively than he could ever hope to do.

SELECTING PRIORITIES FOR GUILD WORK WHILE UNDER ATTACK: THE GINGER STRATEGY
By Leo J. Linder

[In 1955 the Guild was battling for its very survival. Inside the national office a number of options were under consideration. The new administrative secretary, Ann Fagan Ginger, argued for a "concentration policy." Leo Linder recounts his personal objection and subsequent agreement with that decision.]

It was in these circumstances that she undertook her post, quite undaunted and thoroughly imbued with a deep sense of the great need for a Bar association devoted to the protection of civil liberties and social welfare, and thoroughly convinced that the Guild could make a great contribution. Her task, as she conceived it, was to re-stoke the boiler, to

---

"Report of the Administrative Secretary," by Jessica Davidson, *Lawyers Guild Review* 14:4 (Winter 1954–55).

"Selecting Priorities for Guild Work While under Attack: The Ginger Strategy," by Leo J. Linder, *Guild Lawyer* (May 1959).

serve as a catalytic force which would stimulate the leadership and membership of the Guild into greater activity.

The "concentration program" of the Guild, the concentration of the energies of the Guild on a limited number of projects and the avoidance of the diffusion of those energies in more than the chosen projects, was one of her organizational devices. I must confess that I was unhappy at what seemed to me to be a tactical retreat and a contraction, even temporarily, of our activities, although I abided by the program as a matter of organizational discipline. I must confess, too, that she was probably right in her insistence upon this program, and I must pay her the deserved tribute due her for the way she fought for the program and then endeavored to make it a success.

THE GUILD HONORS DEFENDERS OF THE BILL OF RIGHTS
By The New York Guild Lawyer

[On October 25-26, 1957, over a year before the Brownell case was resolved, the Guild sponsored a conference and banquet in New York City. It was an occasion to assess the impact of recent Supreme Court decisions affecting civil liberties and an opportunity to honor its own members who had been in the midst of these struggles.]

The National Lawyers Guild's banquet of October 25, 1957 has a two-fold aspect.

The banquet was inspired by the epoch-making decisions of the 1956-1957 term of the United States Supreme Court in the civil liberties field. The Court's rulings have stayed the erosion of individual rights in the arid decade through which the American nation has passed. They have planted roots which, when nurtured, bear promise of growth and bloom. To those reflective citizens, lawyers and non-lawyers, who viewed the restrictive trends of recent years with misgiving and concern, the occasion is indeed one to be marked.

These decisions were the end result of long years of litigation in which many members of the Bar honorably served in the lawyer's historic role of the defender of liberty. Many of them labored valiantly, often at great personal sacrifice, in keeping alive the best traditions of the bar.

In reviewing the cases in the area of civil liberties during the past ten years, we are proud to find that so many of the lawyers who served the cause of freedom in them are members of the National Lawyers Guild.

"The Guild Honors Defenders of the Bill of Rights," by *The New York Guild Lawyer* (Oct. 1957).

The Guild tenders this banquet to honor those of our members who persevered over the years in the defense of the Bill of Rights. The American people owe a profound debt of gratitude to all members of the bar who participated in the defense of our liberties. For the victories that were won were won for all our people.

CONFERENCE PROGRAM
OCTOBER 26, 1957

Morning Session

Opening Remarks:

Osmond K. Fraenkel, Chairman—Vice President, National Lawyers Guild—One of General Counsel, American Civil Liberties Union.

I. The Impact of the Recent Decisions of the United States Supreme Court on the Smith Act.

Discussion Leader—Mary Kaufman—of the New York Bar.

"In my judgment the statutory provisions on which these prosecutions are based abridged freedom of speech, press, and assembly in violation of the First Amendment to the United States Constitution." —Black, J.: Yates.

II. The Impact of the Recent Decisions of the United States Supreme Court on Aspects of Due Process—Jencks Case, etc.

Discussion Leader—David Rein—of the District of Columbia Bar.

"For the interest of the United States in a criminal prosecution . . . is not that it shall win a case, but that justice shall be done."—Brennan, J.: Jencks.

Afternoon Session

III. The Impact of the Recent Decisions of the United States Supreme Court on Admission to the Bar and the Right to Practice Law.

Discussion Leader—Benjamin Dreyfus—of the California Bar.

"A Bar composed of lawyers of good character is a worthy objective but it is unnecessary to sacrifice vital freedoms in order to obtain that goal. It is also important both to society and the bar itself that lawyers be unintimidated—free to think, speak, and act, as members of an Independent Bar."—Black, J.: Konigsberg.

IV. The Impact of the Recent Decisions of the United States Supreme Court of Congressional Committee Investigations.

Discussion Leader—Victor Rabinowitz—of the New York Bar.

"We have no doubt that there is no Congressional power to expose for the sake of exposure."—Warren, C. J.: Watkins.

A TESTIMONIAL TO THE STRUGGLE FOR CIVIL LIBERTIES
By The New York Guild Lawyer

[The following list provides a remarkable visual account of Guild involvement in important Cold War cases. The * designates representation by individual Guild lawyers. The † indicates that the Guild submitted amicus curiae briefs. All cases in italics resulted in victories for the parties raising a civil liberties issue; some pending cases were won at a later date.]

INDEPENDENCE OF THE BAR

†In re Anastaplo, 3 Ill. 2d 471, 121 N. E. 2d 826 (1954), cert. den. 349 U. S. 903 (1955).
*Bouslog v. Bar Assn. of Hawaii, pending 9th Cir.
*Braverman v. Bar Assn. of Baltimore City, 121 A. 2d 473 (Md. 1956); In re Braverman, 148 F. Supp. 56 (DC Md. 1957).
Cammer v. U. S., 223 F. 2d 322, reversed 350 U. S. 399 (1956).
*Gladstein v. McLaughlin, 230 F. 2d 762 (9th Cir. 1955).
*Hallinan v. California State Bar, 43 Cal. 2d–, 45 Cal. 2d–.
*In re Isserman, 9 N. J. 316, 88 A. 2d 199, cert. den. 345 U. S. 927 (1953).
**In re Isserman,* 345 U. S. 286, set aside 348 U. S. 1 (1954).
Konigsberg v. State Bar of California, Comm. of Bar Examiners, 353 U. S. 252 (1957).
Application of Levy, 348 U. S. 978 (1955).
Patterson v. Oregon State Bd. of Bar Examiners, 302 P. 2d 227, 353 U. S. 952 (remanded).
†*Sacher v. U. S., 182 F. 2d 416, cert. den. 341 U. S. 952, cert. granted 342 U. S. 858; aff'd 343 U. S. 1.
**In re Sacher,* 206 F. 2d 358 (2d Cir. 1953), Sacher v. Assoc. of the Bar of the City of New York, 346 U. S. 894, reversed 347 U. S. 388 (1954).
In re Schlesinger, pending (Sub-Comm. of Comm. on Offenses, Common Pleas Ct., Pa.).
Schware v. Bd. of Examiners of New Mexico, 353 U. S. 232 (1957).
†*Sheiner v. Florida,* 82 So. 657 (Fla. S. Ct. 1955).
*Shibley v. U. S., 236 F. 2d 238, cert. den. 352 U. S. 873.
In re Steinberg, pending (Sub-Comm. of Comm. on Offenses, Common Pleas Ct., Pa.).

CONGRESSIONAL COMMITTEE CASES, GRAND JURY CASES (AND STATE INVESTIGATING COMMITTEES)

Alexander v. U. S., 181 F. 2d 480 (9th Cir.).
*Barenblatt v. U. S., 240 F. 2d 875, 354 U. S. 930 (1957), remanded to CA DC.
†*Barsky v. U. S., 167 F. 2d 241 (DC Cir. 1948), cert. den. 334 U. S. 843 (1948).

"A Testimonial to the Struggle for Civil Liberties," by *The New York Guild Lawyer* (Oct. 1957).

A Testimonial to the Struggle for Civil Liberties / 153

*Bart v. U. S., 349 U. S. 219 (1955), reversing 203 F. 2d 45 (1954).
*Blau v. U. S., 340 U. S. 159, 332 (1951).
Bowers v. U. S., 202 F. 2d 447 (DC Cir. 1953).
*Christoffel v. U. S., 338 U. S. 84 (1949).
Deutch v. U. S., 98 U. S. App. D. C. 356, 235 F. 2d 853 (1956).
†*Eisler v. U. S., 170 F. 2d 273 (DC Cir. 1948), cert. dismissed 338 U. S. 883 (1949).
*Emspak v. U. S., 349 U. S. 190 (1955).
*Fayerhaugh v. U. S., 232 F. 2d 803 (9th Cir. 1956).
*Flaxer v. U. S., 235 F. 2d 821, 354 U. S. 929 (1957), remanded to CA DC.
*Grossman v. U. S., 229 F. 2d 775 (DC Cir. 1956).
*Healey v. U. S., 186 F. 2d 164 (9th Cir.).
*Jones v. Commonwealth, 327 Mass. 491, 99 NE 2d 456.
Kamp v. U. S., 176 F. 2d 618 (DC Cir. 1948), cert. den. 339 U. S. 957 (1950).
*Kasinowitz v. U. S., 181 F. 2d 632 (9th Cir.).
†*Lawson v. U. S., Trumbo v. U. S., 176 F. 2d 49 (DC Cir. 1949), cert. den. 339 U. S. 934 (1950).
*Marshall v. U. S., 176 F. 2d 473 (DC Cir. 1949), cert. den. 339 U. S. 933 (1950).
*McKenzie v. U. S., unrep. (9th Cir. 1957), pending in U. S. S. C.
*Morford v. U. S., 176 F. 2d 54 (DC Cir. 1949).
*Morgan v. Ohio, 164 Ohio St. 529, 354 U. S. 929 (1957), (remanded to Ohio S. Ct.).
*Quinn v. U. S., 349 U. S. 155 (1955).
*Rogers v. U. S., 340 U. S. 367 (1951).
*Sacher v. U. S., 139 F. Supp. 853, 240 F. 2d 46, 354 U. S. 930 (1957), (remanded to CA DC).
*State ex rel. Benemovsky v. Sullivan, 37 So. 2d 907.
*State ex rel. Feldman, et al. v. Kelly (Florida), 76 So. 2d 798.
*Sweezy v. New Hampshire, 354 U. S. 234 (1957).
*U. S. v. Abe, 85 F. Supp. 991.
*U. S. v. Arguimbau, unrep. (DCDC 1956).
*U. S. v. Brown, pending in U. S. S. C.
*U. S. v. Bryan, 339 U. S. 323 (1950).
*U. S. v. Dennis, 339 U. S. 162 (contempt case).
*U. S. v. Dunham (DCDC).
*U. S. v. Fitzpatrick, 96 F. Supp. 491 (DCDC 1951).
*U. S. v. Fleischman, 339 U. S. 349 (1950).
U. S. v. Furry, unrep. (DC Mass. 1956).
*U. S. v. Gojack, unrep., pending in CA DC.
U. S. v. Hoag, 142 F. Supp. 667 (DCDC 1956).
*U. S. v. Jackins, unrep. (9th Cir. 1957), pending in U. S. S. C.
U. S. v. Jaffe, 98 F. Supp. 191 (DCDC 1951).
†*U. S. v. Josephson, 165 F. 2d 82 (2d Cir. 1947), cert. den. 333 U. S. 838 (1948).
U. S. v. Kamin, 136 F. Supp. 791 (DC Mass. 1956).
*U. S. v. Keeney, 111 F. Supp. 233, reversed 218 F. 2d 843 (DC Cir. 1954).

U. S. v. Knowles, 147 F. Supp. 19, 148 F. Supp. 832 (DCDC 1957).
U. S. v. Lamont, 18 F. R. D. 27, reversed 236 F. 2d 312 (2d Cir. 1956).
U. S. v. Miller, unrep. (DCDC).
*U. S. v. Nathan, unrep. (DCDC 1957).
**U. S. v. Nelson,* 103 F. Supp. 215 (DCDC 1952).
**U. S. v. O'Connor,* 135 F. Supp. 590, reversed 240 F. 2d 404 (DC Cir. 1956).
U. S. v. Peck, unrep. (DCDC 1957).
**U. S. v. Raley,* 96 F. Supp. 495 (DCDC 1951).
U. S. v. Rumely, 345 U. S. 41 (1953).
*U. S. v. Seeger, unrep. (DC NY).
**U. S. v. Shadowitz,* 236 F. 2d 312 (2d Cir. 1956).
U. S. v. Shelton, 148 F. Supp. 926 (DCDC 1957).
*U. S. v. Starkovich, 231 F. 2d 411 (9th Cir. 1956), pending in U. S. S. C.
*U. S. v. Sullivan, unrep. (SD NY).
*U. S. v. Ullman, 350 U. S. 422.
**U. S. v. Unger,* 236 F. 2d 312 (2d Cir. 1956).
*U. S. v. Watson, unrep. (DCDC 1957).
*U. S. v. Yarus aka Tyne, unrep. (SD NY).
Watkins v. U. S., 354 U. S. 178 (1957).
*Wollam v. U. S., unrep. (9th Cir. 1957), pending in U. S. S. C.

ATTACKS ON ORGANIZATIONS

*Adler v. Bd. of Education, 342 U. S. 485 (1952), affirming 301 N. Y. 476, affirming 276 App. Div. 527.
**Albertson v. Millard,* 345 Mich. 519, 77 NW 2d 104 (1956).
†*American Communications Assn. v. Douds, 339 U. S. 382 (1950).
**Association of Lithuanian Workers v. Brownell,* unrep., listing withdrawn by Attorney General.
*Brownell v. American Committee for Protection of Foreign Born, SACB.
*Brownell v. American Peace Crusade, SACB #117-56.
*Brownell v. American Slav Congress, SACB #112-53.
*Brownell v. California Emergency Defense Committee, SACB.
*Brownell v. California Labor School, SACB.
*Brownell v. Civil Rights Congress, SACB #106-53.
Brownell v. Independent Socialist League (Dept. of Justice).
*Brownell v. Intl. Union of Mine, Mill & Smelter Workers, SACB.
*Brownell v. Joint Anti-Fascist Refugee Committee, SACB.
*Brownell v. Labor Youth League, SACB #102-53.
*Brownell v. National Council of American-Soviet Friendship, SACB.
*Brownell v. United Electrical Workers, SACB #119-56.
Brownell v. Washington Pension Union, SACB #114-55.
Bryan v. Austin, 354 U. S. 933 (1957).
*Bryson v. U. S., cert. denied, unrep. U. S. S. C. (1957).
**Chicago Housing Authority v. Blackman,* 4 Ill. 2d 319, 123 NE 2d 522.
**Commonwealth v. Hood,* 134 N. E. 2d 12 (Mass. 1955).
†**Communist Party v. Subversive Activities Control Board,* 351 U. S. 115, reversing 223 F. 2d 531 (1956); now pending CA for D. C.

*Dressler v. Wilson, pending (DCDC).
**Farmer v. United Electrical Workers*, 110 F. Supp. 220, 211 F. 2d 36 (DC Cir. 1953), cert. den. 347 U. S. 943 (1954).
*Friedman v. Schwellenbach, 159 F. 2d 22 (CA DC 1946, cert. den. 330 U. S. 838 1947).
*Gerende v. Bd. of Supervisors of Elections of Baltimore, 341 U. S. 56 (1951), affirming 78 A. 2d 660.
**Housing Authority of Los Angeles v. Cordova*, 130 Cal. App. 2d 883.
**Imbrie v. Marsh*, 3 N. J. 578, 71 A. 2d 352 (1950).
*Joint Anti-Fascist Refugee Committee v. McGrath, 341 U. S. 123 (1951), 215 F. 870 (DC Cir. 1954).
Kreznar v. Wilson, pending (DCDC).
Kutcher v. Gray, 199 F. 2d 783.
**Lawson v. Housing Authority of City of Milwaukee*, 70 N. W. 2d 605 (Wis. 1955), cert. den. 350 U. S. 882.
**Leedom v. Intl. Union of Mine, Mill & Smelter Workers*, 352 U. S. 145 (1956).
**Lithuanian Literary Assn. v. Brownell*, pending in U. S. S. C.
*Methodist Federation for Social Action v. Eastland, 141 F. Supp. 729 (DCDC 1956).
**Nash-Kelvinator Corp. v. Webb & Industrial Comm. of Wisconsin*, 266 Wis. 81 (1954).
Natl. Assn. for Advancement of Colored People v. Alabama ex rel. Patterson, pending in U. S. S. C.
*National Council of American-Soviet Friendship v. Brownell, 148 F. Supp. 94 (DCDC 1955).
*National Council of the Arts, Sciences and Professions, Inc. v. Brownell (DCDC).
*National Lawyers Guild v. Brownell, 225 F. 2d 552, cert. den. 351 U. S. 927 (1955), pending before Attorney General.
N. L. R. B. v. Highland Park Mfg. Co., 341 U. S. 322 (1951).
*N. L. R. B. v. Lannom Mfg. Co., 352 U. S. 153 (1955), reversing 226 F. 2d 194.
**Peters v. NYC Housing Authority*, 307 NY 519 (1954).
**Rudder v. U. S.*, 226 F. 2d 51 (DC Cir. 1955).
*Scott v. RKO Radio Pictures, 240 F. 2d 87 (9th Cir. 1957).
*Shub v. Simpson, 76 A. 2d 332 (Md. 1950), 340 U. S. 881 (1950).
Thorp v. Bd. of Trustees, 6 N. J. 498, 79 A. 2d 462 (1951).
**Travis v. U. S.*, unrep. (10th Cir.).
*Twentieth Century Fox Film Corp. v. Lardner, 216 F. 2d 844 (9th Cir. 1954).
*United Electrical Workers v. Brownell, 232 F. 2d 687 (DC Cir. 1955).
*United Electrical Workers v. General Electric Co., 127 F. Supp. 934 (DCDC 1954).
*United Electrical Workers v. Lilienthal, 84 F. Supp. 640 (DCDC 1949).
**United States v. Killian*, unrep., 7th Cir. (1957).
*United States v. Pezzati, et al., pending, DC Colo.
United States v. Remington, 342 U. S. 895, 343 U. S. 907.
**Weixel v. NYC Housing Authority*, 143 NYS 2d 589 (1955).

Wieman v. Updegraff, 344 U. S. 183 (1953).
*Wilkinson v. Bd. of Education, 125 Cal. App. 2d 100.
*Re Worthington Corp., 24 L. A. 1 (1955).

CASES UNDER THE SMITH ACT AND SIMILAR STATE ACTS

*Blumberg v. U. S., 136 F. Supp. 269, pending in 3rd Cir.
*Cole v. Arkansas, 333 U. S. 196.
*Commonwealth v. Hood (Massachusetts) 134 NE 2d 12.
†*Dennis, et al. v. U. S., 341 U. S. 494 (1951).
*Flynn, et al. v. U. S., 130 F. Supp. 412, 216 F. 2d 354, cert. den. 348 U. S. 909 (1955).
*Frankfeld, et al. v. U. S., 103 F. Supp. 48, 198 F. 2d 679, cert. den. 344 U. S. 922 (1953).
*Fujimoto, et al. v. U. S., 102 F. Supp. 890, pending in 9th Cir.
*Huff, et al. v. U. S., unrep., pending in 9th Cir.
Kentucky v. Braden, 291 SW 2d 843.
*Lightfoot v. U. S., 228 F. 2d 861, 350 U. S. 992.
*Massachusetts v. Hood, — Mass. —.
Massachusetts v. Struik, — Mass. —.
*Mesarosh, et al. v. U. S., 223 F. 2d 449, reversed on other grounds, 352 U. S. 1 (1956).
*Pennsylvania v. Nelson, 350 U. S. 497 (1954).
*Scales v. U. S., 227 F. 2d 581, 350 U. S. 992.
*Sentner, et al. v. U. S., unrep., pending in 8th Cir.
*U. S. v. Bary, et al., unrep., pending new trial, DC Colo.
U. S. v. Blum, pending trial, SD Ind.
*U. S. v. Brandt, et al., 139 F. Supp. 349, 362, 367, pending in 6th Cir.
*U. S. v. Forest, et al., unrep., pending in 8th Cir.
U. S. v. Hellman, pending trial, DC Mont.
*U. S. v. Jackson, et al., unrep., pending in 2nd Cir.
U. S. v. Kuzma, et al., 141 F. Supp. 91 (DC Pa. 1954), pending in 3d Cir.
U. S. v. Noto, unrep., pending in 2d Cir.
*U. S. v. Russo, pending trial in DC Mass.
*U. S. v. Russo, et al., pending trial in DC Mass.
*U. S. v. Silverman, et al., 129 F. Supp. 496, 132 F. Supp. 820, reversed and acquitted (2d Cir.) Sept. 1957.
*U. S. v. Stone, indictment dismissed, DC Conn. 1956.
U. S. v. Weiss, pending trial in ND Ill.
*Wellman, et al., v. U. S., 227 F. 2d 757, cert. granted and remanded, 354 U. S. 931 (1957).
*Yates. et al. v. U. S., 354 U. S. 298 (1957).

DUE PROCESS OF LAW

*Abramowitz v. Brucker, pending in U. S. S. C.
*Adler v. Board of Education, 276 App. Div. 527, 301 N. Y. 476, 342 U. S. 485 (1952).

*Alesna v. Rice, 74 F. Supp. 865, aff. 172 F. 2d 176, cert. den. 338 U. S. 814.
Bailey v. Richardson, 182 F. 2d 46 (D. C. Cir. 1950) affd. without opin. 341 U. S. 918 (1951).
*Barsky v. Board of Regents, 347 U. S. 442 (1954).
*Bernstein v. Herren, 141 F. Supp. 78, 234 F. 2d 434 (2d Cir. 1956) cert. den. 352 U. S. 840.
†*Black v. Cutter Laboratories, 43 Cal. 2d 789, 351 U. S. 292 (1956).
*Boudin v. Dulles, 235 F. 2d 532 (DC Cir. 1956).
*Briehl v. Dulles, pending in U. S. S. C.
Burns v. Wilson, 346 U. S. 137 (1953).
*Carlson v. Landon, 342 U. S. 524 (1952).
Cole v. Young, 351 U. S. 536 (1956).
Dayton v. Dulles, 237 F. 2d 43 (DC Cir. 1956).
*Dulles v. Nathan, 223 F. 2d 29 (DC Cir. 1955).
*Galvan v. Press, 347 U. S. 522 (1953).
*Garner v. Bd. of Public Workers of Los Angeles, 341 U. S. 716 (1951).
*Gold v. U. S., 77 S. Ct. 378 (1957).
*Harisiades v. Shaughnessy, 342 U. S. 580 (1952).
Harmon v. Stevens, 137 F. Supp. 475 (DCDC 1955), pending in U. S. S. C.
*Heikkinen v. U. S., pending in U. S. S. C.
*I. L. W. U. v. Wirtz, 37 Haw. 404, 170 F. 2d 183, cert. den. 336 U. S. 919, 971.
*I. L. W. U. v. Ackerman, 82 F. Supp. 65, rev. 187 F. 2d 860, cert. den. 338 U. S. 814.
In re Murchison, 340 Mich. 140, 151, 349 U. S. 133 (1955).
*Jay v. Boyd, 351 U. S. 345 (1956).
*Jencks v. United States, 353 U. S. 657 (1957).
*Kent v. Dulles, pending in U. S. S. C.
*Kremen v. U. S., 353 U. S. 346.
*Kwong Hai Chew v. Colding, 344 U. S. 590 (1953).
*Lerner v. Casey, pending in U. S. S. C.
*Loew's, Inc. v. Cole, 185 F. 2d 641 (9th Cir. 1950).
*Marshall v. Brucker, 243 F. 2d 834, pending in U. S. S. C.
*Nishikawa v. U. S., pending in U. S. S. C.
†*Nowak v. U. S., pending in U. S. S. C.
*Orloff v. Willoughby, 345 U. S. 83.
*Palakiko v. Harper, 39 Haw. 141, 167, 209 F. 2d 75, cert. den. 347 U. S. 956.
*Parker v. Lester, 227 F. 2d 708 (9th Cir. 1955).
*Perez v. Brownell, pending in U. S. S. C.
*Peters v. Hobby, 349 U. S. 331 (1955).
*Reinecke v. Loper, 77 F. Supp. 333.
*Robeson v. Dulles, 235 F. 2d 810, cert. den. 77 S. Ct. 131.
*Rochin v. California, 342 U. S. 165 (1952).
†*Rowoldt v. Perfetto, pending in U. S. S. C.
Shachtman v. Dulles, 225 F. 2d 938 (1955).
Shaughnessy v. U. S. ex rel. Mezei, 345 U. S. 206 (1953).
Shepherd v. Florida, 341 U. S. 50 (1951).
Slochower v. Board of Higher Education of New York City, 350 U. S. 551 (1956), mod. on rehearing 351 U. S. 944 (1956).

Stewart v. Dulles, —F. 2d—(DC Cir. 1957).
*Trop v. Dulles, pending in U. S. S. C.
**United States v. Coplon,* 191 F. 2d 749, cert. denied 342 U. S. 926 (1952).
*United States v. Green and Winston, pending in U. S. S. C.
**United States v. Bridges,* 199 F. 2d 811, 201 F. 2d 254, 346 U. S. 209.
*United States v. Phillips, pending in CA 9.
*United States v. Spector, 343 U. S. 169 (1952).
**United States v. Witkovich,* 353 U. S. 194 (1957).
Washington v. McGrath, 182 F. 2d 375 (D. C. Cir. 1950), affd. without opin. 4-4 341 U. S. 923 (1951).
*Wilson, et al. v. Loew's, Inc., pending in U. S. S. C.
Wolf v. Colorado, 338 U. S. 25 (1949).
*Yates v. U. S., pending in U. S. S. C.

THE JUSTICE DEPARTMENT ENDS *BROWNELL V. NLG*

[On September 11, 1958, more than five years after Attorney General Herbert Brownell sought to place the Guild on the subversive list, his successor, William Rogers, dropped the case rather than present an answer to the Guild's lawsuit. Guild President John Coe and Executive Secretary Royal W. France called the decision "another notable victory for freedom of speech and the independence of the Bar." The Justice Department letter was addressed to Osmond Fraenkel, chief counsel in the fight-back defense.]

DEPARTMENT OF JUSTICE

Washington

Certified Mail
Return Receipt Requested

September 11, 1958

Osmond K. Fraenkel, Esquire
Attorney at Law
120 Broadway
New York 5, New York

Re: The National Lawyers Guild

Dear Mr. Frankel [sic]:

The Attorney General proposed to designate the National Lawyers Guild under the provisions of Executive Order No. 10450 on

---

"The Justice Department Ends *Brownell v. NLG*," *New York Guild Lawyer* (Sept. 1958).

August 27, 1953, and soon thereafter served the Guild with a Statement of Grounds and Interrogatories. On November 30, 1953, the Guild initiated in the courts an unsuccessful attack upon the Executive Order and procedures thereunder, which effort delayed the administrative proceedings for nearly three years. On June 14, 1956, the Guild answered the Statement of Grounds, objected to 43 of the 64 Interrogatories and failed to answer any of them. The Guild was afforded a hearing on the propriety of the Interrogatories on April 22, 1957, and the Hearing Officer's recommended decision and the exceptions thereto were filed by October 8, 1957.

The Attorney General has been actively considering the recommendations of the Hearing Officer as well as reappraising the entire case in view of the non-availability, due to death or other causes, of some of the witnesses considered important to establishing the Statement of Grounds. A comprehensive analysis of the entire case having now been completed, it is concluded that the evidence available for a hearing on the merits of this matter fails to meet the strict standards of proof which guide the determination of proceedings of this character.

Accordingly, and without in any manner endorsing the organization, the proposal to designate the National Lawyers Guild is hereby rescinded.

For the Attorney General,

J. Walter Yeagley
Acting Assistant Attorney General
Internal Security Division

A PROMISE AND A PROPHECY
By the Board of Editors, Lawyers Guild Review

[The editors of the *Lawyers Guild Review* took a momentary respite from their work to present this collective assessment of the victory.]

In October 1950, when the hysteria whipped up by McCarthy, McCarran, Rankin, and the other bogus patriots was rising to its crescendo, there appeared in the *Guild Lawyer* a statement of principles under the title "For This We Stand." It set out the things the Guild and its members believed in and what they proposed to do. The years have not diminished its worth and force, and we wish we could spare the space to reproduce it. Wanting that, we shall quote two excerpts, one a promise, the other a prophecy.

"A Promise and a Prophecy," by the Board of Editors, *Lawyers Guild Review* 18:3 (Fall 1958).

We, as Americans, who cherish democratic rights and freedoms, and as lawyers, who are aware of the traditional responsibility resting on the Bar to defend them, pledge ourselves to do everything in our power to avert the danger to constitutional liberties. In that cause we shall stand our ground; in that cause we shall not be intimidated and we shall not falter.

In doing these things we believe that we shall be discharging the noblest obligation of lawyers to society. We know that it will not be easy or popular, and that we shall have to endure the slander and opprobrium that the enemies of liberty will hurl at us. But we are not content to pay mere hypocritical homage to the Bill of Rights. We shall defend it at all cost to ourselves and even to our livelihoods. We know that, if not immediately, the American people will in the future be proud, as we are now, that there is a group of lawyers who would not be intimidated.

The Guild and its members have kept their promise. Despite the Un-American Activities Committee's traduction of it, despite former Attorney General Brownell's assault on it, despite every effort to stifle it, the Guild carried on and demonstrated, as in answer to Mr. Brownell it vowed it would, that it is an independent, liberal Bar association acting in the best tradition of American democracy. Its members, some at terrible cost to their livelihood and personal liberty, have been in the forefront in the defense of our fellow citizens whose constitutional rights were threatened. Through their periodicals, pamphlets, studies, briefs, and work in the courts, including the defense of the Guild itself, the Guild and its members have helped to subdue the extravagances of the earlier years and to create a climate in which, though our civil liberties have not yet been fully restored and the Bar's independence is not yet wholly secure, there is ground for hope that they soon will be.

The promise has been kept. What of the prophecy? One cannot yet say that it has been fulfilled. But evidence is accumulating that fulfillment is on its way. New members are joining. The devotion of its old members—hundreds of brave and fine people from Florida to California, from Louisiana to New York—is more intense than ever. The Guild, which has always been a rallying point, is becoming a symbol of the good fight.

In the fall of 1953 issue of this journal, in the dark after-hours of Mr. Brownell's attack on the Guild, we appealed to the many men and women of good will, in and out of the profession, to join us in the struggle to restore the America of Paine and Jefferson, Holmes and Brandeis, Fighting Bob LaFollette and Franklin Delano Roosevelt. Some battles have been won since then. But the struggle is by no means over; recruits are badly needed. At this moment of victory, not for the Guild so much as for American freedom, we repeat our appeal: Join us; it is a bracing experience to be part of such a struggle.

■ ELEVEN

Moving from Victory to Affirmative Action (1958–1961)

THE GUILD FACED 1959 as a victor in its suit against the Attorney General of the United States and a supporter of the United States Supreme Court. The entire Court was now under attack from the Right for its civil liberties decisions on what was being called "Red Monday," June 17, 1957. The Chief Justice was under intense personal attack, with the John Birch Society and others putting up billboards printed with "IMPEACH EARL WARREN" and picketing his public appearances. From his first days on the Court, Warren had decided cases as Bob Kenny, but few others, had expected. He had worked slowly to achieve a unanimous decision in *Brown v. Board of Education,* and had kept the justices together as desegregation led to integration orders in virtually every aspect of Southern life.

When the ABA and champions of judicial restraint attempted to restrict the Court's appellate jurisdiction, the Guild sponsored mass admissions to the Court and continued to submit *amicus curiae* briefs to bolster the liberal majority. In taking such steps, the Guild also increased its own prestige and visibility at the very time the FBI had targeted it as a COINTELPRO target.

The Guild's history during these years is one of steady but cautious advance. Even though there was never enough money to do everything the organization wanted, significant innovations were initiated. Publication of *The Civil Liberties Docket,* beginning in 1955, was both a scholarly and political milestone. The Guild had survived the Cold War precisely because its members engaged in both legal research and political action.

THE ROLE OF THE UNITED STATES SUPREME COURT
By John M. Coe

[John M. Coe, the Guild's president from 1957–1960, practiced law in Pensacola, Florida. During the height of the McCarthyite attacks on civil rights and

---

"The Role of the United States Supreme Court," by John M. Coe, *Lawyers Guild Review* 18:4 (Winter 1958).

civil liberties, he stepped forward to defend the oppressed. This excerpt from his keynote address at the 1958 convention captures his spirit and integrity.]

Let's see the concrete things that the Supreme Court has done in that period of stress.

Now, if you were a reactionary and wanted to have a made-to-order situation so that you could keep labor of your country divided, so that you could keep your country divided against itself, so that you could set up a group, a bloc of kept senators and members of the House of Representatives who had a semi-eternal tenure and a seniority situation consistent therewith, and if you wanted that kind of setup, you would create the condition of the Negro people that has existed from the time of the Emancipation Proclamation to the time of the decision of the *Brown* case in 1954.

And the Supreme Court, after a delay of 91 years, announced with the voice of the highest tribunal of the United States that liberty, equality, and all of those things that go with them were the right and property of the Negro people, and that they should have them in the future; that we should no longer look upon the Constitution of the United States and the Declaration of Independence as a piece of hypocrisy that applied to us but didn't apply to our brethren of another color; that we should with sincerity apply ourselves to the implementation of both.

And, now that the Supreme Court has done a great service for American liberty, let's for a moment turn aside to count the cost. It is not a light thing to antagonize the secret police of a nation that has dossiers no doubt upon many members of the Senate and House of Representatives, and we of the Guild are surely honored with being numbered among those dossiers.

It is not a light thing to antagonize and prejudice a reactionary group, conscious of itself, that has maintained itself in violation of law for the past 90 odd years; and it is not a light thing to see the witch hunt developed, to see anti-Communists build up a devil image of the Communist that would make Hitler's international Jew look like a saint by comparison, and then for the Supreme Court to come along and proclaim that Communists are people, and that they may not all be conspirators, and they might actually be a political party, and in any event that they have rights.

The Supreme Court doesn't stand by its strength alone; it stands only by its moral strength and the moral support and the politically organized support that the people of the United States can give it.

The opposition to it is powerfully organized, closely knit, and obstinate. The powers supporting it, the people of our country, are vastly greater numerically, but vastly less organized. The Supreme Court, like any other tribunal of moral strength alone, can stand momentarily against the waves of public opinion, but it cannot stand against the tides.

But it is we, the citizens of the United States, like the droplets of water that constitute the ocean, that make the tides. And it is the duty of every organization, the duty of every man, the duty of every woman, to lift his hand and raise his voice and swell the tide that will support the great tribunal, that had the courage and spoke for democratic liberty when everyone else in high official places spoke against it.

I am proud today that the Guild has performed that duty through the difficult period in the past, and the Guild hopes to perform that duty in the somewhat less difficult period of the future, and in conjunction with the liberty-loving, and right-minded, people of the United States of America to bring our political state back to the faith of our fathers where we can love it, revere it, and support it as our fathers did.

Friends, we have revered our government in the past, but I am sorry to say we have not been able to do so with our whole heart in the period that has just elapsed. But the morning I believe is dawning and the opportunity of the future is to go forward in justice, in democracy, and to hold up one's head with pride as an American citizen. But it is only if every American citizen heeds the call of duty and bears the responsibility that goes therewith, that the great people of the United States can maintain their position and adhere to their duty and that this will be and remain the great democratic nation invisioned by our fathers whose principles are written in the Constitution, but which can only be made to live if written too in letters of living light upon the hearts and lives of men.

ATTACK BY UN-AMERICAN COMMITTEE ON GUILD
By The Guild Lawyer

[On February 16, 1959, HUAC released a report entitled "Communist Legal Subversion, The Role of the Communist Lawyer." The Committee charged that an "elite corps" of Communist lawyers was guilty of abuse of the courts, misbehavior before Congressional committees, circumvention of the law, and even espionage. *The Guild Lawyer* offered this response.]

It is hardly surprising that the Committee which has unremittingly waged war on the Bill of Rights should have seized an opportunity to attack the court by maligning the lawyers who appeared before it in important civil liberties cases. With unconscious candor the report complains that "In the past decade alone, identified Communist lawyers

---

"Attack by Un-American Committee on Guild," by *The Guild Lawyer* (March 1959).

appeared in person before the United States Supreme Court or were on the principal brief in at least thirty-two important cases adjudicated by the Court on some vital issue affecting the operations of the Communist Party, itself." Obviously the Committee's concern is not with the fact that the lawyers have appeared before the Court, but rather with the fact that they have succeeded in vindicating the constitutional liberties of all Americans.

The report disavows any purpose to attack or undermine the right of legal representation for Communists or other unpopular groups. Yet this pious protest is belied by the body of the report which almost in every instance places enormous emphasis upon the clients of the accused lawyers. The report comes at a time when American lawyers, sometimes unfortunately reluctant in the past to defend the rights of the unpopular and despised, have come to a greater realization of the obligation imposed upon them by their calling. The report warns such lawyers who now feel freer than ever before to defend unpopular clients that the judgment of "subversion" might reward their efforts.

Because the Guild is such an important touchstone of subversion in the committee's report, it is useful to note that one of the committee's less skillful uses of the technique of suppression occurs in connection with the Guild. In order to establish what a fearful organization the Guild really is, the report lists the following as evidence of its "subversion"— the fact that it has campaigned for:

1. Abolition of congressional committees assigned to the task of coping with subversion in the United States;
2. Curbing of the investigative powers of the Federal Bureau of Investigation;
3. Emasculation of the recent statute which grants immunity to any witness called before a committee or a federal grand jury if the witness furnishes information regarding subversive activities;
4. Repeal of the Smith Act prohibiting teaching or advocacy of forceful overthrow of the United States Government;
5. Discontinuance of the Attorney General's listings of subversive organizations;
6. Repeal of the Internal Security Act and the Walter-McCarran Immigration Act;
7. Unrestricted issuance of passports to subversive individuals;
8. Repeal of the federal employees loyalty-security program;
9. Limitations on the right of the Defense Department to discharge subversives from the Armed Forces.

We hardly need belabor the absurdity of the committee's proof of the Guild's "subversion."

Finally, only the naive will fail to recognize that the report is the committee's latest contribution to a campaign to discredit and undermine the Supreme Court. The decisions of the Court are intolerable to the committee, and the Court's libertarian views are offensive to it. What better way to strike at the Court than to suggest that the Court has either sanctioned or been victimized by "Communist legal subversion?" Nor can any thoughtful American ignore the even wider implications of the report that Americans who attack as tyrannical and repressive a committee of Congress, can suffer the lash of official condemnation and attack.

REPORT OF THE NATIONAL LAWYERS GUILD ON THE RECOMMENDATIONS OF THE AMERICAN BAR ASSOCIATION
By the National Executive Board

[On February 24, 1959, the ABA, acting on the recommendation of its Special Committee on Communist Tactics, Strategy, and Objectives, adopted a series of proposals purporting to deal with internal security. Underlying these recommendations was the belief that Communists represent a threat to national security and that recent Supreme Court decisions further weakened the nation.]

The Recommendations come at a time when the Supreme Court has been the subject of sharp attack by the most reactionary opponents of civil rights and civil liberties. The ABA, while paying lip service to the independent role of the judiciary as the "ultimate guardians of the Bill of Rights and the protectors of our freedom" and the "duty of the members of the Bar to defend the institutions of the judiciary from unfair and unjust attacks," allied itself with these critics of the Court by the Recommendations which it adopted.

The right to criticize decisions of the Supreme Court is as fundamental a right of American democracy as is the right to criticize policies of the executive and legislative bodies. However, the recent attack on the Supreme Court in which the ABA has now joined transcends the bounds of mere criticism. It constitutes a grave threat to the civil rights and liberties of the people. It is marked by an alliance between opponents of civil liberties and of the segregationist critics of the Court who are now engaged in a vigorous campaign to set back much needed progress in realizing the civil rights and liberties guaranteed under our Constitution. One has but to examine the roster of sponsors of legislation now pending in Congress designed to halt this progress to note the alliance.

It is at such a time, when such strong forces seek a reversion to McCarthyism, that a special responsibility is placed upon the lawyers of

---

"Report of the National Lawyers Guild on the Recommendations of the American Bar Association," by the National Executive Board, *Lawyers Guild Review* 19:1 (Spring 1959).

this country, not to guard the Court against criticism, but to use their particular abilities, their power of objective evaluation, their knowledge of the law, to make sure that the people of this country are not misled by rabble-rousers, are not inundated by hysteria, but are put in possession of the facts which will enable them to form the kind of calm judgment which must be expected from citizens of a healthy democracy.

We believe that the fatal defect of the ABA's Recommendation is in its use of the term "internal security" without once defining and discussing what it means. Plainly, the ABA would have it that internal security is inconsistent with constitutional liberty and civil rights and would abandon the latter.

What is internal security? It is, at least, the concern of the people of the United States to be secure in the possession of their rights and opportunities, economic, political, social, and cultural, as free citizens. These they have the right to expect their government to protect, not to encroach upon; to defend them in their exercise, not to attack them therefor. Internal security is endangered, to the lasting damage of the country, when government encroaches upon the area of the people's domain of political opinion and association, and the ABA multiplies that danger when it permits, and even encourages, that invasion.

The past ten years and more have proven the validity of these general principles, which are only a reiteration of the ideas of American democracy. The danger to "Internal Security" has been equated with "Communism," when that equation has not been proven. To deprive Americans of their rights and liberties on the basis of an unproved assumption is too costly a sacrifice, and the sacrifice has indeed been a heavy one. In order to stifle the ideas of Communism and to prevent the American people from hearing and evaluating them in the market place of ideas, the Constitution is abridged, reckless laws are enacted, insecurity is spread in public and private employment, witch hunts are indulged in, harmless persons are imprisoned, and the American reputation is disgraced throughout the world.

THE GUILD AND THE COURT:
MASS ADMISSIONS AND AMICUS BRIEFS
By The Guild Lawyer

[Two events in 1960 symbolized the importance of the Supreme Court in Guild activities. The first was Guild sponsorship of the group admission of sixty lawyers to practice before the Court. The second was the Guild's long-standing

---

"The Guild and the Court: Mass Admissions and Amicus Briefs," by *The Guild Lawyer* (May and Oct. 1960).

practice of submitting amicus curiae briefs on issues of vital importance such as First Amendment rights, internal security, and independence of the Bar.]

Dr. Royal W. France, National Secretary of the National Lawyers Guild, moved the admission before the United States Supreme Court of 60 lawyers in a group admission sponsored by the Guild on April 21, 1960.

Chief Justice Earl Warren graciously received each of the applicants as they appeared before the Court in a moving and solemn ceremony held in the spacious courtroom of the highest Court of the land. The group then took the oath as members of the Bar of that Court in the presence of a large audience among whom were many of the applicants' wives and children who were seated in the courtroom pursuant to special arrangements made with the Clerk of the Court.

The Guild has filed a series of amicus curiae briefs in important civil liberties cases now pending before the United States Supreme Court. The four areas touched by these amicus briefs are Internal Security—*Communist Party v. SACB;* Independence of the Bar—*Konigsberg* and *Anastaplo;* the Privilege Against Self-Incrimination—*Albert Cohen v. Hurley;* and First Amendment Rights against Congressional investigations—*Wilkinson v. U.S.*

In *Communist Party v. SACB,* the Guild amicus brief, written by Professor Thomas I. Emerson of Yale Law School, points up the clash between the Internal Security Act and the mandate of the First Amendment forbidding the government from interfering with a political association in its normal and legitimate forms of political activity. The brief also points out that the standards as to what constitutes a "Communist front" under the Internal Securities Act "are so broad that any association or individual dealing with problems with which the Communist Party is also concerned, and not differing sharply from the Communist Party position on that problem, operates under the shadow of the Act and has reason to fear its possible application."

The *Albert Cohen v. Hurley* case concerns an appeal from an order of disbarment of an attorney solely for pleading the privilege against incrimination in a judicially instituted investigation of improper solicitation of clients. The Guild amicus brief, with Abraham Unger, Herman B. Gerringer, and Jonathan Goldberg, all of the New York Bar, of counsel, stresses the necessity that the highest standards of due process be applied to disbarment proceedings and that no law, rule or canon subjects the attorney to disciplinary action for invoking his constitutional privilege against self-incrimination.

Wilkinson v. United States concerns the power of a Congressional Committee to interrogate an individual solely because of his criticism of the committee. Of counsel on this brief were Lorraine Binder, Louis Berry, David B. Finkel, and Charles Stewart, all of the California Bar. The brief contends that to sanction the committee's action would undermine "the free and sovereign control by the people over all agencies of government." The brief points out that at stake "is the transcendent necessity to secure inviolate the freedom of the electoral process and of the processes of petition, communication, and review, whereby under the Constitution the stewardship of the elected legislature as agent and representative of the people is maintained, accounted and determined." The brief takes issue with the affirmance in the Court of Appeals on the basis of the *Barenblatt* decision, noting that the "right of self-preservation" relied upon in *Barenblatt* has no application to "charge or criticism expressed within the lawful review processes." The brief finally argues that the committee's authorizing statute should be read so as to exclude an investigation based upon criticism of the committee. To permit the interrogation would "set at naught the processes of correction and review."

FACING THE HARD REALITIES: CHAPTER PLEDGES AND PAYMENTS
By David Scribner, NLG Executive Secretary

[Moving from victory to affirmative action cost money and time. While the Guild enjoyed its victory in the Brownell case, additional members and more financial support were needed to move the program forward.]

COMMENTS BY THE EXECUTIVE SECRETARY ON PROPOSED 1960 BUDGET

It is my view that a reasonable and realizable budget for 1960 should not exceed $26,500, taking into consideration the fact that our expenditures paid and incurred for 1959 have by far exceeded the budget for 1959, and at the same time our income from pledges in 1959 may fall short even of the $25,500 which was our estimated 1959 budget figure. This will create a substantial deficit for 1959.

I suggest that the Guild budget be based on probable means and experience rather than on expectations of the success of proposed economies, only because I am convinced that a great resurgence of Guild membership, activities, and influence is in the making, and that we need to marshall our efforts and resources to assure its success. We must "strip for action," to use a banal but descriptive term, and release ourselves wherever possible of financial burdens we cannot now afford. We

---

"Facing the Hard Realities: Chapter Pledges and Payments," by David Scribner (Dec. 1959), in Ann Fagan Ginger Papers, MCLI.

CHAPTER PLEDGES AND PAYMENT, 1959
(AS OF DEC. 18, 1959)

Chapter	Pledge	Paid	Due
Chicago	$ 2,000.	$ 1,906.25	$ 93.75
Detroit	3,000.	1,972.50	1,027.50
Los Angeles	3,600.	3,206.00	394.00
New York	11,000.	11,062.90	
Philadelphia	300.	172.00	128.00
San Francisco	2,600.	2,066.00	534.00
At large	4,000.	1,323.00	2,677.00
Total	$26,500.	$21,708.65	$4,854.25

must take a 20-20 look at the cost of our publications—particularly the *Lawyers Guild Review* and *The Civil Liberties Docket*. And if we cannot agree to extraordinary reduction in the cost of, or even elimination of, the publications, we must necessarily turn to the item on salaries and consider whether the salary of the Executive Secretary is warranted in the light of the Guild's financial picture.

On the other hand, we must consider whether the projected budget for "Guild Activities" is adequate. Note that the proposed budget concerning "Guild Activities" provides for no more than 3 amicus briefs, and has no provision at all for any legislative report or statement.

All Chapters as well as all NEB members should seriously study this financial report and be prepared to advance their points of view at the NEB meeting.

COINTELPRO
By Michael Krinsky, Jonathan Moore, and Ann Mari Buitrago

[COINTELPRO is the FBI acronym for a series of covert action programs directed against domestic groups. In these programs, the Bureau went beyond the collection of intelligence to secret action designed to disrupt and neutralize target groups and individuals. The Guild was a prominent target.]

As the Justice Department's reluctance to proceed with the listing hearing against the Guild became apparent in 1958, the FBI developed

---

"COINTELPRO," by Michael Krinsky, Jonathan Moore, and Ann Mari Buitrago, counsel for plaintiff, in Plaintiff's Principal Factual Papers in Opposition to the Motion of the United States for Partial Summary Judgment Dismissing the Damage Claims Arising from the FBI's Conduct and in Support of Plaintiff's Cross-Motion for Partial Summary Judgment, vol. 1, NLG, Plaintiff, against Attorney General, et al., Defendants, Sept. 26, 1984.

the first COINTELPRO action against the Guild, and there followed a steady stream of COINTELPRO and similar covert disruption efforts for the next seventeen years.

The FBI could achieve its COINTELPRO goals by maintaining the stigma under which the Guild labored and by preventing the Guild from regaining the prestige and influence it once had enjoyed. The evidence presented below of the FBI's campaign to disrupt the Guild demonstrates, in the FBI's own words, a willful, covert campaign effort to deny "prestige" and an "aura of respectibility" to the NLG, so as to hinder its growth and diminish its influence.

[In November 1960, the New York Chapter of the Guild planned a seminar on personal injury claims and obtained permission to hold it at the U.S. Courthouse, Foley Square, New York.]

As part of the process of rebuilding after the designation proceeding had terminated, the Guild turned, as it had numerous times in its history, to holding legal seminars. Such seminars were seen by the NLG as a way of attracting new members, as well as providing a service to its current constituency.

Early in November 1960, the New York [FBI] field office received through a confidential mailbox a letter from the New York Chapter announcing the seminar. Waiting until two days before the seminar was scheduled to begin, the New York field office sent two of its agents to the U.S. Courthouse. The results were reported to the Bureau on December 14, 1960.

Through contacts made at the U.S. Court House, Foley Square, Agents of the N.Y.O. were able to prevent this meeting being held at the Court House. Because of this late change of place for the meeting, it is believed that there were less in attendance at the meeting than there would have been and in addition, *the National Lawyers Guild lost their use of the dignity of the U.S. Court House.*

The FBI secretly moved to defeat Guild members seeking elected office, to deny the organization the same use of civic facilities as others. It encouraged the ABA to attack the Guild and fed the ABA information from supposedly confidential FBI files. It similarly fed friendly press contacts with information to attack the organization. It used the technique of anonymous mailings to create dissension in the organization and to drive a wedge between the organization and other groups. It used the same technique to inflame tensions among members of an important Guild law firm. Informants in the organization created or exacerbated tensions.

LEADING LABOR LAWYER URGES FRESH START IN LABOR LEGISLATION
By Harold Cranefield

[In 1960, a former NLRB official and general counsel to the UAW-CIO looked back on three decades of labor legislation, and told a Guild conference that a new frontier was needed.]

The Taft-Hartley amendments of 1947 proceeded from totally false premises: (1) That unions had grown so huge and powerful under the Wagner Act that the balance of bargaining power was now so weighted in their favor as to require a new redress, and (2) that unions exercised tyrannical and insufferable power over their members and especially over non-members employed in organized shops.

In 1959 came Landrum-Griffin. (1) The first six titles constitute a scheme of far-reaching regulation of the internal affairs of unions, impose a duty of elaborate reporting, and purport to establish a vaguely-defined fiduciary standard of conduct of unions officers. . . . The reporting requirements are oppressive, particularly in smaller unions; the penalties are ferocious and out of all proportion. (2) Title VII contains important and substantial restrictions on the freedom of action in organizing the unorganized and in prosecuting their legitimate claims against employers when organized. . . .

I discern no single point from which we could take off with legislative correction, nor a single area in which progress appears more important than in any other. Nothing short of total repeal of Taft-Hartley and Landrum-Griffin in their entirety will suffice for a beginning. With the decks thus cleared we might be able to construct a new and rational statute for the protection of the right of workers to organize and to compel honest bargaining by their employers. To the extent that workers actually need some governmental protection from racketeers and thieves who have infiltrated a few small corners of the labor movement, a wholly new approach is also required. We should oppose any reenactment of those parts of Taft-Hartley enacted for the protection of employers and industry from the activities of unions.

On no single aspect of labor relations has the American public been so successfully brainwashed as with the idea that there is something inherently anti-social and wrong about the variety of conduct that is described in its generality as "secondary boycott." What all this boils down to is that while railroads and airlines, and doubtless manufacturers

---

"Leading Labor Lawyer Urges Fresh Start in Labor Legislation," by Harold Cranefield, *Guild Lawyer* (Jan. 1961).

in the near future, combine with impunity to insure each other against losses suffered from strikes, workers are forbidden under the penalty of contempt of court to lend one another any assistance whatever in disputes with employers. Such fraternal assistance is enjoined even though it be offered at the risk of the worker's own job.

In concluding, I repeat, we desperately need a wholly fresh start.

CREATIVE LEGAL RESEARCH
By Sam Rosenwein

[Sam Rosenwein presents the kind of advice most law students rarely get in law school. Its appearance in a new Guild publication, *Law in Transition*, was made possible primarily through the efforts of its editor-founder, Laurence R. ("Larry") Sperber, one of the stalwarts of the Los Angeles Guild chapter.]

There is a conception of "legal research" which is as dangerous as it is false. The notion exists that if one knows how to use "Shepard's," or an "ALR," one knows "legal research." There is about as much truth to this as the view that if one knows how to use a hammer, or a chisel, one knows how to build a house.

The point is—to be practical about it—the more you know about *the art* of legal research, *the creative methods* of legal research, the more efficient as well as comprehensive you are going to be. It isn't enough to merely know the available books. You have to learn to think with this material, to analyze a problem, to place your problems in the context of the law generally, and see how your problem perhaps relates to some aspect of the social sciences. What are the substantive problems? What are the procedural problems? What are the trends in this area of the law? Is there a constitutional question involved? How do you raise it? When do you raise it? What are the tax consequences of the estate you are planning for your client, or the contract you are drawing for him? Of course, all legal questions are not of the same importance, and some can be quickly answered. There is "gold" in questions which are tough to answer.

Many lawyers use the gloss of "the practical approach" to cover over their failure to keep up reasonably with developments in the law; a list of two dozen categories of research material elicits an immediate protest from many that they cannot possibly use all that material for a "quick research job." The fact is, that the more material you have, the quicker you can find the answer to your problem. The less you know about legal research material, the longer it will take to answer a legal question, *if you ever answer it.*

"Creative Legal Research," by Sam Rosenwein, *Law in Transition* 21:1 (Spring 1961).

Many lawyers today will avoid a copyright matter or a serious personal injury case because they have developed a serious inferiority complex, believing that legal research is so complicated and esoteric that only the real "intellectuals" can cope with it. It is nonsense to think that legal research is for some small elite. Of course, the native abilities of persons differ, but there are among us very few geniuses. Most lawyers have sufficient talent which, coupled with proper methods of research, can make them equal to any task which client or court can impose on them.

Now a word to newly admitted lawyers. Clients do not give you carefully sorted out problems. One problem may involve negligence, nuisance, and third-party beneficiaries all at the same time. Another may require you to be aware that you are up against a short statute of limitations. You will be required to draw demurrers to indictments, which will require research and analysis, and inventive thinking, [so] continue to be a student of the law and its developments.

To the "idealists," I would add: it is a worthy ambition to want to be a "civil liberties" lawyer or a "labor" lawyer. The opportunities are great; the work extremely satisfying in a personal and social sense. But if you don't want to be a craftsman in the law, if you're not going to develop your knowledge and ability in *every aspect* of the law, please keep away from "the downtrodden." You can't help them; you can do them a great deal of harm.

THE CENTRAL THESIS OF THE FIRST AMENDMENT: ORAL ARGUMENT IN *YELLIN V. U.S.* (1961)
By Victor Rabinowitz

[In April 1962, when Victor Rabinowitz delivered this eloquent argument before the Supreme Court, the First Amendment was far from secure. "Everyone who expresses some opinion," he warned the Justices, "has good reason to fear a subpoena." He won the case on a due process ground.]

The central thesis of the First Amendment is the right of the public to hear what petitioners and many others have to say. The inability of the people of the United States to hear what they have to say is the weakest point in our democracy. Because today there is no free and democratic discussion of the great issues which are confronting the world.

Would you discuss the important issues around the question of peace? Only a year or two ago, about thirty members of the Committee for a

---

"The Central Thesis of the First Amendment: Oral Argument in *Yellin v. U.S.* (1961)," by Victor Rabinowitz (April 1962), 374 U.S. 109 (1963).

Sane Nuclear Policy were subpoenaed to testify before a congressional committee. Would you advocate a change in our policy toward Cuba? Last week this very committee [House Committee on Un-American Activities] issued subpoenas to members of the Fair Play for Cuba Committee in Los Angeles and is at this very moment on its way to the West Coast to conduct an investigation into that subject.

Would you advocate abolition of the House Committee? Who can forget the *Wilkinson* case [365 U.S. 399 (1961)]? Would you advocate a change in our policy toward China? The situation in this regard is so bad that there is no one even left to subpoena. But we can all remember the *Lattimore* prosecutions [215 F. 2d 847 (1954), 127 F. Supp. 405 (1955)], the Amerasia case and the destruction of the Institute for Pacific Relations.

Would you advocate Socialism? We must not forget the Subversive Activities Control Board. Would you teach the theoretical principles of Marxism? Within the past two years there have been two investigations by this committee [House Committee on Un-American Activities], one into a Marxist school in New York and another into an institute which seeks to finance Marxist studies.

Such a situation would have been serious fifty years ago. In the dynamic world of today it poses serious threats to our existence as a democratic nation. There is today a world-wide debate taking place in Viet Nam, in Argentina, in Western Europe, in Africa—a debate which in general terms may be said to be between two great economic systems, the system of free enterprise, capitalism, or a system of planned and controlled Socialism. Unless we too can debate this issue and related questions, we are doomed as a democracy, although we may survive as a military machine.

I cannot say that this Court is responsible for all of this, but certainly it bears its share of responsibility. Beginning with *ACA v. Douds* [339 U.S. 382 (1950)], through *Dennis* [341 U.S. 494 (1951)], *Barenblatt* [360 U.S. 109 (1959)], *Wilkinson, Braden* [365 U.S. 431 (1961)], *Scales* [367 U.S. 203 (1961)], *SACB* [367 U.S. 1 (1961)], and about a dozen other cases, the Court could have thrown its not inconsiderable weight on the side of liberty. It did not do so. Instead, it encouraged and supported the drive to political conformity and gave substance to the black silence of fear.

It will take us a generation or two to recover from this period of repression. I hope it is not too late to begin; certainly it is not too early.

WHO WON THE COLD WAR
By Joseph Forer and the Editors

[In September 1979, at memorial services for David Rein, his law partner of thirty-three years, Washington Guild lawyer Joseph Forer summarized the legal front of the Cold War, and, in the manner of American sports fans, totted up the score for his team.]

In September 1946, David Rein and I left our jobs with the federal government and began a partnership for the private practice of law in Washington. Neither of us had any anticipation or expectation that we would get involved in political cases. Our ambition was to earn our livelihood in the practice of our profession.

The Cold War had already started, and it accelerated, with a governmental attack on the Left in the name of national security. It was the time of Harry Truman. The attack was initiated [not by McCarthy but] by the so-called liberal Democrats, including their folk heroes Harry Truman and Hubert Humphrey. This attack on the Left was unprecedented in American history for its intensity—ferocity is a better word—its variety, its duration, and its traumatic effect on the American mind.

The oppression manifested itself in thousands, many thousands, of actions, seeking to impose sanctions and punishment against individuals and organizations for their beliefs and associations. These included frameup criminal prosecutions, inquisitions before legislative committees, contempt prosecutions, discharges from employment, denials of occupational licenses, deportations, denaturalizations, blacklisting of individuals, blacklisting of organizations, proceedings before the Subversive Activities Control Board, and many others. The victims of these actions desperately needed legal counsel for their defense.

After Dave and I had been in practice a few months, the first one of these legal-political cases came our way. It was a lulu. It was the case of Gerhart Eisler. Thereafter they came by the scores and the hundreds. As it turned out during the period of about twenty years, our firm handled more of these political cases than any other firm in the country. Our firm consisted of two lawyers and a secretary. During this period we had the biggest Supreme Court law practice of any law firm in the country. We had the most petitions for certiorari granted. We argued the most cases before the United States Supreme Court. We had the most cases before the United States Court of Appeals for the District of Columbia Circuit. We represented by far the most witnesses before the several congressional witchhunt committees. We had the most cases before the Subver-

---

"Who Won the Cold War," by Joseph Forer, from a tape of his memorial service speech for David Rein in Washington, D.C., now at MCLI.

sive Activities Control Board. We litigated the most political deportation cases. We were involved in every category of that lugubrious list of sanctions I mentioned a few minutes ago.

With few exceptions, the political victims whom we represented had meager financial resources. Much of our work was free—practically all of it was undercompensated. That created two problems. First, we ourselves were always in a precarious financial position, as Selma can confess, and as my wife can. And, secondly, we had to conduct litigation with a minimum of expense. Let me give an example. About 1954 or 1955, Dave represented the defendant in one of the first two Smith Act membership cases. The case was tried in federal court in Greensboro, North Carolina. Under the court rules—and this is normal—out-of-state counsel had to be accompanied in trying the case by a member of the North Carolina Bar. It turned out that in the whole state of North Carolina, no lawyer could be found to enter the case. The trial judge, a very conservative man, nevertheless directed and permitted Dave to proceed without local counsel. So Dave tried the case for more than three weeks by himself. He not only did not have local counsel, he had no co-counsel. He had no research assistant, he didn't have Fred Soloway as a paralegal, or any other legal worker. He had no jury selection expert. He didn't even have a secretary.

Dave gave the government lawyers—there were three of them in the court—the fight of their lives. But his client was convicted, because the judge put to this jury at that time in Greensboro, North Carolina, that the only factual issue which they had to pass on, all others being admitted, was whether the Communist Party of the United States was dedicated to violent overthrow of the United States government. Well, that's what the jury decided. Dave then had the conviction reversed on appeal because of trial error committed by the judge in denying various requests made by Dave during the trial.

Despite all the difficulties, we did in fact win a great majority of our litigated political cases. It must be about 90 percent. This record attests to Dave's exceptional talents as a lawyer, yet Dave was always modest and unassuming. He was also steadfast in his principles, and his vision of helping to promote a more just and humane society.

The fact is, we were comrades in arms. We fought together, not just in a battle, but in a twenty-year war. It was a war in which we fought on the side of justice, and in which we were vastly outnumbered. We achieved a certain degree of success, and we survived with honor.

[The tactics of Cold War anti-Communists and reactionary elements, in both foreign and domestic policy, was to silence all progressive voices for peace, dissent, and social change. Abroad, this meant unilateral efforts to exercise U.S.

influence over Western Europe in direct contravention of the UN Charter; at home, the Taft-Hartley Act bludgeoned a once powerfully militant labor movement into quiescence. There were some bright spots, however. The Supreme Court became the first governmental agency to say "No" to flagrant abuses of the people's rights. The Court did not outlaw the Communist Party of the United States and did not send all its leaders to prison for peaceful advocacy of Socialism. At the same time, of course, the Court did not outlaw the Smith Act, Taft-Hartley, HUAC, or other Congressional instruments of repression. It did simply, case by case, frequently reverse a conviction for violation of such statutes or committee's orders.

[Cold War foreign policy was similarly inconclusive. The Guild continued its principled criticism of Truman and Eisenhower administration policies. It used its influence in the media to urge a more accurate portrayal of insurgent movements in Latin America, Africa, the Middle East, and Southeast Asia. Such efforts inevitably provoked Red-baiting, but the Guild refused to support a foreign policy predicated on "massive retaliation" and "liberation" by the "Free World."

[The goal of the Cold War was also to destroy the movement against racism and for black liberation. This goal was not achieved, and in this arena progress was made through the civil rights movement of the early 1960s, the black power movement of the late 1960s, and the continuing movement for black liberation. The goal of the Cold War was to destroy the labor movement, and its major successes in that arena were described by Harold Cranefield. The goal was to destroy the peace movement and the movement for women's rights, small as they were at the time. These goals were not accomplished either, and both movements have grown, although both were stopped short for a significant period of time as the need for effective movements for women's rights and for peace mushroomed.

[The role of the Guild and its members in stopping the Cold War has been counted, to the extent this can be done, in the selections above. In round numbers, very few Guild members indeed joined Lee Pressman in naming names, or O. John Rogge in suing a labor defendant convicted on political grounds for his fee. Several liberal lawyers succumbed to McCarthyism by their own hands: Abraham Feller, UN general counsel, suicide after appearance before the Senate Internal Security Subcommittee; Walter Marvin Smith, Justice Department attorney, suicide after being mentioned as a notary in a transaction involving Alger Hiss.]

■ TWELVE

Civil Rights Moves the Guild (1961–1963)

IN 1961, FEW Northern Guild lawyers had ever been to Mississippi unless they had served there in the Army; probably none had been to Albany, Georgia, Hopewell, Virginia, or Neshoba County. While two or three had handled courts martial overseas after World War II, few if any had handled cases in the South or ever thought of doing so. They were busy trying to build, or rebuild, their practices and spent Bar association time on national and international issues.

In the coming period, they were to be changed, changed utterly.

Veteran Guild members knew something about the legal system in the South from the very small and stalwart band of delegates to national conventions— John Coe of Florida, Clifford Durr of Alabama (late of Washington, D.C.), Herman Wright and Arthur Mandell of Texas, Professors Mitchell Franklin and Laurent Frantz of several cities, and Ben Smith of New Orleans. They were nonetheless shocked when they heard details, such as a judge calling an adult Negro plaintiff by her first name.

In October, 1952, the Guild had held a national conference in New York on discrimination and the enforcement of civil rights laws. The 1957 convention in New York featured, not only a Young Lawyers Round Table discussion, but an all-day conference on civil rights and liberties and due process of law. Herman Taylor, a leading black lawyer in North Carolina, described the difficulties faced by Southern lawyers when they tried to implement the Supreme Court's historic decision in *Brown v. Board of Education*. Delegates roundly applauded presentation of the Roosevelt Award to Hubert T. Delany, principled black judge of the New York City Domestic Relations Court. At the 1960 Convention in San Francisco, leading black lawyer and scholar Loren Miller discussed the law and discrimination in housing: "There is need for bold experiment in legal theories designed to compel change. This is no task for the fearful or the faint-hearted...."

The task is enormously complicated by the fact that common law concepts of property rights tend to obscure judicial vision."*

In the fall of 1961, the black president of the San Francisco Chapter, Fred Smith, and the black chairman of the New York chapter Committee on School Integration, Charles E. McKinney, announced programs to sue and abolish de facto segregation in their city schools.

These proved to be quantitative steps leading to the qualitative change in the Guild spelled out in this chapter, based on the philosophical/historical analysis of Professor Mitchell Franklin and the reality described by philosopher/lawyer Edward A. Dawley, both of the South. The power structure responded overtly in Virginia and New Orleans, covertly throughout the country. These events led to one of the stormiest meetings in the history of the National Executive Board, held in November 1963, captured in a few excerpts from the minutes. At the same time, students began sitting-in in the North and West, demanding jobs for Negroes, and putting San Francisco Guild lawyers, among others, to work defending them.

INTERPOSITION INTERPOSED
By Mitchell Franklin †

Although the Supreme Court of the United States has declared the unconstitutionality of interposition by state governments [1] against *Brown v. Board of Education*,[2] which since 1954 requires integration of the public schools, still such interposition continues. In southern states there are at present many modes of interposition: [shown in bad faith regarding their responsibilities under the Constitution, the formalism of token integration, persistent and reiterated evasion of constitutional duties, the consciousness of the southern governmental official, which oscillates between hypocrisy and self-deception]. Above all, interpositionism is demonstrated and maintained through the existing reign of terror.

Meanwhile the national government has remained mute. For eight years President Eisenhower virtually ignored the crisis. The Congress, too, has been silent or indifferent to victory in the integration struggle. The present situation, supposedly arising out of the theory of separation

---

*"The Law and Discrimination in Housing," by Loren Miller, *Lawyers Guild Review* 20:4 (Winter 1960).

"Interposition Interposed," by Mitchell Franklin, from Part I, *Law in Transition* 21:1 (Spring 1961), and Part II, 21:2 (Summer 1961).

† W. R. Irby Professor of Law, Tulane University.

[1] Bush v. Orleans Parish School Board, 364 U.S. 500 (1960), citing *Cooper v. Aaron,* 358 U.S. 1 (1958); later judgments affirmed in *Orleans Parish School Board v. Bush,* 81 S. Cr. 754 (1961).

[2] 347 U.S. 483 (1954).

of powers and of federalism, recalls the struggle between Montesquieu and Rousseau concerning the nature of the state, which culminated in Hegel's presentation that "If the powers . . . become self-subsistent . . . the destruction of the state is forthwith a *fait accompli*."[3]

The legal theorists have in great measure also failed in this crisis. However, they have not been mute. Inspired considerably by the leadership of Judge Learned Hand, they have developed a sort of higher criticism of the Court by means of which they indirectly condemn the general technical competence of the justices who unanimously decided *Brown*. Some of them resent that the Court accepted its responsibility in that case without equivocation or formulating at the same time an escape route from its immediate integrationist position, as is required by the method of American legal pragmatism and of legal realism. They are disturbed because the Court in that case avoided the method of what Hegel called *Verstellung*. This is the method of "shifting" by which the Court would proceed "by fixing definitely one moment, passing thence immediately over to another and doing away with the first," to use the critical language of Hegel. "But, as soon as it has now set up this second moment, it also 'shifts' (*verstellt*) this again, and really makes the opposite the essential element."[4]

Other legal critics of the . . . Court wish more or less to repair the "road to reunion" of Northern and Southern white social forces at the expense of the Negro people which *Brown* had closed.

Interpositionist theory reputes the Fourteenth Amendment, under which *Brown* was decided, as not written . . . either by refusing to recognize its actuality or by depriving the amendment of real legal force. The interpositionists then justify themselves by the Tenth Amendment. But this amendment, which is part of the Bill of Rights, that is, of the Second Constitution, does not support the weight imposed on it by the segregationists. . . . The amendment is concerned with the limited powers both of the United States and of the states, and subordinates both of these to the people. This is certainly true after the introduction of the Third Constitution, founded on the Thirteenth, Fourteenth and Fifteenth Amendments. "Assuming always that the claim of interposition is an appeal to legality," it was said in *Bush v. Orleans Parish School Board,* "the inquiry is who, under the Constitution, has the final say on questions of constitutionality, who delimits the Tenth Amendment. . . . That the final decision should rest with the judiciary rather than the legislature was inherent in the concept of constitutional government. . . ."[5]

---

[3] Hegel, *Philosophy of Right* [Law] 175 (Knox tr. 1942).
[4] Hegel, *The Phenomenology of Mind* 629 (Baillie's tr. 1931).
[5] *Bush v. Orleans Parish School Board,* 188 F. Supp. 916, 924 (E.D., La. 1980).

Although the theory of interposition has been expressed as a theory of interposition by the states against the national government, in reality it is a theory of interposition by the states against the people of such states. It imposes a dictatorship of the segregationists, and, as such, it affronts Constitution art. IV, §4, which requires that "The United States shall guarantee to every State in this Union a Republican Form of Government...."

It is the great historic merit of Justices Black and Douglas that they, like Jefferson, perceived the struggle against racist interposition and against the interposition of the First Amendment merged, and became a struggle for the maintenance and survival of democracy. Black said in *Braden:*

> If the House Un-American Activities Committee is to have the power to interrogate everyone who is called a Communist, there is one thing beyond the peradventure of a doubt—no legislative committee, state or federal, will have trouble finding cause to subpoena all persons anywhere who take a public stand for or against segregation.[6]

Madison interposes the interposers. If a republican form of government is denied through antirepublican interposition by a particular state, the national government has not only plenary, constitutional cassational power to negate or to break such interposition, but it has the positive, plenary power and constitutional duty to introduce republican form of government into such particular state. As Madison said, "it will be, of course, bound to pursue the authority" granted in Constitution art. IV, §4....

As the thought of the Enlightenment concerning republican government developed, there emerged the following conceptions: (1) Republican education must be integrated within an integrated republican state. (2) Republican education must be founded on a principle of equality to achieve unity among the new anti-feudal social forces demanding or insisting on education. Thus, Diderot said, in writing about education, "[E]very system of morality, every political appeal which tends to separate man from man is bad."[7] (3) ... [R]epublican education must be mass, state-controlled public education, rejecting any exclusionary principle. (4) Republican education must be secular ... and the power of the Catholic church over feudal education broken, because the limitations of religion [on] development of science, fettered the anti-feudal social forces. [These] forces under the leadership of the enlightened *bourgeoisie*

---

[6] 81 S. Ct. at 591.

[7] Diderot, *Le père de famille, Comèdie en cinq actes et en prose* (1758), in *4 Oeuvres Completes de Diderot* 237, 246 (1821).

concluded that *republican* education must be equal, mass, *public* education, without any irrational exclusionary principle, and organized by and controlled by the republican state. . . .

"In proposing a system of public education, including every grade of instruction, and which should reach every citizen, Jefferson was advocating nothing essentially new," Arrowood writes.[8]

. . . The constitutional requirement of integrated education reflects eighteenth century ideas of equality in education. If the schools are segregated the Enlightenment believed that the child is deprived of the opportunity to "emulate," that is, "to equal or even to surpass,"[9] other school children competitively. If the Negro child is denied the opportunity to emulate or to compete he is, as Chief Justice Warren said, wounded and denied the equal protection of the laws, as guaranteed by the Fourteenth Amendment. To this may be added Constitution art. IV, §4. . . .

BLACK PEOPLE DON'T HAVE LEGAL PROBLEMS
By Edward A. Dawley

You must realize that my point of view is largely conditioned by the fact that I'm a black lawyer, and that makes a lot of difference.

One of the things that most shocked me when I first visited the offices of black lawyers in Virginia was that they had no books. How could they practice law without books? After practicing a while I could see very well why.

Most of their clients were poor people, and to a large extent poor people do not have legal problems. A person has to have some minimum contact with the mainstream to have a legal problem. He has to be buying something. So, in a community where most of the people are not in the mainstream, most of their problems are not legal problems (except, of course, for the criminal cases). The things the lawyer does for these clients—contacting someone, or giving certain general information—don't require lawbooks, don't even require a lawyer. They require an educated man, that's all.

I am from the South originally. So I went back there to get it out of my system, so I could [leave someday with] a clear conscience.

For me to live up to my vision of what a lawyer should be—accord-

---

[8] Arrowood, *Thomas Jefferson and Education in a Republic* 63 (1930).

[9] 12 *Encyclopedie* 303 (nouvelle éd., 1777); 11 La Bruyère, *Les Caracteres* 85 (1688) (Stott's tr., 194-95, 1890).

"Black People Don't Have Legal Problems," by Edward A. Dawley, from Ann Fagan Ginger, ed., *The Relevant Lawyers* (New York: Simon & Schuster, 1972), pp. 219-26.

ing to what law school, the TV, movies, and the radio had taught me—some conditions had to be changed that kept me from practicing law—the conditions that all the judges were white, all the jurors, court officials, police officers were white. In the police court they would call out the race of the party, "John Jones, defendant, white man on bail," "Bill Smith, black man in custody"—all day long, at the same time claiming that justice was blind and race made no difference. If I wanted to interview a white witness, I could not go into the white section of town or into a white hotel to interview him.

The typical Southern courthouse had signs on the restrooms, "Black Men," "White Men," "White Women," "Black Women," so that even when a black lawyer got in the courtroom and did his thing just like everybody else, when he went out into the hall and saw those signs, they rebutted the whole image he was trying to project of himself.

One of the problems black lawyers have had was that black clients went to white lawyers. Why? I think it was because they did not believe a black lawyer could do as much for them as a white lawyer. Now, that was bad—because it was true. Or if it wasn't true it certainly looked like it. Certainly everyone knew that those signs wouldn't be in the courthouse unless the judge condoned it. So the judge was in effect saying, "There's a difference between a black lawyer and a white lawyer."

It created a vicious circle. Because the lawyers lost clients they weren't getting any money or any practice in their profession. And because they stopped practicing law, they in fact became inferior. All this kept the number of blacks in the legal profession small. It's because the black lawyer has not set a model for youth to imitate. The guys who were prosperous and militant were not the black lawyers.

I suspect that if I had planned to stay in the South I wouldn't have done certain things. I decided to file suits against the judges, challenging various forms of discrimination and segregation in the judicial system. I brought my ideas to the black Bar association, hoping that if it would bring the suits, they wouldn't zero in on any one of us. But unfortunately the rest of the guys planned to stay there, so I could not get them to participate.

The American Civil Liberties Union did not operate in the South very much. The NAACP was concerned mostly with suits on education. It was ironic that the NAACP lawyers were trying to correct segregation and discrimination in the school systems, and they would not participate in these suits to clean up the area in which they practiced.

So I had to file these suits myself, and you can imagine the repercussions: an investigation by the state un-American activities committee, a series of contempt citations, and day-to-day harassment. I couldn't even get a continuance so that I wouldn't have cases going on in two places at the same time. I had to give up any idea of making money. Word gets around—if you need a lawyer, don't get Dawley. Actually, what I was doing was not practicing law; I was crusading. This led me to get a case from the Southern Christian Leadership Conference, when it was first active.

SCLC formed a chapter in Hopewell, Virginia, and when people there began to agitate, the local newspaper wrote an editorial accusing them of being Communists and that type of thing. The SCLC chapter distributed leaflets asking the citizens to boycott the newspaper. So the newspaper brought a libel and slander suit against the leadership of the SCLC. (Remember when Sheriff Bull Connor of Birmingham and a series of other Southern officials sued the *New York Times* and Martin Luther King for slander? They got million-dollar judgments from the trial courts.)

I made up my mind that we were not going to lose this suit. But I could see that the law was not going to apply in this case. I had to ask myself: Do I play the role of lawyer or do I go outside the usual rules of the court system to win?

The lawyer representing the newspaper was going to need the testimony of all the people he was suing, to prove that they had been involved with the leaflets. If they said "Yes," his case was set; if they said "No," he was going to get them for perjury. They would have to appeal to get a reversal and would use all their money defending themselves against perjury. He assumed all these people would be in court, since they were being sued for a tremendous sum of money. But when the case came to trial, there was nobody in the courthouse except me—no defendants. And when it came time to prove that the defendants had written the leaflets, the lawyer for the newspaper had no way to prove it.

If the judge had been fair, he would have dismissed the case, because it was up to the newspaper's lawyer to subpoena the defendants, if they were necessary to his case. Instead, the judge gave the lawyer a series of continuances to find these people. The radio was announcing: "Wanted, So and So; anyone knowing his whereabouts. . . ."

I finally suggested that the newspaper might want to settle the case for twenty-five dollars. You see, the lawyer and the newspaper were being made fools of in the community. Well, he said, "If they will submit an apology, I will settle the case for a small sum." I suggested mutual apologies; so we came out with statements from both sides apologizing, and I gave him twenty-five or fifty dollars. (The *New York Times* eventually won the libel suits against it, too, but it took four years, all the way to the United States Supreme Court, which wrote a very important opinion protecting free press and expression.)

After the order was signed dismissing my case, the judge called me in and asked whether I had anything to do with the defendants being unavailable. Instead of answering his question I asked *him* certain questions: Why was he asking me that, and what were the consequences of saying "Yes" and "No," and of not answering? He refused to answer any of those questions, so I refused to answer his question. Then he had the district attorney draw up an "order to show cause" why I should not be held in contempt of court, and he held a hearing on that order.

It was my position that once he had signed the order dismissing the libel suit he had no more right to make me answer a question than anybody else on the street had.

My case came up for a hearing, and my partner, Len Holt, defended me. The first thing we did was move that the judge disqualify himself from hearing the case, since he was prejudiced against us. He denied that motion. Then we moved to have the case heard somewhere else because we couldn't get a fair trial, even with a jury, in Hopewell. The judge at that point held both of us in contempt for filing the motion for change of venue. Then the judge abandoned the original contempt charge against me, and we appealed the new contempt charge against both of us.

Eventually we got up to the United States Supreme Court, where we won. By that time, of course, both Holt and I had left Virginia.

[Despite the fact that his actions in Virginia had got him branded as a no-good, troublemaking, radical lawyer, Dawley drew up this motion in the most conservative, old-fashioned way, following all the rules, using all the proper language. In fact, the Supreme Court opinion does little more than quote the motion verbatim, to show that the pleading was perfectly proper and that the lawyers shouldn't have been held in contempt for it. See *Holt v. Virginia,* 381 U.S. 131 (1965), reversing 136 SE 2d 809 (Va. Sup. Ct. 1964).]

A CRY FOR HELP:
NORFOLK TO BERKELEY TO NEW YORK TO DETROIT
By the Editors

When the first issue of the *Civil Liberties Docket* appeared in 1955, it defined civil liberties as those guarantees to individuals against government interference in the First Amendment; civil rights as equal protection without regard to race, creed, color, or sex; and due process as those procedural rights (jury trial, right to counsel, etc.) guaranteed in all legal

---

"A Cry for Help" is from material in *Civil Liberties Docket* 7:1 (Nov. 1961); *Guild Lawyer* (Nov.-Dec. 1961); NEB Minutes, Nov. 12, 1961, Maurice Sugar Papers, MCLI; "The NLG, the FBI and the Civil Rights Movement: 1964—A Year of Decision," by Ernest Goodman, from *NLG Practitioner* 38:1 (Winter 1981); and *Guild Lawyer* (March-April 1962).

proceedings. Guild leaders suggested to the editor that the *Docket* be limited to reporting civil liberties cases, many or most of which were handled by Guild members, since it would be difficult to obtain information from non-Guild attorneys handling most of the civil rights and due process cases in the depth of the McCarthy period.

Ann Ginger convinced the Guild that she could solve the problem by sending frequent queries to lawyers handling cases for the NAACP, NAACP Legal Defense and Educational Fund, CORE, and other civil rights organizations. As the *Docket* developed a sizeable list of subscribers, this proved to be true, and, in the fall of 1961, led to one of the first steps in changing the direction and style of Guild work.

Jordan, Dawley, and Holt in Norfolk had a number of cases reported in the *Docket*, including arrests in 1960 of Negro juveniles and ministers sitting in at stores in Petersburg and Hopewell protesting segregation, plus a class action suit to enjoin the Petersburg judge from continuing racial segregation in the courthouse.

Responding to a form letter from the *Docket* editor in Berkeley, Len Holt had written simply: "HELP!" He then described briefly how five officials representing the Virginia Committee on Offenses against the Administration of Justice had entered their law offices in September 1961, demanding all records in four integration cases, and serving them with subpoenas.

Ginger called the new executive secretary of the Guild in New York, Aryay Lenske, recently of the University of California–Berkeley, and urged him to contact Holt to offer whatever assistance was possible. In short order, the Guild filed an *amicus* brief in the federal district court in Norfolk in support of the firm's suit to enjoin the committee, which was part of the massive state resistance to *Brown,* investigating "champerty, barratry, running, and capping"—that is, allegations that civil rights lawyers were ambulance chasing to get Negroes to sign up to sue the power structure for desegregation.

The Detroit Guild Chapter at this time was sponsoring seminars for young lawyers on real-estate closings, criminal law, negligence law, bankruptcy, and probate. The Chicago Chapter was presenting Joseph Forer, of the Washington, D.C., Chapter, discussing the recent Supreme Court decision in his case upholding the Subversive Activities Control Board order requiring the Communist Party to register.

The next Guild National Executive Board meeting was scheduled in New York, and Lenske invited Holt to attend. The day before, the International Law Committee sponsored a conference on the current Berlin dispute, world peace through law, and the representation of China in the UN.

Benjamin Dreyfus, Guild president, convened the NEB on November 12. Visitor Holt met twenty-nine Guild members, all white, including one woman and one other Southerner, Ben Smith, member-at-large from New Orleans. The Chicago, Detroit, San Francisco, Los Angeles, Philadelphia, and New York chapters were also represented, as well as three members-at-large.

After the report of the Auto Accident Compensation Committee, the Independence of the Bar Committee asked Holt to report. He noted that "considerable economic hardship had resulted from the attack by the committee," and thanked the Guild for its timely assistance. In response: "M/S/C—That the Guild continue to provide all necessary legal assistance, and that money be available to pursue this case." Later,

The National Treasurer, Julius Cohen, reported that the chapter pledge payments have been badly lagging. . . . This has put the national office in a precarious financial position. He noted that expenses of the national office had been minimal for this year, but that this was in part due to the fact that there was no executive secretary from January through April.

At the convention in Detroit in February, 1962, six Southern lawyers were honored for their legal fights against segregation: Len Holt and E. A. Dawley of Norfolk, Alexander P. Tureau and Benjamin E. Smith, of New Orleans, Ernest D. Jackson, Sr., of Jacksonville, and John M. Coe, of Pensacola. Ernest Goodman later described the convention from his perspective:

The Detroit Chapter was not as completely knocked out during the McCarthy period as the other chapters; the members did not feel that rebuilding the Guild was as hopeless a task as was felt elsewhere.

This mood was indicated at the 25th Convention of the Guild held in Detroit in 1962. Some of the active participants were the Governor of the state, John Swainson; two judges, particularly Judge Jimmy Montante, who had been president of the Detroit Chapter of the Guild; Michigan Supreme Court Judge Adams; and Harold Cranefield, then General Counsel of the UAW. If the convention had been held in any other state, I doubt whether it would have been possible to have had such broad attendance indicating ties with the labor movement, liberal lawyers, and black lawyers.

Len Holt gave the shot in the arm which really changed the whole complexion of the convention, and, as it turned out, of the Guild itself. He dramatized some of the fighting qualities and activities of the lawyers in the South, and the need for more lawyers to go there to participate in the movement directly.

Nobody who attended that convention will ever forget the drama of the banquet when Holt got up and reiterated his impassioned appeal for help. At the end of his talk, he asked everybody to stand up and join with him to sing "We Shall Overcome."

Most of the guests had never heard this song before. But when Len Holt led that song, everybody soon joined in. Most of us left convinced that "This is *our* struggle."

This led to the drafting of a resolution at the convention to organize a Committee to Assist Southern Lawyers.

The convention also passed resolutions supporting the Mine, Mill, & Smelter Workers union against the Subversive Activities Control Board, calling for abolition of the House Committee on Un-American Activities, for enforcement of existing law against illegal police arrests and detention, for integration in the North, for national health insurance and medical care for the aged, and "firmly" supporting Guild member Martin Popper, who was fighting a contempt citation by HUAC for his use of his passport.

The convention elected twenty-one young lawyers, three women, and eight blacks to join its seventy-one-member Executive Board, three national officers, and fourteen vice-presidents. Of the seventy-seven national Guild leaders, eight were now women and ten were black.

REPORT ON INITIAL ACTIVITIES
By Committee To Assist Southern Lawyers (CASL)

■

REPORT ON HOPEWELL, VIRGINIA CASES
By Ernest Goodman

On March 28, 1962, at Petersburg, a public meeting was held at the First Baptist Church under the auspices of the Southern Christian Leadership Conference. The meeting overflowed the seating capacity into the basement hall. Dr. Martin Luther King was the principal speaker.

Len Holt introduced Richard Scupi, Hal Witt, and myself, the only white persons on the platform. The response from the audience to the announcement of the Guild's action in creating the Special Committee and in bringing us to Hopewell was tremendous. I spoke on behalf of the Guild:

> Any lawyer will know, what everybody knows—white or Negro, Northerner or Southerner—that many states and thousands of counties, cities, and villages are consistently and openly engaged in preventing legal equality. Some even proudly assert that their aim is to deny equality to the Negro people by every means at their command.

"Report on Initial Activities," by CASL, includes reports by Ernest Goodman and Irving Rosenfeld, Ernest Goodman Papers, MCLI.

Now consider this: If the situation were reversed—if the law of our land denied equality and compelled segregation, and the Negro people then sought to obtain the equality denied them under the law, these same officials could, and would, lawfully indict all the Negro leaders as members of a gigantic criminal conspiracy, and legally send them to jail. This is exactly what is now happening in South Africa, which I visited last year. There apartheid—or segregation—is the law of the land. And there the apartheid government acts cruelly and remorselessly to suppress, prosecute, and imprison Africans who even advocate equality. There this suppression occurs under the existing law.

But here in the South, suppression occurs contrary to the law. And I ask: How can we justify the existence, within our country, of a common agreement, by those who possess all political power, under which the right of equality is denied to millions who are entitled to equality under our own Constitution? Is this not, also, a criminal conspiracy?

∎

REPORT ON CASL PARTICIPATION AT TWO
CONFERENCES IN THE SOUTH
By Irving Rosenfeld of Los Angeles

I arrived in Birmingham on April 13, 1962. I met Bruce Waltzer, associate of Ben Smith, at New Orleans. When we arrived in Birmingham we went to the St. Paul Methodist Church for a meeting. We were greeted at the steps of the church by photographers from the Birmingham Police Department and by many parked police cars, each containing a large fierce-looking police dog. I felt like 150 pounds of Dr. Ross dog food at that point. The church was surrounded by many police officers and motorcycle policemen as well as the photographers.

I had never attended a service in a Negro church before and was struck with the beauty and with the great faith exhibited. During the last prayer, a woman with a magnificent voice began singing, "Oh Captain, Help Us Weather the Storm," and the combination of the prayer that God watch over us as we walked through the streets and her voice singing moved me more than I thought was possible. Before leaving the church I had the great pleasure of meeting the Rev. Mr. Fred L. Shuttlesworth. He smiled and said the more lawyers he had around him, the happier and safer he felt.

Bruce introduced me to several of the students from the Student Non-Violent Coordinating Committee charged with criminal anarchy in Baton Rouge, and one acting as SNCC representative to Catholic students.

[Later] we had a very fruitful discussion led by Vic Rabinowitz on *Hague v. CIO* and the deprivation of First Amendment constitutional liberties. Vic discussed ordinances which purport to disallow any picketing, assembly, and outlaw virtually all activities of integration organizations. Vic pointed out that the labor movement had successfully passed through similar problems in the 1930s, and the audience was happy to find that they had some precedent in their favor.

THE FBI INTRUDES ON GUILD-ABA RELATIONS
From the FBI

On March 9, 1960, the Director of the FBI and other high officials of the Bureau met with the ABA President-Elect to discuss ways to attack the Guild [HQ 100-7321-NR, 3/29/60]. John Satterfield indicated he would attempt to reinstitute an ABA policy of making membership in the Guild an automatic bar to joining the ABA and that he wanted to expel from the ABA any attorney who continued to be associated with the NLG. For those purposes, he asked the FBI for "any background information about the NLG concerning its history and current activity." The FBI, through J. Edgar Hoover, indicated that he would be glad "to assist him in these matters wherever possible"; as the FBI emphasized, "much could be accomplished in furnishing Satterfield with pertinent information in our files." [Id.]

Hoover approved the preparation and dissemination to the ABA of a "blind memorandum," 25 pages in length, on the history of the NLG and its current activities. This blind memorandum, along with a photostat of the 1958 NLG Convention program and two HUAC reports mentioning the Guild, were personally delivered by a high-ranking FBI official to Satterfield [HQ 100-7321-2102].

The May 1962 issue of the *American Bar Association Journal* contained a letter to the editor by prominent Guild member Royal France, which was critical of a previous article in the *Journal* by Hoover entitled, "Shall it be Law or Tyranny?" Criticism of the FBI or Hoover was one of the motivating forces which prompted the Bureau to take disruptive action against the Guild on several occasions.

Subsequent to the appearance of France's article, the Bureau dispatched one of its agents to brief confidentially the editor of the *ABA Journal* regarding France's background, utilizing confidential information from Bureau files [HQ 100-157157-45, 5/21/62].

"The FBI Intrudes on Guild-ABA Relations" is based on FBI files released to the Guild in *Guild v. Attorney General,* summarized in "National Lawyers Guild v. Attorney General," *NLG Practitioner* 42:2 (Spring 1985).

A REPORT OF CASL
By George W. Crockett, Jr., and Ernest Goodman

[At the June 1962 NEB meeting, George W. Crockett, Jr., and Ernest Goodman, co-chairmen, and Len Holt and Benjamin Smith, co-secretaries, of the Guild Committee To Assist Southern Lawyers, presented a brief report of their activities since the Convention.]

The Committee is inter-racial. It consists of 22 members from 10 states. Guild members were polled, and 74 lawyers from 33 cities in 14 states sent "Commitment Forms" agreeing to devote at least 40 hours during the year and listing their qualifications, and whether they were willing to go South, if necessary, on a case.

The *Sam Mitchell* case illustrates the problem which faces the Southern Negro lawyer who undertakes desegregation cases. Mitchell has practiced law in Durham, North Carolina, for a number of years and has been one of the few active lawyers in this state who undertook many kinds of cases arising out of segregation. Last year he was indicted for failing to file income tax returns in 1956 and 1957. His failure was undoubtedly related to his non-lucrative, harassing work on desegregation cases. Having no defense, he pleaded guilty, hoping to be able to pay the taxes and penalties out of his current income. The judge, in addition to requiring the payment of taxes and penalties, imposed a fine of $7,500, more than his tax and penalty combined. Mitchell was unable to pay the fine and was prepared to serve a year's imprisonment.

Our Committee was asked to assist. Because we concluded that Mitchell's predicament resulted from his work as a lawyer on desegregation cases, we agreed. Morton Leitson of Flint, Michigan, reported:

> I spent 31 hours in Greensboro, and it turned out to be a most rewarding and gratifying experience to me. In view of the fact that Sam Mitchell received a seven-month extension of time to raise the fine, I am sure that he feels the same. . . .
>
> Mitchell is truly a lawyer's lawyer, whose biggest fault is that he can't refuse to handle cases where the clients can't afford to pay a fee. The result is that his yearly income ranges from $2,200 to $4,300. Every Negro lawyer in North Carolina goes to Sam Mitchell when he has a problem, and we all know that lawyers are the worst paying clients. There were about 20 Negro lawyers present at his hearing and they pledged $1,100 toward his fine.

[The NEB accepted the CASL report. In August, Jordan, Dawley, and Holt and Simon L. Cain of Washington, D.C., filed a history-making complaint in

---

"A Report of CASL," excerpts from Interim Report of CASL approved by NEB June 9, 1960, Ernest Goodman Papers, MCLI. *Guild Lawyer* (Sept. 1962); Call to Nov. 30, 1962, Workshop Seminar, E. Goodman Papers.

the federal district court in Danville, an omnibus integration suit. The Danville Progressive Christian Association, an affiliate of SCLC, and several ministers sued to end discriminatory practices by the local school system, public housing, public buildings, nursing home, cemeteries, parks and playgrounds, city armory, technical institute, civil service, and the memorial hospital.

[On November 30, 1962, the Guild's CASL and the National Bar Association Civil Rights Committee, in cooperation with SCLC, sponsored a Workshop Seminar for Lawyers on Civil Rights and Negligence in Atlanta. (While this was the first Guild meeting there after World War II, in 1945 the NEB had welcomed a new Guild chapter in Atlanta.) On Saturday, the panelists discussed building a negligence practice, investigation and discovery techniques, and the factor of race in trials. On Sunday, panelists discussed criminal prosecutions and constitutional rights, civil remedies and defenses against injunction proceedings. The conference was the first integrated meeting of lawyers in the South since Reconstruction, planned by attorneys Donald Hollowell, Isabell Webster, and the Rev. Mr. Wyatt Tee Walker of Atlanta, CASL, and Professor Charles W. Quick of Detroit. It was addressed by the Rev. Dr. Martin Luther King, Jr., among others.]

TRIBUTES AND DECEPTIONS IN NEW YORK
By Charles McKinney, Hope Stevens, and the FBI

■

[Early in 1963 in New York, tributes were paid to two founding members of the Guild, giants in their contributions to the law, to the Guild, and to civil rights. On the death of Leo Linder, Charles McKinney spoke as chair of the New York Chapter Committee on Integration, on which Linder had worked as a matter of principle, temporarily ignoring the Social Legislation Committee, which had been his life. The young black lawyer described the older white lawyer's "patience and constructive impatience" in working on that committee, comprised in the main of younger members of the Bar.]

By Charles McKinney

Leo was impatient with those of us who became unnecessarily involved with unimportant theoretical formulations to such an extent that they were unable to give practical application to the greater, more important principles with which we were concerned. . . . By his own example, he inspired others to work well beyond what their immediate inclinations would have otherwise permitted.

"Tributes and Deceptions in New York," comments of Charles McKinney, *Guild Lawyer* (Feb. 1963), and of Hope Stevens, *Guild Lawyer* (Nov. 1963); FBI materials from *NLG Practitioner* 42:2 (Spring 1985).

By Hope Stevens

[In May, 1963, Hope Stevens, dean of black lawyers in New York, spoke memorable words at the memorial service for Harry Sacher.]

Is it enough to talk about him; to refer to our love for him when he can no longer help? Is it not better to feel that we will leave here tonight and move out dedicated to the understanding that we have got to implement the love and respect and esteem that we held for him by attempting to reflect in our own lives some of the largeness of his heart? Those of us who are not confronted with a racial question should not feel ourselves so immune, also so secure, because a black neighbor has not moved into our community, . . . because no colored person has asked us for employment in our offices or in our businesses.

. . . I make this specific reference because as a black man I know how Harry felt on this particular point. He was the first man who gave me the opportunity of serving as associate counsel to a non-segregated union. I had been counsel for two Jim Crow unions for many years, but Harry gave me the opportunity of serving with him as an associate counsel of the Transport Workers Union for a short period before he was removed from that very responsible position. I am sure that in the audience tonight there are many lawyers connected with many trade unions in the City of New York, men of goodwill who have not thought about doing something about relieving their law offices of the lily whiteness that pervades and recognizing that they too, like Harry, can do something personal and real in extending their understanding of his personality by attempting to practice the merits of equality and justice for which he gave his life.

From NLG v. FBI

[In June 1963, the New York Field Office directed an anonymous letter to two black members of the New York City Chapter of the NLG. On June 25, 1963, SAC-New York wrote the Bureau enclosing information that the chapter office secretary, Louise Thompson, was the wife of the Chairman of the New York State Communist Party. The following anonymous letter was sent to Edward Cambridge, New York City Chapter president, and Paul Zuber, a member of its Board of Directors:]

Dear Mr. ——,

I believe you should know for the protection of the National Lawyers Guild and yourself, because of your close association with that organization, that Louise Thompson, office secretary of the Guild, is the wife of William Patterson, Chairman of N.Y. State Communist Party [HQ 100-3-104-34-NR, 6/25/63].

THE GUILD PUBLISHES ITS FIRST BOOK
By the Editors

Between the 1962 and 1963 Guild Conventions, Ann Ginger obtained practice materials from forty-five Guild and non-Guild lawyers for inclusion in the Guild's first book, *Civil Rights & Liberties Handbook: Pleadings & Practice* (1963). Twelve Southern lawyers joined thirty-three from the North to provide model complaints, briefs, and other pleadings; thirteen contributors were black, thirty-three white. Artist Barbara Beecher designed the logo, which soon became the official Guild symbol. The editor explained the goal of the *Handbook*: "The resources with which the constitutional lawyer seeks to conduct his campaign seldom match those of his opponent. This *Handbook* is intended to help even the contest by providing a quick source of accurate information. Its looseleaf form permits supplements to be inserted easily."

The *Handbook* used the latest techniques being developed by continuing legal education programs of Bar associations on traditional legal subjects. It emphasized the newest approaches to discovery techniques in proving systematic exclusion of Negroes from juries in state courts. Morton Stavis provided a practical description of how to use habeas corpus in the South. Maurice Sugar described the effective use of the doctrine of unclean hands in anti-union injunction cases that would work equally well in anti-civil rights injunction suits.

ALBANY JOURNAL—SUMMER 1963
By Dennis Roberts

[In the summer of 1963, Dennis Roberts, of the University of California–Berkeley, and William Goodman, of the University of Chicago, were among the first students from Northern law schools recruited by the Guild to work in the South. Goodman worked for Jordan, Dawley, and Holt in Norfolk; Roberts was the first in a string of Boalt Hall students to work for C. B. King in Albany, Georgia. He kept a weekly journal, which he continued when he returned to Albany after graduation. These are excerpts from the early pages.]

June 22: When the bus pulled into the Trailways terminal in Albany, Georgia, a week ago, I immediately phoned Attorney C. B. King at his home, and he said that he would be down to pick me up shortly. A few minutes later a car drove up, and a well-dressed Negro got out and walked into the white waiting room. Physically King is stocky, about six feet one inch tall, of a medium brown color with short curly hair, full

---

"Albany Journal—Summer 1963," by Dennis Roberts, unpublished diary, copyright by Dennis Roberts 1986 and published with permission, in MCLI Archives.

features, and a mustache. He has a deep, booming voice and speaks in a precise, clipped manner. He did his undergraduate work at Fisk and was graduated from Western Reserve Law School at Cleveland, where he was admitted to the Ohio Bar.

Finally I asked him: "Do you think my being white will present any extra problems?"

He said he originally thought it would be safer to have a Negro clerking with him. Therefore he went down the list until he found what he thought might be "a Negro name," and after reading my resume and learning that I had bellhopped, bussed dishes, and served in the merchant marine as a messman, he was convinced. So getting my photograph was quite a surprise. But he feels that this isn't any real problem.

. . .

Wednesday I got down to work in King's office, which is in an old building in the Negro section, which is called Harlem. It is on the second floor above a gin-mill where rock-and-roll music plays all day. At first the surroundings were shocking to my mental image of what the august chambers of an attorney should look like, but now I am used to it, except for the toilets, which I try to avoid using.

June 26: My first experience in a Southern court was an extremely pleasant one. Attorney King wanted me to come up to the Fifth Circuit Court of Appeals in Montgomery so that I would have the experience of being in an excellent federal appellate court to compare with the state trial courts we will be working in for the rest of the summer. The courtroom itself is magnificent: wood-paneled walls and heavy wooden furniture, all lending a somber, dignified air. On the bench is a three-man panel composed of Chief Justice Tuttle and Judges Gewin and Rives. Judge Tuttle is greatly respected throughout the federal court system. Judge Rives also follows the decisions of the U.S. Supreme Court very closely, and his decisions in favor of the movement have earned him the wrath of the racists. I was told that garbage has been dumped on the grave of his son. Judge Gewin generally upholds the "states' rights" position.

We were seeking to get a reversal of the decision by the District Court which denied our suit to desegregate the public facilities in Albany, Georgia. The hearings were carried on in an extremely dignified manner, and I was impressed with the competence of the civil rights attorneys. Some of the attorneys representing the states didn't seem adequately prepared.

At the end of the day, the court promised "emergency action" because of the importance of these cases.

June 28: Today I saw Georgia justice in action. We were up at about seven A.M. We had all the witnesses to John Perdew's arrest meet at Shiloh Baptist Church. . . . One of the kids gave me an announcement of a Klan meeting on July 6 in Albany; the Klan is quite active in this part of the state.

The trials started at nine A.M. The courtroom is upstairs in the city hall, above the jail and police station. It is an old room with uncomfortable wooden benches and ceiling fans.

I sat at counsel table with Attorney King, and before the first case was called, Rawls, solicitor for the city, demanded to know who "the white boy" sitting with King was. C. B. introduced me to the court as his law clerk, and the judge finally decided that I could stay. I think this was the only thing during the day that he decided in our favor.

The clerk called *City v. Willie Ricks*. Ricks, a Negro field secretary with SNCC, was charged with disorderly conduct while attending a mass meeting held in one of the Negro housing projects. The judge said $200 *and* 60 days. . . .

All these cases will immediately have petitions for review to the Superior Court filed. I was supposed to have started working on memoranda for some of the *certioraris* granted since 1961, but with the recent arrests we just don't have time to catch up on old work. These cases just drag on forever, with a fortune in bond money tied up until we can find the time to start working on the appeals.

Every one of the defensive pleadings, which we spent all day and half the night working on, Attorney King hands to the judge, who glances at it, lays it aside, and announces "overruled." . . .

The last case of the day was *City v. Mann, et al.,* which was Wendy Mann, Cathy Cade, and Sue Wender, three white SNCC girls. They had been arrested on suspicion of vagrancy, held 72 hours, and then booked as vagrants. We brought out for the record that they had advised the police they were employed by SNCC (at subsistence wages) and that they also had independent incomes or parental support. The fathers of some of them were in court, including a very proper midwestern law professor. The judge delivered a speech about how they were obviously nice girls from fine upstanding homes and said that they should go back home and not be with these bad associates in Albany. Then he sentenced them to 60 days as vagrants.

June 29: I will have a lot of work Monday because Attorney King is flying to Chicago for a conference. First thing will be to bond out Penny Patch, who is very sick. The fasting has had a shocking physical effect on the SNCC kids. They were at it for at least a week, and they look emaciated.

A really funny thing happened last night. The very proper law professor was picked up by the police for having a faulty muffler. He was handcuffed and brought to the station and told that no charges would be brought if he got out of town immediately and took his daughter. They must have thought he wasn't going to take her out. They left immediately.

[As the summer was ending, Attorney General Robert Kennedy announced in Washington that he was seeking indictments against nine civil rights leaders in Albany—eight Negroes and one white, charging them with conspiracy to obstruct justice, and perjury. Victor Rabinowitz became counsel for Antioch College student Joni Rabinowitz, along with NAACP Legal Defense Fund lawyers representing the Albany Movement defendants. (In 1966, the indictments were dismissed by the Fifth Circuit in *Rabinowitz v. United States,* 366 F.2d 34.)

[The Law Students Civil Rights Research Council, supported by the Guild and many others, was organized in 1963 and began to play a vital role in providing law clerks for embattled lawyers, first in the South, and later throughout the country.]

LAWYERS ARRESTED AT GUILD WORKSHOP IN NEW ORLEANS
By the Editors

On Friday morning, October 4, 1963, Ben Smith presided over the opening session of a civil rights and negligence workshop sponsored by the Guild, the Martinet Society of lawyers, and the Louisiana Civil Liberties Union. Over fifty lawyers from all over the South and parts of the North gathered in the first racially integrated Bar association meeting in Louisiana history. Justice Otis Smith, of the Supreme Court of Michigan, came after reading material from CASL: "The case histories of Southern cases brought back a flood of memories. I called George Crockett and said, 'I wasn't aware of this situation, and I don't think I am unique.'" He was convinced lawyers all over the country would also "want to assist as counsel and also by contributing."

A. P. Tureaud, a leader of the Martinet Society, paid tribute to Louis A. Martinet,

one of the first Negro lawyers admitted to the Louisiana bar. He was also one of the attorneys for and promoter of the case intended to remove the Jim Crow car law, *Plessy v. Ferguson.* He used his newspaper to raise funds to help carry on the fight, and was part of the citizens' committee established to bring the case through the courts and to employ the services of a lawyer.

"Lawyers Arrested at Guild Workshop in New Orleans," quotations from "Highlights of Speeches at New Orleans," *Guild Lawyer* (Feb. 1964); and see "The Dombrowski Case," by Jack Peebles, *NLG Practitioner* 33:3 (Summer 1976).

Plessy v. Ferguson represented the second sit-in in history. The Battle of Jericho represented the first. This case was a planned demonstration. The committee selected the plaintiffs, arranged for their arrest, arranged for their bail long in advance of the demonstration. Mr. Homer Plessy sat in on a railroad train and was arrested by a private detective whom the committee paid to make the arrest in a kind of conspiracy. He went through the courts of this city and state, finally to the United States Supreme Court, and made this bad jurisprudence which we have had to live under.

We honor Louis A. Martinet because he was the first contemporaneous lawyer to challenge these discriminatory laws in the South through a sit-in.

While the meeting at the recently integrated Hilton Inn was in progress, state and city police crowded into the offices of the Southern Conference Educational Fund, arrested the director, James Dombrowski, and spent three hours transporting the files, membership lists, subscription lists, and copies of SCEF's newspaper into a large van, along with inscribed photographs and letters from Albert Einstein, Franklin D. and Eleanor Roosevelt. The police simultaneously raided the offices and homes of Smith and Bruce Waltzer, under the supervision of the staff director and counsel for the Louisiana Joint Legislative Committee on Un-American Activities.

Then they marched into the Hilton and arrested chairman Smith and Waltzer, attorneys and officers of SCEF and the Guild, charging them with criminal conspiracy, i.e., that they "knowingly and willingly participated in the management of a subversive organization, secreted books, records, and files . . . , were members [thereof], . . . and distributed and stored Communist political propaganda in Louisiana."

The constitutional law experts quickly left the conference to discuss legal strategy and tactics. It took several phone calls to find a judge who would release the three on bail, although all had lived in the community for years, Smith had been assistant district attorney, and none had a criminal record.

Conference delegates cheered when Waltzer and Smith appeared the next day. Smith told them:

The charge against me is that desegregation movements in the South are Communist-inspired, the theory being that as long as the Negro can be separated in his struggle from his white allies, the movement forward to constitutional government can somehow be checked.

We cannot desegregate a witch-hunting society; we cannot integrate a silent and fearful nation; we cannot provide equal rights that have any meaning to citizens of a police state.

Later on that contradictory day, Bascom Talley, president of the Louisiana State Bar Association, spoke at the conference:

Bread-and-butter activities such as those discussed here are the finest thing lawyers' organizations can engage in, regardless of their status, interests, area of practice, or color. I hope we can take advantage of some of the things learned from Michigan and that you will take advantage of some things learned in Louisiana. We all have things we can point to with pride and some we would like to kick under the rug.

As lawyers we should emphasize the necessity to live by and observe the rule of law.

Earl Amedee, of New Orleans, summed it up: "The people who arrested Ben Smith and Bruce Waltzer really arrested all of us."

On October 25, 1963, a local judge dismissed the charges against Dombrowski, Smith, and Waltzer; new indictments were expected. The three rejected a wait-and-see approach and decided to take the offensive. They soon filed five suits in federal court: to stop the state criminal prosecution, to return the files and other property taken, and to receive damages for false arrest and illegal seizure of records.

The most important suit was based on the 1871 Civil Rights Act (42 U.S. Code sec. 1983). It alleged that the Louisiana statutes were unconstitutional on their face because they violated the First and Fourteenth Amendment guarantees of freedom of expression and association, giving the federal court jurisdiction to step in immediately. The lawsuit was not unique, but it certainly was not typical. Usually a person charged with a crime in a state court must be tried, convicted, and appeal through the state system before going to the U.S. Supreme Court for a definitive ruling on a claim that the state statute is unconstitutional under the federal Constitution.

Smith and Waltzer tried to continue to earn a living while the cases were pending, and to carry on civil rights activities. Their insurance was cancelled, and Waltzer and his wife were told that final adoption of their child must await the outcome of the case.

A STORMY NATIONAL EXECUTIVE BOARD MEETING IN NEW YORK
By Ernest Goodman

The 1964 Guild Convention was set for the St. Pierre Hotel in New York City in 1963. As we approached that date, the Detroit Chapter began to feel it could not just go ahead in the usual way—holding the

---

"A Stormy National Executive Board Meeting in New York," by Ernest Goodman, from article in *NLG Practitioner* 38:1 (Winter 1981); excerpts from Minutes of NEB, Nov. 10, 1963, by the Secretary, in Maurice Sugar Papers, MCLI.

convention in a status hotel, with a big banquet and speakers and awards. Something new had to be done.

We also probably reacted with a certain degree of resentment that Guild Midwesterners had held for many years with respect to the New York Chapter's dominant role. We felt that many very able New York Chapter members looked down on us, and we were not about to accept the view that the New York Chapter and officers had all the answers to the problems of society and the Guild. We felt we had developed our own answers out of the course of our experience, and we were going to do something about it, not just permit the issue to be evaded.

As a result, it was decided by the national office to delay the convention until after the November 10, 1963, Guild executive board meeting.

■

Minutes of National Executive Board Meeting
Secretary

The meeting was called to order by the President [Benjamin Dreyfus].

Mr. Goodman read the CASL report.

MR. NEUBURGER [NEW YORK] Proposed: that chapters concentrate on: (1) the fight for equality, integration, jobs, and education; (2) CASL as the main, but only one phase, of Guild program. Local CASLs should be set up. Where there is sufficient interest, leadership, and encouragement, there could be activities in other areas: social legislation, labor law, etc. We consider at the convention work on peace and disarmament. Cut out the mechanical approach.

MR. PHILO [DETROIT]: There should be at least 5,000 members because there are that many lawyers that believe in what the Guild stands for. He recommended that the convention be cancelled and a nationwide conference substituted; we should not have a national executive secretary and a national office; instead, a working president to call board meetings from time to time and a minimum national budget; a strong CASL organization with a CASL office in the South. By March first CASL could set up an office in New Orleans with lawyers, secretaries, etc., and start doing everything necessary to collect briefs and distribute them to lawyers; get law clerks for the summer clerkship program; organize and develop CASL in the north, etc. These things would begin to build the Guild. In 2-3 years we would be able to re-establish a national office with an executive secretary, etc.

MR. SMITH [NEW ORLEANS]: We are involved in a great social crisis, and it appears to be primarily in the South. Unless the Guild seeks out the first opportunity to involve itself we will miss the opportunity to grow with the revolution. The Negro revolution will eventually involve itself in all of the other social needs. We can get new members only through personal contacts and by working on the problems. Our structure does not fit the needs of our time.

MR. CROCKETT [DETROIT]: We have not yet licked the problem of the integrated law office in Detroit. The Guild today is not the inter-racial association that it was once. . . . We need a reorientation and rededication. CASL has been able to move people and motivate people. Organizationally, there is no real national organization. The Detroit Chapter is growing because of activity. If we don't have an active growing New York chapter, the Guild is simply a paper organization. [I am] not in accord with Philo's proposals because the New York chapter should be allowed to make an effort to change its functioning.

MR. CONYERS [DETROIT]: What are we planning that makes it necessary for the Guild to continue? I am aware of the interests of lawyers because of the living program that Detroit has. The question of where the money goes in the Guild budget is very paramount. It is difficult to explain, particularly, the lack of Negro members in New York.

MR. SILBERSTEIN [NEW YORK AND DETROIT]: It seems to me wholly incorrect to counterpose the existence of the Guild against the work of CASL. The idea of CASL developed at the last convention in 1962. At that time Detroit was growing rapidly and was doing nothing about the question of civil rights. When I was in Detroit, George Crockett and I addressed ourselves to the question of integration of housing in Michigan. We had tremendous difficulty in finding members who were ready to work on it.

MRS. ABZUG [NEW YORK]: Related to the struggle for integration and its success is the knowledge that it is dependent on other problems in this country, and because we recognize their existence, success can take place only in an organization such as the Guild. The basic problem lies in economic accomplishment. Unless there is a healthy economy based on providing jobs, schools, and other basic needs, other problems won't be solved. Unless we see this relationship and are able to lead the Bar in seeing this, we will not fulfill our function. We have to provide leadership in the area of peace, which will make possible the successful objectives that the integration movement requires. It would be incorrect to place all emphasis and program on CASL. As lawyers, we have a contribution to make in the field of peace and world law, not only in the UN, but in disarmament, planning for peace, etc. In the field of integration, the role we have been playing has been primarily to provide a place for lawyers who are interested to work. We should provide more lawyers to develop the basic conceptual problems which have not been provided by the existing Bar. We have to influence the Bar towards integration.

Mr. Stavis [New Jersey]: The Guild ought to develop a program of going into the law schools and develop an active clerkship program in our own offices. In this way we can make an investment in a more experienced bar among Negro lawyers.

Mrs. Elder [New York]: As young lawyers we resent the top-heavy structure of the New York Guild and mechanical activities. The young people have tried several things in the Guild but, so far, unsuccessfully.

Mr. Cambridge [New York]: The failure of the Guild to recruit Negro lawyers was not due to lack of effort. Within the past five years we have not been able to produce a Negro lawyer to train. Two situations have developed that are seriously threatening the Negro lawyer: (1) Fewer Negro lawyers are coming out. (2) Of those that manage to get through, most do not go into the area of private practice. Of those who have been in practice, for a number of years they had some interest in the Guild, but everyone of them have dropped away.

Mr. Popper: Moved that the primary emphasis of the Guild and of its national offices and officers shall be devoted to the fight for equality throughout the country and that every appropriate means be used.

It was agreed that the main change in Goodman's motion by Popper was to change "75 percent" to "primary emphasis."

Vote: 8 for; 6 opposed. Motion carried.

INTO THE STREETS OF SAN FRANCISCO
By the Civil Liberties Docket

58.15 *California v. Hallinan.* (San Francisco Muni. Ct.) Nov. 2–3, 1963: Negro and white youth (Ad Hoc Comm. To End Discrimination) sat-in at Mel's Drive-In to protest discriminatory hiring practices; 59 arrested: trespass and disturbing the peace. Contract signed between Mel's chain and Ad Hoc Comm: some Negro carhops, bartenders, hired immediately. Defs.' demurrer filed, pending.

"Into the Streets of San Francisco," by the *Civil Liberties Docket* 9:3 (April 1964).

■ THIRTEEN

The Guild Goes South (1964-1965)

WHILE THE NEB was debating the Detroit proposal to concentrate all Guild energies on the South, the Subcommittee on Disarmament of the International Law Committee was completing three years of work on the Guild's second book, *A Summary of Disarmament Documents: 1945-1962* (San Francisco: NLG, 1963). Doris Brin Walker, Malcolm Burnstein, and Harry Margolis presented all disarmament proposals of the Western and Soviet Blocs to encourage further work on this crucial issue. This subject, and Guild member Jerome R. Hellerstein's new book, *Taxes, Loopholes and Morals* (New York: McGraw Hill, 1963) were more familiar, and comfortable, to most Guild members than the subjects on which they were about to embark.

In February 1964, how many Convention delegates had been to Watts? Who had thought of using "affirmative action" in a civil rights context, or of "women's liberation" or "the feminization of poverty"? Who thought the federal government would fund Community Action Programs and Group Legal Services offices to represent indigent clients in civil cases and in suits against welfare departments? Many Guild members had never been abroad, except in the military; many were still unable to get passports, due to the "loyalty" questions still on passport forms. Few had visited Asia or knew Vietnam or Cambodia. Five years after its successful revolution, few Guild lawyers had gone to Cuba. Delano and Pitt River were as far from their consciousness as Puerto Rico, Chile, Nicaragua, El Salvador, and Grenada. The dream of Zimbabwe out of Rhodesia was as distant as an understanding that the transnationals would soon close major Detroit auto factories.

What came to be on every delegate's mind were the facts about the 2,100,000 people living in Mississippi, nearly 1,000,000 Negroes, served by 2,100 white and four Negro lawyers. Many delegates had attended the Guild's conferences in Atlanta and New Orleans in 1963 and agreed with the impassioned speakers that the problem of the civil rights lawyers had reached a totally new stage. This was no longer the era of the occasional test case filed for a few courageous plaintiffs suing to desegregate a school. The arrests of the Freedom Riders marked a new phase in which hundreds of people came to a Southern city to wipe out segregation, which the Supreme Court had declared to be under federal supervision.

Arthur Kinoy, Morton Stavis, Len Holt, and Ed Dawley, among others, pointed out that the lawyers must defend their clients: the movement and individual citizens working for civil rights. The immediate object of the power structure was to stop the movement dead. The lawyers' immediate counter-objective was to keep clients on the streets, where they wanted to exercise their First Amendment liberties to change the pattern and practice of discrimination and segregation.

In Danville the previous summer, they had faced four tactics by the enemy, and had devised a counter-approach to meet each one. (1) Against the state court injunction: a plenary federal civil rights action seeking a temporary injunction to restrain state court proceedings. (2) Against the new ordinances: a plenary federal suit seeking a temporary injunction to restrain enforcement of the ordinances. (3) Against the conspiracy felony indictments: a temporary restraining order holding up prosecutions on state charges until after hearings on federal cases, and a request for a three-judge federal court to hold the state statutes unconstitutional. (4) To ease the immediate pressure, in case of failure in the federal injunction requests: a removal suit to remove from the state court *all* of the pending contempt of court trials coming up in the following days.

The lawyers noted a second forum in which success was indeed possible: the Congress, which inserted in the 1964 Civil Rights Act the right to appeal from remand of a case removed under Title 28 U.S. Code section 1443. This short provision solved a fundamental problem that had been plaguing the movement: how to get demonstrators out of state jails and under federal protection before they were attacked by other racist prisoners.

The lawyers concluded:

We are clearly in for a long siege of civil rights litigation. For example, under the existing law of the Fifth Circuit, there is not a single Negro legally detained in Mississippi because the jury system in state courts has been held totally defective. As things now stand, Mississippi does not have the power to try a single Negro citizen for any offense, civil rights or otherwise.

In order to continue to work on civil rights matters, lawyers must begin to find ways to be reimbursed for their time without taxing the movement beyond its financial capacity. For example, the Fourth Circuit recently awarded attorney's fees to counsel for the civil rights movement in a case in which state officials were following a clear policy of rejecting Supreme Court desegregation decisions.[1]

---

1. From *Civil Rights and Liberties Handbook: Pleadings and Practice* by Ann Fagan Ginger, ed. (Berkeley: NLG, 1964).

THE 1964 CONVENTION AND THE MISSISSIPPI PROJECT
By the Editors

The theme of the Guild convention in Detroit on February 21-23, 1964, was "The Legal Revolution: Challenge to the Legal Profession." In fact, it was a challenge to the Guild. In the end, a number of drastic proposals were agreed upon. The Guild would transfer its national office from New York to Detroit. Ernest Goodman would be president; the executive secretary and treasurer would also be Detroiters. The Detroit program would be adopted; the national office would place its main emphasis on the civil rights movement in the South, with the understanding that any chapter could work on other programs and Bar activities. In the process, CASL became CLAS—Committee for Legal Assistance to the South.

The next *Newsletter*, issued from Detroit, reported the beginning of

what may prove to be one of the most significant projects ever undertaken in the civil rights movement:

The Student Non-Violent Co-ordinating Committee in conjunction with the Mississippi Council of Federated Organizations plans to launch a massive voter registration program this summer. Mississippi Negroes will be registered to the extent possible on county books; at the same time it is hoped to register over 400,000 Negroes on "Freedom Registration" books. These will later be used to challenge the official books of the state and the validity of official elections this fall.

NLG proposes to supplement the legal forces available to defend civil rights suits in the state (three attorneys). The staff will be formed around a full-time corps of two attorneys, two law students, and a secretary. In addition, it hopes to provide a total of sixty "Lawyer Weeks," that is, one lawyer for one week of service to be distributed among the five congressional districts for the full twelve weeks. The program will be initiated by conducting the third NLG Conference for Civil Rights Attorneys in Jackson, Mississippi, on June 6-8, 1964. Registration of Guild attorneys for the summer project is to begin immediately.[2]

The *Newsletter* also proudly announced "New Integrated Firms Formed in Three Cities": by Smith, Waltzer, Jones, & Peebles in New Orleans; by Herbert Fisher of Chicago, who was becoming a partner in Stradford, Lafontante & Lafontante; and by John Cozart, joining Milan & Miller of Detroit.

---

2. *Guild Newsletter* (May 15, 1964).

THE FBI MEETS WITH SOME CIVIL RIGHTS ORGANIZATIONS
By the FBI

[One report, dated 6/10/64, to a Mr. Moore from a Mr. DeLouche of the FBI, referred in considerable detail to a conference held in Washington, D.C., by the FBI with Carl Rachlin, identified as Chief Counsel of the Congress of Racial Equality (CORE); Leo Pfeffer, identified as representing the American Jewish Congress; and Mr. Lukas, identified as the Director of the American Civil Liberties Union.

[Actually, the latter was Edward Lukas, general counsel of the American Jewish Committee, with no organizational ties with the ACLU, according to Prof. John DeJ Pemberton, who was then Executive Director of the ACLU.]

Mr. Rachlin (CORE), a very highstrung individual, did most of the talking in front of the group. He explained that CORE, the American Jewish Congress and the ACLU [sic] had arranged for approximately 100 attorneys to be in the South in key trouble areas between now (6/10/64) and Labor Day . . . to provide legal guidance and counsel to civil rights demonstrators.

Initially Rachlin took pains to point out . . . that he and the ACLU (*sic*) and the American Jewish Congress counsels were perturbed by the plans of the National Lawyers Guild to supply attorneys for civil rights demonstrators in the summer. He knew the NLG was setting up an office in Jackson, Miss., and this was undesirable. He expressed considerable concern that these attorneys were trying to encroach on the role of CORE lawyers in defending civil rights demonstrators. Rachlin indicated that many of their attorneys had not had any experience in opposing the communists such as Messrs. Pfeffer, Lukas and he had encountered during the 1930s.

The participants then made clear to the FBI . . . they wanted some liaison with the FBI, some protection for the safety of their lawyers. . . .

I told Pfeffer that if any of these attorneys were going into a town and he felt concern for their physical safety, that they should . . . go to the local chief of police, inform him of . . . the type of work they were going to be doing, . . . where they were staying, and be completely above board. . . . [They] agreed this was the proper course of action. . . .

I told Rachlin he should feel free to send us a list including data as to where these attorneys were going to be working this summer, and we would see to it that the FBI field divisions were advised. . . .

Mr. Pfeffer (American Jewish Congress) expressed general concern

---

"The FBI Meets with Some Civil Rights Organizations," by the FBI, from "The NLG, the FBI, and the Civil Rights Movement: 1964," by Ernest Goodman, *NLG Practitioner* 38:1 (Winter 1981).

regarding the activities of some of the more active hate groups. I told them that for their own private information, the FBI necessarily possessed sources of information within these groups and that of course it was important to have informant penetration in all organizations which posed an internal security threat. Mr. Lukas pointed out that his organization has some sources within these groups also, and said that a former agent . . . Milton Ellerin handled the sources of information for them.

[The report concluded: "These men said they would like to maintain close contact with my office when difficulties arose and I stressed they should not hesitate to do so, noting of course, that Mr. Jim Farmer of CORE and I were in frequent contact." A further report by the FBI continued:]

Sources 3 through 6 said they personally fear that SNCC and CORE, which form the basic nucleus of COFO, which they termed as immature and irresponsible in many areas, will make no effort to "screen" COFO volunteer workers, . . . accordingly COFO may be infiltrated by Communists, irresponsible agitators who will try to exploit this project for subversive and other ulterior motives.

THE GOODMANS AND SCHWERNERS GO TO THE OVAL OFFICE
With Martin Popper

The Goodman family—Bobby and Carolyn Goodman—were among my dearest friends. . . . Their son Andrew, Andy, was one of the students who went down South in 1964 in the very first group. Before they arrived in Mississippi, they were at an orientation camp, and Andy became friendly with Schwerner and Chaney.

One morning that summer I heard on the radio that these three teenagers were missing. And I went to work troubled. I didn't know quite what to do. That evening my wife and I went over to the Goodmans. The question was what the devil to do, how to find them. We talked about what influential people might be seen or spoken to. And I thought and thought, and I said, "There's only one person in this country who can do anything real about this, and that's whom we're going to see—the President of the United States."

Almost everybody thought that was nice, a good idea.

Then I said, "No, look, we're going to see the President tomorrow." This was about 11 o'clock at night. I said to Bobby Goodman, "I want

---

"The Goodmans and Schwerners Go to the Oval Office," with Martin Popper, Oral History Memoir, MCLI.

you, beginning now, to tell the press you're going to Washington and you're going to see the President of the United States."

By that time Nat Schwerner and his wife had called Bobby.

There were people, even friends of ours, who were opposed to our going to see Johnson. They felt that shouldn't be done. They said, "What you should do is go to court and start a lawsuit." And I had terrible fights, because I said, "What I want is the boys back. I'm not interested in a lawsuit right now."

We got on the plane, and there was at least one reporter with us because of all this getting on the radio. We got to Washington and there was a regiment of media people at the airport. Bobby made a very moving statement.

. . . We were immediately taken to Attorney General Robert Kennedy. Well, I wasn't going to refuse that. I told Kennedy what I thought could be done, should be done. But [he couldn't help us because he and Johnson were not on good terms]. Next we went to see Goodman's Congressman, and then Schwerner's. They called and made an appointment with one of the secretaries to the President. They went with us, and when we got to the White House and saw Lee White, I explained why it was absolutely essential that we see the President, not only for us, but for the President. As I was talking, one of the President's other secretaries, Feldman, came out, and I made what I thought was probably a very effective statement, because, minutes later, there we were in the Oval Room.

We told the President: "You ought to go to Mississippi; you ought to get on television at the airport in Mississippi." We said this was not just another case—the whole world was watching to see whether the United States government was going to live up to its policies in support of civil rights and in defense of the people in the hundreds who were still down there in Mississippi for the rest of the summer. If he failed to act—if the government failed to act—that would be a sign to the whole world about what the government did not stand for, and, if it acted, it would be a sign as to what it did stand for.

Well, the President said, "What about [J. Edgar] Hoover [head of the FBI]?"

I said, "That's not enough."

It was a very good conference, and he ordered the Army and the Navy to really go down there to search. And the next day the papers were full of that.

One of the consequences, but it took some weeks, is that Hoover was ordered to go down there. He did go and opened an office in Jackson. For weeks after that conference, we were down there before the new Attorney General, Katzenbach; he and Burke Marshall and John Doare played an active role, because the administration recognized that the country would support its position to do what it could.

From that moment, we spent day in and day out, reaching everybody we could. I went down to Mississippi, at the suggestion of the Attorney General, to meet with the FBI, to give them what information we could. And I met with George Crockett.

We were down in the White House quite a number of times until they finally found the boys; they didn't find them alive, but they did find them.

MISSISSIPPI AND THE FBI RETALIATE
By the Guild CLAS and from the FBI

■

Report on the Mississippi Summer 1964
By the Guild CLAS

An integrated team of three CLAS lawyers and two law students went to Philadelphia on June 23—two days after the trio's disappearance—to interview the sheriff and inquire into the church burning incidents. "We felt that as attorneys we could accomplish such a routine task without the difficulties encountered by the COFO students, to whom the sheriff had given conflicting stories," said Attorney Anna Diggs, wife of Michigan Congressman Charles Diggs.

Attorney David Finkel of Los Angeles: "We stopped at a filling station on the outskirts to ask our way to the courthouse. A Negro attendant started to tell us something but got so panicky he choked up." Before they could enter the courthouse a crowd of 100 closed in on them. Finkel's way was blocked by a local resident, who demanded his identity, residence, and reason for being there. When George Crockett led the way into the sheriff's office, the townspeople had so filled the hallways of the courthouse and the office itself that, in Mrs. Diggs' words, "We were effectively intimidated by their number and threatening attitude before a word was exchanged with the sheriff."

Nevertheless, Crockett introduced each member of the party to the sheriff, stating their business. The sheriff said there had been no injuries at the church and that the state was investigating. The sheriff gave them

---

"Mississippi and the FBI Retaliate" from Guild CLAS Report, "Summer Project: Mississippi, 1964—An Account of the NLG Program of Legal Assistance to Civil Rights Workers in Mississippi," *NLG Practitioner* 24:2 (Spring 1965); and from FBI files released to the Guild in *Guild v. Attorney General,* summarized in Thomas I. Emerson, Michael Krinsky, Jonathan C. Moore, and Dr. Ann Mari Buitrago, "*National Lawyers Guild v. Attorney General*," *NLG Practitioner* 42:2 (Spring 1985).

directions to the burnt-out church, Finkel related, "but he gave them so loud, he obviously was telling everyone in the courthouse we were going there." They worked their way back to their car, forced to pass through a milling throng, screaming hate-filled epithets. . . .

PRESIDENT LYNDON JOHNSON
IT IS APPARENT THAT WHAT WE EXPERIENCED IS WHAT ALL CIVIL RIGHTS WORKERS FACE IN THEIR EFFORTS TO AID MISSISSIPPI NEGROES STOP IF LAWYERS HAVE NO SAFE ACCESS TO A COUNTY COURTHOUSE IT IS APPARENT THAT THE STUDENTS WHO ARE ARRIVING IN THE STATE WILL NOT BE SAFE WITHOUT FEDERAL PROTECTION STOP
ANNA DIGGS

■

From the FBI

[The FBI learned of the visit of Martin Popper and his clients to the Oval Office from a UPI news release dated June 23, 1964.]

After reading the release, FBI head J. Edgar Hoover queried, "What do we know about Popper?" [HQ 105-1913-362. Bland to Sullivan, 6/24/64.]

A review of Bureau files indicated that Popper was on the Security Index (a list of persons maintained by the FBI for targetting individuals for intensive surveillance and possible harassment) and that he was a past Executive Secretary of the National Lawyers Guild. [Id.] Subsequently, the FBI forwarded information from the Bureau files in "blind memorandum" form to Walter Jenkins of the White House, the Attorney General, the Deputy Attorney General, and Assistant Attorneys General Burke Marshall and J. Walter Yeagley. This memorandum prominently featured Popper's leadership positions in the Guild and continued to promote the stigma that the Guild was a communist-front organization [HQ 105-1913-360, 6/24/64].

RESOLUTIONS BY THE ABA AND MISSISSIPPI BAR ASSOCIATION
By the Committee for Legal Assistance to the South

The ABA's sole contribution to advance the cause of justice in the South consists of resolutions at its 1963 and 1964 conventions urging its members to undertake their professional responsibilities in the "present civil rights controversy." The 1963 resolution states: "In an effort to solve

---

"Resolutions by the ABA and Mississippi Bar Association" from Guild CLAS Report, "Summer Project: Mississippi, 1964," *NLG Practitioner* 24:2 (Spring 1965).

this difficult situation (conflict over civil rights), respect for the Constitution of the United States and of the several states, the various applicable statutes, and the decisions of federal courts and the courts of the various states must be observed, and observed with respect."

This resolution was adopted at a time when thousands of Southern Negroes and civil rights workers were being beaten and jailed because they exercised federal constitutional rights in violation of city ordinances and state statutes, and when the federal government was bringing injunctions suits against state officials for violating federal law.

In the irreconcilable conflict between the federal Constitution, which is intended to guarantee equality to the Negro, and state laws, which are designed to maintain segregation, the Constitution must prevail; and no Bar association can remain aloof from this conflict by calling upon the Negro people to obey both. The ABA has a clear responsibility to act as the Guild pointed out in an August 1964 letter to ABA President Walter E. Craig.

In July 1964, the Mississippi State Board of Bar Commissioners called on the state's lawyers to represent anyone charged with a crime, regardless of the attorney's opinions. . . . It was a step forward, and the Guild applauded—although such a drastic change in attitude must still be seen to be believed.

THE GUILD LOOKS AT ITS BUDGET, CLOSES, AND REOPENS, ITS JACKSON OFFICE
By the Editors

NATIONAL LAWYERS GUILD NATIONAL BUDGET

National Office	1964	Proposed 1965
Salaries	$12,400	$13,500
Rent, Telephone, Printing, General Office Expenses	4,280	8,280
Newsletter and Civil Liberties Docket	3,500	2,500
NEB and Convention	1,000	1,000
Travel	2,000	
Retirement of Past Due Debt		2,000
Miscellaneous	1,000	500
	23,680	25,000
CLAS	15,000	25,000
Total Budget	$38,680	$52,280

Guild Budget from NEB Minutes, Maurice Sugar Papers, MCLI; information on Jackson office from *Guild Newsletter* (Jan. 1965).

[The Guild closed its Jackson office on August 30, 1964, at the end of the Summer Project, out of funds. Within days, new and more serious charges against civil rights workers and Mississippi Negroes were reported. Felony charges of "sedition" for violation of state laws carrying long prison terms supplanted "disturbing the peace." On October 10th, the Jackson office was reopened with the arrival of Claudia Shropshire, director, and Harry Nier of Denver, the first volunteer lawyer for the Guild's winter project.]

THE GUILD GOES TO THE POLLS IN MICHIGAN
By the Guild Newsletter

Despite the fact that their Guild membership was not designated on the ballot, three NLG members managed to be elected to public office this November.

John Conyers was elected to the House of Representatives from Michigan's 1st Congressional district. Conyers is the sixth Negro to be elected to Congress, and, joining Charles C. Diggs, Jr., the second Negro Congressman from Michigan. He worked in the Guild in the Mississippi Project, and is the second Guild member to make the cover of *Jet* magazine in recent months.

Conyers has served as a member of the Executive Boards of both the Detroit chapter and the National organization. His election results partially from a recent redistricting of Michigan Congressional representation. This is a further illustration of the close connection between the Civil Rights struggle, in which Conyers has been active, and the recent developments in reapportionment. It is hoped that his election will give Congressional voice to the problems which exist in Mississippi as well as Michigan, and which Conyers witnessed this past summer.

Roger Craig was elected to the Michigan Senate from Detroit, and Robert Traxler, of Bay City, was elected to the Michigan House of Representatives.

THE MISSISSIPPI FREEDOM DEMOCRATIC PARTY CHALLENGE
By Morton Stavis

The Mississippi challenge followed the frustrations experienced by the Mississippi Freedom Democratic Party at the Democratic Party Convention in Atlantic City in the summer of 1964. Blacks from Missis-

---

"The Guild Goes to the Polls in Michigan," *Guild Newsletter* (dated Oct. 1964; received Dec. 1964).

"The Mississippi Freedom Democratic Party Challenge," by Morton Stavis, from MCLI journal, *Lift Every Voice for Civil Rights 1963* (1983).

sippi felt both ignored and manipulated, and after their return home decided to move on their own to challenge the seating in the House of Representatives of all five Congressmen elected from Mississippi that fall, on the grounds that in practice blacks were being denied the right to vote. The FDP asked a group of attorneys to represent it in the challenge — William Higgs, Arthur Kinoy, William Kunstler, Benjamin Smith (since deceased), and me.

The federal statutes provide specific procedures for a notice of contest, a response, the taking of depositions, and the availability of subpoena (2 U.S.C. §381 et seq.). Accordingly, the attorneys for the challenge sent out a call to lawyers all over the country to assist in the taking of depositions in every one of the five Congressional Districts. The program developed into a massive concentrated turnout of lawyers, working in close cooperation with the movement.

Forty-six lawyers from the San Francisco Bay Area flew to Mississippi, 28 from San Jose and Southern California, 79 from the rest of the country. In the end, 153 lawyers paid their own fares, most put in one-week stints, a few even brought their own court reporters at their own expense. They came from many Bar associations and communities, the majority from the Lawyers Guild.

As coordinator of the challenge, I came to the conclusion that, despite earnest efforts by civil rights workers, advance work would have to be performed by the lawyers themselves. When the first group came from San Francisco, I received a call from Barney Dreyfus, who said they had come in on the "red eye" special and wanted to check into a motel and spend the day swimming and relaxing. He asked that I have everything ready for them the next morning so they could start taking depositions. During a very pleasant meal with a tired group, I calmly announced that they would have to do the preparation, including the location and interviewing of witnesses, as well as the taking of the depositions. There was not a single complaint or recrimination.

And so it was for the entire period and for the whole group of lawyers who came. Lawyers were willing to trudge in the mud to track down witnesses who would be prepared to testify about their difficulties in registering and voting. The positive attitude of lawyers produced a rich working relationship with the civil rights workers as well as the local black people. It also produced 400 depositions taken throughout the state in January and February of 1965.

In accordance with procedures provided for by statute, the depositions were filed with the Clerk of the House, and printed. Every Member of Congress received a set of three volumes, totaling almost 3,000 pages of single-spaced small print, the verbatim copy of the depositions. Thereafter, a team of lawyers, including Dan Crystal of New Jersey, and several law students, prepared a 117-page printed brief with a 99-page appendix [which analyzed contested elections in Congress following the Civil War and until the end of the 19th century, when Congress continued to try to protect black voting rights, despite backsliding by Presidents and the Supreme Court].

With this as precedent, the 1965 contestants—Mrs. Fannie Lou Hamer, Mrs. Annie Devine, and Mrs. Victoria Gray—appeared before the Congressional committee that considered the contest. In accordance with precedents, the three black women contestants were invited to sit on the floor of the House during the debate. On September 17, 1965, 143 Members of Congress voted to deny seats to the regular Democratic Party Congressmen who claimed to have been elected.

The vote was a turning point. The fact that a third of the Members of Congress, on the first try in recent history, were willing to deny seats to their colleagues was an unmistakable sign that Southern political leaders had no choice but to permit blacks to vote. And the challenge did much to sway votes in favor of the Voting Rights Act, passed in August 1965. While it can hardly be said that blacks have full political rights in the South (or, for that matter, the North) today, there is no doubt that the kind of crude, almost total, exclusion of blacks from the electoral process, which was once the practice, is a thing of the past.

STORMING THE PALACE IN SAN FRANCISCO, AND THE GUILD RESPONSE
By Paul Harris and the San Francisco Chapter

■

By Paul Harris

In 1963 and 1964 thousands of young people sat-in at Mel's Drive In, the Sheraton Palace Hotel, and Auto Row to protest racial discrimination in hiring. Later, a few of us went to law school and joined the Lawyers Guild. But in 1964 we had no understanding of the law. Our role was to break the law; to engage in civil disobedience without allowing the fear of jail to deter us. We relied on our lawyers to educate us to our options, and then to step back and allow us to make the decisions. If those decisions meant that we would be prosecuted, we looked to our lawyers to protect us. Frank McTernan was one of a handful of lawyers who gained our respect and admiration. His political experience and

---

"Storming the Palace in San Francisco, and the Guild Response," from Paul Harris, in *San Francisco Chapter Journal Honoring Frank McTernan* (1983); and from "San Francisco Sit-In Trials," by the San Francisco Guild Chapter, *NLG Practitioner* 24:1 (Winter 1965).

humility was as valuable to us as his obvious legal skills. Knowing that we could depend on people like Frank helped to free us from the fear of the state and thereby made us a more powerful movement.

■

By the San Francisco Guild Chapter

Basic Facts on the Trials: 37 misdemeanor trials were held in which defendants were charged with disorderly conduct, disturbing the peace, trespassing, and similar charges. The 474 defendants were mainly young students. Of 369 tried, juries acquitted 48; 89 must be retried a second time and 19 must be retried a third time because the juries disagreed twice.

Several judges required all defendants to be present throughout the trials, including lengthy jury selection. Some forbade students to bring textbooks to court so they could study during recesses; some issued bench warrants for non-attendance. This caused incompletes and lower or flunking grades for some of the students.

Atmosphere in the Community: The governor, the mayor, church officials, and other public figures told the press and TV that the civil rights defendants were all guilty and were attempting to clog the courts by demanding jury trials, although defendants had moved that all persons who demonstrated together should be tried together, and the motion had been denied.

The Guild pointed out that in seven major Southern cities, as soon as desegregation agreements were reached with the demonstrators, all charges were dismissed in Winston-Salem, Nashville, Memphis, Greenville, Atlanta, Baltimore, and New Orleans (1960–1963). This was not done in San Francisco after fair employment practices agreements were signed between the target hotels and auto showrooms and the demonstrators, including several defendants.

The Guild's motion as a friend of the court to postpone the trials or remove them was rejected by the district attorney and judges.

Jury Selection: In 34 of the trials studied, 204 Negroes were called but only 10 actually sat on juries, the majority having been challenged peremptorily by the D.A. Less than 3 percent of the jurors in these 34 cases were Negroes, 10 out of 408, although the population of San Francisco is 10.8 percent Negro.

Contempt Citations: Four lawyers, three of them Negroes, were cited for contempt one or more times during these trials. Four defendants were cited for contempt, and ten were taken into custody by a judge who could not believe he had lost jurisdiction after counsel filed removal petitions to the federal court.

Sentencing: If one compares 150 criminal defendants in San Francisco in the first six months of 1963 with 170 civil rights defendants, only 9 percent of the former received jail sentences for disturbing the peace; 72 percent of the latter got sentences or sentences plus fines. [59 percent got 30 to 90 days, and 3 got 120 to 270 days.]

These sentences were roughly comparable to, although sometimes harsher than, the sentences given to the Freedom Riders in 1961 by Mississippi courts, since 44 percent received fines only and the highest sentence was 120 days. In New York City, sentences on similar charges were much lower.

Appeal: Judges set bonds as high as $350 per defendant, creating a real problem for young student defendants and their movement.

We call on the bar and bench "to reconsider its approach to these defendants and these cases in order to carry out the primary purpose of the judicial system: the equal and even-handed administration of justice without regard to the race of the defendants or the unpopularity of their views."

THE WATTS REVOLT AND THE LOS ANGELES CHAPTER RESPONSE
By the Civil Liberties Docket *and Leo Branton, Jr., Seymour Mandel, and Ben Margolis*

■

WATTS REVOLT (LOS ANGELES, AUG. 11–16, 1965)
By Civil Liberties Docket

[The *Docket* reported the Watts cases in the category on Miscellaneous Violations of Due Process.]

Underlying Conditions: 650,000 Negroes live in the Watts area. Watts is 98 percent Negro. White businessmen own 95 percent of the businesses and property in the 46.5 square mile area. About 10,000 Negro mothers leave the Watts area to work as domestics in white homes in Los Angeles. 34 percent of Watts adults are unemployed, 60 percent are receiving welfare. In Los Angeles there are more than 50,000 unemployed Negroes and Mexican-Americans. Welfare expenditures are $400 million per year. Aid to Families with Dependent Children increased 73 percent between 1960 and 1964. 4 percent of the police force is Negro.

The Revolt: Aug 11–16, 1965: At least 10,000 Negroes from Watts actively

---

"The Watts Revolt and the Los Angeles Chapter Response" from *Civil Liberties Docket* 11:2 (Nov. 1965), p. 34, and from "Watts Riots: Guild Amicus Brief," by Leo Branton, Jr., Seymour Mandel, and Ben Margolis, *NLG Practitioner* 24:3 (Summer 1965).

took to the streets. 934 policemen, 719 Sheriffs, officers, and 13,900 National Guardsmen were on duty. 34 were killed. 32 inquests were held; 26 deaths were labelled justifiable homicide. 26 Negroes, 3 Mexican-Americans, 1 Asian killed, a large percentage by police, National Guard. 1,032 injuries reported and more than $40 million in property damage. Over 600 buildings were damaged, 200 totally destroyed; 1,500 separate fires were set, 300 major fires; 103 squad cars damaged. 12,000 weapons were stolen; 2-3,000 have been recovered.

The Legal Process: Aug 11-16: 4,200 persons arrested including 500 juveniles, 1,500 for misdemeanors, 2,260 for felonies. 80 percent held in jail more than 2 weeks. Oct 20: over 200 persons remained in jail. Charges against 620 dismissed or reduced to misdemeanors before preliminary hearing; of the rest, 320 dismissed at hearing. Dec 6: McCone Commission reported 170 complaints of police malpractice, from verbal abuse to physical harm. Bail was set for felony cases at $5,500, $3,000 above normal. Bail for juveniles was usually $1,500. Only 100 prisoners released on own recognizance. The 5 charges against most misdemeanor Defs: rout, petty theft, violation of curfew, riot, and remaining at scene of a riot.

■

LOS ANGELES CHAPTER RESPONSE
By Leo Branton, Jr., Seymour Mandel, and Ben Margolis

[The Chapter filed an *amicus* brief on the need for release of arrested black people, either on their own recognizance (their promise to show up for legal proceedings) or on low bail.

[The Guild said it had attempted to secure statistical information as to the number of persons allegedly involved in the riot presently in jail, the number charged with felonies and misdemeanors, the number released on bail, and similar facts necessary to give a complete picture of the situation of the incarcerated defendants.]

It has been impossible to obtain such information from any source. It appears in fact that no one knows the answers to these questions because the normal functioning of the jails and the judicial processes have been so overburdened that confusion is the order of the day. . . .

We are dealing here with a situation in which an entire community has been disrupted. The burden that has been placed upon the families of the defendants, upon the counsel to whom they would ordinarily turn for assistance, and upon the courts is so great as to preclude any possibility of protecting the rights of the defendants with that deliberation and care which is essential to a proper representation.

With respect to the ability of the individuals involved to make bail, the deep-seated problem of poverty which was a factor in the riot is an immense obstacle. Add to this the unemployment that has followed the riot, particularly during the period of incarceration, the inability to get paychecks that are due or overdue, the financial problems of the families that have been left without a breadwinner, and the practical impossibility of many of the defendants making bail becomes apparent. It may be urged that private groups are preparing to advance money to post bail. Aside from the fact that long delays are undoubtedly here involved, it would seem clear that a person's availability if he is released on his own recognizance will be as great as if he is released on bail posted by a stranger.

[The Guild brief presented precedents from California and federal law for release on own recognizance, a new remedy for any but the occasional wealthy white criminal defendant. The Guild argued for establishing standards to safeguard the substantive and procedural due process rights of defendants. This brief led to informal conferences and a letter from the chairman of the Court Own Recognizance Committee to the presiding judge, recommending the Guild's proposed procedures. Two hundred copies of the brief were practically snatched from the Guild's table at the State Bar Conference of Delegates, where the Guild's clearly worded resolutions on integration of the Bar, rejected by the Resolutions Committee, were amended and passed.]

PONDERING THE FUTURE: LEN ROSENTHAL, CLAUDIA SHROPSHIRE, AND BEN SMITH
By the Guild Newsletter, *the Editors, and the Subjects*

■

LEN ROSENTHAL

Attorney Leonard H. Rosenthal is truly surprising. He has been a resident of Mississippi and Louisiana since his birth in Mississippi, on January 3, 1940. He went to Mississippi College and Jackson School of Law, and was admitted to the Bar on graduation in 1962. He began practicing as a sole practitioner in Jackson and took civil rights cases from the start.

Len started serving as resident counsel on nearly all Guild cases in Mississippi in the summer of 1964. His landlord kicked him out of his office; a relative chased him with a shotgun; business fell off—but Rosenthal continued to accept Guild cases.

Len's courage is a quiet thing. He does not come on strong as do so many young warriors in the movement. He is not overly outgoing nor

---

"Pondering the Future": Rosenthal from "A Native White Lawyer Struggles for Justice in Mississippi," *Guild Newsletter* (Sept. 1965); Shropshire from *Jet* (July 9, 1964), *Guild Newsletter* (Jan. 1965), and *Guild Newsletter* (Sept. 1965); Smith from "Lawyers in the Great Tradition," by Benjamin Smith, *NLG Practitioner* 24:4 (Fall 1965).

loud-spoken and bold. In fact, he appears quite grim. But, for Len Rosenthal, a white lawyer in his native state, the practice of law is a grim business.

... Certainly the *Newsletter* wishes him and his wife and daughter well.

[The *New York Times* of February 8, 1965, carried an item on the Mississippi Bar Association's approval of a plan for Wall Street firms to send lawyers to Mississippi. This "seemed to reflect an effort to undermine the legal monopoly that the Left-wing Lawyers Guild has had so far in the Mississippi civil rights movement. Sherwood Wise of the Jackson Bar Association said that his group approved of the organized effort to bring lawyers from leading law firms into the state, because it thought that many of the lawyers that had come to Mississippi to help in the civil rights efforts had done more harm than good for all parties concerned. 'If you can keep these zealots off our neck,' Mr. Wise told the bar presidents, 'you will have done Mississippi a great favor.'"]

■

Claudia Shropshire

Claudia Shropshire was born and educated in Detroit, where she has been practicing for nine years. She listened with interest to an offer to be legal counsel for the Council of Federated Organizations (COFO) starting in October, 1964, even though this meant "a definite cut in income" from her position with the Goodman/Crockett firm.

The minute she arrived in Jackson on a Sunday Mrs. Shropshire had to go to work on the cases of eight young people arrested for distributing leaflets on voter registration without a permit, in violation of a city ordinance. Her major work in Mississippi was to provide legal assistance to Negroes seeking to enforce Title 3 of the 1964 Civil Rights Act, which provided for desegregation of public facilities. A second goal was wide distribution of the Guild booklet *Citizen's Guide to the 1964 Civil Rights Act*.

Looking back on her year in Mississippi in January 1966, Mrs. Shropshire said:

People in Detroit think there has been an improvement in civil rights down in Mississippi. This is not so. Only through litigation were we able to get anything accomplished. We challenged the power structure merely to get to the library.... Civil rights has done little for the Negroes in Mississippi. They have to have economic help.

Right now, there is an absolute wall between the races.... The educational setup is particulary bad. Where there is not enough money for one decent integrated system, an attempt is made to have two separate ones, and the result is abysmal.

Claudia Shropshire urged the Guild to pursue its program of neighborhood law offices, started by the Philadelphia chapter twenty-five years ago. "Now let's move back into Watts and similar areas."

∎

Benjamin Smith

[From his address on receiving the Franklin D. Roosevelt Award at the Guild Convention, Nov. 13, 1965.]

I shall hold this honor in trust for all lawyers who place human rights before property rights, who recognize that the real value of this country reposes in the freedom and courage of its people, and not in its awful weapons of destruction and its immense accumulation of capital wealth. . . .

The civil rights lawyer has, through the sheer brilliance of his work and by his total commitment to the rights of man, deeply engaged the national legislature and the judiciary of the several states and of the national government in a tremendous reevaluation of our basic constitutional law. . . .

Lawyers do not make social movements here, but they help to lead them and to give them an historical continuity essential to the story of a people struggling into the future. In this sense the civil rights lawyer, both North and South, has served his country well. Members of this Bar association appear regularly as counsel of record in the most important civil rights cases in this nation. . . .

But what started as a revolution for Negro rights cannot remain only that. It is the first, small opening of the door that leads to a truly constitutional society. Those that protest segregation now denounce the war in Viet Nam that threatens to erase the gains of the Negro revolution. Wars always have as their first victims the rights and the lives of the poor people who fight and pay for them. Our work now, as lawyers, is to preserve, on the one hand, the hard-won gains of the Negro revolt and to extend them to other Negroes and to the poor whites; and, on the other hand, to protect the right of protest against the scourge of war in Viet Nam which is the counter-revolution of our times. Unless we can do this we shall fail.

Those, it is said, who cannot recognize history are condemned to re-live it. We cannot re-live Mississippi 1964—we must enter Oakland in 1965.

As a somewhat down-at-the-heels and slightly battered veteran of the courts of the Fifth Circuit, I say: Do not despair! The goal and the method of achieving a real meaning to the Fourteenth Amendment looked as distant in 1959 and 1960 as do the legal problems of the Peace

Movement today. With the aid of a fearless and tireless civil rights bar, both North and South, we shall prevail.

[On Nov. 12, 1965, Ben Smith appeared amicus for the National Lawyers Guild in federal district court in San Francisco, arguing that the Vietnam Day Committee should be permitted to hold a parade in Oakland.]

WHOSE RIGHTS? WHAT DANGER?
By Michael E. Tigar*

[Excerpts from a review in *Yale Law Journal*; original footnote numbers retained.]

THE LEGACY OF THE CIVIL RIGHTS AND ANTIWAR MOVEMENTS

... The civil rights and free speech cases of the 1950's and 1960's were remarkable because they represented a new vision of federalism, of judicial power, and of the meaning of the Civil War amendments. Almost every expansive Supreme Court opinion on these topics broke new ground on all of these fronts, provided only that the party claiming a federal right was somehow involved in the historic struggle to vindicate the promise of *Brown v. Board of Education*.[19] (Claimants without such an involvement did not uniformly fare well against the competing claims of coordinate branches of the federal government or of the states.)

I consider the proper starting point of this analysis to be *Dombrowski v. Pfister*,[20] decided in 1965. ... The facts are worth recalling. Jim Dombrowski was executive director of the Southern Conference Educational Fund (SCEF). The Louisiana Un-American Activities Committee organized raids, carried out at gunpoint, on the SCEF offices and the homes and law offices of SCEF leaders. Dombrowski, SCEF, and others sued to restrain this sort of conduct, to get back their papers and books, and to inhibit the state authorities from prosecuting them under the Louisiana version of the Smith Act and Communist Control Act.[23]

"Whose Rights? What Danger?" by Michael E. Tigar, excerpted from his review of *Our Endangered Rights: The ACLU Report on Civil Liberties Today*, Norman Dorsen, ed. (New York: Pantheon Books, 1984), appearing in *The Yale Law Journal*. Reprinted by permission of The Yale Law Journal Company and Fred B. Rothman & Company from *The Yale Law Journal*, vol. 94, pp. 970ff.

*B.A. 1962, J.D. 1966, University of California (Berkeley), Raybourne Thompson Centennial Professor of Law, University of Texas. I am grateful for comments and suggestions from my colleagues Douglas Laycock and Lucas A. Powe, Jr., and from my old friend John Mage.

19. 347 U.S. 483 (1954); 349 U.S. 294 (1955).

20. 380 U.S. 479 (1965), *rev'g* 227 F. Supp. 556 (E.D. La. 1964) (three-judge court).

23. While the lawsuit was pending, some of the plaintiffs were indicted under these sedition acts, although they would not have been if Judge Wisdom's restraining order had not been—wrongly, the Supreme Court later said—dissolved.

SCEF and its officers also sued to prevent the Louisiana authorities from transferring the seized records to Senator James Eastland of Mississippi, who had subpoenaed them for use by the Senate Internal Security Subcommittee.[24] ... [T]he three-judge district court ... upheld the laws on their face, and refused to hear evidence on the laws' illegal application.

Justice Brennan, writing for five Justices (Harlan and Clark dissenting, Black and Stewart not sitting) held the challenged provisions of the Louisiana Subversive Activities and Communist Control Laws unconstitutional on their face as overbroad and vague, and remanded the case to the district court to fashion a decree.[25] As for abstention, the Court did not tarry long, for deference to a state court by waiting for it to construe a statute in the first instance is silly when the statute is unconstitutional on any reading. ...

Dombrowski, as one of its wisest critics has put it, led "many litigants" to discern "a major change in federal-state relations."[26] These litigants were doomed to disappointment when in 1971[27] the Court began a retreat from *Dombrowski* that continues to this day.[28]

... In the great debates over the function and power of the Court, *Dombrowski* is a declaration that the Court can decide something important, and that overcoming purported barriers to deciding is not a matter of unprincipled discretion but of closely-argued principle arrayed in the informing light of social conditions.

The historical setting of *Dombrowski* instructs us about the conditions that produce judicial willingness to assert power.[31] Between the

---

24. This aspect of the litigation was mooted by transfer of the records from Louisiana to Mississippi at Eastland's direction, apparently while the lawsuit was pending. My information about the chronology of events is taken largely from 9 CIV. LIBERTIES DOCKET 12–13 (1963); 9 *id.* at 88–89 (1964); 10 *id.* at 30–31 (1964); 10 *id.* at 104 (1965). The Docket is an invaluable resource in revisiting the times of which I am writing. *See also* A KINOY, RIGHTS ON TRIAL: THE ODYSSEY OF A PEOPLE'S LAWYER (1983) (autobiography of leading participant in these struggles).

25. *Dombrowski*, 380 U.S. at 497–98, 496 n.13. ... The equitable principle of noninterference rests upon the theory that a criminal defendant has an adequate remedy at law, by raising the constitutional claim in the criminal case. *See* C. WRIGHT, FEDERAL COURTS § 52A, at 321 (4th ed. 1983). ...

26. *See* C. WRIGHT, *supra* note 25, § 52A, at 322.

27. *See, e.g.*, Younger v. Harris, 401 U.S. 37 (1971).

28. There is a rich and extensive scholarly debate over the meaning of *Dombrowski*. Everybody's favorite is or ought to be Fiss, *Dombrowski*, 86 YALE L. J. 1103 (1977). Douglas Laycock has contributed an important work in Laycock, *Federal Interference with State Prosecutions: The Cases Dombrowski Forgot*, 46 U. CHI. L. REV. 636 (1979). Other commentaries are cited in C. WRIGHT, *supra* note 25, at 320 n.1.

31. Close attention to the constraints of legal ideology is the hallmark of careful judging and an indicium of conscious effort to legitimate a decision by placing it in the context of precedent. Progressive judges and lawyers add to this technical skill a firm appreciation of where the law "must go" if it is to redeem the dominant ideology's promises of freedom and fairness. *See* M. TIGAR, LAW AND THE RISE OF CAPITALISM 20–23 (1977).

filing of the *Dombrowski* appellants' jurisdictional statement in early spring of 1964 and oral argument in January of 1965, the nation had witnessed Freedom Summer—a concentrated effort by civil rights organizations in Mississippi to reform educational opportunities for blacks, register black voters, and unseat the regular Mississippi Democrats at the Democratic Party convention in Atlantic City. During that summer in Mississippi, three civil rights workers were murdered by Klan agents, four were shot and wounded, fifty-two beaten severely enough to warrant reports to the authorities. Two hundred and fifty civil rights workers were arrested by Mississippi authorities. Thirteen black churches were burned to the ground. Seventeen other buildings used by civil rights groups were damaged by arson fires or bombs. Ten automobiles were damaged or destroyed, and there were an additional seven bombings that resulted in no property damage or injury.[32] . . . These events were neither unprecedented nor localized. Leafing through the pages of the *Race Relations Law Reporter* and the Civil Liberties Docket for 1963 through 1965[33] freshens one's recollection.

. . . In sum, the officers of government of the former Confederacy were illegitimate in every juridical sense save only that concerned with their parents' marital status. Despite the unanimous decision in *Brown v. Board of Education,* and the dozens of decrees applying its teaching to particular school systems,[39] segregation of public education was still the rule. Black voters were systematically disenfranchised, and when the overtly racist registration statutes fell before the first wave of civil rights suits, new and ostensibly neutral barriers were erected.[40] These barriers in turn were attacked, with consequent delay in admitting blacks to the political process.

. . . Of course, even had many blacks then registered, the promise of fair representation contained in *Baker v. Carr*[43] and its progeny would not soon be redeemed.

The compelling force of these facts led the great judges of the South —Wisdom, Tuttle, Rives, Johnson, Wright, and others—to their often-repeated conclusion that federal equity power was virtually the only constitutionally based authority in the former Confederacy. . . . I have in mind the desultory performance of the executive branch, even as late as

---

32. N.Y. Times, Aug. 20, 1964, at A1, col. 2. For much of the factual information that follows, I have referred to the Civil Liberties Docket, the Race Relations Law Reporter, and the scripts of my weekly radio program, Mississippi Report, aired over Pacifica Radio stations in the summer of 1964.

33. Race Relations Law Reporter was published by Vanderbilt Law School during this period.

39. These cases are collected in the issues of the Civil Liberties Docket and Race Relations Law Reporter for this period.

40. *See, e.g.,* United States v. Louisiana, 225 F. Supp. 353 (E.D. La. 1963), *aff'd,* 380 U.S. 145 (1965) (striking down ostensibly neutral voter registration provisions).

43. 369 U.S. 186 (1962).

the 1964 Mississippi Freedom Summer. Attorney General Kennedy had no civil rights program and tended to respond to the growing crisis as a series of isolated events, each of which could be "handled" by the Camelot team.[46] Two striking examples deserve mention. When three civil rights workers disappeared on a trip to investigate the burning of a black church, Attorney General Kennedy was reported in the press as having said the federal government lacks power to take "preventive police action" in Mississippi (or, presumably, elsewhere in the South) to aid black citizens seeking to exercise the rights of citizenship. His words brought forth a letter, signed by five members of the Harvard law faculty, terming Kennedy's remark a "facile pronouncement" and pointing to statutes dating nearly to the dawn of the Republic that gave the executive branch precisely such power. The second telling episode was the Democratic party's unedifying compromise with the racist and segregationist Democrats of Mississippi at the 1964 convention in Atlantic City.

Despite calls from members of Congress, however, the Administration intervened only gradually in the South, never becoming a full partner with the courageous and overburdened federal judges. The consequences of inaction included the burnings, bombings, beatings, and deaths. For the civil rights leaders and their lawyers, executive inaction heightened a perceived need for broad equitable relief. . . .

The "judicial era" of *Dombrowski* "was" because courageous judges perceived an imperative need for federal judicial intervention. *Dombrowski* was faithful to the course of decision from *Brown* in 1954 to 1966, when the Court began at last to redeem the promise of the Civil War amendments;[51] it also acknowledged that the movement contending for rights needed at least as much protection as the rights themselves. When, on February 1, 1960, the civil rights movement—in the hands of a new generation—burst out of the courthouses and entered a new phase of direct action,[52] the Court's decisions kept pace while the overworked judges of the Fifth Circuit filled up the interstices with decisions striking at every manner of state interference.

In a string of cases, . . . *Edwards*,[53] *Lombard*,[54] *Hamm*,[55] *Barr*,[56]

---

46. V. NAVASKY, KENNEDY JUSTICE 96–155 (1970).

51. *See generally* Kinoy, *The Constitutional Right of Negro Freedom*, 21 RUTGERS L. REV. 387 (1967) (discussing failure to define substantive rights created by the wartime amendments, and national duty to do so).

52. The first sit-in was February 1, 1960. *See* NATIONAL ADVISORY COMMISSION ON CIVIL DISORDERS, REPORT 226–28 (Bantam ed. 1968) [hereinafter cited as KERNER REPORT].

53. Edwards v. South Carolina, 372 U.S. 229 (1963). I know my list is selective. For a broader, deeper view, see H. KALVEN, THE NEGRO AND THE FIRST AMENDMENT (1966).

54. Lombard v. Louisiana, 373 U.S. 267 (1963).

55. Hamm v. City of Rock Hill, 379 U.S. 306 (1964).

56. Barr v. City of Columbia, 378 U.S. 146 (1964).

Gibson,[57] *Bates*,[58] *Button*,[59] and *Bouie*,[60] the Court recognized that defense of the principles of *Brown* required defense of Black self-organization. These cases not only announced results and rules, but implicitly conceded that in the long run the federal courts could not do this job alone. Seen in this context, *Dombrowski* announced a rule that was as exceptional as the situation it confronted. And one need not have been surprised that in other, less demanding, contexts, a majority of justices could not be summoned to approve a like interference with state procedures for adjudicating claims, or a like skepticism towards the claims of red-baiters. For example, the Court in 1961 had affirmed by a narrow majority the contempt of Congress conviction of SCEF leader Carl Braden for refusing to answer questions concerning anti-House Committee on Un-American Activities organizing.[61] . . . Already by 1964, the majority had begun to waver. *Hamm v. City of Rock Hill*[62] set aside sit-in trespass convictions by a vote of 5 to 4. The basis for Justice Clark's opinion was that the Civil Rights Act of 1964 had abated the prosecutions. This suggested that the occasion for taking to the street was now sharply reduced, given the availability of federal civil remedies for discrimination.

In 1966, it was 5 to 4 the other way, as the Court "stepped back" in *Adderley v. Florida*[63] and, through Justice Black, affirmed trespass convictions that arose from a sit-in at a jail to protest alleged unlawful arrests of civil rights activists. . . . Justice Douglas, writing in dissent, . . . pointed out that jails have traditionally symbolized arbitrary power, and mentioned the Tower of London and the Bastille.[64]

The *Adderley* majority's deference to the state's statute, judicial process, and law enforcement officers, and Black's 1971 majority opinion in *Younger v. Harris*[65] rest on premises that undercut the language, if not the central meaning, of *Dombrowski*. The events that spawned this new-found deference to the state police, courts, and legislatures in First Amendment cases are easy to identify. Racial unrest had led to disorder in the cities and on the campuses of the North.[66] . . . So, despite the

---

57. Gibson v. Florida Legislative Investigation Comm., 372 U.S. 539 (1963).
58. Bates v. City of Little Rock, 361 U.S. 516 (1960).
59. NAACP v. Button, 371 U.S. 415 (1963).
60. Bouie v. City of Columbia, 378 U.S. 347 (1964).
61. Braden v. United States, 365 U.S. 431 (1961).
62. 379 U.S. 306 (1964).
63. 385 U.S. 39 (1966). The phrase is taken from the title of Kipperman, *Civil Rights at Armageddon—The Supreme Court Steps Back*: Adderley v. Florida, 3 LAW IN TRANS. Q. 219 (1966).
64. 385 U.S. at 49 (Douglas, J., dissenting).
65. 401 U.S. 37 (1971).
66. *See* Tigar, *New Frontiers* (Book Review), 78 Yale L. J. at 898–901; Symposium, *Student Rights and Campus Rules*, 54 CALIF. L. REV. 1 (1966).

findings of a distinguished commission in 1968 that American society—North and South—was pervaded with white racism [69] fifteen years after *Brown,* the Court's majority began to recede from the territory it had staked out before 1966. This limited retreat, marked by deep concern with the tactics of some civil rights activists, took place at a time when the civil rights movement itself was riven with controversy over issues of violence, disobedience to law, and the prospect of continued black-white cooperation. The anti-war movement rose, and in its turn faced like disputes.

Some at the center did not abandon their posts: Brennan, Marshall, Douglas, and Skelly Wright spring to mind. But the profound alteration in perceptions of protest and protesters strengthened the hand of the right, and counseled its adherents to regard *Dombrowski,* not as the redemption of a constitutional promise about federalism, but as an extraordinary response to an exceptional and concluded episode. Those who turned away from liberty had been at best its summer soldiers.

The lawyers whose work had brought *Dombrowski* to the Court failed, in some measure, to see this change coming. [T]hey brought affirmative suits in great numbers. These cases mostly foundered.[72] They ... sought to combine the attitude of the early affirmative cases brought in the wake of *Brown* with a confident certainty that *Dombrowski* would be read for all that it might mean. . . . [T]hese lawyers . . . were too confident that . . . most federal judges could survive the shocks of the late 1960's and still pursue the goal of defending the protest and dissent that many began to perceive as imperiling established order.

True, even a relatively conservative Court will respond to genuine constitutional crisis by upholding its own authority: Witness the unanimous decision that President Nixon had to surrender the tapes.[75] Most often, however, the Court has done its great constitutional work in tacit recognition of significant political forces. These forces need not be majorities, but they must at least command support among those with important roles in defining the dominant legal ideology of a particular time.

This analysis suggests that . . . perhaps civil libertarians should have

---

69. KERNER REPORT, *supra* note 52, *passim.*

72. These suits sought every kind of result from receiverships over public institutions to injunctions against prosecutions under laws enforced by states whose policies had not been sullied by the consistent course of conduct that marked the Southern authorities. *See* C. WRIGHT, *supra* note 25, § 52A, at 322-23. I recall the debates at the time over the use of what some perceived as the wonder-working power of *Dombrowski.* Nothing I say here is intended to cast aspersions on Arthur Kinoy, who argued *Dombrowski* in the Court. Arthur and I have disagreed at times over the years, but I remain an unstinting admirer.

75. United States v. Nixon, 418 U.S. 683 (1974).

pressed more for favorable interpretations of state constitutions, which state courts are free to construe as conferring more protection than the federal Constitution.[76]

Dombrowski reminds us of an era that "was" and "can be" because its promise will likely be redeemed only when a movement for change again confronts consistent and implacably lawless hostility, and when judges are willing to perceive what is happening and to act.

There is additional support for this view in the Court's treatment of the Selective Service cases during the Vietnam War, as well as in the eventual reaction of the lower federal courts.[79] The Court, while refusing to confront the issue of the war's legality under international and domestic law,[80] and preinduction judical review in one important case,[81] upheld most registrant challenges in a series of significant decisions. These decisions relied upon a principled theory of judical review and commanded the votes even of those who were later to join the majority in *Younger* and its progeny.[82] In the lower federal courts, the hostility to Selective Service overreaching was even more apparent, as median sentences and conviction rates steadily declined and opinions insisted sharply that the system obey its own rules and honor constitutional commands. . . .

If this analysis is correct, then a study of judicial power in the abstract, or as a matter of the structure of the constitution, does not tell us about the tasks ahead for those who wish to protect and extend democratic rights. We ought to be asking from whence may come the next great movement that will underscore the need for democratic rights. . . . It may be that when such a time comes, the institutions of judicial power will have been so far corrupted and will have committed themselves so deeply to defending power and privilege that the era that "was" cannot then be. That is a question one might profitably raise. . . .

---

76. *See, e.g.,* Pruneyard Shopping Center v. Robins, 447 U.S. 74 (1980) (state may provide more expansive individual liberties in its constitution, not inconsistent with those conferred by federal Constitution); remarks of Justice Brennan, remarks of Judge Wright [on file with the author].

79. For details about this period, including the statistics on the number of prosecutions and the declining rate of convictions and declining median sentence, see the issues of the Selective Service Law Reporter.

80. *See, e.g.,* Mora v. McNamara, 389 U.S. 934, 935 (1967) (Stewart & Douglas, JJ., separately dissenting from denial of cert.).

81. Clark v. Gabriel, 393 U.S. 256 (1968).

82. I have in mind Breen v. Selective Service Board, 396 U.S. 460 (1970) (preventing delinquent induction of student protester who had obtained valid deferment); Gutknecht v. United States, 396 U.S. 295 (1970) (unanimous decision—though different justices had different rationales—striking down delinquency regulations); McKart v. United States, 395 U.S. 185, 192–201 (1969) (excusing failure to exhaust administrative remedies). *See generally* Symposium, *Selective Service* 1970, 17 UCLA L. Rev. 893 (1970). *But see* Asimow, *Introduction,* 17 UCLA L. Rev. 893, 898 (1970) (in protecting registrants court offered "muddy and confusing" rationale for judicial review).

FOURTEEN

Representing "Hell, No! We Won't Go!" (1965-1968)

IN JANUARY 1965, the Guild Executive Board resolved that the United States should withdraw from the war in Vietnam, that the Geneva Conference should be reconvened, and that the Guild should publicize these conclusions. When it did so, the Office of Public Services of the State Department and the Assistant Secretary of Defense promptly took issue with the resolution.

By the time the Guild held its Convention in November 1965, in San Francisco, peace and poverty had joined civil rights as Guild priorities. After the convention panel on "World Peace Through Law," a few lawyers got together to discuss their problems in representing an increasing number of young men who refused to be inducted into the army but resisted going to jail for their beliefs. The Publications Committee soon issued a supplement on Conscientious Objections to War to the *Civil Rights Handbook*, stemming from the work of J. B. Tietz and the Central Committee for Conscientious Objectors.

In March 1966, the Guild's International Law Committee told the press that the ABA resolution supporting the U.S. position in Vietnam was "a miniscule analysis consisting of a distorted excerpting of a few phrases, out of context, from Articles 51 and 52 of the United Nations Charter, and depends upon a total disregard of the text of the SEATO Treaty." The Committee asked Senator Fulbright to call Robert Kenny as a witness to rebut the ABA resolution. In January 1967, the International Law Committee issued a long report on American Foreign Policy and the Rule of Law, concluding that the United States had followed a consistent policy since 1946 of violating the fundamental agreements reached in the Charter and other post-war documents.

In 1967, the Guild published its third book, *The New Draft Law: A Manual for Lawyers and Counselors*, which went through six editions by 1971, used by lawyers, counselors, and draft refusers from coast to coast seeking their way through the maze that was the Selective Service System, depicted on the *Manual*'s back cover (see Figure 2).

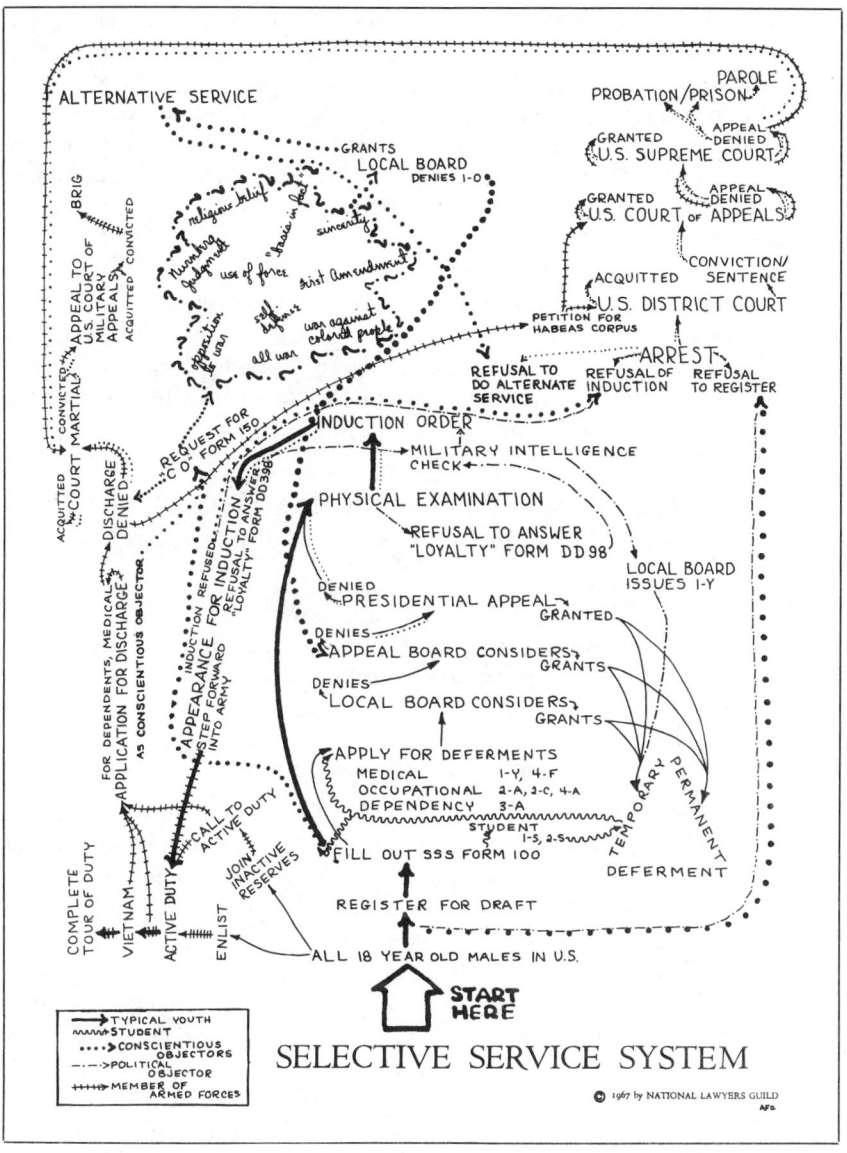

Figure 2.

© 1967 by National Lawyers Guild. Figure by Ann Fagan Ginger.

As Guild chapters, lawyers, and national office learned draft law, they quickly shared it with all interested parties, including counselors who became perhaps the first large generation of "legal workers." As a result of mass indictments of sixty-five young men in San Francisco, instead of the usual one or two a week in other metropolitan centers, the need for the effective assistance of counsel was brought into urgent focus. Leading Guild members, experienced and newcomers, joined forces to build an outstanding Selective Service Panel, proudly described by panel members below.

Mary Kaufman, founding Guild member from New York, used her experience as a prosecutor in the Nuremberg trials of industrialists after World War II to enlarge the approach to the individual's duty in light of United States action in Vietnam, in the selection below, followed by San Francisco Guild lawyer Paul Harris' summary of the Guild's role in that illegal war seen from the vantage point of U.S. foreign policy in 1980.

THE CONSTITUTIONAL RIGHT TO OBJECT TO WAR
By the Civil Liberties Docket *and* The New Draft Law

[In February 1967, the *Civil Liberties Docket* summed up the latest thinking of war resisters and their lawyers, starting with conscientious objector (CO) status, but moving quickly to non-religious objectors to the Vietnam War, and to the rights of militant Negro youth (deleted here, but covered in E. A. Dawley, below).]

OPPOSITION TO WAR IN ANY FORM

Registrants seeking CO status must prove that they are opposed to participation in war in any form, under the present statute. Prof. Malcolm Sharp has taken an interesting look at the definition of "war" and "war in any form" in [the Selective Service law], concluding that the word and phrase may not include "civil war" or even "undeclared war" (*Lawyers Guild Practitioner* 25:4 [Fall 1966]).

Some registrants take the position that they are entitled to CO status because they are opposed to all nuclear wars, which they term a form of mass suicide; that any war in which the U.S. engages may become a nuclear war; that they are therefore opposed to participation in any present or future war in which the U.S. may engage, regardless of their attitude about prior wars. They also maintain that the use of arms or "force" in self-defense is unrelated to the question of opposition to par-

---

"The Constitutional Right to Object to War" from "Opposition to War in any Form," *Civil Liberties Docket* 13 special issue (Feb. 1967); FBI interview in *The New Draft Law: A Manual for Lawyers and Counselors*, by Ann Fagan Ginger (Berkeley: National Lawyers Guild, 1969), pp. 235:85b–:85c.

ticipation in war. By extension, they maintain they are COs despite their willingness to use force to defend the Negro community from racists, for example.

Some registrants explain that they do not believe the U.S. will be attacked during the period of their eligibility for military service. "But if the U.S. were attacked in a non-nuclear war, by an unjustified power, and we came to believe we had a conscientious duty to participate in the defense of the U.S., we would immediately ask to have our draft status changed, and the armed services would have lost nothing by letting us have 1-0 status in the interim."

NON-RELIGIOUS OPPOSITION TO ONE WAR

Attorneys new to Selective Service law are quickly frustrated by the wording of the Act and the Regulations, and the fact that the Service is not amenable to the protections of the Administrative Procedure Act. The philosophical and religious tests on which the CO exemption is based, and the imprecise administrative procedures under which CO status is granted or denied, may nonetheless lead to prosecutions for violation of federal criminal law. Due process requires something more than vague and indefinite standards for conduct which may be prosecuted; the statute and regulations were framed narrowly and on the wrong basis.

Specifically, they maintain that the CO exemption to the draft was originally designed by Quakers and members of other peace churches to protect their members from being forced to violate their religious scruples against participation in war. The exemption was narrowly drawn and the procedures were designed to test "sincerity" of "religious belief," a field in which Congress does not customarily legislate (because of the First Amendment).

According to this view, non-religious men whose whole reason for opposition to war is "political, economic, or based on a purely personal moral code," should nonetheless file form 150 to notify the boards of their conscientious opposition to participation in war and to offer to do alternative service. [So should] men opposed to fighting in the current war in Vietnam, and equally opposed to fighting in Thailand, Cambodia, China, Cuba, the Dominican Republic, and similar places, but willing to fight on U.S. soil in defense of the U.S., or to use armed force to defend the people of Watts or Delano. [This is an era in which] the combined strands of western religion and eastern philosophy affect more American youth each year; the lines between "religious belief" and "philosophy," "morality," "human necessity," "economics," and "the new politics" have become even more blurred than at the time of *Seeger*.

[After discussing five elements of First Amendment rights (under the establishment clause, free exercise, guarantees of free speech, press, association, and assembly), the authors cited recent cases maintaining that:]

(1) Any preference for "believers in a Supreme Being" over non-believers violates equal protection; (2) Any denial of administrative appeals to pacifist non-believers, or to persons who become pacifists at a late stage in the Selective Service process, violates equal protection and the due process clause; (3) Segregation in local draft boards constitutes denial of due process and equal protection voiding induction orders of Negro registrants; (4) The due process requirements in Amendments Four, Five, Six, Seven, and Eight apply to all selective service proceedings, and Congress cannot authorize a system which denies registrants the right to counsel, to a hearing, to bring witnesses, to an accurate transcript of the hearing, or the right to investigation by an impartial body (not the FBI).

[Guild lawyers faced reports of FBI agents concerning the sincerity of their clients' claims of conscientious objection to war. One FBI agent conducting a Department of Justice investigation in 1967 asked a CO claimant's former employer to compare the registrant's religiosity with that of the average person, suggesting these guidelines: Does he attend church once or twice a day? Does he carry a Bible? Does he quote the Bible? The interview occurred long after the Supreme Court, in an opinion by Justice Tom Clark, had laid to rest the old, narrow, Quakers-only definition of a CO, in *Seeger v. United States,* 380 U.S. 163 (1965).]

THE GUILD LEARNS, TEACHES, AND ORGANIZES DRAFT LAW
By the Editors

The national office of the Guild and chapters throughout the country began to get calls for help from people opposing the draft and the Vietnam war. They responded by running draft workshops for attorneys, law students, and non-lawyer draft counselors where new ideas and tactics were proposed, debated, discarded, and integrated into draft law. Each meeting of the National Executive Board was accompanied by a session on draft law for lawyers in the host city, sharing experiences with NEB members from around the country. The San Francisco-Bay Area and Los Angeles chapters were extremely active. The *Guild Practitioner* published a special issue on selective service in the summer of 1967, summarizing speeches at a recent Bay Area draft workshop, including that of draft law specialist William G. Smith of Los Angeles, who discussed the lawyers and the classification process. Los Angeles lawyer

Ben Margolis and Oakland lawyer E. A. Dawley contributed their practice and philosophy at that workshop, excerpted below.

By November 1968, the Southern California Chapters of the Guild were ready to complain to the Board of Governors of the state Bar that the functions of Government Appeal Agents of the Selective Service System involved an important question of conflict of interest contrary to the Canons of Legal Ethics. The Guild convinced the Bar. The Board of Governors sent out a communication on this problem to all members of the California Bar serving as Government Appeal Agents of the SSS.

TRYING A CASE UNDER THE SELECTIVE SERVICE LAW
By Ben Margolis

Perhaps the best way I can tell you about trying a case under the Selective Service Law is to describe two cases we handled recently involving two young Negro men, both under 21. Both were born in the South, but had lived in the Los Angeles area for a number of years.

We decided the best thing we could do [in the short time before trial] was subpoena all the records and all the possible witnesses. We disregarded the advice that this couldn't be done, and it worked. We demanded the production, not only of the individual files of our clients, but every piece of paper from the files of the draft board and of the appeals board that in any way mentioned or related to these two defendants. Some of them turned out to be very valuable indeed.

We subpoenaed every member of the draft board, every member of the appeals board, the secretary of the board, and the Army major who had been in charge for 20 years of the Selective Service processes in Southern California. Then we got the minutes of the local board. We found a very interesting thing: the draft board had sat six and a half hours, and in that period had considered more than 645 cases. We also established that two cases had involved conscientious objector hearings, each of which had taken about an hour. So that in four and a half hours, they had considered 643 cases, one of which was our client's.

Our client had also taken an appeal, so we got into the record on appeal. This summary recognized this as being a hardship dependency appeal, and the form contained a number of questions. We subpoenaed the minutes of the appeal board and learned that the appeal board sat for two hours, in which time it decided 867 cases, one every ten or eleven seconds. They didn't take a deep breath. They didn't leave the room— they all had good kidneys. *One every ten or eleven seconds.*

"Trying a Case under the Selective Service Law," by Ben Margolis, *NLG Practitioner* 26:3 (Summer 1967).

We had previously established what they claimed to be their ordinary procedure in these cases. They not only read the summary, but they read the record. They then discussed it, and after they discussed it, they took a vote in which each one individually expressed his opinion.

As far as the summary was concerned in this case, it wouldn't have taken them very long to read it. But we had established, through the series of questions previously mentioned, that ordinarily if the information is inadequate, the appeal board asks for additional information because they want to be fair and just. They admitted that in order to decide a hardship case, you had to know how much the young man was making, how much he was contributing, what kind of job he was working on, what, if any, earnings his parents had under the circumstances. They didn't have any of this information when they made the decision in the ten or eleven seconds that were allotted.

Incidentally, you can have a lot of fun on these things. These men are distinguished citizens. One of the three men was the former head of the Bureau of Internal Revenue, a very prominent, distinguished and able lawyer in Los Angeles. We asked one of the men, who'd been on the board seven years, "What is II-A?" and he said, "I don't know." The fact of the matter is that they *don't* know. They don't know what they're doing. The whole procedure from beginning to end was a sham.

In the first case the judge gave a directed verdict of acquittal because the government's own records showed the defendant had a dependent child, which entitled him to a III-A deferment. In the second case, tried without a jury, the judge convicted. Since the defendant failed to appear for sentencing, the case at this time is not being appealed.

SPECIAL PROBLEMS OF BLACK DRAFTEES
By E. A. Dawley

BLACK DRAFTEES HAVE NO PROBLEMS, AS SUCH

My controversial proposition and the one in need of support is that the interests of selective service and black draftees do not conflict.

Negroes, who comprise only 10 percent of the population, constitute over 17 percent of the armed forces and 22.4 percent of combat deaths, after 70 percent of those examined (volunteers and draftees) are rejected because of poor education and health. The percentage of Negroes reenlisting is much higher than that of whites; 45.7 percent of Negro servicemen reenlist for additional tours of duty in Vietnam as compared to 17 percent of white servicemen. The percentage of blacks volunteering

---

"Special Problems of Black Draftees," by E. A. Dawley, *NLG Practitioner* 26:3 (Summer 1967).

for initial entry in the military service is three times that of whites. For many Negroes the Army, even with the risk of death, is preferable to the conditions of civilian life, a testimonial to either the U.S. Army or to the deplorable conditions in civilian life for Negroes. For many blacks, military service affords every ingredient of the American dream that the civil rights movement sought for him and the peace movement promises: a reliable income, increased standard of living, prestige, authority, respect, appreciation, recognition, education, recreation, travel, and, all things considered, greater life expectancy.

Because of identity of interest, claimed legal issues, e.g., the denial of due process when a Negro is drafted by a board from which Negroes were improperly excluded, are abstract and not likely to be raised by most black draftees. It might in fact constitute racial and class discrimination in violation of the 14th Amendment to grant deferments to college students, most of whom are affluent white middle class, which results in more Negroes being drafted. But entry into, and not exclusion from, the armed forces solves the black draftee's problem of poverty and ignorance for which his country is responsible.

BLACK RESISTERS HAVE NO PROBLEMS, AS SUCH

It is arguable that conscientious objector status should be automatically granted to any black draftee who claims it; the injustices inflicted on him by his countrymen having failed to provoke him to kill any of them, the sincerity of his dedication to non-violence should be beyond question. Because a draft board or court will be reluctant to expressly base its decision on such a brutally truthful and valid argument, the black draftee should also make the conventional articulation of the conscientious objector position.

The black resister to the draft no doubt may have problems, but they do not flow specifically from his color or his draft status. Such problems as not knowing his rights, not having money to enforce them, or not having sufficient education to exploit his opportunities and articulate his views, may be more frequently faced by the reluctant Negro draftee, but there are thousands of white draftees and black civilians equally disadvantaged.

The number of black draftees opposed to the draft are considerable and should not be underestimated. These numbers are increasing, are likely to accelerate with substantial increases in Vietnam casualties, and are likely to be overwhelming should there be casualties of the magnitude that would probably occur in a war with China. The influential militant Negro leaders' opposition to the draft and the war will also contribute to the increase of opposition by black draftees. Nor should one overlook the number of black soldiers who resist participation in military policies and practices in Vietnam.

IS THERE A "NEGRO" POSITION ON WAR AND PEACE?

Is the Negro pro-war and anti-peace? I recall the widespread and long-held belief of many Negro leaders and many of the rank and file that wars and the Negro's participation in them advances his welfare. This belief is not without substantial factual support. Most of the Negro's advancement has occurred during periods of war, and he has suffered his greatest setbacks and slowest advancement in peacetime. The white man seems able to exhibit more brotherhood towards him when engaged in the slaughter of others. (The same is true of the status of women.) For many years the Negro, with the aid of many of the same liberals and radicals now in the peace and civil rights movements, fought to obtain his acceptance in the armed forces and removal of discriminatory policies and practices that excluded him. The reluctance to accept the conclusion that the Negro is pro-war, especially since most Americans are peace-loving, led me, perhaps for the first time, to seriously ask: What is the peace movement? What is the war movement? What is the civil rights movement? What is the relationship between the three? Once these inquiries are made, many other disturbing questions arise, only a few of which can be stated here.

THE THEORY OF SYMBIOTIC MOVEMENTS

If making the Negro affluent and extending his opportunities will make him more willing to fight for his country, it is a war measure. However, comparing the affluence of the white middle class youth and his unwillingness to fight to the poverty of the Negro and his willingness to fight, can't we conclude that the more one has to fight for, the less willing he is to fight for it, and the less one has to fight for, the more willing he is to fight? Therefore, is it not true that improving the condition of the Negro is a peace measure?

Is it pro- or anti-civil rights, peace, or war to urge Negro youth *not* to enter the military service, resulting in their loss of employment and return to starvation, in their failing to gain knowledge of warfare needed to fight in their home ghettos, losing veterans benefits, going to prison, losing future job opportunities, giving whites an excuse for exterminating them, and for denying their friends and relatives opportunity because of their unpatriotic stand, while whites are entering the service, learning warfare to be used against them, and obtaining all the service and veteran benefits. Are riots pro- or anti-war, peace, or civil rights? If they tend to direct efforts from the war to the ghetto, are they not a peace measure? If they gain additional opportunities for the Negro, are they not pro civil rights? If they are violent can they be pro peace?

Do military expenditures represent a diversion of money from poverty programs and thus are anti-civil rights? Or are they pro-civil rights in that they maintain the war machine that benefits Negroes? Do not most members of the peace movement enjoy the fruits of war prosperity?

WHAT IS THE SHOOTING ALL ABOUT?

Is it possible that the real question is not whether we are for peace, war, or civil rights, or all of them, but who is going to pay for them? May it be that some Negroes see America's answer to be that the Negro, who can least afford it, will pay more than his share for all three? That he will pay for the war with his life, for peace with unemployment and starvation, and for civil rights with humiliation, imprisonment, or death while rebelliously flinging the fiery torch of liberty. May this not explain the birth of the Black Power movement?

CLOSING THE CURTAIN

The hippies, because they cannot stop the world, have gotten off it and now sit in the audience watching the show. Their letter of resignation contains some ideas about every action creating a reaction, that therefore any efforts they might make merely contribute to the revolting energy, and that besides they found it difficult to understand their fellow actors or think while dizzy, turning somersaults, flipping, and falling. One hopes that they will return with new insights when they have rested and been able to observe the show with steady vision and clear heads. Meanwhile, the element of suspense that pervades and sustains the excitement is the point at which the great Director in the Pentagon will suddenly bring down the curtain of nuclear war, destroying the theater, actors, black draftees, hippies, interesting questions, and all. Good actors know and are concerned with more than just their own roles, but know and sympathize with the roles of every other actor. They are also familiar with the entire script and how the play ends. A bad play is sometimes saved when good actors and the critics join to rewrite the script and recast the play. Such plays are sometimes given happy endings.

FORMATION OF THE SAN FRANCISCO SELECTIVE SERVICE PANEL
By the Panel

The San Francisco Selective Service Panel originated when a member of the Bar approached the judge in charge of the Criminal Calendar

---

"Formation of the San Francisco Selective Service Panel," by the Panel, *NLG Practitioner* 27:1 (Winter 1968).

of the U.S. District Court for Northern California and pointed out that (1) there were lawyers capable of providing an adequate defense in Selective Service prosecutions, without fee, and (2) many young defendants charged with such a crime, but not knowing of the availability of these lawyers, would be pleading guilty because they had no means to employ a lawyer, did not realize that there were any defenses available to them, or did not know any way to get in contact with lawyers who would be sympathetic to or understand their position.

Judge Oliver Carter indicated he had already become concerned about this problem, and realized that the lawyers available for appointment lacked the expertise to satisfy the constitutional requirement of effective counsel. He therefore offered, if presented with a list of lawyers willing to serve in such a capacity, to appoint lawyers from that panel in Selective Service cases wherever the defendant met the requirements of the Criminal Justice Act. (This appointment carries with it the payment of a minimum fee under the Act.)

Every lawyer who was then, or had been, acting in draft cases was approached to get his cooperation in accepting appointments. Within two or three weeks Judge Carter was furnished with a list of 50 attorneys, and now, after two months, the panel contains over 80 trial lawyers. In addition, about 15 lawyers agreed to do research, briefing, and ancillary work. The panel is an interesting combination of young and old lawyers. Fifty percent have practiced less than five years, 25 percent less than two years.

The San Francisco experience demonstrates that, given a small core of experienced Selective Service lawyers, it is possible with collective work on motions, exchange of legal memoranda, holding of seminars, and consultation between the experienced and inexperienced lawyers, to obtain many lawyers competent on draft law. In all instances the lawyers have received a great deal more from the panel than they gave, including use of the panel library of briefs and unreported decisions from this area and from all over the country, which is more than any single law firm has at its disposal.

Soon after its establishment the San Francisco Panel felt the need to organize committees to:

1. Prepare joint pretrial motions, including discovery and jury challenges.
2. Begin to prepare on all legal questions expected at trial, and on trial tactics; and to plan all-day seminars.
3. Prepare a check list on SSS Regulations and due process issues for trial lawyers and to go over the SSS file in each case, to find what the trial lawyer might have missed.

4. Advise men who have not yet reached the indictment stage, and hopefully, even the induction stage.
5. Deal with cases of men in the military (AWOL), habeas corpus, and refusal of orders.

The panel began holding regular meetings and publishing a bulletin.

The panel has decided to set up teams of a more and a less experienced lawyer and, it is hoped, also a law student. The panel is also seeking the cooperation and assistance of law professors, and has found some who will act as trial counsel, and others who will do research and brief work.

The San Francisco panel has concluded, because of the large number of prosecutions involved and the need for collective legal work and the exchange of ideas, briefs, forms and memoranda, that the only possible organizational form to meet the problem is the development of Selective Service panels in every district court.

THE INDIVIDUAL'S DUTY UNDER THE LAW OF NÜRNBERG
By Mary Kaufman

Some twenty years ago a world horrified by the barbarities of the Nazi regime and in the terrifying glare of the atom bomb's fire fashioned the Nürnberg principles in the hope that those who used military might for conquest might be deterred by the threat of punishment.

Nürnberg defined three categories of crimes and made them crimes under international law: the crime against peace, war crimes, and crimes against humanity. The relevant principle of Nürnberg is the obligation of the individual to refuse to commit an act that he knows is a crime under international law, even if he is ordered to do so by the laws of his country or the command of his government. The individual's international duties transcend his national obligation of obedience. If a nation engages in an illegal war or in war crimes and crimes against humanity, each of its citizens who is aware of the violation is under the obligation to disobey the command and to refrain from this illegal conduct.

This law was stated in the London Agreement and Charter under which the major Nazi war criminals were tried, as it was construed by the International Military Tribunal, as it was stated by the United Nations General Assembly after the trial in a resolution unanimously adopted affirming the principles of the London Agreement and Charter

---

"The Individual's Duty under the Law of Nürnberg," by Mary Kaufman, *NLG Practitioner*, special issue on Nuremberg, 27:1 (Winter 1968).

and the Tribunal's judgment as principles of international law, and as these principles were defined by the International Law Commission.

Even while the Nürnberg principles were being fashioned, the seeds of our foreign policy of cold and hot war were planted and made known in unmistakable terms to the world by our use of the atomic bomb on the Japanese people—a use we would not have dared to make on a people with whom white America could racially identify.

The Nürnberg principles failed to act as the hoped-for deterrent. Today these principles are being raised by men and women as a symbol of their conscience, an affirmative statement of the responsibility of the individual to himself, to the people of this country, and to the world; they are being invoked in protest against the inhumanity of the war in Vietnam to justify refusal to obey laws that aid in the prosecution of that war.

In essence, what the young men who say "No" on the basis of Nürnberg, and those who join them in public complicity, seek to do is to embody the Nürnberg principles in the principles of our national law and to make them the operative rules of this time.

It is our task as lawyers to help in the radical development of the rules of law to support the effective utilization of the Nürnberg principles. We cannot be fettered by archaic precedents applicable to other times and conditions. We must unfreeze them, discard what is inhumane in them, and use in creative fashion those parts that serve the interests of mankind. As was said concerning the First Amendment, we cannot define the limits of the Nürnberg principles by their application to the conditions of that time....

As lawyers we must give legal validity to this moral "No." We have precedent for effectuating change through civil disobedience when the laws are unjust and violate higher laws.

Some of the significant questions raised by the application of the principles in our courts were framed by Justice Douglas in his dissent to the denial of certiorari in *Mitchell v. U.S.* (1967) 386 US 972. There the claim was made in support of Mitchell's refusal to be drafted that our war in Vietnam was a war of aggression in violation of our treaty obligations, especially the London Agreement, described there as a treaty. Douglas pointed to the assurance given by Justice Jackson, the U.S. prosecutor at Nürnberg, that "if certain facts in violation of treaties are crimes they are crimes whether the U.S. does them or whether Germany does them and that we are not prepared to lay down a rule of criminal conduct against others which we would not be willing to have invoked against us."

Douglas, noting that "there is a considerable body of opinion that our actions in Vietnam constitute the waging of aggressive war," stated that the case presents "sensitive and delicate" questions which the Supreme Court should consider," . . .

A strong case can be made to support the proposition that the London Agreement has the force of a treaty within the meaning of [U.S. Constitution] Article VI. Although executive agreements are not made the supreme law of the land as are treaties, for some purposes at least executive agreements have been held in equal dignity. *U.S. v. Pink* (1942) 315 US 203; *U.S. v. Belmont* (1937) 301 US 224. A further argument could be made that the London Agreement was regarded as expressing and implementing the Kellogg-Briand Treaty, to which we were a party.

The principles codified in the London Agreement and applied by the International Military Tribunal at Nürnberg were so widely affirmed by many nations as principles of international law that their status as such is not open to question. Our courts have long recognized the common law development of principles of international law, and that "rules when generally accepted become a universal obligation." We certainly accepted the rules of Nürnberg . . . in our subsequent participation—indeed, in our sponsorship of the resolution before the United Nations.

The regulations of the U.S. Army Field Manual forcefully remind us of our government's recognition that the Nürnberg principles are binding on us; it contains all of them in Section 498, in a section captioned "Crimes Under International Law" [and Sections 500, 510, and 511].

The major problem in cases raising the Nürnberg claim concerning our conduct in Vietnam is whether the courts will treat this question as a justiciable one or as a political one solely within the competence of the executive. Will the courts be willing to make a determination on the legality of our conduct? . . . Although some general standards may be drawn from analysis of all the cases on this question, their application was always based on the context in which each case arose. This can clearly be seen in the analysis of the cases made by the majority, concurring, and dissenting justices of the Supreme Court in *Baker v. Carr* (1962) 369 US 186, and see Fritz Scharpf in the March 1966 issue of the *Yale Law Journal*.

These cases teach that the law does not stand still. When reversals of past decisions become necessary, it will be done directly or by the subtle art of distinction. The key to this delicate question is the political expediency of the moment. At one moment in our history political expediency determined that the judiciary may interfere directly with the executive's power to wage war, as it did in the steel seizure cases during the Korean war. *Youngstown Sheet & Tube Co. v. Sawyer* (1952) 343 US 579. At another moment it may determine, as the Sixth Circuit did in *Farmer v. Rountree* (6th Cir. 1958) 252 F.2d 490, to reject justiciability of the claimed illegality of the Vietnam war as a justification for refusal to pay taxes.

It has yet to be seen whether the courts will remain blind and deaf to the truth, whether they will go the way of those judges and jurists we so vigorously condemned as tools of the Nazi regime, or whether they will select the role our times demand.

The same context is relevant to the next legal questions: At what point in time does the obligation to say "No" arise? Does it begin here at home, or does the obligation under Nürnberg arise only on the battlefield?

Who may raise the claim? Can the soldier, the draftee, the worker in the war machine and in the production of napalm bombs, the taxpayer, be held accountable for war crimes and for the crime against peace?

We will not find the answers to those questions in the application of the Nürnberg principles to the major war criminals tried there in 1945. They were the principal planners of the crime against peace and against humanity. Nor will we find the answers in application of the principles in subsequent trials of the second echelon of planners exculpated of the crime against peace.

The vitality of the Nürnberg principles, and the interpretation of their applicability, lie in the important question of knowledge in the extraordinary compulsions of our times, compulsions qualitatively different from the pre-nuclear age of World War II.

It can no longer be argued, as it was in 1945, that the facts of aggression were known only to a few top leaders, [hidden] in the secret archives of government. The voices charging us with crimes against peace are many and the arguments are well reasoned, based on historical facts fully exposed to public view. Our war crimes have been widely documented by eyewitnesses. They fill the press and television daily. We asked of the German people at the close of World War II, when the full character of the Nazi regime was first disclosed to a horrified world through captured newsreels taken by the victors at the scenes of the crimes: "Where were you when all this happened?" That question is much more appropriately asked of us today, not after the event but while it is happening.

Most of the German people could claim with some justification blindness and deafness. They were to a degree insulated from the truth because the Nazi government established silence of dissent long before the full horrors developed. But we are not insulated from the truth. We see and hear every morning and evening. Whatever responsibility the German individual had to say "No" to his government is a thousand-fold greater for us. The deafness and blindness of an apathetic people is a luxury we cannot claim. The young and not so old who have assumed the responsibility of saying "No" have translated the significance of the Nürnberg principle of responsibility to meet the demands of the present circumstances.

The crime against peace, against humanity, and war crimes are committed when the act is done with knowledge of its illegality. The plea of superior orders or act of state is no defense; no lines were drawn in principle at the Nürnberg trials that free the soldier, the average citizen, or the worker from criminal responsibility for an act of which he has full knowledge. That responsibility extends not merely to the prohibited conduct but also to complicity in it, for Nürnberg designated complicity as a crime. When confronted with orders from above, the test formulated at Nürnberg—not to determine guilt but in mitigation of punishment— was whether moral choice was in fact possible.

Today, in this nuclear age, given the knowledge we have of the awful consequences of this illegal war, moral choice commences with the first act leading to complicity in the conduct of a barbaric war.

SUMMING UP THE GUILD'S ROLE IN THE VIETNAM WAR
By the Guild Convention, Samuel Neuburger, and Paul Harris

■

CONVENTION SCORES WAR, FOES OF SOCIAL CHANGE: GUILD TO EMPHASIZE LAWYER'S ROLE IN CONFLICT, URGES COMMITTEES ON RIGHTS, CITIES, AND DRAFT

[The 1967 Guild Convention projected winds of change in its Statement of Policy and Program, drafted by old Guild leaders and new Guild staff and members.]

Some elements in the movement for social change in the United States today have altered radically their concepts of how the economic and social injustices in this country can be eradicated. In the past, the movement in the area of "civil rights" attempted to gain justice for the black man through legislation, the courts, and massive non-violent demonstrations. The peace movement has also employed these techniques. Today, some activists representing peace, student, and community organizations feel that these techniques brought no more than token success. Many are seeking new approaches—which look toward basic structural changes in society.

"Summing Up the Guild's Role in the Vietnam War," by the Guild Convention, from "Convention Scores War, Foes of Social Change," *Guild Notes* (May 1967); from Sam Neuburger, memo to NEB, Nov. 1968, Maurice Sugar Papers, MCLI; and from "State of the Guild Speech by President Paul Harris," at Los Angeles National Executive Board meeting, *Guild Newsletter* (April 1980).

Lawyers who wish to use their skills effectively to aid these movements must take cognizance of the goals, tactics, and philosophy of the individuals and organizations active in these struggles. Traditional legal representation alone is frequently not adequate to meet the problems created by current social struggles.

■

By Samuel Neuburger

[A few months later, a founding member of the Guild, Samuel Neuburger, urged the NEB to go far beyond the proposal of the Detroit chapter in 1963.]

An Executive Board meeting, a Convention, a meeting of more than two people, or even the cogitations of one person can and must have only one objective: How can we, or I, help stop the war in Vietnam? [Specifically,] it is no answer to have an agenda:
a) Report of Executive Secretary
b) Report of Committees
   1. on the Judiciary
   2. on social legislation . . .

The simple truth is that, in the past few years, the results of all the projects listed have been of little, if any consequence. Nor, in my opinion, will there be nor can there be any progress in any of the described areas until there is an end to the illegal and immoral war in Vietnam.

[The NEB rejected his one-priority approach, but looking back in 1980, Paul Harris, national president of the Guild, described the Guild strategy.]

■

By Paul Harris

Our political approach dictated a strategy of resisting the selective service system, not only on traditional grounds of religious conscientious objection, but with every available legal tactic. Therefore, we dissected the selective service regulations, found due process violations and administrative law loopholes. Our political approach caused us to set up draft counseling centers near induction centers and in some third world communities, staffing them with legal workers, law students, and occasionally volunteer lawyers. We did this while many liberal legal organizations were unable or afraid to serve the people in this direct manner.

Our politics moved the Guild in 1965 to attack U.S. actions in Vietnam as an illegal war. Our left analysis then moved us in 1973 to a point where we supported the NLF, correctly viewing their efforts as an anti-imperialist war.

As the NLF's offensive grew and the war dragged on, soldiers began to avoid combat. G.I.'s needed legal help, and our legal skills were needed. Our political views guided us to set up military law offices in Japan, the Philippines, and around the country.

■ FIFTEEN

Confronting the War at Home (1965–1969)

THE NATIONAL CONVENTION in San Francisco in November 1965 could not be a one-issue convention, an imperative only one year before in Detroit. As Southerner Ben Smith said in accepting the Roosevelt Award for his work on civil rights:

> We must recognize truth when we see it: the moral issue of equality has now been joined by the imperatives of peace and the economic dignity of man. This organization has understood these imperatives—its program for this convention shows this to be the case: the emphasis on world peace through law, the law of the civil rights era, and the law of the war on poverty. This is the program of a modern progressive Bar association. It simply means that this Bar association, which has been my protector and teacher all my professional life, has seen the future and grasped it "entire."[1]

The Convention for the first time in eighteen years honored a woman, not with the Roosevelt Award, but with a special award. She responded by discussing "How Woman's Work Is Sometimes Done." Si Rosenthal lauded the new Legal Services program established by President Lyndon Johnson in response to ghetto revolts in Watts and elsewhere, sparked by massive unemployment, segregation, discrimination, and police brutality. By the time Detroit erupted in 1967 after one more long hot summer of unemployment and frustration, CLAS leader George W. Crockett, Jr., had been elected a judge of the Detroit Recorder's Court, despite some FBI dirty tricks (revealed in the Guild's 1977 lawsuit against the Attorney General). Judge Crockett addressed a conference of the ACLU in April 1968 on the illegal actions of the Recorder's Court during the civil disturbance; excerpts from those remarks are followed by the view from the front-line by a legal services lawyer.

Founding Guild members David Freedman and Victor Rabinowitz, national

---

1. "Lawyers in the Great Tradition," Ben Smith, *NLG Practitioner* 24:4 (Fall 1965).

president, were meanwhile debating the definition of "radical lawyer" in order to find the best approach to recruiting more of them. The winds of change caused other leading Guild members to go outside the Guild to perform functions of low priority in the Guild—filing innovative class action suits against major enemies, publishing a journal on the theory and practice of law, writing scholarly articles on the illegality of U.S. involvement in the Vietnam war for insertion in the *Congressional Record* and use as testimony before legislative committees, and storing the Guild's own rich, but aging, archives. Guild members found non-Guild allies and friends to found the Center for Constitutional Rights and the Lawyers Committee on American Policy Toward Vietnam in New York and the Meiklejohn Civil Liberties Institute in Berkeley.

San Francisco-Bay Area Guild members started the *National Lawyers Guild Practitioner* as a successor to *Law in Transition* and the *Lawyers Guild Review*, without funding from the national Guild. In 1968 the Guild stopped publishing the *Civil Liberties Docket* after thirteen years of recording 9,000 human rights cases brought in U.S. courts.

In 1968, strong winds were loosed at the Santa Monica convention, described here by two student members, Dan Lund and Joan Andersson. Heated convention discussions on "The Movement and the Lawyer" infused Guild participants representing those arrested at the 1968 Democratic Party Convention in Chicago. Charles Garry was busy in San Francisco meanwhile, honing his trial skills in the defense of Black Panther Huey P. Newton, and, coincidentally, providing a new Guild manual on how to pick a jury.

HOW WOMAN'S WORK IS SOMETIMES DONE
By Ann Fagan Ginger

In accepting this special award, I would like to list the things in which I believe. Maybe they are the reasons you selected me for this honor.

I believe in thinking and talking, and especially in the written word. You can reach many more people with the written word than with the spoken word. Until movie, television, and radio audiences can hear what we have to say, we should use the printing press.

I believe that you must walk that lonesome valley; you have to walk it by yourself. You can walk with tens and hundreds and thousands of others so that the valley is not lonesome. But you cannot pay a substitute. You must do these things yourself.

The Lawyers Guild consists of people who do it themselves. If you

---

"How Woman's Work Is Sometimes Done," by Ann Fagan Ginger, from remarks in *NLG Practitioner* 24:4 (Fall 1965).

want your children to know about trade unions, you will have to teach them yourselves; it is not in the textbooks. Your role in the 1930s and 1940s is not written down anywhere, or your role as a trade union lawyer; you won't even find trade unions or SNCC. Your children will not find out about peace or Vietnam, or even about the Constitution and the Bill of Rights and how they are actually enforced in our country.

These things you must teach your children yourself, your nieces, nephews, and the students in college who are looking to us for something. We have a responsibility to walk and talk with them, and teach them whatever it is we have learned in our lives. This includes especially the struggle for peace. I find that if you go talk to teachers who will be talking to students, and if you talk to students, and to parents and administrators and all kinds of people, they will listen. And if you look them square in the eye and smile, they may even get over being so shocked at the content of what you are saying.

I believe in women who try to live in a fourth dimension. They are wives and mothers and home-makers and they also have a job—a job in which they try to use their creativity in a way they cannot in the other parts of their lives. Joining the Lawyers Guild puts a tightrope under a 4-D woman. This tightrope consists of concern for society. When you get the morning mail, with letters asking for money for SNCC and for the Central Committee for Conscientious Objectors and the American Indians and all of the many other groups, or when you read the morning paper and know that you as a lawyer have the power to do something about many of the injustices you read about, this puts a tightrope under you as you juggle the four aspects of your life. There are days when I get up and I don't know whether I should sweep the floor, type words for my husband's music, read over my son's book report, go to my job editing books for California lawyers, or go to work on the *Civil Liberties Docket*.

I might also say to the ladies who are considering becoming lawyers that I urge you to join the Guild. It is a very inexpensive kind of beauty treatment. Your hair grows gray in streaks, you have automatic eyeshadow, and your weight stays down. So, you see, you can do two things at once again.

I would like to mention here those women who are walking this tightrope with me, as wives and mothers and homemakers and also as lawyers. There is no net under us if we fall. If from time to time we drop out of things we will come back—if you help us—we may not otherwise. Each year we lose many women in this way, but Doris Walker Roberson, Eleanor Jackson Piel, Marijana Relich, Jean Kidwell Pestana, Betty Elder are a few of the women in the Guild who are trying to do what I am attempting—none of us with complete success.

I would also like to mention a group of women whom I don't think have ever received any special honor in the Guild but who deserve it. Primarily Carol King, who taught me as much as I know about how to be a woman lawyer, Pearl Hart of Chicago, Harriet Bouslog of Hawaii, Beverly Axelrod of San Francisco, Claudia Shropshire of Jackson, Mary Kaufman, and Gene Ann Condon of New York. There are many others I could name.

I have been criticized sometimes for thinking like a man, and other times for not thinking like a man. I only think the way I think, which is the way I was brought up to think. And I respect my parents for not having taught me there was a different way for men and women to think. Often when we're getting into an argument about a Guild program, my tendency is to say, "But who will really wash the dishes? They won't just go away."

And so I believe in a Guild of lawyers who work in teams to think and to write and to represent clients in court—who are also concerned with each other's personal welfare. Who think it's important when you get married, or when you get divorced, when you have children and when they have grown, who think it's important when you're having financial difficulties and to honestly discuss these things as a Guild, as a family, a group.

In other words, I believe in institutions. This is why my husband and I built the Meiklejohn Civil Liberties Library. It is a building in our backyard to which students come looking for something they do not quickly find in law school.

And last, I believe in the Long View, that there is a continuum, that life does go on through long millions of years and that we have a role to play as fully as we possibly can in the period in which we live.

Bertolt Brecht said this much better in his play "Galileo": "The old says, 'As I am now, it shall always be so.' The new says, 'If you're no good, then go.'"

PIONEER'S REPORTS ON POVERTY LAW
By Simon Rosenthal

[Rosenthal made these remarks in a panel at the 1965 Guild Convention on Legal Services for the Poor.]

I think we should not be describing the OEO [Office of Economic Opportunity] legal services program as a program. Rather, it is a revolution—a legal revolution both for attorneys and for the people.

Many, many people have known for many, many years that they

"Pioneer's Reports on Poverty Law," by Simon Rosenthal, *NLG Practitioner* 24:4 (Fall 1965).

have legal problems. The difficulty is they have never had any place they could go with them. Traditional legal aid societies were charitable organizations which were providing no legal service. The reason for this is complicated and historic. They certainly never had the funds; they never had the staff.

Eight months ago I was the staff attorney in the Alameda County Legal Aid Society. I had 250 new clients a month. Many of these had multiple legal problems: divorce, bankruptcy, creditors dunning them. It was impossible to do anything more than make statistics. I would record the client's problem with a check and a new "case" would be opened. I gave him a little bit of advice and closed the "case." This is a shame both for legal aid societies and for the profession. . . .

When clients become aware that there is a place to go with their legal problems, they go rather rapidly. In the OEO neighborhood offices in Oakland, 80 percent of the people that have come into the multi-service centers requested legal assistance. Each center is operating with two lawyers, family service workers, homemaker services, and visiting nurses. When these legal services are provided, people are able to tell their neighbors that they have received service and their neighbors come in.

This is an exciting thing. Perhaps it is not as dramatic as going down South and fighting for civil rights; but it is fighting for human freedom in another sense. If an individual is denied an attorney, whether in a "small" law suit over a television repossession, or in a suit involving child custody or juvenile court action, this is a tragedy—for the individual, for our society, for the Bar.

In Alameda County, which has approximately one million people, we would need about 25 attorneys to provide minimum legal services in the civil field. If you multiply that by our national population rounded off to 200 million people, you're talking about approximately 5,000 attorneys. If you assume an average $10,000 annual salary for these attorneys and $5,000 in overhead and secretarial expenses, you're talking about approximately $75 million as a national expenditure (from local, state, federal, and private funds) to provide legal services for the poor in civil actions. That would pay for about four planes bombing Vietnam. What does it mean to the people in this country?

It doesn't just mean that they will receive discharge in a bankruptcy, although this is a critical thing, because if they don't, they may be out of work permanently. In the mechanized society we're dealing with, collection agencies have become a second FBI. They will trace people down, attach their wages, and, in doing so, very often break up a family. Many welfare departments have a rule that a family can't live together and draw welfare. If a welfare budget is the only way they can survive when the breadwinner cannot work, very often the man and the woman have to separate. . . .

If you're approaching conservative citizens who will not be enthusiastic about the idealism involved, you can talk about tax budget and welfare costs. It's not just human values we're dealing with. The $75 million to provide civil attorneys for the poor would save many times that amount in reduction of welfare costs. . . .

We now have an opportunity to use the civil law so statutes can be interpreted from the poor person's point of view. If the trial courts are hesitant in buying this, there are opportunities for appellate cases. We have had such already, except that "unfortunately" we won on the trial level. The collection agency stormed out, claiming it was going to appeal. It never did.

The attempt to provide people with attorneys presents dramatic possibilities which parallel anything else Guild members might consider doing. If equal justice is achieved, it will be reflected through every strata of our society.

THE DETROIT RECORDER'S COURT AND THE 1967 CIVIL DISTURBANCE
By George W. Crockett, Jr.

A United States Senate Committee recently suggested that Detroit's Recorder's Court was too lenient in its handling of cases growing out of Detroit's civil disturbance last summer. I assume the Committee had reference to the fact that the large bulk of the 1967 riot cases on our docket have been and are being disposed of as simple misdemeanors instead of felonies; and the sentences generally are limited to the time spent by the defendant in jail while awaiting reasonable bail or the final disposition of the case.

I disagree with the Senate Committee. Instead, I suggest that we judges (perhaps subconsciously) are belatedly endeavoring to make amends for the wholesale denial of the constitutional rights of virtually everyone arrested during that disturbance. I include myself in this indictment. As the report of the President's Commission points out (Chap. 13, note 9), the bails fixed by me were the lowest in the Court; but they still were much higher than they should have been.

Nor am I convinced that there is general appreciation even now of the full extent of the injustices we committed by our refusal to recognize the right to immediate bail and our objection to fixing reasonable bail. Some of the cases which have come before me as a result of the curfew imposed following the death of Dr. King suggest that the prosecutor's

---

"The Detroit Recorder's Court and the 1967 Civil Disturbance," by George W. Crockett, Jr., from remarks reported in *NLG Practitioner* 27:2 (Spring 1968).

office and the policemen in the street have learned nothing from last summer's experience, and this has serious implications for the coming summer.

The situation we faced last summer is authoritatively summed up in the recent Report of the President's National Advisory Commission on Civil Disorders (U.S. Govt. ed., p. 60):

> In all, more than 7,200 persons were arrested. Almost 3,000 of these were picked up on the second day of the riot, and by midnight Monday 4,000 were incarcerated in makeshift jails. Some were kept as long as 30 hours on buses. Others spent days in an underground garage without toilet facilities. An uncounted number were people who had merely been unfortunate enough to be on the wrong street at the wrong time. Included were members of the press whose attempts to show their credentials had been ignored.
>
> People became lost for days in the maze of different detention facilities. Until the later stages, bail was set deliberately high, often at $10,000 or more. When it became apparent that this policy was unrealistic and unworkable, the prosecutor's office began releasing on low bail or on their own recognizance hundreds of those who had been picked up. Nevertheless, this fact was not publicized for fear of antagonizing those who had demanded a high-bail policy.

The Report mentions that at least 83 percent of these 7,200 arrestees were black citizens. I suggest that this fact accounts in large measure for the unconstitutional procedures uniformly followed by the authorities after their arrest—the exceedingly large number of unjustifiable felony charges which have since been reduced to misdemeanors, the insistence upon routine time-consuming clerical and identification procedures as a pretext for holding people in custody, the refusal to utilize the judges and staffs of other courts to expedite the processing of cases and afford time for individual examination at arraignments, and the assessment in mass of exorbitantly high bail which resulted in the exhaustion of our conventional detention facilities.

THE CURFEW CASES

The bulk of the 7,000 arrestees were arrested for being on the streets after the curfew hour. A large portion were juveniles whose cases came before Juvenile Court. . . . This curfew misdemeanor was punishable by fine of not more than $100 and/or a jail sentence of not more than 90 days. It was the equivalent of a traffic violation for which a traffic ticket normally is given and the defendant is not detained. There was then no justification whatever in *detaining* these curfew violators any longer than the time required to obtain and verify their names and correct addresses. . . .

Almost without exception these people did not come before a judge until 24–48 hours after their arrest and their detention in city buses parked in the blazing sun. In most cases they admitted their guilt or were tried by the judge and found guilty. In either event the usual result was a suspended sentence or a sentence to the days already spent waiting to be brought before a judge. The net result is that they were punished by "cruel and inhuman treatment" even before they reached court.

To claim then that our disposition of the curfew cases was too lenient overlooks completely the injustice already visited upon these defendants, as well as the fact that the magnitude of the arrests made any other final disposition impossible in these cases.

THE FELONY CASES

But the real complaint about "the leniency" of Recorder's Court seems to concern our disposition of the felony cases.

The publicity credited to the prosecutor's office and the police department left the public impression that an unusually large number of major crimes were being committed; and there were repeated assurances that "these felons will be prosecuted to the full extent of the law." When the evidence was not forthcoming to support these serious charges, the judges are criticized and the complaint is heard that Recorder's Court judges are too lenient.

The truth is that in the overwhelming majority of the cases the police and the prosecutor simply charged more than they could possibly prove. Much of this was done deliberately for the purpose of having a prohibitive bond placed against the defendant so the defendant could be detained in prison pending examination and trial.

The report of the President's Commission states that 24 percent of those arrested for felonies in the Detroit riots were never prosecuted; of the 76 percent prosecuted, about half (49 percent) were dismissed at the preliminary examination for lack of evidence. Twenty-six persons were charged with sniping but 23 of these charges were dismissed; 34 were arrested for arson, but 21 were never prosecuted; 28 were arrested for inciting to riot but 22 were not prosecuted; and of the 253 assault arrests, 184 were discharged, 11 were convicted, and 58 are still pending.

The statistics from our own Court records are most revealing. Of the 7,200 persons arrested only 4,260 were brought to Recorder's Court. The other 3,000 were juveniles or were discharged by the police or the prosecutor without court appearances.

Of the cases brought to our Court 75 percent of the persons were charged with a felony. So the accused is entitled to counsel, an arraignment on the warrant, a preliminary examination, and an arraignment on the information—three court appearances before his trial date. Since virtually all were indigents, each of these felony cases costs Wayne

County taxpayers a substantial sum in assigned counsel fees, notwithstanding they amounted, at most, to misdemeanors in which there is not a right to assigned counsel. Also an average of six months was required to process these felony charges from warrant to judgment, whereas only days are required for a misdemeanor. Thus, this procedure of uniformly making felony charges has completely disrupted our Court docket and greatly increased the cost of operating Recorder's Court.

In these felony cases, the prosecutor demanded and our Court imposed unconstitutional bail ranging from $10,000 to $200,000! We did it routinely and without making any individual inquiry to determine if such bail could be justified. The asserted justification was: "We have to keep *these people* locked up and off the streets so they won't go out and do the same thing again!" Or "The Prosecutor and the Police Department is waiting for an FBI check so we won't allow any wanted criminals or 'outside conspirators' to escape!"

The Prosecutor knew or should have known—and certainly we judges should have remembered—that reasonable bail before conviction is a matter of constitutional right under our State and Federal Constitutions. As the U.S. Supreme Court said in *Stack v. Boyle* (1951) 342 US 1: "This traditional right to freedom before conviction permits the unhampered preparation of a defense, and serves to prevent the infliction of punishment prior to conviction. . . . Unless this right to bail before trial is preserved, the presumption of innocence, secured only after centuries of struggle, would lose its meaning. . . ."

This "high bail policy" in our Court was followed from Sunday until Friday noon, with hundreds of presumably innocent people with no previous record suddenly finding themselves separated from their families and jobs, incarcerated in our maximum security detention facilities at Jackson and Milan, all without benefit of counsel, examination, [or] the semblance of a trial.

As should have been anticipated, racial tensions mounted to something approaching the explosion point. By Friday noon the prosecutor, . . . the Governor, the Mayor, and the President's personal representative were sufficiently apprehensive that they demanded and received a special audience with our Court, where each asked that we expedite the release of as many arrestees as possible. [And] a sizeable delegation representing Detroit's black community demanded and received a hearing with the judges of our Court and lodged a vigorous protest about the flagrant denials of their civil rights and liberties; the killing of 33 Negroes by police and guardsmen; and the indiscriminate kicking in of doors and searching black people's homes.

It was not until these happenings occurred that we judges returned to our judicial senses. Within a matter of a few hours orders were entered releasing the overwhelming bulk of these defendants on personal bond....

The black citizens of Detroit find it difficult to understand the essential justice of any system that will arrest, charge, and prosecute 3,230 persons with felonies and then dispose of the first 1,630 of these with 961 dismissals, 664 pleas to misdemeanors (trespass, petty larceny, and curfew violations) and only two convictions on the original charge!

It is not surprising that police-Negro tension is almost as high in Detroit today as it was immediately after last summer's events. Detroit's black community knows that the temple of criminal justice has fallen down; they feel the beams resting upon their necks at every turn. What is particularly disturbing is the refusal of the Establishment to open its eyes to this fact.

"WHAT DID YOU DO IN THE RIOTS, DADDY?"
By John Houston

Our special bail program, under which persons meeting certain conditions could be released on their own recognizance, had been authorized to commence on Monday, July 24th [1967], with a case load of 15 per day anticipated. It began on that day with a case load of 1,500 persons, the riot having intervened on Sunday. In its first two weeks the bail program interviewed over 3,000 defendants, in courtrooms, bullpens, Wayne County General Hospital, and the jails of Monroe, Wayne, and Washtenaw Counties, employing three shifts of attorneys and legal interns from the Neighborhood Legal Offices, University of Detroit Urban Law Clinic, and volunteer private practitioners. Over 1,300 interviews were verified by the assistance of many lay persons, including VISTA of Philadelphia, VISTA of Los Angeles, the Protestant Community Service, and members of Wayne University Sociology Department. These case workers are becoming more and more valuable as our efforts continue.

The bail program must be judged a success despite its uneven acceptance by the judges. Over 90 percent of the persons recommended by the program were released on own recognizance. The savings in bond fees to the citizens must run to hundreds of thousands of dollars, money much better spent for food, clothing, and shelter....

A major function of NLSC [Neighborhood Legal Services Center] was as an information center. We answered hundreds of requests for

---

"What Did You Do in the Riots, Daddy?" by John Houston, from shortened version of article for Detroit Neighborhood Legal Service Center *Newsletter*, of which he was editor, in *NLG Practitioner* 26:4 (Fall 1967).

information and location of missing prisoners from anguished, angered, and worried relatives. One mother was assisted in finding her 19-year-old daughter missing for several days. We located her in Wayne County Jail and found that she was supposed to have been released on personal bond. Her release was arranged and the family reunited. A man whose 9-year-old daughter was seriously ill was arrested for curfew violation when he went out one night to purchase desperately needed medicine. Our information service tracked this man down and the bail program arranged for his release.

There were many heroes. Our entire staff—attorneys, interns, clerical, and volunteers—deserve commendation for a tremendous job well done under very difficult circumstances. The police station and Recorder's Court were armed camps, completely surrounded. Soldiers sat in the courtrooms with automatic rifles held at the ready. Even in our offices, there were not adequate numbers of chairs, desks, and especially phones. No line was free for more than three seconds during the first week.

Two major legal actions have grown out of the rioting to date. One is an attempt to have the Governor's Proclamation declared invalid and to attain the release of all curfew violators. This has met with mixed success [in several courts] to date. One judge of the Recorder's Court turned down such a motion. Judge Montane, Wayne County Circuit Court, granted a writ of habeas corpus in a similar case, whereupon the sheriff, prior to the hearing on the writ, released about 70 defendants including the individual named on the writ. . . .

What is most disturbing is our lack of accomplishment following the disturbances. Well over 200 complaints of brutality and excessive force on the part of the police and national guard were made to Representatives Conyers, Diggs, and Del Rio, the Crisis Council, and others. Only two such complaints came to Neighborhood Legal Services.

Our agency and the courts *must* quickly become responsive to the needs of the people of our community. The tension, anger, and mistrust seem greater in Detroit now than before the riot, and yet the prosecutor has announced that he found no grounds for criminal action against 15 policemen and national guardsmen involved in the deaths of seven persons.

It is the last half of the ninth inning, with the score presently about 4,000 to 1 in favor of the police. If the courts do not allow the people their turn at bat, the only alternative to the "Law of the Books" is the "Law of the Jungle."

A DEBATE ON THE DEFINITION OF "RADICAL LAWYER"
By David Freedman and Victor Rabinowitz

[Freedman's remarks at a dinner in his honor, as a founding and continuously active Guild member, led Guild President Rabinowitz to respond in the spring of 1968.]

■

By David Freedman

In my youth, quite a few years ago, we had no confusion about what was meant by being a "radical." There were differences of opinion as to who qualified for the accolade, but, as to what a radical was, there was no doubt. A radical was one who believed that the paramount evils of the society of our times flowed from the very nature of its economic structure and that there was no real cure for them short of transforming our society from one of capitalist exploitation to one where the economy was socially owned and controlled. A radical was a Socialist; his aim was to see our society changed so as to eliminate the exploitation of man by man and thereby put an end to poverty and war, which he believed were the products of our capitalist society. There were great social problems in those days, too. There was massive exploitation, depressions, crises and war—but there was also faith and belief in the future of man.

How is it today? I hear from many young people, faced with the immediate problems caused by our involvement in the evil and horrifying war in Vietnam, and the ever-menacing possibility of atomic annihilation, only pessimistic prophecies. They see no future for themselves, or for mankind in general. When they become "radical," it arises out of this pessimism.

It is quite the contrary with the "radical" of ideology. He tries to relate his activities to an ultimate objective; he selects, as the struggles which currently engage him, those that are steps in that direction; he is animated by an optimistic hope in the ultimate success of his ideology.

The radical of my youth has seen a measure of success of his ideology. In a number of countries, societies, more or less Socialist in content, have come into being, and we have this past year witnessed the 50th anniversary of the founding of the Soviet Union, the first such society. It is regrettably true that evils that have taken place in some of these countries, and that still persist there, have been a cause of bitter disappointment and grief to many who adhere to a Socialist ideology.

"A Debate on the Definition of 'Radical Lawyer,'" from David Freedman, in "The President's Column," *Guild Newsletter* (Jan.–Feb. 1968), and Victor Rabinowitz in the same (May–June 1968).

But, speaking as one who during all his adult life has believed in the desirability of establishing a Socialist society here, I say, that while I, too, abhor and condemn the evils and excesses that have taken place in Socialist countries, my faith in Socialism as a better society for man is unshaken and I remain this kind of radical. We must not become confused and attribute to the institutions the evils that are brought about by those who betray them. . . . I suggest that having a Socialist outlook would help our young radicals to see the various problems that confront them in a context related to an end goal. It would give meaning to the struggles they engage in that is lacking when the struggles are the ends in themselves.

Many young radicals who understand the need for a constructive program are very critical of the ideology in which I was raised and the political institutions which presently are identified with it. It may well be that the ideology and the organizations require some serious overhauling to be adaptable to our present time, I know that efforts in that direction are being made by some younger theoreticians and hopefully they will succeed. . . .

■

THE PRESIDENT'S COLUMN
By Victor Rabinowitz

The radical of today does not think primarily in terms of an economic transformation of the society because his complaints about the society are not primarily economic, nor is it all clear to him that a transformation from Capitalism to Socialism is relevant to the evils which oppress him. Most radicals of today, both white and black, would probably reject Capitalism. But [this] is not really on the current agenda. Perhaps the issue is whether we will live in a dignified society of free men with the power to determine our own destinies or in a conformist programmed society dominated by an overwhelming structure of corporate and governmental power and everlastingly threatened with total annihilation. In their emphasis on the freedom of the individual, perhaps the young are looking to the ultimate goal of Communism rather than to the intermediate station of Socialism. They may have much in common with their contemporaries throughout both Eastern and Western Europe.

. . . [T]he student of the 1960s at Columbia, Berkeley, and elsewhere may well accomplish more to destroy oppressive institutions and to create better ones than his counterpart of 35 years ago, even without an advance blueprint as to what those better institutions will look like.

There is currently a great deal of radical thinking and writing, and it is to be hoped that out of this will come an ideology for the future. But it will be a program for today and will take into account the social and technological structure of the United States in the 1960s.

I am not sure that the radicals of today are pessimistic; but, if they are, it is clear that their pessimism has not driven them to apathy but rather to a resolve to change the world, just as the optimists of David's youth wanted to change the world. In any event, pessimists cannot be turned into optimists by exhortation. If the radical of today is sometimes bitter and frustrated, it may be that the realities of today call forth such attitudes. "Faith and belief in the future of man" is a religious, not a scientific, concept. Those of us who are Marxists should not allow such idealism to blind us to the facts. If an accurate observation of reality leads to pessimism, it is not the fault of the radical but of the reality. In any event, if it is pessimism which leads the young militants of today to action, perhaps we could do with more of it.

NATIONAL OFFICERS AND CHAPTERS OF THE GUILD BEFORE THE 1968 CONVENTION

The following Guild members were elected to office in the National Lawyers Guild:

President	Victor Rabinowitz, New York
Secretary	Herman B. Gerringer, New York
Treasurer	David Scribner, New York
Vice Presidents	Stanley Faulkner, New York
	George Crockett, Detroit
	Max Dean, Flint, Mich.
	Osmond K. Fraenkel, New York
	Ann Fagan Ginger, Berkeley
	Arthur Kinoy, New York
	Doris Brin Walker, San Francisco
	Benjamin Smith, New Orleans
	Herman Wright, Houston
	Robert F. Drinan, Boston
	John McTernan, Los Angeles
Advisory Board	John M. Coe, Pensacola, Fla.
	Earl B. Dickerson, Chicago, Ill.
	Benjamin Dreyfus, San Francisco
	Robert Kenny, Los Angeles
	Malcolm M. Sharp, Albuquerque, N.M.
	Thomas I. Emerson, New Haven, Conn.
	Ernest Goodman, Detroit

"National Officers and Chapters of the Guild," Maurice Sugar Papers, MCLI.

The following were elected to the National Board of Directors:

From New York City Chapter
  Robert Boehm
  Leonard Boudin
  Edward Cambridge
  Julius Cohen
  Bernard D. Fischman
  Lazar Henkin
  Sanford Katz
  Mary Kaufman
  Samuel Koenigsberg
  David Lubell
  I.G. Needleman
  Samuel Neuberger
  Martin Popper
  Barney Rosenstein
  Ralph Shapiro
  Robert Silberstein
  William Standard
  Michael Standard
From San Francisco Chapter
  Allan Brotsky
  Edward Dawley
  Lawrence Duga
  Peter Franck
  Aubrey Grossman
  Jan Hermes
  James Herndon
  Francis J. McTernan, Jr.
  Arthur Schaffer
  John Thorne

From Los Angeles Chapter
  Harriet Buhai
  David Finkel
  Elsa Kievitz
  Ben Margolis
  Jean Kidwell Pestana
  Irving Rosenfeld
  William G. Smith
  Charles B. Stewart
  (one vacancy to be filled later)
From Chicago Chapter
  Irving Meyers
  Charles Markels
  Leonard Karlin
From Detroit Chapter
  Claudia Shropshire
  F. Phillip Colista
  Hon. John J. Conyers, Jr.
  Nathan Conyers
  Don Hobson
  George Downing
  Fred Findling
  David Klein
  James Lafferty
  Dean Robb
  Nedwin Smokler
From Philadelphia Chapter
  A. Harry Levitan
  Erwin Miller

At Large Representatives:

I. Duke Avnet, Baltimore, Md.
John Caughlin, Seattle, Wash.
Len Holt, Washington, D.C.
David Rein, Washington, D.C.
Alan Rosenberg, Boston, Mass.
Morton Stavis, Newark, N.J.
Irwin Gostin, San Diego, Cal.
Bruce Waltzer, New Orleans, La.

Edwin White, Kansas City, Mo.
Maurice Sugar, Onaway, Mich.
Sam Rosenwein, Los Angeles, Cal.
Harry Nier, Denver, Colo.
Rudolph Schware, Denver, Colo.
A. Glenn Epps, Flint, Mich.
Harry Philo, Waughkeegan, Ill. (*sic*)
Morton Leitson, Flint, Mich.

Student Chapters:

Mike Kelly, University of Cal.-Berkeley
Bob Wright, Penn. State University
Bruce Polichar, U.C.L.A.

Dave Needleman, Brooklyn, N.Y.
Barry Williams, Hastings College of Law
Andy Gillen, Chicago

THE CONFRONTATIONAL CONVENTION IN SANTA MONICA, 1968
By Joan Andersson, Dan Lund, David Rein, Bruce Waltzer, James Herndon, Norman Leonard, Rudolph Schware, and Fay Stender

■

By Joan Andersson

It was at the Miramar where, for many of us, it all began. Even those who did not attend have been deeply affected by the 1968 convention, because it was there that the Guild began to take its current form. The convention and all that happened there was the result of a 2- or 3-year period of great upheaval.

[The exuberant] law students were part of the new movement, and they judged any distance from it harshly. So although the Guild had much to attract young members, "We must now begin to re-think and criticize everything. We must re-build the Guild in its entirety" (Exec. Sec'y's report 1967 NEB).

... Those the Guild needed to attract were active in anti-war, anti-draft, and anti-poverty programs. Many were members of SDS, as were the organizers themselves. ...

Internally things were very rocky. "We had to de-emphasize tradition, not scrap it. We had to jostle the Guild and try not to break it. We had to convince people of the necessity of change and prepare them for the slowness of it" (Exec. Sec'y's report, 1968 convention). Many older members felt like a tornado had hit. They distrusted the commitment of the raggedy young people who seemed more interested in being part of the movement than in building the necessary legal skills to defend it.

Students and young lawyers who had taken an oath of poverty for themselves nevertheless demanded financial contributions to an organization which increasingly looked little like the "Bar association" it had been. The young people seemed to reject expertise, while older Guild

---

"The Confrontational Convention in Santa Monica, 1968," based on Joan Andersson, excerpted from *Guild Notes* (Jan. 1980); Dan Lund's description excerpted from "Law for the People" (1983), reprinted in San Francisco Chapter, *Conspiracy* (1986); "The Movement and the Lawyer" excerpts, by David Rein, Bruce Waltzer, James Herndon, Norman Leonard, Rudolph Schware, and Fay Stender, from *NLG Practitioner* 28:1 (1969).

members wanted well-thought-out, legally excellent work. History had taught them the need for such care.

... At times the hostility seemed almost too great for the organization to bear. Yet: "Organizational dissension, factionalism, and disagreement over even basic policy are generally seen as harmful during periods of repression and attack. Whereas they are in fact *necessary* to organizational growth during periods of expansion. Efforts should not be made to hide this disagreement or to cover it up; it represents an aspect of growth in the Guild" (Exec. Sec'y's report Feb. 1968 NEB).

Further, we were advised: "The form of a Bar association need not be contradictory to that of a political association ... most of our limits are self-imposed, arbitrary, and representative of past, not present, needs" (Exec. Sec'y's report 1968 Convention).

■

By Dan Lund

Not since the post World War II generation had law student participation in the NLG been more than minimal. Law students were not voting members of the organization. The National Office staff—Ken Cloke, Bernadine Dohrn, and Alicia Kaplow—had completed travels all over the country, bringing more than fifty law students to the convention, activists fresh from the Columbia strike and years of campus anti-war agitation.

Gathering on the Santa Monica beach, the law students met in caucus. Participating only irregularly in the agenda of the convention, the Law Student Caucus met almost continuously for three days.

[Joan Andersson recalls that when the students began to attend the convention programs, "a grudging respect and awareness of political similarities was apparent. Despite the conflict over the future of the Guild, there began intergenerational friendships that continue today. It was a remarkable event."]

Workshops and panel presentations were electric with the conflict of ideas. Ralph Shoenmann of the Bertrand Russell Tribunal staff challenged the Guild's emphasis on anti-draft selective service counseling and called on us to recognize that military law was essential to protect the sons of the working class who were being drafted. In fact, he urged activists to enter the Army. Michael Tigar, as editor of the *Selective Service Law Reporter*, defended the Guild's work but acknowledged the class bias of much of our effort. Milton Henry, a Guild lawyer from Flint and Vice-President of the Republic of New Africa, called for Guild support to establish a nation in the Black Belt. Judge Jerry Pacht of the Los Angeles Chapter called for continued support for the integration movement.

Innocent vacationers at the Miramar Hotel stared open-mouthed as the lobbies filled with fiercely debating Guild members, sober bodyguards for Milton Henry, and shaggy law students. Bartenders puzzled over this new generation—clearly over 21, but not drinking much.

The specific disputes were often murky, but the general struggle was clear: a majority control of the Guild's boards, staff, and program.

What came of all this? Victor Rabinowitz of New York was re-elected President, as the candidate supporting the program developed by the younger group. The program emphasizing the Guild's role in mass arrest defense and the building of regional offices won. Dennis James of Detroit was named Executive Secretary, and Joan Andersson of Los Angeles became the National Student Organizer. The new NEB, representing old, middle, and young alike, met at the conclusion of the Convention.

[Delegates to the Convention talked fast and furiously at convention sessions on The Movement and the Lawyer.]

■

By David Rein of Washington, D.C.

I won't be modest about it. I think that we have won significant victories in the Supreme Court. One of the reasons is that we felt we were acting as lawyers and consistently confined ourselves to being lawyers and handling legal questions. Where it was possible we have tried to raise constitutional questions. I have heard some criticism about how some cases were tried, for example, that the Spock case was not tried properly because issues other than the legality of the war were introduced. It has always been our feeling, particularly during the McCarthyite period and I think it's still true today, that if the Spock case is won, and if it's won on the ground that the grand jury was not properly selected or the court did not give appropriate instructions, it will be a significant victory. I think every time a political case is won, the government is defeated in its attempt to punish someone for engaging in political dissent, that it's a politically significant victory, even if the opinion does not turn on a fundamental constitutional issue.

■

By Bruce Waltzer of New Orleans

I'd like to comment along some very personal lines, and lay some things out for younger lawyers to consider.

Approximately 18 months ago I withdrew almost entirely from movement activities. I did it because of the fact that I was dead broke—absolutely flat out cold. I did it after seeing a practice completely fall apart. There was no help coming from the people we were helping, and they were taking every bit of their paying business to somebody else whom they thought could do the job for them. It was a terribly hard thing.

Even though I, as an individual, have gotten out of the movement directly, there are so many things that you can do in the day-to-day representation of individuals. You can spend every Monday morning going to court on charges of vagrancy by loitering or having no visible means of support, and get thirty or forty ghetto people acquitted. You can develop a base again and then decide whether to get back in movement work.

■

By James Herndon of San Francisco

When I got involved as a citizen in one of the communities in San Francisco, the Housing Authority was about to evict twelve families. We organized to stop the Authority at least from evicting families with children. Soon a number of other community problems came to the surface. We went from a housing problem into the economic sphere, and started boycotts to get jobs for people from the Negro ghetto. Then the people in the community decided we should own a store, so we started a cooperative which is now in operation. Next people decided that, since our community is going to redevelop, we needed to determine what should be reconstructed. As a lawyer, I was able to help guide the citizens in finding OEO and foundation money for planning grants. This will give us some voice in deciding, on the basis of studies made by our own experts, the kind of community and establishments that should be built in the area. Now we are working on a number of low-rent housing development projects.

As a result of this activity, I have many clients in this community. Almost any citizens' committee that pops up retains me. The housing work will ultimately result in a fee, since the federal housing laws provide for payment of counsel as part of project costs.

■

By Norman Leonard of San Francisco

I, too, have been a "movement" lawyer—for thirty years, not three or four. My "movement" has been the movement of the law as it went, *inter alia* (a good old conservative legal phrase), from *Plessy v. Ferguson* (1896) 163 US 537 to *Brown v. Board of Education* (1954) 347 US 483; from *Schechter Corp. v. United States* (1935) 295 US 495 to *NLRB v. Jones & Laughlin Steel Corp.* (1937) 301 US 1; from *American Communications Assn. v. Douds* (1950) 339 US 382 to *United States v.*

Brown (1965) 381 US 437; from *Betts v. Brady* (1942) 316 US 455 to *Gideon v. Wainwright* (1963) 372 US 335; from *Wolf v. Colorado* (1949) 338 US 25 to *Mapp v. Ohio* (1961) 367 US 643. Like everything else, the law moves! And it has for hundreds of years.

To be a movement lawyer one has, first of all, to be a lawyer. If you are not a sound, capable craftsman—a technician—you are not going to do your client, i.e., the movement, a damn bit of good. If your law training is to have any significance in the struggle for social progress, it is because as a lawyer you have certain technical skills possessed by no one else. If you do not use those skills, if you ignore the intellectual—scholastic, if you will—traditions of your profession, you are not doing that which only you, as a lawyer, can do to support the movement. Others can further social progress as organizers, functionaries, political leaders, and in a variety of other ways. Perhaps you as an individual can do that too—if that is what you want to do. But you are not then acting in your role as a lawyer.

The movement needs people to defend it in court, to use legal creativity so that it can take the offensive in court. "Court" may be, to many of you, a reactionary, capitalistic institution from which can come nothing but harm to the movement; this is at least debatable. More importantly, a good "revolutionary" recognizes the facts of life. He does not ignore them. "Court" is a fact of the movement's life in America in the 1970s. And with the Nixon administration's expected appointments to the Supreme Court, it may not be a very pretty fact of life! Therefore, those of you who by specialized training and skill can deal with "court" can give to the movement something that no one else can give. It may be not as glamorous a role—although the case of Charles Garry proves to the contrary—as that of Fidel or Ché. But it is here, now, and for the foreseeable future, an important one.

This is not to say that lawyers who are thirty years old need act in the same style and manner as lawyers who are fifty or that new methods of work are not called for. But whatever the style, the basic content of a lawyer's work still has to be the most effective and skillful utilization of the tools of his trade to achieve the best results for his client—whether that client be the movement or, as is most likely in the case of any given pragmatic situation, the individual who is facing a criminal prosecution or who is seeking by civil process to turn back the tide of reaction and repression.

■

By Rudolph Schware of Denver

A group of lawyers in Denver have taken the position that whenever anyone in our community does his thing to change this society, regardless of what it is, he is entitled to legal representation, the best he can get. People are entitled to know in advance that there are attorneys who will represent them without any question of how much money will be paid in fees. Of course, it always ends up the other way: we have to go down to the federal building and pay the parking lot; we have to pay the long distance telephone calls.

Our approach is that no attorney will walk into the courtroom alone; there will always be Lawyers Guild attorneys, a minimum of two. The only answer to any one of us having to handle too many free cases is to get more lawyers into the Guild. Building a chapter in Denver is a necessary part of providing adequate legal representation for people in the movement for social change.

■

By Fay Stender of San Francisco

I personally don't have a conflict between economic necessity and movement work because I do a great deal of movement work for the firm that employs me. It is true that situations come up where I find that I want to make a personal commitment, not as a lawyer, but as a citizen. If you do legal work for the movement all of the time, you find a need to make a personal commitment that goes beyond that, expressing your personal feelings as distinct from your professional thing.

I have worked with Charles Garry on the Huey Newton case, which is a good example of a case that has galvanized so much energy and focused so much legal talent and creativity that it will certainly benefit many other poor people and Negroes who challenge the way the grand jury is selected and functions and the way the trial jury panel is selected. We're achieving a great cooperation with lawyers and people in other disciplines (sociologists, psychiatrists) which we hope will not only free Huey, but will result in certain beneficial changes in the legal systems in Alameda County and elsewhere.

GUILD LAWYERS AT THE CHICAGO
DEMOCRATIC CONVENTION OF 1968
By Dan Lund

In the summer of 1968 events moved quickly, and with them, the Guild. Thousands of anti-war activists came to the Chicago Convention of the Democratic Party to demand a stop to the war in Vietnam. They met in the park and on the streets; the whole world was watching as the Chicago Police rioted and the demonstrators were gassed and clubbed.

"Guild Lawyers at the Chicago Democratic Convention of 1968," by Dan Lund, from "Law of the People" (1983), reprinted in San Francisco Chapter, *Conspiracy* (1986).

Much of the defense for the mass arrests was handled by a combination of Guild students, movement organizers, and young local people's lawyers, like Dennis Cunningham, who had a grassroots neighborhood law practice, and Ted Stein, from legal services.

Guild organizing around the mass arrest defense was designed to help reactivate the Chicago Chapter, as well as meet the direct needs of the arrested demonstrators. However, much of the organizing was done by outsiders who did not always understand the local situation. They were often seen as lone rangers riding into town, concerned that the Movement got its cases handled, and then riding out again in a cloud of dust—somewhat before all the work was done. The local legal workers, law students, and lawyers who had to clean up after the national action were not inspired by the work they saw the Guild doing. Therefore, reformation of the Guild Chapter in Chicago, as in other cities later on, was probably retarded rather than encouraged by our inexperience and short-sightedness as organizers.

For some Guild chapters, the primary work in this period was defense of the Black Panther Party. By 1968 they were a national force. Their spirit of militancy and embrace of Marxism made a profound impact on the whole movement. It also made a profound impact on the police. The more the Panthers inspired the movement, the more the police moved. The December 1969 police attacks on the Panthers in Chicago and Los Angeles galvanized significant Guild activity. Out of the repression of the anti-war movement came the trial of the Chicago Eight, represented by William Kunstler of New York, Leonard Weinglass of Newark, and Charles Garry of San Francisco, who became important and controversial models of determined advocacy in the courtroom. These Guild lawyers were important in that they spoke often, traveled widely, and attracted many law students. They were controversial, leading to movement criticism of the traditional male lawyer courtroom role and even of the big Movement trial.

MINIMIZING RACISM IN JURY TRIALS
By Charles R. Garry

[In the introduction to the Guild's fourth book, editor Ann Fagan Ginger described the goal of the manual on jury selection:

Unless a concerted effort is made to challenge grand and trial jury panels, and to challenge individual jurors, there is no possibility of achieving justice in any

---

"Minimizing Racism in Jury Trials" from *Minimizing Racism in Jury Trials: The Voir Dire Conducted by Charles R. Garry in* State of California v. Huey P. Newton, Ann Fagan Ginger, ed. (National Lawyers Guild, 1969).

case in which race, nationality, or class is an issue. And, while it is true that the main character of the *Newton* defense team is unique in his ability to get "into the inwards" of the prospective jurors, every lawyer—however inexperienced or even stiff—must try to follow Garry's example of uncovering prejudiced jurors and getting them off juries.

With the *Newton* model as a starter, every community should develop teams of lawyers, law students and professors, legal assistants, librarians, social scientists, and organizations capable of filing challenges to the method of selecting names for grand jury and trial jury panels, and prepared to conduct extensive voir dire examinations.]

■

VOIR DIRE OF A JUROR IN *CALIFORNIA V. NEWTON*

[Prospective juror Mr. S said he didn't know, and couldn't say, whether he presumed defendant innocent. See the swift surprise ending.]

BY MR. GARRY: We are trying to give you an opportunity to speak so that we will be able to tell whether there is some hidden crevices in your mind that may be an interference in the proper evaluation of that case as the evidence unfolds. You understand that?
A: Yes.
Q: Now, it's a fact, is it not, that you already had an opinion before you came here about this case?
A: Well, to a certain extent, yes.
Q: ... As you sit there right now, do you believe that Huey Newton shot and killed, stabbed, whatever it was, Officer Frey?
A: I don't know whether he shot him or not. That I can't say.
THE COURT: Mr. Strauss, you see, under our law there is a presumption of innocence to start with. ... Do you understand that?
THE JUROR: Yes.
THE COURT: ... [Can] you say to yourself that as far as you are concerned before you hear any evidence that he is not guilty? ...
THE JUROR: I think so.
THE COURT: All right. Go ahead. ...
MR. JENSEN [PROSECUTOR]: As Your Honor said, I think this is a semantic problem.
THE COURT: You may examine further, Mr. Garry.
BY MR. GARRY: Mr. Strauss, again I ask you that same question which you have answered three times to me now—
THE COURT: No. Please ask the question without preface.
MR. GARRY: As Huey Newton sits here next to me now, in your opinion is he absolutely innocent?

A: Yes.
Q: But you don't believe it, do you?
A: No.
THE COURT: Challenge is allowed.

■ SIXTEEN

Movement Lawyers and Clients, and the Courts (1968-1976)

GUILD LAWYERS, LAW students, legal workers, jailhouse writ writers, and clients were ready to try new styles of legal work in the 1960s and 1970s to serve the new and revived movements of students, women, peaceniks, and prisoners, for civil rights, black power, and peace, against the draft and the military. Several styles, and the reasons behind them, are described here.

The Guild opened its Military Law Project office in the Philippines in 1971 to serve the legal needs of U.S. service personnel. Howard DeNike, observing the MLP while working with the Lawyers' Military Defense Committee, liked what he saw, joined the Guild, and became San Francisco Chapter president in the 1980s. His brief description of the MLP catches its essence here.

In April 1972, the National Office launched *Guild Notes*, a newspaper to be circulated to every Guild member, describing the activities of Guild bodies, resolutions adopted, and important cases and movements represented by Guild members as individuals. *Guild Notes* also chronicled attacks on Guild lawyers by judges in contempt proceedings, Bar committees, and other bodies.

Ernest Goodman's lengthy look at two aspects of the Attica case also represents trials in every region in which Guild defense teams struggled through the same basic problems of facts, law, ideology, relationships, financing, and the search for the perfect mix of political and legal action.

NEW STYLE LAW OFFICES
By Anne M. Garfinkle and David Finkel

[Between the July 1968 Convention and the April 1969 NEB meeting in Denver, three new-style firms were opened by Guild members in Detroit, New

---

"New Style Law Offices," described by Anne M. Garfinkle and David Finkel in "The Movement and the Lawyer," Part II, *NLG Practitioner* 28:1 (Winter 1969).

York, and Los Angeles. Partners described the principles and practical problems they faced.]

■

By Anne M. Garfinkle of New York City

We have developed a law commune (although our cards look like any other law firm's). We rented 4,000 square feet at $450 a month in a building owned by the Butchers' Union on Times Square West. We started with four lawyers and now have six; we also have three writers. We planned to be a low-budget operation, but we're making a fortune (due to draft cases mainly). At least half our work goes to the movement.

We each take money from the commune according to need, a fantastic concept for people living in a capitalist system. At first we took according to actual need. When we began to make money, we reevaluated, because you can't consistently make a low salary when, for twenty-six years, you have lived as a middle-class person—it starts to affect your work. We now make about $8,000 take-home annually. (Some people are subsidized by their parents or spouses or have independent incomes and do not need anything from the commune.) We hire one person as a gopher to do the things that take time, like serving papers [at $15–$20 a day on a temporary basis]. We have weekly meetings on political theory and analysis of what we are doing to keep our heads together and to grow together.

Our case load includes: work before draft boards, criminal draft cases, courts martial, a lot of (free) movement criminal cases, obscenity cases (in which we collect reasonable fees when they are not movement cases), landlord-tenant, family court, and advising movement groups, which takes the most time: the Black Student Union, the high-school students union, Newsreel, about where the law is and what the political questions are. Already our writers have prepared *The Bust Book*, with simple explanations about what to do when detained or arrested.

We have a policy of not making decisions for clients. We explain the choices and they decide, whether they want to be political or make money or what.

■

By David Finkel of Los Angeles

We opened a firm in fall 1968, inter-racial, with three Guild members. Our purpose was to enable us to do generally what the Detroit and New York firms are doing. However, we bought ourselves a beautiful, rich, expensive office. This has not increased my net income; it has lowered it. The gross income has increased due to the increased capacity to produce because of the nature of the environment in which we work. We have not had to turn away movement work to pay overhead, but have increased the quantity. Two of us spend more than half of our time on what I would call movement work.

As to maintaining personal integrity, we will not find the answer in our law practice but in the totality of our lives. To the extent that our legal environment itself leads to that goal, fine. But this depends not only on what one does when he practices movement law, but also what he does when he goes home.

[The *Guild Newsletter* issued a supplement to its June 1968 issue to describe "Current Events: Columbia University." The New York City Chapter Mass Defense Office represented many of the 700 students arrested in the April occupation of Columbia and, thereafter, people arrested during demonstrations for school clothing allowances in the Bronx and Brooklyn, picketing welfare centers, and during various activities of the Young Lords and other community groups. It also represented the optimum joint effort by an older Guild member, Mary Kaufman, to teach trial skills to younger members while providing effective, and often inspired, counsel to young and volatile urban movements for change.]

THE ROLE OF THE RADICAL LAWYER AND TEACHER OF LAW
By Arthur Kinoy

[Professor Kinoy, of Rutgers University School of Law, works actively in the Center for Constitutional Rights and the Guild.]

The "radical" teacher of law, the "radical" lawyer, lives, functions, struggles, in the midst of contradictions; his or her life is itself a contradiction. But this should be no shock, no surprise. Every radical who has honestly attempted to study society, as one great student of society once remarked, not for the purpose of understanding it but for the purpose of changing it, knows that "there is nothing that does not contain contradiction; without contradiction there would be no world" (Mao Tse-tung, *On Contradiction*, in Yenan in August 1937).

It should not so disturb us to discover that the role of a radical teacher of law, or a radical lawyer, plays itself out within the framework of a vast contradiction—is itself a contradiction. One of the most honored teachers of all contemporary radicals, Friedrich Engels, wrote over a hundred years ago that

life consists just precisely in this—that a living thing is at each moment itself and yet something else. Life is therefore also a contradiction which is present

---

"The Role of the Radical Lawyer and Teacher of Law: Some Reflections," by Arthur Kinoy, *NLG Practitioner* 29:1 (Winter 1970).

in things and processes themselves, and which constantly asserts and solves itself; and as soon as the contradiction ceases, life too comes to an end, and death steps in (Engels, *Anti-Dühring*).

The role of the radical in the law is the same as the role of the radical in any arena of life. It is to study in depth and in precision the *particularity* of the contradictions he or she operates within in order to understand how best to participate in the resolution of these contradictions in a forward motion; in a manner which assists in the resolution of the principal contradictions of society in the direction of the emergence of a new society free from the oppression, the brutality, the frustration and despair of the old.

Such a study requires first of all an examination of the contradictions within the institutions in which we operate as lawyers and teachers, as they exist *today*, not fifty years ago. It requires an examination of the *particularity* of the contradictions in these institutions in this country at this moment. . . .

A number of radicals have recently clearly recognized the truth which has been apparent for many years to most blacks in this country as well as to large numbers of working people—that the instrumentalities of justice provide justice only for the rich and powerful. This has encouraged useful and helpful probing into the class nature of the system of justice. But this exposure cannot by itself substitute for a fully rounded definition of the role of a radical lawyer or teacher of law at this precise moment in our history. Blacks, browns, and working people, the oppressed sections of society, who daily live with the clubs of the police and the callousness of the courts, rarely need lessons in the "demystification" of the institutions of justice. Their crying need is quite different: what course of conduct will result in a favorable resolution of the fundamental contradictions of the society they live in, a resolution which will once and for all eliminate the oppressive role of present institutions of "justice," and class rule itself.

ANALYSIS OF THE PARTICULARITIES OF THE CONTRADICTIONS

We live today at one of the most historic turning points in American history. The nation is at the edge of events which may shape the destinies of millions for years to come, and we radical lawyers are caught in the very center of the interplay of contradictions which are conditioning this course of developments.

1. *Ruling Powers Edging Toward Open Terrorist Dictatorship*

On the one hand the dominant section of the American ruling circles, represented by the Nixon-Agnew-Mitchell-Pentagon clique, is moving rapidly and openly in the direction of experimentation with sweeping repressive measures of a legal and extra-legal character. These measures range from the nationally directed plan to uproot and destroy the cutting edge of black militancy, the Black Panther Party, through the device of massive frame-up trials, the contrived prosecutions against the national white leadership of the anti-war movement and the expanding youth culture revolt, to the hundreds of local prosecutions in every section of the country of the black and white opposition leaders. The wholesale utilization of "legal" forms of repression of political opposition has now been coupled with extra-legal measures of murder, assassination, and the active encouragement of open vigilantism of a mass character. This all has an ominous and familiar ring.

It is essential, I think, to recognize that the ruling class turns to Fascism, to an open terrorist dictatorship, abandoning its classic form of class domination, bourgeois democracy, out of *fear* and not out of strength.

2. *Growing Radicalization of Vast Numbers of Americans*

The other side of the basic contradiction is the unprecedented and extraordinary growing radicalization of vast numbers of Americans who are experiencing the inability of the rulers to solve any of the immediate problems of this society. There is a new renaissance of black struggle in the heartland of the South . . . coupled with the perspective of black struggles of every form in the Northern urban areas, which will shake the country to its very core. These struggles are merging in time, if not in form.

It is within this context that the role of the radical lawyer or teacher of law begins to emerge more clearly. It is to utilize to the utmost all of his or her skills and energies to assist in a *forward, successful* resolution of the major interacting poles of the central contradictions of the day. On the one hand, the radical lawyer must assist in the increasing and exploding radicalization of masses of people learning from their own political experience. On the other hand, all of the lawyer's skills and energies must be utilized to resist in every way the efforts of the dominant sections of the ruling class to solve their crisis, even if temporarily, by substituting the open terrorist dictatorship for the present forms of bourgeois-democracy, both within the parliamentary and judicial systems. . . .

DISTORTED IMAGE OF A POLITICAL TRIAL TODAY

Today in the United States there is a distorted image of a political trial as primarily a contest between political lawyers and defendants and a "hard-pressed," if "irascible," judge. The development of such a caricature of the radical lawyer or defendant in the present period would be disastrous. It would undermine the effectiveness of radical lawyers and radicals in general in participating in the organizing of powerful movements to oppose the transition measures of repression and reaction. And, most serious of all, it would blunt the radicalization of the millions in struggle, since it would mask the reality of who is the real enemy of the elementary liberties of the people.

SKILL, FLEXIBILITY, PATIENCE AND COURAGE REQUIRED

In *this period* in our history the effective development of a massive defense of the elementary forms of democratic liberties led by radicals is not antithetical to, but in fact accelerates, the radicalization of the millions who are daily being thrown into motion by the attacks and blunders of the governing circles. Such an understanding will permit the radical lawyer, the radical defendant, to become the master, rather than the victim, of the contradictions. It permits the raising of the central political questions: who is conspiring against the liberties of the people? And the answer—that it is the ruling class itself which is moving toward the destruction of the most elementary liberties of the people—is critical to a further radicalization of the people.

YOU DON'T HAVE TO LOVE THE LAW TO BE A LAWYER
By Paul Harris and Gene Ann Condon

■

By Paul Harris

[Paul Harris helped establish the Community Law Firm in San Francisco, one of the longest-lived new-style law offices in the country. This article is based on a speech at the Conference on High School Students' Rights of the San Francisco Guild Chapter in 1969.]

"The law is a ass." "Laws grind the poor and rich men rule the law." "Law flourishes on the corpse of philosophy." These thoughts are expressed by older attorneys escaping into cynicism and self-indulgence and by younger attorneys retreating into pessimism and depression. Yet, the movement cries for more radical attorneys, not only in San Francisco and New York, but in such once quiet places as Santa Barbara and New Haven and in cities throughout this country. And here with us are over a hundred high school students who spend most of their time in the "belly

---

"You Don't Have to Love the Law to Be a Lawyer," by Paul Harris, *NLG Practitioner* 28:4 (Fall 1969); "Comments on You Don't Have To Love the Law To Be a Lawyer," by Gene Ann Condon, *NLG Practitioner* 29:1 (1970).

of the beast." Their strength can be helped by our strength, their emerging power can use our skills.

These statements reflect the tyranny of the law and the disgust of those who work with it. This is a necessary consciousness of a radical lawyer. But it leaves out the analysis of the law which justifies our continuance as attorneys.

IN THE SHADOW OF THE GALLOWS

The legal system is probably the best expression of American capitalist-democracy. The law has as its major purpose the "peaceful" resolution of conflicts for the benefit of the established power in society. This has been its historical function, which can be designated as its thesis. A lesser purpose is the protection of individuals and groups whose actions and ideas are hostile to the status quo. This is the antithesis. As the law successfully protects people from economic and political exploitation, it suggests what complete freedom from such exploitation would be like. In this way the law creates conditions that are antagonistic to its primary purpose of maintaining the American way of exploitation. The thesis is symbolized by the Jail, or ultimately, the Hangman. The antithesis is symbolized by the radical attorney and client.

The classical Marxist synthesis of the preceding dialectic would be a new legal system that would adapt what was constructive in the old legal system to the structure and demands of the revolutionary society.

We are now facing two alternatives: the abolition of the existing oppression which means the radical lawyer remakes the law as a revolutionary, or the temporary victory of the hangman, which means all radical lawyers become clients. Until either one of those extremes, the law continues to express both thesis and antithesis—repression and freedom. Although there have been brief periods in American history where the hangman's shadow has lengthened considerably, on the whole the radical lawyer has maintained his existence and his power. . . .

THE LAW AS PROSECUTOR AND PROTECTOR

The radical lawyer works in a state of perpetual tension or contradiction. On one side is the fact that the law oppresses people in two basic ways (see "In-Laws & Out-Laws: The Community Law Firm," 5 *Lincoln L. Rev.* [Fall 1969]). First, there are penal statutes that make acts illegal and provide for jail sentences. Some express society's moral perversion (prohibiting marijuana, vagrancy, abortion, obscenity, homosexuality, and prostitution). Others express the government's fear of dissent (penalizing the advocacy of revolution, crossing state lines with intent to incite to riot, and conspiracy to overthrow the established order). Another group of directly repressive laws protect society from acts that sometimes are a consequence of political upheaval (trespass, arson, breach of the peace, disorderly conduct, illegal assembly, and assault on a peace officer).

The second, and more subtle means by which the law is an agent of oppression is through its reinforcement of institutions that oppress people, for example, the activism of students in the public high schools. Primarily, this struggle has consisted of minority students challenging curriculum, channeling and tracking, and white students demanding decision-making power and First Amendment rights. The law supports the status quo by authorizing the Board of Education to determine curriculum and to make other basic policy decisions without equal student participation. It also works to keep students from exercising basic rights of association, speech, and dress, and supports the institution by enforcing the authoritarian structure within the school.

The other side of the contradiction is that there are constitutional provisions, court decisions, and legal procedures that can be invoked in the interests of the oppressed. Those legal protections are power in the hands of the attorney. The lawyer can use the test-case approach to challenge and to change laws. The lawyer can use procedural devices to protect the defendant, or may get a hung jury or ultimately gain an acquittal through the use of the jury system.

Where the law supports the institution, the lawyer is not as effective. In the high-school example, the law is not an effective offensive weapon to abolish the tracking system and to secure decision-making power. However, with regard to political rights such as the wearing of armbands, the distribution of leaflets and underground papers, and the creation of free speech areas, the law can be a useful tool. The lawyer must always remember that since the existing legal structure supports the schools' restrictions, before students are vindicated by the higher courts they face the possible destruction of their educational careers through suspensions, expulsions, and juvenile arrest records.

The contradiction of the law as prosecutor and protector is an antagonistic one; it is an irreconcilable contradiction. Yet, this need not breed depression, for it is only the recognition of the existence of a long-term struggle. An acceptance of this fact will help the radical lawyer commit himself to staying in that struggle and using the power the law reluctantly gives him.

LIFESTYLE

The second basic contradiction emerges from the lawyer as priest: that is, his acceptance of a role as interpreter of the dogma and the rituals of the law. . . .

In order to break through the feeling of powerlessness the lawyer must reject many of the doctrines of the legal practice. He must eschew the business rule that a lawyer's time is money; instead, he should spend lots of time discussing the case and the law with his client. He must reject the doctrine that the lawyer runs the case and consider acting as an advisor to his client's self-defense. He must also overcome his professional elitism and recognize that laymen can often offer deep insights into what is normally defined as a "legal" problem.

In the last few years a number of radical attorneys have begun to try to put fundamental changes into practice, such as the placing of the law firm in the community, the residence of the attorneys in the community in which they practice, the development of legal communes, and the establishment of professional-nonprofessional equality within the office.

By these and other means, the client begins to view the lawyer as an equal partner in the struggle. Movement and community groups realize that their power is primarily in their own commitment and organization. They begin to lose their fear of the law and in the absence of fear their potential is unlimited.

This is not to imply that all radical attorneys must change their form of practice; rather, it is to suggest that there are general political effects which flow from accepting the traditional lifestyle of the attorney. It should also be pointed out that this contradiction, unlike the first contradiction, is non-antagonistic. It is to a large degree reconcilable, awaiting only the action of the lawyer.

RIGHT ON

The law is more than an "ass." It is society's sophisticated means of restricting people and repressing revolution. As long as this society maintains its capitalist-democratic approach, the lawyer has power to free people and further the revolution. When the law is replaced by the hangman, there will be sufficient time to throw away the law books and pick up the appropriate tool. We should take note of the following insight of a Russian lawyer who later became one of history's famous revolutionaries: "(R)evolutionaries who are unable to combine illegal forms of struggle with *every* form of legal struggle are poor revolutionaries indeed. It is not difficult to be a revolutionary when revolution has already broken out and is at its height. . . . It is far more difficult—and of far greater value—to be a revolutionary when the conditions for direct, open, really mass and really revolutionary struggle *do not yet exist* to be able to champion the interests of the revolution . . . in non-revolutionary bodies and often enough in downright reactionary bodies . . ." (Lenin, "*Left Wing*" *Communism, an Infantile Disorder*).

For the present you don't have to love the law to be a lawyer. But you do have to love the people.

■

By Gene Ann Condon

[Condon, who practices in New York City, commented on Harris' article immediately.]

I am wrestling with strong feelings of being professionally, emotionally, and physically unable to continue practicing law. My feelings do not come from any sense of division with fellow Guild members or lawyers but from consideration of the question as to whether I, as a lawyer, have any function in our society. There are clients seeking my services and "political cases" of interest, but the question is whether a lawyer, "constitutional" or "radical," has an effective role to play.

Harris in using the term "radical lawyer" does not make it clear if a radical lawyer is a lawyer who represents radicals, a lawyer who is also a radical, or a radical person who uses radical techniques in representing radicals. I am a radical who has represented radicals but has not made use of radical techniques. I must admit I am not quite sure what radical techniques are. . . .

I disagree with Harris that advances made through legal victories are disruptive of American capitalist democracy. In my opinion they are more often placebos. In *Brown v. the Board, Mapp,* and *Miranda,* Warren's decisions are brilliant and, yes, radical, but the application of the decisions on the trial court level is illuminating. Under *Mapp,* a warrantless search may be conducted where the police officer has probable cause to believe a crime is being committed in his presence. The police officer lies through his teeth to establish probable cause; the defendant testifies as to his version of the occurrence; and the court believes the policeman. On appeal, since credibility of witnesses is left to the determination of the trial court, there is no remedy. This does not happen in every case, but it happens frequently enough to make *Mapp,* as a reality, far different from what the Warren court intended and what those who hail it as an advance think it means.

The same applies to charges such as disorderly conduct, unlawful assembly, and others cited by Harris. Each case is decided on its own facts and the courts have little difficulty in convicting when they want to and having the decision upheld on appeal. Thus the test-case approach is not as fruitful as Harris would have us believe, [and is not radical but traditional].

In a court system where 90 percent of defendants in criminal cases, as in New York, are black or Puerto Rican, every criminal case is a political case, and this is a point the radical lawyer must not miss. The New York State prison population runs along the same percentage. In everyday practice it is very easy to see who gets the suspended sentences, who receives Youth Counsel Bureau treatment, and who is acquitted. First it is whites, then middle-class blacks, and very, very rarely a low income minority group defendant. This is a political fact, not a sociological fact, although the sociologists draw conclusions from the statistics by reverse reasoning.

Harris finds encouragement for the radical lawyer who, in the face of adversity, has continued to "exist" and maintain his "power." Of course, we have survived, but I do not know what power we ever had. It was not the kind of power coveted or competed for by lawyers who represented the dominant interests in the society and was minuscule compared to their power. I don't rate this a negative, but I do think it's dangerous to overestimate the power of the radical lawyer. Liberals can afford a rich fantasy life; radicals must be as aware of reality as possible at all times.

The same reasoning applies to decreasing the client's feeling of "powerlessness" in relation to courtroom procedures. The fact is that the client is pretty damned powerless. Any client (or attorney) who sheds his fear (I would rather say appreciation or respect) of the law as it is now administered is walking into open jaws. The administration of justice is a powerful force, and it is now directly aimed against the radical. Most radicals know this, and it is one of the reasons they are radicals rather than reformists.

The "demystification" Harris refers to should be of the client's belief that his case will result in a *meaningful* consequence beyond (maybe) his staying out of jail. The law as now administered in relation to its announced procedures and principles is surrealistic. This reality makes me cynical, pessimistic, and depressed.

Although lifestyle may be important on an individual level, I don't see the relevance in terms of the individual as a lawyer. There is nothing new or radical about practicing in a neighborhood rather than a downtown or mid-town enclave. If you have to live in a slum to want to overthrow the system that perpetuates slums, then you're not a radical to start with. You would have to be a radical lawyer before moving into a slum voluntarily. So it goes around in circles. . . .

I am not convinced that acquittals actually hasten change. I am not talking of creating martyrs but raising the level of consciousness of all the people. One of the most favorable aspects of the past few years, to me, has been the spread of busts into the middle and upper-middle classes. I wouldn't wish being busted on anyone, but it has made the political situation more real to a lot of people who can make use of their experience.

Self-labeling and lifestyle to the contrary, when you step into that courtroom, no matter how radical you and/or your client are, *you, the lawyer, are a part of that system.* It doesn't matter what you wear, say, or do. If you are alienated not from the people but from the system, you will not be able to go into that courtroom. If you do decide to go in, it doesn't matter where your office is or how your personnel are referred to, or how decisions are made in your office; your only job is to be as competent as you are capable of being. This involves professional training and development. When you're there you must be there to win and you don't have to be a radical to win—you have to be the best lawyer you are capable of being. You can be a misanthrope and be an effective lawyer (examples abound); loving people is not a prerequisite to effectiveness. Lawyers are not social workers or encounter group leaders. To the extent that they act as such they potentially diminish their powers as technical instruments, and that's too bad because if you love people you hate to see those prison doors close behind them.

None of this is intended as a put-down of constitutionalists or radicals. I am depressed and negative, and I would love to be proven wrong and distorted in my thinking because whatever the law game is as far as I'm concerned right now it's the only game in town.

THE CLASS ROLE OF U.S. COURTS
By Doris Brin Walker

[This speech was made at a Guild convention panel on democratic rights and the struggle for social change in 1974, after Walker had participated in the Angela Davis case.]

My assigned topic is an historical overview of the class role of the courts, and the key word here is "class," used in its Marxist meaning. It denotes a scientifically established economic group relationship to the means of production.

I am going to spare you discussion of such fascinating matters as the primary role of the working class and the labor theory of value, which underlies all Marxist class analysis, and the concept of "base and superstructure," except to say that that Marxist phrase distinguishes between the economic base of society and the social, cultural, and political superstructure developed on the base, as well as the interaction and effect of each upon the other. The courts and the legal system are a part of the superstructure, not of the base.

It is not necessary to accept all of this Marxist theory in order to understand what follows. What is absolutely necessary in any analysis of

---

"The Class Role of U.S. Courts," by Doris Brin Walker, *NLG Practitioner* 31:2 (Spring 1974).

the class role of the courts is to eliminate as much as possible our own subjectivity and to understand the objective sources of the courts' subjectivity (motivations), whether conscious or not.

Historically, the court's role must be viewed in the context of its institutional origins, including the American Revolution and the Constitution which followed. Lenin described our revolution as "one of those great, really liberating, really revolutionary wars of which there have been so few among the large number of wars of conquest." The eminent American bourgeois historian Charles Beard found from contemporary records that even the drafters of the Constitution recognized the conflicts of economic interests among them and fought out those economic conflicts in their drafting of the Constitution. The drafters were landowners and stockholders, bankers and slaveowners, lawyers, merchants, and speculators. None was a "mechanic," a small farmer, an indentured servant, or a slave.

It is significant that the Constitution and the Bill of Rights, in which rights, duties, privileges, and procedures are written down in a *Document*, is not the amorphous, uncodified, common law principles of the so-called English Constitution. We have in this country legally protected rights of dissent greater than exist anywhere else. We undoubtedly disagree as to the importance of this fact in bringing about revolutionary changes; but it IS a fact, owed in largest part to our revolutionary origins and to our written Constitution.

Engels and Lenin, among many other Marxists, held that the use and protection of legal rights was of great importance in revolutionary struggle. Engels in 1895 called for increasing the development of the mass support and the potential military force for the revolutionary party by "legal methods" rather than "illegal methods and revolt." Lenin agreed, and developed the point further when he called for: "the most thorough . . . and skillful *obligatory* use of . . . even the smallest 'rift' among the enemies, every antagonism of interests among the bourgeoisie . . . taking advantage of every . . . opportunity of gaining a mass ally, even though this ally be temporary, vacillating, unstable, unreliable, and conditional."

We must never have any illusions about the class role of the courts. The judge is not irritable or hostile because he is a personal enemy, or because he is white or a male—or friendly because he agrees with our client's politics or our own. The judge is trying, consciously or not, to do his bit to help the system stick together, in operating order. Judges, like anyone else among the bourgeoisie, are subject to the "rifts" referred to by Lenin. Judges often disagree among themselves and with other elements of their own class as to tactics or the need for reform. But there is virtually no disagreement among them as to their goal: the preservation of the present social-economic order. That was the meaning of *Brown v. Board of Education,* 347 US 483, in 1954, disapproving school segregation, just as it was the meaning of *Plessy v. Ferguson,* 163 US 537, in 1896, upholding the doctrine of "separate but equal" railway coaches. Times change; class lines shift; class composition takes on some new appearances; internal and international pressures alter; an organized, strong Third World movement has developed. But the ruling class follows the iron law of history: they try by any and every means to hold onto their power.

[One example is the] contemporary phenomenon, Judge John Sirica. We saw, at least part, of the consequences of that phenomenon last night when Richard Nixon resigned as President of the United States. Pre-Watergate, Judge Sirica was well known for his severe sentencing of poor criminal defendants; he is conservative. Nixon is very much in the position of those referred to by Engels, who cried "Legality is the death of us!" Too bad for Nixon and his gang of neo-Fascist thugs that Sirica has a different perception of how to save the system! Too bad for Nixon that a unanimous Supreme Court sees only too clearly—as he in his overwhelming venality cannot—the probable consequences of wholesale violation by government officials of dozens of statutes and the destruction of the constitutional separation and balance of powers.

Those probable consequences can only be increased unrest, increased struggle, increased class consciousness. . . . Who knows where it all would end? So the judges hand out relatively light sentences to their class brothers, Erlichman, et al., and do their thing to save the system. The heavy sentences are still saved for the blacks, the Latinos, the poor, the oppressed.

It is not enough, of course, merely to *understand* that courts play a class role. The point is to *use* that understanding in our daily practice. Use requires cool, detached, objective—yes, scientific, analysis of a number of elements:

1) the nature of the case, the issues and the parties;
2) the nature of the historical period—from whence it came and where it is going;
3) the nature of the judge—his background, history, biases, personality, and track record in constitutional law or whatever fields are involved;
4) the role or potential role of a mass movement around the case, including what coalitions are possible;
5) the contradictions inherent in each of these elements and how, and under what circumstances, those contradictions may surface.

The point of all this scientific, objective analysis is TO WIN—at the trial level if possible, and in the Supreme Court if needs be. Victory includes mass education and organization, as well as getting an acquittal or an injunction or damages.

[Walker presented one example in detail, *United States v. Powell and Schuman,* from a 1956 indictment for seditious actions during the "police action" in Korea (publishing articles in Shanghai that the U.S., not Communist North Koreans, had initiated the fighting in Korea, and that the U.S. was using germ warfare weapons) to a successful motion for a mistrial on the fourth day of trial in 1958.]

It has been suggested that the judge deliberately committed error in order to end a trial that could only embarrass the government, and the theory is tenable. Why did he allow the due process that helped produce the embarrassment? Why have the judges (trial or appellate) in the *Huey Newton* case, 8 CA3d 359 (1970), the *Chicago Conspiracy-Dellinger* case, 461 F2d 389 (CA 7 1972), the *Angela Davis* case, and others, made decisions on due process points—discovery, jury selection, jury instructions, exclusion of evidence—which eventually resulted in acquittals or dismissals?

They were acting in the best interests of the system, as they perceived those interests at those points in time. They acted to avert damage—perhaps to the very fabric of society, as they perceived that damage—whether because of mass pressures, the possibility of open and sharpened conflict, the consequences of exposure of corrupt police and prosecution practices, or the influences of our revolutionary origins and Constitution. It is easy to see the class role of the Supreme Court in 1883 in the *Civil Rights Cases,* 109 U.S. 3, which held that businessmen could discriminate on account of race and that Congress had exceeded its powers in forbidding such discrimination. Is it not also easy to see that class role in 1964 in the unanimous opinion, in *Heart of Atlanta Motel v. US,* 379 US 241, which noted "the disruptive effect that racial discrimination has had on commercial intercourse" and upheld the Civil Rights Act of 1964? . . .

It is important to understand the class role of the courts, not merely to use or manipulate legal procedures and proceedings, but rather to help workers and all oppressed people understand how best to support, protect, and extend the bourgeois democratic rights included in our written Constitution and needed by them in their fight against oppression. They need to keep open all options in choosing forms of struggle against the base, against the economic Establishment.

How revolutionaries conduct current struggles will help determine the nature of the eventual victory. We in this country can avoid Fascism and its effects on that eventual victory because of our history as well as because of the victories already achieved by Socialism all over the world.

Thus we have not been considering merely tactics or even merely strategy. The Second American Revolution, when it comes, will be a revolution "American-style." It will grow out of the class struggles in this country, conducted, as necessarily they must be, in the context of our own history and culture, led by workers, not lawyers—by women and men of all colors and ages.

It follows that, in order to make our own peculiar contribution to that revolutionary struggle, rigorous scientific analysis in our own legal work is just as essential as such analysis is to our clients, the working class.

See:

Charles Beard, *An Economic Interpretation of the Constitution of the United States* (1913).

Frederick Engels, *Introduction to Karl Marx "Class Struggles in France"* (1895).

Ann Fagan Ginger, "Due Process in Practice," 25 *Hastings Law Journal* 897 (1974).

Lenin, *Left Wing Communism, An Infantile Disorder* (1920).

Lenin, *Letter to American Workers* (1918).

THE GUILD MILITARY OFFICE IN THE PHILIPPINES
By Howard DeNike and Bob Hilliard

■

SKETCHES FROM THE PHILIPPINES
By Howard DeNike

[Working for the LMDC (Lawyers' Military Defense Committee), not the Guild's Military Law Project, DeNike captures the spirit (and the endless abbreviations) that characterized that place and time. This is one small slice of a major chapter in Guild history that deserves recording.]

Coming from Vietnam, I was greeted at the airport by Barbara Dudley, whom I had first met in Saigon when she stayed with the LMDC. Without pausing, we went to the Manila Press Club, where several sailors and U.S. Air Force enlisted men were in the middle of a press conference called by the Guild, describing their knowledge of nuclear weapons on U.S. ships and planes in Philippine territory. These reports were dramatic news in the Philippines and terribly embarrassing to the U.S. and to President Marcos, who was looking for a way to stay in power as the end of his second four-year term and constitutionally

---

"The Guild Military Office in the Philippines" ("Sketches"), by Howard DeNike, was written for this book; "Government Spied on Guild Military Office," by Bob Hilliard, *Guild Notes* (Jan.-Feb. 1982), was based on information revealed in *Guild v. Attorney General.*

mandated removal from office approached. Within forty-eight hours, the four men who had spoken out at the press conference were transferred to the States.

With massive bases at Subic Bay (Naval) and Clark (Air Force), the U.S. had turned the Philippines into a virtual aircraft carrier for taking part in the Vietnam war. Regularly five, sometimes six, carriers replenished at Subic and then steamed for Yankee Station off the coast of Vietnam to take part in the most ferocious offshore-based bombardment in the history of warfare. Because of Philippine political considerations, no offensive Air Force bombing runs were launched from Clark Air Force Base, but that fact did not prevent Clark from flying a multitude of other support missions.

On the streets of Olongapo and outside Clark Air Force Base, U.S. servicemen wore tie-dyed t-shirts and, in the case of Navy personnel, beards and sideburns, to link them with the movement against the war in Vietnam and the war against authority "back in the world" (the U.S.). Drugs (heroin and marijuana) were plentiful and potent, and the vices of the U.S. Navy's largest port-of-call in the Pacific gaudily available.

The Guild's house on Corpuz Street in Olongapo was a combined residence, law office, and counseling center. In the evenings, counselors from the U.S.-staffed Pacific Counseling Service (PCS) set up discussion groups ("DGs") with as many GIs as could be found. Out came the copies of *Quotations from Chairman Mao Tse-Tung* (the famed "Little Red Book"), and hours were spent pouring over the meaning of key paragraphs. Future cadre for the revolution were being prepared from the ranks of the U.S. Navy.

The New People's Army (NPA) was ever-present in the thoughts of the GI activists. Was there really a parallel between the Philippines and Vietnam? We all thought so. In the meantime, there were veiled suggestions to U.S. sailors and airmen that, if they had any "surplus" medications to donate, there were "forces in the countryside" who could benefit from them.

A familiar part of the regimen in Olongapo were almost daily visits by Barbara, Dan Siegel, and me for a session at the local karate school. The instruction and work-outs gave us contact with a side of Philippine life we needed desperately at times—as when I went outside to collect my wash from the line and discovered all my pants were stolen, or when dozens of small frogs jumped out of the drain in the shower one morning. The high point of our training came shortly before our departure as we stood beside our Filipino friends and proudly received our "green belts" for reaching the first level of competence.

In July 1972, a series of typhoons and tropical storms hit the Philippines, leaving 150 inches of rain in 30 days! Tarlac and Tampanga

Provinces were under water, hundreds were drowning or dying in mudslides, and food shortages were widespread. For the Guild office, the weekly trip to Manila, which usually took four hours by bus, became an ordeal which lasted up to 24 hours. One afternoon, I departed Manila around noon for Olongapo. About 30 miles from the city, it was necessary to change to a dug-out canoe, a *banca* boat, to cross the rice paddies, which had turned into an inland sea. After several hours (and payment of impromptu tolls to property owners whose lands we crossed), we switched to a jeepney and about midnight reached a small crossroads town in Bataan Province, famous for the Death March of allied soldiers during World War II. The street where we had been forced to halt became a quick-paced river, with water waist-high. It might have been that moment I decided the time was right for getting out of the RP. My normal weight of 155 pounds was down to 130, and the nagging infection in my toe would not heal because of the constant water underfoot.

Before departing, however, I had one last court-martial defense of a sailor nicknamed "Frenchie," on trial for taking part in the disappearance of armaments from a Navy magazine at Cubi Point. As the trial approached, the sensation-loving Manila press carried headline stories about a small ship discovered off the coast of Northern Luzon loaded with weapons meant for the NPA. No one knew the destination of the weapons purloined by my client and his friends, least of all Frenchie, who was just eighteen and set up to take the rap for the others, who had rushed to grab immunity in return for their testimony. It would not take much from a prosecutor to plant the suspicion that the grenades from the Cubi Point magazine at Subic would end up with the NPA. (A more plausible explanation was that they were for one of the private armies that the oligarchic plantation owners like to maintain.)

When we could not delay the trial any longer, we were able to convince the court that, compared to the others, the fuzzy-cheeked sailor from the Louisiana bayou was relatively innocent. He was sentenced to nine months in the brig, which severely disappointed the prosecutor, who was asking for six years.

The Judge Advocate General (JAG) Office at Subic Bay was a mixed bag—some Navy lawyers would have nothing to do with the NLG attorneys, some respected their feistiness, and some were openly hostile. The brass were prominent in the last group, and after the base admiral saw Dan Siegel and Barbara Dudley having lunch in *his* Officers' Club with their JAG co-counsel, banned any repetition of such breaches in "decorum."

The element of respect and plain decency reached its height when, after Marcos declared martial law in September 1972, a contingent of the much-feared Philippine Constabulary (PC) came looking for Guild lawyer Doug Sorensen. Lt. Peter C., who lived on base, took Doug into his home, in hopes that Doug could avoid a very uncertain fate. Finally, in violation of U.S. and Philippine law, the PC came to the base and took Doug into custody. In the meantime, the GI counselors from the Pacific Counseling Service had also been arrested.

[While Doug Sorensen and the PCS counselors were being held, a team of Guild lawyers, including Charles Garry, David Rein, and Melvin Wulf, was preparing to fly to Manila to intercede directly on their behalf. On their way to the airport in San Francisco, word was received that Marcos had expelled Doug and the others, thus ending the Guild's fifteen months in the Philippines.]

■

"GOVERNMENT SPIED ON GUILD MILITARY OFFICE"
By Bob Hilliard

[In 1982 some of the revelations from the Guild suit against the Attorney General were reported in *Guild Notes*.]

According to a special report of the U.S. Air Force (August 1972), the Guild "did not pose a serious threat to USAF operations at the moment" but it *did* threaten to create ". . . a more general environment of doubt among servicemen as to the validity of any involvement in Southeast Asia—in effect a mirroring of attitudes prevailing throughout large segments of American society."

From the beginning, Barbara Dudley and Sandy Karp were followed by the CIA in the Philippines. Eric Seitz, National Secretary of the NLG, was followed by the Army. In addition to informants, the United States authorities had phone taps on the [Military Law Office] MLO's operations, making them privy to confidential discussions between attorneys and their clients concerning cases in which the authorities were the adversary.

When it came time to renew the visas of MLO attorneys, Philippine immigration authorities decided this was unauthorized practice of law. The U.S. Embassy issued an "opinion" that this was a proper decision. When the office appealed this decision, the U.S. Embassy tried to influence the Philippine Department of Justice. The MLO won their visa extension.

A U.S. Navy official turned over to a Philippine military liaison officer a flyer the MLO had written, directed toward U.S. military personnel, criticizing the Marcos regime. As the U.S. military well expected, the Philippine authorities used this flyer as an excuse to raid the MLO and arrest and deport the office personnel in October 1972. Immediately after the raid, the Philippine Constabulary invited the U.S. Naval Investigative Service to inspect the GI Center where the MLO operated.

Even while the State Department was saying it was unable to assist the NLG in obtaining return of the MLO's files, the U.S. Navy had its own copy of all the material seized in the raid.

Admiral E. R. Zumwalt, Jr., Chief of Naval Operations, wrote to Acting FBI Director L. Patrick Gray, III, in December 1972: "Thanks to Philippine officials, the Navy has acquired a considerable amount of seized documentary material which implicates . . . the NLG . . . in support[ing] subversion within the U.S. Armed Forces in the Western Pacific." Zumwalt was interested in whether "foreign financial assistance, direct or indirect (e.g., via CP, U.S.A.), has been provided to the NLG in connection with the 'Southeast Asia Military Project.'"

[Even] after the Philippines raid, the Naval Investigative Service asked the San Antonio FBI office to provide it with information on the Guild's 1973 convention in Austin.

WILLIAM O. DOUGLAS: IN RETROSPECT
By Leonard B. Boudin

Justice William O. Douglas was appointed to the Supreme Court at the age of forty and served longer than any other justice in its history until his retirement in 1975. I believe that he was the closest to what we would call "genius" in the history of the Court. He began with a background of poverty, served only two years as an associate in the Cravath firm, and then embarked on a teaching career at Columbia and Yale. His speciality was corporate finance. He served on the Securities and Exchange Commission as member and chairman, and then was President Roosevelt's second appointment, following Justice Black, to the Supreme Court.

With Justice Black, Douglas, during the Cold War period, was an inspiration to those who were the subject of government oppression. . . .

Douglas' contributions to the law were in no way dependent upon his association with Black. . . . Black operated with a certain literalism, both in reading the First Amendment and in insisting upon the legislative role of Congress as a bar to executive assumption of power. His opinions have an almost biblical flavor. Douglas, on the other hand, is blunt, tart, indignant, and at all times realistic.

In *Laird v. Tatum* he dissented from the Court's approval of military surveillance of civilian dissenters: "This case involves a cancer in our body politic. . . . Armed surveillance, like armed regimentation, is at

---

"William O. Douglas: In Retrospect," by Leonard B. Boudin, excerpted from *Guild Notes* (March 1980).

war with the principles of the First Amendment . . . [which] was designed to allow rebellion to remain as our heritage. The Constitution was designed to keep government off the backs of the people."

The uniqueness of Douglas can also be found in his opinions as Circuit Justice. Note the stays granted by him in the *Rosenberg* case, in the Vietnam cases, and in the *Ellsberg* case. His home in Goose Prairie and the District Courthouse in Yakima, Washington, can well be regarded as shrines to the memory of the applications to Douglas for emergency relief.

In terms of creativity, one has only to look at his decision in *Griswold v. Connecticut,* the birth control case, where he enunciated his penumbras theory: "[S]pecific guarantees in the Bill of Rights have penumbras, formed by emanations from those guarantees that help give them life and substance. . . . The right of association contained in the penumbra of the First Amendment is one, . . ."

In terms of my professional relationship, at least three cases stand out: the first was *Kent v. Dulles,* . . . I considered it miraculous that in the Cold War period when constitutional rights were constantly denied by the Court, Douglas was able to enunciate a constitutional right to travel; hence, hundreds of thousands of citizens denied many other rights (such as public and private employment, protection against grand juries) enjoyed this right.

The second case was *Ullman v. United States,* where Douglas wrote a brilliant dissent upholding the Fifth Amendment privilege against self-incrimination against the government's offer of transactional immunity under the Immunity Act of 1954. . . . Ironically, the present Court has accepted testimonial immunity as a sufficient *quid pro quo* for compulsory testimony.

Third, when wiretapping was discovered in the *Ellsberg* case, Douglas heard argument in the district courtroom in Yakima and telephoned his order staying the trial. It was the first time in my recollection that a criminal trial in progress had been stayed by a Supreme Court justice. Although the Court finally denied certiorari, the resulting delay permitted the interaction of Nixon, Watergate and Ellsberg, the combined revelations resulting in a dismissal of the indictment with prejudice.

[Incidentally,] he appeared to be indifferent to the criticism of his enemies, and he survived the efforts of President Nixon and Congressman Gerald Ford and others to secure his impeachment, . . . Nixon's response to the Senate's rejection of Judges Haynsworth's and Carswell's nominations to the Supreme Court. . . .

I pass over the 1,200 Douglas opinions, many of them creative and brilliant, during his long service on the Court. Those who wish to pursue the matter further, and they should, will find most illuminating Vern

Countryman's two books: *The Douglas Opinions* and *Douglas And The Supreme Court.*

BOYCOTTING WINE ON INTERSTATE 99
By Barbara Rhine

I remember getting through all the pain and alienation that was law school by saying it would soon be over. Then when I started on the pain and alienation that was practicing law, I couldn't say it would soon be over any more, and things got scary. This was my life somewhere in here, wasn't it? And all the talk in the world about the "lawyer as organizer" and the "political use of the law" couldn't get around the fact that practicing law was in so many ways deadly, alienating, and lonely. So I quit; spent two years being a carpenter in Berkeley, hanging out with my friends, traveling, trying to learn to give myself a little space. It was one of the best things I ever did, but it didn't solve the problem of how to act on my political principles and try to make my life count for something beyond myself.

Then I came to work for the United Farmworkers Union. I started in July last summer, and worked pretty much the entire time in Livingston (between Modesto and Merced, the first stop light on 99 north of Tijuana, to answer the inevitable question), on the Gallo strike.

I'll never forget the first time I went to court. I hadn't touched a law book for two years, and had never handled an eviction case. A call came: Gallo was moving to evict the first of hundreds from the unbelievably shitty housing they designed to provide for the workers. The trial had already happened and been lost, and this was a motion on a new trial to be heard the next day . . . and no one had located the file yet.

I got up at six the next morning and started to read Moskovitz' handbook madly. I left at noon to drive down and read the court's file by three when the hearing was. Somewhere in the blur one of the people I talked to asked if I wanted people there, and I said "sure, why not?" When I went into court, the room was FULL! In the spectator section, in the jury box, in the aisles, were these silent and dignified workers, sun-rough and brown, the very ones Gallo wanted to evict.

I had promised myself not to be intimidated like the last time I had ventured into the world of men in courtrooms, so I strode up to the silvery-haired, portly gentleman who seemed to embody the corporate opulence of Gallo, and stuck out my slightly shaking hand. As I intro-

---

"Boycotting Wine on Interstate 99," by Barbara Rhine, excerpted from Los Angeles Guild Chapter, *People's Justice* (June–July 1974).

duced myself, he stared in disbelief. Surely, this "girl" couldn't be the lawyer to appear against HIM!

The hearing started, and I asked that the proceedings be translated, first into Spanish, and then into Portuguese.

The judge was not a lawyer, and the other lawyer was arrogant, so, amazingly enough, it turned out I knew as much about eviction law as either of them. I spouted about the Constitution, the right to strike, retaliatory eviction. He spouted about the Constitution, the sanctity of property rights, eviction. The judge looked confused. The people listened intently to every word, translated by members of their own ranks.

At some point in the middle of the hearing my hands stopped shaking, and the Gallo lawyer's started. That was the moment I realized that practicing law would be different this time.

We eventually lost the case, of course. But by that time the people were so together that they were all sitting at the Ramirez' house just waiting for the sheriff to come to evict, ready to go to jail. Gallo was *afraid* to evict because they knew about the publicity and the boycott that was going to start, and they knew that the Union was not powerless. Later, they had tried to evict everyone (over 600) with one injunction in Merced, but when the people, Cesar Chavez, and the press showed up, they had to back off that one, too. So when they couldn't get a continuance (because the judge leaned down to the now-swelled ranks of Gallo lawyers and said, "Really, now, these people have come a long way and you're the ones alleging irreparable injury you know"), they dismissed the complaint. Right there, in front of all those people, though the people already expected to lose and were planning a tent city in Gallo's front yard!

And then I knew I was addicted to the high that can come from practicing law with the people behind you, in front of you, all around you. . . . I worked closely with Aggie Rose, the director of the strike, and we began to understand how intrinsically connected our jobs were.

The excitement of this organization gets me through a lot of hours of boring work, and even makes me interested in understanding farm accounting methods so I can know the enemy.

This is what it means in this country to be a part of an organization with a "mass base" (how many times I heard those words in Guild circles before I quit the law). An organization caught in the midst of a hundred contradictions, that gets everything done with no resources (*i.e.*, money, Xerox machines), full of differences and tensions, making impossible demands on the people that work for it, fighting the most powerful forces in this country, turning people out and fighting back— an organization where even a lawyer can't fool herself that all the responsibility rests in her hands.

THE SHANGO TRIAL:
THE LAWYER, THE CLIENT, AND THE JURY
By Ernest Goodman

[Ernest Goodman, Haywood Burns, and William Goodman were the trial lawyers in the Shango case. The following excerpt focuses on only two of several intriguing aspects of the Attica uprising cases; others are discussed in the manuscript from which this excerpt is taken.]

I have always wanted to handle my own cases in my own way, without having to wrestle with other people's ideas as to procedure, strategy, and tactics. I changed for the first time in the Detroit Black Panther trial, where we had a defense team. But the trial of Shango, one of the key Attica cases in 1975, went far beyond that. A group of people did the research, helped on the briefs, secured and talked to witnesses, helped in jury selection, raised community support, and dealt with the personal problems that arose during the case. For the first time I saw how it was possible to work as a team for a common cause—lawyers, non-lawyers, law students, legal workers, investigators.

My client was an important part of this team. I've never worked for a client who contributed so much and was such a remarkable person. Indicted as Bernard Stroble, he had adopted the name Shango Bahati Kakawana and preferred to be called that. Shango was a tall, well-built, bearded, handsome, black man. On first sight, he gave an impression of great dignity, strength, alertness, and intelligence. After I had explored his personality, I found that this external impression truly reflected his character. Shango acted as pro se—his own attorney—on one of the three indictments against him. I was his attorney on the murder charge. (Later Haywood Burns became his attorney on one of the felony murder charges.)

I expected this to present great difficulties. The time element alone would be a real problem. Well, it was a difficulty, but there was a process of mutual education that became very valuable. Sometimes I had strong ideas on one approach or strategy, and Shango would come up with an opposite idea. I tried consciously to keep my mind open. Shango not only spoke well but also was very thoughtful; his views were based on reason and logic. I learned to respect his judgment. Many of his views that I originally rejected I eventually accepted. I avoided a number of mistakes by doing that, and we developed ideas I could not have developed on my own. When I felt I was right about something, I fought

---

"The Shango Trial," by Ernest Goodman, from an unpublished work, MCLI; concluding editors' note from "Attica Lives: Reflections on the Dismissal of the Attica Indictments," by Ernest Goodman, *Guild Notes* (May 1976).

for my position. There were many things that Shango didn't know about trying lawsuits, of course. But I found that he, too, kept an open mind and could change his position.

The prison uprising began on Thursday morning, September 9, 1971, when there were approximately 2,000 prisoners at Attica. Of these, 1,200 eventually grouped themselves in D yard. They had about 40 hostages. . . . The first official reports from prison authorities asserted that the throats of hostages had been slit and that they had been brutalized by the prisoners. But when the bodies were taken to Rochester for autopsies, the pathologist, Dr. Edland, reported that they had been shot. . . . Since the troops were the only ones who had guns, this proved that they—not the prisoners—had killed the hostages. . . .

It was clear that Shango had had a good deal to do with the events following the uprising. He was involved in the prisoners' security force and was part of the group that brought the two white prisoners, Hess and Schwartz, to D block. We denied that the two had been tried and sentenced to death; they had been sent to D block by the leadership to protect them from other prisoners in the yard who might want to harm them. It was true Shango was present when Schwartz and Hess were assaulted in the cell on Company 42 in D block. But it was not true Shango had killed Schwartz or had approved of or wanted to have him killed by someone else. . . .

Shortly after the pre-trial hearing ended, the three defendants had a substantial disagreement on issues central to the entire case: where was the real fight? Could a political battle be fought successfully in the courtroom? Big Black publicly took the position that a political struggle, such as Attica, could not be fought in a courtroom. Shango disagreed: one must fight where the enemy is; you can't always choose the place of battle, and in this case there is no choice; and there's no reason you can't win the courtroom fight. It ended when Big Black announced in court, "I'm leaving. I'm not coming here any more."

This incident caused a rift between Shango and Big Black and had a deep impact on the whole defense effort in Buffalo.

I'd seen a great deal of controversy about this question over the years, particularly in the Lawyers Guild. Our defense team tried to work on a highly political level but nevertheless within the context of a courtroom fight. We decided to try to win over the jury and the public by the manner in which we developed and presented the defense. . . .

Shango was in jail all during the trial, of course, but the judge was careful to have him brought into the courtroom so that the jury wouldn't see him in handcuffs. Many of the jurors didn't realize he was in custody. He wore good clothes and looked great when he came into the courtroom. The impression the jury had of him had a bearing on the outcome of the case. . . .

We were able to show the jury that Shango had been specifically selected for prosecution, not just because he was an inmate and inmates were prosecuted for homicides while the state police were not. He had been purposely prosecuted even though the prosecution knew that another person was responsible. To the extent that we proved this, it was obvious that Cryan, the prosecuting attorney, was involved in the selection of Shango.

We had another advantage over Cryan. Most prosecutors don't take a broad view of a case. They tend to make mistakes in both strategy and tactics by failing to understand the broader implications of a case. Take the race issue. Cryan had no real conception about race relations in the United States or in prisons, the nature of race prejudice, or of his own prejudices. This became apparent as he tried to deal with the issue when we raised it.

We were constantly developing an overall strategy, building areas of defense that were not apparent at first. The prosecution seemed completely unaware of these. We were able to develop a strong, forward-looking, consistent, logical attack from the beginning to the end of the case. The jury understood it and saw it developing in the courtroom. The prosecution had very little success in diverting or undermining it. At the same time we were able to undermine the prosecution's case and ultimately make it unbelievable.

Cryan was a competent lawyer in the courtroom, but he didn't seem to feel the emotions that an ordinary person would be moved by. He never developed a personal relationship with many of the jurors. On the other hand, we made every effort to show the jurors we were humane and concerned, that this wasn't a game to us, that we were personally, intimately, and fully committed to the defense of a person and a cause we believed in. At the end, some of the jurors commented on this distinction between the defense and the prosecution. They also noticed the young people working with us so intensely, and the spectators who came over to talk to Shango during recesses.

In other Attica cases the defense called for picket lines outside the courtroom. That must be done in some cases, but we didn't do it that way. We approached the jury on the basis of our understanding of their backgrounds. (Some time before our trial started, the defense had won a challenge to the Buffalo jury selection process as a whole, particularly as to underrepresentation of youths and women. As a result of the new process, several good juries had been selected in earlier trials. This gave us a good basis for our jury work.) . . .

Some people on the defense team wanted to keep jurors who appeared to be not as bad as most. Shango was opposed to this and argued strongly against it. I soon came over to this point of view and, in the end, this strategy prevailed. We decided we'd take our chances on getting *good* jurors. . . .

The prosecutor excused the only black person on the first panel of fifty for no apparent reason other than race. From then on, he excused every black person, over our protests. Finally, ten jurors had been selected, and there wasn't a black person among them. When the DA peremptorily excused a young black woman who seemed suitable in every sense, except the color of her skin, we really raised hell! We made motions to the court, issued statements to the press, and prepared an interlocutory appeal on this issue to a higher court. Representatives of community organizations protested the DA's attitude.

Then two more jurors were called and one was a black man, the strongest black person yet called. He was the president of a local union, an independent guy, and we found out from our "network" enough to decide he would be a very good juror. The white man looked as though he might be more helpful to the prosecution, but we didn't know anything really bad about him. The prosecutor had *voir dired* the two prospective jurors and it then became our turn to question them.

At Shango's suggestion, we announced we would not put a single question to either juror. We were saying we would accept the white juror if the prosecutor would accept the black juror—anything to avoid an all-white jury. The pressure was on the prosecutor. He finally announced he was satisfied with the jury.

Shango's brilliant strategy had paid off! Then the first alternate was a black woman, solid, strong, a church person. The prosecutor accepted her. After a few weeks of trial, the Chicano woman had to attend a funeral in New Mexico and was excused, so the black woman took her place. We had two strong, black jurors when we came to the verdict. . . .

We decided to tell the jury who killed Schwartz, although it was not necessary. We pointed out that the state had, in effect, recognized that the uprising was unplanned and had arisen out of miserable prison conditions, for no one had been indicted for bringing it about. The state itself was responsible for the result of its own actions and neglect. The inmates caught up in the events, including Shango, had to be judged in the context of the circumstances in which they found themselves. We were able to bring out on cross-examination that all the guards and officials at Attica were white, whereas about eighty percent of the prisoners were black, and other facts on the underlying racial prejudice.

After the prosecution had put in its case, Shango was anxious to put on witnesses and even to testify himself. So many of the witnesses had lied, he wanted witnesses to tell the jury what the truth was. I tried to convince him that to prove the truth, the defense would undertake a burden it didn't have to sustain. Almost the only witnesses we could put on were prisoners, under the same pressures and promises from the prosecution that the others had succumbed to. There was no assurance they would stick to a story.

Because of Shango's strong feelings, we agreed to investigate other possible witnesses. So we argued on a hot, miserable Sunday in the hot, miserable jail. We finally agreed to call only three witnesses, including Dr. Edland, who had done the autopsies. We also agreed I would argue on the murder charge and prosecutorial misconduct. Shango would then project his ideas about prison life, the problems arising when 1,200 prisoners suddenly obtained relative freedom, and the role he had played in the leadership. He would try to get the jury to understand what it is like to be a prisoner under these circumstances. Haywood would argue what remained of the former kidnap-murder charge, the background of the uprising, and the racial issues.

Shango made a very personal argument, yet it was objective in many ways. The jury could not help but be impressed with the man as an intelligent human being, a person of dignity. He had been accused of horrible crimes, had been in prison all these years after conviction of a felony, and yet he approached this long and difficult case in a very fair way. He never pushed the jurors, never assumed too much, and always dealt with them rationally and intelligently. Shango's argument was very impressive.

Prosecutor Cryan made an effective closing argument. The only thing lacking was a sense of being a concerned human being.

The jury started deliberating at about one o'clock. They continued to deliberate with time out for dinner. At nine o'clock that night the jury was ready to give their verdict. The courtroom was filled. It was very quiet. After six months, here was the end. The foreman arose and said, "On the charge of murder, we find the defendant not guilty." Pandemonium broke out—not stamping or yelling, but just the release of tension and happiness.

"On the count of unlawful imprisonment, not guilty," he announced.

I never felt such a surge of absolute happiness as I did at that moment....

Later, as I came down the steps alone, I saw everyone who had been in the courtroom. They started to applaud. It was a remarkable feeling of oneness. We had put up a defense jointly that had been able to overpower the state and to bring some justice to that courtroom. It never could have occurred without everyone's help. I put down my briefcase and in the gesture I had learned in the Socialist countries, I applauded them as they applauded me.

The only element missing was Shango. He had already been taken back to the jail. So all of us walked around the jail and shouted the chant of the Attica defense movement: "ATTICA MEANS—ATTICA MEANS—"

Back from the jail came the shout: "FIGHT BACK! FIGHT BACK!"

Again: "ATTICA MEANS—"

And back from the jail, not just one voice, but many: "FIGHT BACK!"

What a moment!

Struggles of oppressed peoples were going on all over the world. This was just a small part of that movement but at that moment I felt that struggle was not only possible but could ultimately result in victory. They might be limited victories, but they would lead to more lasting victories. We felt a part of those millions who were struggling everywhere, and of those who had died in such struggles long before we had come on the scene.

[When Governor Rockefeller of New York ordered police to retake Attica by force, rather than acknowledge the validity of the demands of the prisoners in September 1971, he set the stage for conscientious local attorneys to represent inmates and to form the Buffalo Chapter of the Guild.

[On February 26, 1976, a Special Deputy Attorney General, recently appointed by Governor Carey, moved to dismiss all but two indictments against Attica prisoners. Ernest Goodman found "a sweet taste in the spectacle of the last of the special prosecutors who had tried so hard to convict, being castigated by others appointed to create a new image of state concern with justice." Shango wrote in *Guild Notes* to thank the many who had worked on his case, from Don Jelinek, who headed the effort during 1972 and 1973, when the state set out to prosecute 62 inmates on 42 separate criminal indictments, to Linda Borus, who acted as investigator and whose "substantial communication . . . allowed me to participate in my own defense in as full a manner as I was capable," and Beth Bonora, Mike Laine, Eric Swanson, Devon Hodges, Carrie Curry, Brian Strait, Stu Cohen, and John Stewart in Buffalo; Neal Bush, Ken Mogill, Dick Skutt and Sid Rosen in Detroit. He mentioned especially his mother, the Rev. Mrs. Mozie Lee Stroble-Smith, who "dedicated herself to the freedom for all those who have been wronged," whose "spirit of unceasing resistance has sparked mine."]

■ SEVENTEEN

Young Lawyers Take Hold (1970–1979)

INTERNAL STRUGGLES IN the Lawyers Guild from 1967 to 1979 deserve long and careful description and analysis because the Guild is one of the few national organizations that survived the shift in membership and leadership from the Depression/New Deal/World War II era to the Vietnam/black power/New Left era. Fascinating novels and histories are yet to be written about the results of changed habits—from reading *State and Revolution* by Lenin to *The Little Red Book* by Chairman Mao, from reading about Clarence Darrow and Eugene V. Debs to watching TV newsclips of William Kunstler and Abbie Hoffman.

This chapter does not purport to provide such a detailed analysis or even description. Excerpts from a much longer history by Dan Lund provide a contemporaneous whiff of the 1970 and 1971 conventions; Guild president Doris Walker provides a counterpoint. The fact that the FBI was meanwhile limiting Guild membership by preventing some Guild members from being admitted to practice was suspected, but not proved until considerably later.

Throughout this period, Guild members continued to work in their specialized fields, from labor law to affirmative action in education and employment, a record reflected here in briefs filed in state and federal courts. But the internal struggles kept coming to the fore during the presidencies of James Larson, Doron Weinberg, William Goodman, and Henry diSuvero. They are described here in the words of others, and sometimes their own.

THE 1970 CONVENTION IN WASHINGTON
By Dan Lund

At the Guild Convention in Washington, D.C., in February 1970, nearly every aspect of the agenda was touched in one way or another by

---

"The 1970 Convention in Washington" from Dan Lund, "Law for the People" (1983), reprinted in San Francisco Chapter, *Conspiracy* (1986).

the debate over women's roles and male chauvinism. The entire convention of 350 attended the panel presentation on women. All the uncomfortable challenges of men's leadership which had been growing in the movement came home to the Guild. Flo Kennedy from New York made a vigorous challenge of many of the sexist assumptions in the practice of law. Jean Kidwell of Los Angeles criticized many aspects of the traditional family roles and of the practice of family law. To many men, everything seemed topsy-turvy. It was no longer simply young versus old. . . .

It had been generally agreed before the convention that it was at long last time to have a woman as president of the Guild and that the woman was to be Doris Walker of San Francisco. Then the law student issue emerged in a new form, and everything was up in the air.

Most of the students of 1968 were now lawyers, engaged in opening offices, working for the Guild, and taking jobs with legal services. The new group of law students, led by people like Bonnie Brower of New York, demanded full voting membership in the Guild, commensurate with the work they did in the organization. While such a step threatened the strict "Bar association" definition of the Guild, a majority of the convention participants were clearly lining up to support the motion, including many of the older members. Charles Garry of San Francisco spoke passionately about the tremendous assistance that law students had given him in his work. Doris Walker rose to urge defeat of the motion, on the ground that the Guild would be better able to serve the movement and more attractive to lawyers if it remained a lawyers' group with a law student section.

Immediately, small knots of convention participants asked: How can we have a president on the "wrong" side of the law student question? The vote was taken and law students were admitted by a lopsided margin.

Who could be nominated in opposition to Doris Walker? Jennie Rhine, a young lawyer from San Francisco and a leader of the Law Student Caucus? The Guild has a tradition of resolving these conflicts before an election. Under the circumstances, only one group was politically able to make such a decision—a women's caucus. It convened and met for hours, leaving the men to roam about. At last, the caucus chose Walker, with the understanding that she would look for assistance from the new young active women. The decision was confirmed on the floor. . . .

Many of the graduates of the Santa Monica Law Student Caucus gathered with other young new left lawyers and constituted a Radical Caucus at the convention. This group participated in the "Banquet Dinner Riot," which arose when fifty delegates could not afford the traditional banquet. While three hundred sat down in the chandeliered hall, the fifty waited outside for the program to begin. Hungry activists eventually acted. Someone crept inside and stole a huge platter of dinner rolls. It was felt necessary for a group of young Guild lawyers to guard the doors so that participants without tickets could not rush in and get the Guild in hot water with the hotel management, who would serve dinner only to paid ticket holders. William Kunstler of New York came outside, made a rabble-rousing speech and publicly burned his ticket.

Before the formal program began, a designated spokesperson for the fifty, Dan Siegel of Berkeley, took the microphone and called for future Guild conventions to be conducted in a place and style in conformity with the new membership. His speech was cheered by all.

THE PRESIDENT'S ANALYSIS
By Doris Brin Walker

Any evaluation of the state of the Guild must be set within the framework of the state of the nation: the state of our comrades in the movement for social change, and the state of our enemies, whose criminal activities are all too familiar. On these questions we have been in substantial agreement. The trends continue to develop: the U.S. widens its aggression in Indochina and elsewhere; the Burger Supreme Court continues its repudiation of established concepts of due process and of other constitutional rights and liberties; and the people increase their resistance and struggle.

Since the last convention, our membership has grown, in absolute numbers and in number of chapters, among both lawyers and law students. Our national reputation is good. Our chapters appear to be in their best shape in years in volume of organizational and substantive work, including demonstrations, conferences, workshops, finding counsel in political cases, and in thinking about and discussing seriously the role of the radical lawyer today. Our national organization has been tightened by our efforts to implement the new dues schedule and by increased attention to organizational details. . . .

We must recognize, however, that our substantive work has not measured up to the goals implicit in our self-defined role of the "legal arm of the movement." Both nationally and locally we have failed to confront the enemy or to assist our clients to do so with maximum effectiveness and clarity. Only two major legal issues have been dealt with nationally in anything approaching the style of which the Guild is capable: new problems of grand jury subpoenas and litigation use of

---

"The President's Analysis," by Doris Brin Walker, from *NLG Practitioner* 29:2 (Spring 1971).

the Nuremberg principles in the light of the Calley conviction and its sequelae.

SOME "THOUGHTS OF CHAIRWOMAN WALKER"

1. On My Own Role

Like many of us, I learned very early that basic social change will never be achieved by lawyers. The job will be done by the decisive masses of the people, of our clients. Maximum assistance to those who are really making the revolution thus requires the lawyer to sharpen professional skills and make them accessible. Impelled by my view of the lawyer's role, my style in working in the Guild as president has been to try to force members to face up to the implications of their own attitudes and actions. I engaged and encouraged others to engage in political struggle involving members representing various tendencies within the Guild on as many occasions and to the greatest extent possible. I tried to see to it that every political position within the Guild had an opportunity to be expressed with enough authority to help make policy, at the price of endless confrontations, interruptions and highly charged emotional scenes. My hope has been that in the long run there would result a worthwhile degree of increased learning, maturity, and cooperative participation.

[As a result] I have a report primarily of struggle and of relatively few accomplishments. It is too early to say whether [my] choice was correct. We have not had a functioning National Defense Committee, nor have we had a much needed Lawyers Defense Committee. We have not had regular issues of the *Guild Practitioner* or of any Newsletter. The International Law Committee has barely functioned. We have had too little contact with other U.S. lawyers and Bar associations on matters on which we could have sought their involvement and support. We made no effort to prevent passage of even the worst of the new repressive legislation, the Omnibus Crime Control Act of 1970.

There has been no time to initiate work with Guild law professors, to help them understand the nature of the crisis in their own classrooms and to go through the same process with their students that we have been going through in the Guild.

2. On Women's Liberation

This has been an important issue in Guild debates in the past year for the first time. However, it must be subdivided in order to be understood, because there has not been one attitude by one group toward another, but something much more complicated. Each of several groupings manifests its own form of sexism: Young and older men toward all women with whom they work; young women (lawyers, students, and legal workers) toward each other and toward older women lawyers and legal workers; older women lawyers toward each other and toward younger women.

It would be useful to identify and study these manifestations, as well as those very specifically directed by each group toward the Guild's first woman president. My own study has led me to conclude that the rights of women and the struggle for those rights have been used by many for manipulative purposes. Concern for women has been put on and taken off depending on the political line of the opponent on other issues.

3. On Criticism and Self-Criticism (or Let's Self-Criticize You)

Can we all recognize now that when we go to a meeting, many things are said by each side which are taken by the other as put-downs, as unjustified and even destructive, vicious criticism? For example, the new lawyers believe that the older lawyers are pulling rank (professionalism) and are denigrating their political, legal, and organizational skills and understanding. The older lawyers believe that the young reject as bad and corrupt all of the political and professional lessons learned by the old in their long years of practice. A double standard seems to have developed that is particularly infuriating to older members: Just as sexism, in the eyes of some (younger lawyers), is expressed only toward legal workers and young women lawyers and students, so collective work in the eyes of some (younger lawyers) is work which they do only among themselves. They seem to reject collective work which involves in-put from the entire membership. (This attitude does not extend to the question of collecting money for the Guild.)

[Walker called older and younger practitioners to the coming Convention, and concluded:]

VENCEREMOS

Let us work together truly to serve the people—who are our clients.

THE 1971 CONVENTION IN BOULDER
By Dan Lund

[This is excerpted from the history of this period by Dan Lund, followed by comments of the Editors.]

In the summer of 1971, 700 Guild people converged on Boulder for the national convention by plane, bus, car, camper, motorcycle, bicycle,

---

"The 1971 Convention in Boulder" from Dan Lund, "Law for the People."

foot, and thumb—twice as many as had attended the convention in Washington the year before. A single issue came increasingly to dominate the discussion in the halls and on the floor: the proposed admission of legal workers, people working in the law but not admitted to practice and without law school training.

The pro-legal worker people wanted to reshape the Guild into more of a movement organization, not a professional group that served the movement. Some New York Guild members had also recently faced legal secretaries attempting to organize into worker bargaining units. Fay Stender, busy with prison work in San Francisco, added a second issue: admission of "jailhouse lawyers" into full Guild membership.

For many older lawyers, the Left excesses of the period confirmed their fear that the Guild was being transformed into some kind of movement organization soon to consume itself in militant fury. For example, in Boston, young members developed a "NGL progressive income tax" for dues, which included a 33 percent bit of a lawyer's income in certain categories. In San Francisco, a group of young members attended a formal NLG-hosted dinner at the California State Bar Convention by eating on the floor out of brown bags. In Chicago, a group of young liberal lawyers anxious to help out doing legal work on Panther cases were told that only Marxist-Leninists need apply.

After considerable discussion, it was agreed that in California and Michigan and any other state with an integrated Bar, any chapter would have the option of forming a coordinate but not separate lawyers group solely for the purpose of participating in state Bar activities. ("Integrated," in this context, means a state Bar association to which every lawyer in the state must belong.) With this compromise, the vote for admission of legal workers was even more certain. . . .

A weakness reflected in any Guild debate from this period forward was the almost complete absence of a middle generation in the membership, those who came of lawyer age in the 1950s—a tangible sign of the success of the McCarthy-period repression.

The proposal for jailhouse lawyer membership reflected a significant development of systematic Guild prison work in several areas of the country, and a newly acquired respect for the work of the writ writers. The lack of deep debate probably reflected a certain "why not" attitude after legal worker admission was approved. A tired, talked-out bunch of delegates confirmed the result. The Guild now included as full members: lawyers, law students, legal workers, and jailhouse lawyers.

Catherine Roraback of New Haven, attorney for Black Panther leader Erica Huggins and a respected independent radical, a part of the small middle generation in the Guild, was seen as the kind of president who could bind the legal worker controversy wounds. She was well known to the older membership, respected as a feminist fighter, and had consistently supported legal worker admission. My name was urged by a California radical caucus as a young lawyer with a relatively long history as a local and national Guild organizer. Finally it was decided we would urge her nomination as president, with me to assume a national organizing role as executive vice-president.

Most of the participants in the convention spent most of their time seeking out other Guild people doing similar work in other regions. The increased specialization of interest and skill affected prison law work and the newly emerged group of activists relating to rank-and-file labor struggles and grand jury work, in the face of Nixon's traveling coordinator of movement harassment. . . .

The Guild since Santa Monica had shown a propensity for getting deeply into whatever struggle was current, becoming over-committed, and then backing off when a new struggle demanded our attention. This is, perhaps, an overly harsh judgment on our work. However, the consistency with which we have received criticism on this score cannot be ignored. Establishing a set of priorities and learning to say "no" as well as "yes" required of us a common set of political assumptions we hadn't acquired. . . .

After the convention, for a month and a half in the spring of 1972, Jim Larson and I traveled through Florida, Georgia, and Alabama, parts of Texas, Oklahoma, New Mexico, and Colorado. Chapter formations were begun in Atlanta, Austin, Houston, and Norman. That summer, the Guild undertook a new approach to educational organizing by having teams of travelers from the NLG Grand Jury Office and other Guild organizers do four travel circuits to teach people grand jury skills, and to introduce people to the Guild generally. . . .

Since Santa Monica the numbers and proportion of active older members had declined from a majority to a token. The political fights had been intense, even bitter and mean at times. The style of work and meeting was new, even confusing or alarming to older more orderly minds.

[In this period, some older Guild members got in the habit of taking Lenin's *Left-Wing Communism: An Infantile Disorder*, or its equivalent, to read on the plane to prepare them for the meetings that lay ahead. When defeated for office on chapter boards, older black and white men and women took different paths. Some found a corner in which they could work on Guild projects they believed in where they would be left alone—state Bar committee work, publications, etc. Others got active in black or women's Bar associations, in community work, parent-teacher associations, their own practices, and, occasionally, gardening.

[Most older members were slow to use the words "red baiting," "opportunism," or "ageism" to describe the treatment they felt they received. Well-to-do older lawyers were soon sought after, as younger lawyers learned that it takes money to fuel a new Guild program, and that there was an occasional job opening for a young lawyer who seemed bright as well as brash. But what could one learn from a lawyer who had only survived McCarthyism? What could be learned from a poverty lawyer who had not consciously chosen that role, before that term was coined in the 1960s, but had worked into it naturally while representing working class and union clients?]

THE FBI BLACKLIST OF BAR APPLICANTS
By the Editors

Documents uncovered in 1985 in the Guild suit against the Attorney General showed that the FBI routinely shared information about Guild members with the National Conference of Bar Examiners (NCBE), which investigates applications to the Bar in all state jurisdictions, and particularly when a lawyer admitted in one state moves for admission in a second state. This practice started in 1945 and apparently continued until 1985. While the FBI made every effort to conceal its hand, a 1961 FBI document makes clear that the FBI was interested in passing along "information indicating some Communist or subversive affiliation on the part of the applicant." In the eyes of both the FBI and NCBE, Guild membership fitted within this category.

Through burglaries of the Guild office, and the use of informants at mailing houses and in the Guild, the bureau always managed to obtain complete Guild membership lists and a fair picture of members' activities. (In California, the state Bar regularly gave the FBI copies of the list of Bar members who designated the Guild as their organization for purposes of representation at the State Bar Conference of Delegates.) The 42 pages released from the bureau's NCBE liaison file indicate that the FBI maintained direct relationships with the character committees in New York, the District of Columbia, Michigan, and California. When a 1972 Justice Department ruling limited the FBI's dissemination of Bar applicants' arrest records to NCBE, the bureau continued dissemination of information of a political character.

In 1985, as a result of disclosures in the Guild suit, NCBE adopted a resolution not to exchange information with the FBI and to investigate past practices. When the Guild publicly complained, the California state Bar stopped its practice.

One example of information on a Bar applicant sent by the FBI to the Bar Examiners of California in 1972 is reproduced in Figure 3. This page surfaced as part of the discovery in *National Lawyers Guild v.*

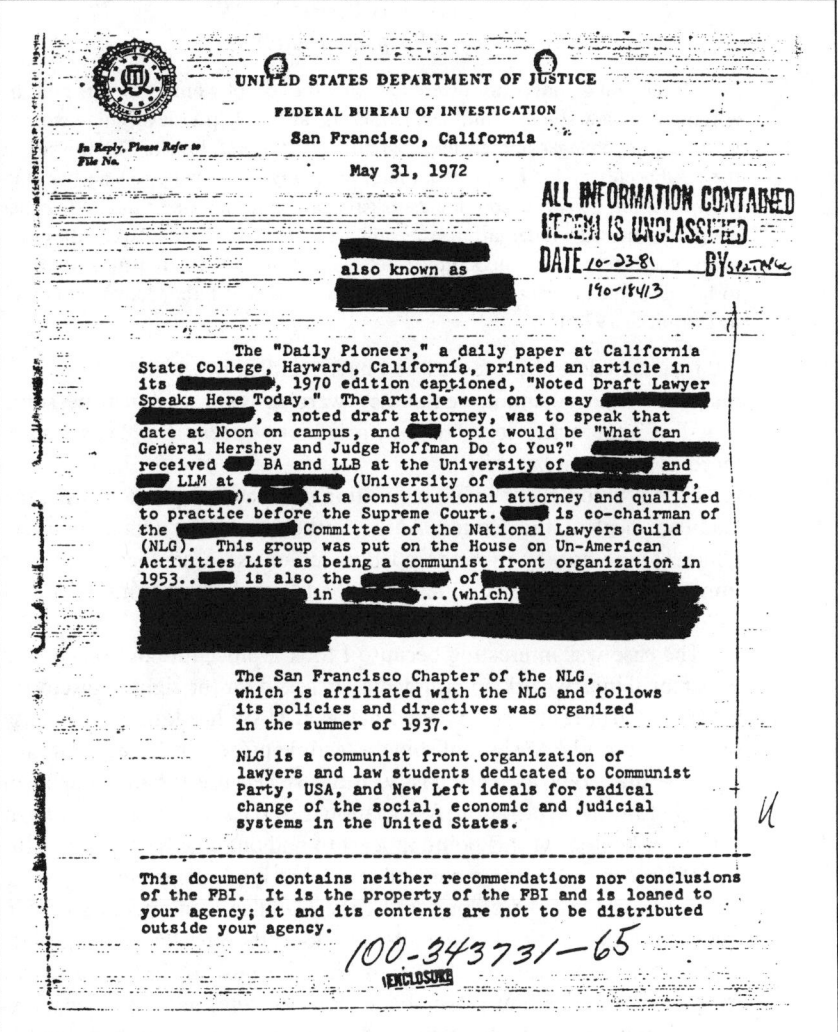

Figure 3.

Attorney General. Nothing was blacked out when the FBI made their reports to the National Conference of Bar Examiners or when this page was turned over to the Guild. The name has been blacked out by the editors to protect, at least in this book, the Bar applicant's First Amendment rights.

PRACTICING LABOR LAW
By Marijana Relich

[While Guild conventions were debating the role of women lawyers and the admission of law students and legal workers, at the chapter level some women were making changes in their lives, typified by Marijana Relich. She worked as the legal secretary for Ernest Goodman for many years while raising her children, keeping active in community organizations in her free time. When her daughter entered kindergarten, she quit work and entered college. After two years, she entered law school, graduated, joined the Goodman firm, and began to handle some labor cases, as she described at a Guild Labor Law Conference in Detroit in 1972.]

I want to describe a few cases I have handled in which sex discrimination or internal union democracy were at issue, to illustrate some practical approaches to labor law, and some special problems I have faced as a woman lawyer.

I got a union client in an arbitration case involving two unions, the Cadillac local of the United Auto Workers, and the Office Workers Union. One attorney represented both unions so a conflict of interest immediately arose, and Cadillac local had to seek another attorney and called me.

The case was interesting because I took a procedure our office uses in personal injury work and immediately asked for the right of discovery before the arbitrator. This created havoc at UAW headquarters because they were afraid I was establishing a terrible precedent for arbitrations, and one that could be very costly. But just because it had never been done before in Arbitration Association cases I saw no reason why it could not be done at this point, at least to find out who the witnesses for the office workers union would be and what kinds of proofs they were going to establish. I was present at the Cadillac local meeting on the question, and I noticed that half-way along the line the International stepped in, took over the chairmanship, and pushed through a settlement. I've got to admit it was by a majority vote, but I was very disturbed because I felt that certainly each local is autonomous and that the rights of the membership of the union should be determined by the members, without the heavy hand of the International.

I am fairly new to the labor field, having been an attorney not quite nine years. I only represent two unions. One is unique in that it is headed by a woman president, a woman financial secretary, and two-thirds of its business agents are women, although its membership includes more men than women. I also represent the tree trimmers, maintenance people, housekeepers, and canteen workers at Wayne State University. Within

---

"Practicing Labor Law," by Marijana Relich, from *NLG Practitioner* 30:1 (Winter 1972).

those unions on rare occasions problems of internal union democracy have arisen. The business agent for a unit doesn't let the workers know the terms of the contract, although it is now spelled out in Landrum-Griffin that union members have a right to receive a copy of the contract that covers them.

[In another case,] we had four hearings before the appeal board of the [Unemployment Compensation] Commission. Each time two lawyers appeared for the General Motors Corporation. At no time did the union representative appear with this worker. I just could not believe that General Motors was paying two high-priced lawyers for four sessions of four hours each to get $106 back in their unemployment rating account. (At one point I commented that it just did not stand to reason that a corporation whose gross national income exceeds the gross national product of South America should be here fighting about $106. The Commission reprimanded me for this.)

After the fourth session, and just prior to my taking an appeal to the Circuit Court, as I had threatened to do, the Commission finally agreed that without the worker's agreement, the union did not have the right to transform a layoff to a leave of absence, thereby depriving him of his rights.

These are some of the ways that lawyers can help workers. But you've got to have a good physical constitution.

I'm a peculiar kind of lawyer, for which I sometimes get criticized by my male partners. Incidentally, I'm the only female lawyer in the office of Goodman, Eden, Millender, Goodman, and Bedrosian; I think people ought to know that. And consequently much of the criticism—I think the females in the audience will appreciate this—is "Marijana, you're too damn subjective. You can't get yourself all wrapped up in your client's problems, because you're going to get ill. You've got to be a little more aloof."

And I have a problem: I can't get aloof. I *do* get very involved. That might be why I have ulcers. I only represent the two unions I mentioned. I usually represent dissident workers against big, powerful unions. And it's a problem.

THE NATIONAL LAWYERS GUILD AS AN ALL-WHITE ORGANIZATION
By William Goodman

[Detroit trial lawyer William Goodman made this speech at a Midwest Regional Guild Meeting in Cleveland in January 1973. He began Guild work as a

---

"The National Lawyers Guild as an All-White Organization," by William Goodman, from *NLG Practitioner* 30:2-3 (Spring-Summer 1973).

student sent to Norfolk in the summer of 1963 to assist Jordan, Dawley, and Holt.]

It is difficult to discuss racism and racialism without immediately striking chords of guilt. However, any organization worthy of survival must openly face and discuss these questions, and must do so in as healthy and positive a manner as possible. While it is easy to accuse an organization like the Guild of being racist and while that charge may indeed be true in some degree or another, we would not continue to belong to an organization which was predominantly or even significantly racist. Therefore it is possible to take certain affirmative steps to strengthen our organization so that black legal people can feel comfortable either as members of the Guild or working in conjunction with it.... If we are committed to basic social change in this multi-national country, we must eliminate racist behavior and thinking in our lives so that we can go forward with black and other Third World people to achieve that goal.

I. AN ANALYTICAL PERSPECTIVE

At the present time the Guild is almost entirely white; most of the organizing is directed toward white legal workers, law students, and lawyers; there is and has been an absence of black leadership. (E. A. Dawley, editor of *The Guild Practitioner*, is a notable exception.) Ironically, history and society may dictate the racial composition of the Guild more than our subjective feelings. [But] we can control Guild programs. Is the Guild pursuing programs or policies oriented toward the needs and demands of the white Left, giving insufficient attention to the demands of blacks?

II. A STATISTICAL PERSPECTIVE

The number of black lawyers who join the Guild must be related to the total number of black lawyers in the country. Today there are fewer than 5,000 black and other Third World lawyers out of approximately 350,000 lawyers: slightly more than one percent. If Guild membership is around 3,000 now, 43 black members nationally would give us the same proportion as in the profession. If we limited the figures to lawyer members, then fewer than 40 black lawyers would give us the same proportion.

These figures counter the idea that the Guild is a racist organization. However, they raise the question: Does the Guild have a duty, not only to be free of racism, but not to *appear* to be racist?

And they suggest several other ideas. First, that there are now, in this country, fewer than 10,000 women lawyers out of the same 350,000.

If the Guild had the same proportion of women lawyer members as the profession as a whole, it would have fewer than 85.

Why do we have about the same proportion of blacks as in the profession and many more than the proportion of women? Perhaps we need to study the correlation, if any, between these statistics and the positions and concern of Guild chapters on problems of blacks and women. (And, of course, the Guild has a much higher proportion of young lawyer members than there are young lawyers in the legal population as a whole.)

Second, many of the 5,000 black and Third World lawyers hope to or even expect to become judges or government officials at some point in their careers. This is not an illogical assumption, since blacks are so underrepresented in the legal profession. There were, in 1972, fewer than 300 black judges out of a total of more than 16,000. Either 10 percent of 16,000 judges should be black, or at least 10 percent of 5,000 black lawyers should be judges. How many white lawyers join the Guild while harboring hopes of becoming judges? (Detroit is obviously an exception on this question.) Certainly in most parts of the country Guild membership will not be an asset in being appointed a judge or in winning at the polls.

Third, the annual income of the average black lawyer is considerably below the annual income of the average white lawyer, although there are a few conspicuous exceptions. The Detroit Chapter verified these statistics in a study some years ago. Black lawyers have fewer clients paying monthly retainers than white lawyers and firms. Most of their clients are black and are poorer than most white clients. Since Bar association participation does not bring in clients or get legal work done, only lawyers with fairly secure incomes and clientele can afford to participate, regardless of color. Sole practitioners and lawyers in small firms tend to limit their meetings to organizations that will bring in clients or build a political base.

Many of the 5,000 black and Third World lawyers come from lower middle or working class families. The particular attitudes we call "humanitarian" or "political" or "pro bono publico" that have emerged from a certain stratum of upper middle class white families could not be expected in precisely the same degree in other classes and races, or at this juncture. As E. A. Dawley says, "It takes a couple of generations of prosperity to get the pro bono spirit."

III. AN HISTORICAL PERSPECTIVE

One of the reasons for founding a second national Bar association in the mid-1930s was that the American Bar Association simply did not admit black lawyers to membership. Throughout its early history the

Guild was very conscious of racism in the profession and worked actively at the local and national levels to combat it. . . .

The Detroit Chapter has come closer than any other to having a large active membership among black lawyers and has also had the closest relationship with the local black (Wolverine) Bar association. This came about when the chapter, in the late 1940s and early 1950s, consciously turned to bread-and-butter issues and away from other activities. One of its most successful programs was a long course on how to handle personal injury cases, which was the first opportunity many black lawyers had had to gain skills normally learned in large PI offices. This very practical approach to economic problems of black lawyers led to close ties that lasted for many years and also led many white lawyers to join and remain in the Guild. Whenever the Guild has focused on problems in the black community, black lawyers, judges, and Bar associations have worked with the Guild and some black lawyers have become Guild members.

Despite these important exceptions, the Guild could be characterized throughout its history as being predominantly white, with predominantly white leadership. This appeared to be changing during the early 1960s as the Guild became deeply involved in the civil rights movement in the South and Len Holt became a staff member. Many Southern black lawyers began to view the Guild as *their* organization.

Even then, a number of black lawyers did not actually sign membership cards. They would speak at Guild conferences, publish articles in Guild publications, and welcome Guild lawyers into their communities. But concern about bearing the double burden of being black and red restrained them.

The Guild civil rights program was given leadership by two black attorneys from Detroit—George Crockett and Claudia Shropshire. Thus there were two very important simultaneous developments: the apparent rapid development of many active Guild members who were black, and the apparent development of black leaders within the Guild.

During this period the Guild was the most important legal organization working on civil rights. While other groups [late-comers] in developing an interest in civil rights, were better financed and more "prestigious," the Guild and Guild lawyers developed the most imaginative and creative tactics.

While it is historically possible to locate the point at which blacks assumed control of the civil rights movement itself and whites became irrelevant to and unwelcome in the civil rights movement in the South, it is by no means so easy to locate this point with reference to legal support for the civil rights movement. Indeed, white lawyers were always welcomed and many stayed with southern civil rights struggles throughout the 1960s and into the 1970s. The Guild, however, seemed to draw away after 1964 and move on to the Vietnam war, professionalism, lifestyle, grand juries, and a wide spectrum of issues with little relevance to or interest for many private black attorneys.

Soon after the closing of the Guild office in Mississippi, as the Guild turned to building student chapters for the first time since the McCarthy period, a proposal that recruitment of black lawyers also be a priority was defeated at an NEB meeting.

Another force was at work within the Guild. During the ghetto revolts, Guild lawyers played a variety of roles. They filed suits for personal injuries against the Detroit police department that, years later, forced the payment of large damages to a few victims and educated the department to beware of open law violations by its officers. But the Guild did not respond as widely or as meaningfully in its local ghettoes as it had in Mississippi. Ties that might have been forged with black lawyers and Bar associations for common work barely got warmed up.

By the time the Kerner Commission Report on Civil Disorders was published in March 1968, some chapters were ready to move. Spurred by the organization of, and attacks against, the Black Panther Party for Self-Defense and other events in black communities, Guild chapters in San Francisco and Detroit held conferences on Racism in the Law, and the *Guild Practitioner* published a special issue on the subject. The conferences were well attended by black and white attorneys, law professors, and students, and frank exchanges took place on the failure of white lawyers to assist black lawyers in the day-to-day struggle to survive in a racist system and particularly within the racist court structure. California Guild chapters proposed a resolution to the Conference of State Bar Delegates that the Bar establish a Committee on Racism in the Law to study and act on racial discrimination in the legal system. The resolution was defeated in 1968, but passed in 1969. (The committee, retitled Special Committee on Disadvantaged Persons of Special Concern to the Bar, has yet to appoint one Guild member to serve.)

The Santa Monica convention of 1968 listened with excitement to Milton Henry of Pontiac discuss black separatism, but that was the last treatment of any black question at a national convention, and Henry's selection as a vice-president did not result in his working actively in the Guild or bringing in other black lawyers.

At the same time strong feelings of nationalism and self-determination manifested themselves amongst all segments of the black community, including black professionals. Black Bar groups increased their participation on social and political issues.

The National Conference of Black Lawyers was organized to use legal skills in the service of the community. The Conference participated in the defense of the Attica prisoners; organized the defense of H. Rap Brown and the students at Southern University; organized the original, New York, defense of Angela Davis; and is working on problems of justice in the military.

As a result, the possibilities of the 1960s evaporated. The Guild returned to its former condition of being predominantly all white. The Detroit Chapter, previously an exception to the national picture, today appears to be an almost all-white organization.

IV. GUILD POLICY AND QUESTIONS OF STYLE

Why are so many current civil rights issues not acted on by the Guild, or even discussed? I cannot recollect one Guild discussion of busing, except for the resolution opposing anti-busing legislation proposed by the San Francisco Chapter to the 1972 Conference of California Bar Delegates. (The Conference defeated the resolution.) It may indeed be impossible to resolve the questions without some input from black clients or black legal people; this does not mean the question cannot or should not be discussed. While many civil rights attorneys work on housing, health care, welfare benefits, and nutrition, these subjects have been apparently abandoned by the Guild as an organization.

Clearly the style of Guild members, meetings, and the Guild as an organization have changed drastically over the last ten years. So-called lifestylism, youth culturalism, and cultural revolutionalism have had a profound effect. While in many respects this has been healthy, it has tended to create a cultural chauvinism. Those who are more openly middle class in style and taste, particularly older members, have tended to be excluded or openly disdained at meetings. These attitudes carried over in relationships between younger Guild members and black lawyers. Many black attorneys possess conventional middle-class lifestyles.

These people were simply made to feel unwelcome at Guild meetings because of how they dressed, in what kinds of cars they rode, and what they drank as opposed to what they smoked. . . . This is not intended as an attack on any particular lifestyle or cultural attitude. In attempting to rebuild the Lawyers Guild along multi-racial lines, we must not implicitly exclude certain groups due to standard and conventional forms of living.

[Goodman concluded with proposals for informal discussion and action based on his presentation. In 1979, these proposals led to a resolution and action discussed in Chapter 19 by Fania Davis and Kathleen Herron.]

SKETCHES OF GUILD PRESIDENTS LARSON, WEINBERG, AND diSUVERO
By the National Guild Banquet Committee

[In 1980, the Guild Convention honored the living members who had served as president and executive secretary from its founding. The Convention Journal described three presidents who served in the 1970s.]

JIM LARSON (1973-1974)

Jim Larson, who primarily practices criminal law with another former Guild president, Doron Weinberg, has been counsel in such political cases as Wendy Yoshimura, Moody Park 3 and Graham & Allen. One of the most organizationally active younger members, Jim was chosen at the Austin convention to preside over "the cataclysmic merger of old and new left politics" in the Guild. He worked hard at developing a new form of collective leadership. From the experience he joined leading Guild delegations to North Vietnam and Cuba. [Later] he became chairperson of the International Committee.

DORON WEINBERG (1974-1976)

After retiring from three years as staff person of the Guild Regional Office, Doron began his practice as a criminal lawyer in San Francisco in 1972. He rapidly earned a reputation of not only being a people's lawyer but also a lawyer's lawyer. He has taught at Stanford and Boalt and is currently teaching at New College School of Law. Doron was president during a time marked by intense political disagreements. Debates over the Guild's position on undocumented workers and the Middle East characterized many of our local and national meetings. However, throughout his term, Doron successfully promoted the development of programmatic work in keeping with his vision that the Guild must strive to remain a broad-based organization.

HANK DISUVERO (1977-1979)

Hank was one of the "lost generation" of the Guild—those few people willing to risk joining the Guild while still in law school, despite the threat of McCarthyism. His legal work has reflected many of the struggles of the last period. He defended people charged in the 1967 Newark rebellion, dissident GI's, grand jury witnesses, prisoners, and many others. Hank also worked as staff counsel for the ACLU and

---

"Sketches of Guild Presidents Larson, Weinberg, and diSuvero" appeared in the 1980 Convention Journal, *Our Legacy, Our Future.*

ECLC [Emergency Civil Liberties Committee], and was the leading force in the creation of the multi-racial coalition which led to the formation of "People's College of Law" in Los Angeles in 1973. Hank is currently living in Sydney, Australia.

Hank was president at the time when the Guild was facing a great deal of internal division. The long period of study, debate, compromise, and ultimate unity over the Guild's position on the Middle East was the most significant accomplishment. Hank also devoted much time and energy to initiating the National Labor Law Center and the Southern Regional Office. We are still emulating his creative efforts to create a sound financial base for the first time in many years.

LIMITING ACCESS TO FEDERAL COURTS
By Frank Askin

[In August 1976, the Guild held a panel in New Brunswick on the Burger-Nixon Court and what to do about it. Askin was then working as special counsel to the House Labor-Management Subcommittee, on leave from Rutgers University Law School.]

I assume I do not need to spell out in detail the ways in which the new Court majority has greatly reduced the power and jurisdiction of the federal courts by manipulation of concepts like standing, justiciability, equitable jurisdiction and remedies, case and controversy, and comity, and by a narrow approach to class actions. I assume we are in fundamental agreement on the nature of the problem and are seeking ways to deal with it.

I have two messages, and they are rather contradictory. One has to do with finding ways to live with the Burger Court decisions limiting access to the federal courts—the traditional lawyer's role of narrowly construing hostile law. The other message is that these Burger Court decisions are really so egregious that we cannot afford merely to play the traditional lawyer's role; we must wage an ideological and political battle against the Burger-Rehnquist Court itself and the new majority's narrow view of the role and function of the federal courts in our constitutional system. We must go out and convince the people and through them the Congress of the need for legislation to restore the federal courts to their proper role as primary guardian of constitutional liberties. . . .

I don't believe we can make Burger and Rehnquist go away or change their plans by hiding our heads in the sand. They are embarked on a program of giving maximum protection from judicial interference

---

"Limiting Access to Federal Courts," by Frank Askin, from *NLG Practitioner* 33:4 (Fall 1975).

to government officials, particularly those engaged in law enforcement functions. They intend to dismantle all of the constitutional protections constructed by the Warren Court and even earlier Courts over the previous thirty years. The Burger-Rehnquist Court goal of emasculating the federal court was probably most bluntly, maybe inadvertently, revealed in *Laird v. Tatum,* 408 US 1 (1972). In dismissing for lack of a justiciable controversy the plaintiff's systemic attack on the Army's domestic surveillance program, Chief Justice Burger stated, in apparent horror:

> ... what respondents appear to be seeking is a broad-scale investigation, conducted by themselves as private parties armed with ... subpoena power ... and the power of cross-examination, to probe into the Army's intelligence-gathering activities, with the district court determining at the conclusion ... the extent to which those activities may or may not be appropriate to the Army's mission.

Well, of course, Burger was right: that was precisely the aim. I suggest it was a proper aim, under a constitutional system that promises political freedom as part of the social compact. It was an aim and goal recognized as appropriate by the Warren Court. And it is the apparent Burger-Rehnquist plan to obliterate these gains of the Warren era.

Unless these plans are exposed, they will erode our constitutional bulwarks one by one. By publicly attacking and exposing their plans, we can explain to the public at large and to a legal community that has been indoctrinated in the importance of judicial review just exactly how the Burger-Rehnquist Court is undermining our constitutional system of checks and balances and making it easy for mistrusted government officials to take away our rights. Even if we don't accomplish legislative reform, and that is going to be very difficult, we may build up enough public pressure on the Court that, if not Burger and Rehnquist, then some of their more flexible and less committed colleagues, may jump off their express before its final destination.

[Professor Askin analyzed the recent decision in his case, *Rizzo v. Goode,* 423 U.S. 362 (1976), and concluded:]

[We] probably should move on to another topic on our agenda—the utilization of state forums in constitutional cases. One of the legacies of the Warren era is strong doctrine that state courts have a firm duty to enforce federal constitutional rights and remedies. (*Sullivan v. Little Hunting Park,* 392 U.S. 657 (1967), is probably the best authority.) And remember, state courts have that obligation without the baggage that enforcement of rights now carries with it in the federal courts: state courts cannot abstain or dismiss on comity grounds! And, in some states, justiciability and standing requirements are less stringent. Maybe federal law requires state equity courts to issue *Dombrowski* injunctions in appropriate circumstances?

... While Burger and Rehnquist have temporarily sealed off the federal courts for some purposes, we must keep as our goal their restoration as the prime protector of the constitutional system. I am convinced we can eventually prevail over Burger and Rehnquist in this most important ideological contest.

[During this period, the Guild also had to attend to some old business: the application for reinstatement to the federal Bar by Guild member Maurice Braverman. In 1974, Braverman had been readmitted to the Maryland state Bar by the Maryland Court of Appeals after being convicted under the Smith Act in 1952 and sentenced to three years and fined $1,000 for alleged conspiracy to organize the Communist Party in order, at some time in the future, to advocate the overthrow of the United States government by force and violence. In 1975, the NEC passed a resolution supporting this reinstatement.]

WHEN THE DEFENDANTS ARE FOXES TOO: THE NEED FOR INTERVENTION BY MINORITIES IN "REVERSE DISCRIMINATION" SUITS LIKE *BAKKE*
By Charles Lawrence

[This is a shortened version of an article based on the NAACP brief as friend of the court in *Bakke*. Lawrence was assistant professor at the University of San Francisco Law School, teaching constitutional and education law, and a member of the National Conference of Black Lawyers and the steering committee of the Third World Coalition for Justice in the Legal System.]

> One day Brother Fox caught Brother Goose and tied him to a tree.
> "I'm going to eat you, Bro' Goose," he said, "You've been stealing my meat."
> "But I don't even eat meat," Bro' Goose protested.
> "Tell that to the judge and jury," said Bro' Fox.
> "Who's gonna be the judge?" asked Bro' Goose.
> "A fox," answered Bro' Fox.
> "And who's gonna be the jury?" Bro' Goose inquired.
> "They all gonna be foxes," said Bro' Fox, grinning so that all his teeth showed.
> "Guess my goose is cooked," said Brother Goose.
>
> —African-American slave folktale

"When the Defendants Are Foxes Too," by Charles Lawrence, from *NLG Practitioner* 34:1 (1976).

OUR GOOSE IS COOKED

In the recent rash of anti-affirmative action, so-called "reverse discrimination," cases that have come fast and furious in the wake of *DeFunis v. Odegaard,* 416 U.S. 312 (1974), black people and their third world brothers and sisters have found themselves in an even more precarious position than that of Brother Goose. Not only are the judges and juries foxes but the *defendants* are foxes, too. In the civil litigation that seeks to destroy existing affirmative action programs in education, employment, and industry, minorities have not even been allowed the opportunity to appear in court in their defense. Most often the defendant is a university, an employer, or some governmental entity. The defendants are rarely if ever the parties most concerned with the program under attack. Typically they have instituted such programs only after being subjected to considerable moral and political pressure or threatened with litigation, and their commitment to the programs is at best suspect.

The real parties in interest are the minority communities who have fought for the establishment of affirmative action programs and who benefit by their existence. Yet a motion to intervene in the trial court filed by minorities in *De Ronde v. Board of Regents,* a reverse discrimination attack on University of California at Davis Law School special admissions program, has been denied. Similarly blue-collar women and men workers were not parties to the suit that abolished statutory protection for premium pay for overtime work, *California Industrial Welfare Commission v. Homemakers, Inc,* 509 F 2d 20 (9th Cir, 1974), *cert den,* 423 U.S. 1063 (1976). See Ginger and Mischel, "Which Side Are You On?" 1 *Women's L. Jour* 27 (1977).

Our Constitution requires that issues be presented within the context of a real "case or controversy" before they will be heard by a federal court. Case law requires that a plaintiff have standing or demonstrate actual injury that is a direct result of the challenged provision to insure that the plaintiff vigorously and conscientiously litigate the legal issues in their most complete and thorough form. There is no similar requirement to insure aggressive advocacy on the part of the defendant other than the provisions in state and federal rules for intervention of interested parties at the discretion of the court, and the constitutional prohibition against collusive suits. (Only the most extreme conspiratorial designs have been held "collusive".)

Bakke v. Regents of the University of California, 132 Cal Rptr 680 (1976), is a prime example of what happens when minorities are unrepresented in the litigation of constitutional issues that directly affect them. . . . Affirmative action programs are a relatively recent phenomenon. With the riots of the 1960s and the assassination of Martin Luther

King, it became evident that this society could not continue to exist as two societies—one black and one white. This awareness, combined with political pressure from minority groups who refused to continue to be excluded from the mainstream of American life, forced universities to re-evaluate their policies and criteria that had served to block minority group entry into professional careers.

Members of the minority community and some white civil rights advocates have recognized the need to maintain a constant vigil over university administrations for fear they would not continue these programs. [Yet] minorities, on first hearing of the *Bakke* suit, assumed that the University would vigorously pursue the legal defense of the program.

The failure to seek intervention at an earlier state was also due to a scarcity of legal resources. The few minority attorneys who expressed a concern with whether the case would be properly handled could not find time in their already overburdened schedules to handle it themselves. It is ironic that the very programs necessary to fulfill the need for persons capable of representing minority communities are destroyed in part because of that need.

The opinion in *Bakke* confirmed our worst fears. It became clear that the rights and interests of those persons for whom affirmative action was instituted had not been adequately represented. The record produced in the trial court was wholly inadequate. Counsel for both parties stipulated that the matter be heard on the pleadings, declaration, interrogatories, and the deposition of the Chairman of the Admissions Committee at UC Davis Medical School, together with attached exhibits. No oral testimony was taken from expert witnesses, students, or members of the minority communities to be served. (Compare the 477-page trial transcript of ten witnesses in *DeFunis,* and the 62 court days, 250 exhibits, and testimony of 43 witnesses in *Serrano v. Priest,* 5 Cal 3d 584 (1971).)

The detrimental impact of the inadequacies of the record became especially clear on reading the majority opinion, based on several key aspects of the trial court's findings of fact that can be traced directly to the defendant's failure to make a proper record. Had the case been handled differently, the issues would have come before the court in an entirely different and more enlightening factual context that would have compelled a different result. Compare *Alevy v. Downstate Medical Center of New York, Inc,* 384 NYS 2d 82 (Ct of Appeals, 1976).

[Lawrence listed specific types of evidence that would have been presented by minority students if they had been part of this lawsuit in support of arguments, some of which were made by the defendants, but without evidence to support them.]

REMAND TO PERMIT INTERVENTION BY THE GOOSE

It is no wonder that on learning of the California Supreme Court decision in *Bakke,* the minority communities felt they had been sold down the river by a less than sympathetic University. There were cries of "conspiracy" and "collusion."

We are no more easily fooled by sham justice than our slave ancestors. Until minorities are truly represented in "reverse discrimination" litigation, we will understand that the litigation is merely preparatory ritual for the foxes' barbecue. We can not be expected to come back to court but so many times.

It would seem that the best approach is to attempt to convince the Supreme Court, perhaps by way of amicus briefs, to deny certiorari because *Bakke* is inappropriate to adjudicating such a significant issue.

[This approach was not followed. Bakke was decided by the United States Supreme Court on the record prepared by the University; see *Regents of University of California v. Bakke,* 438 U.S. 265 (1978). In the next big affirmative action case, *United Steelworkers v. Weber,* 443 U.S. 193 (1979), the Guild joined with sixty-two national and local organizations as friends of the court, arguing that the Thirteenth Amendment protects efforts to overcome badges and incidents of slavery and that institutional discrimination against racial minorities as currently manifested in their disproportionate underrepresentation in the skilled trades is a badge and incident of slavery. The authors of this brief, published with other amicus briefs in *The Guild Practitioner,* were Victor Goode, Denise S. Carty-Bennia, Alfred A. Slocum, Jack P. Harris, Arthur Kinoy, Doris Peterson, and Jeanne Mirer, members of the Guild and of NCBL.]

INTERNAL STRUGGLES
By William Goodman

[In his Officers' Column in May 1976, Guild president William Goodman reminded members:]

The Guild was initially formed as an alternative to the ABA. We have lost sight of that role, and it is time we reclaimed it. We should be leading the attack on the ABA for its role in the selection of recent members of the Supreme Court. In addition, the ABA has consistently been fighting affirmative action within the Bar, law schools, and private industry. It has been leading the attack on the jury system. It has either remained silent or joined in the attack on the attorneys for their vigorous

---

"Internal Struggles," by William Goodman, from Officers' Columns, *Guild Notes* (May 1976 and May 1977).

representation of clients in both political cases and nonpolitical criminal trials.... Furthermore, we should be involved in a program of press releases and press conferences which permit us to speak out on significant matters of day-to-day concern.

[In his Officers' Column in May 1977, President Goodman discussed "an important and intensely political fight" being waged in the Guild.]

At the recent NEB in Norman, Oklahoma, the Anti-Imperialist Caucus met and informally organized in the Guild around slogans: "Oppose the Two Super Powers" and "Oppose the CPUSA!" The formation of this caucus, which in my opinion represents a distinct minority, is a good thing because it brings into the open differences which have been veiled and unclear. The people in this group put forward two strategies in resolutions to the plenary. They wanted to amend the Guild's resolution acknowledging the importance of involving ourselves in the Gary Tyler case with a precondition recognizing the existence of a separate Black Nation in the South, and acknowledging the leadership of one group around the case.... This amendment was soundly defeated.

Those who claim that our membership should be narrow and small, united around opposition to the CPUSA, similarly argue that our program should be severely limited, to avoid any building of incorrect reliance on the state. This view would ultimately restrict the program and membership of the Guild to people who are able to unite around a fairly narrow set of political principles. Amy Gladstein claims that the price we must pay for purity of politics will be our inability to organize members from the ACLU and liberal members of state bar associations.

The other position has been consistently put forward by a majority in the Guild, recently by Bonnie Brower, Jeanne Mirer, and Mary Alice Theiler. Jeannie argues that, to be effective, we must reach out to others, make alliances with liberals and progressives in other groups and thereby, as Guild members, provide progressive leadership in other Bar associations and coalition efforts....

[T]he Caucus put forward programmatic strategy for the Guild also in a proposed amendment to the resolution on South Africa. The original resolution called for an end to U.S. intervention in South Africa. The proposed amendment deleted the reference to "U.S. intervention" and instead spoke in terms of "foreign intervention." Supporters spoke of Soviet gunboats in the Indian Ocean. Thus, we are asked to base our support for African liberation on sentiments and language which objectively are supportive of the South African government. Could we seriously maintain ties with the African National Congress, Mozambique, Angola, and the majority of African liberation solidarity movements in this country were we to adopt such an amendment? This amendment also was soundly defeated.

... We will not be able to organize people into the Guild, and in fact we will lose much of our membership, if we promote slogans of opposing the Soviet Union and opposing the Communist Party. These are slogans which perhaps could organize George Meany, Daniel Moynihan, Henry Jackson, or Albert Shanker into the Guild, but are not likely to see us move forward.

Those amongst us who view themselves as revolutionaries or Marxist-Leninists have a responsibility to act in a disciplined (as opposed to infantile) fashion if what we desire is a stronger and healthier Guild. Mass work needs recruitment and program-building rather than constantly pushing for unity around issues which are essentially party issues and not mass issues.

For us, there is no dichotomy between program and politics. Whenever the Guild's program has been effective, whether around mass defense efforts or the development of movement law offices (i.e., in the South and in Puerto Rico), many new people have been organized to do legal/political work; political consciousness and dialogue have been healthy within the organization because political struggle has occurred in the context of program. When politics are advocated which are abstracted from our program, they promote programmatic sluggishness and narrowness of membership. Those politics are reactionary for this organization.

■ EIGHTEEN

Let Theory and Practice Bloom (1977–1980)

GUILD MEMBERS WANTED the Guild to address a series of major issues during the last half of the 1970s: U.S. government actions abroad, the rights of women and racially oppressed minorities, attacks by the radical Right, and how best to enlarge the Guild and strengthen its work. Questions of economic rights were muted, and the work of the Labor Law Committee tended to focus on representation of emerging rank-and-file caucuses.

During this period, membership grew, chapters multiplied, law students became lawyers; some faced new features of traditional constitutional problems while others faced new features in the emerging field of peace law, discussed in the last two selections.

MAMMON AND CAESAR
By Peter Weiss

[In January 1976, New York lawyer Peter Weiss made a brief investigation and proposal concerning the juridical regime of multinational corporations at the second Bertrand Russell Tribunal in Rome, based on his work in private international law and his work in the Guild and the Center for Constitutional Rights. The opening and closing of his address follow.]

I will attempt to analyze the activities of multinational corporations in Latin America and other parts of the world from a juridical point of view and to make suggestions for establishing a modicum of control over their worst abuses and for assigning both individual and corporate responsibility for such abuses. I shall assume the following propositions to be true for this purpose:

"Mammon and Caesar," by Peter Weiss, from *NLG Practitioner* 34:3 (Summer 1977).

(1) That multinationals are an essential fact of life of the contemporary period and will, for the foreseeable future, continue to play a dominant part in economic relations between the industrialized and nonindustrialized world.
(2) That there is a close interplay between the activities of multinationals and governments, both in their countries of domicile, particularly the U.S., and, for the most part, in the so-called host countries. In fact, it is often difficult to perceive where multinational activities begin and where government activities end. For example, the credit squeeze against the Allende government was part of a grand design and required the active participation of the Export-Import Bank, an organ of the U.S. government, as well as of numerous private banks and manufacturing companies.
(3) That, at present, both the concepts and the instruments of domestic and international law are grossly inadequate to cope with the noxious activities of the multinationals.

The panoply of objectionable activities by multinationals ranges all the way from what we may call ordinary economic offenses and ordinary crimes, through activities inflicting harm on the economic, political, social, and cultural systems of peoples, to massive crimes cognizable by the Nuremberg principles.

The first category would include such offenses as tax evasion, restraint of trade, fraud upon the public, and interference with labor organizing and collective bargaining, which, depending on their gravity and the legal system of the particular country, may constitute either civil or criminal violations.

Illustrative of the third category would be the activities of an East India Company in the 18th century, an I.G. Farben before and during World War II, or an IT&T during the contemporary period. All of these can be said, with considerable justification, to have engaged in crimes against the peace and crimes against humanity in the Nuremberg sense.

But it is in the middle category, where most of the damage is being inflicted, that the conceptual and definitional framework is most inadequate. It is here that juridical life can—and must—be breathed into the inchoate expressions of collective frustration and anger represented by a whole series of resolutions adopted in recent years by the UN and its subsidiary organs.

Without destroying the principle of individual rights and responsibilities which is the cornerstone of the edifice of procedural justice—what we in the U.S. call due process of law—we must find a way to conceptualize, codify, and implement the principle of collective rights and responsibilities without which there can be no economic justice, no genuine sovereignty, no true self-determination.

UN RESOLUTION

Let us pass from the general to the specific. On November 21, 1975, the General Assembly of the UN, by an overwhelming vote, adopted Resolution No. 3398 (XXX) entitled "Activities of Foreign Economic and Other Interests Which Are Impeding the Implementation of the Declaration on the Granting of Independence to Colonial Countries and Peoples in Southern Rhodesia and Namibia and in All Other Territories under Colonial Domination and Efforts to Eliminate Colonialism, Apartheid, and Racial Discrimination in Southern Africa."

This resolution reads, in part:

> The General Assembly reaffirms that, by their depletive exploitation of natural resources, the continued accumulation and repatriation of huge profits and the use of those profits for the enrichment of foreign settlers and the entrenchment of colonial domination over the territories, the activities of foreign economic, financial, and other interests operating at present in the colonial territories of Southern Africa constitute a major obstacle to political independence and to the enjoyment of the natural resources of those territories by the indigenous inhabitants.

If we substitute "foreign companies" for "foreign settlers," "neocolonial" for "colonial," and "developing countries" for "Southern Africa," we have as good a definition as any of the crimes of multinational corporations which the Third World seeks to outlaw. Such a definition would merely be a restatement of the rights repeatedly enumerated in many UN documents and particularly the Charter of Economic Rights and Duties of States, which, in Chapter I, states that: "Economic as well as political and other relations among States shall be governed *inter alia* by the following principles":

> [The author lists fourteen principles, from "(a) Sovereignty, territorial integrity and political independence of states," through "(d) Nonintervention," and "(l) No attempt to seek hegemony and spheres of influence," through "(n) International cooperation for development."]

Increasingly, attempts are being made to urge the multinationals to abide by these principles, in "codes of conduct" formulated by various UN or regional bodies. These codes, however, are mere exhortations to good behavior. They do not carry with them the threat of sanctions.

The task of translating these principles—these rights of peoples—into legal, prescriptive terms, is not an easy one, but it is manageable. "Intervention" as such cannot very well be defined as a crime, because it is impossible for a multinational to function in a given country without interfering in its affairs in some way. But activities which have the purpose or effect of "undermining or destroying the sovereignty of the state" or "the right of the people to self-determination" or "the integrity of public administration" are concepts rising to the dignity of legally enforceable definitions. They are no more vague than the concept of "abuse of a dominant position" found in Article 86 of the Rome Treaty establishing the European Economic Community, which the courts of the Community and its member countries have repeatedly had occasion to interpret.

JURISDICTION: FOR EXAMPLE—SOUTH AFRICA

It is well known that the Nuremberg principles, which, like the cases mentioned above, are concerned with crimes against groups rather than individuals, have never been effectively applied except by victors against vanquished. With economic crimes, the situation is different. If the spirit of solidarity running through the Economic Charter and similar documents has any substance, a crime against a developing country should be considered and treated as a crime against all developing countries, punishable in any country which has ratified an appropriate convention which has entered into force.

A UN document concerned with Southern Africa points the way. Article I of General Assembly Resolution 3068 (XXVIII) of November 30, 1973, entitled "International Convention on the Suppression and Punishment of the Crime of Apartheid," states that "apartheid is a crime against humanity" and declares "criminal those organizations, institutions and individuals committing the crime of apartheid." Article V provides that persons charged under Article II may be tried by a competent tribunal of any state party to the convention which may acquire jurisdiction over the accused or by an international penal tribunal having jurisdiction due to a state party having accepted its jurisdiction.

The advantage of this approach is that it does not require the consent of states in which multinationals are incorporated or domiciled, but is capable of being implemented by any two or more countries in which they operate. Another advantage, and one which may be appreciated by the more sophisticated multinationals themselves, is that it introduces an element of notice, definition, and certainty into their relations with the developing countries, which may serve as a more official guideline to permanent, and therefore profitable—but justly profitable—operations than the vague and unenforceable "codes of conduct" which are the fashion today. . . .

IN CONCLUSION

Two observations: (1) It seems paradoxical in the extreme that, while corporate managers are among the leading advocates of capital punishment against individuals as an alleged deterrent to crime, there is no capital punishment for corporations, which have been known from time to time to commit crimes against entire peoples or classes, dwarfing anything of which a single person is capable. There is nothing unjust in penalizing such extreme crimes with the ultimate punishment, which is the death of the offender through nationalization or revocation of its charter.

(2) One of the greatest crimes against humanity is the enormous waste in human resources involved in the application of some of the finest and most educated brains operating today to such totally unproductive tasks as tax evasion, maximization of profit, corruption and the other daily tasks of meanness which grease the wheels of the system. There is reason to believe that, at least in the lower ranks of corporate management, there are many who would rather apply their talents and energies to serving the people than be hatching sordid plots with the CIA or the local exploiting classes.

They, too, need to be liberated for human, dignified, and productive work. An effective scheme of control may point the way to such liberation.

RESOLUTION ON THE MIDDLE EAST
By the 1977 National Convention and the Middle East Task Force

[In 1975, the International Committee of the Guild took the unusual step of proposing that the national Guild membership study a question and then act on the knowledge gained. The subject: "the many complex historical/political/social issues flowing from the Palestinian-Israeli conflict." Chapters were to organize educational programs, including debates and teach-ins and "in preparing educational programs, the positions of the various Israeli political parties, as well as member organizations of the Palestinian Liberation Organization be adequately reflected. . . . " This work led to passage of the following resolution by the 1977 Convention.]

BE IT RESOLVED THAT the National Lawyers Guild:

1. Calls for the cessation of all Israeli settlement in the occupied territories and effect a complete withdrawal from all territories occupied in 1967.

2. Recognizes the right of self-determination and national independence for the Palestinian people.

3. Recognizes the Palestine Liberation Organization as the sole legiti-

---

"Resolution on the Middle East," by the 1977 National Convention, from *Guild Notes* (Oct. 1977); "Treatment of Palestinians in Israeli-Occupied West Bank and Gaza," by the Middle East Task Force, from Guild book by that name (New York: NLG, 1978), pp. 119-20.

mate representative of the Palestinian people and its right to participate on an equal footing as a principal party in any discussion of the Palestinian Israeli conflict.

4. Recognizes the right of return or compensation for all Palestinians displaced or dispossessed in the creation of Israel in 1948 pursuant to the United Nations resolution #194.

5. Calls for the elimination in all the states in the Middle East of laws, institutions, regulations, and practices which have the purpose or effect of discriminating on the basis of religion, national or ethnic origin, sex or sexual orientation, or race.

6. Calls on the Palestine Liberation Organization and the state of Israel to commit themselves to the exchange of mutual recognition between an independent sovereign Palestinian state and the state of Israel, and the development of a full program of peace between them.

■

Treatment of Palestinians in Israeli-occupied West Bank and Gaza
By the Middle East Task Force (Majority Report, 1978)

The delegation spent three weeks in the Middle East to learn about the situation there, especially the allegations of violations by Israeli authorities of the human and political rights of the Palestinian people in the West Bank and Gaza Strip.

Based on observations and interviews, as well as examination of relevant studies and documents, the delegation concludes that many of the allegations commonly made are valid. Repression is a fact of life in an occupation; Israel's occupation is no different. Israel has violated the rights of West Bank and Gaza Palestinians in a variety of ways, all aimed at incorporating the West Bank and Gaza into Israel and at suppressing resistance to that goal.

Many of these practices, and others noted in this report as well, violate the explicit provisions of the Fourth Geneva Convention, which has been formulated by the nations of the world to protect populations in precisely the situation in which West Bank and Gaza Palestinians find themselves—military occupation.

Israel has violated the Palestinians' territorial rights in the West Bank and Gaza, first by maintaining its presence in those areas in violation of international law prohibitions against acquisition of territory by force. In addition, Israel has endeavored to solidify its control over the West Bank and Gaza by promoting settlement of those areas by its own citizens, by illegally annexing East Jerusalem into Israel, by resettling Gaza residents into the Sinai, and by refusing to permit the return of Palestinians displaced from the West Bank and Gaza during the 1967 fighting. The following provisions of the Convention have been violated by these Israeli practices: Articles 47 and 49.

A major Israeli stratagem for strengthening its control over the West Bank and Gaza has been its efforts to suppress self-determination of the local population by rendering the economies of these territories dependent on the Israeli economy and by restricting development of local institutions that might form the basis for self-governance: municipal councils and medical and educational institutions. The following provisions of the Convention have been violated by these Israeli practices: Articles 51, 52, 54, 56, 57.

In addition, Israel has used harsh methods to suppress manifestations of resistance to its continued hold on the West Bank and Gaza. It has imposed severe limitations on political activity by outlawing any anti-occupation activities. It has punished whole populations for the resistance activity of individuals. Israeli authorities have expelled many Palestinians from their native West Bank and Gaza when they have voiced opposition to Israeli rule. Another repression technique has been to hold Palestinians without charge for substantial periods of time, on mere suspicion of anti-Israel activity. The following provisions of the Convention have been violated by these Israeli practices: Articles 27, 33, 49, 53, 68, 78.

Those Palestinians convicted by Israeli courts are sent to prisons which are among the most overcrowded in the world. And substantial evidence exists that Israeli police, military, and intelligence interrogators have, on numerous occasions, tortured West Bank and Gaza detainees. The following provisions of the Convention have been violated by these Israeli practices: Articles 30, 31, 32, 66, 71, 72, 76.

One of the intended consequences of the totality of oppressive conditions in the West Bank and Gaza is to encourage Palestinians to leave by emigration. Israel does not want the West Bank and Gaza with its people; this would change the demographic composition of Israel. Thus, Israel has sought to create circumstances which would make emigration an attractive alternative to the hardships that a Palestinian under occupation faces daily. Torture, arrests, curfews, economic and psychological pressures, blowing up of houses—all have the objective of impelling the Palestinians to leave their land by the force of the converging factors of fear, insecurity, and destitution. Persecution is deliberately used by the Israeli authorities as a political weapon to intimidate the population into leaving the occupied areas.

It is not necessarily cruel deeds that lead the delegation to condemn the Israeli occupation, but, rather, the humiliation and harassment that are imposed upon the population. No authority exists to which Palestinians can appeal, no protection which they can invoke. Their every movement and action is subject to the arbitrary authority of the occupying force. Their very right to live in the area is questioned by the Occupying Power. This Report is intended to be part of the considerable international pressure which must be exerted upon Israel to curtail those violations of the Palestinians' human rights which can be remedied short of Israel's total withdrawal from the West Bank and Gaza. But the violations by Israel of the Palestinians' human and national rights cannot be terminated so long as Israel occupies the West Bank and Gaza. One professor at Bir Zeit University told the delegation:

We are trying to live normally while living under an abnormal state. We are living under conditions of total insecurity as a people. Even the concept of self-government is denied us—and so it is not a question of timetables, as in South Africa. And we are living under conditions of total insecurity as individuals—there is no definition of right or wrong, no constitution, no basic law. . . .

The professor's statement is, unfortunately, all too true. The rights of West Bank and Gaza Palestinians will be realized only when they control their own destiny in an independent state. This Report will have served its purpose if it assists, however marginally, in achieving that end.

THE RIGHT TO EQUALITY: A MARXIST ANALYSIS
By Barbara Wolvovitz and Jules Lobel

[In 1979, the authors, then members of the New York City Chapter, wrote a longer version of this article with Peter Avenia, as the Guild's Theoretical Studies Committee and the Conference on Critical Legal Studies blossomed.]

Recently, there has been a growth of interest in Marxist legal analysis in the Guild. Similar tendencies have developed in economics, sociology, and history, due to the present stage of the mass movement. The tremendous mass struggles of the 1960s have temporarily receded. Activists and intellectuals are attempting to understand and draw lessons from these movements to guide our practice in current and future struggles.

This article will analyze the struggle of oppressed nationalities for equality from a Marxist perspective through a general analysis of the nature of bourgeois democratic rights, in particular the right to equality and the work for affirmative action.

EQUALITY UNDER LAW

In capitalist society, the fundamental unit of economic life is the commodity; the basic unit of law is a "right." Marx started by analyzing

---

"The Right to Equality: A Marxist Analysis," by Barbara Wolvovitz and Jules Lobel, from Part One, of a two-part article, on which Peter Avenia also worked, *Guild Notes* (Jan. 1979).

the nature of a commodity; we must begin with an analysis of the nature of a "right."

A right to equality is susceptible to two contradictory definitions. First: equal treatment under law. This defines a negative right, affecting only state action and not relations between private individuals; all must be treated by the same "neutral" standard, *as if* they were equal. See the 14th Amendment and the U.S. Constitution generally for this formal, political right.

Second: the social right, guaranteeing equality in fact, not simply equal treatment under law; not a negative right prohibiting governmental discrimination, but mandating an affirmative duty on all levels of society to achieve actual socio-economic equality.

The social right treats individuals who have different class and racial backgrounds differently. The demand for affirmative action is a demand for a social right, acknowledging existing social reality by applying an unequal standard to individuals who are in fact unequal, looking to equality in fact and not under law.

In bourgeois society, these two conceptions are not posed as distinct or contradictory. Bourgeois ideology puts forward the notion that equal opportunity, the formal right to equality, leads to social and economic equality. This ignores and obscures the contradiction between these two conceptions of equal right.

However, the formal right, guaranteed by the 14th Amendment, contains a fundamental contradiction. On the one hand, formal equality is not simply a ruse, but a tremendous victory won by the masses of people which serves as a foundation and steppingstone for their struggles for social and economic equality. On the other, it serves as a mechanism limiting the struggle for real equality and social rights. When, spurred on by formal rights, the masses of people demand social rights, formal equality turns into its opposite and becomes a major bulwark of reaction, providing the ideological and legal handle for stifling the struggle and perpetuating inequality.

Thus, the formal right to equal treatment under law contradicts the social right to equality in fact. First, by outlawing only state discrimination, and refusing to impinge on "private" discrimination, the state presupposes and reinforces the existing inequality. . . .

Man proclaims private property is *overcome politically* once he abolishes the *property qualification* for active and passive voting. . . . Yet the political annulment of private property not only does not abolish it but even presupposes it. The state abolishes distinctions of *birth, rank, education, and occupation* . . . when it declares them to be *non-political* distinctions, when it proclaims that every member of the community *equally* participates in popular sovereignty without regard to these distinctions. . . . Nevertheless the state permits private property, education, and occupation to *act* and manifest their particular nature as private property, education, and occupation in their *own* ways. Far from overcoming these *factual* distinctions, the state exists only by presupposing them . . . (Marx, *On the Jewish Question*).

Second, when the state does impinge on the social sphere it does so through application of a "neutral" standard. However, to treat people who come from different class and racial backgrounds as if they were equal only perpetuates the existing inequality [citing Marx, *Critique of the Gotha Program*].

Formal rights and social rights are therefore not merely two supplementary conceptions, but are contradictory. The formal right is both a progressive step in the direction of equality which gives rise to the demand for social rights, and a force perpetuating inequality which is used to stifle the demand for social rights. This contradiction only arises with the emergence of capitalism but can not be solved by that system. Capitalism both needs yet can not go beyond the formal right to equality, due to the contradiction in the social relations of production and exchange under capitalism.

THE MATERIAL BASIS OF THE CONTRADICTION IN BOURGEOIS RIGHT

The concepts of equality and freedom are not absolutes, or eternal truths, but arise out of the mode of production of material life. Bourgeois law develops out of the social relations which exist under capitalism. "Right can never be higher than the economic structure of society and the cultural development conditioned by it" (Engels, *Anti-Dühring*).

Under slavery or feudalism, formal political equality was inconceivable. The economic status of blacks as slaves directly mandated that they were to have no political rights.

However, capitalism forces an individual to lead two contradictory lives. First, as a private individual, with particular economic and social characteristics. In this realm, which Marx and Hegel termed Civil Society, there exist rich and poor, black and white, capitalist and worker. Our modern individual also has a second life—a political life as a citizen, in which all individuals are equal, regardless of economic status. In this realm, all the lofty ideals of bourgeois society—freedom, democracy, and equality—flower. To maintain these ideals, the state must view each person individually and abstractly, denuded of real class and racial attributes.

Why does capitalism, unlike slavery or feudalism, develop a political superstructure which contains the notion of equal treatment under law? Why can't bourgeois democracy go beyond formal equality to grant actual social and economic equality?

Unlike prior economic systems, capitalism bases itself on the exchange of commodities, i.e., an exchange of equivalent amounts of socially necessary labor. Underneath this exchange lies a social relation between the owners of commodities who meet in the marketplace as equals, enter into social relations by exchanging commodities which have equivalent amounts of labor abstracted from its private, individual character and reduced to a standard of homogeneous human labor.

The most important commodity under capitalism is the commodity of labor-power. In selling labor-power, the worker, like every other commodity owner, receives, in general, an equivalent value in the form of wages (measured not by how much value the worker produces, but by how much is needed to reproduce her or him). For the laborer to sell his commodity, labor-power, he and the capitalist must be able to meet in the market and deal with each other as equals under law. Otherwise, the laborer would be a slave, who *is* a commodity.

This social relation between commodity owners, based on the exchange of equivalent amounts of socially necessary labor time, provides the material basis for the formal right to equality under capitalism. The human labor on which the exchange of commodities is based is labor abstracted from its particular useful characteristics. Likewise, the citizen on whom political equality is based is the "abstract individual" denuded of class or racial background.

Once we leave the marketplace, where automobiles and human labor-power is bought and sold, the worker descends into the factory. In the sphere of production we find an altogether different situation. Once the worker sells her labor to the capitalist, the boss is no longer concerned with exchanging equivalent for equivalent. He wants to expand value, to produce surplus value; all ideas of equality vanish. The social relations of production also demand that the worker be "freed" from ownership of the means of production. The worker approaches the capitalist without any means of survival, except that of selling the ability to labor. While the laborer, as a commodity owner, may get the value of his commodity labor-power, the very act of being forced to sell it to another stems from and perpetuates an essential inequality.

Thus, the contradiction in the nature of the bourgeois right to equality is not simply a distortion, nor is it caused by conservative judges. It is rooted in and reflects a basic contradiction between the relations of production and exchange under capitalism. This tension between production and exchange is in turn based on a fundamental duality inherent in each commodity; between value (exchange value) and use value. The contradiction in the concept of equal right—between formal and social rights—is a reflection of the contradiction between value and use value inherent in every commodity. Value rests on *abstract human labor time*, while use value reflects a *particular* type of labor which produced a *particular* item of utility. Similarly, formal rights rest on the abstract citizen, while social rights rest on the particular citizen, with particular class and racial characteristics. Capitalist production is of necessity production for value (exchange value) and not for use. Capitalist rights are similarly formal rights and not social rights.

The contradiction between production and exchange relations, between value and use value, finds its outlet in the business cycle of capitalism with periodic depressions during which goods produced cannot be sold. The tension between formal rights and social rights has its outlet in the political struggles of the masses of people. By tracing the dialectical twists and turns produced by this duality in the nature of bourgeois rights we can understand the great struggles of the past decades for equality.

Several important political lessons for our mass work can be drawn from this analysis:

1. Formal rights are not just a hoax on the people, but represent a step toward equality. This is not a scheme hatched by the capitalists but stems from the social relations of exchange of commodities. Moreover, the grant of formal rights sets in motion the demand for social rights.
2. Formal, political rights cannot lead to social and economic equality. The political task is not simply to give content to the existing rights which are formal, nor to extend bourgeois democratic rights. The task is to struggle for and win a new kind of right, antithetical to and opposite of formal rights. Such a social right is in essence inconsistent with capitalist relations of production, e.g., a right to affirmative action. The current attack on affirmative action brings out the contradiction inherent in the bourgeois notion of equal rights.
3. The relationship between the struggle for democratic rights and for Socialism is reflected in the relationship between the demand for formal rights and for social rights. A study of the concrete struggles for equality and the relationship between these two demands is critical to the development of political strategy.

[In 1985, the co-authors presented testimony for the Guild regarding the enforcement of civil rights by the Civil Rights Division of the Justice Department before the House Committee on the Judiciary Subcommittee on Civil and Constitutional Rights—turning theory into practice.]

NATIONAL LAWYERS GUILD V. ATTORNEY GENERAL
By 1986 Guild Annual Report and Michael Krinsky

[The Guild provided a brief overview of this suit in the 1986 Guild Annual Report.]

In 1977, we filed suit against the attorney general, the FBI, and other agencies, to determine the extent of government activities over the years—and to seek damages and an injunction against future disruption. What the Guild has uncovered over the past eight years is astounding: More than 300,000 pages of documents produced by the FBI show that, since 1941, the FBI has used well over 1,000 informants to report on NLG activities, and to disrupt Guild meetings, press conferences, and seminars. Informants sat on the policy-making bodies of chapters and of the national organization. FBI agents repeatedly broke into the NLG national office and into private law offices of key NLG members. They directed efforts to defeat members' political and judicial candidacies. The bureau secretly released derogatory and misleading information about the Guild to judges, the media, and the public.

■

By Michael Krinsky

[Lead counsel in the Guild litigation, Michael Krinsky, set the context of the suit in an essay from which the following excerpt is taken.]

The immediate catalyst was the Guild's inadvertent discovery that the FBI had approached an Atlanta hotel clerk for information about an NEB meeting. The Guild was shocked and outraged and, as it turned out, it also was pretty naive. This sort of thing and much worse had been going on for forty years on a systematic basis. In a more general sense, the Guild launched its case in the wake of Watergate and, more particularly, the revelations of government misconduct by the Senate's Select (Church) Committee to Study Governmental Operations with Respect to Intelligence Activities in its Final Report in 1976, Rpt. No. 94-755, 94th Congress, 2d Session (1976). The Guild hoped to move beyond momentary apologies for illegality and to consolidate in law at least some of the lessons the public had been willing to draw from the Church Committee Report.

The temper of the times was apparent in the court's attitude to the case. It was willing to allow broad discovery of FBI conduct on the basis of comparatively few hard facts and at this time the government was

---

"*National Lawyers Guild v. Attorney General,*" by Michael Krinsky, was written for this book.

apologetic, defensive, although not obliging. But, during the first six years of litigation, the government chose to fight the case out on the facts and discovery, not caring to join issue on the law, on the extent of the FBI's legal authority to spy on citizens and to disrupt their activities. . . .

[We learned that] finally, in March 1975, the FBI ran out of time and Attorney General Levi ordered a close to the "internal security" investigation of the Guild. Even so, large loopholes were left to the FBI—investigations aimed at the Guild's international work or nominally aimed at individual Guild members but not at the Guild itself. There is reason to believe that the FBI has used these loopholes effectively to continue at least some surveillance of the organization.

In 1983, after seven years of litigation, the administration took a remarkable step: It filed a motion to dismiss. The motion was not based on the Guild's lack of a sound case. Rather, the government argued, the forty-year investigation of the NLG was carried out on the basis of "national security," and should therefore not be subject to judicial review. The brief put it baldly: "Decisions relating to this investigation were made by high-level officials. . . . Whether each of these was wise or even constitutionally valid is not the point."

On the Guild's damage claims, the government argued that the federal government is immune from suit for conduct taken in the defense of the nation against threats of subversion, terrorism, or unrest. The argument, in form anyway, is statutory. The Federal Tort Claims Act is the waiver of the government's sovereign immunity from damage claims. That statute provides for a broad waiver of immunity, but with a few exceptions; one is the "discretionary function" exception. The Attorney General said the identification of threats to national security and the determination of how to meet those threats is a discretionary function.

He made similar arguments to our demand for injunctive relief. Reagan's Justice Department said that a court cannot issue an injunction in this area, not a broad one anyway, because it would have to draw the line between what is permissible and impermissible in meeting national security threats, and that is a question which cannot be resolved by reference to the Constitution. There remains only a political question for Congress and the executive to work out, and they have not worked it out: there is no FBI charter or statutes binding us, no law for the courts to apply.

With some irony but also with some logic, the Attorney General offers us the assurance that the government's argument would not leave citizens without a remedy, for there is the "Nixon remedy": If the FBI is doing things you don't like, go to Congress and try to get us impeached. . . .

We are now in the Age of Reagan, and the government is increasingly bold. The FBI and its advocates in the Justice Department think they have ridden out the storm created first by the Watergate scandal and then by the Church Committee. And, indeed, they have played a pretty masterful waiting game. Nothing of substance has developed in Congress; Reagan has been triumphant at the polls. Now they are trying to win big in the courts and to restore that degree of unreviewable discretion which they enjoyed in fact, though not through formal judicial decision, prior to Watergate and the Church Committee. . . .

Protracted and important as this suit has been, no doubt it will not be the Guild's last battle against the FBI, whatever its outcome.

OPPOSING RIGHT-WING WHITE SUPREMACIST GROUPS
By Fania Davis, Doris Brin Walker, Ann Fagan Ginger, and the National Executive Board

[In the wake of Klan attacks on the Communist Workers Party in Greensboro, North Carolina, and of the increased visibility of the KKK, White Confederacy, National Caucus of Labor Committees, U.S. Labor Party, National States Rights Party, National Socialist White People's Party, and the American Nazi Party, the Guild debated the proper role of the Guild and of Guild lawyers. Jim Reif and Michael Avery wrote articles on the First Amendment and the Nazis for *Guild Notes;* Jim McNamara and a group of three San Francisco-Bay Area lawyers each proposed resolutions for adoption at the February 1980 NEB. The latter resolution was based on discussions in the National Conference of Black Lawyers as well as the Guild.]

■

Proposed Resolution on the American Nazi Party and the Ku Klux Klan

WHEREAS (A) All Guild members can agree that the Guild should play its special role in entering fully into the struggles against the American Nazi Party, the Ku Klux Klan, and similar groups, and (B) We recognize that the primary and major arena in this struggle is political-economic, not legal.[1] [O]ur specific problem is how to add legal tools to the other weapons in the people's arsenal against these groups.

"Opposing Right-Wing White Supremacist Groups," the proposed resolution by Davis, Walker, and Ginger, was published (along with a proposed resolution of Jim McNamara) in *Guild Notes* (Jan. 1980). The actual adopted resolution was published in *Guild Notes* (April 1980).

1. For this reason, Oliver Wendell Holmes' writings will not provide us with the proper questions to ask or with the realistic frame of reference, let alone a complete answer. He was a member of the Brahmin caste who, as a Justice of the Supreme Court, invented a phrase narrowing the First Amendment coverage by making an exception in the event of a "clear and present danger" while he affirmed the conviction of Socialist Eugene V. Debs for making a speech against U.S. entry into World War I. Earlier, Holmes took a backward view on federal protection of the rights of blacks struggling for voting rights. What he wrote that is helpful we, of course, will continue to use.

RESOLVED that the National Lawyers Guild agrees to pursue the following tactics:

1. To place work against the Nazi-KKK as a priority.
[2-5. List organizational steps, including cooperation with other groups, collecting information from members on each case, building a speakers bureau, etc.]
6. To continue to use the Civil Rights Act of 1964 (especially Title 7) and other statutes to defeat white chauvinist attacks on jobs, education, voting, and other civil rights of minorities and women.[2]
7. To increase the use of the anti–Ku Klux Klan Act of 1871, when appropriate in both civil and criminal cases [Quoting 42 U.S.C. §1985(3) and 18 U.S.C. §§241 and 242].
[8-10. Urge ratification of the Convention on the Prevention and Punishment of the Crime of Genocide, the International Covenant on Civil and Political Rights, and the International Convention on the Elimination of All Forms of Racial Discrimination, all then pending before the U.S. Senate Committee on Foreign Relations.]
11. To establish a committee to study national and international tools and tactics to defeat the Nazis and the Klan, to hold seminars and conferences for Guild members and others and to produce written material on this subject.

By using today the legal weapons forged in the Civil War and Reconstruction Period and in World War II and the UN, and by using that law to the utmost, we will be able to wage a major and effective struggle and to attract (or shame into cooperation) the maximum number of allies.[3]

■

RESOLUTION ADOPTED BY NEB, FEBRUARY 16, 1980
By the National Executive Board

[After a series of Whereas clauses describing specific acts of Right-wing white supremacist groups:]

WHEREAS, although the National Lawyers Guild realizes the inherent limitations of the First Amendment under bourgeois democracy

---

2. As Engels recommended, we should, at every opportunity, force the bourgeoisie to obey their own laws. Twenty-four years after the smashing of the Paris Commune, he wrote that "The irony of world history turns everything upside down. We, the 'revolutionaries,' the 'rebels'—we are thriving far better on legal methods than on illegal methods and revolt.... And if we are not so crazy as to let ourselves be driven into street fighting in order to please them, then nothing else is finally left for them but themselves to break through this legality so fatal to them" (Introduction to *Class Struggles in France* by Karl Marx).

3. These tactics will contribute to building a climate of mass opinion against Fascism and racism and in support of the civil rights and liberties of minorities.

we also recognize its usefulness and potential for helping to build progressive movements; and. . . .
THEREFORE BE IT RESOLVED: . . .

2. The National Lawyers Guild shall seek to expose the activities of all Right-wing white supremacist groups, especially the Ku Klux Klan and Nazis, and shall also expose the relationships between these groups and other more moderate Right-wing groups and the police, corrections officers, the military, and all other state and federal agencies; and
3. The National Lawyers Guild shall participate when it is practical and opportune to do so, in lawsuits under the Civil Rights Act, e.g., 42 U.S.C. § 1985 and other appropriate legislation to obtain compensation for the victims of organized Right-wing violence, and in order to enjoin violent acts and conspiracies to commit violent acts by these groups. The Guild shall also encourage prosecution under state statutes when appropriate. . . .
5. Members of the National Lawyers Guild should not represent Right-wing white supremacist groups or individuals in legal proceedings which would advance their Right-wing white supremacist ideology.
6. Opposition to the organized Right-wing white supremacist groups . . . shall be an organizational priority. . . .

STATE OF THE GUILD SPEECHES
By Paul Harris and Mary Alice Theiler

[In State of the Guild speeches as president, and in Officers' Columns in *Guild Notes*, Harris and Theiler in 1979 and 1980 touched on a series of their concerns.]

■

By Paul Harris at the Los Angeles NEB, December 1979

There has been a change in the relations of power in the world. And it is a change which is causing the ruling forces in the United States to argue among themselves as they grope for a strategy which will assure them the power they exercised prior to their defeat in Vietnam. . . .

The last few years we have also seen a socialist world split both theoretically and militarily. We have seen the explosive power of nationalism. The world will be in turmoil in the coming years and U.S. foreign

---

"State of the Guild Speeches," from Paul Harris, Officers' Columns, *Guild Notes* (Jan. 1980) and (June 1980); and from "The Deep Traditions of Domestic Debate in the National Lawyers Guild," by Mary Alice Theiler, *NLG Practitioner* 37:3 (Summer 1980), and *Guild Notes* (Nov.–Dec. 1980).

policy is in flux as it tries to meet these changes. In these circumstances, we should not be smugly certain of our analysis while the world is in rapid motion. Our conventions should be a time of education for us, not a catharsis of international resolutions. . . .

The American imperial eagle can no longer fly unrestrained. But it has begun to spread its ugly wings and its vicious talons. For the Guild, U.S. imperialism should continue to be the main focus of our international work. The role of U.S. multinational corporations, the action of the U.S. government abroad—these are our responsibilities, as we live in what Che Guevara accurately called "the belly of the beast."

[Harris described an example of the weakness, and strength, of the Guild: the fight against nuclear power plants as a threat to the ecology. In 1969, Guild member David E. Pesonen, who went to law school after defeating the building of a nuclear power plant on an earthquake fault at Bodega Bay, wrote on "Lawyers and the Environmental Crisis" in the *Guild Practitioner*. But Harris pointed out that this was not an issue as late as the February 1979 Convention, one month before Three Mile Island and the movie "China Syndrome."]

But we were saved by our very nature. Guild members on the local level in New Hampshire, Massachusetts, Portland, and South Carolina had been involved in that work since 1977. Therefore, it was no accident that in the significant Rancho Seco anti-nuke trial all four lawyers were young Guild members and the Guild was able to set up a national network within a few months of Three Mile Island. . . . We have members doing important work in areas, which on first analysis do not seem to be key areas, but which in fact become so notwithstanding our lack of theoretical foresight.

Let me highlight some of the organizational factors which will influence our work. We have 86 chapters and 6,000 members. Our membership is made up of 55 percent lawyers, 35 percent law students, 6 percent legal workers, 4 percent jailhouse lawyers, and a growing number of law teachers. We are primarily white, but we are seriously addressing the subtle racism and stereotyping within the Guild, as well as attacking racism in the outside world. We have also been striving to combat the anti-gay feelings and theories prevalent in society and on the Left.

We are a firmly sexually integrated organization. We have 60 percent men and 40 percent women. Women outnumber men in national and regional leadership. Our organization has the potential of creating a model of men and women working together [as equals and fighting] our own sexism and the sexism of our society. The fact that we are seriously discussing pornography and violence against women reflects the composition and politics of the Guild. . . .

[The most effective way] priorities get translated to the membership, bound to a large degree in their local concerns and weighted down by their case loads, is through you, the NEB delegates and national activists. You have the role of linking the local to the national. It is time to shed our new Left aversion to taking leadership. We should maintain the new Left stress on leadership which is collective, not sexist and authoritarian, and which does not develop a cult of personality. But you should accept the responsibilities of being teachers and leaders. . . .

Why do you think 500 people joined in 1979? They were getting ready for 1980. It's going to be a busy period for the Guild because conditions in the world will force people into motion; and people in motion run smack into the law and will turn to us for help.

We Are Family. Look at us—we have disagreements, adolescent rebellions, trial separations, and reunions. We share our work, and we care about each other's lives. The 1980s will be a time to test our commitment, a time of pain and a time of love. As the man said, there's plenty of both in this war we are fighting. We Are Family, and we can be proud to be part of it.

■

By Paul Harris in June 1980

The state of the Guild survey, just completed, showed one startling change in our composition: one out of every three members works for a government agency: legal services, public defenders, and labor-related agencies. This change has a number of consequences. People are making a more consistent and higher salary than those in small private practices. We are spread out in rural areas, cities, and even states where there has been no previous Guild presence. We are in a position to reach out to more of the liberal legal community and in some areas to affect policy of the institutions we work in.

Unfortunately, it also means we are more vulnerable to red-baiting. . . . We must remember that this organization is rooted in the four slogans put forth at the Austin convention: Anti-Racism, Anti-Sexism, Anti-Capitalism, and Anti-Imperialism. We are a Left organization. Whether we call ourselves radical or progressive, in fact, the government will define us as a Left organization.

■

By Mary Alice Theiler

[Mary Alice Theiler, a Seattle attorney and outgoing chairperson of the Guild International Committee, gave this acceptance speech as president at the Boston convention in August 1980.]

Several months ago a letter was received by the government of Argentina protesting the increasing repression against progressive attorneys who represent the labor movement and others who have been singled out. The letter came from the U.S., from a national legal organization, and it showed that the people of this country were watching those in Argentina who sought to extinguish the flame of resistance. We have been told by someone who recently left that country that it caused a considerable stir and had a significant impact. The letter was from the National Lawyers Guild.

I share this story with you because in the recent period there has been a discounting of the importance of international work in the Guild. As outgoing chairperson of the International Committee, I have come to believe firmly in its place in the organization and have deepened my understanding of its importance.

The starting point of our international work is that we must take ourselves seriously. We can have a tremendous impact. If this were not true, we would not have the opportunity to engage in the types of efforts which we do. Delegations such as the one we sent to Guatemala and will be sending to El Salvador pose substantial security and logistical problems for our hosts. We would not be invited if there were not something important to be gained from our investigation and report.

In a more fundamental way, there is another reason we have historically been involved in international work. It has to do with the economic crisis in this country, with the draft, with the attempt to seize the mineral-rich lands of the Native American people; it has to do with the attempt to lift restrictions on the intelligence agencies and the nurturing of ties by these agencies between Right-wing Latin American governments and the white-ruled South Africa.

In the final analysis, we can't do our very best work in our other areas of involvement without an understanding of the general crisis of U.S. imperialism at home and the way this translates into the international context....

We have survived because we have a deep tradition of democratic debate and because we had more in common than we didn't. We shouldn't be afraid of differences, and we shouldn't be afraid to take positions and vote after full discussion and then move on even if we haven't reached consensus. We need to keep in mind that, despite our differences, we belong to a unique organization [with a] heritage of commitment to struggle; we have a responsibility to make that organization stronger and better than when we found it.

HANDLING MY FIRST CONSTITUTIONAL LAW CASE—1981
By Colleen Rohan

[A young lawyer in private practice in San Francisco describes one of the ways a new practitioner starts practicing constitutional law.]

One has a tendency to think of representing a client in a case involving constitutional law as a ponderous, weighty process, involving learned lawyers of high repute, fat books, lengthy legal briefs, and ultimate victory (if one is an optimist) in the highest court of the land. Certainly, law review articles and amicus briefs wait upon the constitutional law case, even as the law students who read them wait upon the Supreme Court.

So my new lawyer illusions ran one day when I was told I had a phone call from my sister.

"Colleen," she said, "Kristine (my niece) brought some books home from school, and I wanted to ask you something. You won't believe this, but they say there's no scientific support for Darwin's theory! I'm going to talk to the principal about them. Do you know anything about these publishers? Are they a religion? What should I do? You can't teach religion in public schools, can you?"

We talk for an hour and I promised to find out who "Creation Life Institute" is. Two hours later I've gathered some information. The Institute is located in El Cajon, California. The corporation is not a California corporation. Names of various directors, presidents, and officers people my legal tablet. My friends in Del Mar are fine and getting suntans. (This may seem somewhat irrelevant, but was necessary to gather in the course of convincing them to drive to El Cajon to surveil the Institute.) I even discover that a state lawsuit is pending regarding these books, including *Dry Bones*, the book that had upset my sister so. Creation Life Publishers were suing the state to get their books accepted as part of the state science curriculum.

Thrilled with my own importance and success, I call my sister back. But she had much more to tell me than I had to tell her. Parents were calling other parents about the books. Visits had already been made to the principal. The books had been taken out of my niece's classroom, made a brief reappearance in censored form, and then mysteriously disappeared.

"What should we do? I want to show it to the principal and the school board, but now, all of a sudden, the books can't be found!"

"Handling My First Constitutional Law Case—1981," by Colleen Rohan, from *NLG Practitioner* 38:4 (Fall 1981).

"They can't do that!" I say (in a lawyerlike fashion).

"There are going to be meetings here about this," my sister says. "Teachers, parents, the school board. The 'creationists' claim the Bible theory of the creation of the world can be supported by scientific evidence, and should be taught as science in public schools! Now some people claim the Education Code allows for this. Where do I get a copy of the Education Code?"

"It's a whole set of books," I say. "I'll check it. I don't suppose anyone mentioned what section of the Code allows for this?"

"No."

Hours of research too gruesome to recount followed. I work in a criminal and civil litigation office. I'd never even looked at the Education Code before. Needless to say, no ready index reference led me to an answer. I found nothing. On to the state Constitution. A few references to prayer in schools, Bibles in school libraries, Darwinism.

"Sheila," I explained in our next phone conference, "science can be taught in school. Your fight is to demonstrate that this isn't science, but religion. You do that, and you'll keep it out of the schools."

Days passed and the phone continued to ring, sometimes midmorning at the office; sometimes midnight at home. I felt I had few, if any, "legal" answers for my sister. I would be consulted on strategy and organizational tactics. She had organized a whole group of parents and had begun keeping files. She spoke out at community meetings, attended all the discussions, sought to persuade reluctant friends to speak out along with her.

I sat at home one glorious evening, watching my sister on the 6 o'clock news, making a strong and intelligent statement of her side. "I'm not 'representing' a client here," I mused. "The truth is, my 'client' is representing me!"

A few days later articles about the pending state lawsuit began to appear in the newspapers, and my sister's local school board scheduled a special meeting.

A frantic phone call came at 7:30 A.M. "Colleen, they've set up the meeting in a room that can't hold more than fifty people. Everyone in town wants to be there!"

[I gave advice on the First Amendment rights of the public and the media, and pointers on how to present "our" case.]

The resolution of this controversy? The school board voted to do nothing until the state lawsuit was resolved. In the meantime, the books were to stay out of the classrooms. . . .

Though this resolution was not the resounding victory we envisioned, it was also most assuredly not a defeat. That is, until a family dinner some weeks later. My niece listened quietly to the excited discussions of creationism and its fallacies, then intelligently repeated the "creationist" theories she had been taught at school. The doubts and confusions my niece expressed that evening were disturbing indeed. Even more disturbing perhaps were the doubts of her mother and aunt, barely admitted, that we had not fought back soon enough, or long enough, or in the proper manner.

I told this story to a lawyer friend of mine, a woman experienced in the field of constitutional law. "Congratulations," she said. "You've defended your first constitutional law case."

I hadn't remotely perceived the situation in exactly that manner until she made the remark. "I don't really think I can make that claim," I said. "I just made phone calls and read some statutes and thought up strategies. I didn't even charge a fee, not that I would from my sister, and not that anyone involved would have had the money to pay anything anyway."

"That's what I mean," she said.

THE LEGAL RIGHT TO PEACE DEMANDED BY OUR CLIENTS
By Ann Fagan Ginger

[In response to some of the work of the critical studies group, and to calls for help from clients, Ginger wrote a long laundry list of the economic, social, and political rights of people in the United States. This excerpt discusses only the basis for defining a legal right to live in peace and the responsibility of lawyers to struggle for enforcement of this right.]

People come to lawyers when they think their rights have been denied. If they are simply angry, but doubt that anyone can help them by means of the judicial system, they seek redress by some form of direct action, or they do nothing. Experienced lawyers have learned that it pays to listen to what clients say, and to pursue the clients' insights about their own cases. So we need to ask ourselves: What are the fundamental rights of people living in the United States today? How did they develop? Where can they be found in the law? And how can lawyers make use of them? . . .

The liberal approach (mindful of the Cold War period) poses a definition of constitutional rights based almost exclusively on the First Amendment. Civil liberties, due process of law, and equal protection are compartmentalized, and changes in the economic system in the United

---

"The Legal Right to Peace Demanded by Our Clients," by Ann Fagan Ginger, from "The Economic, Social, and Political Rights of Our Clients," *NLG Practitioner* 37:4 (Fall 1980).

States since 1791 are largely ignored, particularly the Great Depression; also the rise of Fascism in the 1930s, and the development of public international law since 1945. This approach is often accompanied by an unspoken distrust of "the people," and the assumption that the majority would abolish the First Amendment if it came to a vote today. Nor does it take into account the widespread feeling (particularly among those not covered by the First Amendment when it was written, i.e., blacks and women) that the First Amendment has not proved sufficient to stop the rise of racist and sexist violence in this country in this era.

[So far the new critical theory has] paid little attention to the rich lessons we have learned from practicing social change law. Many clients today are asking lawyers to file a "class action suit" or "a Title Seven case," approaches as well known since the civil rights and legal services movements as *Dred Scott* and *Brown v. Board of Education.*

With this stimulus, many general practitioners, public defenders, pragmatic poverty lawyers, and public-interest law firms keep trying to represent their clients' specific interests and to earn their livings by doing so. They formulate their clients' problems in complaints stating causes of action that sound traditional but actually move one step beyond current law.

These lawyers tend to scorn ideology for practice because the ideology they read does not fit the practice they know. Many are first-generation professionals whose parents were blue-collar workers or small farmers. A few are black, Hispanic, Asian, or Native-American. An increasing number are women. They have learned to fight to win their cases before juries of their peers. Most are pragmatists and will scorn theory until it is proved in practice. . . .

Only the broadest definition of "fundamental rights of the people" will meet the needs and demands of our clients, who have been taught that this country is a democracy run by the people "with liberty and justice for all." The list of fundamental rights is more extensive than we sometimes realize. They grew out of demands of the people to settle economic, social, and governmental grievances in five historic epochs: (1) the Revolutionary War/Articles of Confederation/Constitution-writing period; (2) the Shays Rebellion/Bill of Rights period that followed immediately thereafter; (3) the Civil War/Reconstruction period; (4) the Great Depression/New Deal period (preceded by the Populist 1890–1915 period); (5) the World War II/United Nations period. In the process of spelling out these fundamental rights of the people of the United States, the nature of law comes clearer, as procedural and substantive rules rooted in the actual use of law at all levels and in all departments of the governmental system. The process of change in law emerges as the product of the people's struggles. . . .

THE RIGHT TO LIVE IN PEACE

One more set of basic rights belong to people in the United States today. They are part of the supreme law of our land. These rights, like those in the Constitution and Bill of Rights, and in the Reconstruction Amendments, arose out of a major war—World War II. The U.S. played a significant role in drafting the basic document in which they appear. That document was ratified by the U.S. Senate and is the United Nations Charter.

Although they are thirty-five years old, U.S. lawyers have only begun to think about using the rights in the Charter in their day-to-day litigation, as they commonly consider using the First Amendment, due process, and the equal protection clause. Yet these rights are based on the commitments the United States made when it signed and ratified the United Nations Charter as a treaty, and the U.S. became a member state of the United Nations. Our government committed itself to "settle" our "international disputes by peaceful means in such a manner that international peace and security, and justice, are not endangered," and to "refrain" in our "international relations from the threat or use of force against" other nations. (UN Charter, Art. 2, sections 3 and 4.)

The U.S. government also committed itself to "promote ... solutions of international economic, social, health, and related problems; and international cultural and educational cooperation," in Article 55 of the Charter. And our government pledged to promote "universal respect for, and observance of, human rights and fundamental freedoms for all without distinction as to race, sex, language, or religion" (Art. 55). In Article 56, as a member state, we "pledge[d]" ourselves "to take joint and separate action in cooperation with the Organization for the achievement of the purposes set forth in Article 55."

These are affirmative pledges of action by the signatory governments, and differ from the many negative pronouncements in the U.S. Constitution (that "Congress shall make no law ..."; "... nor shall [any person] be deprived of ... due process of law ... "). As in previous periods, the writing down of these rights in the U.N. Charter, and their ratification by the U.S. government, came long after people had been demanding and seeking to exercise them.

On this issue, as on many issues in the past, the leadership in the strengthening and broadening of fundamental rights has been taken by black people, by women, and by intellectual workers. Very early, black leaders filed a petition with the United Nations against the government of the United States charging violation of international human rights in the form of genocide. At that time, Eleanor Roosevelt chaired the commission that drafted the Universal Declaration of Human Rights, from which the two enforceable documents were drawn: the Covenant on Economic, Social, and Cultural Rights, and the Covenant on Political and Civil Rights. Soon after, Dr. Linus Pauling, Nobel scientist, filed suit claiming that his right to become a grandparent was endangered by U.S. testing of nuclear weapons, which also endangered world peace.

THE RESPONSIBILITY OF LAWYERS TO FIGHT FOR PEACE

Traditional U.S. constitutional lawyers may argue that there can be no "right" without a cause of action to enforce it, which is the flip side of the maxim: No wrong without a remedy. Under this theory, "international human rights" are no more than unenforceable declarations of our aspirations.

Whether the limited view of these scholars is correct will depend on the will of the people of the United States. If they continue to organize and go to lawyers seeking redress, and if the lawyers continue to seek relief from judges, administrators, and legislators, then some of the declarations of international human rights will become "law" by the same process that has occurred in other areas of law. (See *Filartiga v. Pena-Irala,* 630 F.2d 876 (2d Cir. 1980.)

Our clients today ask us to fight for them . . . when they demand liberty, justice, equality, security, and peace. This may actually be easier than to secure each right individually, since it is impossible, now, to have liberty or justice unless we also have racial, national, and sexual equality. It is impossible to have liberty unless we have economic security. And none of these rights has any meaning unless we have peace.

■ NINETEEN

The Challenge of the Eighties (1981–1984)

TENS OF THOUSANDS of students decided to become lawyers in the 1970s and early 1980s, to follow in the footsteps of Charles Garry, Fay Stender, Susan Jordan of San Francisco, Leo Branton and John McTernan of Los Angeles, Dean Robb and Richard Goodman of Michigan, Walter Gerash of Denver, and other Guild lawyers across the country handling front-page, big-verdict, political and personal injury cases. Additional thousands of professionals, seemingly settled in teaching, social work, nursing, engineering, and other fields, decided to go to law school by day or night in order to change careers, or to add law to the tools at their command that were not strong or deft enough to accomplish the goals they had set for themselves. They were motivated by the success of suits to protect the environment, to obtain affirmative action in employment, to challenge unsafe products in "class action suits," making that a household phrase.

In both of these developments, Guild lawyers were more important than their mere numbers. They were the models; they made the waves. It was their image that got students through the Law School Admission Test and their first-year courses in contracts, torts, and civil procedure.

Between 1960 and 1984, the number of lawyers more than tripled, from 205,515 to 678,000.[1] Between 1964 and 1984, ABA-approved law schools increased from 134 to 175, increasing their student seats from 54,265 to 125,698, and unaccredited law schools mushroomed.[2] Guild lawyers began teaching in many law schools and setting up practice clinics to help prepare students for the realities of practice that, for most, would not include lengthy apprenticeships in Wall Street firms, although some might have to work there, at least briefly, to pay

---

1. Department of Commerce and Bureau of the Census, *Statistical Abstract of the United States* (1964), p. 229, and (1986), p. 402.

2. "Review of Legal Education for the United States" (Chicago: American Bar Association, Section of Legal Education and Admission to the Bar, 1984), p. 66.

off up to $50,000 in student loans from college and law school. In 1986, Professor Debra Evenson of DePaul University helped create an organization of Guild professors.

As Ronald Reagan was settling into the Oval Office, the Guild was growing so dramatically in numbers and in geographical spread that no short list could be made of Guild bodies and their work. Barbara Dudley, becoming the first full-time working president of the Guild in 1983, and continuing as full-time executive director under succeeding presidents, prepared comprehensive annual reports of Guild activities, starting in 1985. They present an accurate overview of national Guild work not discussed here, including: projects in Puerto Rico; work against repressive legislation and violations of civil liberties; delegations to meetings of the International Association of Democratic Lawyers and the American Association of Jurists; testimony before Congressional committees, state agencies, and the UN; work on electoral issues and on a myriad of local grassroots problems, and on impact litigation.

Some intriguing examples of Guild work follow, on diverse subjects. David Rudovsky of Philadelphia, vice president in 1980, set the context:

[I]t is our experience that forceful, principled political and legal advocacy need not relegate us to a status of insignificance. We are and will continue to be listened to by the courts, Congress, local legislatures, and other legal people, if we understand that insurgency is not incompatible with skilled and effective legal advocacy.[3]

RETHINKING INDIAN LAW
By Steven Tullberg and Robert T. Coulter for the Guild Committee on Native American Struggles (CONAS)

[In 1982, CONAS published an anthology entitled *Rethinking Indian Law*, based on the work of Committee members over several years. One section discussed, in detail, "The Failure of Indian Rights Advocacy: Are Lawyers to Blame?" This segment is from that section.]

With increasing frequency, Indians are asking why the lawyers representing Indians in court battles over Indian rights have had such little success in gaining legal protection for the most important Indian rights: the sovereign rights to self-determination and to ownership and control of Indian land and resources. A close look at some of the Indian rights advocacy in the courts today suggests that lawyers representing Indians are in significant part responsible for this failure.

Many had hoped that the past two decades of Indian activism in

---

3. David Rudovsky, Officers' Column, *Guild Notes* (July–Aug. 1980).
"Rethinking Indian Law," by Steven Tullberg and Robert T. Coulter, from the book by that name (CONAS of NLG, 1982).

United States courts would lead to a new era in which these fundamental rights would finally be given the strongest legal protection available under federal law and the United States Constitution. Instead, the Supreme Court has issued a series of decisions which dramatically undercut Indian sovereignty and which reaffirm broad, unrestrained powers of Congress to expropriate Indian property. The Court has even gone out of its way to announce the chilling news that the power to terminate Indian governments is still "legal" under United States law, and that Indian land rights and land claims are not protected by the Fifth Amendment to the Constitution from confiscation by the federal government.

In the adversary system of justice, the arguments made by the lawyers for each side are critical to the outcome of the case. Seldom does a court give that which is not requested, and if the lawyers for the two sides agree on an issue—if one lawyer concedes a point made by his opponent—the court almost always accepts that agreement and incorporates it into the final decision.

A review of some of the transcripts of oral arguments made before the Supreme Court in Indian rights cases decided during the past few years shows that lawyers representing Indians have time and again given away at least half of the legal battle and have actively favored a "handout" theory of Indian sovereignty which helps erode Indian rights. It is not likely that these concessions have been authorized by the Indian peoples whose cases were being heard, and they certainly have not been authorized by all the other Indian tribes, who find the concessions used as precedents to deny their rights as well. . . .

[To argue] that Indian peoples have fundamental rights to self-determination and to ownership and control of their lands and resources, rights which arise from the history, separate existence, and will of sovereign Indian peoples, rights which cannot be lawfully divested or impaired by the United States or by any other sovereign, is not far-fetched or difficult to conceive. It takes no special brilliance or creativity to fashion strong legal support for such argument from the early Indian rights decisions of Chief Justice John Marshall and from the body of constitutional law developed during the past several decades by advocates for civil rights, aliens' rights, women's rights, mental patients' rights, juveniles' rights, and so forth. And a growing body of international law (which is applicable in United States courts), developing human rights standards during the post-colonial era of the United Nations, is also available to support fundamental Indian rights. . . .

The totally unsatisfactory state of United States Indian law will continue until Indian peoples and others become aware of its failings and work to bring about the law reform so sorely needed.

FROM NATIONAL COMMITTEE TO COMBAT WOMEN'S OPPRESSION (NCCWO) TO ANTI-SEXISM TASK FORCE
By Elizabeth Schneider, Patti Roberts, and Barbara Dudley

[Guild committees, projects, task forces, subcommittees, and regions find it useful to meet each time the Guild convenes an NEB or Convention. This permits participation by delegates from throughout the country, including those unable to attend committee meetings and those too busy with other Guild work to focus on the work of a group, even though it represents one of their interests. At an NEB meeting in New York in 1983, NCCWO presented a panel to review the past seven years of work. The panel included Liz Schneider, on the faculty at Rutgers Law School, representing the perspective of a woman active in the Guild and in women's rights work, but who did not relate to NCCWO on an ongoing basis; Patti Roberts, practicing in San Francisco, representing a woman active in the Guild and women's rights work, who did work actively in NCCWO; and Barbara Dudley, then practicing in San Diego, representing a woman who did not choose to do women's rights work in the Guild but who did other types of Guild political work.]

LIZ SCHNEIDER: The women's caucuses in the Guild led to creation of NCCWO. A lot of younger women came into the Guild in the 1970s out of the new Left and went to law school specifically to work on women's legal issues. . . . We were also involved in the women's movement, so we felt there was a need for a separate women's presence in the organization. That need was not clearly articulated. The experience of women meeting together was more support-oriented, a consciousness-raising function: talking in a more open way about the sexism we experienced in the Guild, the predominance of male approaches (emphasis on rhetoric), styles of lawyering (emphasis on criminal law and so-called heavy political defense work), and emphasis on a more top-down approach to decision-making.

PATTI ROBERTS: Even though it's rather slow, there have been a lot of changes. There is NCCWO; it meets regularly; when issues come up, NCCWO deals with them; there is some programmatic work, networking, and support work. What is pathetic is that in 1983, why don't we have more? Why don't we have an impact on Washington? Organizationally, the movement is pretty big. This is only a small part of the Guild women's experience; we only represent the last bit of history.

"From National Committee to Combat Women's Oppression (NCCWO) to Anti-Sexism Task Force" includes panel excerpts from "Women's Issues in the Guild—A Retrospective," Part One, *NCCWO Bulletin* (1983); New York Chapter, *Blind Justice*, February 1982, on the Fighters for Reproductive Rights; National Guild Office, Guild Annual Reports, on the Anti-Sexism Task Force and other Guild activities, 1985–1987.

Those women active in the Guild before 1969 don't happen to be here and we only remember our little piece and the rest gets lost. There have always been a lot of women active in the Guild, and always a lot of women's work, feminist work—maybe in the thirties it was called work on the woman question. On the counterside, there has always been that struggle about who does it, and are we really putting the kind of resources we should be putting behind that kind of work? There still are not a lot of other progressive, Socialist, or quasi-Socialist or anti-imperialist Left perspective organizations that deal with work around women's issues, hopefully gay issues, but also other issues. . . .

In the late 1960s in the conflict over priorities, class and race were always in the front. Women's issues came next, and people could never figure out how to put in gay issues.

BARBARA DUDLEY: One of the things that has changed in the Guild and I'm not sure it has changed for the better, is that we no longer have anything very concrete we can react to because people have learned the right words. You rarely now find a panel that is all men; they notice a panel is all men and say to themselves, "Oops, we'd better get a woman." . . . I firmly believe that I am the "girls' vice-president."

Being back in the Guild with responsibilities of the national organization, I'm back in a scene I left in 1972, and now I remember why I left. I don't mean history has stood still, it hasn't; but a whole lot of things came back to me in terms of the role of women and men in this organization.

LIZ: Why have many of the active women—doing feminist work in the Guild—shifted their focus to doing women's rights work outside the Guild? Local chapters have made efforts to have active anti-sexism committees, but they have not taken off in the Guild.

BARBARA: I've found confusion about NCCWO's identity: is it a women's caucus or a committee to work externally on political issues which particularly affect women?

PATTI: I think NCCWO plays both roles. And all these problems are multiplied a thousandfold when we talk about gay and lesbian issues. You can't have any analysis or work that is narrowed to women's issues that doesn't deal with lesbian concerns, but the Gay Rights Task Force has a tremendous problem surviving.

BARBARA: I perceive NCCWO as a programmatic committee which is more successful than most Guild committees.

LIZ: We are not talking about enormous progress over the last few years but different stages of the struggle. The first stage was that nobody at all thought about this. Now there is a need to overtly recognize that women's issues are important and part of the litany of things that progressive people are supposed to include. But we are frequently bogged down with having to raise anti-sexism issues within the organization. This diverts energy from developing affirmative and conscious programs which are useful for making ties with groups outside the organization. . . . Since 1978, I have had two children and that has been the major factor affecting my life. I have continued to work full time and have found it extremely difficult to stay nearly as involved in Guild work as I would like. It has made an enormous difference in the focus of the issues I feel concerned about. I feel much more deeply perplexed about the role of the family in general, and angrier than I might have been before about the extent to which the pro-family movement in the Left has been pushing that as our way of unifying with the Right. I feel more limited and tired in terms of taking on organization work. It is a funny, ironic, and trite dilemma that I am laying out—it is more difficult to connect my experiences to active political work.

PATTI: "Tired" is the word which most fits. I have been very active, but now I feel less willing to do the organizational work of the Guild. Is that because it feels like the same thing again or am I just going through a little swing? Newer people in the organization have a lot more energy and enthusiasm. They aren't part of the "old girls network" in the Guild. What I can do in the Guild now is work on specific tasks, like the Gay Rights Litigation Manual.

BARBARA: My personal life has not influenced my attitude toward the Guild. What brought me back was Reagan's election and living in San Diego. I really needed to connect politically with people who were not part of the Right. For all the years I was not active in it, it was still my organization.

[In the late 1970s, young Guild leaders in several chapters quietly reverted to the practice of sponsoring annual banquets at fancy hotels honoring prominent members and raising money for the chapter coffers. In 1981, the San Francisco chapter thus honored the first woman national president, Doris Brin Walker. In 1982, the New York chapter honored "fighters for reproductive rights": Catherine Roraback, the second woman national president, Judith Levin, Nancy Stearns, and Rhonda Copelon, all active in the New York City chapter, as well as in litigation on women's rights. The Chapter newspaper, *Blind Justice*, described not only their innovative work as litigators, but more about their personal traits than had been written about many male honorees in the past. In 1983, the Buffalo chapter honored Barbara Ellen Handschu. From then on, women became frequent honorees at local and national events.

[At the Guild's Atlanta convention in 1985, a renewed commitment to anti-sexist work resulted in the merger of the National Committee to Combat Women's Oppression and the Gay Rights Task Force into a new Anti-Sexism Task Force. The quarterly *Task Force Newsletter* analyzes legislation and litigation and describes Guild work on pornography, domestic violence, anti-choice violence, repression of gay men and lesbians in the military, affirmative action, comparable worth, and anti-sexist resources. After the 1985 convention, the Guild formed an AIDS network to educate members and combat widespread misinformation about AIDS, and to assist members working to help AIDS victims and to defeat anti-AIDS legislation and litigation.]

LOOKING BACK AND LOOKING FORWARD
By Gerald Horne and Doris Brin Walker

[In the 1980s, younger Guild members with a sense of history referred, from time to time, to events in the Guild predating their own membership. Paul Harris quoted long-time Guild president Robert Kenny concerning his representation of the Hollywood Ten: "There was a period in the late forties and fifties when it wasn't clear whether membership in the Communist Party of the United States was a felony, a misdemeanor, or just economic suicide."

[Dr. Gerald Horne, attorney and historian, discussed "Our Common Struggles — Past, Present, and Future" in the 1984 banquet journal honoring Haywood Burns. He focused, in these excerpts, on three incidents significant in Guild history. Doris Brin Walker, in remarks at the 1981 San Francisco chapter banquet in her honor, looked back to 1941, and to the difficult period in the early 1970s.]

■

By Gerald Horne

It was more than serendipitous that the National Lawyers Guild was involved in the critical event which marked the beginning of the end of McCarthyism in this country. It was the spring of 1954 and the televised hearings of McCarthy's investigation of the U.S. Army and its alleged Communist ties were brought into living rooms across the country. It was quite a spectacle. Aides Roy Cohn and Robert Kennedy sat snarling like watchdogs. The Senator himself was posing questions in a sanctimonious voice dripping with unctuous insincerity. The Senator wanted to know if a member of the law firm of Army counsel Joseph Welch had ever been a member of the Guild, the "legal bulwark of the Communist Party." In one of those snatches of dialogue that has become immortalized, Welch plaintively answered, "Have you left no sense of decency, sir, at long last? Have you left no sense of decency?"

This moment, poignantly captured on television and underscored by the major news media, marked a turning point in the nation's perception of McCarthy. But somehow forgotten in the deluge of publicity was

---

"Looking Back and Looking Forward" from Gerald Horne, "Our Common Struggles — Past, Present, and Future," in New York City Chapter banquet journal, 1984; and from Doris Brin Walker, remarks made at her testimonial dinner, June 6, 1981, on file at MCLI.

Welch's comment that the young attorney's membership in the Guild was his "one mistake" in life. The notion that joining one of the most progressive, anti-racist, and forward-looking organizations in the U.S. could be deemed a "mistake" not only dramatized the distorted perspectives inherent in Welch's question, but also how widely his statement was believed, as revealed by the disunity which permeated the Guild ranks in the 1950's.

Thirty years later, the Guild is now as strong as it has been in a long time. Not the least reason for its revitalization has been its ability to maintain unity and to tolerate a diversity of viewpoints while adhering to principle. This has not been an easy task. Indeed, maintaining unity between black and white in the most racist society this side of South Africa has at times required herculean skill. . . .

The chilling winds of the Cold War and anti-Communism had a devastating effect on the blooming relationship between the black legal community and the Guild. Louis Redding, who contributed significantly to the *Brown v. Board of Education* victory, and was one of the most eminent black NLG members, resigned after his home state, Delaware, enacted a law requiring members of organizations deemed to be subversive "to register with the state police." . . .

We study the past to understand the present and to make projections for the future. We can profit by examining the Progressive Party campaign of 1948 and the subsequent history of this historic organization in which NLG stalwarts like Earl Dickerson and John Abt played such prominent roles. The very creation of the PP compelled the two major parties to become more responsive to the needs of the nation's majority —national minorities and women—and its existence helped to shape and alter the prevailing political agenda. . . .

In 1949 the FBI attempted to split the tie between the Guild and the International Association of Democratic Lawyers over the events then occurring in Yugoslavia. One FBI memo predicted confidently, "it is believed that considerable dissension in the ranks of the National Lawyer's Guild" could be engendered by this conflict. Murray Kempton's column in the *New York Post* of May 8, 1950 highlighted this conflict. . . .

To ensure the Guild's growth and its ability to make steely-eyed projections for the future, the recent trend of elevating the peace question must be continued. Those black and white, male and female attorneys who created the Guild almost fifty years ago—just prior to a war which killed 50 million people—would have it no other way. The soundest policy to insure that we will have a future can be articulated in three simple words: UNITY, UNITY, UNITY.

By Doris Brin Walker

The Guild has helped change my professional life. Probably every Guild member here can say the same. And those of you who are our clients have much for which to thank the Guild: it has helped to educate us and to train us, and has given us a place in which to clarify our own thinking as your lawyers about the causes for which you fight. It has helped to build and to provide for you as well as for us the professional and community support and strength we so often need with clients like you.

Still, although I have been a Guild member since 1941, I would never have believed tonight was possible. In the 1950s, during the first Cold War, the Guild was fighting government suppression and losing members by the thousands. In the 1960s we were fighting the weariness caused by that struggle and trying to hold the organization together for the day when young lawyers and their clients would come looking for us. In the 1970s, after young lawyers and law students and legal workers had found us, and after, for historical and other reasons, we had succumbed temporarily to racism and become an all-white organization, we were fighting among ourselves, fiercely, over what we then called the "fight for basic social change" and over who was leading it. Was it students? Was it prisoners? Was it the working class, people who really worked for their livings, earning a wage or a salary? Was there even a working class—or were workers so middle-class in their lives and in their view of the world that the old-fashioned working class of Eugene Debs and the organization of the CIO no longer existed? And we fought over what was racism anyway, and where did it fit into the "fight for basic social change"? And what kind of social change did we want?

It was during this period, at the 1971 convention in Boulder, that the Guild refused to adopt a resolution of support for Angela Davis when she was on trial for her life. But that was ten years ago, and here is Angela, our honored guest and main speaker. And once again people of color are members and among our leaders.

I have asked myself repeatedly, and I asked many of you: how can I best use this wonderful occasion, with a captive and friendly audience, to say effectively what I want most to say, even if it does stir up a bit of trouble—in a constructive way, of course?

Shall I talk about the working-class struggle internationally, and about the fallacies in the views of those who deny the existence of the international working class, who refuse to acknowledge the class role of the Socialist countries? Shall I point out to them that the people of El Salvador do not equate the United States with the Soviet Union?

I thought about the fact that during my own lifetime I have seen hundreds of millions of people take the road to Socialism. I thought about the fact that Japan and most of Western Europe have been drawing away from the biocidal foreign policy of the Reagan administration. The international ruling class *is* divided over what methods are most effective to keep hold of as much as possible of what they have, for as long as possible, and a large section of the ruling class is not rushing to embrace nuclear holocaust as a "viable" method. And I thought about what a fascinating, exciting, terrifying, and hopeful period we live in. (Marxists are generally hopeful and optimistic.)

I finally decided that there is one thing I must say, especially to my younger Guild colleagues: Working class struggle—for a decent life, for peace and security, for equality and against racism, and sexism, and ageism, and for political and social and economic justice for every person—studying, supporting, and aiding working class struggle, as an individual citizen and as a lawyer—that has been both the keystone of my adult beliefs and the touchstone of my professional and organizational life. It is this commitment which makes me so proud to be a member of the Communist Party; and it is this commitment which has brought me here tonight—a Guild activist as a student and as a lawyer.

ECONOMIC RIGHTS AS HUMAN RIGHTS
By Ramsey Clark, Arthur Heitzer, Melinda R. Bird, and Sam Rosenwein

■

By Ramsey Clark

That we question whether economic rights are human rights reflects both the power of culture and the weakness of intellect. Conditioned from earliest awareness to consider the struggle for human rights in terms of traditional civil liberties—freedom to think and communicate, freedom from certain excessive government conduct, due process of law —affluent America has put economic issues in a separate epistemological category. Trapped by this differentiation, we think of freedom and human rights as political liberty.

"Economic Rights as Human Rights" from Ramsey Clark, guest editorial, *Guild Notes* (Sept.-Oct. 1982); "Outline for a Campaign for an Economic Bill of Rights," by Arthur Heitzer, *Guild Notes* (Jan.-Feb. 1983); "Toward an Economic Bill of Rights," by Melinda R. Bird, a speech at NLG Regional Conference, March 1983, in *NLG Practitioner* 40:2 (Spring 1983); "Toward an Economic Bill of Rights—Some Legal Bases," by Sam Rosenwein, *NLG Practitioner* special issue, 41:1 (Winter 1984).

Then to stand history and actuality on their heads, it is hypothesized that only political liberty requires a guarantee. The theory holds that when political rights are assured, they afford equal opportunity for all, resulting in economic well being in accordance with just desserts. Magna Carta was for the Lords. Patrick Henry did not include Nat Turner when he cried for liberty or death. Most growth of the idea of political rights has been among those sharing economic power and designed for their own benefit.

Political liberty depends on economic power. The very rule of law is largely a reflection of the allocation of powers, among which economic power is principal.

After thousands of executions and lynchings, the U.S. Supreme Court in 1932 accorded "Scottsboro Boy" Powell a court appointed attorney because he was a pauper in a capital case and ". . . incapable adequately of making his own defense because of ignorance, feeble-mindedness, illiteracy, or the like. . . ."

And today nearly half a million Americans, practically all poor, waste in prison while more than a thousand, all poor, wait on death row to die.

No political freedom, no human rights, not even legal justice, can be assured to people who do not have economic rights. The human rights guaranteed by the Bill of Rights in the U.S. Constitution cannot be fulfilled unless economic rights are fulfilled. To arbitrarily exclude economic rights from definitions of human rights is worse than illogical. It is false, because it implies that all human rights are achievable by political fiat and sets us on a vain pursuit that defies reality. *Gideon*, the Legal Services Corporation and any prodigious progeny they may produce cannot achieve equal justice under law, even in criminal prosecutions, in the absence of economic and social justice for the general population.

The Great Writ, habeas corpus, run to a pile of bones, has neither virtue nor utility. A child, brain damaged by malnutrition, can only be tormented by the awesome right to read, access to great libraries and wise teachers, freedom of speech and faith.

Economic rights are the first and most essential among all human rights. Franklin D. Roosevelt added freedom from want to the American definition of human rights as the U.S. approached entry in World War II.

In the wake of that terrible war, the Universal Declaration of Human Rights included basic economic rights. The International Covenant on Economic, Social and Cultural Rights of 1966 showed an expanded human imagination seeking to enlarge economic rights. The Algiers Declaration of 1976 presented a powerful third world people's perception of the human need for freedom from economic exploitation, foreign intervention and domination, multinational corporate abuses including manipulation through corrupt local officials. It included affirmative rights to scientific knowledge, beneficial development of national resources, and the fundamental right to choose national economic and social systems.

Economic rights are internationally recognized fundamental human rights . . . essential to the effective exercise of psychological, social, cultural, and political freedom. A poor nation forced to choose between bread in tryanny and hunger with political liberty will choose to eat.

[Sam Rosenwein (below) added that the fundamental economic rights are enshrined in the treaty known as the UN Charter, passed by the Senate in 1945 and part of the supreme law of the land, including particularly Articles 55 and 56, in which the United States pledged to "promote . . . full employment" individually and through the UN.

[As successive regional vice presidents working with the Economic Rights Task Force, Arthur Heitzer, a labor lawyer from Milwaukee, and Melinda Bird, a legal service lawyer from Los Angeles, spoke and wrote extensively in 1983 and thereafter on a campaign for an economic bill of rights.]

■

By Arthur Heitzer

REALISTIC SOLUTIONS

Clearly, while there is great potential for Left liberal forces and for the Guild in this period, there are also great dangers. Despite many initiatives by progressive forces in this country in recent years, a candid appraisal reveals that many times the far Right has tactically outperformed us, giving at least the mass media in this country the impression that the country has "moved to the right." . . .

One task for us, then, is to succeed in not only raising the right issues, but in popularizing them. The people in this country can then recognize the realistic solution which the Guild and its allies could offer. This realistic solution could be posed in terms of transferring wealth from the wealthy to the poor and working class and rebuilding the cities at the expense of the military, thereby really addressing the cause of crime and other social ills. This solution should be opposed to the "social issues" which have fairly effectively been used by the Right in recent years, such as fear of crime, high taxes, allegedly excessive welfare expenditures and often blatant racist and anti-Semitic scapegoating.

WHAT WOULD IT INCLUDE?

Clearly, an economic bill of rights would begin assuring the right to meaningful and remunerative employment. Virtually all draft statements of economic rights being circulated also include a guaranteed income at a reasonable standard for all those who are unable to work, whether due to plant closings and layoffs; any kind of disability or infirmity; the need to be at home, such as for raising minor children and for those who have retired after a normal work life. [I] favor greater emphasis on high quality day care centers as a right, in order to assure utilization of full employment opportunities, as opposed to a presumption that women (parents) with minor children would automatically be relegated to the present type of AFDC welfare system, outside the job market.

[I applaud the new rule giving non-union workers protection from discharge at will, not only because it helps them, but because] a better bargaining climate exists for unionized workers where the base level of benefits and security for all workers is increased, and such a view was expressed at the AFL-CIO Lawyers' Conference of May 1982 in Minneapolis by a major presenter, Michael Gottesman, affiliated with the AFL-CIO's Industrial Union Department.

■

By Melinda R. Bird

Just as the right to vote is constitutionally protected because of its significance in guarding all other rights (*Harper v. Virginia Board of Elections*, 383 US 663, 667 (1966), *Doe v. Plyler*, 457 US 202, (1982) note 15), subsistence is necessary to the enjoyment of all other fundamental rights. An assurance that one can obtain the means to survive is "implicit in the concept of ordered liberty" (*Palko v. Connecticut*, 302 US 319 (1937)) and important both to the individual and to society (*Serrano v. Priest*, 5 Cal 3d 584, 605 (1971)), two hallmarks which define a fundamental right. Recognition of subsistence as a fundamental right for all would also command strict judicial scrutiny when government fails to protect and safeguard this right.

Presently, at most, the state is required merely to refrain from interfering with those struggling to survive, with no legal or even moral duty to assist. As progressives or socialists, we see the proper role of the state as guaranteeing a basic, minimum package of goods and services to ensure a decent and adequate standard of living for all, and our task as legal workers is the achievement of this goal.

Existing statutory programs do not provide benefits to all those in need, but only to those who meet stringent eligibility conditions. The "fortunate" who qualify have an entitlement interest which is constitutionally protected, in part because the denial of aid renders the poor so desperate. (*Goldberg v. Kelly*, 397 US 254, 264 (1970)). But as the massive cutbacks in federal and state health and welfare programs demonstrate, this entitlement to subsistence can be wiped out at the whim of the legislature. Moreover, even these fragile guarantees do not exist for the millions of people who may be equally or more desperate, who cannot meet their basic human needs, but who do not fit the statutory pigeon holes to qualify for aid. The goal of both political and judicial advocacy must be a universal entitlement which guarantees that none will suffer from an inability to meet their basic human needs.

[Bird stressed that entitlement must include two-thirds of the poor who are women and children. They turn not to unemployment insurance or pension plans for their economic rights, but to the welfare system. In the meantime, we must pay close attention to welfare advocacy.

[As national Guild president, Michael Ratner added his voice to the call for the recognition of economic rights, which, he pointed out, are contained in the constitutions of all Socialist countries.]

■

By Sam Rosenwein

[This is a very short excerpt from a long, heavily footnoted article on some legal bases for an economic bill of rights.]

If 10,000 workers are one day laid off by GM, US Steel, International Harvester, or any other supercorporation, without any possibility of resort to the due process or equal protection provisions of the 5th and 14th Amendments, who is enjoying "freedom"—the workers or the corporations?

When the highest officials of government announce that private power, not government, should deal with deprivation of livelihoods, economic decay in the cities, social and racial tensions, and all the misery created by that same private power, while the said government systematically uses tax and budget policy to redistribute income so that the rich get richer and the poor poorer, has such government been "instituted among men . . . to secure these rights . . . life, liberty, and the pursuit of happiness" as the founding fathers declared when they initiated the revolution? . . .

SUGGESTED PROGRAMS

We have enough proposals to protect the economic and social welfare of the populace against the "supply side" practices of the dominant elements in present-day society. The problem is how to achieve the goals set forth in these many meritorious programs. The legal front is only one area of struggle.

It is possible to glean from the varied specific proposals an overview of a definitive program: total employment—everyone who desires a job assured of finding one that reasonably satisfies his or her needs, thus, an unqualified guarantee of full employment; an incomes policy based on mandatory controls over prices set by large corporations; redistributive taxation on grounds of equity and controlled inflation; income maintenance at decent levels for individuals unable to work; for everybody—a national health care system, decent housing, an accessible mass transportation system, a continuing education program from childhood through life, consumer protection, access to civil justice, recognition by the public and private sectors that all persons are entitled as a matter of legal and constitutional right to wages, food, health, housing, education. (The word "everybody" means the elimination of all forms of discrimination.)

Any claim that private investment would be discouraged by such a program is met by the further suggestion that a growing portion of the private sector be socialized with an expansion of the public economy.

THE ARGUMENT

(1) Government (federal and state) has the power to maintain economic justice and freedom for the people of the U.S.; (2) Government has an affirmative obligation to achieve such justice and freedom; (3) People have a constitutional right to obtain the ingredients that constitute economic justice and freedom; (4) Government possesses ample power to curb the external activities of corporations and their internal governance.

Before we take up these specific arguments, however, some background is needed.

CONSTITUTIONALIZING THE SUPERCORPORATION

The federal and state governments clearly have ample power to curb corporate activities. Now the time has arrived to recognize that the supercorporations must be constitutionalized. Sovereignty today is shared by public government and the private governments of the corporations. The influence and pressure corporations put on government is well known. They dominate the economic, social, and political activities of the entire population—making binding decisions, planning (legislating), enforcing, adjudicating—a continuous process that determines domestic as well as foreign policy.

Government acquiescence in the actions of these corporate powers amounts to ratification of those actions and is subject to constitutional claims. Tolerance of such actions constitutes "state action." These corporations perform public functions and are clearly affected with a public interest. Any activity engaged in by corporations in a state, or in the nation, or in the world, is done with the active aid, subsidy, and protection of government. The two governments, one public, the other economic, are bound together in unholy wedlock. The Supreme Court knows this and should not deny as judges what it knows as men and women.

CONCLUDING OBSERVATIONS

The power of government to exercise eminent domain, the power to take private property for a public use with compensation, and sometimes without compensation, should be utilized by government when necessary. There is no reason why a government cannot use its eminent domain power to take over an abandoned plant and run it with the workers to produce needed goods. In the crisis the country now faces, there is good reason for declining to compensate the private owners in the light of the emergency.

Secondly, the doctrine of "unconstitutional conditions" should be considered. Government cannot state that welfare funds will be denied to blacks, or Republicans, or Jews, because this would place an unconstitutional burden on the right to subsistence, the right to life itself. The burden is no less when government refuses to raise or spend funds for such welfare purposes, or cuts funds below the existence level. Is not willful inaction really a species of deliberate action?

Finally, we must acknowledge the United Nations Charter, ratified as a treaty in 1945, and the Universal Declaration of Human Rights, adopted in 1948. We must ratify the Covenant on Civil and Political Rights, the Covenant on Economic, Social and Cultural Rights, and the Genocide Convention, all pending in the U.S. Senate. We must incorporate in our law the UN treaties on forced labor, abolition of slavery, protection of stateless persons, refugees, racial discrimination, and apartheid. The United States commitment to these agreements has been minimal. It would not be amiss at this juncture for a government which prides itself on being a "world power" dedicated to "peace and freedom" to begin to seriously conduct itself in accordance with the principles of the UN Charter, the principles of international law, and the Law of Nations. The security of the nation—economic, social, political—depends on the observance of those principles intended for the maintenance of a decent and civilized world.

[In 1984, the Economic Rights Task Force produced "A How-to Guide: Starting an Unemployment Benefits Clinic," surveying fourteen existing Guild-supported clinics nationally. While the University of Pennsylvania Law students opened a new food stamp clinic, the South Florida Guild provided services through Lawyers Nights at the Miami NAACP office, and Chicagoans staffed the People's Community Law Center at the Rudy Lozano Justice Center. The Guild filed an amicus brief that supported the National Association of Social Workers in opposing a decrease in welfare payments in a county with an increasing cost of living.

[The Labor Committee, Chapters, and ERTF activists, fueled by scholar/lawyer Staughton Lynd's writings, and desperation, went to work in the Steel Valley and elsewhere to fight plant closures. They maintain that the government has the power of eminent domain to take over privately owned plants and run them for the public good under the public Steel Valley Authority of Pennsylvania and similar agencies, to fulfill the government purpose of providing jobs and producing goods and services.]

WAGING THE WAR AGAINST UNION SECURITY
By Barbara Kraft

[The Guild National Labor Committee, with an office in Washington, D.C., and a publication, *Labor Update*, published a litigation manual, *Employee and Union Member Guide to Labor Law* (1982). After the office was closed and the Reagan anti-union campaign got into full swing, the Committee produced a comprehensive article, *White Paper on the NLRB*, containing a thorough analysis of the board's anti-union rulings, distributed widely among union attorneys, submitted in the oversight hearings conducted by the Labor Management Subcommittee of the House Committee on Education and Labor, and reproduced in full in the *Congressional Record*. The committee sent a delegation to Nicaragua and countered the American Institute for Free Labor Development (AIFLD AFL-CIO) report, making known its findings at the fourth annual meeting of AFL-CIO lawyers. Local Labor Committees sponsored forums for lawyers and union members on basic union issues, and jointly sponsored seminars with the Guild Immigration Committee on the rights of undocumented workers.

[Washington labor lawyer Barbara Kraft in this selection from the *Labor Update* discusses the continuing so-called "right to work" movement against union security.]

The 1947 Taft-Hartley amendments to the National Labor Relations Act includes section 8(b)'s prohibitions against union unfair labor practices and section 14(b), which allows states to outlaw the union shop and other forms of union security even though section 8(a)(3) expressly permits employers and unions to negotiate union security in collective bargaining agreements. President Truman vetoed the amendments because he opposed section 14(b). Nevertheless, 14(b) forces prevailed and, since 1947, have sought to enact state and national legislation prohibiting union security. The professed goal of "right to work" adherents is a U.S. Supreme Court decision eliminating the requirement of non-member financial support of the union as a condition of employment in both the private and public sectors.

The National Right to Work Committee is the most well organized, well funded, and outspoken critic of union security in all its forms, and

---

"Waging the War Against Union Security," by Barbara Kraft, *Labor Update* (July–Aug. 1982).

of unions in general. Conservative media spokespersons, and some unions, credit Committee President Reed Larson's multi-million dollar direct mail campaign with defeat of Labor Law Reform in 1977. In spite of its incredible resources, however, the committee has succeeded in adding only three state "right to work" laws to the seventeen that existed at the time of the Committee's formation. The National Right to Work Legal Defense Foundation claims ongoing litigation in five areas: (1) "misuse of compulsory union dues for political and ideological purposes"; (2) "violations of the Constitutional right of free speech, assembly and other civil rights"; (3) "violations of the merit principle in public employment and academic freedom in public education"; (4) "injustice of the compulsory union hiring hall 'referral system'"; and (5) "violations of existing protections against compulsory unionism." [In 1982 the Foundation claimed to be representing employees in 250 cases.] In Maryland, Foundation attorneys brought suit against the Communication Workers of America (CWA), which resulted in a hearing before a special master on the union's expenditures (*Beck v. CWA*, D. Md., Civ. No. M-76-839). As a result of the special master's decision that CWA had not met its burden of proving its expenditures and justifying the fair share fee, CWA instituted a record-keeping system which will allow it to determine, at the end of an accounting period, which expenditures are chargeable to non-members. . . .

The unions are attempting to prove that all, or nearly all, of their expenditures are in fact related to collective bargaining, contract administration, and grievance adjustment. On the issue of political expenditures, unions point out that the costs of their political action committees are in no case chargeable to non-members who object to such expenditures. And, as a result of the internal rebate procedures adopted since *Abood*, some unions currently rebate 10–15 percent of their annual expenditures to non-members who file timely objections under those procedures.

CARRYING OUT THE GUILD RESOLUTION ON FIGHTING RACISM IN THE GUILD
By the 1979 Guild Convention

[The 1979 Guild Convention resolved to take a number of specific steps to fight racism in the Guild, building on proposals by William Goodman when he was national president. The resolution includes, in the Whereas clauses:]

Whereas, to develop a solution to these problems requires the implementation of a program of Affirmative Action within the Guild which means a deliberate effort on the part of leaders and members of the

National Lawyers Guild to develop a program, practices, and structures which increase minority participation within the Guild, develop good joint programmatic work with progressive minority legal organizations, and at the same time, respect the organizational integrity of these organizations."

[The resolved clauses include:]

(1) The NLG shall continue its participation in the Affirmative Action Coordinating Center (AACC), which is a key aspect of the Guild's affirmative action work and is jointly sponsored with NCBL and the Center for Constitutional Rights.

(2) The NLG through the AA/AD Committee working with the NO shall initiate discussions with NCBL, La Raza Legal Alliance, La Raza Law Students Association, Puerto Rican Law Students Association, BALSA, LSCRRC, and various progressive Asian and Indian Legal organizations on other areas of joint programmatic work, including future summer projects [and, through the Travel Subcommittee of the International Committee, jointly sponsor delegations abroad.] . . .

(3) The NLG and its chapters shall provide legal and political support for minority legal organizations and their members and other lawyers who come under attack for vigorously advancing the interests of minorities. . . .

(6) Local chapters and regions initiate discussions about the various factors, including white chauvinist errors which have hindered our work, have limited active minority participation within the Guild, and have prevented good joint work with progressive minority legal organizations on a local and regional level. . . .

(9) Dues-paying members of progressive minority legal organizations with which the NLG has established a working relationship be allowed to join the NLG [on payment of] the cost of a subscription to *Guild Notes* [and (5), shall be invited to attend national and regional meetings at reduced fees and to plan and participate in workshops and skills seminars]. . . .

(11) Guild lawyers shall make concerted effort to build multiracial law practices, offer law student clerkships to minority law students, and make case referrals to minority lawyers.

[Sensitive to the charge that the Guild resolved about every subject, but did not carry out most of its resolves, after adopting 283 resolutions between 1975 and 1982, the Guild adopted stringent requirements for all resolutions, including provisions for implementation. The Steering Committee of AA/AD Committee, with a member of the NO, was given responsibility for implementing the Fighting Racism in the Guild resolution, and was to report to the NEC every three months on the progress being made.

[To carry out some of the purposes of this resolution, the Affirmative Action/ Anti-Discrimination Committee of the Seattle Chapter of the Guild called for a national, free, and unfettered sharing of thoughts and feelings as a means of collectively "identifying and reversing" racist conditioning that adversely affects the personal, professional, and political lives of Guild members. Such sessions were held at the 1982 Santa Fe Convention, and Fania E. Davis, of Oakland, California, attended from her perspective as a private practitioner and member of the National Conference of Black Lawyers. In her critique of the personal racism workshops, Davis maintained that "the tested and surest path to 'identifying and reversing' racist conditioning is to work day-by-day, side-by-side, with lawyers and other people of color as equal partners in struggle. French Algerians came to grips with their own racism in the crucible of common struggle. So it is with white South Africans."[1]

[Kathleen Herron of the Portland chapter responded from her perspective: "I am a white, 35-year-old, with a working-class background. I have been active in the Guild for eight years." She found that, at their best, workshops helped her "to work effectively with third world people here in a recent struggle over establishing a non-racist day-care center and with the Black United Front on various issues."[2]]

SKETCH OF PEOPLE'S LAWYER R. SAMUEL PAZ
By Roberto Velasquez-Rodriguez

[The Los Angeles Chapter has honored its leading members in a series of banquets in recent years, publishing brief biographical sketches in banquet journals. In 1983 it was the turn of R. Samuel Paz, selected for his work in the Guild, and particularly in the People's College of Law, founded in 1974 by the Guild and other local progressive legal organizations.]

Seymour Myerson v. City of Los Angeles is one of the latest triumphs of R. Samuel Paz. What turned out to be the leading case in political spying was undertaken in 1977. The settlement in May 1982 for $27,500 was an admission of fault by the city that agents of the Police Department Intelligence Division had been involved in using illegal tactics toward Myerson and had harassed him. This is what is called "impact litigation" and this is "Sam."

Born in Los Angeles, Samuel was raised in South Central Los Angeles, Lincoln Heights, and Banning, California. He received his undergraduate degree from UCLA and his law degree from USC in

---

1. "National Lawyers Guild Personal Racism Workshops: A Critique," by Fania E. Davis, *NLG Practitioner* 39:4 (Fall 1982).

2. "On Fania Davis and Guild's Personal Racism Workshops," by Kathleen Herron, *NLG Practitioner* 40:2 (Spring 1983).

"Sketch of People's Lawyer R. Samuel Paz," by Roberto Velasquez-Rodriguez, Peoples College of Law *Journal* (April 1983).

1974. As a recipient of the Reginald Heber Smith Post-Graduate Fellowship, he spent one and a half years working for the Legal Aid office in El Monte, California.

He strongly feels that attorneys should be people's advocates and truly represent their needs; to do this one must make oneself accessible to the people. With this as his goal, he opened an office with some former schoolmates in 1976, located in the heart of downtown Los Angeles.

He says his law firm is proof that the people of the communities, of the "barrios" and "ghettos" can be a base of support.

[Paz and Linda Ferguson, the other 1983 honoree, were members of a broad array of organizations: National Conference of Black Lawyers and La Raza Legal Alliance, Mexican American Bar Association, Black Women Lawyers, State and County Bar Associations and their committees, and numerous civic groups working on civil liberties, police misconduct, drug treatment, battered women, and other human rights issues.]

THE STATUS OF NUCLEAR WEAPONS UNDER INTERNATIONAL LAW
By Elliot L. Meyrowitz

POST-WORLD WAR II LEGAL DEVELOPMENTS

Our examination of nuclear weapons in the context of the norms of international law builds a very solid case for prohibiting the use and possession of nuclear weapons based on the analogy of nuclear weapons to a poison and poisoned gas, the inability of nuclear weapons to restrict their impact to military targets, the unnecessary and cruel suffering produced by nuclear weapons, and the indiscriminate nature of the effects of such weapons.

The position that nuclear weapons are illegal is strengthened further by evaluating the effects of such weapons under the Nuremberg Principles, the UN Charter, the Genocide Convention of 1948, the Geneva Convention of 1949, and various United Nations General Assembly Resolutions.

The Nuremberg Charter defined "crimes against peace" as the "planning, preparation, initiation or waging of a war of aggression, or a war in violation of international treaties, agreements or assurances." This definition was based on already existing legal obligations to settle dis-

---

"The Status of Nuclear Weapons under International Law," by Elliot L. Meyrowitz, *Guild Notes* (June 1980), and *NLG Practitioner* 38:3 (Summer 1981).

putes peacefully and to renounce the threat of force. The intentional destruction of a group of people because of their race, religion, or nationality—crimes against humanity—was logically derived from the "principles of humanity" and the "dictates of the public conscience," enumerated in the IVth Hague Convention of 1907.

The primary function of international law is the elimination of the arbitrary use of force and violence in international relations. Consequently, there exists a legal duty under international law to afford primary respect for those agreements which seek to establish peace. Furthermore, such agreements are but part of a wider international legal duty to refrain from the use of force in international relations, except in self-defense or under the authority of the United Nations. The General Treaty for the Renunciation of War (Treaty of Paris or Kellogg-Briand Pact) is a fundamental assertion of these legal duties. Article I specifically renounces war as an instrument of national policy. Nuremberg Article VI (a) defines Crimes against the Peace as "... planning, preparation, initiation or waging of a war of aggression." Finally, the obligation to renounce war as an instrument of national policy has its most authoritative enunciation in the United Nations Charter, Article 2(4). The U.S. Senate ratified the UN Charter in 1945 as a treaty, making it part of "the supreme law of the land" under the U.S. Const, Art VI Sec 2.

"Crimes against humanity" found further formal expression in the Convention on the Prevention and Punishment of the Crime of Genocide, enacted by the UN General Assembly in 1948. Article I prohibits acts that have the intention of destroying, in whole or in part, national, ethnic, racial, or religious groups.

As a result of technological developments in military weaponry during the 20th century, the range and destructive power of new weapons has enlarged the geographic limits of the traditional battlefield and made the civilian population the object of military attack. Military theoreticians believed that by making war unbearable for the civilian population, the belligerent government would be forced to capitulate. Instead, the practice of using new weaponry to break the will of a nation by attacking its civilian population has become the basis for the concept of "total war," and the theory of nuclear deterrence/massive retaliation.

Since 1945 the strategic nuclear policy of the United States has been "deterrence": in order to deter a nuclear attack, the U.S. must have the ability to mount a massive retaliatory second strike against populations and industrial centers. The primary object is to destroy the morale of a civilian population, similar to the goal of strategic bombing during World War II.

However, nuclear weapons are clearly distinguishable from the conventional weapons used during World War II. Not only do nuclear weapons initially create human and geographic destruction greater than any conventional weapon or bomb ever developed, but, more importantly, such weapons initially create uncontrollable radioactivity which threatens the very survival of human species and its environment. Their efficiency results inevitably in genocide and ecocide. In fact, the massive retaliation theory relies on this potential genocidal effect for its alleged credibility. Thus, it is an inescapable conclusion that such weapons would result in wars of extermination, thereby violating the prohibitions in Article 6(c) of the Nuremberg Charter and the Genocide Convention.

The four Geneva Conventions of 1949 offer a further yardstick to measure the illegality of nuclear weapons. Their primary objective is to assure that "disinterested aid (is) given without discrimination to all victims of war who on account of their wounds, capture or shipwreck cease to be enemies and become suffering and defenseless human beings." Consequently, these conventions, formulated soon after the first use of atomic weapons, represent not only a reaffirmation of the fundamental protection afforded non-combatants, but also offer additional proof that the international community considers the principles of humanity and the dictates of the public conscience of continuing validity.

The effects resulting from the use of nuclear weapons are incompatible with the character of protection afforded the various categories of people enumerated in the Geneva Conventions. As the radioactive effects of nuclear weapons contaminate vast geographic areas, conditions will be created that will expose the wounded, sick, and civilians to contagion and infection and will prevent efforts to provide adequate medical assistance. Moreover, they will eliminate locations sufficiently safe for a prisoner of war camp, a hospital, or safety zones for civilians. Thus, the neutralized zones created by the Conventions will be subject to direct military attack.

Another important international legal source useful in evaluating the status of nuclear weapons is the United Nations. As early as 1946, the General Assembly recognized that nuclear weapons potentially undermine the laws and therefore must be brought under international control. By creating the Commission on Atomic Energy, the United Nations hoped to formulate proposals for the elimination of nuclear weapons. However, the events of the Cold War overtook this sentiment, and the Commission was dissolved.

By 1959 opinion had grown among the non-nuclear states that the use of nuclear weapons should be forbidden because they were a threat to the survival of mankind. As a result the General Assembly adopted Resolution 380 (XIV) prohibiting any further proliferation of nuclear weapons. Even more significant was Resolution 1653 (XVI), adopted in 1961 by the General Assembly, which declared that "any state using nuclear and thermo-nuclear weapons is to be considered as violating the Charter of the United Nations, as acting contrary to the laws of humanity, and as committing a crime against mankind and civilization." The General Assembly in 1966 adopted Resolution 2126A (XXI) authorizing the Secretary General to assess the effects of nuclear weapons. The Secretary General's report concluded that the use of nuclear weapons would threaten the existence of life on this planet as we know it. The Treaty of Tlatelolco of 1967 further reflects the conclusions reached in that report. It prohibits the use, manufacture, production, or acquisition of nuclear weapons in Latin America. UN Resolution 2936 (XXVII), adopted in 1972, not only renounces the use of force in international relations, but also permanently prohibits the use of nuclear weapons. The 1960 Antarctic Treaty denuclearized Antarctica. The 1966 Treaty on Principles Governing the Activities in Exploration and Use of Outer Space creates a nuclear-free zone in outer space. The Treaty Banning Nuclear Weapons from the Sea-Bed and Ocean Floor (1970) prohibits the installation or testing of nuclear weapons in the world's oceans.

CONCLUSION

While it has been argued throughout this article that the laws of war prohibit the use of nuclear weapons, a formal convention specifically prohibiting the manufacture, stockpiling, and use of nuclear weapons would be an important step in the disarmament process.

CIVIL DISOBEDIENCE: DEFENSES THAT KEEP ISSUES AT THE FORE
By Peter Goldberger

American legal principles can be creatively used in the defense of anti-nuclear weapons activists charged with crimes or otherwise cast in the role of defendants in five basic kinds of cases:

1. Peaceful entry, such as vigils or sit-ins, on the property of weapons-making or storage facilities.
2. Actual property destruction at these facilities, as occurred in the Plowshares Eight case.
3. Refusal to pay federal taxes either entirely or in a proportional amount representing the Pentagon budget or some other benchmark, or refusal to participate voluntarily in the tax collection process.

"Civil Disobedience: Defenses that Keep Issues at the Fore," by Peter Goldberger, from remarks at International Symposium on the Morality and Legality of Nuclear Weapons, in *Guild Notes* (Nov.–Dec. 1982).

4. Resistance to military service and draft registration.
5. Civil suits brought against anti-nuclear protesters attempting to restrain their activities or to collect damages from them, as has happened to a group of religious activists in Philadelphia, and to the Diablo Canyon protestors in California.

The ideal legal strategy for such cases would be designed not just to win the case, but also to take a bold, affirmative stance in support of the defendants' actions, to keep the real issues at the fore and in the public eye, rather than to have the case bog down, as court cases too often do, in irrelevancies. . . .

In its pure sense, civil disobedience involves the decision to break a law that is unjust or immoral, while accepting the legitimacy of the legal system in general and so accepting the punishment which comes from breaking the law. This is not the usual position taken by activist protests in the U.S. today. It was not to protest the existence of the laws against burglary and criminal mischief that the Plowshares 8 entered the General Electric nuclear weapons facility at King of Prussia, Pa., hammered on Mark 12A missile nose cones with hammers, and poured blood on blueprints. The purpose of their protest was not to make a public statement that the burglary law was unjust; but rather their point concerned individual responsibility and the threat of nuclear weapons.

A few fundamentals of our legal system should be recalled. Our Constitution is enforceable as law and operates as a limit on the interpretation and application of all other laws: nothing is a crime unless it is written in the statute books. Anyone charged with a crime is entitled to a trial in which the prosecutor bears the burden of proof beyond a reasonable doubt; this trial must usually be held before a jury if the defendant chooses. These principles apply no matter how guilty the defendants may seem to be and without regard to public statements the accused may have made virtually proclaiming guilt. We also have (theoretically, at least) an independent judiciary. The judge should decide every case in accordance with law, even if the decision does not foster official national policy. Juries have a legal power to find a defendant not guilty, and no judge may overturn their verdict.

DEFENSES

Three kinds of defenses can be raised to bring the real issues of nuclear activist cases into the courtroom:

(1) Protest, even illegal protest, involves the expression of political and religious views and lends itself to a defense on First Amendment grounds. Many of the other doctrines of constitutional law can also be used effectively in the defense of these cases.

(2) Many crimes which protestors are charged with involve an element of willfulness or specific intent to achieve a criminal purpose. All kinds of evidence, even expert testimony, are admissible to prove or raise a reasonable doubt about a defendant's specific intent or state of mind in the commission of a crime. This is a difficult theory to prove and to win on, but it provides an extremely effective vehicle by which the political, religious, and moral issues can be presented.

(3) Justification is a broad concept and generally refers to any situation in which the defendant may claim that his or her actions were required or authorized by conditions which made the commission of an act, which would have otherwise been a crime, the correct choice under the circumstances. This includes not only self-defense, but also necessity or choice of a lesser evil. Alternatively, action which violates the criminal law is justifiable when it is taken to comply with another law.

The exact contours or elements of these defenses vary from jurisdiction to jurisdiction.

LAW OF WAR

The Pennsylvania Crimes Code explicitly acknowledges the defense of justification for action required or authorized by "the law of war." This should allow to be raised, as incorporated under state law, the various treaties, Hague conventions, and Nuremberg doctrines of international law. This justification language also comes from the Model Penal Code.

Another statute taken from the Model Code makes it a felony to "risk a catastrophe" by any means capable of causing widespread destruction, including explosion, fire, collapse of buildings, and release of radioactive material or poison gas. This statute could describe a nuclear explosion. A companion statute penalizes anyone who fails to take measures to prevent a catastrophe when he or she has responsibility to do so.

[It can also be argued] that the use of reasonable force, including force against property, is permissible to prevent the commission of crime. This contention would arguably permit the offer of evidence that the manufacture of nuclear weapons is a crime such as "risking catastrophe," or "possessing lethal weapons having no lawful purpose," and a crime against peace and humanity as defined by the Charter of the International Military Tribunal at Nuremberg.

I am not claiming that there are no theoretical or practical problems with these arguments or that they lead to miraculous courtroom victories. Rather, they provide a means of putting the real issues in a case before a jury and the public by saying, "What the defendants did was right, and the law recognizes that this is so."

GUILD PRESIDENTS SOUND THE ALARM
By Michael Ratner and Barbara Dudley

■

By Michael Ratner

[Moving from his litigation work at the Center for Constitutional Rights, Michael Ratner began sounding the alarm against Reagan initiatives on taking the Guild presidency in 1982.]

The chief feature of many of the Reagan proposals for the National Lawyers Guild's work is that those proposals and the changes that have already occurred change dramatically the usefulness of law as a social tool in the ways in which the Guild has traditionally used it. No longer can we simply use law the way we have used it in the last number of years, as a progressive social force. We must begin to change our thinking and develop new forms. Essentially Reagan has taken from us the forums where we will litigate—the courts. He's taken away the lawyers to enforce the rights of people. And he's taking away the rights themselves. . . . We must create a very strong national and local voice to expose, fight, and ultimately stop what is occurring. . . . It first means having a strong educational presence. Secondly, we must take every opportunity to write, speak, and use the media. Thirdly, we must emphasize national and local legislative work.

[On November 29, 1982, the Guild and the Center filed a federal lawsuit to stop the U.S.-sponsored "secret" war against Nicaragua, *Sanchez Espinoza v. Reagan,* alleging damages and seeking injunctive relief from U.S. military activities which terrorize and injure the civilian populations of Nicaragua. Ratner participated in the suit and told Guild members: "WE CANNOT BE BLIND TO WAR IN NICARAGUA."]

■

By Barbara Dudley

[Moving from Vice President to President in 1983, and from San Diego to New York, Barbara Dudley called for broadening Guild work on nuclear disarmament, and began tightening up Guild administrative procedures to better serve the almost 7,000 members and the movements with which they work.]

"Guild Presidents Sound the Alarm" contains excerpts from "Toward a Guild Response for the Reagan Era," by Michael Ratner, *Guild Notes* (March–April 1981); "Lawsuit Filed to Stop 'Secret' War Against Nicaragua," by Michael Ratner; "We Cannot Be Blind to War in Nicaragua," Ratner, *Guild Notes* (Jan.–Feb. 1983); and "Call for Broader NLG Work on Disarmament," by Barbara Dudley, *Guild Notes* (Jan.–Feb. 1983).

BEYOND MERE GADFLIES

"[R]aising issues" can become a meaningless intellectual exercise, if we think of ourselves as mere gadflies. It is unlikely that LANAC [Lawyers Alliance for Nuclear Arms Control], because of its constituency, nor the Lawyers Committee [on Nuclear Policy], because of its focus on international law, can be moved to broaden their appraoch to nuclear disarmament. To play a broader role we have to bring the pariah Guild out of the closet. Many local Guild chapters have become involved in the freeze movement, but primarily their role, as in New York and Seattle, has been as legal defense for those who are undertaking militant resistance or civil disobedience to call attention to the issue. These efforts are necessary and in keeping with one of the Guild's traditional roles in many "movements."

However, with a functioning national committee we could do much more. We could, as the Guild, enter into the current national discussions about the future direction of the freeze movement, in coordination with our work on the Middle East, on Central America, on labor, energy, and the economy. For example, in pushing forward the notion of an economic bill of rights, the Guild should include the proposition that the people of the U.S. should have a direct voice in not only the size and uses of the military budget, but the objectives of any weapons buildup. An approach such as this could bring many otherwise single issue freeze advocates into the struggle for comprehensive, people-oriented economic planning, as a political platform. The Guild is also in a unique position, because of the breadth of our international work, to develop the ties that so desperately need to be developed with anti-nuclear groups throughout the world. The first step is obviously the formation of a nuclear disarmament committee within the Guild, one with the initiative to develop and implement a plan of action.

[The Peace and Disarmament Subcommittee of the International Committee was established after this proposal.]

■ TWENTY

The Future Lies Ahead (1984–   )

IN ONE DAY'S mail in 1986, the president of a California Guild chapter was asked to notify members of two openings for young lawyers with a private chainstore-type corporation "formed to deliver qualitative legal services," and her spouse was invited to join the Montgomery Ward Enterprises Legal Services Plan. Ward's bulk mailing warned that a study sponsored by the ABA found "the average law-abiding American citizen has a 37 percent chance of having a legal problem during the next 12 months. . . . According to a recently published survey in Illinois, the median rate [charged] for family law and personal matters is $70 an hour."

These two solicitations highlight basic changes in law practice from fifty years ago when the Guild was founded. Then all group legal services programs were deemed unethical by the ABA, and state Bar associations would discipline a lawyer for overt advertising.

The picture of a typical ABA member has not changed that much since 1936, according to the *ABA Journal* for September 1986. In its report on a recent study of 317 *Journal* readers, men made up 85 percent of all practicing ABA lawyers in 1986; their median age was 38 years and two months; their median income was $64,448 and average income was $104,625. Lawyers had an average household income of $121,913; almost 23 percent worked in firms that billed between $1 million and $2.9 million in 1985. About 33 percent practiced personal injury and property damage law; 44 percent practiced business and corporate law; the median firm had eight lawyers. And 8.9 percent had personal incomes of $25,000–$34,999, and 6.9 percent had incomes of less than $24,999. Like their predecessors, none of them listed specialties in labor, criminal, constitutional, poverty, or peace law.

While the Guild has conducted no similar study of its members, it is clear that typical Guild members continue to work in the fields shunned by ABA members as they did fifty years ago, but the traditional Guild law firm that survived the early decades is becoming extinct. It was financed by three kinds of cases: plaintiffs' personal injury (PI) contingent-fee wins, criminal law immediate-fee cases, and small retainers for cases on family, civil, labor, and small business law. This mix gave lawyers maximum independence. They did not have to rely on keeping one major client happy, and they did not have to bring the same kind of case before the same (sometimes hostile) judge every day. These firms could absorb law students and train new lawyers in the course of handling their occasional mammoth PI or product liability cases.

Today's Guild lawyers who handle criminal cases often work as full-time public defenders (PDs); some represent injured plaintiffs as members of a consumer protection unit of a district attorney's office. Their problems, and their future, are different from those of early Guild lawyers. They work in large offices within a bureaucratic structure and must appear daily before the same judges, representing clients on the same side of the same kinds of cases. This limits their choices of action. On the other hand, they receive regular paychecks from the government, and some are even protected by union contracts.

Since 1937, the number of government lawyers paid to represent indigent defendants in felony and misdemeanor cases has risen from a handful of public defenders in California to thousands throughout the country. The number indirectly paid by the federal government to represent indigent civil claimants has risen from virtually zero to 4,500 working for local nonprofit corporations funded to a great extent by the Legal Services Corporation. Another 1,000 are funded by state and local Bar associations, attorneys' trust funds, United Ways, etc. Some additional lawyers work for other non-profit corporations on a series of human rights concerns, facing a growing number of lawyers working for non-profit corporations to protect property rights.

Other qualitative changes affect the Guild's activities today and its plans for the future. While the population of the country has almost doubled since the New Deal, the legal profession more than tripled since 1960, from 205,515 to 678,000 in 1984.[1] In 1951, 5,500 women comprised 2.5 percent of the total lawyers; by 1984, 83,000 women comprised 12.8 percent.[2] The Bureau of the Census recorded 2,575 "non-white" lawyers in 1960, or 1.3 percent; in 1984, they recorded 2.6 percent Black and 2.0 percent Hispanic.[3] Many of these women and some of these people of color joined the Guild and assumed positions of leadership, including eight women and four Blacks or Asians serving as national officers or vice-presidents in 1986–1987.

Some statistics confirm one's suspicions as to the rate of actual change.

---

1. *Statistical Abstract of the United States*, 1964 and 1986 (U.S. Dept. of Commerce and Bureau of the Census), pp. 229 and 402 respectively.

2. *The Lawyer Statistical Report*, by Barbara A. Curran (Chicago: American Bar Foundation, 1985), p. 10.

3. *Statistical Abstract* (1964), p. 229; (1986), p. 402.

INCOME BY RACE, SEX, AND AGE IN 1979 OF LAWYERS AND JUDGES

	35–44 Yrs. old		45–54 Yrs. old	
	Number	Mean annual earnings	Number	Mean annual earnings
White male	108,135	$46,632.	68,988	$54,981.
Black male	2,337	29,930.	1,314	39,322.
White female	11,147	20,285.	4,915	20,768.
Black female	755	18,493.	338	19,242.

Source: 1980 Census of Population (U.S. Dept. of Commerce and Bureau of the Census, May 1984), pp. 301, 342.

While women and blacks still lag behind in earnings, the number and distribution of Guild members has expanded dramatically. In 1986, the Guild boasted 83 lawyer chapters, 102 law student chapters, and 12 jailhouse lawyer chapters stretching from one end of the country to the other. Many members have higher and more stable earnings than their predecessors, and an earnest desire to meet and share experiences. This has resulted in a distinctive method of fund-raising developed by the National Finance Committee in the 1970s, after it was taken over by the new generation. The custom is that anyone can speak to the assembled multitude at the Guild Convention banquet in the process of making a donation or pledge to the Guild. It is an impressive sight, at 11 P.M. after a long day of conventioneering, to see people lined up around the room for their chance to get to the microphone to describe what they have been doing in practice recently, how the Guild helped them in their work, or to honor a particular client, movement, or colleague, as a prelude to giving money. Many express their need for the Guild as a place to exchange ideas with others in the same field, to learn about other parts of the law—and the world, to take positions on critical issues, and to find support in the event of problems with the establishment—bench, bar, or prosecution. More and more lawyers bring their babies and young children to conventions, using the daycare provided.

Today's Guild members reflect a deep concern with international developments, and it has been suggested that during the Reagan Administration, some Guild leaders know more movement leaders on the West Bank or in El Salvador than in the barrios and ghettoes of their own communities, where less seems to be happening.

At the same time, in this vast country with its many constituencies, eight to ten million people are officially unemployed (8 to 10 percent), with the real figure closer to twice that number (compared to 15 million unemployed in the Great Depression). Once again thousands of black and white families are being evicted from their homes and forced off their farms by foreclosures for nonpayment of debts. Native Americans are again being forced off their treaty lands. These people are becoming refugees in their own country. Over 35 million people live below the poverty line, most of them women and children.[4] Tens of thousands of homeless men and women, and especially young people, roam the streets of the nation's cities in desperate but futile pursuit of food and shelter, as immigration agents round up and deport thousands to Mexico and neighboring countries. Emaciated Americans scavenge in restaurant garbage cans and city dumps and return to the entryways of skyscrapers, where they sleep under cardboard boxes. Hungry children stand silently in lines at churches and charities, waiting for free meals while their parents grimly gather at factory gates and cross picketlines anxiously awaiting the chance for a day's pay. Disabled people and seniors wait in line for food stamps and free cheese. Those fortunate enough to find jobs are victimized by low wages, long hours, unhealthy working conditions, and organized union-busting tactics; their strikes are met by sweeping labor injunctions and plant closures. In many families, women are the only breadwinners, working long hours and then facing long commutes. They return to children they feel they are neglecting, often without partners to share the family chores. 500,000 people live in prisons, some of which have been turned over to private companies to be run for profit.[5]

Primarily concerned with survival, these men and women also have legal problems. They do not need lawyers to write wills or contracts. They do need lawyers at bankruptcy, eviction, and deportation proceedings, in negligence and worker's compensation cases, and as speakers and organizers, but few can afford to pay a fee. Millions of citizens are discovering, some for the first time, that they have few legally-recognized economic rights, and that they need lawyers to find and complete the forms to obtain the economic benefits for which they do qualify. Many have heard of "PDs" and poverty lawyers, but have been taught that such services, being free, will not be effective.

Additional millions of people are determined to do something to prevent another war—nuclear or conventional, against the Soviet Union or Nicaragua. They find that they need lawyers to help them get permits for demonstrations, to formulate the legal bases for their actions under the Constitution and international law, and to represent them when they are arrested for civil disobedience or other actions against the military/industrial complex.

This is the context in which the Guild and its members work in the 1980s. Further parallels and differences from the period of its birth are suggested by the selections below. One overriding problem facing Guild lawyers is the determination of the New Right and the Reagan administration to turn many government agencies into their opposites, through changes in personnel, budgeting, regulation, and deregulation. Lawyers face an anti-labor NLRB, an anti-minorities and anti-women Civil Rights Commission and Civil Rights Division, an anti–student-aid Education Department, a warlike Defense Department, and an anti-protectionist

---

4. *Statistical Abstract*, 1983 (U.S. Dept. of Commerce and Bureau of the Census, 1985), p. 454.

5. 1980 Census of Population (U.S. Dept. of Commerce and Bureau of the Census, Oct. 1984), p. 4. In 1980, 466,371 persons were in correctional institutions, according to the Census.

Environmental Protection Agency. It is almost as if the Reaganites wanted to provide a caricature of the textbook example of Hegel's (and later Marx's) thesis that things are turned into their opposites.

LEGAL SERVICES FOR THE POOR
By Simon Rosenthal

[Periodically since 1969, Guild members in private practice have been asked by Guild members in Legal Services to lobby Congress to preserve Legal Services or to support union organizing among Legal Services workers that proved successful in Chicago, West Texas, and elsewhere. For an overview of President Johnson's highly touted war on poverty, one must go elsewhere. For a short overview of Legal Services, its longest-lived component, here are excerpts from a 1986 interview with a Guild lawyer who was deputy director and director in two California counties, "did six months in some wasted, burned out East Coast cities where I would come in as a consultant to help reorganize the program and find a permanent director," and was also national director of evaluations out of Washington, D.C., visiting 100 programs across the country. (For his views in 1965, see Chapter 15.)]

Q: You told the Guild Convention in 1965: "We should not be describing the OEO legal services program as a program. . . . It is a legal revolution both for attorneys and for the people." So what about the legal revolution, the ultimate impact of Legal Services from the perspective of 1986?
ROSENTHAL: Lawyers in general tend to overestimate the law, especially bourgeois middle-class lawyers, which is almost synonymous. In the 1960s, a lot of us who helped get the Legal Services program going really thought that microcosm could be on the cutting edge of social change; it could change society. I guess you need the kind of idealism and energy reflected in that thinking to get anything done. And that was a time when political activism was not an uncommon phenomenon—in the movements for civil rights, civil liberties, and other aspects of social change, at a time of opposition to the atrocious war in Vietnam. Legal Services blossomed as one element of a broader movement.

In retrospect you may come to the conclusion that to speak of law and revolution in the same phrase is a little silly. Law is a microcosmic part of our society excessively emphasized by lawyers. The concept of equal justice is also a law-school phrase, meaning what? Social justice? economic justice? political justice? legal justice?

But we did accomplish. We got some thousands of lawyers representing poor people winning significant test case victories, although implementation was often difficult. You could win a case, win a point, but having that trickle down and be implemented on the local level as

---

"Legal Services for the Poor," by Simon Rosenthal, from interview with Ann Fagan Ginger, Aug. 1986, MCLI.

applied to individual human beings wasn't always so easy. But changes have occurred.

One accomplishment has been to make government bureaucracies more responsive to their clients' rights. When the program first started in Oakland, three social workers asked to meet privately with me outside their building, and explained how certain categories of disabled people were not receiving any money, completely against their own regulations, because the administrator didn't want to spend the money so he would look good with the board of supervisors. In 1965, the welfare department in Alameda County, as in almost every city and county, had never been sued. I called the director of the department and asked him to remedy the situation or face litigation. Within ten minutes, the department had phoned my boss to complain about this outrageous lawyer. That sort of thing couldn't happen today.

It wasn't long before the tripartite concept of law reform evolved: litigative advocacy, legislative advocacy, and community education. It was cost effective because, by handling one test case, you might help establish or protect rights of large numbers of people. . . .

We had gained control of policy really in the beginning. Then in the early years of the Nixon administration, class actions became a point of controversy. The Right wing thought it smacked of Communism: "class," "group," "collective"—there was a natural flow, and the end seemed to be a red flag. It's funny how they focused on it. The difference between a class action and a certain kind of test case/precedent-setting appeal may be miniscule in ultimate result. But the class action became the focal point and they had heated debates in Congress whether to try to prohibit class actions, when really precedent-setting change was the issue they were concerned about.

Q: What about back-up centers, one of the ideas of genius of Legal Services?

ROSENTHAL: The concept was to provide one place funded by Legal Services on each field of poverty law—welfare, housing, senior citizens, education, juvenile rights. You put together specialists—in litigation, legislative advocacy, administrative advocacy, maybe some sort of education component—as a resource to programs around the country. They can be brought in as co-counsel for free, and on matters pending before state or federal legislatures. They have libraries somewhat similar to Meiklejohn Civil Liberties Library, where you can get briefs or other written materials. They were a focal point of attack from the beginning by the Right wing, who very correctly viewed them as a vehicle expediting social change in the courts and other forums. They are under very severe attack at this moment; I can't say whether they will exist in another year.

Q: How did Legal Services survive Nixon and Reagan?

ROSENTHAL: We developed a lot of skills in networking. There is no county in the United States where you have a Congressperson or Senator who can't be reached by lawyers. All you have to do is find which lawyers can and will work on your behalf. We have thousands of Legal Services lawyers plus alumni, and thousands who are or have been on local boards of directors. Then you put together thousands of lawyers sincerely interested in saving the program, and they know other lawyers who will do them a favor. We have local Bar association contacts, state Bars, the ABA, plus the minority and progressive Bars. We also had the editorial support of a vast number of newspapers, including, at the time, the *Wall Street Journal*. (Editorials are often a result of lobbying, too.)

There was serious conservative thought that Legal Services was a traditional classical bourgeois concept: If the poor are cut off from the law, they will use other vehicles to address their grievances. This is not the hypocrisy of the new Right, which favors intrusion on your sexual privacy, intrusion on abortion, and implementing governmental intrusion on the rights of the people. . . .

Certainly we had problems in Legal Services with quality control, inadequate resources, burnout, bureaucracy, and factional disputes. But there are more people from the disinherited or the powerless going to law school today because they at one time got the idea that law could do something. Legal Services helped advertise law as a good thing for progressive people. That had never been done on a national scale before. The fact of survival of Legal Services, whether it's going to be 95 or only 82 percent effective, is really quite a remarkable accomplishment. There are people being served out there every day of the week, who never would have been.

One of the facts of life is that the law is often a mirror of society, and there has been a significant loss of idealistic energy and political activism in the 1980s compared to the 1960s. Legal Services is not going to emerge in some sort of leadership progressive role for the country as an isolated microcosm. But hopefully the country will move forward, and Legal Services with it.

IMMIGRANT RIGHTS AND SANCTUARY
By Susan Gzesh and Marc Van Der Hout

[Most of the founders of the Guild were the grandchildren or children of immigrants, or themselves refugees from foreign oppression and economic want.

"Immigrant Rights and Sanctuary" from "The Defense of Dennis Brutus: Apartheid on Trial," by Susan Gzesh, in NLG National Immigration Project *Immigration Newsletter* (Jan.–Feb. 1984); and from interview with Marc Van Der Hout at MCLI (for a longer profile, see *Los Angeles Daily Journal*, May 27, 1985).

During every period of repression, Guild lawyers worked individually and collectively to help individual aliens and the class they represent. In 1971, the National Immigration Project of the Guild inaugurated the *Immigration Newsletter* and in 1979 produced "Immigration Law and Defense."

[In the Reagan administration, issues facing immigration lawyers were inextricably linked to issues facing Guild International subcommittees on Central America and South Africa, and the Labor Committee.]

■

By Susan Gzesh

[Chairperson of the Guild National Immigration Project, Susan Gzesh simultaneously represented Dennis Brutus in her Chicago law practice.]

Dennis Brutus was a dual national of South Africa and Zimbabwe whose poetry was banned in South Africa when he left for England in 1965 following release from Robben Island prison. In 1970 he came to the United States to teach, write, and work against apartheid. In September 1981, the U.S. Immigration Service began deportation proceedings against him; he sought political asylum here. There were three main issues to be tried in the asylum case in 1983: whether Brutus had a well-founded fear of persecution in South Africa and [also] in Zimbabwe; and whether he had been firmly resettled in England.

At the opening of the hearing in July, we were successful in persuading the immigration judge that all South Africa–related evidence was relevant to show the motivation of the South Africans to pursue Brutus into Zimbabwe. We had to build a factual case to show that Dennis Brutus' work in the anti-apartheid struggle and in the U.S. divestment movement presented such a threat to the South Africans that they would try to kill him were he to be found within their reach. (In the preceding two years, two close comrades of Brutus' from South Africa had been killed by South African agents in frontline countries.)

The political problem with this issue was that the Reagan State Department, with its policy of "constructive engagement" toward South Africa, was never going to acknowledge publicly that a U.S.-supported regime invaded neighboring countries in order to murder its opponents....

Dennis Brutus' anti-apartheid activities in the U.S. grouped themselves in three broad categories: sports, divestment, and poetry. To educate the judge, the public, and the press about the critical nature of Brutus' work, we needed to present the entire history of U.S.–South Africa relations and to demonstrate the importance of sports and divestment of U.S. capital. This was a large, complex undertaking to which many would contribute. [Gzesh describes how Brutus helped organize the international boycott against South African participation in sports.

Eight organizations helped Brutus, from the Subcommittee on Africa of the House of Representatives and the Guild to the Peoples Law Office in Chicago, which designated Peter Schmiedel to work on the case.]

When we came into court on September 6, 1983, the government called Brutus as a witness and questioned him again regarding his residence in the United Kingdom. The only exhibits the government introduced were Brutus' applications for visas [stating his place of residence was Britain].

We entered into the record all of Brutus' nine published volumes of poetry, over the objection of the Service. After Brutus testified that all his books were banned in South Africa, that possession of his poetry was a crime there, and that all of his poetry dealt with apartheid, the judge ruled the poetry relevant. We were ultimately unable to persuade the judge to accept hundreds of support letters, including one personally signed by 50 members of the House of Representatives. The judge did accept into evidence affidavits from Congressman Howard Wolpe, chairman of the House Subcommittee on Africa, and an ex–South African secret service agent who formerly spied on Brutus.

The government's case lasted only two hours; both sides made closing arguments. We asked the judge to rule from the bench. Judge Schwartz granted Dennis Brutus political asylum, [finding] that South Africa was heavily dependent on billions of dollars of U.S. investment; that South Africa's image in international sports was of great importance to the government; that Brutus' successful efforts in the anti-apartheid movement made him hated by the South African government; and that South Africa, with the largest military force in southern Africa, could and would send military personnel or death squads to strike at him in Zimbabwe.

The victory, and our ability to present a case that put apartheid on trial, were due in large part to the tremendous public support shown in the thousands of letters that poured into the immigration court, the packed courtroom, and extensive favorable press coverage. The victory for Brutus was a victory for the struggle of the people of South Africa.

■

By Marc Van Der Hout

[When Guild president Marc Van Der Hout went to the federal courthouse in San Francisco in May 1985 to file suit against the Reagan administration, he nearly didn't get in the door. He was leading a group of lawyers suing Attorney General Edwin Meese to halt prosecutions of members of the church-led movement offering sanctuary to refugees from the civil wars in Central America. In one of those contradictions Guild members face more often than their colleagues, Van Der Hout had to explain his purpose to U.S. marshals, who were guarding the entrance to the building during a civil disobedience demonstration to protest the same U.S. policies in Central America.]

I felt a little trepidation in going into a building that was being blockaded and there was a touch of irony, but I had spoken to organizers a couple of days earlier when we realized they would be there on the same day, so we had no problem with them in going in.

My experience in talking to people is that they are convinced, once they hear the types of asylum and refugee cases that are being denied and the types of cases that are being approved. They realize that the refugees are really pawns in a foreign policy game, and it's not for economic reasons that people come here. When I say many of my clients are teachers, doctors, and lawyers who had very good jobs in El Salvador or Guatemala and are here washing dishes or cleaning floor or unemployed, . . . the myth that the Reagan administration puts forward is blown.

One reason the administration has decided to attack the sanctuary movement is exactly because it has been effective in raising the consciousness of average, church-going Americans about Reagan's Central American policies. . . . Bringing these lawsuits is important because it means people just aren't going to sit by and watch the government break the law. It also serves educational purposes, even if the court ultimately rules against us.

RESPICE, ADSPICE, AND PROSPICE
By Haywood Burns, introduced by Leora Mosston

■

By Leora Mosston

[When the New York Guild Chapter named Haywood Burns its honoree for 1984, the Associate Director of the Max E. and Filomen M. Greenberg Center for Legal Education & Urban Policy at City College, Leora Mosston, wrote "An Open Letter to the Director." Herself "a civil rights and civil liberties attorney, member of the NLG and National Conference of Black Lawyers, and past, present, and future activist," Mosston's biographical essay included the following facts about the man elected national president of the Guild in 1986.]

Haywood was born in June 1940 in Peekskill, New York, "the first Yankee born to [his] family in recorded history." His family is a southern

---

"Respice, Adspice, and Prospice" from "An Open Letter to Haywood Burns," by Leora Mosston, from New York City Chapter *Banquet Journal*, 1984; and from remarks made by Haywood Burns at banquet (typescript at MCLI).

black family, "from a wide place in the road known as Clover, Virginia." He is of "African, Native American, and Scotch Irish descent." His father began his working life on his parents' tobacco farm and held all the jobs "you can imagine that require strong arms and a broad back." His father's last job was that of a taxi driver-owner whose assets included one taxi and two sons, Haywood and his brother.

Haywood's mother grew up an orphan in the same small town as his father. They were childhood sweethearts. She was forced to drop out of Hampton College during the Depression. She worked all her life, in and out of the family home, raising a daughter and two sons and several foster children. "A major influence" in Haywood's life, she fanned his love of learning, taking him to the library from the earliest years, stretching his vision of what he could be and do.

■

By Haywood Burns

[The following excerpts from Haywood Burns' remarks cover the first two of his three topics. The third appears at the end of this chapter.]

The great seal of the great institution of excellence and opportunity that I serve, the City College of New York, has three faces—Respice, Adspice, and Prospice. For those whose Latin is a little rusty, that's looking backwards, looking present, and looking forward. This might be a good way for me to approach sharing my thoughts with you concerning our common struggle, our common goals.

Looking backward, I see a proud history of struggle in which I was fortunate enough to play a very small part. A marvelous coming together of people in this country who dared America to be what it said it was already, people who challenged this country with its own Jeffersonian ideals, and in many ways won because of the strength of mass movements, coupled with an excellent use of the legal system.

Looking back, I remember it was not all glory, not all triumph. We often felt afraid, and if we didn't feel afraid, we didn't understand the situation. We were a non-violent army, often isolated, sleeping on pallets on the floor, and living on butter beans and fatback and whatever courageous local people had in their pots. When I left to go to the South from the District of Columbia, I did not know whether I would ever come back. Many were lost along the way: Chaney, Schwerner and Goodman, Ralph Featherstone, Lemuel Penn, Viola Liuzzo, the students at Kent State, Jackson State, and Orangeburg, and Southern, Fred Hampton, Mark Clark, the Brothers at Attica, Malcolm, and Martin.

But we did experience many gains. The passage of the Civil Rights Act of 1964 and all that it portended for public accommodations and employment; the Civil Rights Act of 1965 and its impact on the franchise, and of 1968, and its impact on housing. The political power in this country changed and it is still changing the face of American politics, putting black people in positions where they can have more say over decisions that intimately affect their lives, putting black mayors at the helms of Los Angeles, Chicago, Detroit, New Orleans, Atlanta, Philadelphia, Newark, Cleveland, Richmond, and many other U.S. cities.

Yes, new movements were spawned. . . . But the gains have not really been that many. Racism still rots the body politic. Old attitudes die hard, and sometimes not at all. . . .

Our movement has been caught in the terrible turbulent tide of history, and has foundered because of the people's fear, in some quarters, of sharing power. In a nation founded on white power people recoil from the very phrase "Black Power." People did not really appreciate the process of decolonization of the mind, or the redefinition of the terms on which black and white interaction should take place. The movement foundered and fragmented as it moved north and many of us found there was considerable truth in Malcolm's adage that "south of Canada it's all Mississippi." The movement foundered as we made economic demands, not just for a hamburger at a lunch counter, but for jobs, for true economic equality; as we moved from making domestic demands to global demands and would not segregate our morality between domestic and international. This process has been aided and accelerated by the Nixon and Reagan years—COINTELPRO, preventive detention, no-knock laws, inter-state riot act, mass arrest without probable cause, Supreme Court changes, both in personnel and in substantive direction.

. . . I began to practice *before* the Supreme Court in 1968, when I had only been out of law school a couple of years. I mean literally before the Supreme Court—on the steps. My responsibility was to represent the people in Resurrection City, the Poor People's Campaign—Martin Luther King's last great campaign before he died. This particular day, people were coming up out of the tents of Resurrection City to protest at the United States Supreme Court a decision that had been made that greatly undermined the historic treaty rights of Native Americans. As I stood there on the steps, I was overwhelmed. If you know that scene in Washington—you can see the Washington Monument in the background and it looked like something out of a Cecil B. DeMille movie—people coming out of the valley with Native American headdresses on and Chicanos from Colorado, white people from Appalachia, black people from the South.

As they approached I rushed out to meet Ralph Abernathy, who was leading the group, trying to give some legal advice on the hoof because I knew that there were literally hundreds of police waiting in the wings to break heads. Just as I did that, behind me the great bronze doors of the Supreme Court rumbled noisely shut. To me, this has always been emblematic of what we are experiencing—the courts closing off access to the people.

In the face of all this, we have lost the unity and drive of our earlier movement. And as we look at the present, we have come to a sorry pass. We see the civil rights gains of the past being taken apart, a Justice Department making a charge to the rear, a Meese being appointed Attorney General. We see assaults on affirmative action—the rights of black people and women. And we see attacks on the poor, the poor getting poorer, and the 26 million poor people in this country in 1979 now number 34 million. And we see them in our cities, sleeping on our sidewalks, and huddled in our doorways. We see it in the cutting off of government benefits, the attacks on students who want nothing more than to get an education, in the criminal justice system that is often more criminal than just.

We see it in the way people, in a national hysteria, are getting angry about crime instead of getting smart. And we have a vacuum in progressive leadership in this area. We need to speak to a wider public to explain the real problems of crime, not to try to pass over them, not to lack compassion for the victim, but to understand that the victims are many, including sometimes the perpetrators. We have to address this hysteria that looks for quick fix solutions, that would "solve" the problem of crime by killing hundreds of people by the gas chamber, the electric chair, the gallows. Of the hundreds of people awaiting death, vast numbers are black and Hispanic; almost all are poor. And we're getting numbed by executions that are beginning to get more and more common in America, 1984.

Looking at the present, we have to take into account what's happening with racially motivated violence and para-military training camps. The violence at home has a mirror image in the violence abroad, [and in] the military spending that drains our resources and cheats the crying social needs of our people, while at the same time, building a nuclear stockpile that threatens the very existence of the species.

What are we to do about our present state? Are we too soft, too comfortable, too tired, to carry on? Have we forgotten the injunction of Frederick Douglass, "without struggle there is no progress"? It is well amid the grandeur of the Grand Hyatt to remember that those who comfort the afflicted still afflict the comfortable and ask ourselves, "Where do we stand? What are we doing?"

1980s CIVIL RIGHTS WORK
By Tom Meyer and Ann Noel

[When Tom Ginger left California and Antioch College in 1972 to attend Ole Miss Law School, as the first step toward becoming a Mississippi lawyer, he said he heard and found no overt signs that the Guild had been there before him in 1964 and 1965. In fact, the immediate consequence of the work of the Guild's Committee to Assist Southern Lawyers was an absolute decline in the number of Guild lawyers in the South, as white and black lawyers were run out of state after state—by overt, covert, and especially economic pressures. But by 1973 Guild lawyers had opened an office in Hattiesberg; soon others were working for Northern Mississippi Rural Legal Services, and some graduates of Guild programs to encourage black lawyers in the South began to practice there. In the 1980s, Northern and Western Guild lawyers continued to be called to the South in emergency situations to defend some of the gains made in the heady days of the civil rights movement. Tom Meyer and Ann Noel, both of San Francisco and the national Affirmative Action/Anti-Discrimination Committee of the Guild, describe aspects of current Guild work in this field.]

■

By Tom Meyer

For decades, the white southern power structure employed every conceivable device to keep blacks disenfranchised. *Smith v. Allwright,* abolishing the white primary election and the voting provisions of the 1957, 1960 and 1964 Civil Rights Acts, had little impact on black voter registration. Black access to the ballot became a reality when the Voting Rights Act of 1965 replaced reliance on judicial enforcement with direct intervention by federal registrars and observers.

Absentee ballots have been particularly significant in the 10 Black Belt counties of western Alabama, because the population in these counties is sparse, and many voters either are elderly or work outside the county. When blacks started participating in local politics, a pattern arose: Blacks would win narrowly at the polls, only to lose when absentee ballots were tallied. Once rural black politicians themselves began to master the strategic use of the absentee ballot—by canvassing the elderly and invalids for absentee votes—blacks began getting elected to local office in striking numbers. By 1984, they were in political control of five counties.

In response, white politicians entered into coalitions with opportunistic blacks. Complaints of voter fraud originated with these coalitions.

"1980s Civil Rights Work" from "Voting Rights Workers Vindicated: Justice Department Convicts Just One in Alabama," by Tom Meyer, *Guild Notes* (Winter 1986), and from "National Day for Racial Justice: Guild & NCBL Commemorate Martin Luther King, Jr.," by Ann Noel, *Guild Notes* (Winter 1986).

Through the intervention of politicians like U.S. Senator Jeremiah Denton (who faces an uphill battle for reelection in 1986 in a district where a strong black showing could make a difference), the Justice Department, setting the Voting Rights Act on its head, began to monitor Black Belt elections for *black* voting abuses.

Immediately following Jesse Jackson's sweep of the 1984 Democratic primary, 80 FBI agents descended, seizing ballots and questioning over 1,000 Black Belt voters. Agents visited the homes of elderly people, intimating that they may have been involved in illegal voting. Many were transported under state trooper escort to be photographed, fingerprinted and questioned before an all-white grand jury. Voting violations by those supporting coalition-backed candidates were systematically ignored. Against this background, indictments were returned.

Thirty years after the Montgomery bus boycott launched the civil rights movement, Albert Turner was indicted, a former chief aide to Martin Luther King, Jr., his wife Evelyn, and co-worker, Spencer Hogue, Jr. [Then indictments were handed down against] Spiver Gorden, a Eutaw city council member and statewide leader of the Southern Christian Leadership Conference, James Colvin, mayor of Eutaw, and Bobbie Nell Simpson, a white woman who has supported the black empowerment movement despite almost total ostracism from the white community.

The outcome of the trials hinged largely on the racial composition of the juries. Seven blacks and five whites took only four hours to acquit the Turners and Hogue of all charges in July 1985. The cases of Simpson and Colvin ended in mistrials after juries containing one black and two blacks, respectively, deadlocked along racial lines. On retrial, Simpson was acquitted by a jury of seven whites and three blacks.

The government secured its sole conviction to date only after using all six of its peremptories to secure an all-white jury in the trial of Spiver Gorden. Even then, the jury took five full days before convicting Gorden of four counts and acquitting him of 14. The jury's verdict at first contained a stipulation that Gorden be granted clemency, which the judge rejected. Following this conviction, the only indictee whose case had yet to go to trial, pled guilty to a single misdemeanor charge and was given two years probation. The Colvin case was not retried; rather, he also entered a plea to a misdemeanor. How the Gorden conviction will affect the prospect of further indictments remains unclear.

Defense teams have included lawyers from the Guild, the NAACP Legal Defense Fund, the Center for Constitutional Rights, and the Southern Poverty Law Center, and several private attorneys. Participating on behalf of the Guild were: Bill Goodman, Tom Meyer, Jonathan Moore, Lewis Pitts and Len Weinglass.

By Ann Noel

The National Lawyers Guild's Affirmative Action, Anti-Discrimination Committee and the National Conference of Black Lawyers jointly sponsored a National Day for Racial Justice on January 20, 1986, the first federal holiday to commemorate Martin Luther King, Jr.'s birthday. Guild and NCBL chapters in ten cities, working with other civil rights organizations, held a variety of conferences, forums, demonstrations, and marches. The events were intended to focus national attention on King's dream of racial justice, in the context of current attacks by the Reagan administration on affirmative action, voting rights, and civil rights in general. For example:

The Justice Department is attempting to overturn 53 affirmative action consent decrees around the country. The Equal Employment Opportunity Commission plans to abolish goals and timetables from its regulations. President Reagan has proposed eliminating Executive Order 11246, which requires all federal contractors (including most large American corporations) to obey government rules against discrimination, and to adopt goals and timetables. In San Francisco, the Guild, NCBL, and numerous other civil rights and public interest groups organized a major conference on "Civil Rights on the Rebound," attracting union members, community leaders, students, professors, corporate affirmative action officers, and attorneys. In Seattle, Guild and NCBL attorneys appeared on local television to discuss the future of the movement for black empowerment, and members of both organizations took part in a civil rights rally. The Baltimore NLG chapter sent op-ed pieces on Executive Order 11246 to local newspapers and spent a day lobbying the House of Representatives. Progressive Chicago lawyers helped organize an all-day forum on civil rights and yet another rally in King's honor. National Day for Racial Justice activities were also held in Portland, San Diego, Durham, and Boston.

STATE OF CALIFORNIA V. STEPHEN BINGHAM
By Stephen Bingham

[When Berkeley poverty lawyer Steve Bingham became a defendant in a criminal case in August 1971, he joined a long narrow line of Guild lawyers who have found themselves clients—in civil and criminal cases, in contempt cases, and in proceedings before Bar disciplinary committees—for their beliefs, actions,

---

"*State of California v. Stephen Bingham*," by Stephen Bingham, from the Friends of Stephen Bingham Defense Committee at MCLI.

and representation of unpopular clients and causes. The line is 90 to 100 persons long, from Edward Lamb in Ohio and Leo Gallagher in Berlin in the early days, to Harry Margolis in California, Kiko Martinez in Colorado, Barry Wilson and Robert Doyle in Boston, Lennox Hinds in New Jersey, and Susan Tipograph in New York in recent times. Each case was hard fought, both for the principle and for the person. Some were ultimately won in whole or in part; some were lost. They helped build a tradition of uncompromising advocacy of clients' causes.

[When Steve Bingham became a fugitive, and remained on the wanted list for thirteen years in Paris, he was traveling uncharted territory as a Guild lawyer. Returning in July 1984, he made a statement to his friends, the media, and the public, from which the next selection is taken.]

I am not guilty of the charges against me, and I have come back to gain my acquittal.

First I want to say very personally to the families of the six human beings killed that day that I feel a deep sorrow for the senseless deaths. My politically active life has always been dedicated to the idea that change can come about without violence, that violence tends to poison otherwise good motives.

What I would like to convey to you is a sense of why I left, even though I am not guilty.

George Jackson was one of the most closely watched prisoners in the annals of California prison history. It is simply not believable that a large, nine-millimeter gun *plus* two clips of ammunition *plus* a wig could enter the prison, let alone be turned over to Jackson, without the knowledge and complicity of prison authorities. Personally I know nothing at all about how those items entered the prison. I never smuggled a gun nor anything else into San Quentin, and I intend to testify under oath to that effect.

Why then did I leave if I had nothing to run from? Three black prisoners, two of whom were actively working against Soledad's institutionalized racism, had been murdered by a gun-tower guard at Soledad in early 1970. The county grand jury declined to indict the guard or anyone in the prison command for these deaths, for which the prison was held civilly liable years later. George Jackson, also a prison activist, and two others were charged with retaliatory killing of a guard. So hated was Jackson that the prison authorities tried to persuade a white prisoner to kill Jackson. The prisoner's affidavit to that effect was perhaps the key thing which first caused me to ponder seriously what had in fact happened to Jackson on August 21.

What frightened me even more in its implications was the fact that I did not have a tape recorder on August 21, but the guard on duty asked me if I wanted to take a tape recorder into the visiting room. The legal investigator there to see Jackson offered her tape recorder, which the guard had me sign for. The state authorities told the press that the gun was smuggled in the tape recorder. Why then was the legal investigator never seriously interviewed by the state authorities, nor called to testify before the grand jury or at the trial? The only conceivable answer is that the authorities knew that she was not guilty of anything; yet, the authorities did accuse *me* of smuggling a gun in that very same tape recorder, even though it was not mine, and I had not brought it to the prison.

If you question the likelihood of government officials trying to neutralize their enemies, [see] the instruction given the FBI to its agents at the outset of their counterintelligence program in 1967: "The purpose of this new counterintelligence endeavor is to expose, disrupt, misdirect, discredit, or otherwise neutralize the activities of black nationalist hate-type organizations and groupings, their *leadership, spokesmen,* membership and supporters."

Later it was learned that in January 1971, California and FBI authorities had reported finding an exchange of messages purportedly between Jackson and his friend Jimmy Carr. The letter was clearly about an escape plan for Jackson. California's leading documents examiner later testified that the portion of the message supposedly written by Carr was not in his handwriting. FBI informer Mosher had admitted an intimate association with Carr and his friends. Could the FBI have initiated this exchange of messages? How Jackson was in fact killed may never become known. That the prison officials were happy at his death was too hard to conceal. Warden Park was quoted as saying that "the only good thing that happened all day is that we got George Jackson. Killed him. Shot him in the head."

I was afraid that day precisely because of my position as a lawyer visiting a prisoner. In the late sixties and early seventies the effort by prisoners organizing against medieval prison conditions had reached its peak. As national, even world, attention was spotlighted on California's prisons, lawyers became involved in helping to reform this inhuman system. Prison authorities were only too anxious to discredit these attorneys. Both as governor and as president, Reagan led the attack on legal services attorneys. Reagan's aide Ed Meese organized the Uhler Commission to seek to show that federally financed attorneys for California Rural Legal Assistance were fomenting disorder in California's prisons. A peaceful hunger strike at Folsom was characterized as the "brainchild of a small group of lawyers who were feverishly involved with left-wing activities throughout the state." This strike was supported by the Lawyers Guild, of which I was an active member.

This Uhler report was so damaging to the reputations of the accused attorneys that [the] federal commission formed to review it concluded that the report "subjected many able, energetic, idealistic, and dedicated

California Rural Legal Assistance attorneys to totally unjustified attacks upon their professional integrity and competence." These attorneys had filed two suits against the California Department of Corrections, charging conspiracy to kill inmates.

I had been employed by Berkeley Neighborhood Legal Services on landlord-tenant problems. However, I *had* visited George Jackson four or five times to discuss the filing of a federal civil rights suit charging inhuman conditions at the infamous San Quentin Adjustment Center, including 23½-hour lockup, use of tear gas, shackling, strip cells. Such a suit was eventually filed and was ruled upon favorably.

Was it rational for me to believe that I might be a victim of a careful cover-up as to what really happened to George Jackson, and the scapegoat of a prison system bent on discrediting lawyers? I certainly believed so on August 21, 1971, and I think so even more strongly today [based on newspaper stories including a statement by Warden Park that "We are not going to have a goddamn parade of lawyers coming in here anymore," and "radically altered" descriptions of how Jackson was killed].

What has changed to encourage me to come back now? I believe today I *can* get an open, fair trial. I am convinced that most Americans reflecting back on the late sixties and early seventies are now willing to accept that the government has at times engaged in illegal, excessive, and immoral practices to discredit those who have been working actively for change.

The indictment of officials for the murders of Chicago Black Panthers Fred Hampton and Mark Clark (whose families received nearly $2 million stemming from a civil suit), the acquittal of two American Indian movement leaders of murder when massive evidence of FBI misconduct was finally admitted into evidence, the far-reaching implications of Watergate indicate a new public awareness of official violations of the public trust. The verdict in the original San Quentin Six case was hardly a victory for the state prosecutors. The 6 counts (out of 46) sustained against Spain, Pinell, and Johnson were brought in by a jury tainted by the presence of a prejudiced juror. . . .

I am confident today that I will be acquitted.

[After a very long preliminary hearing, in which Leonard Weinglass, Paul Harris, and Rich Ingram participated, the trial began April 7, 1986, with Guild lawyers M. Gerald Schwartzbach, Susan Rutberg, and Bruce Eric Cohen, law student Matthew Menzer, and legal worker Wendy Morrison. After hearing 61 witnesses in the ten-week trial, the jury deliberated more than 23 hours over five days. They voted only once, 12-0 for acquittal.

["It's clear that this case represented something much larger and more important than myself," Bingham told the *San Francisco Chronicle*. "I'm just glad to be able to be part of that again." Charles Garry returned to the underlying issue: "The public has forgotten very quickly. The prison system is still a cesspool."]

NLG LEADS BATTLE AT CALIFORNIA STATE BAR
By the Los Angeles Chapter State Bar Committee

[After Royal W. France and William L. Standard, long-time members of the American Bar Association, succeeded in getting their views published, at least once, in the *ABA Journal* during the Cold War, the Guild did not find time to work further in that arena. The occasional effort to get the ABA to support human rights in the 1970s and 1980s, to vote for ratification of the Genocide Convention, for example, was made without Guild participation.

[The arena in which the Guild most consistently confronted open advocates of property rights before human rights was the Conference of Delegates of the State Bar of California. The Conference provides clear-cut procedures for accredited Bar associations to propose specific statutory or constitutional changes of concern to the Bar, but victories in the Conference do not become Bar policy without much further work in the Board of Governors. Guild Conference delegates must be prepared for an occasional resounding victory—as when just resigned President Nixon decided he better resign from the California State Bar before he was pushed out by the Conference then assembled; and for an occasional outburst of old-fashioned red-baiting—as in the Conference debate rejecting Guild resolutions on U.S. policy in Nicaragua and El Salvador right after the "007" incident in 1984.]

For more than twenty-five years our chapter has worked actively at the annual conventions of the state Bar. At these annual events, libations flow in many "hospitality" suites. Meanwhile, Guild members have labored for progressive resolutions on the floor of the Conference of Delegates.

In the last years, we have been particularly successful. It is, therefore, a high compliment that conservative forces now seek to change the rules under which we have worked. The Guild has been successful in placing before the Conference issues involving sexism, the death penalty, due process for poor people, and other progressive causes. The 1,000 delegates to the annual event have increasingly given the Guild a fair hearing, and have adopted a surprising number of Guild proposals. Most recently, the Guild led a successful six-year campaign to get the Conference to endorse sanctions against South Africa [and then to urge] the Bar itself to withdraw funds from institutions doing business with South Africa. The California state Bar became one of the first prominent

---

"NLG Leads Battle at California State Bar," by Los Angeles Chapter State Bar Committee, *Los Angeles Chapter News* (Sept. 1986).

non-black institutions in the country to put itself on record and take action on this issue.

Understandably, the conservatives have been increasingly frustrated. For years, they have argued that NLG and progressive resolutions were beyond the "purview" of appropriate action. Such "purview" objections were heatedly debated, and repeatedly rejected by the Conference. The argument that lawyers are inevitably involved with issues of social justice and substantive due process has been persuasive. Finally, the conservative forces, withdrawing from the field of battle at the Conference, adopted other strategies of collateral attack . . . appealing to the legislature to limit Conference activities, and to the courts to obtain the same end. Unfortunately, both of these "end runs" have been partially successful.

At the end of the 1985 session, a minority of legislators were able to block passage of the dues bill, which provides all the funds for operation of the state Bar bureaucracy. Representatives of the state Bar were then forced to go to the legislature and wheel and deal to get funding. In this climate, the Executive Committee of the Conference and Board of Governors passed new and restrictive rules concerning the purview of Conference resolutions. The second line of attack utilized a court challenge by several individual State Bar members complaining that their mandatory dues were being utilized to promote "ideological" causes with which they disagreed. They complained about some of the resolutions the Conference had considered. Predictably, many of their complaints were directed at our resolutions.

Our chapter is not about to accept these new conservative assaults placidly. We are participating in counter attacks on each of the two fronts. . . . Given our history we can take the long view. We were surprisingly successful under the old rules. Even if the rules are somewhat modified, there is no reason to believe we will not continue to have success.

[At the 1986 Conference, San Francisco and Los Angeles Guild chapter delegates joined in the successful attack on the new purview rules. The Conference almost unanimously adopted a new category of permissible resolutions dealing with the science of jurisprudence. Delegates then heard Chief Justice Rose Bird, six weeks before the November retention election in which her position was under massive, well-financed attack. She praised the remarkable heritage of our legal system, in which the rich and powerful are as accountable before the Bar of justice as the poor and weak, and concluded: "If we judges and lawyers are not to be popular, let it be because we are standing on the forefront of protecting people's rights during a time of transition."]

INTERNATIONAL WORK
By the International Committee

[Summarized in the *New York Chapter Journal* for 1986 honoring the International Committee.]

In response to the serious threat to the rule of international law which the Reagan Administration poses, new alliances are forming and resistance is growing. The Guild's response, both legally and politically, has intensified. We raise our voices in opposition to intervention and repression and in support of national liberation movements throughout the world.

1984

Over 30 Guild members join 300 activists in mass civil disobedience at Federal Building in N.Y.C. in opposition to U.S. sponsored mining of Nicaraguan harbors.

Guild delegates—Vicki Erenstein, Franklin Siegel, Jeffrey Haas—travel to Vietnam and Kampuchea at invitation of Association of Vietnamese Jurists.

Guild members organize War Crimes Tribunals on Central America and the Caribbean in NYC and 12 other cities to investigate the legality of U.S. government's actions.

Jennifer Garvey presents Guild testimony before New York State Assembly Banking Committee in support of legislation on divestment of state funds from corporations and banks doing business in southern Africa.

Guild forms Visa Denial Project in response to political denial of visas by Reagan Administration to individuals whose views are opposed by U.S.

1985

Guild helps form Lawyers Against Apartheid to galvanize the legal community against racist South African regime and for abolition of constructive engagement.

Guild representative visits Angola to investigate U.S. and South African collaboration in the attempt to overthrow the Angolan government.

Guild helps form Lawyers Committee to Free Nelson Mandela. Drafts resolution for introduction to legislatures calling for an immediate end to apartheid and freedom for political prisoners.

"International Work" from summary of work by International Committee, in New York City Chapter 1986 Banquet Journal.

Guild sends emergency delegation to Chile to investigate newly imposed state of siege and forms Chile Task Force to investigate condition of political prisoners in Chile.

Central America Task Force members quickly respond to economic embargo against Nicaragua, defend scores of demonstrators in civil disobedience, and join CCR in legal challenge to embargo in *Beacon Products v. Reagan.*

Guild delegation to Nicaragua organizes material aid campaign to assist Nicaraguan National Assembly in preparing country's first Constitution.

NYC Chapter members join in the fight to keep the U.S. Navy from "homeporting" nuclear weapons on Staten Island.

THE PRIORITY OF WORK ON PEACE LAW
By 1986 National Convention

Whereas, the most critical issue facing the peoples of the world is the survival of the planet, which is endangered by the threat of nuclear annihilation; and

Whereas, it is becoming universally recognized that the survival of life itself requires peace and that peace requires nuclear disarmament; and

Whereas, in our legal work in the U.S. on a wide range of people's concerns we see the connection between economic despair, governmental repression and personal powerlessness, and the drive toward domination and nuclear war, yielding superprofits for weaponry, menacing national chauvinism, and massive cuts in spending for people's needs; and

Whereas, our professional responsibility includes a commitment to act against war crimes, crimes against peace and crimes against humanity under the Nuremberg Principles, which are part of U.S. law; and

Whereas, we can make a unique contribution to the work for peace by building a body of peace law demonstrating that, as human rights come before property rights, so peaceful solutions come before military actions; and

Whereas, the government of the U.S. is growing increasingly isolated in the international community for its refusal to renounce the first strike use of nuclear weapons, its unilateral continuation of nuclear testing,

---

"The Priority of Work on Peace Law" from "Resolution On the Priority of Work on Disarmament and Peace" adopted at 1986 Guild National Convention, in *Guild Notes* (Fall 1986).

threats to renounce the restraints contained in the SALT and A.B.M. treaties, and its announced intention to attempt the militarization of space;

Therefore be it resolved that:

1. The peaceful resolution of disputes between nations is essential to the survival of the planet and is a priority in our political and programmatic work, including support for the United Nations;
2. Working to stop the march towards nuclear conflagration is our professional responsibility;
3. In all our work we raise the connections between the government's wartime budgets, its rejection of proposals to reverse the arms race, end nuclear testing and militarize space with the disastrous effects on the economy of massive military spending, U.S. intervention abroad, and cuts in vital social programs;
4. Each Guild committee and task force study ways to make connections between its specialized fields of law and work and the fields of nuclear disarmament, peace law, and peace work;
5. In all our work, we constantly search for allies in labor unions, churches, movements of Blacks, Hispanics, Native Americans, Asian Americans, the women's movement, gay liberation movement, and allies in other Bar associations and professional organizations, scientists, law professors, and other groups and persons, even in ruling circles, who are working toward the prevention of nuclear annihilation by supporting disarmament;
6. We demand that our government join with the U.S.S.R. in a moratorium on nuclear testing;
7. We demand that our government honor the provisions of the SALT and ABM treaties, which require abandonment of the Star Wars program to militarize space;
8. We support Rep. Schroeder's bill to cut off funding for nuclear testing for six months if the Soviets also do not test;
9. We support efforts to reverse the decision to Homeport nuclear warships in New York, San Francisco, Florida, and other cities;
10. We support local legislation creating Nuclear Weapons Free Zones, and requiring public education on the dangers of nuclear war;
11. The NLG start immediately preparing and holding discussions at all levels in the Guild on nuclear disarmament and make this a major subject at the next Convention; . . .

Passed June 15, 1986, by the NLG Convention Plenary.

FREEDOM IS A CONSTANT STRUGGLE
By the Editors

The Guild of 1937 was intimately concerned about the day-to-day problems of organized workers. The general counsels of the old AFL and the new CIO were both founders of the Guild, and were often quoted in the press as important leaders of important organizations. The national CIO made annual contributions to the Guild, as did other unions whose leadership had benefited from Guild work and whose attorneys were Guild members. In the 1980s, Guild members representing AFL-CIO unions have become a presence at annual meetings of AFL-CIO lawyers. Some Guild lawyers have joined unions of government workers representing public defenders and prosecuting attorneys. Guild lawyers working for the Legal Services Corporation have taken the lead in organizing their fellow lawyers and legal workers. But fewer Guild members today have relatives active in unions than was typical in 1937. Probably fewer Guild members have participated in a strike in the United States than have participated in almost any other kind of demonstration in this, or another, country. Younger Guild members have been in struggles for participatory democracy and against war, racism, and sexism. They have more limited experience with what their older colleagues call the class struggle, although this is changing in the new wave of strikes against take-away demands in the 1980s.

This situation is related to changes in the work force and in the labor movement. It is also part of another problem: the economics of practice seem to require specialization. Labor law has become a specialty, like bankruptcy, Native American rights, police misconduct, discharges at will, and employment discrimination. There is so much paperwork to deal with in each field, after the basic law has been learned, that there are more specialists and fewer generalists to draw the connections between developments in one field and another. When it takes a lawyer or legal worker fulltime—and overtime—to represent human rights over property rights in a particular field, where can s/he find time to see the larger picture and to work for basic change through the Guild?

The time factor is part of the broader financial problem arising as the cost of being active in the Guild, like all other costs of practice, goes up. To be effective on the national scene requires long-distance phone calls, several long trips per year, the secretarial work needed for correspondence, minute-taking, and filing, and the efficient use of time in a busy law practice. Effective work at the national level often leads to invitations to become active on the international level, with its higher phone bills, airline ticket costs, and need to write bilingually. Guild members also find it difficult to sit at a meeting where funds are being raised for an urgent project without pledging some money, and difficult to find the money to bring a spouse along, or to justify repeated travel without the family.

The economic problems of the profession merge into the economic problems of the nation, worrisome subjects receiving inadequate study and analysis. Each time the movement and its lawyers have approached an effective campaign for economic rights, it has been derailed by other problems that take precedence because they involve the very survival of the people. In the 1930s, the New Deal had only begun to address the basic economic problems when the United States had to turn to the defeat of Fascism abroad. After the war, the movement faced strikebreaking and Taft-Hartley Act enforcement at home, followed by Cold War here and hot war in Korea. These brought jobs in the military/industrial complex that muted more basic economic demands for thirty-five years. The civil rights movement, having made some gains on social and political rights, was derailed as it moved toward economic demands in the late 1960s. The new wave of political repression unleashed by Richard Nixon, and nurtured by the FBI, CIA, COINTELPRO, and others into the Reagan era, kept the movement from priority work on economic rights in the 1970s and 1980s, as obscenely high military spending pumped up parts of the economy.

Now economic realities are hitting the people of the United States who have always had jobs since the Great Depression: white, male, hardhat union members, and white-collar workers with large corporations. Plant closings, bankruptcies, runaway shops, mergers, and cost-cutting have taught every working person at every level that there is no economic security, as the facts of the nuclear age have taught every conscious person that there is no security in militarism.

These hard facts touch the lives of every Guild member as the Reagan administration policies and Gramm-Rudman-Hollings budget cuts take hold. Many Guild lawyers face serious economic problems. There are staff cuts and no hiring in some Legal Service, public defender, consumer fraud, and affirmative action offices; labor law firms are cutting staffs as legal problems mount but per capita dues payments decline. Some older lawyers, after decades of excellent work, must scramble for new clients while watching some of their ex-clients graduate and open their own law offices. The lure of efficiency in research through computer technology and word processors adds to the skyrocketing cost of law books and malpractice insurance, forcing many Guild members onto credit card payments that never cease.

But Guild lawyers retain, as their basic tool or tactic, belief in the people who sit on juries and in their ability to convince jurors of the righteousness of their clients' cause, or, if that is too much on the particular facts, at least to convince jurors that the other side has not proved its case. They faced the open attacks by Chief Justice Burger on jury trials in civil cases, and his attacks on extensive *voir dire* in criminal cases in order to select juries that can be fair. Now they face Chief Justice Rehnquist's open hostility to federal protection of the constitutional rights of people who are black, poor, or women.

These attacks force all Guild members to spend some of their time defending the constitutional right to trial by jury, no unreasonable search and seizure, and other basic legal rights. They must respond to well-funded insurance company campaigns against "outrageous recoveries by lawyers" in PI cases, leading to efforts in several states to change tort law to limit liability for admitted injuries. They must defend against Reagan administration attacks on attorney-fee awards, provided for in the Civil Rights Acts in meritorious cases, and respond to the appointment of "barely competent" men to federal judgeships, and to open administration attacks on Justice William Brennan, one of the remaining Supreme Court justices from the Warren Court with a New Deal approach to law. Guild lawyers have their work cut out for them as the Supreme Court closes the doors of the federal courts to many classes of claimants from the poor and working classes, and local Reagan supporters seek to turn out of office state court justices who stick to Warren Court precedents, starting with Rose Bird in California. They are under added pressure at every stage in every criminal case as they face strident advocates of capital punishment.

These attacks on specific legal rights were accompanied by the Reagan administration's open defiance of the rule of law in general. Internationally, the White House turned its back on the 150-page opinion and decision of the World Court in *Nicaragua v. United States,* and undertook the privatization of U.S. foreign policy, ignoring laws passed after Watergate requiring Congressional oversight of certain foreign policy decisions. Within the United States, the White House turned its back on the Constitution, with its limitations on the powers of the President and its requirement of openness in government, so that the people can ultimately decide which policies they favor. While establishment lawyers tried to cope with the constitutional crisis created by Iran/contragate, Guild members asked themselves: "How can I help my clients participate most effectively in reversing illegal courses of action by the government?" The quick answer of the 1960s, "Sue the bastards!" does not suffice in this era.

The Nixon/Reagan/Rehnquist Supreme Court does not appeal to Guild lawyers as the best place for a final decision on the most critical problems facing this nation. If the fundamental problems are economic, older Guild lawyers can attest that the courts have never been the source of long-range plans or basic answers. Today Guild members face frightened clients, some without work or hope of work, as they observe the destruction of many basic segments of the economy of the United States, the permanent closing of steelmills, mines, auto factories, railroads, and of banks, credit unions, and savings and loan associations.

Where were the decisions made that led to these closings? Not in Congress or the courts, but at meetings of the boards of directors of transnational corporations, apparently unconstrained by concern for their fellow citizens, and holding themselves above the resolutions of the United Nations General Assembly on trade and development. Guild members see decisions being made by private banks, the World Bank, and International Monetary Fund that tighten the noose on developing nations and breed the terrorists they decry. They see Congress pass tax bills that encourage corporations to build new plants abroad rather than renewing plants, and other facilities, at home. They see Congress fund the Department of Defense without being able to find out how as much as 35 billion dollars is being spent annually on so-called "secret" budget items, for which no accounting will ever be made to Congress or the people. Some Guild members learned in litigation, even before Iran/contragate, that Congressional oversight has not kept the actions of the Central Intelligence Agency and the National Security Council within legal limits. Recent presidents have sworn to uphold the checks and balances written into the U.S. Constitution, the UN Charter, and treaties limiting nuclear arms, while seeking an imperial presidency within the country and the mirage of an American Century abroad.

Guild members in 1937 thought they could change the United States, as part of a massive popular movement. They were right. They did make a difference, individually, collectively, and through the power of their work, analysis, advocacy, and negotiating ability.

Guild members today find themselves working on a global stage helping to prevent international economic disaster, war, and the ecocide resulting from use of nuclear weapons.

They were not trained for such work, either in law school or in their practice since. But their service on the Guild's Economic Rights Task Force, the Labor Committee, and on Guild delegations abroad, seems to have opened a path toward such local and global work with a broad movement, a rainbow coalition. Guild people are learning to work in many forums, from the streets to courtrooms and Congress, from administrative agencies to UN agencies, from school boards to press conferences, in order to guarantee that human rights come before property rights. They are talking about the right to earn a living in the United States, and the right to peace. They are experimenting with many legal tools, especially the ancient power of eminent domain and the new peace law. They represent clients who want courts to condemn closed factories so the government can take them over and run them, producing needed goods and saving local jobs. They represent clients seeking to enforce the Ethics in Government Act, the Neutrality Act, the UN Charter, and the Nuremberg Principles.

Looking back and looking forward, the Guild celebrated its fiftieth anniversary during the 42nd year of the United Nations and the 200th year of the United States Constitution. In 1984, Haywood Burns pointed the way for the Guild in concluding his remarks on its past, present, and future.

LOOKING AHEAD
By Haywood Burns

Looking ahead I stand foursquare with those who would come together to build a new movement, who would pick up the old questions on which we foundered—black/white alliance, economic justice, domestic and international peace and justice and their relationship—and make a renewed effort to work them out in pursuit of our shared goals for a just society, realizing that there are many here we can reach. Even if we are a minority on these shores, we are part of a worldwide majority that seeks to end the scourge of poverty, racism, and injustice.

A new coming together, yes, but it cannot be in a vertical relationship. A civil rights activist of the sixties observed that "integration is an insidious subterfuge for white supremacy." Unless there is reciprocity and mutuality of respect, integration just serves to recreate, in another form, a relationship of white over black. A new coming together, yes, but it cannot be a hypocritical alliance. The white progressive legal community, individuals, firms and organizations have achieved much and have come a long way, but they still have a long way to go. You cannot be in favor of affirmative action in the society but not in your office. You cannot champion the cause of workers in general, while treading upon rights of your employees in particular.

We need to realize that we cannot afford to be a progressive Bar that is two nations, one rich, one poor, one black, one white. Resource-strong groups cannot stand idly by while resource-weak groups wither and die. The Guild has provided an excellent example in the assistance that it has given to the National Conference of Black Lawyers. We need more actions of this type—truly shared power and goals, and the concomitant

---

"Looking Ahead," from conclusion of Haywood Burns' speech at New York City Chapter banquet, 1984 (typescript at MCLI).

ability to take leadership from the right quarter at a given time on a given issue. Yes, even leadership that is female, that is non-white.

As lawyers we must realize that the law is no panacea in addressing the range of issues that face us. But it does have a role to play, and it is much too important a role for us to neglect if we truly want to seek change. . . .

There are those who say that our triumph is inevitable, that the forces of history are on our side and that they will vindicate us. There are those who say we will not win, that we are Don Quixotes tilting at windmills; that we are Sisyphus interminably pushing that rock up the hill, only to have it roll back down again.

As for me, I don't know. But it seems to me that principled people have no choice but to struggle.

I do believe we can win if we just keep pushing that rock. . . .

And as we toil in the field together, that day will come, when the people will come out of the fields and the factories, the mines and the mills, the steel and glass office towers, out of the ghettos, the barrios, and the reservations, out of the muck and the mire of despair, of hopelessness, and rise up out of the valley. Red people and black people and white people and yellow people and men and women, old and young, and go to the court—to the citadel of justice, and sit down in their rightful places, and the doors will fling open before them. And they will sit in a court of law that is also a court of justice.

Appendix A

GUILD NATIONAL CONVENTIONS AND NATIONAL OFFICERS

National Conventions, National Presidents	*National Executive Officers*	*National Treasurers*
1936 PreConvention		
Frank P. Walsh		
1937 Washington, D.C.		
John P. Devaney	Mortimer Riemer*	Pearl Hart
1938 Washington, D.C.		
Ferdinand Pecora		Julius I. Peyser
1939 Chicago		
John Gutknecht		Charles MacPhee Wright
1940 New York City		
Robert W. Kenny*	Martin Popper	Ruth Weyand
1941		George Slaff
1942		Benedict Wolf*
1943 Chicago		
Robert W. Kenny		
1944 Cleveland		
Robert W. Kenny		
1946 Cleveland		
Robert W. Kenny		Frank Donner
1947	Robert J. Silberstein	Abraham Pomerantz
1948 Chicago		
Clifford J. Durr		Nathan B. Kogan

*Spaces following names indicate continuing office.

National Conventions, National Presidents	National Executive Officers	National Treasurers
1949 Detroit		
Thomas I. Emerson		
1950 New York City		
Thomas I. Emerson		
1951 Chicago		
Earl B. Dickerson		William L. Standard
1952		Joseph Crown
1953 New York City		
Earl B. Dickerson		
1954 Chicago		
Malcolm Sharp	Jessica Davidson*	
	Ann Fagan Ginger†	
1956 Detroit		
Malcolm Sharp	Royal W. France	Julius Cohen
	Ann Fagan Ginger†	
1957 New York City		
John M. Coe		
1958 Chicago		
John M. Coe		
1959	David Scribner	
1960 San Francisco		
Benjamin Dreyfus		
1961	Herman Gerringer*	
	Aryay Lenske	
1962 Detroit		
Benjamin Dreyfus		Samuel A. Neuburger
1963	David Rynin	
1964 Detroit		
Ernest Goodman	James T. Lafferty	Bernard Fieger
1965 San Francisco		
Ernest Goodman		Harry Margolis, Chair, National Finance Comm.
1966		David Scribner
1967 New York City		
Victor Rabinowitz	Kenneth Cloke	
1968 Santa Monica		
Victor Rabinowitz	Dennis James	Ralph Shapiro
1970 Washington, D.C.		
Doris Brin Walker	Eric Seitz	National Finance Comm.

*Secretary
†Administrative Secretary

Appendix C

WINNERS OF NATIONAL GUILD AWARDS

Franklin D. Roosevelt Awards

Claude Pepper (1946)
Adolph J. Sabath (1948)
J. Waties Waring (1949)
Osmond K. Fraenkel (1950)
Delbert E. Metzger (1953)
Thomas I. Emerson (1954)
Patrick H. O'Brien (1956)
Hubert T. Delany (1957)
Mitchell Franklin (1958)
Alexander Meiklejohn (1960)
Louis Redding (1962)
Benjamin E. Smith (1965)
George W. Crockett, Jr. (1967)
Arthur Kinoy (1968)

Special National Lawyers Guild Awards

Leonard W. Holt (1962)
Edward Dawley (1962)
Ernest D. Jackson, Sr. (1962)
Alexander P. Tureaud (1962)
Benjamin E. Smith (1962)
John M. Coe (1962)
Ann Fagan Ginger (1965)

Guild Law Student (1946)	Editorial Board
(1953)	Rhoda Hendrick
Guild Student Bulletin (1947)	Editorial Board
(1950)	Alan Westin
(1967)	Editorial Board
Law Students in Action Newsletter	
(1986–)	Penny Pahl

Appendix B

NATIONAL GUILD JOURNALS AND NEWSLETTERS

National Law Journals	*Editors*
National Lawyers Guild Quarterly (1937–39)	George Bronz (1937–39)
	Samuel Frankel (1940)
Lawyers Guild Review (1940–59)	Benjamin Algase (1940–47)
	Nathan Greene (1943–47)
	Robert B. Seidman (1948)
	Emanuel Gordon (1950–53)
	David Weissman (1950–59)
Law In Transition (1961–63)	Laurence R. Sperber (1961–63)
Guild Practitioner (1965–)	Marvin Stender (1965)
	E. A. Dawley (1965–)

National Newsletters	
Guild Lawyer (1938–51)	Simon Schachter (1938–39)
	Benjamin Algase (1939–40)
	Elliott L. Biskind (1940–45)
	Simon Schachter (1946–51)
New York Guild Lawyer (1943–58)	Simon Schachter (1943–58)
Guild Lawyer (1959–64)	Arthur Schutzer
Guild Newsletter (1964–69)	David Y. Klein (1964)
	William Goodman (1964–66)
	David G. Lubell and William H. Shaap (1967–69)
Guild Notes (1971–)	Editorial Board (1971–81)
	Maritza Arrastia (1982–84)
	Editorial Board (1985–)

National Conventions, National Presidents	National Executive Officers	National Treasurers
1971 Boulder		
Catherine Roraback		Neal Gantcher
1973 Austin		
James Larson	National Office Collective	National Finance Comm.
1974 Twin Cities		
Doron Weinberg		Jeanne Mirer and National Finance Comm.
1976 Houston		
William Goodman		
1977 Seattle		
Henry diSuvero		Judy Mead
1979 San Francisco		
Paul Harris		Steve Saltzman
1980 Boston		
Mary Alice Theiler		
1982 Santa Fe		
Michael Ratner		Joe Lipofsky
1983 Chicago		
Barbara Dudley		Tim Plenk
1985 Atlanta		
Mark Van Der Hout	Barbara Dudley	Rudolph Schware
1986 Denver		
Haywood Burns		William Goodman
1987 Washington, D.C.		
Haywood Burns	Michael Cowan	Cathleen Connealy

Appendix D

NATIONAL OFFICERS, CHAPTERS, PROJECTS, COMMITTEES, TASK FORCES, AND CAUCUSES (1986–1987)

President: Haywood Burns
Vice Presidents: Debra Evenson, John Brittain
Treasurer: Bill Goodman
National Vice Presidents: D'Ann Johnson, Marilyn Johnson, Julie Shapiro, Roberto Soto, Bill Tamayo
Regional Vice Presidents:
Mideast: Rich McHugh
    Chapters: Ann Arbor, Buffalo, Cincinnati, Cleveland, Columbus, Dayton, Detroit, Flint, Lansing, Ohio River Valley, Pittsburgh
    Law School Chapters: Buffalo, Case Western, Cleveland-Marshall, Detroit College of Law, Ohio State; Universities of Cincinnati, Dayton, Michigan, Pittsburgh, Wayne State
Midwest: Peter Erlinder
    Chapters: Central Indiana, Champaign-Urbana, Chicago, Iowa City, Kansas City, Lawrence, Lincoln, Madison, Milwaukee, St. Louis, Southern Illinois, Twin Cities
    Law School Chapters: Chicago-Kent, DePaul, Drake, Marquette, Southern Illinois; Universities of Chicago, Illinois, Iowa, Kansas, Minnesota, Missouri-Kansas City, Missouri-Columbia, North Dakota, Wisconsin, Washington University, William-Mitchell
Northeast: Jim Klimaski
    Chapters: Albany, Baltimore, Ithaca, Maine, Massachusetts (Boston), Mid-Hudson, New Hampshire, New Haven, New Jersey, New York City, Northern Connecticut, Philadelphia, Pioneer Valley, Syracuse, Vermont, Washington, D.C., Western Massachusetts
    Law School Chapters: Albany, American, Antioch, Boston College, Boston

University, Brooklyn, Cardozo, Columbia, Cornell, CUNY, Fordham, Franklin-Pierce, Georgetown, Harvard, Hofstra, Howard, New England, New York Law School, NYU, Northeastern, Pace, Rutgers-Camden, Rutgers-Newark, Seton Hall, Suffolk, Syracuse, Temple, Touro; Universities of Baltimore, Bridgeport, Connecticut, Maine, Maryland, Pennsylvania, Western New England, Yale

Northwest: Eva Kutas
    Chapters: Eugene, Portland, Salem, Seattle
    Law School Chapters: Lewis & Clark; Universities of British Columbia, Oregon, Puget Sound, Washington, Willamette

South: Sandy Mayes
    Chapters: Alabama, Athens, Atlanta, Charlottesville, Eastern Kentucky, Eastern Tennessee, Louisville, McCain, Mississippi, New Orleans, North Carolina, North Florida, South Carolina, South Florida, West Virginia
    Law School Chapters: Emory, Loyola, Marshall-Wythe, Nova, Tulane; Universities of Florida, Louisville, Miami, North Carolina, South Carolina, Virginia, West Virginia

Southwest: Ann Hopfenbeck
    Chapters: Central Arizona, Colorado, New Mexico, Northern Arizona, Salt Lake City, Southern Arizona
    Law School Chapters: Arizona State, Brigham Young; Universities of Arizona, Colorado-Boulder, Denver, New Mexico

Texhoma: Virginia Raymond
    Chapters: Austin, Dallas-Fort Worth, East Texas, Houston, Oklahoma, San Antonio, Southern Texas, Western Texas
    Law School Chapters: Baylor, University of Texas

Far West: Philip Brimble
    Chapters: Hawaii, Los Angeles, Sacramento Valley, Salinas/Monterey, San Diego, San Francisco Bay Area, San Joaquin/Bakersfield, Santa Clara, Santa Cruz, Whittier
    Law School Chapters: Golden Gate, McGeorge, New College, People's College, Southwestern; Universities of California-Boalt Hall, -Davis, -Hastings, -Los Angeles, Hawaii, San Diego, San Francisco, Southern California, Western State

National Finance Committee Representative: Joe Lipofsky
Transitional Representative: Marc Van Der Hout
50th Anniversary Liaison: Martin Popper
Jailhouse Lawyer Chapters:
  Attica, N.Y.; Dannemora, N.Y.; Stormville, N.Y.; Dallas, Pa.; Angola, La.; Jackson, Miss.; Stateville, Ill.; Graham, Ill.; Leavenworth, Kan.; El Reno, Okla.; Tennessee Colony, Tx.; Huntsville, Tx.

PROJECTS, COMMITTEES, TASK FORCES, CAUCUSES, AND CONTACT PERSONS

Affirmative Action/Anti-Discrimination Committee: Ann Noel
Anti-Sexism Task Force: Abbe Smith

Gay Rights Subcommittee: Paula Ettelbrick
  AIDS Network: Paul Albert
Civil Liberties Committee: David Rudovsky, Chip Berlet
  Anti-Repression Task Force: Linda Backiel
Committee on Native American Struggles: Rex Friend
  Rethinking Indian Law: Wendy Eaton
Criminal Law Committee: Carla Hagen
Economic Rights Task Force: Mark Greenberg
  Work & Welfare: Martha Easter-Wells
Faculty Network: Debra Evenson
Grand Jury Project: Robert Boyle
International Committee: Ellen Ray, Michael Tigar
  Central America Task Force: Jody LeWitter, Cathy Potler
  Chile Task Force: Laura Safer
  Cuba Subcommittee: Bill Montross, Emily Yozell
  Disinformation & Information Restriction: Ann Marie Buitrago, Bill Schaap
  International Debt Crisis Subcommittee: Ellen Chapnick
  International Law Subcommittee: Michael Krinsky, John Mage
  Ireland Task Force: Jack Kilroy
  Middle East Subcommittee: John Quigley, Terri Waller
  Peace & Disarmament Subcommittee: Ted Dzielak, Brian Spears
  Philippines Subcommittee: Jack Waterman
  Puerto Rico Subcommittee: Michael Deutsch
  Relations with International Organizations: Reed Brody, John Privitera
  International Association of Democratic Lawyers Representative: Michael Ratner
  Southern Africa Subcommittee: Vicki Erenstein, Tim Wright
National Immigration Project: Dan Kesselbrenner, Kip Steinberg
  Central America Refugee Defense Fund: Dan Kesselbrenner
  Visa Denial Project: Claudia Slovinsky
Labor Committee: Bob Gibbs
Law Students in Action: Karol Heppe
Military Law Task Force: Kathy Gilberd
Movement Support Network: Adelita Medina
National Prison Network: Debreh Gilbert
Rural Justice Committee: Libby Cooper
Summer Projects Committee: Ted Dzielak
Theoretical Studies Committee: David Kairys
Third World Caucus: Marilyn Johnson
50th Anniversary Committee: Martin Popper, Mary Alice Theiler, Corinne Rafferty
Toxics Committee: Vicki Laden

Appendix E

BOOKS PUBLISHED BY THE NATIONAL LAWYERS GUILD

Bonora, Beth, and Elissa Krauss, eds. *Jury Work: Systematic Techniques.* Berkeley: National Jury Project, in cooperation with the National Lawyers Guild and the National Conference of Black Lawyers, 1979.

Ginger, Ann Fagan, ed. *Civil Liberties Docket, Volumes 1-13.* Berkeley: National Lawyers Guild, 1955-1969.

———. *Civil Rights & Liberties Handbook: Pleadings & Practice* (with supplements). Berkeley: National Lawyers Guild, 1963-1972.

———. *Minimizing Racism in Jury Trials.* Berkeley: National Lawyers Guild, 1969.

———. *The New Draft Law: A Manual for Lawyers and Counselors.* Berkeley: National Lawyers Guild, 1969.

Kairys, David; Jay Schulman; and Sid Harring, eds. *The Jury System: New Methods for Reducing Prejudices.* Cambridge: National Lawyers Guild, 1975.

National Lawyers Guild. *Citizens' Guide to the 1964 Civil Rights Act.* Detroit: National Lawyers Guild, 1965.

National Lawyers Guild-Grand Jury Defense Office. *Representation of Witnesses Before Federal Grand Juries.* San Francisco: National Lawyers Guild, 1974.

National Lawyers Guild-Immigration Project. *Immigration Defense Manual.* Los Angeles: National Lawyers Guild, 1977.

National Lawyers Guild-International Law Committee. *A Summary of Disarmament Documents, 1945-1962.* San Francisco: National Lawyers Guild, 1963.

National Lawyers Guild-Middle East Delegation. *Treatment of Palestinians in Israeli-Occupied West Bank and Gaza.* New York: National Lawyers Guild, 1978.

National Lawyers Guild-National Immigration Project. *Immigration Law and Defense.* New York: C. Boardman Co., 1979.

National Lawyers Guild-Special Projects Staff. *Raising and Litigating Electronic Surveillance Claims in Criminal Cases.* San Francisco: Lake Law Books, 1977.

NATIONAL LAWYERS GUILD: BOOKS IN PRINT, 1987

Achtenberg, Roberta (ed.), and SF Bay Area Anti-Sexism Committee. *Sexual Orientation and the Law.*
Avery, Michael; David Rudovsky; and Civil Liberties Committee. *Police Misconduct: Law and Litigation.*
Lobel, Jules (ed.), and Civil Liberties Committee. *Civil Rights Litigation and Attorney Fees Annual Handbook.*
National Lawyers Guild–Immigration Project. *Immigration Law and Crimes.*
National Lawyers Guild–Immigration Project. *Immigration Law and Defense.*
National Lawyers Guild–Labor Law Center. *Employee and Union Member Guide to Labor Law.*

Index

Abernathy, Ralph, 389, 401
ABM (Antiballistic Missile Treaty), 401
Abraham Lincoln Brigade, 6, 30
Abrahams, Robert D., 38–40, 101
Absentee ballots, 391–92
Abstention doctrine, 222, 317
Abt, John, 357
Abzug, Bella, 201
Acheson, Dean, 94
Achtenberg, Roberta, 419
Adderley v. Florida, 225
Ad Hoc Committee to End Discrimination, 202
Administrative Procedure Act, 231
Affirmative Action, 203, 355, 390, 393; ABA against, 321; in education, 318–21; in employment, 350; in NLG, 367; work for, 331–35
AFL-CIO Industrial Union Department, 362
AFL-CIO Lawyers' Conference, 362, 366, 402
African-American slave folktale, 318
African National Congress, 322
Ageism, 306, 359
Agricultural Adjustment Administration (AAA), 5
Agrin, Gloria, 96, 101
Aid to Families with Dependent Children (AFDC), 362
Alabama, 391–92
Alameda County Legal Aid Society, 250
Albany, Georgia, 178, 194–97
Albany movement, 197
Albert, Paul, 417
Albert Cohen v. Hurley, 167

Alevy v. Downstate Medical Center of New York, 320
Algase, Benjamin, 412
Algerians (French), 369
Algiers Declaration of 1976, 360
Allende, Salvator, 325
Amedee, Earl, 199
American Association of Jurists, 351
American Bar Association (ABA): against affirmative action, 321; attacks New Deal, 4; calls for loyalty oaths, 138–39; on civil rights, 210–11; excludes blacks, 5, 9–10, 311; expels advocates of Marxism-Leninism, 114; and FBI, 190; group legal services program, 384; *Journal*, 190, 397; on jury system, 321; 1936 convention, 16; opposes mandatory social security for lawyers, 107–9; and Supreme Court, 165–66, 321; typical member, 378; on Vietnam, 228
American Civil Liberties Union (ACLU), 6, 183, 206, 246, 317, 322
American Committee for the Protection of the Foreign Born, 6, 20
American Communications Association v. Douds, 133, 174
American Indian movement, 396
American Institute for Free Labor Development, 366
American Jewish Committee, 206
American Jewish Congress, 206
American Labor Party, 6
American Nazi Party, 338–40
American Revolution, 282, 363; second, 285

421

422 / INDEX

American Trial Lawyers Association, 100
Amicus briefs, 186, 215, 217–18, 318, 321, 365
Anarchy, criminal, 189
Anderson, Charles, 89
Andersson, Joan, 261–63
Anglo-American Committee of Inquiry (Palestine), 80–82
Angola, 322, 399
Antarctic Treaty, 1960, 373
Anti-apartheid, 385–86
Anti-busing, 314
Anti-capitalism, 342
Anti-Communism, 86–99, 113–35, 322–23
Anti-draft, 261
Anti-Düehring (Engels), 333
Anti-gay feelings, 341
Anti-imperialism, 342
Anti-imperialist caucus, 322
Anti–Ku Klux Klan Act of 1871, 339–40
Anti-lynching bill, 10, 68–69
Anti-sexism, 341–42, 402
Anti-war movement, 221, 227, 261, 402
Apartheid, 189, 327, 399
Appalachia, 389
Argentina, 343
Arms race, 401
Arnold, Thurman, 6, 26
Arrastia, Maritza, 412
Asian Americans, 401
Askin, Frank, 316–18
Association of the Bar of the City of New York, 126, 128
Association of Vietnamese Jurists, 399
Asylum case, 385
Atomic bomb, 240
Attica uprising cases and Shango trial, 293–98
Attorney-fee awards, 204, 404
Attorney General's list of subversive organizations, 136–38, 158–59. *See also* Executive Order 10450
Avery, Michael, 338, 419
Avnet, I. Duke, 260
AWOL cases, 239
Axelrod, Beverly, 249

Backiel, Linda, 417
Bail, 183, 217–18; right to, 254; special bail program, 255–56; unreasonable in Detroit riots (1967), 251–55
Baker v. Carr, 223, 241
Bakke v. Regents of the University of California, 318–21

Bankruptcy proceedings, 250, 381, 402–3
Bar: applicants to, 306–7; integration of, 218
Bar associations: for blacks, 313; disciplinary committees of, 393–94; for legal services, 384; NLG as, 246, 261–62, 300, 304; poverty law offices in, 379; for women, 305
Barenblatt v. U.S., 168, 174
Barratry, 186
Barrios, 380, 406–7
Bataan Province, 287
Beacon Products v. Reagan, 400
Beard, Charles A., 282, 285
Beck v. Communications Workers of America, 367
Beecher, Barbara, 194
Berkeley, 185, 291, 396
Berle, Adolf A., Jr., 6, 34–35
Berlet, Chip, 417
Berry, Louis, 168
Bertrand Russell Tribunal, 262, 324
Bible, 232, 345
Biddle, Francis, 48–49, 51, 53–54
Bill of Rights, 180, 248, 282, 290, 347, 360
Binder, Lorraine, 168
Bingham, Stephen, 393–97
Bird, Melinda R., 361–63
Bird, Rose, 398, 404
Birmingham, Alabama, 189
Birth control, 290
Biskind, Elliott L., 412
Black, Hugo L., 67, 126–27, 143; quoted, 151, 181, 222, 225, 289
Black American Law Students Association (BALSA), 368
Black Belt, 262, 391–92
Black Panthers, 267–68, 304
Black Power movement, 237, 389
Blacks, 182–85, 389; bar associations of, 313; churches of, 188, 189, 223; as conscientious objectors, 235; as draftees, 234; as mayors, 389; as national officers in NLG, 187–88, 259–61; as Southern lawyers, 182–85; in Vietnam War, 235–37; voting rights of, 205, 212–14, 391–92; as women lawyers, 370. *See also* Negroes
Black Student Union, 271
Black United Front, 369
Black-white alliance, 406
Bloch, Emanuel, 96
Block, S. John, 10
Blue-collar workers, 319
Bodega Bay, 341
Boehm, Robert, 260

Bone, Homer T., 9
Bonora, Beth, 298, 418
Borus, Linda, 298
Boudin, Leonard, 117, 260, 289–91
Boudin, Louis B., 18–19
Bourgeois democratic rights, 274, 284, 331–35, 338–40
Bouslog, Harriet, 98, 249
Bowie, Robert R., 89
Boycotts, 264, 291, 385
Boyle, Robert, 417
Braden, Carl, 225
Braden v. U.S., 181, 225
Branton, Leo, Jr., 216–18, 350
Braverman, Maurice, 318
Bread-and-butter issues, 100–12, 199
Brecht, Bertolt, 249
Brennan, William, 151, 222, 226, 404
Bridges, Harry Renton, 20, 51–53
Brief banks, 383
Brimble, Philip, 416
Brittain, John, 415
Brodsky, Joseph, 10
Brody, Reed, 417
Bronx Women's Bar Association, 40
Bronz, George, 412
Brooklyn Women's Bar Association, 40
Brotsky, Allan, 260
Brower, Bonnie, 300, 322
Brown, Alan, 49–50
Brown, Ernest J., 90
Brown, H. Rap, 314
Brownell, Herbert, Jr., and NLG, 136–44, 158, 160
Browns, 273
Brown v. Board of Education, 18, 161, 178–80, 186, 221–26, 264, 279, 283, 347, 357
Brutus, Dennis, 385
Bryce, Lord James, xvii
Budget policy, 405
Buhai, Harriet, 260
Buitrago, Ann Marie, 417; analyzes FBI operations toward NLG, 36–38, 75, 169–70
Burden of proof in civil disobedience cases, 374
Burger, Warren E., 317–18, 404
Burger court, 301, 316–18
Burger-Rehnquist Court, 316–18
Burns, Haywood, 293, 297, 356, 387–90, 406–7, 411, 415
Burnstein, Malcolm, 203
Burton, Harold H., 143
Bush, Neal, 298

Bush v. Orleans Parish School Board, 179–80
Bust Book, The, 271
Butchers' Union, 271

Cade, Cathy, 196
Cain, Simon L., 191
California, University of: Berkeley, 194, 258; Hastings College of Law, 91; Law School at Davis, 319
California Department of Corrections, 396
California Education Code, 345
California Industrial Welfare Commission v. Homemakers, Inc., 319
California Rural Legal Assistance, 395–96
California State Bar, 233, 304, 306, 316; attacks on, 398; Conference of Delegates, 218, 397–98; and NLG resolution opposing anti-busing laws (1972), 314; and NLG resolutions on racism in the law (1968–1969), 313; and NLG supports broad purview, 398; resolutions on sanctions against South Africa, 397
California v. Graham and Allen, 315
California v. Hallinan, 202
California v. Newton, 267–69
California v. Stephen Bingham, 393–97
Calley conviction, 302
Cambodia, 231
Cambridge, Edward, 193, 202, 260
Canons of Professional Ethics, 138, 233
Capitalism, 258, 333–35
Carey, Hugh, 298
Carr, Jimmy, 395
Carswell, G. Harrold, 290
Carter, Oliver, 238
Carty-Bennia, Denise S., 321
Case or controversy, 316, 319
Castro, Fidel, 265
Catholic Church, 181
Catholic students, 189
Caughlan, John, 260
Cavers, David F., 90
Center for Constitutional Rights, 324, 376, 392, 400; founding of, 247
Central America, 386–87
Central Committee for Conscientious Objectors, 228, 248
Champerty, 186
Chaney, James, 207–9, 388
Chapnick, Ellen, 417
Character Committees, 306
Chavez, Caesar, 292
Chicago Conspiracy–Dellinger case, 267, 284

424 / INDEX

Chicago Red Squad, 129–30
Chicanos, 296, 389
Child care, 55–57, 362
Child labor amendment, 4, 10
Chile, 203
China, 186, 231, 235
"China Syndrome," 341
Churchill, Winston, 65
CIA (Central Intelligence Agency), 288, 328, 403, 405
Citizen's Guide to the 1964 Civil Rights Act, 219
City College of New York, 387–88
Civil disobedience, 214–16, 373–75, 381, 399; defenses, 374–75; defined, 374
Civil law from poor person's perspective, 251
Civil liberties, 89–90; Cold War cases, 152–58, 185–86, 359
Civil Liberties Docket, The, 161, 169, 185–86, 223, 247–48
Civil rights, 204; act of 1871, 199; act of 1957, 391; act of 1960, 391; act of 1964, 204, 219, 225, 284, 339, 388, 391; act of 1965, 214, 389, 391–92; act of 1968, 389; definition of, 185; movement, 184–92, 194–216, 218–27, 236, 243, 312, 391, 403
Civil Rights and Liberties Handbook, 194, 228
Civil Rights Cases, 284
Civil War amendments, 68–69, 180, 182, 199, 220–21, 224, 235, 321, 332, 347, 363
Clark, Charles C., 126, 140
Clark, Mark, 388, 396
Clark, Ramsey, 359–61
Clark, Tom C., 61, 66–67, 222, 225, 232
Clark Air Force Base, 286
Class action suits, 226, 247, 316, 347, 350, 383
Clients, 183, 264; Spanish-speaking, 292
Cloke, Ken, 262, 410
Coe, John M., 158, 161–63, 178, 187, 259, 410, 414
Cohen, Bruce Eric, 396
Cohen, Felix, 6, 10
Cohen, Julius, 187, 260, 410
Cohen, Stu, 298
Cohn, Roy, 356
COINTELPRO, 161, 169–70, 389, 403
Cold War, 86–99, 113–60, 186, 263, 289–90, 372, 397, 403
Colista, F. Phillip, 260
Columbia University: Oral History Collection, 24; School of Law, 90–91; students, 258, 262, 272
Colvin, James, 392

Committee to Assist Southern Lawyers (CASL), 92, 188–89
Communications Workers of America, 367
Communist Control Act, 221
Communist Party, 15, 113, 115–19, 133–35, 167, 186, 193, 318, 322–23, 356, 358
Communist Party v. Subversive Activities Control Board, 167, 174
Communist Workers Party, 338
Community Action Programs, 203
Community Law Firm, 276
Comparable worth, 356
Condon, Gene Ann, 249, 279–81
Congress, 179; CIO (Congress of Industrial Organizations), 22, 30–31, 358; general counsel in NLG, 402; Judiciary Subcommittee on Civil and Constitutional Rights, 335; Labor Management Subcommittee, 366; lobbying and testifying before, 316, 335, 351, 366, 376, 382–84; role to bar executive assumption of power, 289; Subcommittee on Africa, 386
Connealy, Cathleen, 411
Connor, T. Eugene ("Bull"), 184
Conscientious objectors: blacks as, 235; status of, 229–31
Consciousness raising, 353
Conspiracy, 189; criminal, 198, 204
Constitution (U.S.), 179, 181–82, 189, 211, 241, 352
Constitutional law, 344–46; fees in cases, 346
Contempt citations against lawyers, 124–28, 215, 391–92
Contradictions, 272, 276–79, 332–35; in court system, 283–84
Conyers, John J., Jr., 110, 201, 212, 256, 260
Conyers, Nathan, 110, 260
Cooper, Libby, 417
Cooper v. Aaron, 179
Copelon, Rhonda, 355
Coplon, Judith, 92
CORE (Congress of Racial Equality), 186, 206–7
Coulter, Robert T., 351–52
Council of Federated Organizations (COFO), 205, 207, 209–10, 212–14, 219, 223
Counsel, right to, 121, 185, 360
Countryman, Vern, 289–90
Court packing bill, 10, 12
Courts: class role of, 281–85; as superstructure, 281
Cowan, Michael, 411

Cox, Hugh B., 53–54
Cozart, John, 205
Craig, Roger, 212
Craig, Walter E., 211
Cranefield, Harold, 171–72, 177, 187
Cravath firm, 289
Creation Life Institute, 344
Crime: fear of, 361, 390; against humanity, 239, 243, 325, 371; against peace, 239, 242–43, 325, 370
Criminal Justice Act, 238
Crockett, George W., Jr., 191, 197, 201, 209, 246, 251–55, 259, 312, 414
Crown, Joseph H., 54–55, 410
Crum, Bartley, 73, 80–82, 118
Crystal, Dan, 213
Cuba, 203, 231
Cuneo, Ernest, 33
Cunningham, Dennis, 267
Curfew cases, 252–55
Curry, Carrie, 298

Danville, 192, 204
Darrow, Clarence, 7, 299
Darwin's theory, 344–46
Davidson, Jessica, 149, 410
Davis, Angela, 281, 284, 358
Davis, Fania E., 338–39, 369
Dawley, Edward A., 179, 182–85, 187, 204, 234–37, 260, 310–11, 412, 414
Dawsey Report, 37. *See also* FBI (Federal Bureau of Investigation)
Dean, Max, 259
Death penalty, 360, 390, 397, 404
Debs, Eugene V., 299, 358
Defense teams, 270, 293–98
DeFunis v. Odegaard, 319–20
Delano, 203, 231
Delany, Hubert T., 30, 178, 414
Democratic Party: 1964 Atlantic City convention, 212; 1968 Chicago convention, 247, 266–67
Dennis case, 124, 127–28, 134, 174
Denton, Jeremiah, 392
Department of Defense (U.S.), 228, 381
Department of Education (U.S.), 381
Department of Justice (U.S.): Alien Enemy Control Unit, 53–54; Civil Rights Division, 335, 381, 392; Custodial Detention List, 37; ends effort to list NLG, 158–59; under Reagan, 337–38
Deportation, 381

De Ronde v. Board of Regents, 319
Desegregation suits, 195
Detroit, 185, 202, 205, 246, 251–56, 313; black community of, 254–56; neighborhood legal service center, 255–56; 1943 race riot, 49–50; NLG chapter, 49–50, 110–11; Recorder's Court, 251–55; urban law clinic at University of, 255–56
Deutsch, Michael, 417
Devaney, John P., 9, 409
Devine, Annie, 214
Dickerson, Earl B., 43, 45–47, 143–44, 259, 357, 410
Dies, Martin, 30
Diggs, Anna, 209–10
Diggs, Charles C., Jr., 209, 212, 256
Disabled people, 362, 381, 383
Disarmament and peace law, NLG priority work on, 400–1
Discovery, 308
Discrimination: basis of race, 246, 284; private, 332; reverse, 319–21; state, 332
diSuvero, Henry, 315–16, 411
Divestment movement, 385, 397, 399
Divorce cases, 250
Dmytryk, Edward, 122
Doare, John, 208
Doe v. Plyer, 362
Dohrn, Bernadine, 262
Dombrowski, James, 198–99, 221
Dombrowski v. Pfister, 199, 221–27, 318
Domestic violence, 355
Dominican Republic, 231
Donner, Frank, 115, 409
Donner, Isaac C., 101
Douglas, William O., 6, 126–28, 144, 181, 225–26, 240, 289–91
Douglas and the Supreme Court (Countryman), 291
Douglas Opinions, The (Countryman), 291
Douglass, Frederick, 390
Downing, George, 260
Doyle, Robert, 394
Draft: boards, 229, 233–34; cases, 271; counselors, 232; law, 229–44; registration, 229, 374
Draftees: black, 233–39; refusers, 229–34
Dred Scott case, 347
Dreyfus, Benjamin ("Barney"), 151, 186, 213, 259, 410
Drinan, Robert F., 259
Drugs, 286

Dry Bones, 344
Du Bois, W. E. B., 68–69
Dudley, Barbara, 285–88, 351, 353–55, 376–77
Due process, 231–34, 284, 325, 346, 348, 363; definition of, 185; for poor people, 397
Duga, Lawrence, 260
Durr, Clifford J., 91, 93–94, 118, 178, 409
Dzielak, Ted, 417

Easter-Wells, Martha, 417
Eastland, James, 222
Eaton, Wendy, 417
Ecocide, 405
Economic Bill of Rights, 361, 377
Economic rights, 381, 403; defined as, 362–64; demands for, 389; dignity of, 246; as human rights, 359–66; justice of, 406; necessity of, 219
Economics, 201, 231, 405
Eighth Amendment, 232
Einstein, Albert, 198
Eisenhower, Dwight D., 179
Eisler, Gerhart, 175
Elder, Betty, 202, 248
Ellerin, Milton, 207
Ellsberg, Daniel, 290
El Salvador, 203, 358, 380, 387, 397
Elson, Alex, 101
Emergency Civil Liberties Committee (ECLC), 316
Emerson, Joan P., 24–26
Emerson, Thomas I., 23, 87, 91, 167, 259, 410, 414; and HUAC report (1950), 117–19; as president of NLG, 113–14; service of, with NLRB, 24–26
Eminent domain, 365–66, 405–6
Employment: discrimination in law offices, 193; full, 361, 363; in San Francisco, 214–15
Endo, Mitsuye, 60
Engels, Friedrich, 272–73, 282–83, 285, 333
England, 385–86
English constitution, 282
Enlightenment, 181–82
Enlistment in Foreign Service Act, 36
Environmental crisis, 341
Environmental Protection Agency, 382
Epps, A. Glenn, 260
Equal Employment Opportunity Commission, 393
Ernst, Morris L.: leads anti-Communist element in NLG, 31–35; as New Deal insider, 12–13; refuses membership in segregated ABA, 9–10
Equality, 246; under law, 331–33; Marxist analysis of, 331–35; material base for, 333–35; right to, 331
Equal protection, 182, 185; definition of, 232, 346, 363
Erenstein, Vicki, 399, 417
Erlichman, John D., 283
Erlinder, Peter, 415
Ethics in Government Act, 406
Ettelbrick, Paula, 417
European Recovery Program, 84–85
Evenson, Debra, 351, 415, 417
Eviction proceedings, 264, 291–92, 380
Evolution, 344–46
Exchange value, 334–35
Executive Order 8802, 46–47. *See also* Fair Employment Practices Committee (FEPC)
Executive Order 9835, 86–88, 143
Executive Order 10450: and NLG, 136–38, 141–44. *See also* Attorney General's list of subversive organizations
Executive Order 11246, 393
Ex Parte Endo, 60
Expert testimony, 375
Export-Import Bank, 325

Fahy, Charles, 23
Fair Employment Practices Committee (FEPC), 43, 45–47, 49, 69
Family law cases, 250, 300
Farben, I. G., 76–78, 325
Farmer, James, 207
Farmer v. Roundtree, 241
Farms, foreclosures on, 381
Fascism, 31–34, 274, 284, 403
Fasting, by civil rights prisoners, 196
Faulkner, Stanley, 259
FBI (Federal Bureau of Investigation): agents of, 232, 392, 399; attacks on NLG, 190, 289, 306–7, 336, 357; broad discovery of conduct, 246; call for investigation of, 52–53; charter of, 337; COINTELPRO, 169–70; dirty tricks of, 246, 336; informants of, 336, 395; relations with civil rights groups, 206–7, 392; surveillance of NLG (1940–1941), 36–38; at U.N. San Francisco conference, 75
Featherstone, Ralph, 388
Federal courts, limited access to, 316–18
Federalism, 180, 221

Federal Tort Claims Act, 337
Feller, Abraham, 177
Feminization of poverty, 203
Ferguson, Linda, 370
Fieger, Bernard, 410
Fifteenth Amendment, 180
Fifth Amendment, 144–45, 232, 290, 363
Fifth Circuit Court of Appeals, 190, 204, 220, 223–24
Filartiga v. Pena-Irala, 349
Findling, Fred, 260
Finkel, David B., 168, 209–10, 260, 271–72
First Amendment, 167, 181, 185, 231, 240; and civil disobedience, 374; liberties, 189, 199, 204, 277, 289–90, 345–47; and the Nazis, 338–40
Firstenberg, Sol L., 101
Fischman, Bernard D., 260
Fisher, Herbert, 205
Food stamps, 365–81
Ford, Gerald R., 290
Forer, Joseph, 104–6, 143–44, 175–76, 186
Fortas, Abe, 35
Fourteenth Amendment, 68–69, 180, 182, 199, 220, 235, 332, 363
Fourth Amendment, 232, 279
Fourth Circuit Court of Appeals, 204
Fraenkel, Osmond K., 10, 33, 82, 89, 118, 143–44, 151, 158–59
France, Royal W., 137, 158, 167, 190, 397, 410
Franck, Peter, 260
Frank, Jerome, 6, 34–35, 126
Frankel, Samuel, 412
Frankfurter, Felix, 6–7, 126–28, 143
Franklin, Mitchell, 178–82, 414
Frantz, Laurent, 178
Freedman, David, 246–47, 257–58
Freedom Riders, 204, 216
Free speech, 221, 232
Freund, Paul A., 90
Frey, Alexander, 6, 32
Friend, Rex, 417
Fulbright, J. William, 228

Gallagher, Leo, 394
Gallo strike, 291–92
Gantcher, Neal, 411
Garfinkle, Anne M., 270–71
Garrison, Lloyd K., 23
Garry, Charles, 247, 265–69, 288, 300, 350, 397

Garvey, Jennifer, 399
Gays. *See* Homosexuals
Gaza, 329–31
Gellhorn, Walter, 6
Geneva Convention, Fourth, 329–30, 370, 372
Genocide, 348
Gerash, Walter, 350
Germany, 240, 242
Gerringer, Herman B., 167, 259, 410
Gewin, Theodore, 195
Ghettos, 380, 406; revolts, 216–18, 225, 246, 251–56
GI activists, 286–87
Gibbs, Bob, 417
Gideon v. Wainwright, 265, 360
Gilberd, Kathy, 417
Gilbert, Debreh, 417
Gillen, Andy, 261
Ginger, Ann Fagan, 186, 194, 259, 285, 410, 414, 418; argues for "concentration" policy, 149–50; discusses NLG origins, 9–11; on 1939 NLG convention, 31–34; on 1946 convention, 65–67; opposes right-wing groups, 338–39; proposes anti-sexism resolution (1950), 111–12; on right to peace, 346–49
Ginger, Tom, 391
Gladstein, Amy, 322
Gladstein, Richard, 51–52
Goldberg, Jonathan, 167
Goldberg v. Kelly, 362
Goldberger, Peter, 373–75
Goode, Victor, 321
Goodman, Andrew, 207–9, 388
Goodman, Bobby, 207–9
Goodman, Carolyn, 207–8
Goodman, Ernest, 36–37, 188–89, 191, 199–200, 205, 259; as defense lawyer in Shango trial, 293–98, 308, 410
Goodman, Richard, 350
Goodman, William, 194, 293, 309–14, 321–23, 392, 411–12, 415
Goodman-Crockett firm, 219, 308
Goose Prairie, 290
Gorden, Spiver, 392
Gordon, Emanuel, 412
Gostin, Irwin, 260
Gottesman, Michael, 362
Gramm-Rudman-Hollings, 403
Grand jury: challenge, 266–67; improper selection, 263; subpoenas, 301, 305; witnesses, 317

Gray, L. Patrick, 289
Gray, Victoria, 214
Great Depression, 3–21, 347, 380, 388, 403
Greenberg, Mark, 417
Greene, Nathan, 27–29, 412
Greensboro, North Carolina, 338
Greenville, South Carolina, 215
Grenada, 203
Griswold, Erwin, 131
Griswold v. Connecticut, 290
Grossman, Aubrey, 51–52, 260
Group Legal Services, 203
Guaranteed Income, 361
Guatemala, 387
Guevara, Ché, 265, 341
Gutnecht, John, 34, 409
Gzesh, Susan, 384–86

Haas, Jeffrey, 399
Habeas corpus, 194, 360
Hagen, Carla, 417
Hague conventions, 371, 375
Hague v. CIO, 22, 189
Hamer, Fannie Lou, 214
Hamm v. City of Rock Hill, 225
Hampton, Fred, 388, 396
Hand, Augustus N., 126, 128
Hand, Learned, 180
Handschau, Barbara Ellen, 355
Harlan, John Marshall, 222
Harper, Fowler V., 121–222
Harper v. Virginia Board of Elections, 362
Harring, Sid, 418
Harris, Jack P., 321
Harris, Paul, 214–15, 275–79, 340–42, 356, 396, 411
Hart, Pearl M., 19, 249, 409
Harvard Law School, 89–90
Hastie, William H., 43, 44–45
Haynesworth, Clement, 290
Heart of Atlanta Motel v. U.S., 284
Heitzer, Arthur, 361–62
Hellerstein, Jerome R., 203
Hendrick, Rhoda, 413
Henkin, Lazar, 260
Henry, Milton, 262–63, 313
Heppe, Karol, 417
Hermes, Jan, 260
Herndon, Angelo, 6
Herndon, James, 260, 264
Herndon v. Lowry, 20

Herron, Kathleen, 369
Higgs, William, 213
High school students' rights, 275, 277
Hilliard, Bob, 288–89
Hincks, Carroll, 127
Hinds, Lennox, 394
Hispanic lawyers, 379
Hiss, Alger, 177
Hobson, Don, 260
Hodges, Devon, 298
Hoffman, Abbie, 299
Hollowell, Donald, 192
Holly, William H., 26
Hollywood Ten, 114, 356
Holt, Len, 185–88, 191, 204, 260, 313, 414
Holt v. Virginia, 184–85
Homeless, 381
Homeporting nuclear war ships, 400–1
Homosexuals: issues, 354–55; liberation movement, 401; in the military, 355; prohibiting, 276
Hoover, John Edgar, 36–37, 53–54, 190, 208
Hopewell, Virginia, 178, 184, 186, 188
Hopfenbeck, Ann, 416
Horne, Gerald, 356–57
House Committee on Un-American Activities (HUAC), 30, 179, 181, 188, 190; labels NLG "legal bulwark" of Communist Party, 113, 115–19; testimony of Ben Margolis before, 122–24; testimony of Mortimer Riemer before, 14–17; testimony of Ruth Weyand before, 130–31
Housing: discrimination in, 178, 314; integration of, 201
Houston, Charles H., 18
Houston, John, 255–56
Howard University School of Law, 18, 90
Howe, Mark De Wolfe, 89
Human rights cases, 247
Humphrey, Hubert H., 177

Immigrant rights, 384–86
Immigration Service, 385–86
Immunity Act of 1954, 290
Impeachment, 337
Independence of the Bar, 26–27, 132–39, 144–45, 152, 167
Indian law, 351–52. *See also* Native Americans
Ingram, Rich, 396
Injunction suits: anti-civil rights, 194, 204; anti-labor, 381

Integrated Bar Association, definition of, 304
Integrated law offices, 193, 201, 205, 271
Integration movement, 178–82, 184–92, 194–216, 218–25, 262, 406
Intellectual workers, 331, 348
Intent, specific, 375
Inter-American Bar Association, 58
Internal union democracy, 308–9
International Association of Democratic Lawyers (IADL), 79–80, 94–95, 351, 357
International Convention on the Elimination of All Forms of Racial Discrimination, 339
International Convention on the Suppression and Punishment of the Crime of Apartheid, 327
International Covenant on Civil and Political Rights, 339, 349, 365
International Covenant on Economic, Social, and Cultural Rights, 349, 360, 365
International debt crisis, 405, 417
International Juridical Association (IJA), 6, 29
International Juridical Association Bulletin, 18, 28
International Labor Defense, 6, 10
International law, 241, 325, 347; nuclear weapons under, 370–73
International Military Tribunal, 239–43
International Monetary Fund, 405
International Telephone and Telegraph Company (ITT), 325
International Workers Order, 10
Interposition, 179–82
Iran contragate, 404–5
Israel: occupations by, 329–30; recognition of, 329
Isserman, Abraham, 22, 124–28

Jackson, Ernest D., Sr., 187, 414
Jackson, George, 394–96
Jackson, Henry, 323
Jackson, Jesse, 392
Jackson, Robert H., 35–36, 76, 240; calls for a liberal bar, 23–24; defends Edward Lamb, 26–27
Jackson Bar Association, 219
Jackson State College, 358
Jailhouse lawyers, 270, 304
James, Dennis, 263, 410
Japan, 359
Japanese Americans, 60
Jefferson, Thomas, 181–82, 388
Jelinek, Don, 298

Jenkins, Walter, 210
Jernagin, W. H., 105
Jim Crow, 193, 197
Johnson, D'Ann, 415
Johnson, Frank M., 223
Johnson, Lyndon B., 207–8, 210, 246
Johnson, Marilyn, 415–17
Joint Anti-Fascist Refugee Committee v. McGrath, 138, 143
Jordan, Dawley, and Holt, 186, 191, 194
Jordan, Susan B., 350
Judicial system: class nature of, 273, 282–85; power of, 180, 211, 221–22
Jurisdiction of courts, 316
Jurors: belief in, by NLG lawyers, 403; black, in Shango trial, 296
Jury: instructions, 263; system, 204; trials, 185, 404
Jury selection: absentee voter case, 392; Attica Shango case, 295–96; *Newton* case, 247, 266–69; San Francisco sit-in trials, 215; systematic exclusion of blacks, 194
Justiciability, 241, 316–18
Justification, 375
Juvenile rights, 383

Kairys, David, 417–18
Kakakawana, Shango Bahati, 293–98
Kampuchea, 399
Kaplow, Alice, 262
Karlin, Leonard, 260
Karp, Sandy, 288
Kassner, Minna F., 40
Katz, Sanford, 260
Katzenbach, Nicholas de B., 208
Kaufman, Mary, 76–78, 151, 230, 239–43, 249, 260, 272
Kellogg-Briand Pact, 241, 371
Kelly, Mike, 260
Kempton, Murray, 357
Kennedy, Flo, 300
Kennedy, Robert F., 197, 208–9, 224, 356
Kenny, Robert W., xviii, 228, 259, 356, 409; assumes NLG presidency, 35–36; investigates Los Angeles riot (1943), 48–49; receives letter from FDR, 59; role of at UN and Nuremberg, 73–76; testifies before HUAC (1947), 114–15
Kent State University, 388
Kent v. Dulles, 290
Kenyon, Dorothy, 41

Kerner Commission Report on Civil Disorders, 251–53, 313
Kesselbrenner, Dan, 417
Kievitz, Elsa, 260
Kilroy, Jack, 417
King, C. B., 194–96
King, Carol Weiss, 18, 20, 51, 249; looks forward to 1946 NLG convention, 65–66
King, Martin Luther, Jr., 188, 192, 389, 392–93; death of, 251–52, 319–20, 388; and *New York Times* suit, 184
Kinoy, Arthur, 204, 213, 259, 272–75, 321, 414
Klein, David Y., 260, 412
Klimaski, Jim, 415
Koenigsberg, Samuel M., 138–39, 260
Kogan, Nathan B., 409
Konigsberg v. California, 132–34
Korean War, 94–96, 241, 284, 403
Kraft, Barbara, 366
Krauss, Elissa, 418
Krinsky, Michael, 417; analyzes FBI operations directed at NLG, 36–38, 75, 91–92, 137–38, 169–70, 336–38
Kross, Anna Moskowitz, 41
Ku Klux Klan (KKK), 196, 223, 338–40
Kunstler, William, 213, 267, 299, 301
Kutas, Eva, 416

Labor law: practicing, 248, 305, 308–9, 402; and Reform Act of 1977, 367
Labor theory of value, 281, 334
Laden, Vicki, 417
Lafferty, James, 260, 410
La Follette, Philip F., 9
La Follette Civil Liberties Committee, 10, 23
Laine, Mike, 298
Laird v. Tatum, 289–90, 317
Lamb, Edward, 23, 26–27, 394
Landrum-Griffin Act, 171, 309
Lane, Mark, 103
La Raza Law Students Association, 368
La Raza Legal Alliance, 368, 370
Larson, James, 305, 315, 411
Larson, Reed, 367
Law communes, 271, 275
Law in Transition, 172
Law offices: affirmative action in, 406; building multiracial practices, 368; integrated, 193, 201, 205, 271
Law professors, radical, 272–75, 302
Law reform, 383

Lawrence, Charles, 318–21
Law School Admission Test, 350
Law students, 232, 270; in clerkship program for minorities, 202, 368; and MFDP challenge, 213–14; at 1968 NLG convention, 261–63; number of, 350
Law Students Civil Rights Research Council, 197, 368
Lawyers: and advertising, 378; income of black, 311; black women, 370; civil rights, 186–87, 220–21; criticism of, 351–52; earnings of, 271–72, 304, 306, 380; fees of, 309, 378; in government agencies, 342, 379, 382, 402; Hispanic, 379; lifestyle of, 277–78, 280–81, 301; as members of Legal Services Workers, 402; movement, 264–65, 301; number and age of, 303, 305, 350, 403; pro bono draft work, 238–39; relations with clients, 271, 278, 293–94, 296–97, 351–52; Southern black, 182–85
Lawyers Against Apartheid, 399
Lawyers Alliance for Nuclear Arms Control (LANAC), 377
Lawyers Committee on American Policy Toward Vietnam, 247
Lawyers Committee on Nuclear Policy, 377
Lawyers Committee to Free Nelson Mandela, 399
Lawyers Military Defense Committee, 285
Lawyers Security League, 3, 15–16
Lazarus, Isidor, 34
"Left Wing" Communism, an Infantile Disorder (Lenin), 278, 305
Legal Aid Society, 250
Legal arm of the movement, 301
Legal fees, 378
Legal pragmatism, 180
Legal profession: growth of, since 1960, 379; percentage of non-whites in, 379; women in, 379–80
Legal realists, 6, 180
Legal representation, entitlement to, 250–51
Legal research back-up centers, 383
Legal secretaries, 304, 308
Legal services, 100–2; back-up centers, 383; NLG lawyers for, 342, 379; for the poor, 249–51, 382–84; programs, 246, 249–51, 267, 382–84; union organizing among, 402
Legal skills, 261, 264–65
Legal workers, 230, 270, 304–5
Leitson, Morton, 191, 260
Lenin, V. I., 278, 282, 285, 299, 305

Lenske, Aryay, 186, 410
Leonard, Norman, 264–65
Lesbians. *See* Homosexuals
Levi, Edward, 337
Levin, Judith, 355
Levitan, A. Harry, 260
LeWitter, Jody, 417
Libel suits, 184
Lie, Trygve, 82
Linder, Leo J., 62, 107–9, 149–50, 192
Lipofsky, Joe, 411, 416
Little Red Book, The, 286, 299
Liuzzo, Viola, 388
Llewellyn, Karl, 6, 9
Lobbying, 316, 335, 351, 366, 376, 382–84
Lobel, Jules, 331–35, 419
London Agreement and Charter, 239, 241
Los Angeles: Police Department, 369; race riot (1943), 48–49; and Watts, 216–18
Louisiana: Civil Liberties Union, 197; Joint Legislative Committee on Un-American Activities, 198, 221; State Bar Association, 198; Subversive Activities and Communist Control laws, 221–22
Lowenthal, Max, 36
Loyalty oath, 10, 121–22; ABA version of, 138–39
Loyalty program (post–World War II), 86–88. *See also Executive Order 9835*
Lozaro Justice Center, 365
Lubell, David, 260, 412
Lukas, Edward, 206–7
Lund, Dan, 262–63, 266–67, 299–301, 303–6
Lynd, Staughton, 366

McCarran Internal Security Act, 87, 167
McCarthy period, 86–99, 186, 263, 289–90; Army hearings and NLG, 356–57; effects of on NLG, 113–60, 304
McClain, Elmer, 21
McCone Commission, 217
McGrath, J. Howard, 120
McHugh, Rich, 415
McKinney, Charles, 179, 192
McNamara, Jim, 338
McTernan, Francis J., Jr., 214–15, 260
McTernan, John T., 132–35, 259, 350
McWilliams, Carey, 48–49
Madden, Warren, 23
Madison, James, 181
Mage, John, 417

Magna Carta, 360
Malcolm X, 388–89
Male chauvinism, 300
Malnutrition, 360
Mandel, Seymour, 216–18
Mandel, Vivian, 145–46
Mandell, Arthur, 178
Mann, Wendy, 196
Mao Tse-tung, 272, 299
Mapp v. Ohio, 265, 279
Marcos, Ferdinand, 285, 287
Margolis, Ben, 122–24, 216–18, 233–34, 260
Margolis, Harry, 203, 394, 410
Marijuana, prohibition of, 276
Markels, Charles, 260
Marshall, Burke, 208, 210
Marshall, John, 352
Marshall, Thurgood, 43, 44–45, 226
Marshall Plan. *See* European Recovery Program
Martinet, Louis A., 197
Martinet Society of Lawyers, 197
Martinez, Kiko, 394
Marx, Karl, 332–33, 382
Marxism, 267; analysis of, 276, 281–85, 331–35; lawyers and, xviii, 259
Marxist-Leninists, 139, 304, 323, 359
Mass arrest defense, 272
Mayes, Sandy, 416
Mead, Judy, 411
Meany, George, 323
Medical care, 362, 364
Medina, Adelita, 417
Medina, Harold R., 124–28
Meese, Edwin, 386, 390, 395
Meiklejohn, Alexander, 414
Meiklejohn Civil Liberties Institute, xxi–xxii, 247, 249
Mel's Drive In, 214
Menzer, Matthew, 396
Metzger, Delbert E., 98–99, 414
Mexican American Bar Association, 370
Mexican-Americans, 369–70
Meyer, Tom, 391–92
Meyers, Irving, 260
Meyrowitz, Elliot L., 370–73
Michigan, University of, law school, 90
Middle East, NLG position on, 315
Milan & Miller, 205
Military: budget, 377, 400; law, 262; repression of homosexuals in, 355
Miller, Erwin, 260

Miller, Loren, 178
Mine, Mill, & Smelter Workers, 188
Minority communities, 379
Miranda v. Arizona, 279
Mirer, Jeanne, 321, 322, 411
Mississippi, 178, 203–4, 208–9, 220; law school at University of ("Ole Miss"), 391; lawyers in, 203
Mississippi Bar Association, 219
Mississippi Freedom Summer (1964), 205, 223
Mississippi Freedom Democratic Party (MFDP), and congressional challenges, 212–14, 223–24
Mississippi State Board of Bar Commissioners, 211
Mitchell, Sam, 191
Mitchell v. U.S., 240
Model Penal Code, 375
Mogill, Ken, 298
Montante, Jimmy, 187, 256
Montesquieu, 180
Montgomery Bus Boycott, 392
Montgomery Ward Enterprises Legal Services Plan, 378
Montross, Bill, 417
Moody Park, 3, 315
Moore, Jonathan, 392; analyzes FBI operations directed at NLG, 36–38, 75, 169–70
Morality, 181, 231, 247
Moratorium on nuclear testing, 401
Morgan, Edmund, 89
Morris, Charles J., 90
Morris, Newbold, 48
Morrison, Wendy, 396
Mosston, Leora, 387–88
"Movement and the Lawyer, The": discussion of, at Santa Monica convention (1968), 247, 261–66; 1970 convention, 300; 1971 convention, 304–5
Movement disinformation, 417
Movement lawyer, 264–65, 301
Movement work: economic problems of, 263–64, 271–72; legal skills needed in, 264–65; NLG responsibility in, 265–66; style, 265–67, 270–81, 304; United Farmworkers Union and, 291–92
Moynihan, Daniel Patrick, 323
Mozambique, 322
Multinational corporations, 324–28, 341; crimes of, 325–26, 360–61; economic offenses of, 325

Murphy, Frank, 67
Murray-Kilgore bill, 62
Myerson v. City of Los Angeles, 369

NAACP (National Association for the Advancement of Colored People), 183, 186, 318, 365; legal defense and educational fund of, 186, 392
Napalm bombs, 242
Nassau County Women's Bar Association, 40
National Advisory Commission on Civil Disorders report, 251–53, 313
National Association of Social Workers, 365
National Association of Women Lawyers, 40
National Bar Association, 30; Civil Rights Committee, 192
National Caucus of Labor Committees, 338
National Conference of Bar Examiners, 306–7
National Conference of Black Lawyers, 313–14, 318, 321, 338, 368–69, 387, 393, 406
National Day for Racial Justice, 393
National health care system, 188
National Industrial Recovery Act, 22
National Labor Board, 22
National Labor Relations Act, 22, 26–28; Taft-Hartley amendments to, 366. *See also* Wagner Act
National Labor Relations Board (NLRB), 5, 22–23, 24–29, 130–31
NLRB v. Jones and Laughlin Steel Corporation, 24, 28
National Lawyers Guild (NLG): ABA recommendations criticized by, 165–66; anti-Communist split, 31–36; Asian national officers, 379; attacked by HUAC, 163–65; award winners, 246–47, 414; black members in, 202, 310–11, 313; black national officers, 187–88, 259–61; books published by, 418–19; budget, 187, 211; burglary of, 37, 306, 336; concern of all-white organization, 309–310; constitution of, 11–12; conventions, 409–11; as defenders of Bill of Rights, 150–52; delegations to Cuba and North Vietnam, 315; and FBI, 92–93; fighting racism, 367–68; fights listing as subversive organization, 136–44, 158–59; at founding of UN, 72–75; internal struggles (1971–1973), 302–306; internal struggles (1976), 321–23; internal struggles (1977–1979), 316; Jackson, Mississippi, office, 206, 211–12; journals by, 412; during Korean war, 94–96; labeled

"Communist front" by HUAC, 113–21; law student chapters, 89–91, 262–63, 300, 341; leadership (non-white and women), 407; for mandatory social security for lawyers, 107–9; members employed by government agencies, 342, 379, 393–94; membership statistics, 341–42, 380; minority participation in, 187–88; national officers, 259–61, 409–11; newsletters, 412–13; origins of, 7–11, 16–17; prohibits sex discrimination, 111–12; projects (1986), 416–17; qualitative changes in, 179, 261–63, 270–79, 301–3; questions of style, 261–67, 270–81, 304; radical caucus in, 300; strategy of, 68, 261–63; tax program (World War II), 54–55; woman president of, 301–303, 355; women lawyer members, 40–41, 188, 246; women national officers, 187–88, 259–61; Young Lawyers Round Table (1952), 178; young v. old in, 300–301, 402

National Lawyers Guild chapters: Atlanta, 192, 305; Austin, 305; Boston, 393; Buffalo, 355; Chicago, 186–87, 267; Denver, 265–66; Detroit, 186–87, 199–201, 312, 314; Houston, 305; Los Angeles, 187, 216–18, 232–33, 369, 397–98; New York City, 179, 187, 192, 272, 387; Norman, 305; Philadelphia, 187; Portland, 393; San Diego, 393; San Francisco Bay Area, 179, 187, 214–16, 232, 270, 307, 393, 397–98; Seattle, 369, 393; South Florida, 365; Washington, D.C., 186

National Lawyers Guild committees, networks, task forces: Affirmative Action/Anti-Discrimination Committee, 368–69, 391–93; AIDS Network, 356; Anti-Sexism Task Force, 353–56; Auto Accident Compensation Committee, 187; Central America Task Force, 400; Chile Task Force, 400; Committee for Legal Assistance to the South (CLAS), 205, 209, 211; Committee on Native American Struggles (CONAS), 417; Committee to Assist Southern Lawyers (CASL), 188–90, 191–92, 197, 200–1, 391; Economic Rights Task Force, 361, 365, 405; Faculty Network, 351; 50th Anniversary Committee, 406; Grand Jury Office, 305; Immigration Committee, 366; Independence of the Bar Committee, 187; International Committee, 315, 328, 343; International Committee delegations to Chile, 400; International Committee delegations to El Salvador and Guatemala, 343; International Law Committee Subcommittee on Disarmament, 203; International Subcommittee on Central Africa, 385; International Subcommittee on South Africa, 385; Labor Committee, 366, 385; Labor Committee delegation to Nicaragua, 366; Middle East Task Force, 328–31; Military Law Project, 205, 209–12; National Committee to Combat Women's Oppression (NCCO), 353–56; National Finance Committee, 380; National Immigration Project, 385; National Labor Law Center, 316; Peace and Disarmament Subcommittee, 377; Puerto Rico Movement Law Office, 323; Social Legislation Committee, 192; Visa Denial Project, 399; Women's Caucus, 300

National Lawyers Guild conferences, conventions, workshops: banquet dinner riot in Washington D.C., 300–1; Conference for Civil Rights Attorneys, 192, 197, 203, 205; on discrimination (1952), 178; labor law (1972), 308; 1957 convention, 178; 1958 convention and FBI, 190; 1960 convention, 178; 1964 convention, 199, 204–5; 1965 convention, 228; 1967 convention, 243–44; 1968 convention in Santa Monica, 247, 261–66; 1970 convention, 299–300; 1971 convention in Boulder, 303–5; 1973 convention, 342; 1974 convention, 281; 1979 convention, 367; 1982 convention, 369; personal racism, 369; racism and the law, 313; 25th convention in Detroit (1962), 187–88

National Lawyers Guild National Executive Board (NEB): anti-imperialist caucus, 191–92, 322–23; meetings of, 179, 186–87, 200–2, 244; older members' composition in 1961, 187; older members' composition in 1962, 188; resolutions (1965), 228, resolutions (1975), 318

National Lawyers Guild publications, 228; *Blind Justice*, 355; "Employee and Union Member Guide to Labor Law," 366; *Gay Rights Litigation Manual*, 355; gay rights *Task Force Newsletter*, 355–56; *Guild Notes*, 270; "A How-to Guide: Starting an Unemployment Benefits Clinic," 365; "Immigration Law and Defense," 385; *Labor Update*, 366; *Law in Transition*, 247, 302, 310, 341; "The New Draft Law: A Manual for Lawyers and Counselors," 228; "A Summary of Disarmament Documents: 1945–1962," 203; *White Paper on the NLRB*, 366

National Lawyers Guild v. Attorney General, xx, 246, 288, 306–7, 336–38
National liberation movements, 399
National Recovery Administration, 5
National Right to Work Committee, 367
National Right to Work Legal Defense Foundation, 367
National security, 337
National Security Council, 405
National Socialist White People's Party, 338
National States Rights Party, 338
Native Americans, 248, 343, 351–52, 380, 389, 401–2
Natural resources, 341
Naval Intelligence Service, 288
Nazi war criminals, 239–42
Needleman, Dave, 261
Needleman, I. G., 260
Negligence cases, 192, 197, 313, 350, 381, 404
Negroes: church, 188–89; community, 264; exclusion from juries, 235; in ghetto. *See* Watts; jobs demanding, 179; killing of in Detroit (1967), 254; position on war and peace, 234–37; rights revolution, 201, 220; separated from white allies, 198. *See also* Blacks
Neighborhood law offices, 38–40, 220, 267
Neshoba County (Mississippi), 178
Neuburger, Samuel, 200, 244, 260, 410
Neutrality Act, 406
Newark, 1967 rebellion in, 317
New College School of Law, 315
New critical theory, 347
New Deal, 4–5, 347, 403–4
New Jersey Women's Lawyers Club, 40
New Left, 257–67, 270–80, 299–305, 321–23, 353
New Movement, 406
New Orleans, 179, 215
New People's Army, 286
New Right, 361, 381, 384
Newton, Huey P., 247, 266–69, 284
New York City, 185
New York County Lawyers Association, 126
New York State Assembly Banking Committee, 399
New York Times, 184
New York University School of Law, 90, 103
New York Women's Bar Association, 40
Nicaragua, 381, 397, 400; secret war, 376, 399
Nicaragua v. U.S., 404

Nier, Harry, 212, 260
Nixon, Richard M., 92, 403; administration of, 273, 305, 383–84, 389; presidential resignation, 283; resignation from the California State Bar, 397; and Watergate, 226, 290
NLF (National Liberation Front, Vietnam), 244–45
Noel, Ann, 393, 416
No-knock laws, 389
Norfolk, 185
Norris, George W., 13, 36
Norris, Harold, 110–11
Northern Mississippi Rural Legal Services, 391
North Korea, 284
North Vietnam, 315
Nuclear deterrence, 371
Nuclear disarmament, 376–77, 400–1
Nuclear freeze movement, 377
Nuclear holocaust, 257, 400
Nuclear power plants, 341
Nuclear testing, 373, 400–1
Nuclear war, 230, 237
Nuclear weapons: first strike, 400; in free zones, 401; under international law, 370–73; in Philippine territory, 285
Nuremberg charter, 76–82, 375; crimes against humanity, 239, 243, 325, 371, 400; crimes against peace, 239, 242–43, 325, 370, 400; war crimes, 400
Nuremberg principles, 239–43, 302, 327, 370–72, 400
Nuremberg trials, 230

Oakland, 220–21
O'Brien, Patrick H., 33–34, 50, 414
Obscenity, 276, 271
Office of Economic Opportunity (OEO), 249–50, 264; legal services, 249–51
Office of War Information, 48–49
Office Workers Union, 308
Old girls network, 355
Olshausen, George, 60, 101
Omnibus Crime Control Act of 1970, 302
On the Jewish Question (Marx), 332–33
Orangeburg, 388
Orleans Parish School Board v. Bush, 179
Outer space treaty, 373

Pacht, Jerry, 262
Pacific Counseling Service, 286
Pahl, Penny, 413

Palestine, 80–82
Palestine Liberation Organization (PLO), 328
Palestinian-Israeli conflict, 328–31
Palko v. Connecticut, 362
Para-military training camps, 390
Park, Warden, 395–96
Parker, Cornelia Straton, 41
Participatory democracy, 402
Passports, 203
Patch, Penny, 196
Patterson, William, 193
Pauling, Linus, 349
Paz, R. Samuel, 369–70
Peace: and disarmament, 200–1; law, 400–1; movement for, 236, 243; right to, 346–49; struggle for, 247, 357, 406
Pecora, Ferdinand, 32–34, 409
Pemberton, John DeJ, 206
Penn, Lemuel, 388
Pennsylvania, University of, Law School, 365
Pension plans, 363
Pentagon budget, 401, 405
Penumbra theory, 290
People's College of Law, 316, 369
People's Community Law Center, 365
People's Law Office, 386
Pepper, Claude, 414
Perdew, John, 196
Personal injury (PI) cases, 192, 197, 313, 350, 381, 404
Pesonen, David E., 341
Pestana, Jean Kidwell, 248, 260, 300
Petersburg, Virginia, 186, 188
Peterson, Doris, 321
Peyser, Julius I., 409
Pfeffer, Leo, 206–7
Philadelphia, Mississippi, 207–10
Philippines, 285–89; Department of Justice of, 288
Philo, Harry, 110, 200–1, 260
Piel, Eleanor Jackson, 248
Pinell, Hugo, 396
Pitt River, 203
Pitts, Lewis, 392
Plant closures, 366, 403
Plenk, Tim, 411
Plessy, Homer, 198
Plessy v. Ferguson, 197–98, 283
Plowshares Eight case, 373–74
Police: brutality, 246, 256; misconduct, 188, 267, 402

Polichar, Bruce, 260
Polier, Justine Wise, 17–18
Polier, Shad, 67
Political asylum, 384–87
Political cases, 263, 265, 283–84
Political prisoners, 399
Political theory, 271
Political trials, 274–75, 284. *See also specific case names*
Pollak, Walter, 24
Poll taxes, 10
Pomerantz, Abraham, 409
Poor people, 182, 390, 397
Poor People's Campaign, 389
Popper, Martin, 188, 202, 207, 210, 260, 409, 416–17; addresses 1943 NLG war convention, 42, at creation of International Association of Democratic Lawyers, 79–80; at founding of UN, 73–75; as NLG executive secretary, 34–36; at war crimes trials, 75–76
Pornography, 355
Potler, Cathy, 417
Poverty, 406; line, 381; war on, 246, 249–50
Poverty law, pioneer's reports on, 249–51, 382–84
Powell, Ozie ("Scottsboro Boy"), 360
Powell, Thomas Reed, 6, 89
Powell v. Alabama, 24
Prayer in schools, 344–46
Pressman, Lee, 23, 177
Presumption of innocence, 268–69
Preventive detention, 389
Prison conditions, in West Bank and Gaza, 330
Prisoners, 381; rights movement, 270. *See also* Shango trial
Prison uprising, 294. *See also* Attica uprising cases and Shango trial
Privitera, John, 417
Pro bono spirit, 311
Progressive party, 357
Prosecutor's office and overcharging of offenses, 252–55
Protestant Community Service, 255
Public defenders, 342, 379
Puerto Rican defendants, 279
Puerto Rican Law Students Association, 368
Puerto Rico, 203, 323

Quakers, 231–32
Queen's County Women's Bar Association, 40
Quick, Charles W., 192

Quigley, John, 417
Quotations from Chairman Mao Tse-tung, 299

Rabinowitz, Joni, 197
Rabinowitz, Victor, 69–71, 151, 173–74, 189–90, 197, 246–47, 258–59, 263, 410
Rabinowitz v. U.S., 197
Race Relations Law Reporter, 223
Rachlin, Carl, 206
Racism, 310, 406; appearance of, 310; fighting in NLG, 367–69
Radical caucus, 300–1
Radical lawyer: debate on definition of, 257–59; work of, 272–81, 283–84
Rafferty, Corinne, 417
Ratner, Michael, 376, 411, 417
Ray, Ellen, 417
Raymond, Virginia, 416
Reagan, Ronald W., 351, 359, 376, 381, 383–86, 389, 393, 395, 399, 403
Red-baiting, 305, 397
Redding, Louis, 357, 414
Reed, Stanley, 67
Reginald Heber Smith Post-Graduate Fellowship, 370
Rehnquist, William H., 404
Reif, Jim, 338
Rein, David, 90, 131, 151, 175–76, 260, 263, 288
Reinhardt, Gunther, 36
Release on own recognizance: Detroit Neighborhood Legal Services, 255–56; Los Angeles Court Committee, 218
Relich, Marijana, 248, 308–9
Religious belief, 229, 231–32; in schools, 344–46
Repression, 273–74, 276–77, 399, 403
Reproductive rights, 355
Republic of New Africa, 262
Republic Steel Corporation, 28
Resurrection City, 389
Rethinking Indian Law, 351–52
Reverse discrimination, 318–21
Rhine, Barbara, 291–92
Rhine, Jennie, 300
Rhodesia, 203
Ricks, Willie, 196
Riemer, Mortimer, 14–17, 409
Rights: collective, 325; to counsel, 121, 185, 360; individual, 325; relation between formal and economic, 331–35; to strike, 381; to travel, 290; to work, 366–67

Rights of Undocumented Workers, 366
Right-wing white supremacist groups, 338–40
Rives, Richard, 195, 223
Rizzo v. Goode, 317
Robb, Barbara, 110
Robb, Dean, 110, 260, 350
Roberson, Doris Walker. *See* Walker, Doris Brin
Roberts, Dennis, 194–97
Roberts, Patti, 353–55
Robinson, Thomas R., 104
Rockefeller, Nelson A., 48, 298
Rogers, William, 158–59
Rogge, O. John, 90, 177
Rohan, Colleen, 344–46
Rome Treaty, 327
Roosevelt, Eleanor, 198, 348
Roosevelt, Franklin D., 3, 198, 289, 360; corresponds with NLG leaders, 12–14, 59
Roosevelt Award, 178, 220, 246
Roraback, Catherine, 304–5, 355, 411
Rose, Aggie, 292
Rosen, Sid, 298
Rosenberg, Alan, 260
Rosenberg case, 96–98; stays in, 290
Rosenfeld, Irving, 189–90, 260
Rosenstein, Barney, 260
Rosenthal, Leonard H., 218–19
Rosenthal, Simon, 246, 249–51, 382–84
Rosenwein, Sam, 20–21, 172–73, 260, 361, 363–65
Rudovsky, David, 351, 417, 419
Ruling class, 274–75
Runaway shops, 403
Running and capping, 186
Rural Justice Committee (NLG), 417
Rutberg, Susan, 396
Rutledge, Wiley, 67
Rynin, David, 410

Sabeth, Adolph J., 414
Sacher, Harry, 34, 42, 193; biographical sketch of, 19–20; contempt charges and disbarment proceedings against, 124–28
Safer, Laura, 417
SALT (Strategic Arms Limitation Treaty), 401
Saltonstall, John L., Jr., 89
Saltzman, Steve, 411
Sanchez Espinoza v. Reagan, 376
Sanctions, 385, 397, 399
Sanctuary movement, 386–87
San Francisco, 202, 214–16, 264
San Quentin Adjustment Center, 394–96

San Quentin Six case, 394–96
Santa Monica: 1968 NLG convention, 261–66
Satterfield, John, 190
Schachter, Simon, 412
Schaffer, Art, 260
Schapp, Bill, 412, 417
Scharpf, Fritz, 241
Schmiedel, Peter, 386
Schneider, Elizabeth, 353–55
School integration, 179
Schroeder, Patricia, 401
Schulman, Jay, 418
Schutzer, Arthur, 412
Schware, Rudolph, 260, 265–66
Schware v. New Mexico, 132–34
Schwartzenbach, M. Gerald, 396
Schwerner, Bobby, 207–9, 388
Schwerner, Nat, 208
Schwerner, Mrs. Nat, 208
Scottsboro boys, 6, 20, 24
Scribner, David, 168, 259, 410
Scupi, Richard, 188
SDS (Students for a Democratic Society), 261
SEATO (Southeast Asia Treaty Organization), 228
Securities and Exchange Commission (U.S.), 289
Sedition charges, 212
Seeger v. United States, 231–32
Segregation, 204, 246; de facto in schools, 179
Segregationists, 181
Seidman, Robert B., 412
Seitz, Eric, 288, 410
Selective Service: administrative loopholes, 244; law, 229; system, 229–34; trying a case, 233–34; Vietnam war cases, 227–44
Selective Service Law Reporter, 262
Selective Service Panel, of San Francisco, 230, 237–39
Senate (U.S.): Church Committee to Study Governmental Operations, 336–38; Committee on ghetto revolts, 251
Seniors, 381, 383
Separation of powers theory, 179–80
Serrano v. Priest, 320, 362
Seventh Amendment, 232
Sex discrimination cases, 308
Sexism, 402
Shango trial, 293–98; defendant's role, 293, 296–97; jury selection, 296–97; political courtroom defense, 294–96; team defense, 293–94, 296–98. *See also* Prisoners

Shanker, Albert, 323
Shapiro, Julie, 415
Shapiro, Ralph, 260, 410
Sharp, Malcolm P., 6, 33, 147–48, 230, 259, 410
Shay's Rebellion, 347
Sheiner, Ada, 147
Sheiner, Leo, 144–45
Sheraton Palace Hotel, 214
Shiloh Baptist Church, 196
Shoenmann, Ralph, 262
Shropshire, Claudia (Morcom), 212, 219–20, 249, 260, 312
Shuttlesworth, Fred L., 189
Siegel, Dan, 286–87, 301
Siegel, Franklin, 399
Silberstein, Robert J., 86–87, 91, 101, 104, 136, 201, 260, 409–10
Simpson, Bobbie Nell, 392
Sirica, John J., 283
Sit-ins, 389
Sixth Amendment, 121–22, 232
Skehan, Vesta J. C., 41
Skutt, Dick, 298
Slaff, George, 409
Slander, 184
Slavery, 333
Slocum, Alfred A., 321
Slovinsky, Claudia, 417
Smith, Abbe, 416
Smith, Benjamin, 178, 187, 189, 191, 197–99, 200–1, 213, 220–21, 246, 259, 414
Smith, Fred, 179
Smith, Lawrence M. C., 37, 53
Smith, Otis, 197
Smith, Walter Marvin, 177
Smith, Waltzer, Jones, & Peebles, 205
Smith, William G., 232, 260
Smith Act, 156, 221, 318
Smith v. Allwright, 391
Smokler, Nedwin, 49–50, 260
SNCC (Student Non-Violent Coordinating Committee), 189, 196–97, 205, 207, 249
Socialism, 284, 335
Socialist, 257, 340, 354, 358, 363
Social rights, 331–35
Social scientists, 266, 268
Social Security, 10, 62–65, 106–9
Social workers, 383
Soledad brothers, 394
Sorenson, Doug, 288
Soto, Roberto, 415

South, 178, 182–85; lawyers in, 178, 191; segregation in courthouses, 183
South Africa, 189, 322, 343, 357, 369, 385–86
Southern Africa, 399; UN resolution on, 326
Southern Christian Leadership Conference (SCLC), 192, 392; in Hopewell, Virginia, 188; libel and slander suit against, 184
Southern Conference Educational Fund, 198, 221
Southern Poverty Law Center, 392
Southern University, 388
South Korea, 284
Soviet Union, 257, 322–23, 358, 381, 401
Space: militarization of, 401; treaty, 373
Spears, Brian, 417
Sperber, Laurence R., 172, 412
Stack v. Boyle, 254
Standard, Michael, 260
Standard, William L., 23, 260, 397, 410
Star wars, 401
State action, 332
State and Revolution (Lenin), 299
State bar, 109–10, 306
State bar committee work, 304
State constitutions, 227
State courts, 317
State Department (U.S.), 228, 288–89, 385
Stavis, Morton, 138–39, 194, 202, 204, 212–14, 260
Stearns, Nancy, 355
Steel Valley Authority, 366
Stein, Annie, 104–5
Stein, Jack, 267
Steinberg, Kip, 417
Stender, Fay, 266, 304, 351
Stender, Marvin, 412
Stettinius, Edward R., Jr., 43
Stevens, Hope, 192–93
Stewart, Charles B., 168, 260
Stewart, John, 298
Stewart, Potter, 222
Stradford, Lafontante & Lafontante, 205
Strait, Brian, 298
Strikebreaking, 403
Strikes in the 1980s, 402
Stroble, Bernard, 293. *See also* Shango trial
Stroble-Smith, Mrs. Mozie Lee, 298
Student deferments, 229, 235
Subic Bay Naval Base, 286
Subpoena power, 184, 233
Subversive Activities Control Act. *See* McCarran Internal Security Act
Subversive Activities Control Board, 186, 188
Sugar, Maurice, 7–9, 23, 194, 260
Sullivan v. Little Hunting Park, 317
Supercorporation, 363–65
Superstructure, 281
Supply side practices, 363
Supreme Court (U.S.), 126, 128, 179, 185, 198, 204, 221–26, 232, 254, 283, 321, 352, 389–90; civil rights decisions, 221–26; criticism of, 180, 195; criticized by ABA, 165–66, 177; independence of the bar, 132–35; Nixon appointees on, 265; NLG, relationship to, 161–63, 166–67; Selective Service decisions, 227
Surplus value, 334–35
Surveillance, domestic, 317
Swainson, John, 187
Swanson, Eric, 298
Symonds, Myer, 98

Taft-Hartley Act, 171, 177, 366, 403
Talley, Bascom, 198
Tamayo, Bill, 415
Taxes: failure to file returns, 191; redistribution of, 364; refusal to pay for Pentagon, 373
Taxes, Loopholes and Morals (Hellerstein), 203
Taylor, Herman, 178
Tenth Amendment, 180
Terrell, Mary Church, 105
Terrorism, 179
Test-case approach, 277
Thailand, 231
Theiler, Mary Alice, 322, 342–43, 411, 417
Third World Coalition for Justice in the Legal System, 318
Third World Movement, 283
Thirteenth Amendment, 180, 321
Thompson, Louise, 193
Thompson restaurant case, 104–5
Thorne, John, 260
Three Mile Island, 341
Tietz, J. B., 228
Tigar, Michael E., 221–27, 262, 417
Tipograph, Susan, 394
Tocqueville, Alexis de, xvii
Torture, 330
Trailways, 194
Transnationals, 203, 405
Transportation Workers Union, 19, 193
Traxler, Robert, 212

Truman, Harry S., 86–87, 91, 177
Tullberg, Steven, 351–52
Tureaud, Alexander P., 187, 197, 414
Turner, Albert, 392
Turner, Evelyn, 392
Turner, Nat, 360
Tuttle, Elbert P., 195, 223
Tyler, Gary, 322

Uhler Commission, 395
Ullman v. U.S., 290
Unanimity formula, 83
Unclean hands, doctrine of, 194
Unconstitutional burden, 365
Undocumented workers, 315
Unemployment, 3, 219–20, 246, 380
Unemployment Compensation Commission, 309
Unger, Abraham, 167
Unions, 292; members of, 403; non-member financial support, 367; nonsegregated, 193; security, 366–67
United Automobile Workers, 22–23, 187, 308
United Farmworkers Union, 291–92
United Nations (UN), 186, 201, 228, 326–27, 329, 347–48, 352, 401, 406; Bar Association, 57–59; charter, 348, 361, 365, 370–71, 406; commission on atomic energy, 372; General Assembly, 239, 372–73, 380, 405; genocide convention, 339, 365, 370–72, 397
United Steel Workers v. Weber, 321
Universal Declaration of Human Rights, 348–49, 360, 365
U.S. Air Force, 285–88
U.S. Army intelligence gathering activities, 241, 317
U.S. Civil Rights Commission, 381
U.S. Labor Party, 338
U.S. v. Belmont, 241
U.S. v. Pink, 241
U.S. v. Powell and Schuman, 284
U.S. v. Spock, 263

Vagrancy, 196
Valasquez-Rodriguez, Roberto, 369–70
Vallance, William Roy, 58
Vallat, Francis, 104
Vanderbilt, Arthur T., 22
Van Der Hout, Marc, 384, 386–87, 411, 416
Vietnam War, 221, 227–45, 248, 313, 340, 399; black soldiers in, 235–37; illegality of U.S. involvement in, 227–29, 240–44, 247; NLG role in, 243–45, 266–67, 285–89
Violence against women, 390
Virginia, 179, 182; Committee on Offenses against the Administration of Justice, 183, 186
VISTA (Volunteers in Service to America), 255
Voir dire examinations, 404
Voter registration, 205, 391–93
Voting Rights Act (1965), 214, 389, 391–92

Wagner Act, 22. *See also* National Labor Relations Act
Wagner-Murray-Dingell Social Security bill, 63–65
Wainger, Morris, 63
Walker, Doris Brin, 203, 249, 259, 281–85, 300–3, 338–39, 358–59, 410
Walker, Wyatt Tee, 192
Waller, Terri, 417
Walsh, Frank P., 6–7, 9, 12–14, 409
Waltzer, Bruce, 189, 198–99, 260, 263–64
War, and individual responsibility, 239–43
War crimes, 239, 242–43, 399
War on poverty, 246, 249–50
Waring, J. Waties, 414
Warren, Avra, 75
Warren, Earl, 151, 161, 182
Warren Court, 317, 404
Watergate, 336, 338, 396
Waterman, Jack, 417
Watts, 203, 216–18, 220, 231, 246
Wayne State University: law school, 91; sociology department, 255
Webster, Isabell, 192
Weinberg, Doron, 315, 411
Weinglass, Leonard, 267, 392, 396
Weiss, Peter, 324–28
Weissman, David, 104, 412
Welch, Joseph, 356–57
Welfare, 250–51, 363, 383
Wender, Sue, 196
"We Shall Overcome," 187–88
West Bank, 329–31, 380
Westin, Alan, 413
Weyand, Ruth, 130–31, 409
White, Edwin, 260
White, Lee, 208
White House, 207–10
White supremacy, 406
Wilkinson v. U.S., 167–68, 174

Williams, Barry, 261
Wilson, Barry, 394
Wilson, Charles E., 90, 104
Winchell, Walter, 36–37
Winston-Salem, 215
Wiretapping, 288, 290
Wirin, A. L., 60
Wisdom, John Minor, 223
Wise, Sherwood, 219
Witt, Hal, 188
Witt, Nathan, 23
Wolf, Benedict, 23, 409
Wolf, Henry, 101
Wolpe, Howard, 386
Wolverine Bar Association, 50
Wolvovitz, Barbara, 331–35
Women's issues, 203, 247–49, 302–3, 353–56, 362, 401
Worker's compensation cases, 381
Working class, 319
Works Progress Administration, 3
World Bank, 405
World War II, 42–59, 178, 192, 239, 242, 287, 348–49, 371

Wright, Bob, 260
Wright, Charles MacPhee, 409
Wright, Herman, 178, 259
Wright, Skelly, 223, 226
Wright, Tim, 417
Wulf, Melvin, 288

Yale Law School, 6, 104
Yeagley, J. Walter, 158–59, 210
Yellin v. U.S., 173–74
Yoshimura, Wendy, 315
Younger v. Harris, 225, 227
Young lawyers, 271
Young Lords, 272
Youngstown Sheet and Tube Co. v. Sawyer, 241
Yozell, Emily, 417
Yugoslavia, 94–95, 357

Zimbabwe, 203, 385–86
Zoot-suiters, 49. *See also* Los Angeles, race riot (1943)
Zuber, Paul, 193
Zumwalt, E. R., Jr., 289